BRUSSELS II-TER

BRUSSELS II-TER

Cross-border Marriage Dissolution,
Parental Responsibility Disputes
and Child Abduction in the EU

Nigel Lowe
Costanza Honorati
Michael Hellner

Cambridge – Antwerp – Chicago

Intersentia Ltd
8 Wellington Mews
Wellington Street | Cambridge
CB1 1HW | United Kingdom
Tel: +44 1223 736 170
Email: contact@larcier-intersentia.com
www.larcier-intersentia.com

Distribution for the UK and
Rest of the World (incl. Eastern Europe)
NBN International
1 Deltic Avenue, Rooksley
Milton Keynes MK13 8LD
United Kingdom
Tel: +44 1752 202 301 | Fax: +44 1752 202 331
Email: orders@nbninternational.com

Distribution for Europe
Lefebvre Sarrut Belgium NV
Hoogstraat 139/6
1000 Brussels
Belgium
Tel: +32 (0)2 548 07 13
Email: contact@larcier-intersentia.com

Distribution for the USA and Canada
Independent Publishers Group
Order Department
814 North Franklin Street
Chicago, IL 60610
USA
Tel: +1 800 888 4741 (toll free) | Fax: +1 312 337 5985
Email: orders@ipgbook.com

Brussels II-ter. Cross-border Marriage Dissolution, Parental Responsibility Disputes and Child Abduction in the EU
© Nigel Lowe, Costanza Honorati, Michael Hellner 2024

The authors have asserted the right under the Copyright, Designs and Patents Act 1988, to be identified as authors of this work.

No part of this book may be reproduced, stored in a retrieval system, or transmitted, in any form, or by any means, without prior written permission from Intersentia, or as expressly permitted by law or under the terms agreed with the appropriate reprographic rights organisation. Enquiries concerning reproduction which may not be covered by the above should be addressed to Intersentia at the address above.

Artwork on cover: © Oxanaso/Shutterstock

ISBN 978-1-78068-844-2
D/2024/7849/7
NUR 822

British Library Cataloguing in Publication Data. A catalogue record for this book is available from the British Library.

To Madoc, Mostyn and Maya
Marco, Gregorio and Guglielmo
Ann and Jacob

PREFACE

Council Regulation (EU) No 2019/1111 of 25 June 2019, referred to in this work as 'Brussels II-ter', is the pre-eminent EU cross-border family law instrument. It provides the EU's rules on jurisdiction, recognition and enforcement of matrimonial matters, matters of parental responsibility and international child abduction, and governs the placement of children between Member States.

Brussels II-ter is the third and latest version of the so-called 'Brussels II Regulations', which originated as the Brussels II Convention of 28 May 1998. This Convention never entered into force. Instead, following the Amsterdam Treaty and the communitarisation of judicial cooperation in civil matters, the Commission's proposal made in 1999 was converted, remarkably quickly, into a Regulation (Council Regulation (EC) No 1347/2000 of 29 May 2000) which came fully into force in March 2001. It was the EU's first entry into mainstream cross-border family law matters.

So far as matters of parental responsibility were concerned, the 2000 Regulation only applied to children of both spouses on the occasion of matrimonial proceedings. It contained no specific provisions concerning international child abduction (although it was expressed to take precedence over the 1996 Child Protection Convention). It did not deal with placements of children from one Member State to another and it contained no provisions for cooperation between Member States. These restrictions and omissions were addressed by Council Regulation No 2201/2003 ('Brussels II-bis'), but only after protracted and hard-fought negotiations (particularly in relation to child abduction). Brussels II-bis became fully applicable on 1 March 2005. In 2016, after ten years of application and with 13 Member States applying a Regulation to which they had not been party in relation to its drafting, the EU Commission published its Proposal for recasting Brussels II-bis. There followed lengthy negotiations which resulted in Brussels II-ter, which became fully applicable on 1 August 2022.

Brussels II-ter has made substantial and, at times, fundamental changes with regard to matters of parental responsibility. None is more fundamental than the abolition of the need for an *exequatur* for *all* decisions on matters of parental responsibility. Alongside this development, Brussels II-ter makes major, but complicated, changes to the recognition and enforcement provisions (see further below).

Another important change made by Brussels II-ter concerns the jurisdictional rules on parental responsibility with regard to choice of court, transfer of jurisdiction and jurisdiction to take provisional measures in urgent cases. Key changes, too, are made in relation to international child abduction on which there is now a separate chapter rather than a single article, as was the case previously. Of particular note are the new provisions concerning the timing of abduction proceedings, the more limited application of the 'override provision' and clarifying that a return order ranks as a 'decision' for the purposes of the Regulation. The importance attached to international child abduction is reflected by the fact that it is now included in the title of the Regulation.

Other notable changes include: making express and separate provision for listening to children in proceedings concerning matters of parental responsibility; having a separate chapter (rather than a single article, as was the case previously) dealing with authentic instruments and agreements; enhancing the provisions concerning cooperation between Central Authorities; introducing express provision for cooperation and communication between courts; and substantially revamping the provisions governing the placement of children from one Member State to another. Finally, mention should be made of the new provisions that helpfully clarify the relationship between Brussels II-ter and the 1996 Hague Child Protection Convention.

Welcome though most of these changes are, they come at a cost, not least in the sense that Brussels II-ter now comprises 105 Articles and 98 Recitals compared to 72 Articles and 33 Recitals in Brussels II-bis. But on top of this expansion, Brussels II-ter has become more complex, particularly following the decision to maintain the distinction between what are now termed privileged and non-privileged decisions with regard to recognition and enforcement. While the pros and cons of this decision can be debated, what cannot be justified is the convoluted structure of Chapter 4, which is hard to negotiate.

It cannot go without comment that in contrast to all the changes made to matters of parental responsibility, Brussels II-ter makes no substantial changes with regard to matrimonial matters. Indeed, the provisions concerning matrimonial matters have essentially remained the same since the 2000 Brussels II Regulation. Notwithstanding the criticisms that it is unsatisfactory to have multiple non-hierarchical grounds of jurisdiction and that there is no power of the parents to agree on jurisdiction or of the courts to transfer proceedings, in its 2016 Proposals to recast Brussels II-bis, the Commission refrained from making any recommendations for substantive changes with regard to matrimonial matters. This was not because the Commission necessarily considered the provisions relating to matrimonial matters to be beyond reproach, but, rather, because it did not want to run the risk of opening up the whole topic of matrimonial matters, given the probable divergent views of the new Member States that had not been party either to the 2000 Brussels II Regulation or the Brussels II-bis negotiations, in particular concerning same-sex marriages. It is suggested that when Brussels II-ter next comes to be reviewed, the EU legislature must bite the bullet about re-examining the provisions relating to matrimonial matters.

The book aims to provide an in-depth discussion of this complex Regulation. It endeavours to provide not only a clear exposition of the Regulation's provisions but also a critical evaluation of them. Rather than an article-by-article analysis, the book comprises separate chapters on discrete parts covered by the Regulation, namely: the history and scope of Brussels II-ter, common rules on court proceedings, jurisdiction in matrimonial matters, jurisdiction in matters of parental responsibility, coordination of proceedings, international child abduction, the hearing of the child, recognition, enforcement and authentic instruments and agreements, and cooperation in matters of parental responsibility. The book concludes with a chapter on the relationship between the EU and the UK following Brexit. This chapter discusses, among other issues, the often problematic inter-relationship between Brussels II-ter and the 1996 Hague Child Protection Convention.

The book was originally planned by Nigel Lowe and Costanza Honorati, who participated in the Expert's Group supporting the Commission in the preparatory work. Nigel drafted Chapters 1, 6, 7, 11 and 12, and Costanza drafted Chapters 2, 3, 4 and 5. Michael Hellner joined at a later stage and drafted Chapters 8, 9 and 10. All the authors have read and commented on each other's chapters and have had the benefit of a fruitful and stimulating debate and exchange of views, which they hope will be transferred to the reader.

We have sought to consider the law as we understand it to be as of 31 July 2023.

Like Brussels II-ter itself, the book has been a long time in its preparation and the authors are grateful to Intersentia for their patience and commitment to the work.

Nigel Lowe
Costanza Honorati
Michael Hellner

10 November 2023

CONTENTS

Preface vii
List of Cases: Chronological xv
List of Cases: on Brussels II-bis, by Article xix
Correlation Table between Articles and Recitals in the Brussels IIb Regulation xxv
List of Legislation xxxiii

Chapter 1. History and Scope of Brussels II-ter 1

    I.   Introduction 2
    II.   Material Scope of Application 9
    III. Relationship with Other International Instruments. 29
    IV. Relationship with States that are not Bound by Brussels II-ter. 42
    V.   Transitional Provisions 44
    VI. Monitoring and Evalutation. 47

Chapter 2. Common Rules on Court Proceedings 49

    I.   Seising of a Court: Article 17 50
    II.   Examination as to Jurisdiction: Article 18 58
    III. Examination as to Admissibility: Article 19 63

Chapter 3. Jurisdiction in Matrimonial Matters 71

    I.   Introduction 72
    II.   The General Framework 73
    III. The General Ground for Jurisdiction in Divorce and Separation:
         Article 3. 78
    IV. No Transfer of Proceedings in Matrimonial Cases 94
    V.   Jurisdiction on the Conversion of Legal Separation into Divorce:
         Article 5. 94
    VI. Residual Jurisdiction: Article 6 98

Chapter 4. Jurisdiction in Matters of Parental Responsibility 109

    I.   Introduction 110
    II.   The General Rule on Jurisdiction: Article 7 111
    III. Continuing Jurisdiction in Relation to Access Rights: Article 8 123
    IV. Choice-of-Court Agreements: Article 10 126

V.	Jurisdiction Based on the Child's Presence: Article 11	147
VI.	Transfer of Jurisdiction: Articles 12 and 13	152
VII.	Residual Jurisdiction under Article 14	171
VIII.	Provisional and Protective Measures	172

Chapter 5. Coordination of Proceedings ... 193

I.	*Lis Pendens* and Dependent Actions: General Notions	194
II.	Common Procedural Issues	201
III.	*Lis Pendens* in Matrimonial Matters Cases	212
IV.	*Lis Pendens* in Parental Responsibility Cases	214

Chapter 6. International Child Abduction ... 219

I.	Introduction	220
II.	An Overview of the Application of the 1980 Hague Convention to Return Applications	224
III.	Applying Brussels II-ter to Child Abduction	226
IV.	Expediting the Processing and Hearing of Return Applications	239
V.	Alternative Dispute Resolution	245
VI.	The Right of the Child to Express His or Her Views in Return Proceedings	247
VII.	The Procedure for the Return of the Child	248
VIII.	Enforcing Decisions Ordering the Return of the Child	255
IX.	Refusing to Order a Child's Return – The Override Mechanism: Article 29	257

Chapter 7. The Hearing of the Child ... 271

| I. | Introduction | 271 |
| II. | The Position under Brussels II-ter | 275 |

Chapter 8. Recognition of Decisions ... 287

I.	Introduction	288
II.	The Meaning and Effect of Recognition	290
III.	The Procedure for Recognition	299
IV.	Partial Recognition	311
V.	Refusal of Recognition	312
VI.	The Special Regime for Privileged Decisions	327

Chapter 9. Enforcement of Decisions ... 331

| I. | Introduction | 332 |
| II. | The Procedure for Enforcement | 333 |

III. Refusal of Enforcement. 341
IV. Partial Enforcement 350
V. Adaptation 352

Chapter 10. Recognition and Enforcement of Authentic Instruments and Agreements. 355

I. Introduction. 355
II. Scope. 357
III. Conditions for Recognition and Enforcement 361
IV. Procedure for Recognition and Enforcement 364
V. Grounds for Refusal 365

Chapter 11. Cooperation in Matters of Parental Responsibility. 371

I. Introduction. 371
II. Central Authorities 374
III. Cooperation between Courts and Competent Authorities 385
IV. Placement of a Child in Another Member State: Article 82 386

Chapter 12. The Relationship between the EU and the UK. 399

I. Introduction. 400
II. The Withdrawal Agreement. 401
III. The Post-Transition Position 407

Index. 427

LIST OF CASES: CHRONOLOGICAL

EUROPEAN UNION

ECJ, 22 November 1977, *Industrial Diamond Supplies*, 43/77 .... 8.60
ECJ, 16 June 1981, *Klomps*, 166/80 .... 2.18, 8.95
ECJ, 24 June 1981, *Elefanten Schuh*, 150/80 .... 8.91
ECJ, 15 July 1982, *Pendy Plastic*, 228/81 .... 8.96, 8.97
ECJ, 6 October 1982, *Srl CILFIT*, 77/83 .... 3.30
ECJ, 18 January 1984, *Ekro BV Vee-En Vlees Handel*, 327/82 .... 1.23
ECJ, 10 April 1984, *Sabine von Colson and Elisabeth Kamann*, 14/83 .... 6.62
ECJ, 11 June 1985, *Debaecker*, 49/84 .... 8.94
ECJ, 8 December 1987, *Gubisch Maschinenfabrik*, 144/86 .... 5.66
ECJ, 4 February 1988, *Hoffmann*, 145/86 .... 8.4, 8.47, 8.86
ECJ, 26 March 1992, *Reichert and Kockler*, C-261/90 .... 4.196
ECJ, 2 June 1994, *Solo Kleinmotoren*, C-414/92 .... 10.28, 10.34
ECJ, 15 September 1994, *Magdalena Fernández*, C-452/93 P 3.33, 4.10
ECJ, 6 December 1994, *Tatry*, C-406/92 .... 1.187, 5.63, 5.66
ECJ, 13 July 1995, *Hengst*, C-474/93 .... 8.95
ECJ, 10 November 1998, *Van Uden*, C-391/95 .... 4.196
ECJ, 19 November 1998, *Nilsson*, C-162/97 .... 1.19
ECJ, 17 June 1999, *Unibank*, C-260/97 .... 1.54, 10.11
ECJ, 25 November 1999, *Swaddling*, C-90/97 .... 3.33
ECJ, 28 March 2000, *Krombach*, C-7/98 .... 8.54, 8.86
ECJ, 9 December 2003, *Gasser*, C-116/02 .... 5.36–5.38
ECJ, 1 July 2004, *Wallentin*, C-169/03 .... 3.33
ECJ, 25 January 2007, *Finanzamt Dinslaken*, C-329/05 .... 3.33
ECJ, 27 November 2007, *C*, C-435/06 .... 1.23, 1.37, 1.40, 1.41,
                                                                        1.51, 11.41
ECJ, 29 November 2007, *Sundelind Lopez*, C-68/07 .... 1.56, 2.37, 3.27, 3.72
ECJ, 6 March 2008, *Nordania Finans and BG Factoring*, C-98/07 .... 1.23
ECJ, 11 July 2008, *Rinau*, C-195/08 PPU 6.105, 6.126, 7.33, 8.43
ECJ, 19 September 2008, *Hampshire County Council*, C-325/18 PPU and
   C-375/18 PPU 1.37
ECJ, 2 April 2009, *A*, C-523/07 .... 1.23, 1.41, 3.30, 3.45, 4.5, 4.7,
                                               4.9, 4.11, 4.24, 4.27, 4.181, 4.183, 12.55
ECJ, 28 April 2009, *Apostolides*, C-420/07 .... 8.28
ECJ, 16 July 2009, *Hadadi*, C-168/08 .... 3.7, 3.25, 3.50
CJEU, 23 December 2009, *Detiček*, C-403/09 .... 4.5, 4.181–4.182, 4.184, 4.189
CJEU, 1 July 2010, *Povse*, C-211/10 PPU 4.123, 6.26, 6.117, 6.127, 7.33, 9.35, 9.60
CJEU, 15 July 2010, *Purrucker I*, C-256/09 .... 4.176, 4.177, 4.181, 4.201,
                                                         4.205, 4.206, 4.210, 11.69
CJEU, 5 October 2010, *J McB*, C-400/10 PPU 6.33, 6.44, 12.64
CJEU, 9 November 2010, *Purrucker II*, C-296/10 .... 5.19, 5.23

CJEU, 22 December 2010, *Aguirre Zarraga*, C-491/10 PPU 6.72, 6.122, 7.9, 7.10, 7.23, 7.31, 7.32, 7.53, 8.89, 8.134
CJEU, 22 December 2010, *Mercredi*, C-497/10 PPU 3.45, 4.17, 4.18, 6.47, 6.58, 12.64
CJEU, 12 April 2011, *DHL Express France*, C-235/09 . . . . 8.12, 9.79
CJEU, 26 April 2012, *Health Service Executive*, C-92/12 PPU 6.122, 9.26, 11.16, 11.41, 11.43, 11.47, 11.49, 11.55, 11.62, 11.64, 11.67
CJEU, 21 June 2012, *Wolf Naturprodukte*, C-514/10 . . . . 1.58
CJEU, 6 September 2012, *Trade Agency*, C-619/10 . . . . 8.134
CJEU, 15 November 2012, *Gothaer Allgemeine Versicherung and Others*, C-456/11 . . . . 2.42, 8.27, 8.55
CJEU, 21 March 2013, *Novontech-Zala*, C-324/12. . . . . 6.57
CJEU, 1 October 2014, *E v. B*, C-436/13 . . . . 4.85
CJEU, 9 October 2014, *C v. M*, C-376/14 PPU. 4.21, 6.36, 6.39, 6.40, 6.42, 6.95
CJEU, 23 October 2014, *flyLAL-Lithuanian Airlines*, C-302/13 . . . . 8.119
CJEU, 12 November 2014, *L v. M*, C-656/13 . . . . 4.55, 4.68
CJEU, 9 January 2015, *RG*, C-498/14 PPU 6.116
CJEU, 16 July 2015 (order), *P*, C-507/14. . . . . 2.9, 2.14
CJEU, 16 July 2015, *Diageo Brands*, C-681/13 . . . . 8.53, 8.86, 8.88, 8.125, 10.46
CJEU, 9 September 2015, *Bohez*, C-4/14. . . . . 1.39, 9.14, 9.80
CJEU, 6 October 2015, *Matoušková*, C-404/14 . . . . 1.45, 1.48, 8.48
CJEU, 6 October 2015, *A*, C-489/14 . . . . 5.3, 5.5, 5.9, 5.31, 5.39–5.42, 5.60
CJEU, 21 October 2015, *Gogova*, C-215/15 . . . . 1.40, 4.70
CJEU, 19 November 2015, *P*, C-455/15 PPU 2.33, 8.53, 8.84, 8.86, 8.125, 10.45, 10.46
CJEU, 22 June 2016 (order), *M.H*, C-173/16 . . . . 2.11, 2.22, 2.24
CJEU, 13 October 2016, *Mikołajczyk*, C-294/15 . . . . 1.35, 3.5, 3.7, 3.22, 8.48
CJEU, 27 October 2016, *Child and Family Agency*, C-428/15 . . . . 4.115, 4.127, 4.136, 4.137, 4.140, 4.142, 4.146, 12.58
CJEU, 9 February 2017, *MS*, C-283/16 . . . . 11.17
CJEU, 15 February 2017, *W and V*, C-499/15 . . . . 4.22–4.23, 4.85
CJEU, 9 March 2017, *Pula Parking*, C-551/15 . . . . 10.19
CJEU, 8 June 2017, *OL*, C-111/17 PPU. 4.20, 4.21, 4.27, 4.101
CJEU, 20 December 2017, *Sahyouni*, C-372/16 . . . . 1.32, 1.56, 1.57, 1.89, 10.11, 12.45
CJEU, 20 December 2017, *Schlomp*, C-467/16. . . . . 2.20
CJEU, 19 April 2018, *Saponaro*, C-565/16 . . . . 1.45, 1.48, 4.61, 4.65, 4.70, 4.80
CJEU, 31 May 2018, *Valcheva*, C-335/17 . . . . 1.39
CJEU, 5 June 2018, *Coman and Others*, C-673/16. . . . . 1.29, 813
CJEU, 28 June 2018, *HR*, C-512/17 . . . . 4.12–4.16
CJEU 19 September 2018, *Hampshire County Council*, C-325/18 PPU and C-375/18 PPU 1.37
CJEU, 4 October 2018, *IQ*, C-478/17. . . . . 3.54, 4.115, 4.119–4.121, 4.147, 5.56
CJEU, 17 October 2018, *UD*, C-393/18 PPU 1.56, 1.89, 4.22, 4.98, 12.44
CJEU, 16 January 2019, *Liberato*, C-386/17 . . . . 5.3, 5.9. 5.17, 5.30, 5.34, 5.60, 8.84, 8.88, 8.125
CJEU, 23 May 2019, *WB*, C-658/17. . . . . 10.21
CJEU, 10 July 2019 (order), *EP*, C-530/18 . . . . 4.115, 4.127, 4.143, 4.144
CJEU, 15 September 2019, *R*, C-468/18 . . . . 1.85
CJEU, 3 October 2019 (order), *OF*, C-759/18 . . . . 1.50, 4.69

CJEU, 7 November 2019, *K H K*, C-555/18 .... 6.57
CJEU, 24 March 2021, *SS*, C-603/20 PPU 1.73, 4.167, 6.18, 12.62
CJEU, 25 November 2021, *IB*, C-289/20 .... 3.5, 3.19, 3.29, 3.36, 3.37, 3.39,
3.43, 3.46, 3.49–3.50, 4.10, 4.29
CJEU, 14 December 2021, *Stolichna obshtina, rayon 'Pancharevo'*, C-490/20 ..... 1.29, 8.13
CJEU, 7 April 2022, *H Limited*, C-568/20 .... 8.67
CJEU, 1 August 2022, *MPA*, C-501/20 .... 3.29, 3.32, 3.37, 3.41, 3.78, 3.82, 3.84, 4.167
CJEU, 10 February 2022, *OE*, C-522/20 .... 3.5, 3.19, 3.46
CJEU, 12 May 2022, *WJ*, C-644/20 .... 4.19
CJEU, 14 July 2022, *CC*, C-572/21 .... 1.70–1.74, 4.3, 12.44, 12.46, 12.54
CJEU, 15 November 2022, *Senatsverwaltung für Inneres und Sport*,
  C-646/20 .... 1.32–1.33, 1.51, 1.54–1.55, 1.93,
10.13, 10.20–10.21, 12.38
CJEU, 16 February 2023, *T.C., and Others*, C-638/22 PPU 1.93, 6.1, 6.56, 6.64, 9.46
CJEU, 27 April 2023, *CM*, C-372/22 .... 4.41, 4.129
CJEU, 6 July 2023, *BM*, C-462/22 .... 3.15, 3.19, 12.35
CJEU, 13 July 2023, *TT*, C-87/22 .... 4.131, 6.13, 6.16–6.17

COUNCIL OF EUROPE

ECtHR, 25 April 1978, *Tyrer v. United Kingdom* App No 5856/72 .... 1.30
ECtHR, 23 June 1993, *Hoffmann v. Austria*, App No. No 12878/87 .... 8.108
ECtHR, 21 December 1999, *Salgueiro da Silva Mouta v. Portugal*,
  App No. 33290/96 .... 8.108
ECtHR, 20 July 2001, *Pellegrini v. Italy*, App No. 30882/96 .... 8.85
ECtHR 16 December 2003, *Palau-Martinez v. France*, App No. 64927/01 .... 8.108
ECtHR 22 January 2008, *EB v. France*, App No 43546/02 .... 1.30
ECtHR, 3 December 2009, *Zaunegger v. Germany*, App No. 22028/04 .... 8.108
ECtHR, 30 November 2010, *P.V. v. Spain*, App No. 35159/09 .... 8.108
ECtHR, 12 July 2011, *Šneersone and Kampanella v. Italy*, App No. 14737/09 .... 1.74
ECtHR, 26 July 2011, *Shaw v. Hungary*, App No. 6457/09 .... 6.62
ECtHR, 12 February 2013, *Vojnity v. Hungary*, App No. 29617/07 .... 8.108
ECtHR, 26 November 2013, *X v. Latvia*, App No. 27853/09 .... 7.27, 8.90
ECtHR, 18 June 2014, *Povse v. Austria*, App No. 3890/11 .... 6.117
ECtHR, 28 April 2015, *Ferrari v. Romania*, App No. 1714/10 .... 6.62
ECtHR, 3 September 2015, *M and M v. Croatia*, App No. 10161/13 .... 7.6
ECtHR, 2 February 2016, *NTS and Others v. Georgia*, App No. 71776/12 .... 7.6
ECtHR, 1 March 2016, *KJ v. Poland*, App No. 30813/14 .... 6.62
ECtHR, 11 October 2016, *Iglesias Casarrubios and Cantalapiedra
  Iglesias v. Spain*, App No. 23298/12 .... 7.6
ECtHR, 21 May 2019, *OCI and Others v. Romania*, App No. 49450/17 .... 6.83
ECtHR, 18 February 2020, *Cînța v. Romania*, App No. 3891/18 .... 8.108

LIST OF CASES:
ON BRUSSELS II-BIS, BY ARTICLE*

Article 1 (see Article 1 Brussels II-ter)[1]
ECJ, 27 November 2007, *C*, C-435/06
ECJ, 2 April 2009, *A*, C-523/07
CJEU, 26 April 2012, *Health Service Executive*, C-92/12 PPU
CJEU, 6 October 2015, *Matoušková*, C-404/14
CJEU, 21 October 2015, *Gogova*, C-215/15
CJEU, 13 October 2016, *Mikołajczyk*, C-294/15
CJEU, 31 May 2018, *Valcheva*, C-335/17
CJEU, 19 September 2018, *Hampshire County Council*, C-325/18 PPU and C-375/18 PPU
CJEU, 17 October 2018, *UD*, C-393/18 PPU
CJEU, 19 April 2018, *Saponaro*, C-565/16
CJEU, 3 October 2019 (order), *OF*, C-759/18
CJEU, 2 August 2021, *A*, C-262/21 PPU

Article 2 (see Article 2 Brussels II-ter)
CJEU, 5 October 2010, *J McB*, C-400/10 PPU
CJEU, 9 October 2014, *C v. M*, C-376/14 PPU
CJEU, 21 October 2015, *Gogova*, C-215/15
CJEU, 8 June 2017, *OL*, C-111/17 PPU
CJEU, 31 May 2018, *Valcheva*, C-335/17
CJEU, 3 October 2019 (order), *OF*, C-759/18
CJEU, 2 August 2021, *A*, C-262/21 PPU
CJEU, 15 November 2022, *Senatsverwaltung für Inneres und Sport*, C-646/20

Article 3 (see Article 3 Brussels II-ter)
ECJ, 16 July 2009, *Hadadi*, C-168/08
CJEU, 13 October 2016, *Mikołajczyk*, C-294/15
CJEU, 16 January 2018 (order), *PM*, C-604/17
CJEU, 3 October 2019 (order), *OF*, C-759/18
CJEU, 25 November 2021, *IB*, C-289/20
CJEU, 10 February 2022, *OE*, C-522/20
CJEU, 1 August 2022, *M P A*, C-501/20
CJEU, 6 July 2022, *BM*, C-462/22

---

*   At the time of going to press no decision has yet been given by way of preliminary ruling on Brussels II-ter.
[1] It should be noted that although corresponding Articles in Brussels II-ter are given, these might have changed quite substantially in relation to their counterparts in Brussels II-bis.

List of Cases: on Brussels II-bis, by Article

Article 6 (see **Article 6(2)** Brussels II-ter)
ECJ, 29 November 2007, *Sundelind Lopez* C-68/07

Article 7 (see **Article 6(1) and (3)** Brussels II-ter)
ECJ, 29 November 2007, *Sundelind Lopez*, C-68/07
CJEU, 1 August 2022, *M P A*, C-501/20

Article 8 (see **Article 7** Brussels II-ter)
ECJ, 2 April 2009, *A*, C-523/07
CJEU, 23 December 2009, *Detiček*, C-403/09 PPU
CJEU, 22 December 2010, *Mercredi*, C-497/10 PPU
CJEU, 1 October 2014, *E v. B*, C-436/13
CJEU, 9 October 2014, *C v. M*, C-376/14 PPU
CJEU, 15 February 2017, *Wand V*, C-499/15
CJEU, 8 June 2017, *OL*, C-111/17 PPU
CJEU, 28 June 2018, *HR*, C-512/17
CJEU, 17 October 2018, *UD*, C-393/18 PPU
CJEU, 14 July 2022, *CC*, C-572/21
CJEU, 1 August 2022, *M P A*, C-501/20

Article 9 (see **Article 8** Brussels II-ter)
CJEU, 27 April 2023, *CM*, C-372/22

Article 10 (see **Article 9** Brussels II-ter)
ECJ, 2 April 2009, *A*, C-523/07
CJEU, 1 July 2010, *Povse*, C-211/10 PPU
CJEU, 22 December 2010, *Mercredi*, C-497/10 PPU
CJEU, 9 October 2014, *C v. M*, C-376/14 PPU
CJEU, 10 April 2018 (order), *CV*, C-85/18 PPU
CJEU, 17 October 2018, *UD*, C-393/18 PPU
CJEU, 24 March 2021, *SS*, C-603/20 PPU

Article 11 (see **Articles 22, 23 and 26** Brussels II-ter)
ECJ, 11 July 2008, *Rinau*, C-195/08 PPU
CJEU, 1 July 2010, *Povse*, C-211/10 PPU
CJEU, 9 October 2014, *C v. M*, C-376/14 PPU
CJEU, 9 January 2015, *RG*, C-498/14 PPU
CJEU, 8 June 2017, *OL*, C-111/17 PPU
CJEU, 2 August 2021, *A*, C-262/21 PPU
CJEU, 16 February 2023, *T.C. and Others*, C-638/22 PPU

Article 12 (see **Article 10** Brussels II-ter)
CJEU, 1 October 2014, *E v. B*, C-436/13
CJEU, 12 November 2014, *L v. M*, C-656/13
CJEU, 21 October 2015, *Gogova*, C-215/15
CJEU, 15 February 2017, *W, V*, C-499/15
CJEU, 16 January 2018 (order), *PM*, C-604/17

CJEU, 19 April 2018, *Saponaro*, C-565/16
CJEU, 3 October 2019 (order), *OF*, C-759/18

Article 13 (see Article 11 Brussels II-ter)
CJEU, 22 December 2010, *Mercredi*, C-497/10 PPU

Article 14 (see Article 11 Brussels II-ter)
CJEU, 24 March 2021, *SS*, C-603/20 PPU
CJEU, 1 August 2022, *M P A*, C-501/20

Article 15 (see Articles 12 and 13 Brussels II-ter)
CJEU, 27 October 2016, *Child and Family Agency*, C-428/15
CJEU, 4 October 2018, *IQ*, C-478/17
CJEU, 10 July 2019 (order), *EP*, C-530/18
CJEU, 27 April 2023, *CM*, C-372/22
CJEU, 13 July 2023, *TT*, C-87/22

Article 16 (see Article 17 Brussels II-ter)
CJEU, 22 December 2010, *Mercredi*, C-497/10 PPU
CJEU, 16 July 2015 (order), *P*, C-507/14
CJEU, 6 October 2015, C-489/14
CJEU, 22 June 2016 (order), *MH*, C-173/16

Article 17 (see Article 18 Brussels II-ter)
ECJ, 29 November 2007, *Sundelind Lopez*, C-68/07
CJEU, 16 January 2019, *Liberato*, C-386/17
CJEU, 3 October 2019 (order), *OF*, C-759/18

Article 19 (see Article 20 Brussels II-ter)
CJEU, 9 November 2010, *Purrucker II*, C-296/10
CJEU, 22 December 2010, *Mercredi*, C-497/10 PPU
CJEU, 6 October 2015, *A*, C-489/14
CJEU, 16 January 2019, *Liberato*, C-386/17

Article 20 (see Article 15 Brussels II-ter)
ECJ, 2 April 2009, *A*, C-523/07
CJEU, 23 December 2009, *Detiček*, C-403/09 PPU
CJEU, 15 July 2010, *Purrucker I*, C-256/09
CJEU, 9 November 2010, *Purrucker II*, C-296/10
CJEU, 26 April 2012, *Health Service Executive*, C-92/12 PPU
CJEU, 19 September 2018, *Hampshire County Council*, C-325/15 PPU and C-375/18 PPU

Article 21 (see Article 30 Brussels II-ter)
ECJ, 11 July 2008, *Rinau*, C-195/08 PPU
CJEU, 9 November 2010, *Purrucker II*, C-296/10
CJEU, 26 April 2012, *Health Service Executive*, C-92/12 PPU
CJEU, 15 November 2022, *Senatsverwaltung für Inneres und Sport*, C-646/20

Article 22 (see Article 38 Brussels II-ter)
CJEU, 16 January 2019, *Liberato*, C-386/17

Article 23 (see Article 39 Brussels II-ter)
ECJ, 11 July 2008, *Rinau*, C-195/08 PPU
CJEU, 22 December 2010, *Aguirre Zarraga*, C-491/10 PPU
CJEU, 19 November 2015, *P*, C-455/15 PPU
CJEU, 16 January 2019, *Liberato*, C-386/17

Article 24 (see Article 69 Brussels II-ter)
CJEU, 15 July 2010, *Purrucker I*, C-256/09
CJEU, 16 January 2019, *Liberato*, C-386/17

Article 26 (Article 71 Brussels II-ter)
CJEU, 9 November 2010, *Purrucker II*, C-296/10
CJEU, 19 September 2018, *Hampshire County Council*, C-325/15 PPU and C-375/18 PPU

Article 28 (no corresponding provision in Brussels II-ter)
CJEU, 26 April 2012, *Health Service Executive*, C-92/12 PPU
CJEU, 9 September 2015, *Bohez*, C-4/14

Article 31 (no corresponding provision in Brussels II-ter)
ECJ, 11 July 2008, *Rinau*, C-195/08 PPU

Article 33 (no corresponding provision in Brussels II-ter)
CJEU, 19 September 2018, *Hampshire County Council*, C-325/15 PPU and C-375/18 PPU

Article 40 (see Articles 42 and 47(1) Brussels II-ter)
ECJ, 11 July 2008, *Rinau*, C-195/08 PPU
CJEU, 19 September 2018, *Hampshire County Council*, C-325/15 PPU and C-375/18 PPU

Article 41(1) (see Article 43(1) Brussels II-ter)
CJEU, 9 September 2015, *Bohez*, C-4/14

Article 42 (see Articles 43(1) and 47(3) Brussels II-ter)
ECJ, 11 July 2008, *Rinau*, C-195/08 PPU
CJEU, 1 July 2010, *Povse*, C-211/10 PPU
CJEU, 22 December 2010, *Aguirre Zarraga*, C-491/10 PPU

Article 46 (see Article 65 Brussels II-ter)
CJEU, 15 November 2022, *Senatsverwaltung für Inneres und Sport*, C-646/20

Article 47 (see Article 51 Brussels II-ter)
CJEU, 1 July 2010, *Povse*, C-211/10 PPU
CJEU, 22 December 2010, *Aguirre Zarraga*, C-491/10 PPU
CJEU, 9 September 2015, *Bohez*, C-4/14

Article 55 (see Article 79 Brussels II-ter)
ECJ, 2 April 2009, *A*, C-523/07

Article 56 (see Article 82 Brussels II-ter)
CJEU, 26 April 2012, *Health Service Executive*, C-92/12 PPU

Article 59 (see Article 94 Brussels II-ter)
ECJ, 27 November 2007, *C*, C-435/06

Article 61 (see Article 97(1) Brussels II-ter)
CJEU, 24 March 2021, *SS*, C-603/20 PPU
CJEU, 14 July 2022, *CC*, C-572/21

CORRELATION TABLE BETWEEN ARTICLES AND RECITALS IN THE BRUSSELS IIB REGULATION*

Article	Recital(s)	Topic
–	Recital 1 Recital 3 Recital 90	The need to recast Brussels IIa Regulation
ARTICLE 1(1)	Recital 2 Recital 4 Recital 5 Recital 8	Scope of the Regulation, the notion of 'civil matters' – general
ARTICLE 1(1)(a)	Recital 9 Recital 12	Scope of matrimonial matters
ARTICLE 1(1)(b), 1(2)	Recital 4 Recital 5 Recital 7 Recital 10 Recital 11 Recital 17 Recital 18 Recital 92	Scope of matters of parental responsibility
ARTICLE 1(3)	Recital 2 Recital 5 Recital 16 Recital 17 Recital 40 Recital 73	The circulation of return decisions
ARTICLE 1(4)	Recital 11 Recital 12 Recital 13 Recital 92	Matters falling outside the scope
ARTICLE 2(1)	Recital 14 Recital 16 Recital 59	Definition of 'decision'
ARTICLE 2(2)(1)	Recital 7 Recital 14	Definition of 'court'

---

* The Correlation Table is provided in Annex I to the *Practice Guide for the Application of the Brussels IIb Regulation*.

Correlation Table between Articles and Recitals in the Brussels IIb Regulation

Article	Recital(s)	Topic
ARTICLE 2(2)(2)	Recital 5 Recital 14 Recital 15	Definition of 'authentic instrument'
ARTICLE 2(2)(3)	Recital 5 Recital 14	Definition of 'agreement'
ARTICLE 2(2)(4), (5)	–	Definitions of 'Member State of origin' and 'Member State of enforcement'
ARTICLE 2(2)(6)	Recital 7 Recital 17	Definition of 'child'
ARTICLE 2(2)(7)	Recital 7 Recital 10 Recital 11 Recital 16 Recital 18	Definition of 'parental responsibility'
ARTICLE 2(2)(8)	Recital 18	Definition of 'holder of parental responsibility'
ARTICLE 2(2)(9)	Recital 18	Definition of 'rights of custody'
ARTICLE 2(2)(10)	Recital 18	Definition of 'rights of access'
ARTICLE 2(2)(11)	Recital 16 Recital 17	Definition of 'wrongful removal or retention'
–	Recital 19	Notion of 'best interests of the child'
ARTICLE 3	Brussels II Regulation Recital 8 and Recital 12	General jurisdiction in matrimonial matters
ARTICLE 4	Brussels II Regulation Recital 8 and Recital 12	Counterclaim
ARTICLE 5	Brussels II Regulation Recital 8 and Recital 12	Conversion of legal separation to divorce
ARTICLE 6	Brussels II Regulation Recital 8 and Recital 12	Residual jurisdiction
ARTICLE 7	Recital 19 Recital 20 Recital 21	General jurisdiction in matters of parental responsibility
ARTICLE 8	Recital 20	Continuing jurisdiction in relation to access rights
ARTICLE 9	Recital 22	Jurisdiction in cases of the wrongful removal or retention of a child
ARTICLE 10	Recital 20 Recital 22 Recital 23 Recital 24 Recital 38 Recital 43	Choice of court

Correlation Table between Articles and Recitals in the Brussels IIb Regulation

Article	Recital(s)	Topic
ARTICLE 11	Recital 25	Jurisdiction based on presence of the child
ARTICLES 12 AND 13	Recital 21 Recital 26 Recital 27 Recital 28 Recital 37 Recital 79	Transfer of jurisdiction
ARTICLE 14	Recital 29 Recital 34	Residual jurisdiction
ARTICLE 15	Recital 30 Recital 31 Recital 44 Recital 46 Recital 59 Recital 79	Provisional, including protective, measures in urgent cases
ARTICLE 16	Recital 32 Recital 33	Incidental questions
ARTICLE 17	Recital 35 Recital 36 Recital 38	Seising of a court
ARTICLE 18	Recital 31 Recital 37	Examination as to jurisdiction
ARTICLE 19	Recital 36	Examination as to admissibility
ARTICLE 20	Recital 35 Recital 38 Recital 79	*Lis pendens* and dependent actions
ARTICLE 21	Recital 39 Recital 53 Recital 57 Recital 71	Right of the child to express his or her views
ARTICLE 22	Recital 16 Recital 40 Recital 73	Return of the child under the 1980 Hague Convention
–	Recital 41 Recital 43	Concentration of jurisdiction for return proceedings
ARTICLE 23	Recital 73	Receipt and processing of applications by Central Authorities
ARTICLE 24	Recital 41 Recital 42	Expeditious court proceedings
ARTICLE 25	Recital 42 Recital 43	Alternative dispute resolution
ARTICLE 26	Recital 39 Recital 53	Right of the child to express his or her views in return proceedings
ARTICLE 27(1)	Recital 53	The right of the person seeking the return of the child to be heard
ARTICLE 27(2)	–	Access arrangement during return proceedings

Correlation Table between Articles and Recitals in the Brussels IIb Regulation

Article	Recital(s)	Topic
ARTICLE 27(3), (4)	Recital 44 Recital 45 Recital 46 Recital 79	Adequate arrangements
ARTICLE 27(5)	Recital 30 Recital 44 Recital 45 Recital 46 Recital 59 Recital 79	Provisional measures to protect the child from grave risk
ARTICLE 27(6)	Recital 47 Recital 66	Provisional enforceability of a return decision
ARTICLE 28	Recital 60 Recital 65 Recital 66 Recital 67	Enforcement of decisions ordering the return of a child
ARTICLE 29(1)	Recital 48 Recital 49	Scope of the 'overriding mechanism'
ARTICLE 29(2), (3), (4)	Recital 49 Recital 50	'Overriding mechanism' where parental responsibility proceedings are pending
ARTICLE 29(2), (5)	Recital 49 Recital 51	'Overriding mechanism' where no parental responsibility proceedings are pending
ARTICLE 29(6)	Recital 52	Overriding effect
ARTICLE 30(1), (2), (3)	Recital 54	Recognition of a decision
ARTICLE 31	–	Documents to be produced for recognition
ARTICLE 32	–	Absence of documents
ARTICLE 33	–	Stay of proceedings
ARTICLE 34(1)	Recital 58 Recital 66	Enforceable decisions
ARTICLE 34(2)	Recital 66	Provisional enforceability of decisions granting rights of access
ARTICLE 35(2)	–	Documents to be produced for enforcement
ARTICLE 36	Recital 64	Issuance of the certificate
ARTICLE 37	–	Rectification of the certificate
ARTICLE 38	Recital 54 Recital 55 Recital 56	Grounds for refusal of recognition of decisions in matrimonial matters
ARTICLE 39	Recital 54 Recital 55 Recital 56 Recital 62	Grounds for refusal of recognition of decisions in matters of parental responsibility
ARTICLE 39(2)	Recital 39 Recital 57	Ground for refusal of recognition of decisions in matters of parental responsibility where the child did not have an opportunity to express his or her views

Correlation Table between Articles and Recitals in the Brussels IIb Regulation

Article	Recital(s)	Topic
ARTICLES 40	Recital 54 Recital 6	Procedure for refusal of recognition
ARTICLE 41	Recital 54 Recital 55 Recital 62	Grounds for refusal of enforcement of decisions in matters of parental responsibility
ARTICLE 42	Recital 52 Recital 58	Scope of privileged decisions
ARTICLE 43	Recital 52	Recognition of privileged decisions
ARTICLE 44	–	Stay of proceedings
ARTICLE 45	Recital 66	Enforceable privileged decisions
ARTICLE 46	–	Documents to be produced for enforcement
ARTICLE 47	Recital 52	Issuance of the privileged certificate
ARTICLE 48	–	Rectification and withdrawal of the privileged certificate
ARTICLE 49	–	Certificate on lack or limitation of enforceability
ARTICLE 50	Recital 38 Recital 52 Recital 56	Irreconcilable decisions
ARTICLE 51	Recital 60 Recital 65 Recital 6	Enforcement procedure
ARTICLE 52	Recital 60	Authorities competent for enforcement
ARTICLE 53	–	Partial enforcement
ARTICLE 54	Recital 61	Arrangements for the exercise of rights of access
ARTICLE 55	Recital 64	Service of certificate and decision
ARTICLE 56(1)	Recital 64 Recital 67	Suspension of enforcement proceedings where enforceability is suspended in the Member State of origin
ARTICLE 56(2)(b) AND ARTICLE 56(3)	Recital 67 Recital 68	Suspension of enforcement proceedings due to appeal
ARTICLE 56(4)–(6)	Recital 67 Recital 69	Suspension and refusal of enforcement due to exposure of the child to grave risk
ARTICLE 57	Recital 62 Recital 63	Grounds for suspension or refusal of enforcement under national law
ARTICLES 58–60	Recital 62 Recital 63	Procedure for refusal of enforcement
ARTICLE 61	–	Challenge or appeal
ARTICLE 62	–	Further challenger or appeal
ARTICLE 63	–	Stay of proceedings
ARTICLE 64	Recital 5 Recital 6 Recital 14 Rectal 15	Scope of authentic instruments and agreements

Correlation Table between Articles and Recitals in the Brussels IIb Regulation

Article	Recital(s)	Topic
ARTICLE 65	Recital 55 Recital 70	Recognition and enforcement of authentic instruments and agreements
ARTICLES 66–67	–	Issuance, rectification and withdrawal of the certificate
ARTICLE 68(3)	Recital 55 Recital 71	Grounds for refusal of recognition or enforcement of authentic instruments and agreements
ARTICLE 69	–	Prohibition of review of jurisdiction of the court of origin
ARTICLE 70	–	Differences in applicable law
ARTICLE 71	–	Non-review as to substance
ARTICLE 72	–	Appeal in certain Member States
ARTICLE 73	–	Costs
ARTICLE 74	–	Legal aid
ARTICLE 75	–	Security, bond or deposit
ARTICLE 76	Recital 72 Recital 73 Recital 74	Designation of Central Authorities
ARTICLE 77(3)	Recital 74 Recital 86	General tasks of Central Authorities and EJN-civil
ARTICLE 78(1)–(2)	Recital 74 Recital 75 Recital 80	Requests through Central Authorities
ARTICLE 78(2) – (3)	Recital 74 Recital 75 Recital 76 Recital 78	Applicants
ARTICLE 78(4)	Recital 77	Agreements between Central Authorities
ARTICLE 79	Recital 78 Recital 79 Recital 80	Specific tasks of Central Authorities, discovering the whereabouts of a child
ARTICLE 80	Recital 75 Recital 76 Recital 81 Recital 84 Recital 85	Cooperation on collecting and exchanging information relevant in procedures in matters of parental responsibility
ARTICLE 81	Recital 82	Implementation of decisions in matters of parental responsibility in another Member State
ARTICLE 82	Recital 11 Recital 77 Recital 83 Recital 84 Recital 85	Placement of a child in another Member State
ARTICLE 83	Recital 72	Costs of Central Authorities
ARTICLE 84	Recital 86	Meetings of Central Authorities
ARTICLE 85		Scope of general provisions

Correlation Table between Articles and Recitals in the Brussels IIb Regulation

Article	Recital(s)	Topic
ARTICLE 86	Recital 75 Recital 79 Recital 80	Cooperation and communication between courts
ARTICLE 87	Recital 85	Collection and transmission of information
ARTICLE 88	Recital 87	Notification of data subject
ARTICLE 89	Recital 88	Non-disclosure of information
ARTICLE 90	–	Legalisation or other similar formality
ARTICLE 91	–	Languages
ARTICLE 92	Recital 89	Amendments to Annexes
ARTICLE 93	Recital 89	Exercise of the delegation
ARTICLE 94	Recital 90	Relations with other instruments
–	Recital 90	The continuity with the Brussels II Convention, the Brussels II and Brussels IIa Regulations
ARTICLE 95	Recital 91	Relations with certain multilateral conventions
ARTICLE 96	Recital 2 Recital 5 Recital 16 Recital 17 Recital 30 Recital 40 Recital 72 Recital 73	Relation with the 1980 Hague Convention
ARTICLE 97	Recital 17 Recital 25 Recital 72 Recital 92	Relation with the 1996 Hague Convention
ARTICLE 98	Recital 91	Scope of effect
ARTICLE 99	–	Treaties with the Holy See
ARTICLE 100	Recital 90	Transitional provisions
ARTICLE 101	Recital 93	Monitoring and Evaluation
ARTICLE 102	–	Member States with two or more legal systems
ARTICLE 103	Recital 94	Information to be communicated to the Commission
ARTICLE 104	–	Repeal
ARTICLE 105	–	Entry into force
–	Recital 95 Recital 96	Protocols on the positions of the UK, Ireland and Denmark
–	Recital 97	Consultation of the EDPS
–	Recital 98	Subsidiarity

LIST OF LEGISLATION

COUNCIL OF EUROPE

European Convention of 4 November 1950 for the Protection of Human Rights and Fundamental Freedoms (ECHR) 6.62, 6.64, 7.3, 7.27
Article 6. . . . . 5.37, 7.22, 8.85
Article 8. . . . . 7.3, 8.13, 8.108
Article 14. . . . . 8.108
European Convention of 20 May 1980 on Recognition and Enforcement of Decisions concerning Custody of Children and on Restoration of Custody of Children (1980 European Convention on Recognition and Enforcement of Decisions Concerning Custody of Children and on the Restoration of Custody of Children). 1.60
European Convention of 25 January 1996 on the Exercise of Children's Rights. 7.4
Article 3. . . . . .7.4
Article 6. . . . . .7.4
European Convention of 15 May 2003 on Contact Concerning Children 4.167

EUROPEAN UNION

EU BASIC TREATIES

Treaty establishing the European Economic Community (Treaty of Rome)
Article 220. . . . . .8.2
Treaty on European Union (1992 version – Maastricht Treaty)
Article K.1. . . . . .8.2
Treaty of Amsterdam of 2 October 1997 amending the Treaty on European Union, the Treaties establishing the European Communities and certain related Acts (Treaty of Amsterdam) 9.5
Treaty on European Union (Lisbon Treaty, i.e. present version – TEU)
Article 4(3) 9.79
Treaty on the Functioning of the European Union (TFEU) 8.2
Article 18. . . . . 3.88
Article 20. . . . . 8.13
Article 21. . . . . 8.14
Article 81. . . . . 11.41
Article 81(3) 1.13
Article 258. . . . . 6.62
European Union Charter of Fundamental Rights. . . . 1.79, 7.20, 12.19
Article 7. . . . . .8.13, 8.108
Article 21. . . . . .1.30, 8.108
Article 24. . . . . .6.44, 6.118, 7.7, 7.11, 7.32, 8.106, 10.41
Article 24(1) 7.2
Article 24(3) 6.78, 11.37, 11.53
Article 47. . . . . 3.87
Agreement of 24 January 2020 on the withdrawal of the United Kingdom of Great Britain and Northern Ireland from the European Union and the European Atomic Energy Community (EU Withdrawal Agreement). 12.1–12.2, 12.18, 12.20
Article 2(e) 12.1
Article 67. . . . . 1.99, 12.6–12.9
Article 67(1) 12.10
Article 67(2)(b) 12.13
Article 126. . . . . 12.1
Trade and cooperation agreement of 30 December 2020 between the European Union and the European Atomic Energy Community, of the one part, and

EU PIL CONVENTIONS

Convention of 27 September 1968
on jurisdiction and the enforcement
of judgments in civil and commercial
matters (1968 Brussels
Convention)[1] 1.6, 3.88,
5.36, 8.129,
10.1–10.2
Article 19...................... 5.66
Article 21...................... 5.37
Article 24..................... 4.196
Article 26.................. 8.32, 8.37
Article 27(4) 8.129
Article 29..................... 8.132
Article 30...................... 8.57

Convention of 16 September 1988
on jurisdiction and the enforcement
of judgments in civil and commercial
matters (1988 Lugano
Convention) 8.129

Convention of 28 May 1998 drawn
up on the basis of Article K.3 of
the Treaty on European Union, on
Jurisdiction and the Recognition
and Enforcement of Judgments in
Matrimonial Matters (1998
Brussels II Convention) 1.6, 1.34,
1.73, 3.56, 3.62,
4.201, 6.4, 8.13,
8.128, 10.1, 10.13
Article 2........................ 3.1
Article 13(3) 10.3
Article 14..................... 8.32

Convention of 30 October 2007 on
jurisdiction and the recognition
and enforcement of judgments in
civil and commercial matters
(2007 Lugano Convention)....... 8.129
Article 30...................... 8.57

the United Kingdom of Great Britain
and Northern Ireland, of the other part
(EU-UK Trade Agreement) 12.2

EU REGULATIONS

Council Regulation (EC) No 1347/2000
of 29 May 2000 on jurisdiction and
the recognition and enforcement of
judgments in matrimonial matters and
matters of parental responsibility for
children of both spouses
(Brussels II)......... 1.7–1.8, 1.19, 3.29,
3.88, 4.201, 6.4–6.6,
7.6, 8.39, 11.4, 11.42
Article 2........................ 3.1
Article 4........................ 6.4
Article 9...................... 2.28
Article 11(4) 2.3
Article 13(3) 10.3
Article 14..................... 8.32

Council Regulation (EC) No 44/2001
of 22 December 2000 on Jurisdiction
and the Recognition and Enforcement
of Judgments in Civil and
Commercial Matters (Brussels I).... 1.6,
2.44, 3.88, 4.201, 8.27
Article 27....................... 5.3
Article 30....................... 2.3
Article 37..................... 9.25

Council Regulation (EC) No 1206/2001
of 28 May 2001 on cooperation between
the courts of the Member States in the
taking of evidence in civil or commercial
matters (2001 Taking of Evidence
Regulation) 7.23

Council Regulation (EC) No 2201/2003
of 27 November 2003 concerning
jurisdiction and the recognition of
judgments in matrimonial matters and
the matters of parental responsibility,
repealing Regulation (EC) 1347/2000
(Brussels II-bis) 1.2, 1.9, 1.19, 1.57,
1.64, 1.88, 1.91, 1.93–1.94,
1.96, 1.99, 4.3, 4.168, 4.204,
6.7, 6.9, 6.35, 6.54, 6.62, 6.74,
6.88, 6.92, 6.107, 6.116, 6.127,
7.7, 7.33–7.34, 8.116, 8.118, 8.135,
9.5–9.6, 9.14, 10.5, 11.2, 11.4, 11.6,

---

[1] Strictly speaking not an EU convention but entered into between the (then) Member States of the EU and those States that were then members of the EFTA. In addition Poland acceded to the Convention before becoming an EU Member State.

11.10–11.11, 12.1, 12.3–12.4,
12.6–12.9, 12.13, 12.17–12.18,
12.21, 12.33–12.34, 12.45
Recital (3) 11.69
Recital (12) 4.10
Recital (33) 7.7
Article 1(2) 1.40
Article 1(4) 1.49–1.50
Article 2....................... 1.18
Article 3.....3.1, 3.73, 4.12, 12.33, 12.35
Article 3(1) 3.7, 3.73
Article 3(1)(b)................... 1.86
Article 6....................3.10, 3.68
Article 6(b) 3.83–3.84
Article 7...................3.68, 3.73
Article 7(1) 3.73, 3.83
Article 8......1.90, 4.9, 4.11–4.12, 4.177
Article 9...................4.162, 4.177
Article 10............ 4.177, 6.17, 6.27
Article 10(b)(iii).................. 6.25
Article 10(b)(iv) 6.26
Article 11.............1.95, 4.177, 6.7,
12.15, 12.65
Article 11(1) 6.29
Article 11(2) 6.29
Article 11(3) 6.29
Article 11(4) 6.29, 6.81
Article 11(5) 6.29, 6.75
Article 11(6) 6.29
Article 11(7) 6.29, 6.112, 6.116
Article 11(8) ...6.29, 6.116–6.117, 6.119
Article 12.............4.42, 4.55, 4.78,
4.82, 4.177
Article 12(1) 4.48, 4.55, 4.86, 4.120
Article 12(1)(a).................. 4.56
Article 12(1)(b) 1.77
Article 12(2) 4.69, 4.86–4.87
Article 12(3) 1.48, 4.46, 4.48,
4.55, 4.68, 4.81, 4.86, 4.114
Article 12(3)(b) 4.65
Article 12(4) 4.97
Article 13............ 4.99, 4.103, 4.177
Article 14.................4.177, 4.204
Article 14(3) 8.42
Article 15.......... 4.81, 4.111–4.112,
4.116–4.120, 4.124,
4.134, 4.136, 5.56, 10.45
Article 15(1) 4.114
Article 15(2) 4.154
Article 16......2.3, 2.23–2.24, 5.42, 12.9
Article 16(1)(a)................. 2.24
Article 16(1)(b) 2.24
Article 17...................... 2.28
Article 19...1.81, 5.3, 12.10, 12.12, 12.20
Article 19(1) 5.42
Article 19(2) 5.24
Article 20.............. 4.169, 4.179,
4.181, 4.183, 4.188,
4.190, 4.194, 4.201,
4.203, 4.205–4.206, 4.210
Article 20(2) 4.207
Article 21...................... 8.32
Article 22..................1.95, 12.14
Article 23..................1.95, 12.14
Article 23(b) 7.14
Article 24..............8.123, 10.45
Article 25..................... 8.123
Article 26..................... 8.123
Article 28(1) 9.19
Article 35...................... 9.25
Article 40...................... 9.24
Article 41..................... 12.15
Article 42..................7.32, 12.15
Article 46........... 10.3–10.4, 10.23
Article 42(2) 7.32
Article 47(2) 9.60
Article 53..................... 11.5
Article 54..................... 11.15
Article 55................. 1.98, 11.3,
11.21, 11.35
Article 55(a) 11.23, 11.28
Article 55(b) 11.26
Article 56................ 1.98, 8.115,
11.42–11.44, 11.47–11.48,
11.55, 11.57, 11.67
Article 56(2) 11.67
Article 57...................... 11.17
Article 58..................... 11.12
Article 60(e) 6.4
Article 61(a) 1.82, 12.20
Article 64..................... 12.13
Article 65...................... 1.11
Article 105..................... 1.14

Regulation (EC) No 1393/2007 13
November 2007 on the service in
the Member States of judicial and
extrajudicial documents in civil
or commercial matters (service
of documents) (the 2007 Service
Regulation) 2.44, 2.53, 2.55

Article 2 . . . . 2.25
Article 19 . . . . 2.54

Council Regulation (EC) No 4/2009 of 18 December 2008 on jurisdiction, applicable law, recognition and enforcement of decisions and cooperation in matters relating to maintenance obligations (EU Maintenance Regulation) 1.4, 8.79, 9.76

Article 2(3)(b) 10.16
Article 3(a) 1.86
Article 3(c) 3.51
Article 5 . . . . 1.86, 4.71
Article 7 . . . . 3.87
Article 13 . . . . 1.87
Article 19 . . . . 8.98
Article 21(3) 8.57, 8.62
Article 23(2) 8.37
Article 25 . . . . 8.57, 8.59, 8.62
Article 41(2) 9.20
Article 42 . . . . 8.132
Article 49 . . . . 11.4
Article 50 . . . . 11.4
Article 51 . . . . 11.4
Article 52 . . . . 11.4
Article 53 . . . . 11.4
Article 54 . . . . 11.4
Article 55 . . . . 11.4
Article 56 . . . . 11.4
Article 57 . . . . 11.4
Article 58 . . . . 11.4
Article 59 . . . . 11.4
Article 60 . . . . 11.4
Article 61 . . . . 11.4
Article 62 . . . . 11.4
Article 63 . . . . 11.4

Council Regulation (EU) No 1259/2010 of 20 December 2010 implementing enhanced cooperation in the area of the law applicable to divorce and legal separation (Rome III) 1.4, 3.8, 5.62, 8.130

Article 9 . . . . 3.66

Council Regulation (EU) No 650/2012 of 4 July 2012 on jurisdiction, applicable law, recognition and enforcement of decisions and acceptance and enforcement of authentic instruments in matters of succession (Succession Regulation) 1.4, 1.19, 8.59

Article 11 . . . . 3.87
Article 31 . . . . 8.11
Article 39(2) 8.37
Article 41 . . . . 8.132
Article 42 . . . . 8.57, 8.61
Article 43 . . . . 9.4
Article 45 . . . . 9.4
Article 46 . . . . 9.4
Article 47 . . . . 9.4
Article 48 . . . . 9.4
Article 49 . . . . 9.4
Article 50 . . . . 9.4
Article 51 . . . . 9.4
Article 52 . . . . 9.4
Article 53 . . . . 9.4
Article 54 . . . . 9.4
Article 55 . . . . 9.4
Article 56 . . . . 9.4
Article 57 . . . . 9.4
Article 58 . . . . 9.4

Council Regulation (EU) No 1215/2012 of the European Parliament and the Council on jurisdiction and the recognition and enforcement of judgments in civil and commercial matters (Brussels I-bis) 1.42, 1.56, 8.4, 8.39, 8.67, 9.6, 10.19, 10.35

Recital (23) 3.34
Article 2(c) 10.6
Article 26 . . . . 2.44, 4.71
Article 28 . . . . 2.44
Article 30 . . . . 1.87
Article 30(3) 5.11
Article 31(3) 5.14
Article 32 . . . . 2.3
Article 36(2) 8.37
Article 36(3) 8.49
Article 38 . . . . 8.62
Article 41(3) 9.20
Article 44 . . . . 9.25
Article 45(1)(b) 8.92
Article 45(1)(e) 8.125
Article 45(3) 8.125
Article 48 . . . . 9.44
Article 52 . . . . 8.132
Article 54 . . . . 8.11, 9.78
Article 66(1) 12.9

Regulation (EU) No 606/2013 of the European Parliament and of the Council of 12 June 2013 on mutual recognition of protection measures in civil matters
  Article 11 .... 11.51
Council Regulation (EU) No 2016/1103 of 24 June 2016 implementing enhanced cooperation in the area of jurisdiction, applicable law and the recognition and enforcement of decisions in matters of matrimonial property regimes (Matrimonial Property Regulation). 1.4, 1.19, 8.59, 9.76
  Article 5 .... 3.51
  Article 11 .... 3.87
  Article 36(2) 8.37
  Article 37 .... 8.98
  Article 40 .... 8.132
  Article 41 .... 8.57, 8.62
  Article 42 .... 9.4
  Article 44 .... 9.4
  Article 45 .... 9.4
  Article 46 .... 9.4
  Article 47 .... 9.4
  Article 48 .... 9.4
  Article 49 .... 9.4
  Article 50 .... 9.4
  Article 51 .... 9.4
  Article 52 .... 9.4
  Article 53 .... 9.4
  Article 54 .... 9.4
  Article 55 .... 9.4
  Article 56 .... 9.4
  Article 57 .... 9.4
Council Regulation (EU) No 2016/1104 of 24 June 2016 implementing enhanced cooperation in the area of jurisdiction, applicable law and the recognition and enforcement of decisions in matters of property consequences of registered partnerships (Partnership Property Regulation) 1.4, 8.59
  Article 11 .... 3.87
  Article 36(2) 8.37
  Article 40 .... 8.132
  Article 41 .... 8.57, 8.62
  Article 42 .... 9.4
  Article 44 .... 9.4
  Article 45 .... 9.4
  Article 46 .... 9.4
  Article 47 .... 9.4
  Article 48 .... 9.4
  Article 49 .... 9.4
  Article 50 .... 9.4
  Article 51 .... 9.4
  Article 52 .... 9.4
  Article 53 .... 9.4
  Article 54 .... 9.4
  Article 55 .... 9.4
  Article 56 .... 9.4
  Article 57 .... 9.4
Council Regulation (EU) No 2019/1111 of 25 June 2019 on jurisdiction, the recognition and enforcement of decisions in matrimonial matters and the matters of parental responsibility, and international child abduction (Brussels II-ter) 1.1, 1.4–1.6, 1.14–1.15, 1.29, 1.31–1.32, 1.34–1.36, 1.58, 1.88–1.89, 1.92, 1.94, 1.96, 1.99, 3.61, 4.1, 4.45, 4.47, 4.77, 4.93, 4.98, 4.103, 4.105–4.106, 4.113, 4.115, 4.168, 4.203–4.204, 4.206, 5.11, 5.30–5.31, 5.36, 5.38, 5.62, 6.2–6.3, 6.8–6.10, 6.18, 6.20, 6.29, 6.31, 6.41, 6.48, 6.53–6.54, 6.74, 6.92, 6.94–6.95, 6.99, 6.107–6.108, 6.112, 6.118, 6.127, 7.8–7.9, 7.22, 7.27, 7.31, 7.34, 8.1, 8.4, 8.10, 8.12, 8.17, 8.21, 8.48, 8.60, 8.79, 8.97, 8.116, 9.2, 9.6–9.7, 9.11, 9.13–9.15, 9.27, 9.37–9.39, 9.46, 9.49, 9.57, 9.60, 9.72, 9.76, 9.78, 10.5, 10.11, 10.13, 10.15–10.16, 10.22–10.23, 10.25, 10.35, 10.41, 11.1, 11.3–11.4, 11.6, 11.17, 11.35, 11.50–11.51, 11.60, 11.71, 12.34, 12.45, 12.55
  Recital (2) 8.82
  Recital (3) 1.3, 8.2, 8.82, 11.69
  Recital (5) 1.19, 1.23, 1.25, 9.16
  Recital (6) 8.82
  Recital (7) 1.37
  Recital (9) 1.26, 5.54, 8.31
  Recital (10) 1.42
  Recital (11) 1.41
  Recital (12) 1.50

Recital (14)	1.19, 1.33, 1.51, 7.11, 10.20
Recital (16)	6.92
Recital (17)	1.35
Recital (18)	6.45, 8.19
Recital (19)	4.5, 4.12, 8.106
Recital (20)	4.5, 4.10
Recital (21)	4.129
Recital (22)	6.27
Recital (23)	4.49, 4.59, 4.61, 4.72
Recital (25)	4.105, 4.107, 4.112
Recital (26)	4.112–4.113, 4.152
Recital (27)	4.112
Recital (29)	4.167
Recital (30)	4.199–4.200, 4.211–4.212, 4.215, 9.16
Recital (32)	1.45
Recital (33)	1.45
Recital (34)	3.76–3.78
Recital (35)	2.14
Recital (39)	1.19, 7.2, 7.18, 7.20, 7.23–7.24
Recital (41)	1.20, 6.52–6.53
Recital (42)	6.56–6.59
Recital (43)	6.66, 6.68, 6.70–6.71
Recital (45)	6.82–6.83
Recital (46)	6.86
Recital (47)	6.93
Recital (48)	6.104
Recital (50)	6.111
Recital (51)	6.111
Recital (53)	7.24
Recital (54)	8.32, 8.37, 8.83
Recital (56)	8.84, 8.112
Recital (57)	7.19, 8.120
Recital (59)	9.16
Recital (62)	9.36
Recital (63)	9.34, 9.68
Recital (67)	9.27
Recital (68)	9.28
Recital (69)	9.31, 9.65, 9.70
Recital (71)	7.11, 10.41
Recital (72)	11.7–11.8, 11.10
Recital (73)	11.1
Recital (74)	11.14
Recital (76)	11.19–11.20
Recital (81)	11.31
Recital (82)	11.38
Recital (83)	11.57, 11.61–11.62, 11.64
Recital (84)	11.48–11.49, 11.52–11.54
Recital (85)	11.31, 11.66
Recital (86)	11.12
Recital (90)	1.16–1.17, 1.21, 1.30
Recital (92)	1.85
Recital (96)	1.21
Article 1	1.22
Article 1(2)	1.38, 7.12, 8.14
Article 1(2)(d)	1.38, 1.41
Article 1(3)	1.65, 6.31, 7.12
Article 1(4)	7.12
Article 1(4)(a)	8.34, 8.79
Article 1(4)(e)	8.79
Article 2	1.18, 10.17
Article 2(1)	1.52, 4.200, 4.205, 9.17
Article 2(1)(a)	6.31, 6.92, 9.15
Article 2(1)(b)	9.16
Article 2(2)(1)	8.62, 10.19
Article 2(2)(2)	10.6
Article 2(2)(3)	10.8
Article 2(2)(7)	1.37, 6.32, 8.110
Article 2(2)(9)	1.38, 8.16
Article 2(2)(10)	1.38
Article 2(3)	1.55
Article 2(7)	5.55
Article 2(8)	11.18
Article 2(9)	6.42
Article 2(11)	6.33–6.35, 6.39, 6.45, 12.63
Article 2(11)(a)	6.42
Article 2(11)(b)	6.46
Article 3	1.27, 1.56, 1.90, 3.6, 3.10, 3.12, 3.19, 3.58, 3.71, 3.74, 3.77, 3.80, 3.85, 4.4, 4.45, 4.98, 5.20, 8.125, 10.45
Article 3(a)	3.18–3.19, 3.22, 3.26, 3.51
Article 3(a)(ii)	3.11
Article 3(a)(iii)	3.75
Article 3(a)(iv)	3.19
Article 3(a)(v)	3.11, 3.15, 3.19, 3.21, 3.75, 12.35
Article 3(a)(vi)	3.11, 3.15, 3.21, 3.75, 12.35
Article 3(b)	3.18, 3.23–3.24, 3.26
Article 4	3.10, 3.71, 3.74–3.75, 3.77, 3.85, 5.20, 5.51, 8.125, 10.45
Article 5	3.10, 3.55, 3.58, 3.61, 3.63, 3.66, 3.71,

3.74–3.75, 3.77, 3.85, 5.20,
5.51, 8.125, 10.45
Article 6 . . . . 1.27, 2.35, 3.10,
3.67–3.68, 3.80, 3.89,
5.20, 8.125, 10.45
Article 6(1) 2.36, 3.69, 3.71,
3.74–3.75, 3.80, 3.83, 3.90
Article 6(2) 3.68, 3.70, 3.79,
3,80–3.81, 3.83–3.86, 3.90
Article 6(3) 3.88, 3.90–3.92
Article 7 . . . . . 1.56, 1.69, 1.90, 2.37, 3.16,
4.4, 4.7, 4.33–4.34, 4.45,
4.121–4.122, 4.127, 4.129,
4.135, 4.166, 4.176, 4.208, 5.20,
6.16, 8.125, 10.45, 12.44
Article 7(1) 1.72, 2.4, 3.17, 4.3
Article 8 . . . . . . 1.56, 4.3, 4.25, 4.33–4.39,
4.41, 4.129–4.130, 4.166,
4.208, 5.20, 6.32, 8.125,
10.45, 12.44
Article 8(1) 4.33
Article 8(2) 4.34, 4.40
Article 9 . . . . 1.56, 4.3, 4.36,
4.166, 4.208, 5.20, 6.16–6.19,
6.27, 6.33, 8.125, 10.45, 12.62
Article 9(a) 6.20
Article 9(b) 6.21–6.22, 6.24, 12.62
Article 9(b)(i) 6.21–6.22
Article 9(b)(ii) 6.21–6.22
Article 9(b)(iii) 6.21–6.22, 6.24
Article 9(b)(iv) 2.4, 6.21–6.22, 6.25
Article 9(b)(v) 6.21–6.22, 6.26, 6.117
Article 10 . . . . 1.56, 1.78, 2.34, 4.3,
4.42, 4.47, 4.98, 4.102,
4.114, 4.121–4.122, 4.166,
4.172, 4.176, 4.208, 5.20,
5,43, 5.45, 6.16, 8.30, 8.125,
10.10, 10.45, 11.50, 12.57
Article 10(1) 4.51
Article 10(1)(a). 4.52, 4.98
Article 10(1)(b) 4.56, 4.63–4.64,
4.114
Article 10(1)(b)(i) 4.56, 4.72–4.74,
4.76, 4.93
Article 10(1)(b)(ii) 4.56, 4.62,
4.71–4.74, 4.76
Article 10(1)(c). 4.78, 4.91
Article 10(2) 4.61, 4.82, 5.44, 10.10
Article 10(3) 4.69, 4.84,
4.86–4.88, 4.158

Article 10(4) 4.74, 4.76
Article 11 . . . . 1.56, 2.37, 4.36,
4.99–4.107, 4.109–4.110,
4.122, 4.166, 4.172,
4.176, 4.208, 5.20,
8.125, 10.45
Article 11(2) 4.108
Article 12 . . . . 1.56, 2.4, 4.93, 4.111,
4.116–4.119, 4.122–4.123,
4.154, 4.163, 4.208, 5.17,
5.20, 5.55–5.56, 6.16, 8.125,
10.45, 11.40, 12.58
Article 12(1) 4.133, 4.135,
4.140, 4.149–4.150
Article 12(1)(a). 4.151,
4.155, 4.160
Article 12(1)(b) 4.152,
4.154–4.155, 4.160
Article 12(2) 4.135, 4.149, 4.151
Article 12(3) 4.53, 4.64, 4.140,
4.149, 4.160
Article 12(4) 4.54, 4.127–4.128,
4.133, 4.163, 12.58
Article 12(5) 4.74, 4.91–4.93,
4.114, 4.122
Article 13 . . . . 1.56, 2.38, 4.93,
4.103, 4.111, 4.116–4.119,
4.123, 4.162, 4.208, 5.17,
5.20, 5.55–5.56, 8.125,
10.45, 11.40, 11.50, 12.58
Article 13(2) 4.165
Article 14 . . . . 1.56, 2.35–2.36,
3.69–3.70, 4.101,
4.106, 4.166, 4.208,
5.20, 8.125, 10.45
Article 15 . . . . 1.53, 1.56, 1.75, 4.38,
4.109, 4.168–4.170,
4.173–4.176, 4.178, 4.180,
4.183, 4.193, 4.195,
4.199–4.200, 4.204–4.206,
4.210–4.211, 4.214–4.215,
5.7, 5.20–5.22, 5.26–5.27,
6.77, 9.16, 11.40, 11.50, 12.56
Article 15(1) 4.173, 4.185
Article 15(2) 4.212, 4.214
Article 15(3) 4.197, 4.205,
4.207–4.208,
4.210–4.212, 4.215
Article 16 . . . . 1.43–1.44, 1.48, 8.45
Article 16(2) 1.47, 8.51

Article 16(3)	1.42, 1.45, 8.48
Article 17	1.93, 2.2, 2.6–2.8, 2.20, 2.65, 3.15, 5.12, 6.58
Article 17(a)	2.17, 2.24
Article 17(b)	2.24
Article 17(c)	2.3, 2.12
Article 18	2.2, 2.27, 2.29, 2.31–2.32, 2.35–2.36, 2.40–2.42, 2.45, 2.47, 2.65, 3.13, 3.71
Article 19	2.2, 2.26, 2.43–2.45, 2.47–2.48, 2.51, 2.54–2.55, 2.57, 2.60, 8.93
Article 19(1)	2.17, 2.53, 2.62, 2.64
Article 19(2)	2.44, 2.53, 2.55
Article 19(3)	2.44, 2.53
Article 20	1.81, 2.4, 2.41, 4.208, 5.3–5.4, 5.9, 5.16, 5.22, 5.34, 5.53, 5.55, 5.64, 5.66–5.68, 8.101, 8.103, 8.125, 11.40, 12.12
Article 20(1)	5.4, 5.6, 5.16–5.17, 5.60, 5.71
Article 20(2)	5.4, 5.7, 5.16–5.17, 5.22, 5.60, 5.65
Article 20(3)	5.31–5.32, 5.47–5.48, 5.50, 5.52
Article 20(4)	4.89, 5.3, 5.14
Article 20(5)	4.89, 5.3, 5.14–5.15, 5.44, 5.46
Article 21	6.72, 7.1, 7.8–7.13, 7.20, 7.34, 8.72, 8.117, 8.119–8.120, 10.27, 10.41, 12.66
Article 21(1)	7.10, 7.14–7.15, 7.17, 7.21, 7.24–7.25
Article 21(2)	7.10, 7.25, 7.27
Article 22	6.16, 6.28–6.30, 6.47
Article 23	6.28, 12.66, 12.68
Article 23(1)	6.49
Article 23(2)	6.49
Article 24	6.28, 6.55–6.56, 6.60, 6.62, 12.66, 12.68
Article 24(1)	6.61
Article 24(2)	6.55
Article 24(3)	6.55–6.56, 6.59
Article 25	6.28, 6.66–6.67, 6.69
Article 26	6.28, 6.72, 8.117, 8.119, 10.27, 12.66
Article 27	6.28, 12.66
Article 27(1)	6.75
Article 27(2)	4.178, 6.77–6.79
Article 27(3)	6.81–6.82, 6.84, 6.89, 6.103, 12.68
Article 27(4)	6.83, 6.87, 6.89
Article 27(5)	1.53, 4.168, 4.178, 4.200, 4.205, 4.211, 6.79, 6.85, 6.88–6.89, 6.94, 9.16, 9.22
Article 27(6)	6.60, 6.93, 6.95
Article 28	6.28, 6.60, 6.91
Article 28(1)	1.101, 6.90
Article 28(2)	6.63–6.64, 6.90
Article 28(6)	9.44
Article 29	2.4, 6.28, 6.100, 12.66
Article 29(1)	6.101, 6.103
Article 29(3)	6.108, 6.114–6.117
Article 29(5)	6.109, 6.114–6.116
Article 29(6)	6.117, 6.119, 6.126–6.127, 7.29, 8.112, 9.63, 9.74
Article 30	11.69, 12.59
Article 30(1)	8.32, 10.29
Article 30(2)	8.34–8.35, 9.20
Article 30(3)	8.36, 8.42–8.43, 8.46, 8.61, 8.68, 8.82, 8.132, 8.136, 9.19
Article 30(4)	8.41
Article 30(5)	8.45, 8.47, 8.49, 8.68, 8.82, 8.132, 8.136, 10.29
Article 31	8.67–8.68, 10.29
Article 31(1)	8.67
Article 31(2)	8.74, 8.139
Article 31(3)	8.75, 8.139
Article 32	8.77
Article 32(1)	10.26
Article 33	8.56, 8.65
Article 33(a)	8.59, 8.60, 8.64
Article 33(b)	8.61
Article 34	9.3, 9.45
Article 34(1)	9.7, 9.12, 12.15
Article 34(2)	9.13
Article 35	9.3
Article 35(1)	9.21, 11.37
Article 35(2)	9.22
Article 35(3)	9.23
Article 35(4)	9.23

Article 36. . . . . .7.28, 8.71, 8.74, 8.76–8.77, 8.134, 9.3, 9.21	Article 47. . . . . .6.124, 6.126, 7.28, 8.137, 8.139, 9.3, 9.28, 9.47
Article 36(3) 7.30	Article 47(2) 6.123
Article 37. . . . . .7.30, 9.3	Article 47(3) 2.17, 6.121
Article 38. . . . . .1.95, 8.53, 8.82, 8.85, 8.105, 8.110, 12.14	Article 47(4) 6.121
	Article 48. . . . . 7.30, 7.34, 8.137, 8.141, 9.3, 9.28, 9.47
Article 38(a) 8.53, 8.86	
Article 38(b) 2.17, 2.46–2.47, 2.51, 2.65, 8.89, 8.91–8.94, 10.32	Article 49. . . . . .9.3
	Article 50. . . . . .8.140, 9.3, 9.34, 9.49–9.50, 9.57–9.59, 9.61–9.63, 9.66, 9.69
Article 38(c) . . . 8.89, 8.101, 8.104, 10.34	
Article 38(d) 8.54, 8.89, 8.103, 8.114, 10.34	Article 50(a) 9.59
	Article 50(b) 9.59
Article 39. . . . . .1.95, 8.53, 8.82, 8.85, 8.105, 8.141, 9.37, 9.49, 9.56, 9.69, 11.69, 12.14, 12.60	Article 51. . . . . .9.3
	Article 51(1) 9.77
	Article 51(2) 9.20
	Article 52. . . . . 9.3, 9.18
Article 39(1) 1.95, 8.85, 8.121	Article 53. . . . . 8.78, 9.3
Article 39(1)(a). 8.53, 8.105	Article 53(1) 9.72
Article 39(1)(b) 2.17, 2.65, 8.105, 8.109, 9.55	Article 53(2) 9.72
	Article 53(3) 9.74
Article 39(1)(c). 8.110, 10.39	Article 54. . . . . .9.3
Article 39(1)(d) 8.105, 8.112, 9.59, 10.40	Article 55. . . . . .9.3
	Article 56. . . . . .9.3, 9.24, 9.34, 9.69–9.70
Article 39(1)(e). 8.54, 8.105, 8.114, 9.59, 10.40	
	Article 56(1) 9.26, 9.40
Article 39(1)(f). 8.115, 11.69	Article 56(2) 9.28, 9.31, 9.48
Article 39(2) 8.72, 8.80, 8.85, 8.117, 8.122, 10.41, 10.42	Article 56(2)(c). 9.53
	Article 56(3) 9.28, 9.48
Article 39(2)(a). 1.95, 7.19, 8.122, 10.42	Article 56(4) 6.90, 9.29, 9.31, 9.33
	Article 56(5) 9.30–9.31
Article 39(2)(b) 1.95, 7.19, 8.122, 10.42	Article 56(6) 9.30–9.31, 9.49–9.50, 9.54, 9.56–9.57, 9.64, 9.67, 9.70, 9.73
Article 40. . . . . 1.101, 8.42–8.43, 8.132, 8.136, 9.52, 9.54, 10.29	
	Article 57. . . . . 9.3, 9.34–9.35, 9.48–9.50, 9.54–9.57, 9.68, 9.70
Article 40(1) 8.46, 8.52, 8.61, 8.68, 8.82, 9.39	Article 58. . . . . .1.101, 9.3
	Article 58(1) 9.37
Article 40(2) 8.43, 9.67	Article 59. . . . . .8.36, 9.3, 9.38, 9.54
Article 41. . . . . .9.3, 9.34, 9.36, 9.49–9.50, 9.69	Article 59(1) 9.40
	Article 59(2) 9.41
Article 42(1)(a). 9.62	Article 59(3) 9.42
Article 42(2) 6.120, 8.137	Article 59(4) 9.42
Article 43. . . . . 8.136	Article 59(5) 9.41, 10.26
Article 43(2) 8.139	Article 59(6) 9.43
Article 44. . . . . 8.137	Article 60. . . . . .8.36, 9.3, 9.44, 9.46
Article 44(b) 8.137–8.138	Article 61. . . . . 1.101, 8.36, 9.3, 9.71
Article 45. . . . . 9.3, 9.8	Article 61(2) 9.71
Article 46. . . . . .9.3	Article 62. . . . . 1.101, 8.36, 9.3

Article 63	9.3, 9.25, 9.47, 9.71	Article 79(a)	11.22, 11.24
Article 63(2)	9.47	Article 79(b)	11.25
Article 64	10.5, 10.11, 10.17, 10.18	Article 79(c)	11.26
		Article 79(d)	8.25, 11.25
Article 65	1.55, 10.5, 10.11–10.12, 10.17, 10.44	Article 79(e)	11.25
		Article 79(f)	11.25
Article 65(1)	10.28	Article 79(g)	11.27
Article 65(2)	10.23, 10.30	Article 80	11.9, 11.16, 11.21, 11.28, 11.54
Article 66	10.5, 10.11, 10.29		
Article 66(2)(a)	10.18	Article 80(1)	11.29
Article 66(5)	10.17, 10.25	Article 80(1)(a)	11.29–11.30
Article 67	10.5, 10.11	Article 80(1)(b)	11.29–11.30
Article 68	9.49–9.50, 10.5, 10.11, 10.31	Article 80(1)(c)	11.29–11.30
		Article 80(2)	11.32–11.33
Article 68(1)	10.32	Article 80(3)	11.31
Article 68(1)(a)	10.33, 10.45	Article 80(4)	11.31
Article 68(1)(b)	10.34	Article 81	11.2, 11.9, 11.36–11.38
Article 68(1)(c)	10.34	Article 82	8.115, 11.2, 11.9, 11.16, 11.45, 11.48–11.49, 11.52, 11.67, 11.69
Article 68(2)	10.37		
Article 68(2)(a)	10.39, 10.45		
Article 68(2)(b)	10.39	Article 82(1)	11.45–11.46, 11.49, 11.55, 11.57, 11.59
Article 68(2)(c)	10.40		
Article 68(2)(d)	10.40	Article 82(2)	11.48, 11.58
Article 68(3)	10.17, 10.27, 10.37, 10.41	Article 82(3)	11.54, 11.56
		Article 82(4)	11.59
Article 69	2.33, 5.30, 8.84, 8.88, 8.123–8.124, 9.51, 10.43–10.45	Article 82(5)	8.115, 11.55
		Article 82(6)	8.116, 11.65–11.66
		Article 82(8)	11.57
Article 70	8.87, 8.123, 8.128, 8.131, 10.48	Article 83	11.10, 11.71
		Article 83(1)	11.71
Article 71	4.176, 8.71, 8.119, 8.122–8.123, 8.130, 8.132, 8.134, 9.33, 9.51, 10.48	Article 84	11.12
		Article 86	11.2, 11.19, 11.39
		Article 86(2)	11.40
Article 72	8.59	Article 86(2)(a)	4.153
Article 73	8.68, 9.75	Article 86(2)(b)	4.214
Article 74	8.68	Article 87	11.2, 11.34–11.35
Article 76	11.5–11.6	Article 87(1)	11.34
Article 77	11.13–11.14	Article 87(2)	11.34
Article 77(1)	11.15	Article 87(3)	11.34
Article 77(2)	11.16	Article 87(4)	11.34
Article 77(3)	11.16	Article 91	8.76
Article 78	11.9, 11.17	Article 91(1)	8.76
Article 78(1)	11.18	Article 91(2)	8.76
Article 78(2)	11.18, 11.22	Article 91(3)	11.9
Article 78(3)	11.18	Article 91(4)	8.76
Article 78(4)	11.19	Article 94	6.32
Article 78(5)	11.18	Article 94(1)	1.59
Article 78(6)	11.21	Article 95	1.73
Article 79	1.67, 11.9, 11.21, 11.26	Article 96	1.64–1.65, 6.30–6.32
		Article 97	1.68, 1.73, 1.75, 4.106

Article 97(1) 1.68–1.70,
1.72–1.73, 1.76,
1.79, 4.98, 4.106
Article 97(1)(a). . . 4.95, 4.97–4.98, 4.107
Article 97(2) 1.68–1.69,
1.74–1.81, 1.83
Article 97(2)(a). 4.94, 4.96–4.97
Article 97(2)(b) 4.123
Article 97(2)(c). 5.2, 12.20
Article 98. . . . . 1.66, 1.85
Article 98(1) 1.61, 1.67
Article 99. . . . . 1.63
Article 100. . . . . 2.4, 12.9
Article 100(1) 1.93, 1.97,
1.100, 12.13
Article 100(2) 1.93, 1.97–1.98, 1.101
Article 101(2) 1.102
Article 103. . . . . 1.55, 7.28,
9.37, 9.71, 10.7,
11.16, 11.55, 11.58
Article 103(1)(b) 8.71
Article 103(1)(c). 8.41
Article 103(1)(d) 9.18
Article 103(1)(f). 11.9
Article 103(1)(h) 11.9
Article 105. 1.14
Annex II 8.67
Annex III. 7.29, 8.16,
8.19, 8.67,
8.118, 9.21
Annex IV. 7.29, 8.139, 9.22
Annex V 7.29, 8.139
Annex VI. 7.29
Annex VIII 10.17, 10.25
Annex IX. 10.17, 10.25

Regulation (EU) 2020/1783 of the
European Parliament and of the
Council of 25 November 2020 on
cooperation between the courts
of the Member States in the taking
of evidence in civil and commercial
matters (taking of evidence) (recast)
(2020 Taking of Evidence
Regulation) 6.76, 6.128, 7.23

Regulation (EU) 2020/1784 of the
European Parliament and of the
Council of 25 November 2020 on the
service in the Member States of judicial
and extrajudicial documents in civil
or commercial matters (service of
documents) (recast) (2020
Service Regulation) 2.25, 2.44,
2.53–2.57
Article 3. . . . . 2.25
Article 12(1) 8.99
Article 22. . . . . 2.54, 2.57, 2.60
Article 22(1) 2.57
Article 22(2) 2.58, 2.62
Article 22(3) 2.58, 2.62
Article 22(4) 2.58
Article 22(5) 2.58
Article 63. . . . . 2.55
Article 63(2) 2.55

EU DIRECTIVES

Directive 2004/38 on the Rights of
Citizens of the Union and their family
members to move and reside freely
within the EU 1.29

HAGUE CONFERENCE FOR PRIVATE INTERNATIONAL LAW

Convention of 5 October 1961
concerning the Powers of Authorities
and the Law Applicable in respect
of the Protection of Minors (1961
Hague Protection of Minors
Convention) 1.60, 4.167

Convention of 15 November 1965 on
the Service Abroad of Judicial and
Extrajudicial Documents in Civil or
Commercial Matters (1965 Hague
Service Convention) 2.53, 2.59, 2.64
Article 15. . . . . 2.54, 2.59

Convention of 1 June 1970 on the
Recognition of Divorces and Legal
Separations (1970 Hague Divorce
Convention) 1.60,
12.23–12.24, 12.37
Preamble 12.26
Article 1. . . . . 12.26

Article 2 . . . . 12.27
Article 3 . . . . 12.28
Article 7 . . . . 12.29
Article 8 . . . . 12.29
Article 9 . . . . 12.29
Article 10 . . . . 12.29
Article 17 . . . . 12.26

Convention of 25 October 1980
on the Civil Aspects of International
Child Abduction (1980 Hague
Abduction Convention) 1.2, 1.35,
1.59, 1.64, 1.66–1.67,
1.96, 4.4, 4.28–4.29,
5.68, 6.2–6.8, 6.10,
6.15–6.17, 6.30–6.33, 6.48,
6.50–6.51, 6.65, 6.70, 6.74,
6.78, 6.90, 6.96, 7.7–7.8, 7.12,
7.29, 7.32, 9.5, 9.15, 11.1, 11.7,
11.11, 12.15–12.17, 12.47,
12.50, 12.56, 12.64–12.67
Article 3 . . . . 6.35, 12.63
Article 7(a) 11.23
Article 7(d) 11.28
Article 7(e) 11.28
Article 7(f) 11.37
Article 11 . . . . 12.66
Article 12 . . . . 6.12, 6.14
Article 12(2) 6.23–6.24
Article 13 . . . . 1.95, 6.5, 6.12, 6.96,
6.101–6.102, 12.16
Article 13(1)(a) 1.95, 6.20, 6.101
Article 13(1)(b) 1.95, 4.168, 4.199,
4.211, 6.21, 6.24, 6.78,
6.81–6.82, 6.84–6.85, 6.89,
6.100–6.101, 6.103–6.105,
6.107, 6.121, 6.125, 9.22,
9.33, 12.66–12.68
Article 13(2) 1.95, 6.21, 6.24,
6.100, 6.103–6.105, 6.107,
6.121, 9.63, 12.66
Article 16 . . . . 6.15, 6.73
Article 19 . . . . 6.15
Article 20 . . . . 6.13, 6.24, 6.104
Article 21 . . . . 1.67, 6.32
Article 29 . . . . 6.11, 6.29

Convention of 29 May 1993 on
Protection of Children and Co-operation
in Respect of Intercountry Adoption
(1993 Hague Adoption Convention)
Article 7(1) 11.16

Convention of 19 October 1996
on Jurisdiction, Applicable Law,
Recognition, Enforcement and
Co-operation in Respect of Parental
Responsibility and Measures for the
Protection of Children (1996 Hague
Child Protection Convention) 1.17,
1.35–1.36, 1.59, 1.68, 1.70,
1.72, 1.74, 1.76, 1.79, 1.82,
1.88, 1.92, 4.4, 4.57, 4.94–4.98,
4.105–4.107, 4.123, 4.167,
5.2, 6.43, 8.21, 9.60, 11.2, 11.7,
11.11, 11.33, 11.38, 12.23–12.24,
12.43–12.47, 12.49–12.52,
12.54–12.55, 12.64
Article 1(1)(a) 12.49
Article 5(2) 1.73
Article 5(3) 1.73
Article 6 . . . . 4.99, 4.103–4.105
Article 7 . . . . 6.17, 12.62, 12.64
Article 7(1)(b) 12.62
Article 7(2) 12.63
Article 8 . . . . 1.80, 4.111, 4.123, 12.58
Article 8(2)(c) 12.58
Article 9 . . . . 1.80, 4.111, 4.123,
4.162, 12.58
Article 10 . . . . 1.77, 4.94, 12.44, 12.57
Article 10(1) 1.77
Article 11 . . . . 1.75, 4.171, 4.199,
4.202, 6.88, 12.56
Article 12 . . . . 4.169, 4.171,
4.199, 12.56
Article 13 . . . . 1.82–1.84, 5.2,
12.20, 12.44
Article 15(1) 1.85
Article 15(2) 8.25
Article 15(3) 8.22
Article 16 . . . . 4.57
Article 16(1) 8.22
Article 23 . . . . 12.60
Article 23(1) 12.59
Article 24 . . . . 12.59
Article 26 . . . . 9.4, 12.60
Article 27 . . . . 8.132
Article 28 . . . . 12.60
Article 30 . . . . 11.16
Article 31(c) 11.23
Article 33 . . . . 11.42, 11.45,
11.60, 12.53
Article 35(1) 11.37

Article 35(2) 11.37
Article 36 .... 11.33
Article 52(2) 4.107
Article 52(3) 1.73, 4.107
Convention of 13 January 2000
on the International Protection
of Adults 1.35

INTERNATIONAL COMMISSION ON CIVIL STATUS

Luxembourg Convention of 8 September 1967 on the Recognition of Decisions Relating to the Validity of Marriages (1967 Luxembourg Convention) 1.60–1.61

UNITED NATIONS

Vienna Convention of 24 April 1963 on Consular Relations
Article 37(b) 11.54

Convention of 20 November 1989 on the Rights of the Child (UNCRC) 1.79, 7.2, 7.4, 7.20, 8.106
Article 8 .... 11.53
Article 9 .... 6.78, 11.53
Article 9(3) 11.37
Article 10 .... 11.37
Article 11 .... 6.2
Article 12 ..... 7.2–7.3, 7.11, 10.41, 12.66
Article 12(2) 7.14
Article 20 .... 11.53

MISCELLANEOUS INTERNATIONAL AGREEMENTS

'Concordato lateranense' of 11 February 1929 between Italy and the Holy See, modified by the agreement with additional Protocol signed in Rome on 18 February 1984 .... 1.63

Convention of 6 February 1931 between Denmark, Finland, Iceland, Norway and Sweden comprising international private law provisions on marriage, adoption and guardianship (1931 Nordic Convention) 1.59, 1.62

Agreement between the Holy See and Spain on legal affairs of 3 January 1979 .... 1.63

Agreement between the Holy See and Malta on the recognition of civil effects to canonical marriages and to decisions of ecclesiastical authorities and tribunals on those marriages of 3 February 1993, including the Protocol of application of the same date, with the third Additional Protocol of 27 January 2014 .... 1.63

International Treaty (Concordat) between the Holy See and Portugal, signed at the Vatican City on 18 May 2004 .... 1.63

NATIONAL LAWS

FRANCE

Code Civil (France)
Article 14 .... 3.92
Article 388-1 .... 10.41

IRELAND

Withdrawal of the United Kingdom from the European Union (Consequential Provisions) Act 2020 (Parts 17, 18, 19 and 20) (Commencement) Order 2020 (Ireland)
Article 2 .... 12.31

Withdrawal of the United Kingdom from the European Union (Consequential Provisions) Act 2020 (Ireland) 12.1
Section 125 .... 12.31
Section 126 .... 12.31

UNITED KINGDOM

European Communities Act 1972 .... 12.48
    Section 1(2).................... 12.47
Domicile and Matrimonial
    Proceedings Act 1973 .... 12.32
    Section 5 .... 12.33
    Section 5(2).................... 12.34
    Section 5(2)(a) 12.33
    Section 5(2)(d) 12.35
    Section 5(2)(e) 12.35
    Section 5(2)(f) 12.34
    Section 5(3).................... 12.33
    Section 7 .... 12.36
Matrimonial Causes (Northern Ireland)
    Order 1978 .... 12.32
    Article 49...................... 12.36
Civil Jurisdiction and Judgments
    Act 1982....................... 12.48
Family Law Act 1986 .... 12.37–12.38,
                   12.47, 12.49, 12.51
    Section 2 .... 12.49
    Section 19 .... 12.49
    Section 46 ....12.38–12.39
    Section 46(2)................... 12.40
    Section 48 .... 12.38
    Section 51 .... 12.41
    Section 51(3)(a) 12.41
    Section 51(3)(b) 12.41
    Section 54(1)................... 12.38
    Section 55(2)................... 12.42
Parental Responsibility and Measures
    for the Protection of Children
    (International Obligations
    (England and Wales and Northern
    Ireland) Regulations 2010........ 12.47
    Regulation 8 .... 12.60
Parental Responsibility and
    Measures for the Protection
    of Children (International
    Obligations (Scotland)
    Regulations 2010 .... 12.47
European Union (Withdrawal)
    Act 2018.................12.19, 12.48
    Section 1A(6) 12.1
    Section 6(1).................... 12.19
    Section 6(2).................... 12.19
    Section 7A..................... 12.19
Jurisdiction and Judgments (Family)
    (Amendment etc) (EU Exit)
    Regulations 2019
    Regulation 8 .... 12.19
Schedule to the Jurisdiction and
    Judgments (Family) (Amendment etc)
    (EU Exit) Regulations 2019
    Paragraph 7.................... 12.34
Jurisdiction and Judgments (Family,
    Civil Partnership and Marriage
    (Same Sex Couples)) (EU Exit)
    (Scotland) (Amendment etc)
    Regulations 2019 .... 12.49
    Regulation 4 .... 12.36
    Regulation 6 .... 12.19
Jurisdiction, Judgments and Applicable
    Law (Amendment) (EU Exit)
    Regulations 2020
    Regulation 5 .... 12.19
Civil and Family Justice (EU Exit)
    (Scotland) (Amendment etc)
    Regulations 2020
    Part 6 .... 12.19
European Union
    (Withdrawal) Act 2020
    (United Kingdom) 12.18–12.19
Private International Law
    (Implementation of Agreements)
    Act 2020......................12.48, 12.51

CHAPTER 1

HISTORY AND SCOPE OF BRUSSELS II-TER

I. Introduction.. 2
   A. Background and History of Brussels II-ter......................... 3
      1. The Original Provenance of Brussels II-ter...................... 3
      2. Brussels II-bis... 4
      3. Recasting Brussels II-bis.................................... 6
   B. A Brief Overview of Brussels II-ter............................... 8
II. Material Scope of Application....................................... 9
   A. Definitions, Recitals and Interpretation........................... 9
   B. Civil Matters.. 11
   C. Matrimonial Matters... 12
   D. Matters of Parental Responsibility.............................. 17
      1. Meaning of 'Child'... 17
      2. Meaning of 'Parental Responsibility'.......................... 18
   E. Incidental Competence on Preliminary Questions................. 21
   F. Matters Falling Outside the Scope of the Regulation............... 24
   G. Application to Decisions, Authentic Instruments and Agreements ... 25
      1. Decisions.. 25
      2. Authentic Instruments and Agreements....................... 26
   H. Personal, Geographical and Temporal Application................ 27
III. Relationship with Other International Instruments.................... 29
   A. The General Rule.. 29
   B. Exceptions to the General Rule................................. 30
   C. Relations with the 1980 Hague Abduction Convention............. 31
   D. Relations with the 1996 Hague Child Protection Convention........ 33
      1. The Application of Article 97(1).............................. 33
      2. The Application of Article 97(2).............................. 37
          i) Prorogation/Choice of Court............................ 37
          ii) Transfer of Jurisdiction................................ 38
          iii) *Lis Pendens*.. 39
      3. Applicable Law... 40
   E. Relationship with Other EU Regulations......................... 41

IV. Relationship with States that are not Bound by Brussels II-ter.......... 42
V. Transitional Provisions... 44
VI. Monitoring and Evalutation.. 47

I. INTRODUCTION

1.1. Council Regulation (EU) No 2019/1111 of 25 June 2019 on jurisdiction, the recognition and enforcement of decisions in matrimonial matters and the matters of parental responsibility, and international child abduction (recast) is the pre-eminent EU family law instrument. The 2019 Regulation is variously known as 'Brussels II recast', 'Brussels IIb' or 'Brussels II-ter'. In this work it is referred to as 'Brussels II-ter'.

1.2. Like its predecessor, the revised Brussels Regulation of 2003 (also known as 'Brussels IIa' or 'Brussels II-bis'), Brussels II-ter is a private international law instrument governing jurisdiction, recognition and enforcement of judgments in matrimonial matters and in matters of parental responsibility, and complements the application of the 1980 Hague Abduction Convention as between Member States. It also deals with the placement of children in another Member State. **It does not govern applicable law, nor does it provide substantive rules governing private law.** To facilitate the working of the Regulation with regard to matters of parental responsibility, Member States are obliged to designate a Central Authority, the tasks of which are set out by the Regulation.

1.3. Brussels II-ter is the cornerstone of judicial cooperation in family matters in the European Union (EU). As Recital (3) states:

> The Union has set itself the objective of creating, maintaining and developing an area of freedom, security and justice, in which the free movement of persons and access to justice are ensured. With a view to implementing that objective, the rights of persons, in particular children, in legal procedures should be reinforced in order to facilitate the cooperation of judicial and administrative authorities and the enforcement of decisions in family law matters with cross-border implications. The mutual recognition of decisions in civil matters should be enhanced, access to justice should be simplified and exchanges of information between the authorities of the Member States should be improved.

1.4. Brussels II-ter is not the only EU Regulation dealing with family law.[1] **Separate Regulations** govern **maintenance**,[2] the applicable law on divorce

---

[1] For a general introductory discussion of the overall scheme and strategy of the European Family Law Regulations, see U. MAGNUS and P. MANKOWSKI, 'Intro Brussels IIter' in U. MAGNUS and P. MANKOWSKI (eds), *Brussels IIter Regulation*, OttoSchmidt, 2023, pp. 21–28.

or separation,[3] jurisdiction, the applicable law and the recognition and enforcement of decisions in matters of matrimonial property regimes[4] and in matters of registered partnership property regimes.[5] There is also a separate Regulation dealing with **succession**.[6] As discussed later in this chapter,[7] the relationship between Brussels II-ter and the above-mentioned Regulations can sometimes be problematic.

1.5. Brussels II-ter came into force on 1 August 2022, is part of the EU *acquis* and, being an EU Regulation, is directly applicable.[8] **It applies in all Member States**[9] **except Denmark.**[10]

A. BACKGROUND AND HISTORY OF BRUSSELS II-TER

1. *The Original Provenance of Brussels II-ter*[11]

1.6. Brussels II-ter originated as a Convention (the Brussels II Convention of 28 May 1998),[12] negotiations for which began in 1992 when Germany proposed that the 1968 Brussels Convention on Jurisdiction and Enforcement of Judgments in Civil and Commercial Matters ('Brussels I'), which provided a general framework for jurisdiction and the recognition and enforcement of judgments in civil and commercial matters, should be extended to include

---

[2] Council Regulation (EC) No 4/2009 of 18 December 2008 on jurisdiction, applicable law, recognition and enforcement of decisions and cooperation in matters relating to maintenance obligations.
[3] Council Regulation (EU) No 1259/2010 of 20 December 2010 implementing enhanced cooperation in the area of the law applicable to divorce and legal separation.
[4] Council Regulation (EU) No 2016/1103 of 24 June 2016 implementing enhanced cooperation in the area of jurisdiction, applicable law and the recognition and enforcement of decisions in matters of matrimonial property regimes.
[5] Council Regulation (EU) No 2016/1104 of 24 June 2016 implementing enhanced cooperation in the area of jurisdiction, applicable law and the recognition and enforcement of decisions in matters of property consequences of registered partnerships.
[6] Council Regulation (EU) No 650/2012 of 4 July 2012 on jurisdiction, applicable law, recognition and enforcement of decisions and acceptance and enforcement of authentic instruments in matters of succession.
[7] See 1.86 et seq.
[8] Article 288 of the Treaty on the Functioning of the European Union (TFEU).
[9] For the Regulation's application to overseas territories of certain Member States, see Article 349 TFEU. Brussels II-ter only applies to those areas of Cyprus that the government of that Member State exercises effective control.
[10] See Recital (96).
[11] See also M. WILDERSPIN, *European Private International Family Law. The Brussels IIb Regulation*, Oxford University Press, 2023, pp. 3–20, paras 1-001–1-080; and U. MAGNUS and P. MANKOWSKI, above, n. 1, pp. 28–35.
[12] The Convention on Jurisdiction and the Recognition and Enforcement of Judgments in Matrimonial Matters 1998 (OJ C221, 16.7.1998, p. 1).

family law.[13] The 1968 Brussels Convention (which subsequently became a Regulation)[14] expressly excluded matters of status and rights of property arising from marriage because it was considered too difficult to unify the applicable jurisdiction rules of the then six Member States.[15]

1.7. The original German proposal was confined to divorce, separation and annulment, but in 1995 France and Spain proposed that matters relating to children of married parents should be included, in part because a divorce judge would normally have competence in such litigation and that it would be unduly complicated to have different rules dealing with these issues. Given the relevance of divorce to the structure of the proposed Convention, its application was confined to parental responsibility issues relating to children of both spouses in the course of matrimonial proceedings. Negotiations proved protracted and the Convention was not concluded until May 1998. However, the Convention never entered into force. Instead, following the Commission's proposal made in 1999,[16] it was converted, remarkably quickly, into a Regulation in May 2000,[17] and brought into force in March 2001.[18]

2. Brussels II-bis

1.8. Even before Brussels II had entered into force in July 2000, France presented a proposal principally aimed at facilitating, through the abolition

---

[13] Family law is, of course, civil law, but was – with the exception of maintenance – excluded from the scope of the Brussels Convention. A general background to the genesis of the Brussels II Convention is given in the explanatory report by A. BORRÁS *Explanatory Report on the Convention, drawn up on the basis of Article K.3 of the Treaty on European Union, on Jurisdiction and the Recognition and Enforcement of Judgments in Matrimonial Matters (approved by the Council on 28 May 1998)* (the Borrás Report), OJ C221, 16.7.98, p. 27, paras 1–10.

[14] Viz. Council Regulation (EC) No 44/2201 of 22 December 2000 on Jurisdiction and the Recognition and Enforcement of Judgments in Civil and Commercial Matters. Although this is commonly known as 'Brussels I', it came into force one year *after* 'Brussels II'. This instrument was later recast as Regulation (EU) No 1215/2012 of the European Parliament and of the Council of 12 December 2012 on jurisdiction and the recognition and enforcement of judgments in civil and commercial matters ('Brussels I-bis'). From 2011, private international law issues on maintenance have been regulated by Council Regulation (EC) No 4/2009 of 18 December 2008 on jurisdiction, applicable law, recognition and enforcement of decisions and co-operation in matters relating to maintenance obligations. This instrument has replaced the maintenance provisions in Brussels I.

[15] See the Jenard Report (the Explanatory Report on the Convention) OJ C59, 5.3.79, p. 1, 10, which singled out divorce as 'a problem which is complicated by the extreme divergences between the various systems of law'.

[16] COM(1999) 220 final, 26 May 1999, OJ C247, 31.8.1999, p. 1. This proposal was grounded in the belief that the changes made by the Amsterdam Treaty empowered the Community to adopt measures in the field of family law.

[17] Following approval by the European Council; see OJ 2000 L 160/19.

[18] Council Regulation (EC) No 1347/2000 of 29 May 2000 on jurisdiction and the recognition and enforcement of judgments in matrimonial matters and matters of parental responsibility for children of both spouses, Article 46.

of *exequatur* with regard to the exercise of cross-border rights of access to children.[19] In September 2001, the Commission proposed that Brussels II be extended to all decisions on parental responsibility based on common rules of jurisdiction and on reinforced cooperation between authorities.[20] It was subsequently resolved to amalgamate the two proposals and thus to entirely replace Brussels II, but without changing the provisions on matrimonial matters. To this end, the Commission presented a new proposal in May 2002.[21]

1.9. Subsequent negotiations were hard-fought, controversial at times (particularly in relation to child abduction)[22] and protracted. Nevertheless, aided by a compromise over abduction, ironically brokered by Denmark (which, as already noted, is not bound by the Regulation), a revised Regulation ('Brussels II-bis') was finally concluded on 27 November 2003 and was applied from 1 March 2005.

1.10. At the time of negotiations and when Brussels II-bis came into force, there were 15 Member States, 12 of which became automatically bound by the Regulation. Both Ireland and the United Kingdom (UK) opted in and were accordingly bound by the Regulation. The position with regard to Denmark was more complicated, the net result being that it became the only Member State that was not bound by the Regulation.[23] However, because Brussels II-bis was part of the *acquis* the 14 States which became Member States after the conclusion of the Regulation automatically became bound by it. This meant that half the Member States bound by Brussels II-bis had not been party to its drafting. This was not without significance when it came to negotiating the revision of the instrument (see 1.13 below).

---

[19] Initiative of the French Republic with a view to adopting a Council Regulation on the mutual enforcement of judgments on rights of access to children (OJ 2000 C 234 15.8.2000, pp. 7–11). Because the proposal aimed at amending the Brussels II Regulation, it became known as 'Brussels IIA' or 'BII-bis', an epithet that continued to be applied to the eventual revised Regulation, notwithstanding that it repealed the original Regulation.

[20] Proposal for a Council Regulation on jurisdiction and the recognition and enforcement of judgments in matters of parental responsibility OJ No C 332 of 27.11.2001.

[21] Proposal for a Council Regulation on jurisdiction and the recognition and enforcement of judgments in matrimonial matters and in matters of parental responsibility repealing Regulation (EC) No 1347/2000 and amending Regulation (EC) No 44/2001 in matters relating to maintenance, Brussels, 3.5.2002 COM(2002) 222 final).

[22] The proposal, which was prompted by the French dissatisfaction with the German performance under the 1980 Hague Abduction Convention, would have effectively disapplied the Convention in intra-Community cases of refusals to return.

[23] According to Protocol 25 to the EC Treaty (ECT) on the position of Denmark, it did not have a right of opt-in, but according to the subsequent Protocol 22 to the TFEU, it does have a right to opt in to instruments adopted under civil law cooperation (see Articles 3–4 of the Protocol). This Protocol did not enter into force until 1 December 2009, so when Brussels II-bis came into force, Denmark could not opt in. Subsequent referenda rejected proposals that it should opt into the Regulation.

3. Recasting Brussels II-bis

1.11. Although under Article 65 Brussels II-bis the Commission had an obligation to present a report to the European Parliament, the European Council and the European Economic and Social Committee (EESC) on the application of the Regulation no later than 1 January 2012,[24] it was not until 2014 that such a report was presented.[25] This Report concluded that while Brussels II-bis was a well-functioning instrument, there were indications that the existing rules could be improved. The Commission accordingly announced its intention to conduct a full-scale review of the working of the Regulation. Pursuant to that review, it conducted an extended public consultation, commissioned various studies *inter alia* to collect specific data concerning parental responsibility decisions, and appointed a separate expert group to discuss problems and potential solutions for revising the Regulation.

1.12. Following these investigations, the European Commission published its reform proposals in June 2016.[26] According to the Explanatory Memorandum to the Proposal:

> The objective of the recast is to further develop the European area of Justice and Fundamental Rights based on Mutual Trust by removing the remaining obstacles to the free movement of judicial decisions in line with the principle of mutual recognition and to better protect the best interests of the child by simplifying the procedures and enhancing their efficiency.[27]

1.13. Although the 2014 Report noted some criticisms of the provisions relating to matrimonial matters (the multiple non-hierarchical grounds of jurisdiction and the absence of any power of the parents to agree on jurisdiction or of the courts to transfer proceedings),[28] in its 2016 Proposals,[29]

---

[24] It is standard practice to include a provision to review the operation of a Regulation. See, for example, Article 79 of Brussels 1 recast; Article 74 of the Succession Regulation; and Article 74 of the Maintenance Regulation. For the obligation to review Brussels II-ter, see Article 101, discussed at 1.100 below.

[25] Report from the Commission to the European Parliament, the Council and the European Economic and Social Committee on the application of Council Regulation (EC) No 2201/2003 concerning jurisdiction and the recognition and enforcement of judgements in matrimonial matters and the matters of parental responsibility, repealing Regulation (EC) No 1347/2000, COM(2014) 225 final.

[26] Proposal for a Council Regulation on jurisdiction, the recognition and enforcement of decisions in matrimonial matters and the matters of parental responsibility, and on international child abduction (recast) COM(2016) 411.

[27] Ibid, p. 2.

[28] In fact, the jurisdictional rules in matrimonial matters was the first topic of discussion of the Expert Group. For further discussion of these rules, see Chapter 3.

[29] Above, n. 26.

the Commission refrained from making any recommendations for substantive changes with regard to matrimonial matters. This was not because the Commission necessarily considered the provisions relating to matrimonial matters to be beyond reproach,[30] but rather because it did not want run the risk of opening up the whole topic of matrimonial matters, given the likely divergent views of the new Member States that had not been party to the Brussels II-bis negotiations, in particular concerning same-sex marriage.[31] To that end, the 'recast' formula was chosen deliberately as it meant that neither the European Council nor the European Parliament could make proposals on the Articles that the Commission had not proposed to change. It is worth bearing in mind that because the proposals concerned family matters, they required unanimous approval.[32]

1.14. These proposals were the subject of extensive discussion and negotiations between Member States and at various stages the proposals were scrutinised by the European Economic and Social Committee (EESC) and by the European Parliament, whose Opinions were taken into account in the final version.[33] The final version of Brussels II-ter was concluded on 25 June 2019 and published in July 2019. Under Article 105, the Regulation entered into force on 22 July 2019 and became applicable from 1 August 2022.[34] Useful, but non-binding guidance on the application of Brussels II-ter, *Practice Guide for the Application of the Brussels IIb Regulation* (hereinafter the *2022 Practice Guide*) has been published by the European Commission.[35]

---

[30] But see its defence of the position under Brussels II-bis in the 2014 Report: above n. 25, at pp. 4–6. However, it may be noted that the Commission itself had some time before that, sought to address concerns about the rules leading to a 'rush to court' in its Proposal for a Council Regulation amending Regulation (EC) No 2201/2003 as regards jurisdiction and introducing rules concerning applicable law in matrimonial matters COM(2006) 399 final, but dropped its proposal in 2008, acknowledging that the opposition was too strong to achieve the necessary unanimity. Subsequently, however, a small group of States (originally just nine) asked the Commission to ask the Council to authorise enhanced cooperation, which was the first time that enhanced cooperation, which was provided for in the 1997 Amsterdam Treaty was used. This subsequently led to the Proposal for a Council Regulation (EU) implementing enhanced cooperation in the area of the law applicable to divorce and legal separation COM(2010) 105, which only concerned applicable law and omitted amendments to the rules on jurisdiction, which, when approved, became Regulation No 1259/2010 (Rome III), which only deals with conflict-of-law provisions.

[31] For a criticism of this approach, see M. WILDERSPIN, above n. 11, pp. 18–19, para. 1-068.

[32] Article 81(3) TFEU.

[33] See in particular the EESC's Opinion of 26 January 2017 (OJ C125, 21.4.2017, p. 46) and the European Parliament's Opinion (OJ C125, 19.12.2018, p. 499).

[34] With the exception of Articles 92, 93 and 103, which became applicable from the date of entry into force in 2019. The two former Articles concern delegated instruments to be adopted by the Commission and the latter information to be given by the Member States to the Commission. Both needed to be put in place before Brussels II-ter could be applied in full in 2022.

[35] European Union, 2022.

B. A BRIEF OVERVIEW OF BRUSSELS II-TER

1.15. The title of Brussels II-ter has been expanded to include 'international child abduction', which reflects the importance attached to the issue. Brussels II-ter is substantially longer than Brussels II-bis. There are now 105 Articles compared to the former 72 and 98 Recitals compared to the former 33. As before, Chapter 1 covers scope and definitions and Chapter II covers jurisdiction. However, there is now a separate Chapter III, dealing with international child abduction, which means that the two successive chapters on recognition and enforcement and on cooperation in matters of parental responsibility are now Chapters IV[36] and V respectively. There are separate chapters on general provisions (Chapter VI) and delegated acts (Chapter VII). Chapter VIII deals with relations with other instruments, while Chapter IX is entitled 'Final Provisions' and deals with transitional provisions, monitoring and evaluation (Article 101), Member States with two or more legal systems (Article 102), information to be communicated to the Commission (Article 103) and finally the repeal of the 2003 Regulation and the entry into force of Brussels II-ter (Articles 104 and 105). There are extensive Annexes. Annex 10 provides a useful correlation table comparing the numbering of Articles between Brussels II-bis and Brussels II-ter.

1.16. The historical provenance of Brussels II-ter is relevant to its interpretation since there is, as Recital (90) states, a principle of continuity of interpretation of provisions that have remained unchanged from previous versions. As discussed below (see 1.30), Recital (90) should be borne in mind when determining in particular whether or not Brussels II-ter applies to same-sex divorces or to private divorces.

1.17. The more general application of Recital (90) is to preserve the authority of both the former Court of Justice (ECJ) and of the Court of Justice of the European Union (CJEU) decisions on the ambit of previous versions of the Regulation. That will include interpretations made upon a reference from the UK. The UK had been a fully participating Member State to the two previous versions of the Regulation and indeed played an active role in the negotiations leading to the present Regulation. Having left the EU, the UK is not bound by the current Regulation and must instead be regarded as a third State just like any other non-Member State.[37] Nevertheless the UK's extensive experience of and well-developed jurisprudence on the application, particularly of Brussels II-bis and especially in the context of child abduction, while of course not binding, may continue to be of relevance

---

[36] The structure of Chapter IV is particularly complicated; see further the discussion in Chapter 8 at 8.3.
[37] The application of the Regulation to third States is discussed at 1.88 et seq.

in pointing out problems and possible solutions to applying Brussels II-ter. On the other hand, the UK courts are likely to have regard to (but without being bound by) future CJEU decisions on the application of Brussels II-ter when applying similar concepts, for example, 'habitual residence' under the 1980 Hague Abduction Convention and the 1996 Hague Child Protection Convention.

II. MATERIAL SCOPE OF APPLICATION

A. DEFINITIONS, RECITALS AND INTERPRETATION

1.18. An indispensable aid to the interpretation and application of the Regulation are the definitions provided by Article 2 and the Recitals. The former are clearly authoritative and for the most part repeat, though not necessarily in the same order, those provided by Article 2 Brussels II-bis. Some key differences are as follows:

- Defining 'child' – meaning a person under the age of 18.
- Substituting 'decision' for 'judgment' (which is reflected throughout the Regulation) and providing a more extensive definition of that term.
- Defining 'authentic instrument' and 'agreement'.
- One definition omitted from that provided by Brussels II-bis is that of 'Member State', which excluded Denmark. Instead, the non-application of Brussels II-ter to Denmark is now mentioned in Recital (96).
- Another definition omitted is that of 'judge'.

1.19. The number of Recitals has grown exponentially: whereas there were only 33 in Brussels II-bis (and 25 in the 2001 Regulation), there are now 98. This increase, though dramatic, reflects a trend in more recent Regulations to be accompanied by expansive Recitals[38] and, as a result, more closely resemble Explanatory Memoranda attached to Council of Europe Conventions. Many of the Recitals set the provisions in their context and provide information about the thinking behind them, which of course is a useful adjunct to interpreting the Articles themselves. Others usefully augment the substantive provisions.[39]

---

[38] See, for example, Council Regulation (EU) No 650/2012 of 4 July 2012 on Succession, which has 83 Recitals, and Council Regulation (EU) No 1103 of 24 June 2016 on Enhanced co-operation in matters of matrimonial property regimes, which has 73 Recitals. The Recitals were of particular concern to the European Parliament; see its Opinion (OJ C125, 19.12.2018, p. 499).
[39] See Chapter 10 of the Joint Practical Guide of the European Parliament, the Council and the Commission for persons involved in the drafting of European Union legislation

In these respects the Recitals are an integral part of the Regulation and they were frequently cited by the Court of Justice when interpreting Brussels II-bis. Some Recitals (for example, Recitals (5), (14) and (39))[40] refer to EU court decisions[41] on the former Regulation. While some might think this is helpful, others may think that it goes too far and strays into the territory that is more properly dealt with by guidance, particularly as, unlike Articles, Recitals are not binding and cannot be relied upon in terms of derogating from the actual provisions in the Regulation.[42]

1.20. Some Recitals represent a compromise between imposing a binding obligation under the Regulation and having an aspiration. A classic example is Recital (41), which in effect encourages Member States to concentrate jurisdiction to deal with child abduction cases rather than, as originally proposed, to have an obligation to do so.[43] Other Recitals deal with points not mentioned in the Articles at all – for example, that in Recital (96), which explains that Denmark is not bound by Brussels II-ter.

1.21. Another example of a Recital dealing with an issue not directly mentioned in the substantive text is Recital (90), which, as noted earlier, provides for continuity of interpretation, including the application of Court of Justice decisions on provisions in the previous Brussels II Regulations to the extent that these provisions have remained unchanged.

1.22. By Article 1, Brussels II-ter applies in civil matters of:

(a) divorce, legal separation or marriage annulment;
(b) the attribution, exercise, delegation, restriction or termination of parental responsibility.

The matters listed in (a) are collectively referred to as 'matrimonial matters'. The matters referred to in (b) are further augmented by Article 1(2)–(4) (discussed in 1.37 et seq below).

(2016), https://data.europa.eu/doi/10.2880/5575, which describes the function of Recitals.

[40] Which deal respectively with the meaning of 'civil matters', the meaning of 'court' and the requirement to give the child the opportunity of being heard in abduction cases.

[41] These references stop short of citing the particular decision.

[42] See, e.g., ECJ, 19 November 1998, Nilsson, C-162/97, para. 54. For an interesting discussion of the general use of Recitals in EU legislation, see L. Humphreys, C. Santos, L. di Caro, G. Boella, L. van der Torre and L. Robaldo, 'Mapping Recitals to Normative Provisions in EU Legislation to Assist Interpretation' in A. Ratolo (ed.), Legal Knowledge and Information Systems, JURIX, 2015 28th Annual Conference, IOC Press, p. 41. Note also some specific criticisms by C. González Beilfuss, 'Regulation (EU) No. 2019/1111 (Brussels II-ter) and Third States: relations with other instruments' in Festskrift till Maarit Jänterä-Jareborg, Iustus Förlag, 2022, pp. 129, 141.

[43] See proposed Article 22.

B. CIVIL MATTERS

1.23. In *all* the above cases Brussels II-ter applies to 'civil matters', which, as Recital (5) says, includes civil court proceedings and the resulting decisions as well as authentic instruments and extra-judicial agreements in matrimonial and parental responsibility matters. **In line with the general approach when interpreting concepts in the Regulation,**[44] the term 'civil matters' has an **autonomous or independent meaning** such that it should be interpreted not by reference to internal laws of the States involved, but rather, as the Court of Justice put it in the case of *C*,[45] by reference to the objectives and scheme of the Regulation and to the general principles which stem from the corpus of the national legal systems. On this basis, it ruled that civil matters 'must be interpreted as capable of extending to measures which, from the point of view of the legal system of a Member State, fall under public law'.[46] The Regulation consequently applied to the enforcement of a single decision ordering a child to be taken into care and placed outside his original home in a foster family.

1.24. In *C* itself, a Finnish mother was living with her two children in Sweden. The local Swedish social welfare authority ordered that the children be taken into care and placed in a foster family immediately, but the decision could not be implemented until it had been confirmed by the county administrative court. However, before that confirmation, the mother had moved with her children to Finland and had registered there. Nevertheless, following confirmation of the order by the Swedish authorities, the Swedish police asked the Finnish police at the children's new place of residence in Finland for cooperation in the enforcement of the decision. The Finnish police duly complied and ordered that the children be taken into care and handed over to the Swedish social authorities. The mother appealed and the Finnish court made a reference to the Court of Justice on whether a public law decision in connection with child welfare such as taking children into care and placing them with a foster family fell within the definition of 'civil matters' for the purposes of what was then Brussels II-bis. It was ruled that it did for the reasons already stated.[47]

1.25. According to Recital (5), 'civil matters' also covers

> applications, measures or decisions as well as authentic instruments and certain extra-judicial agreements concerning the return of a child under the 1980 Hague

---

[44] ECJ, 2 April 2009, *A*, C-523/07, para. 34, citing ECJ, 18 January 1984, *Ekro BV Vee-En Vlees Handel*, C-327/82, para. 11 and ECJ, 6 March 2008, *Nordania Finans and BG Factoring*, C-98/07, para. 17.
[45] ECJ, 27 November 2007, *C*, C-435/06, para. 40, and repeated in Recital (4).
[46] Ibid, para. 51.
[47] This meant that the Swedish judgment could no longer easily be enforced according to harmonised intra-Nordic rules, but was instead subject to the *exequatur* procedure as then provided for by Brussels II-bis.

Convention, which, according to the case-law of the Court of Justice and in line with Article 19 of the 1980 Hague Convention, are not proceedings on the substance of parental responsibility but closely related to it and addressed by certain provisions of this Regulation.[48]

C. MATRIMONIAL MATTERS

1.26. As Recital (9) explains, the Regulation only applies to the dissolution of matrimonial ties and to the consequential effect on the civil status of the former spouses. It **does not deal** with issues such as the grounds for divorce (including the consequences of a divorce based on the fault of one of the parties), applicable law in **divorce**, property consequences of the marriage or any other ancillary measures, such as maintenance obligations, or matters of succession.[49] Furthermore, decisions **refusing** the dissolution of matrimonial ties fall outside the Regulation's provisions on recognition.[50] This exclusion is justified on the basis that such a refusal does not alter the marital status. Consequently, recognising such a refusal is tantamount to recognising the marriage which falls outside the scope of the Regulation.

1.27. The Regulation only applies to the dissolution, etc. of **marital ties**. It has **no application to the termination of registered or civil partnerships** (whether between same-sex or different-sex couples). This seems clear from the structure and wording of Chapter II, Section 1, which refers to 'matters relating to divorce, legal separation or *marriage* annulment' (emphasis added) and to the references to 'spouses' rather than to 'partners' in, for example, Articles 3 and 6.[51] Given that civil or registered partnerships are permitted in most Member States[52]

---

[48] For a more detailed discussion, see Chapter 6 at 6.92.
[49] These matters are the subject of other Regulations referred to in nn. 2–6 above.
[50] See Recital (9), which was amended in this respect during the negotiations and below at Chapter 5, n. 37.
[51] It is also implicit in Recital (9), which says that the Regulation only applies to the dissolution of *matrimonial* ties. Notwithstanding this seemingly clear position, it seems that some States applied Brussels II-bis to the dissolution or annulment of civil or registered partnerships; see M. ŽUPAN, 'Scope of Application, Definitions and Relations to Other Instruments' in C. HONORATI (ed.), *Jurisdiction in Matrimonial Matters, Parental Responsibility and International Abduction*, Giappichelli/Peter Lang, 2017, 2.1 (p. 13). See further W. PINTENS, 'Art. 1 Brussels IIter' in U. MAGNUS and P. MANKOWSKI (eds), *Brussels IIter Regulation*, above, n. 1, pp. 76–80, paras 34–43.
[52] At the time of writing, six Member States do not permit civil partnerships: Bulgaria, Latvia, Lithuania, Poland, Romania and Slovakia. The position in Sweden is more complicated: same-sex registered partnerships were permitted between 1994 and 2009, when marriage became also available to same-sex couples. After that date, no new same-sex registered partnerships could be entered into, but those already entered into continue to exist for those couples who have chosen not to convert their partnership into a marriage. A similar position exists in Ireland and in Germany following the availability of same-sex marriage in 2015 and 2017 respectively.

and given the increasing number of dissolution of such partnerships, it seems a major gap in the coverage of the Regulation not to include them within its scope.

1.28. While it is clear that Brussels II-ter does not apply civil partnerships, a different problem arises from the fact that some but not all Member States permit **same-sex couples to marry**. This may be problematic for same-sex couples either seeking a divorce or having a divorce recognised in a Member State which does not permit same-sex marriage. Take, for example, the case of a same-sex couple who are habitually resident in Member State A that does not permit same-sex-marriages, but who validly marry in Member State B that does. They now wish to divorce in Member State A of their habitual residence. Alternatively, suppose the couple validly marry in Member State B and later divorce there. One of the spouses subsequently becomes habitually resident in Member State A where same-sex marriages are neither permitted nor recognised. In each of these scenarios, is a court in Member State A **bound by the Regulation** to hear the divorce application or to recognise 'divorce' granted in Member State B and, if not, what remedy (if any) does the individual have?

1.29. The question of whether the Regulation applies to the dissolution of **same-sex marriages** is hotly debated. The lack of clarity in this respect was a particular concern of the EESC, which commented that what was meant by 'marriage' was 'not defined, but assumed' in the proposed recast Regulation.[53] Despite this concern, the final version of Brussels II-ter has not clarified the position, no doubt because of the political sensitivity of the issue. It remains the case that 'divorce' is not defined, nor does the reference to 'spouses' in Chapter II, Section 1 settle the position, particularly following the CJEU ruling that for the purposes of Directive 2004/38 on the Rights of Citizens of the Union and their family members to move and reside freely within the EU, the term 'spouses' is gender-neutral.[54] Therefore, read literally, Brussels II-ter could be considered to apply to divorces of same-sex married couples. On the other hand, having regard to the overall context (see 1.30 below), the Regulation can plausibly be interpreted as not applying to divorces of same-sex marriages.

1.30. One argument for saying that Brussels II-ter should be interpreted as applying to the dissolution of same-sex marriages is, as the EESC pointed out, that following the *Coman* case,[55] Member States are required to comply with Article 21 of the European Union Charter of Fundamental Rights, which prohibits

---

[53] See its Opinion of 26 January 2017 (OJ C125, 21.4.2017, p 46) para. 3.2.
[54] CJEU, 5 June 2018, *Coman and Others*, C-673/16. See also CJEU, 14 December 2021, *Stolichna obshtina, rayon 'Pancharevo'*, C-490/20, para. 67.
[55] See its Opinion of 26 January 2017, above n. 53, para. 3.2. The Committee recommended that compliance with Article 21 of the Charter should be mentioned in the Recitals. But, of course, the fact that it is not does not alter Member States' obligation to comply with that Article.

discrimination on the grounds of sexual orientation. Such discrimination could impede the ability of same-sex couples to move and freely reside within the EU. A counter-argument is Recital (90), which provides for continuity of interpretation with previous versions 'to the extent that the provisions have remained unchanged'. As the provisions dealing with matrimonial matters have not been materially changed compared to those provided in the original 2000 Regulation, applying the current Regulation to same-sex couples implies that both the 2000 Regulation and Brussels II-bis would have been so applied. Given that no Member State permitted same-sex marriage when the 2000 Regulation came into force[56] and only Belgium and the Netherlands did so when Brussels II-bis came into force,[57] it seems unlikely that the issue was even contemplated, let alone covered. Some might argue that reliance on Recital (90) is too static and restrictive an approach and would be out of kilter with the international trend to interpret international instruments following the evolution of the law.[58]

1.31. How the CJEU might apply Brussels II-ter to 'divorces' of same-sex couples is hard to predict. It could simply rule that the Regulation has no application to same-sex marriages, which would reflect the original perspective of the instrument.[59] On the other hand, it could apply an autonomous meaning to 'divorce' such that it means the ending of a marriage as understood by the Member State in which it was granted. The advantage of this approach is that it avoids having directly to consider what is meant by 'marriage', which, in any event, lies outside the scope the Regulation. However, while this approach might work for recognition, it is less appropriate in terms of jurisdiction, since it is open to the objection that the CJEU will be seen as implicitly entering into the sensitive and forbidden field of defining 'marriage'. Another approach is to apply the *lex fori* such that if the forum considers 'marriage' to include same-sex relationships, it must apply Brussels II-ter (failure to do so would be to discriminate against same-sex couples whose marriage has been celebrated abroad), but if it does not, then it is under no obligation to apply the Regulation.

---

[56] Although the Netherlands did so from 1 April 2000.
[57] Although Spain permitted same-sex marriage in July 2005. Even when Brussels II-ter came into force on 1 August 2022, five Member States (Croatia, Hungary, Latvia, Lithuania and Poland) neither permitted nor recognised same-sex marriages.
[58] According to the International Court of Justice (ICJ), for example, there is a presumption that the interpretation of international treaties 'follow the evolution of the law and … correspond with the meaning attached to the expression by the law in force at any given time'; see *Aegean Continental Shelf (Greece v. Turkey)*, Judgment, [1978] ICJ Reports 32, para. 77. See also concerning the evolving interpretation of the European Convention on Human Rights (ECHR), particularly concerning discrimination based on sexual orientation by the European Court of Human Rights (ECtHR) in, for example, ECtHR, 25 April 1978, *Tyrer v. United Kingdom* App No 5856/72, para. 31 and ECtHR 22 January 2008, *EB v. France*, App No 43546/02.
[59] An argument convincingly rejected by M. WILDERSPIN, above, n. 11, p. 93, para. 3-029.

While this approach avoids having to define 'marriage', its drawback is that the outcome will vary according to the forum. Which (if any) of these approaches is preferable can be debated. Nevertheless, in the authors' view, even as it is currently worded,[60] Brussels II-ter ought to be interpreted as applying to divorces of same-sex couples.[61]

1.32. Brussels II-ter does not apply to unilateral divorces such as *Talaqs*[62] or to so-called private divorces, even if agreed upon by both spouses. On the other hand, as the CJEU held in *Senatsverwaltung für Inneres und Sport*,[63] there is a clear distinction between agreed mutual divorces that have been registered by a public authority and those that are purely private or purely religious. In the former case, provided the public authority empowered by national law to grant divorce retains control over its granting, which means, in the context of divorces by mutual consent, that 'it examines the conditions of the divorce in the light of national law and the actual existence and validity of the spouses' consent to divorce',[64] the divorce constitutes what is now a 'decision' under Brussels II-ter[65] and, as such, must be recognised in other Member States. *Senatsverwaltung für Inneres und Sport* concerned the status of a divorce certificate issued by the civil registrar at the Italian civil register at the end of divorce proceedings through extra-judicial means in accordance with Italian national law. The CJEU held under what was then Brussels II-bis that the Italian divorce had to be recognised in Germany.

1.33. Although *Senatsverwaltung für Inneres und Sport* specifically concerned the granting of a divorce by a civil registrar, it seems clear from the ruling, not least given the CJEU's reference to Recital (14) Brussels II-ter,[66] that notaries registering agreements can qualify as a 'public authority' even, to quote the Recital, 'where they are exercising a liberal profession'. Given the introduction in some Member States of a non-judicial or extra-judicial divorce process by

---

[60] It is understood that the Commission is working on a proposal for the circulation of status which, ultimately, should provide the best solution.
[61] For a similar conclusion, see M. WILDERSPIN, above, n. 11, pp. 93 et seq, paras 3–029 et seq. After extensive discussion, W. PINTENS, above, n. 51, pp. 73–75, paras 24–30 seems to favour interpreting Brussels II-ter as applying to same-sex marriages.
[62] See CJEU, 20 December 2017, *Sahyouni*, C-372/16 – a private divorce before a religious court held to be outside the substantive scope of Council Regulation (EU) No 1295/2010 and by implication outside Brussels II-ter; see, for example, the comments by A. DUTTA, 'Private Divorces outside Rome III and Brussels II bis. The Sahyouni Gap' CMLR 2019, no. 6, 1661–1672.
[63] CJEU, 15 November 2022, *Senatsverwaltung für Inneres und Sport*, C-646/20. This case was determined under Brussels II-bis, but the CJEU's reasoning clearly applies to Brussels II-ter.
[64] Ibid, para. 54.
[65] The term 'decision' has replaced 'judgment' in Brussels II-bis. The meaning of 'decision' is further discussed below at 1.51 et seq.
[66] Paragraph 58.

which divorce by mutual consent is obtained from a notary,[67] this application of the Regulation is important. Following the CJEU's ruling, whether or not a 'notarial divorce' ranks as a 'decision' for the purposes of Brussels II-ter will depend on the degree of control that a notary has in a particular Member State. However, where there is thought to be insufficient control for these purposes, the divorce can still be as a recognised as an authentic instrument or agreement (discussed below at 1.54). While it is clearly right that these decisions on matters of status should freely circulate among Member States, it seems unsatisfactory, not to say unnecessarily complicated, that how the Regulation applies depends on the degree of control that a particular national scheme vouchsafes to notaries.

1.34. Another area of uncertainty with regard to the application of Brussels II-ter is in relation to 'marriage annulment'.[68] Although 'marriage annulment' must have an autonomous meaning,[69] in the absence of any definition in the Regulation and of any CJEU ruling, precisely what it covers is a matter of speculation, particularly as there is considerable divergence among Member States in terms of how their national laws treat defective marriages.[70] It was no doubt with this in mind that, as the Borrás Report explained,[71] when drafting the original Brussels II Convention, the concern was to establish grounds of jurisdiction in matrimonial proceedings without becoming involved in any examination of the situation in which the validity of the marriage needs to be considered as part of the annulment proceedings. The Report took the view that **marriage annulment proceedings after the death of one or both spouses** fell outside the scope of the Convention and therefore what would now be Brussels II-ter.[72] But not everyone now accepts that position.[73]

---

[67] As in France (by Article 229-1 to 229-4 of the French Civil Code), Greece (by Article 1441 of the Greek Civil Code) and Spain (by Articles 82 and 87 of the Spanish Civil Code).

[68] Marriage annulment is known in all Member States, save for, until 2023, Finland (the concept has been reintroduced in the case of forced marriages; see further Chapter 8 at 8.9, n. 10) and Sweden, where divorce is the remedy used for those who marry contrary to marriage law (for example, because they are siblings).

[69] See, for example, M. WILDERSPIN, above n.11, pp. 99–101, paras 3–053–3–056; W. PINTENS, 'Marriage and Partnership in the Brussels IIa Regulation' in J. ERAUW, V. TOMLJENOVI and P. VOLKEN (eds), *Liber Memorialis Šarčević – Universalism, Tradition and the Individual*, Sellier, 2006, pp. 335, 336 seq.

[70] For a succinct summary, see W. PINTENS, above n. 51, p. 84, para. 62.

[71] Above n. 13, para. 27.

[72] As the Report explained, in the majority of cases, these situations arise as preliminary questions relating to succession and that they will be resolved by international instruments such as the 1970 Hague Convention on the Recognition of Divorces and Legal Separations or according to national law.

[73] See the arguments by W. PINTENS, above n. 51, p. 85, para. 66 and with reference to CJEU, 13 October 2016, *Mikolajczyk*, C-294/15, which established that what was then Article 1(1)(a) Brussels II-bis made no distinction on the basis of the date on which the action is brought in relation to the death of one of the spouses or the identity of the person entitled to bring the action.

It is the authors' view that on the basis that the Regulation is only concerned with the dissolution of marital ties and not its establishment, **declaratory actions concerning the validity of the marriage fall outside the scope of Brussels II-ter.**

D. MATTERS OF PARENTAL RESPONSIBILITY

1. Meaning of 'Child'

1.35. Brussels II-ter breaks new ground in defining what is meant by 'child', namely, that it is 'any person under the age of 18'.[74] It was a shortcoming of Brussels II-bis and its predecessor that 'child' was left undefined and the inclusion of the definition in Brussels II-ter is a welcome improvement. The definition in Brussels II-ter is in line with the 1996 Hague Child Protection Convention and, as Recital (17) says, it applies the Regulation to *all* children up to the age of 18[75] 'even in cases where they have acquired capacity before that age under the law of their personal status, for example through emancipation through marriage'. The exception to this age limit is in relation to Chapter III of the Regulation (discussed in Chapter 6 at 6.29), which complements the application of the 1980 Hague Abduction Convention in relations between Member States, and which continues to apply to children up to the age of 16.[76] The definition avoids an overlap with the 2000 Hague Convention on the International Protection of Adults and, at the same time, 'prevents gaps between those two instruments'.[77]

1.36. Brussels II-ter is silent on whether it applies to an unborn child, but given that the intention is to bring Brussels II-ter into line with the 1996 Hague

---

[74] Article 2(6).
[75] As the *2022 Practice Guide*, p. 42, para. 3.1.1.1 says, this includes children born in or out of wedlock. The point has been made (by M. WILDERSPIN, above n.11, pp. 114–15, para. 3-119) that measures taken before the child has become 18 probably cannot be enforced *after* the child has reached the age of 18. This would be in line with the position taken, by the courts in England and Wales at any rate, that the 1980 Hague Abduction Convention ceases to apply once the child has reached the age of 16, even where the application was brought before then: *Re H (Abduction: Child of 16)* [2001] 2 FLR 51.
[76] The EU has no power to alter the terms of the 1980 Hague Abduction Convention. One consequence of this limitation is that in the relatively unusual case of abduction of 16 or 17 year olds, one must look to the 1996 Hague Child Protection Convention for any international redress.
[77] See Recital (17). The 2000 Convention is designed to avoid conflicts between the legal systems of Contracting Parties in respect of jurisdiction, applicable law, recognition and enforcement of measures for the protection of adults (defined in Article 2 as 'a person who has reached the age of 18 years').

Convention, which clearly does not apply to unborn children,[78] there is no reason to suppose that the Regulation has a wider application. Even so, it would have been preferable if, like the 1996 Convention, the Regulation had been expressed to apply to children 'from the moment of their birth until they reach the age of 18 years'.

2. Meaning of 'Parental Responsibility'

1.37. Although the concept of parental responsibility is commonly used in international instruments, it is not known to every national legal system and, indeed, for some it is a difficult concept to translate.[79] Nevertheless, it has always been used in the Brussels II Regulations and remains integral to Brussels II-ter. As Recital (7) says:

> In order to ensure equality for all children, this Regulation should cover all decisions on parental responsibility, including measures for the protection of the child, independent of any link with matrimonial proceedings or other proceedings.

Parental responsibility is accordingly defined widely. By Article 2(2)(7) it means 'all rights and duties relating to the person or property of a child which are given to a natural or legal person by a decision, by operation of law or by an agreement having legal effect including rights of custody and rights of access'. The Court of Justice held in C[80] that it does not matter whether parental responsibility is effected by a protective measure taken by the State or by a decision which is taken on the initiative of the person or persons with rights of custody.

1.38. Further guidance can be derived from Article 1(2), which **includes** within the concept of parental responsibility:

(a) rights of custody and rights of access;
(b) guardianship, curatorship and similar institutions;

---

[78] A proposal that it should, was decisively rejected; see the Explanatory Report on the 1996 Convention by P. LAGARDE, HCCH, 1998, para. 15 (the Lagarde Report); see further N. LOWE and M. NICHOLLS, *The 1996 Hague Convention on the Protection of Children*, Jordan Publishing, 2015, para. 2.2.
[79] See, for example, W. PINTENS, above n. 51, p. 86, para. 67.
[80] ECJ, 27 November 2007, C, C-435/06, at [50]. See also ECJ, 19 September 2008, *Hampshire County Council*, C-325/18 PPU and C-375/18 PPU, in which the ECJ ruled that an English decision making children wards of court (which thereby placed control of the children in the court) and directing that those children be returned related to the attribution and/or exercise and/or restriction of parental responsibility, within the meaning of Article 1, and that it therefore dealt with 'rights of custody' and/or 'guardianship' within the meaning of Article 1(2).

(c) the designation and functions of any person or body having charge of the child's person or property, representing or assisting a child;
(d) the placement of a child in institutional or foster care;[81]
(e) measures for the protection of the child relating to the administration, conservation or disposal of the child's property.

Apart from some linguistic tweaking, the above definition is the same as under Brussels II-bis. Similarly, Article 2(2)(9) defines '**rights of custody**' as including 'rights and duties relating to the care of the person of a child and in particular the right to determine the place of residence of a child', while Article 2(2)(10) provides that **rights of access**' means 'rights of access to a child, including the right to take a child to a place other than his or her habitual residence for a limited period of time'.

1.39.   So far as **rights of access** are concerned, in *Valcheva*[82] the CJEU ruled that the concept must be interpreted as including rights of access of grandparents to their grandchildren but its reasoning went further than that, commenting that the concept of rights of access:

> must be understood as referring not only to rights of access of parents to their child, but also to the rights of access of other persons with whom it is important for the child to maintain a personal relationship, among others, that child's grandparents, whether or not they are holders of parental responsibilities.[83]

1.40.   In *Gogova*[84] separated Bulgarian parents and their child lived in Italy. The mother wanted to renew the child's passport, which, under Bulgarian law, required an application by both parents to the competent administrative

---

[81]   Note: Article 1(2)(d) does not adopt the recommendation of the Study *Cross-border placement of Children in the European Union* commissioned by the Policy Department for Citizens' Rights and Constitutional Affairs Directorate-General for Internal Policies, at the request of the JURI Committee and written by L. Carpaneto (European Union, 2016, http://www.europarl.europa.eu/supporting-analyses) para. 5.3.1, p. 57 (hereinafter 'the Cross-Border Study') that it should provide: 'The placement of the child in a foster family or in institutional care, as well as placement accompanied by measures involving deprivation of liberty for a specified period, ordered to protect the child.' Nor does it adopt the suggestion (at para. 5.3.1.1, at p. 59) that, like the 1996 Hague Child Protection Convention, it should include 'kafalah and analogous institutions'.

[82]   CJEU, 31 May 2018, *Valcheva*, C-335/17. The Court accepted (at para. 32) the Advocate General's point that it was clear in the light of the *travaux préparatoires* that it was contemplated that Brussels II-bis extended to all decisions concerning parental responsibility and therefore concerning rights of access, 'irrespective of the nature of the persons who may exercise those rights and without excluding grandparents'.

[83]   Paragraph 33. Note also CJEU, 9 September 2015, *Bohez*, C-4/14, in which it was held that the imposition of a penalty payment to ensure that the holder of rights of custody complied with an order for access, fell within what was then Brussels II-bis.

[84]   CJEU, 21 October 2015, *Gogova*, C-215/15, para. 26.

authorities. However, the father did not agree and the mother applied to the district court in Bulgaria to resolve the matter. The question was whether the district court was right to hold that as the child was habitually resident in Italy, it had no jurisdiction under what was then Brussels II-bis, since the issue before it was a matter of parental responsibility within the meaning of the Regulation. On these facts the CJEU ruled that the issue of a child's passport fell within the Regulation's scope. It did not matter that the issue of a passport was an administrative act, since the Regulation applies whatever the nature or the court or tribunal. Nor did it matter that the issue of the passport was not specifically covered in Article 1(2), since the list therein contained was intended to be illustrative and not exhaustive.[85] Here, the child's need to obtain a passport and the parent's right to apply for the passport and travel abroad without the other parent's agreement was manifestly within the scope of parental responsibility for the purposes of the Regulation. *Gogova* shows that when determining whether a matter qualifies as parental responsibility, regard is to be had to the object of the application rather than looking at the action in isolation.[86]

1.41. With regard to 'the **placement of a child** in institutional or foster care' as provided for by Article 1(2)(d), it had been clearly established both by ECJ rulings in *C*[87] and in *A*[88] that it covers single decisions ordering a child to be taken into care and placed outside his or her original home and that it was irrelevant that that might be regarded as a 'public law' measure according to domestic law. As Recital (11) says:

> Any type of placement of a child in foster care, that is, according to national law and procedure, with one or more individuals, or institutional care, for example in an orphanage or a children's home, in another Member State should fall within the scope of this Regulation unless expressly excluded, which is for example the case for placement with a view to adoption, placement with a parent or, where applicable, with any other close relative as declared by the receiving Member State.

The Recital accordingly suggests that 'educational placements' ordered by a court or arranged by a competent authority with the agreement of the parents or the child or upon their request following deviant behaviour of the

---

[85] Following, in this respect, ECJ, 27 November 2007, *C*, C-435/06; and CJEU, 26 September 2012, *Health Service Executive*, C-92/19 PPU. Note also the English decision *Health Service Executive of Ireland v. Z* [2016] EWHC 784 (Fam), in which it was held that an order authorising the transfer of a child to a hospital unit and authorising that unit to treat her and, where necessary and appropriate, to use proportionate and reasonable force, and restraint in the course of the treatment fell within the concept of parental responsibility.
[86] See the *2022 Practice Guide*, p. 43, para. 3.1.1.2.
[87] ECJ, 27 November 2007, *C*, C-435/06.
[88] ECJ, 2 April 2009, *A*, C-523/07.

child falls within the Regulation. However, 'a placement – be it educational or punitive – ordered or arranged following an act of the child which, if committed by an adult, could amount to a punishable act under national criminal law, regardless of whether in the particular case this could lead to a conviction' falls outside the Regulation.[89]

1.42. With regard to the **property of the child**, Recital (10) helpfully explains that the Regulation:

> should apply only to measures for the protection of the child, namely the designation and functions of a person or body having charge of the child's property, representing or assisting the child, and the administration, conservation or disposal of the child's property.

On this basis, the Recital suggests that whereas Brussels II-ter should apply in cases where the object of the proceedings is the designation of a person or body administering the child's property, measures relating to the child's property which do not concern the protection of the child should continue to be governed by the Brussels I-bis Regulation. However, the Recital adds that it should be possible for the provisions of Brussels II-ter on jurisdiction over incidental questions to apply in such cases.[90]

E. INCIDENTAL COMPETENCE ON PRELIMINARY QUESTIONS

1.43. Notwithstanding the scope of application as defined above, there are situations where an issue which falls within the scope of Brussels II-ter will nevertheless be decided by a court which is not competent under the Regulation. This is the effect of the new rule on **incidental questions** provided by Article 16.[91] Article 16 states that:

> If the outcome of proceedings in a matter not falling within the scope of this Regulation before a court of a Member State depends on the determination of an incidental question relating to parental responsibility, a court in that Member State

---

[89] Cf. the Cross-border Study's (above n. 81) recommendation that a recital should expressly take the CJEU case law achievements into account, by saying 'Placement accompanied by measures involving deprivation of liberty for a specified period, ordered to protect – and not to punish' was not adopted.

[90] See also Article 16(3), discussed at 1.45 below.

[91] Having a specific provision dealing with incidental questions had first been included in the Commission's Proposal, above, n. 26 (see the proposed Article 16), but Article 16 Brussels II-ter significantly expands the proposed provision.

may determine that question for the purposes of those proceedings even if that Member State does not have jurisdiction under this Regulation.

1.44. The case envisaged by the rule is one where, in order to decide a matter falling outside the scope of Brussels II-ter (for example, in succession matters), it is first necessary to **preliminarily** decide an issue concerning parental responsibility (for example, the appointment of a guardian). In such a case it might happen that the court seised for the principal question (succession) is in principle not competent to hear the preliminary issue on parental responsibility (for example, because the child is habitually resident in a different State). Article 16 now allows such a court to expand its competence and to **incidentally decide** on issues of parental responsibility for which, in principle, it would not be competent. With a view to an efficient way to administer justice, the rationale of the rule is to allow the Member State having jurisdiction for the dispute on succession to appoint the guardian for the pending proceedings. In other words, Article 16 does **not provide an autonomous ground of jurisdiction**, but refers to other rules – both of a national and an international nature – conferring jurisdiction in matters outside the scope of application of Brussels II-ter and extends the competence of such rules to encompass issues falling under Brussels II-ter.

1.45. What is an 'incidental question' is not defined. However, some indication as to its meaning is provided by Article 16(3). This provision mentions the case where the validity of a legal act undertaken or to be undertaken on behalf of a child in succession proceedings requires permission or approval by a court, and clarifies that in such case this court may decide on this issue, even if it does not have jurisdiction under Brussels II-ter. Further examples, both drawn from cases decided by the CJEU,[92] are provided by Recitals (32) and (33). Recital (32) refers to the question regarding the appointment of a guardian, or a legal representative of the child in the context of a succession dispute; Recital (33) refers to the case where, in succession proceedings, permission or approval from the court is required for the validity of a legal act to be undertaken on behalf of a child. Recital (33) further clarifies that the term 'legal act' should include the acceptance or rejection of inheritance or an agreement between the parties on the sharing-out or the distribution of the estate. All the examples mentioned so far refer to succession matters, but similar preliminary issues are also likely to occur in other matters, for example, in relation to parenthood, maintenance obligations, change of names or marriage of the minors,[93] or migration.

---

[92] That is, CJEU, 6 October 2015, *Matoušková*, C-404/14; and CJEU, 19 April 2018, *Saponaro*, C-565/16, discussed below at 1.48.

[93] For these examples, see *Practice Guide 2022*, p. 53, para. 3.1.1.6.

1.46. As the above examples show, 'incidental' questions concern the competence of the court which is not seised with the matter, but which needs to decide the matter in order to solve the principal issue for which it was seised. From the point of view of the decision-making process, the 'incidental' question is a preliminary one, as it will not be possible to decide the principal question without having first determined this question.

1.47. As the decision on parental responsibility is given by a court which does not have full competence under Brussels II-ter, the **legal effects of such decision are limited to the proceedings** for which it was made (see Article 16(2)). The matter is thus not solved *erga omnes* and the incidental decision will not amount to *res judicata*. Furthermore, because effects are limited to one single proceeding, the incidental decision is not a ground for opposing the recognition in the forum of a foreign decision on the same question. However, it should be noted that the limited effects are the consequence of the lack of a full ground of competence and not of the preliminary nature of the issue. This means that where the court seised with the principal matter *also* has competence on the preliminary issue under general grounds (for example, because the child is habitually resident in that State), the decision on such a point will be a full decision producing its normal effects, notwithstanding its being a preliminary question in another subject's proceedings.

1.48. The choice to insert a new rule in Article 16 is the reaction to the approach previously taken by the CJEU in Brussels II-bis cases. In *Matoušková*,[94] the Polish court was seised with a succession proceedings involving the surviving spouse and two minors habitually resident in the Netherlands. When an agreement on the sharing-out of the estate by the guardian *ad litem* of the children was concluded, the decision was brought to the court for approval. The question thus arose as to whether this issue fell within the scope of application of what was then Brussels II-bis and, further, whether the Polish court had jurisdiction over it. The CJEU held that the legal capacity of minors and the associated representation issues were not to be regarded as preliminary issues dependent on the legal acts in question and must be assessed in accordance with their own criteria.[95] As a consequence, the fact that the approval of an act concluded by a guardian *ad litem* is requested in succession proceedings does not lead to classifying that measure as falling within the law on succession. On the contrary, the need to obtain approval from the court is a direct consequence of the status and capacity of the minor children, and is to be classified as a protective measure relating to the administration of the child's property in the exercise of parental

---

[94] CJEU, 6 October 2015, *Matoušková*, C-404/14.
[95] Ibid, para. 30.

responsibility. Following this approach, the Court applied Brussels II-bis and found that Polish competence could be granted on prorogation of competence pursuant to what was then Article 12(3) Brussels II-bis, given the substantial connection of the child with that State.[96] Along similar lines, in *Saponaro*[97] the CJEU argued that an application lodged by parents in the name of their minor child for authorisation to renounce an inheritance concerned the status and capacity of the child did not fall within the law on succession. In that case too, the court seised with the succession was found to have competence on the renouncement of inheritance based on Article 12(3) Brussels II-bis. While the solution offered by the Court in the above-mentioned cases might have been appropriate, it appeared to be too formalistic and, on a more general scale, not a complete solution, given that the requirements under Article 12(3) could not always be met. For these reasons, the insertion of a rule based on the opposite principle of a joint assessment of the competence on the preliminary question with the competence on the principal question is a welcome one.

F. MATTERS FALLING OUTSIDE THE SCOPE OF THE REGULATION

1.49. Article 1(4) **excludes** from the Regulation's application:

- the establishment or the contesting of a parent–child relationship;
- decisions on adoption, measures preparatory to adoption,[98] or the annulment or revocation of adoption;
- the names and forenames of a child;
- emancipation;
- maintenance obligations;
- trusts or succession; and
- measures taken as a result of criminal law offences committed by children.

1.50. Article 1(4) is intended to be exhaustive of what is excluded. The rationale for these exclusions varies. In some cases – namely, adoption, maintenance obligations,[99] succession and trusts – they are matters already covered by other Conventions or EU Regulations. In others – namely, the

---

[96] Ibid, paras 36–37.
[97] CJEU, 19 April 2018, *Saponaro*, C-565/16, para.18.
[98] Note: in an English decision, *Re N (Adoption: Jurisdiction)* [2015] EWCA Civ 1112, it was held that an order placing a child in care, even where the local authority plan is for the child to be adopted, is not a measure 'preparatory to adoption'. The cut-off is placement for adoption proceedings.
[99] As Recital (13) explains, maintenance obligations are excluded because they are already covered by Council Regulation (EC) No 4/2009. In addition to the courts of the place where

establishment of the parent–child relationship,[100] names and emancipation – they are excluded because they fall within the domain of national law and where the EU has not yet adopted legislation. A final group of exclusions (education, health, immigration and measures taken following the commission of penal offences by the child) are excluded because they are public law matters over which States would not give up control. These exclusions are not always straightforward as cases can involve mixed issues, though, as discussed above (at 1.43 et seq), Article 16 confers limited competence to determine incidental issues, even where there is no competence to do so under Brussels II-ter.

G. APPLICATION TO DECISIONS, AUTHENTIC INSTRUMENTS AND AGREEMENTS

1. Decisions

1.51. Brussels II-ter applies to decisions, authentic instruments and agreements. With regard to the former, following the CJEU ruling in *Senatsverwaltung für Inneres und Sport*,[101] it is clear that the term 'decision'[102] must be given an autonomous and uniform interpretation. Article 2(1) Brussels II-ter defines a 'decision' as that of a court of a Member State. In turn, Article 2(2)(1) defines a 'court' as 'any authority in any Member State with jurisdiction in the matters falling within the scope of this Regulation'. Reflecting earlier Court of Justice case law,[103] Recital (14) augments this definition by saying that the term 'court' 'should be given a broad meaning so as to also cover administrative authorities,

---

the defendant, or the creditor, is habitually resident, the courts having jurisdiction under Brussels II-ter in matrimonial matters should generally have jurisdiction to decide on ancillary spousal or post-marital maintenance obligations by application of Article 3(c). The courts having jurisdiction under Brussels II-ter in matters of parental responsibility generally have jurisdiction to decide on ancillary child maintenance obligations by the application of Article 3(d). Note also CJEU (order), 3 October 2019, OF, C-759/18, in which the Court ruled that the concept of 'parental responsibility does not include parental contributions towards the costs of the child's care and upbringing, which is covered by the concept of 'maintenance obligations' and comes within the scope of Regulation No 4/2009.

[100] As Recital (12) explains, Brussels II-ter should not apply to the establishment of parenthood, since that is a different matter from the attribution of parental responsibility, nor should it apply to other questions linked to the status of persons (although, of course, divorce and marriage annulment are questions of personal status). Another reason for the exclusion is that the issue is commonly regarded as a matter of national sovereignty.

[101] CJEU, 15 November 2022, *Senatsverwaltung für Inneres und Sport*, C-646/20, para. 41. For a critical comment of this ruling, see E. BARGELLI, 'Reshaping the Boundaries between "Decision" and Party Autonomy: The CJEU on the Extrajudicial Italian Divorce' (2023) *European Forum* x, 8. See also Chapter 10 at 10.13–10.14 and 10.21.

[102] As noted, Brussels II-ter now refers to 'decisions' rather than, as previously, to 'judgments'.

[103] See ECJ, 27 November 2007, *C*, C-435/06, in which it was said that Brussels II-bis applied 'whatever the nature of the court or tribunal'.

or other authorities, such as notaries, who or which exercise jurisdiction in certain matrimonial matters or matters of parental responsibility'. In the former case, Recital (14) was referred to by the CJEU in *Inneres und Sport*[104] when ruling that a divorce certificate issued by a civil registrar in Italy came within the definition of 'court'. In the case of parental responsibility matters, child protection/welfare authorities that have power to place children would fall within the definition of 'court'.[105]

1.52. Article 2(1) further defines a 'decision' as including 'a decree, order or judgment, granting divorce, legal separation, or annulment of a marriage, or concerning matters of parental responsibility'. Recital (14) extends the definition still further by saying that any agreement approved by the court following an examination of the substance in accordance with national law and procedure should be recognised or enforced as a 'decision'.

1.53. In the context of international child abduction, for the purposes of recognition and enforcement under Chapter IV,[106] a 'decision' includes 'a decision given in one Member State and ordering the return of a child to another Member State pursuant to the 1980 Hague [Abduction] Convention which has to be enforced in a Member State other than the Member State where the decision was given'.[107] In the context of return orders made under the 1980 Convention, it also includes 'provisional, including protective, measures ordered by a court which by virtue of this Regulation has jurisdiction as to the substance of the matter or measures ordered in accordance with Article 27(5) in conjunction with Article 15'. However, it does not include such measures ordered by such a court without the respondent being summoned to appear, unless the decision containing the measure is served on the respondent prior to enforcement.[108]

2. *Authentic Instruments and Agreements*

1.54. Brussels II-ter has a wide application inasmuch as it applies not just to court decisions (which, as just discussed, is itself a wide concept), but also to authentic instruments and agreements. 'Authentic instruments' are documents that have 'been formally drawn up or registered as an authentic instrument in any Member State in matters falling within the scope of this Regulation and the authenticity of which: (a) relates to the signature and content of the instrument and (b) has been established by a public authority or other

---

[104] Paragraph 58.
[105] See also Chapter 11 at 11.47 on the meaning of 'competent authority'.
[106] Discussed in Chapters 8 and 9.
[107] See further Chapter 6.
[108] See further Chapter 6.

authority empowered[109] for that purpose'.[110] Commonly, such instruments are those drawn by or before notaries.[111] In the context of divorce, at any rate, divorces granted after an examination as to the substance of the matter, even those issued by a civil registrar or notary, are considered to be 'decisions' and not authentic instruments (or, indeed, 'agreements').[112] This distinction is explored in more detail in Chapter 10 (at 10.6 et seq).

1.55. 'Agreements', on the other hand, are newly defined by Article 2(3) as documents that are not authentic instruments, but have been 'concluded by the parties in the matters falling within the scope of this Regulation[113] and have been registered by a public authority as communicated to the Commission by a Member State in accordance with Article 103 for that purpose'.[114] The critical, new and sole condition is that such agreements must be appropriately registered, which means that for recognition purposes, for the first time, duly registered private agreements on legal separation and divorce fall within the scope of Article 65 Brussels II-ter,[115] regardless of whether they are enforceable in the State of origin.[116] Recognition and enforcement of authentic instruments and agreements is governed by Chapter IV, Section 4, which is discussed in Chapter 10 (at 10.17 et seq).

H. PERSONAL, GEOGRAPHICAL AND TEMPORAL APPLICATION

1.56. Provided the jurisdiction criteria under Article 3 (in matrimonial matters) or Articles 7–15 (in matters of parental responsibility) are satisfied,[117]

---

[109] As Recital (15) states: 'Empowerment' in this context 'is to be interpreted autonomously in accordance with the definition of "authentic instrument" used horizontally in other Union instruments and in the light of the purposes of this Regulation'.
[110] Article 2(2).
[111] For a general indication of the meaning of 'authentic instrument', see ECJ, 17 June 1999, *Unibank*, C-260/97. See also the definition in Article 2(3) of the Maintenance Regulation for the purposes of maintenance. For a detailed discussion on the application of Brussels II-ter to authentic instruments, see Chapter 10.
[112] See CJEU, 15 November 2022, *Senatsverwaltung für Inneres und Sport*, C-646/20, para. 60.
[113] But they must all fall within the scope of Chapter IV, that is, essentially they must concern the substance of the dispute. Consequently, they do *not* include prorogation agreements (discussed in Chapter 4). See M. WILDERSPIN, above, n. 11, p. 114, para. 3-116.
[114] Article 2(3).
[115] That is, those agreements that are not considered 'agreements' as interpreted by CJEU, 15 November 2022, *Senatsverwaltung für Inneres und Sport Standesamtsaufsicht*, C-646/20, discussed above.
[116] See Article 65(1). Cf. authentic instruments and agreements in matters of parental responsibility (for example, a registered agreement on child custody and/or access) which *do* need to be enforceable in the State of origin, both for recognition and enforcement purposes: Article 65(2). See further Chapter 10.
[117] Discussed respectively in Chapters 3 and 4.

and provided the proceedings fall within its scope, Brussels II-ter applies regardless of any personal connection of the respondent with a Member State.[118] There is no requirement, for example, as under Article 4(1) of Brussels I-bis, that the defendant be domiciled in a Member State. Similarly, there is no requirement that any of the parties be EU nationals. This means, therefore that **provided the jurisdictional rules are satisfied, Brussels II-ter applies to non-EU nationals**. So, for example, an Italian court would have jurisdiction to hear divorce proceedings brought by a Russian wife who has been habitually resident in Italy for more than a year[119] against her Russian husband in respect of a marriage celebrated in Russia.[120] As the CJEU observed in *UD*[121] in relation to the application of Brussels II-bis, Article 1 specifies the civil matters to which the Regulation does and does not apply, but it does not make any reference to any limitation of the **territorial scope** of the Regulation.

1.57. Unlike matters of jurisdiction, **Brussels II-ter has no application** with regard to the **recognition and enforcement of decisions made in a third State**. This was clearly established in *Sahyouni*,[122] in which it was held that what was then Brussels II-bis did not apply to the recognition of a divorce granted in a third State. In other words, in this respect there is a **geographical limitation** on the application of the Regulation. Given that under the Regulation, the simplified and automatic recognition and enforcement procedures are based on common rules of jurisdiction and mutual trust, it is clearly right that these rules should not be applied to decisions given in third States which are not so bound.

1.58. Brussels II-ter has **a temporal element** inasmuch as it only applies as between Member States (except Denmark). Consequently it does not apply, for example, to the recognition of divorces granted in a Member State before its accession to the EU.[123] Conversely, Brussels II-ter does not apply to the recognition and enforcement of orders made after a State has left the EU. In the

---

[118] See CJEU, 17 October 2018, *UD*, C-393/18 PPU. See also ECJ, 29 November 2007, *Sundelind Lopez*, C-68/07, para. 24.
[119] Jurisdiction is conferred by Article 3(a)(v); see Chapter 3 at 3.19 et seq.
[120] This clear position is often misunderstood; see the discussion by M. ŽUPAN, above n. 51, para. 2.4. However, it should be noted that the Regulation does not apply to the recognition or enforcement of orders made outside the EU; see CJEU, 20 December 2017, *Sahyouni*, C-372/16, discussed below at 1.57 and 1.91.
[121] CJEU, 17 October 2018, *UD*, C-393/18 PPU, para. 31.
[122] CJEU, 20 December 2017, *Sahyouni*, C-372/16.
[123] This issue has been of relevance with regard to Croatia, which only became a Member State in 2013; see M. ŽUPAN, above n. 51. For a case under the Brussels I Regulation, see CJEU, 21 June 2012, *Wolf Naturprodukte*, C-514/10 and, in relation to Regulation 4/2009, CJEU, 15 April 2021, *TKF*, C-729/19.

case of the UK, this means that, subject to the transitional provisions,[124] orders made after 31 December 2020 fall outside the scope of the Regulation.

III. RELATIONSHIP WITH OTHER INTERNATIONAL INSTRUMENTS

A. THE GENERAL RULE

1.59. The relationship between Brussels II-ter and other international instruments is governed by Chapter VIII.[125] The general rule under Article 94(1) is that as between Member States (other than Denmark), Brussels II-ter supersedes those conventions existing at the time that Brussels II-bis entered into force,[126] 'which have been concluded between two or more Member States and relates to matters governed by this Regulation'.[127] This rule, which is grounded in the general priority of EU law as between Member States over international Conventions, is subject to some exceptions to accommodate a well-established 1931 Nordic Convention (see 1.62 below) and pre-existing Treaties with the Holy See. Separate provisions deal with the 1980 Hague Abduction Convention and the 1996 Hague Child Protection Convention, in relation to both of which the EU has a special link.

1.60. In pursuance of the general rule, Article 95 provides that as between Member States (other than Denmark), Brussels II-ter takes precedence over:

- the 1961 Hague Protection of Minors Convention;
- the 1967 Luxembourg Convention on the Recognition of Decisions Relating to the Validity of Marriage;[128]
- the 1970 Hague Convention on the Recognition of Divorces and Legal Separations; and

---

[124] See Article 67(2) and (3) of the EU Withdrawal Agreement (2019/C 384 (1)) referred to at 1.90 and discussed in detail in Chapter 12. The transitional provisions under Brussels II-ter are discussed at 1.93 et seq.
[125] For a general discussion of this chapter, see M. WILDERSPIN, above n. 11, Chapter 11; C. GONZÁLEZ BEILFUSS, above n. 42, pp. 130 et seq.
[126] Article 94(1) is written in the same terms as Article 59(1) Brussels II-bis and Article 36(1) of the 2000 Regulation.
[127] Note also Article 98(1), which provides that such Conventions 'shall continue to have effect in relation to matters not governed by this Regulation'.
[128] Only the French original of this International Commission on Civil Status (ICCS) Convention is authentic, but the French 'Convention sur la reconnaissance des décisions relatives au lien conjugal' is translated into 'Convention on the recognition of decisions relating to the matrimonial bond' by the ICCS itself.

- the 1980 European Convention on Recognition and Enforcement of Decisions Concerning Custody of Children and on the Restoration of Custody of Children.

1.61. This precedence extends only insofar as these Conventions concern matters governed by Brussels II-ter, which means, as Article 98(1) states, that these Conventions continue to have effect in relation to matters not covered by Brussels II-ter. In this respect it may be noted that the 1967 Luxembourg Convention on the recognition of decisions relating to the matrimonial bond also covers the non-validity of marriages.

B. EXCEPTIONS TO THE GENERAL RULE

1.62. One exception to the general rule is that the Convention of 6 February 1931 between Denmark, Finland, Iceland, Norway and Sweden comprising international private law provisions on marriage, adoption and guardianship, together with the Final Protocol thereto apply in full in relations between Finland and Sweden in place of the Regulation.[129] Orders made in Finland or Sweden under that Convention must be recognised and enforced in other Member States in accordance with Chapter IV of the Regulation, provided jurisdiction was taken on grounds corresponding to those laid down in Chapter II of the Regulation.[130]

1.63. A second exception is, as Article 99 provides, Brussels II-ter applies without prejudice to the following Treaties:

- the 2004 Concordat between the Holy See and Portugal;
- the 1929 Concordato Lateranense between Italy and the Holy See as modified by the 1984 Protocol;
- the 1979 Agreement on legal affairs between the Holy See and Spain; and
- the 1993 Agreement, including the 1993 and 2014 Protocols, between the Holy See and Malta on the recognition of civil effects to canonical marriages and to decisions of ecclesiastical authorities and tribunals on these marriages.

---

[129] This is the consequence of the declaration that Finland and Sweden had made pursuant to the Brussels II-bis (see Annex VI) at the time of its entry into force, which is preserved by Article 94(2). Note: Denmark is not included because it is not bound by Brussels II-ter (see Recital (96), discussed above at 1.10). Iceland and Norway are not Member States. For further discussion, see C. González Beilfuss, above n. 39.
[130] Article 94(5).

C. RELATIONS WITH THE 1980 HAGUE ABDUCTION CONVENTION

1.64. The EU has special links with the 1980 Hague Abduction on the Civil Aspects of International Child (hereinafter the 1980 Hague Convention) to which all Member States are Contracting Parties[131] with many being so for a long time.[132] Reflecting this connection, Brussels II-ter (like Brussels II-bis) makes special provision for its relationship with the Convention. In particular, Article 96 provides that in the case of a wrongful removal to or retention in another Member State other than the Member State where the child was habitually resident immediately before the wrongful act, the provisions of the Convention continue to apply 'as complemented' by Chapters III and VI of Brussels II-ter.[133] This wording better reflects the position than simply saying, as Brussels II-bis did,[134] that the Regulation takes precedence over the 1980 Hague Abduction Convention in so far as they concerned matters governed by the Regulation.[135] The continued application of the 1980 Convention as complemented by Chapter III does not create new law, but the application of Chapter VI, which deals *inter alia* with the collection and transmission of information, is new.[136]

1.65. Article 96 also provides, and this is also new:

> Where a decision ordering the return of the child pursuant to the 1980 Hague Convention which was given in a Member State has to be recognised and enforced in another Member State following a further wrongful removal or retention of the child, Chapter IV shall apply.

This provision complements Article 1(3), which applies Brussels II-ter to return orders made under the Hague Convention.

---

[131] Under Article 38 of the 1980 Hague Convention, only States that were members of the HCCH at the time of the 14th Session when the Convention was concluded are entitled to ratify, but any other State can accede. The critical difference is that all existing Contracting States have to accept a ratification, but can choose whether or not to accept an accession. It is established that Member States no longer have individual competence to accept accessions; see 14 October 2014, Opinion 1/13, Convention on the civil aspects of international child abduction – Accession of third States – Regulation (EC) No 2201/2003 – Exclusive external competence of the European Union.

[132] Two of the first three States in which the Convention came into force (in 1983) were France and Portugal. All Member States had either ratified or acceded to the Convention by 2003. All such accessions have been accepted by all other Member States.

[133] For a detailed discussion of child abduction, see Chapter 6.

[134] See Articles 60(e) and 62(1).

[135] See also Article 98, discussed at 1.66 below.

[136] Chapter VI is discussed in Chapter 11.

1.66. Under Article 98,[137] the 1980 Hague Convention (among other Conventions) continues to have effect in relation to matters not governed by Brussels II-ter. Given, as already discussed, that Brussels II-ter makes clear provision for the continued application of the Hague Abduction Convention to applications for the return of abducted children, albeit as complemented by the Regulation, for the most part Article 98 adds little, save perhaps with regard to Central Authorities.[138] In this respect, two points may be made. First, those Member States[139] that have chosen to designate separate Central Authorities for the Regulation and the Convention can continue to do so. Even where the same Central Authority is designated, there are obligations placed upon them by the Convention that are not so placed by Brussels II-ter. For example, under the Convention, but not under the Regulation, Central Authorities must take all appropriate measures 'to prevent further harm to the child or prejudice to interested parties by taking or causing to be taken provisional measures' and to 'provide such administrative arrangements as may be necessary and appropriate to secure the safe return of the child'.[140] They continue to be under these obligations.

1.67. Notwithstanding that the statistical survey of all applications made under the 1980 Hague Convention in 2021[141] found that a significant number of access applications being made between Member States,[142] it is difficult to see on what basis the Convention rather than the Regulation was being (or could now be) invoked. Clearly, the Regulation must be invoked to recognise or enforce an access decision. Although Article 98(1) Brussels II-ter could possibly be interpreted as permitting applications to be made to a Central Authority under Article 21 of the 1980 Hague Convention for arrangements to be made for organising or securing the effective exercise of rights of access, particularly

---

[137] Article 98(2) effectively repeats Article 96 that in intra-Member State applications for the return of the child, the 1980 Convention is to be applied as complemented by Brussels II-ter.
[138] For a general discussion of Central Authorities under Brussels II-ter, see Chapter 11.
[139] That is, Bulgaria, Hungary, Lithuania and the Netherlands; see M. ŽUPAN, above n. 51, p. 273 and Annex.
[140] See Article 7(b) and (f) of the 1980 Convention.
[141] See N. LOWE and V. STEPHENS, 'A Statistical Analysis of Applications Made in 2021 under the Hague Convention of 25 October 1980 on the Civil Aspects of International Child Abduction', Preliminary Documents Nos 19A and 19B (October, 2023), http://www.hcch.net/index_en.php?act=progress.listing&cat=7.
[142] According to the 2021 Study, above, 62 of the 137 access applications received by Member States (45%) came from States bound by Brussels II-bis. For an analysis of the not dissimilar findings by the 2015 Study (by N. LOWE and V. STEPHENS, 'A Statistical Analysis of Applications Made in 2015 under the Hague Convention of 25 October 1980 on the Civil Aspects of International Child Abduction', Preliminary Documents Nos 11B (Revised, 2018) http://www.hcch.net/index_en.php?act=progress.listing&cat=7., see N. LOWE and V. STEPHENS, 'How are the Access Provisions under the 1980 Hague Abduction Convention Working?' [2019] Child and Family Quarterly 3, 21.

where no court order or agreement has been made since that is not expressly provided for by Article 79,[143] the better view is that Brussels II-ter excludes even that possibility.

D. RELATIONS WITH THE 1996 HAGUE CHILD PROTECTION CONVENTION

1.68. As before,[144] Brussels II-ter deals separately with the inter-relationship with the 1996 Hague Convention on Jurisdiction, Applicable Law, Recognition, Enforcement and Co-operation in Respect of Parental Responsibility and Measures for the Protection of Children (hereinafter the 1996 Hague Convention), to which all Member States are a party.[145] Although, when first recommending Member States be authorised to become Contracting Parties to it, the European Council commented[146] that it is 'widely recognised that the Convention would make a valuable contribution to the protection of children in situations that transcend the boundaries of the Community and thus usefully complement existing and future Community rules in the same area', in fact, as between Member States, the scope for applying the 1996 Convention is limited and at times problematic. The operative provision is Article 97. Article 97(1) sets out when Brussels II-ter is to be applied, while paragraph (2), which is designed to afford better coordination with the Convention, sets out when the 1996 Convention, rather than the Regulation, applies.

1. *The Application of Article 97(1)*

1.69. In line with the general priority of EU law over international Conventions, where the child is habitually resident in a Member State (other than Denmark), Article 97(1)(a) gives, subject to paragraph (2), general priority to Brussels II-ter over the 1996 Convention. This means that with regard to jurisdiction, recognition and enforcement in matters of parental responsibility, it is incumbent on courts of Member States (except Denmark) to apply

---

[143] The role of Central Authorities under Brussels II-ter is discussed in Chapter 11.
[144] That is, Article 61 Brussels II-bis.
[145] The history of EU-wide membership of the 1996 Convention is interesting: although the implication of Opinion 1/13, above, n. 131, was that individual Member States (that had not already done so) had no individual competence to ratify or accede to the 1996 Convention, an EU procedure for ratification, etc. was subsequently authorised by Council Decision 2008/431/EC of June 2008. It was intended that all Member States (except Denmark) would have ratified or acceded with a view to the Convention entering into force throughout the EU by September 2010, but that process was only fully achieved on 1 January 2016, when Italy's ratification took effect.
[146] See Proposal for a Council Decision authorising the Member States to sign in the interest of the European Community the 1996 Hague Convention, COM(2001) 680 final, para. 2.

Brussels II-ter rather than the 1996 Convention. Further, and in line with the general rule that all decisions taken by an EU court under the Regulation should circulate freely between Member States, Article 97(1)(b) applies the Regulation to the recognition and enforcement of a decision made in a Member State, even where the child is habitually resident in a State that is a Contracting Party to the 1996 Convention, but is not bound by Brussels II-ter – that is, Denmark or a non-EU Hague Convention State.

1.70. Unlike Article 7, which grounds jurisdiction on the basis of the child's habitual residence *at the time the court is seised*, Article 97(1) does not state when the child's habitual residence has to be established. However, in *CC*,[147] the CJEU ruled that what is now Article 97(1)(a) applied up to the time of the order. Consequently, if, during the proceedings, the child's habitual residence *lawfully* changed to that of a third State that was a party to the 1996 Convention, the court ceases to have jurisdiction over matters of parental responsibility.

1.71. *CC* concerned a child born in Sweden and in respect of whom the mother had been granted sole custody from birth. Until October 2019, the child had always resided in Sweden, but then began attending a boarding school in Russia. In December 2019, the father applied to a Swedish court, *inter alia*, seeking sole custody. The court granted the father sole custody on a provisional basis after dismissing the mother's plea that it had no jurisdiction on the ground that the child had not yet transferred his habitual residence to Russia. Although the custody decision was set aside on appeal, the decision on jurisdiction was upheld. On a further appeal, the Swedish Supreme Court, having been informed by the mother that she had made a custody application before a Russian court which, in November 2020, had held that it had jurisdiction in any matter relating to parental responsibility with respect to the child, stayed the proceedings. It sought a preliminary ruling on whether the court of a Member State retained jurisdiction if the child concerned changes his or her habitual residence during the proceedings from a Member State to a third State that is a party to the 1996 Convention.

1.72. The Court ruled that although what is now Article 7(1) Brussels II-ter embodies the principle of *perpetuatio fori*, such that the court does not lose jurisdiction even where the habitual residence of the child concerned changes during the proceedings, and applies where the dispute involves a third State, this had to be read subject to what is now Article 97(1)(a).[148] This Article had to be interpreted as governing relations between the Member States,

---

[147] CJEU, 14 July 2022, CC, C-572/21.
[148] Formerly, Article 61(a) Brussels II-bis. Note: there is no substantial difference in the wording of Articles 8(1) and 61(a) Brussels II-bis and Articles 7(1) and 97(1(a) Brussels II-ter.

which have all ratified or acceded to the 1996 Hague Convention, and third States which are also parties to that Convention, in the sense that the general rule of jurisdiction laid down in what is now Article 7 ceases to apply where the habitual residence of a child has been lawfully transferred, during the proceedings, from that of a Member State to that of a third State which is a party to that Convention.

1.73. In so ruling, the Court noted[149] that unlike Article 95,[150] Article 97 does not state that its scope is limited to relations between Member States, nor, as already noted, unlike Article 7(1), does Article 97(1)(a) refer to the child's habitual residence 'at the time the court is seised'. Given these differences, it was held that if, when the court having jurisdiction gives its ruling, the child's habitual residence is no longer established in a Member State, but in a third State that is a party to the 1996 Hague Convention, the Convention and not the Regulation applied. This interpretation was supported by Article 97(1)(b),[151] which applies the Regulation to recognition and enforcement of a judgment given in a court of a Member State in another Member State even if the child concerned is habitually resident in a third State which is a Contracting Party to the 1996 Hague Convention. It was also consistent with the intention of the EU legislature not to undermine the provisions of the 1996 Convention. In that respect, note was taken of Article 5(2) of the Convention, which provides that following a change of the child's habitual residence to another Contracting State, the authorities of the State of the new habitual residence have jurisdiction, and of Article 52(3), which expressly precludes, as regards matters within the scope of the Convention, the concluding of another Convention between two or more Contracting States from affecting, in the relationship of such States with other Contracting States, the application of the provisions of the 1996 Convention. As the Court pointed out,[152] that provision resulted from a compromise between EU Member States which were also all parties to that Convention, which wanted to be able to enter into separate agreements in that field, such as (at that time) the 'Brussels II' Convention, and that of the other States that were parties to the 1996 Hague Convention, which feared that such separate agreements may have resulted in those States considering themselves to be free from their obligations towards other Contracting States, thereby weakening the Convention. The Court noted[153] that interpreting the Regulation as applying the *perpetuatio fori* rule even where the child's habitual residence changed during the proceedings to that of a non-EU Hague Convention State would run

---

[149] Paragraphs 34–38.
[150] Formerly Article 60 Brussels II-bis.
[151] Formerly Article 61(b) Brussels II-bis.
[152] See para. 41, relying on the Lagarde Report, above n. 78, paras 170–173.
[153] Paragraph 42.

counter to both Articles 5(2) and 52(3) of the 1996 Convention and would lead Member States to act in a way that was incompatible with their international obligations.[154]

1.74. CC, taken together with the ruling in SS,[155] underlines the CJEU's concern to interpret the Regulation in a way that promotes a harmonious relationship with the 1996 Convention rather than to undermine it – a policy further extended by Article 97(2) (discussed below). In that sense the ruling is to be welcomed. However, as a matter of practicality, the ruling is not without its difficulties, since it means that the court of the Member State that initially has jurisdiction has continually to monitor the position in case the child's habitual residence changes. The longer the proceedings take, the more likely there could be an issue. Moreover, as the ruling only applies to lawful changes, the court may become embroiled in disputes over whether the change was lawful or not.

1.75. The priority provided for by Article 97(1)(a) only applies where the child concerned is habitually resident in a Member State (other than Denmark) and the implication of Article 97(1)(b) is that with regard to jurisdiction, the 1996 Convention takes precedence over Brussels II-ter where the child is habitually resident in Denmark or a non-EU Hague Convention State, even if the child is present in a Member State (other than Denmark).[156] However, this latter interpretation does not exclude the possibility of jurisdiction being assumed under Brussels II-ter to take provisional (including protective) measures in urgent cases on the basis of the child's presence, pursuant to Article 15.[157] However, there is also jurisdiction to 'take necessary measures of protection' in urgent cases on the basis of the child's presence under Article 11 of the 1996 Convention. Furthermore, under the Convention, such measures have extra-territorial effect, whereas under Brussels II-ter, save when making return orders under the 1980 Hague Abduction Convention, they do not.[158] Although it might seem sensible to take measures under the 1996 Convention rather than the Regulation, as they would be recognisable and enforceable in the non-EU Hague Convention State, it is doubtful whether this is permitted under Brussels II-ter.[159] Jurisdiction under Brussels II-ter is only derogated from in favour of the 1996 Convention to the extent expressly provided for by Article 97,

---

[154] Cf. CJEU, 24 March 2021, SS, C-603/20 PPU, para. 56, discussed in Chapter 6 at 6.18.
[155] CJEU, 14 July 2022, CC, C-572/21.
[156] See M. ŽUPAN, above n. 51, p. 33.
[157] Nor does it exclude the possibility of Brussels II-ter applying in cases where parties agree on a Member State having jurisdiction in respect of a child habitually resident in a third State; see Chapter 4 at 4.94 et seq. Article 15 is discussed in detail in Chapter 4 at 4.169 et seq.
[158] Article 27(5), Brussels II-ter, discussed in Chapter 6 at 6.85 et seq.
[159] A similar question arises with regard to jurisdiction to take provisional measures, etc. based on the location of the child's property, which is another matter not dealt with by Article 97.

and no mention is made of the power to make provisional protective measures under the 1996 Convention.

2. *The Application of Article 97(2)*

1.76. The general rule under Article 97(1) is subject to three exceptions set out by Article 97(2),[160] namely, where: (i) the parties have agreed upon the jurisdiction of a court of a State Party to the 1996 Convention to which the Regulation does not apply; (ii) the transfer of jurisdiction between a Court of Member State a court of a State Party to the 1996 Convention to which the Regulation does not apply; and (iii) there are pending proceedings relating to parental responsibility before a State Party to the 1996 Convention to which the Regulation does not apply. In each of these cases it is the relevant provisions of the 1996 Convention rather than those of Brussels II-ter that apply. These exceptions are new to Brussels II-ter.

i) Prorogation/Choice of Court

1.77. The first of the exceptions is where the parties have agreed upon the jurisdiction of a court of a State Party to the 1996 Convention to which the Regulation does not apply. Article 97(2)(a) provides that Article 10 of the 1996 Convention applies. Article 10(1) of the Convention permits authorities exercising jurisdiction to decide on an application for divorce, legal separation or annulment of marriage, to take measures to protect children if their domestic law so permits, providing that, at the time of the commencement of proceedings: (a) one of the child's parents is habitually resident in that State and one of them (but not necessarily the parent just referred to) has parental responsibility; *and* (b) the parents and anyone else with parental responsibility agree to such jurisdiction being so exercised *and* that it is in the child's best interests to do so. These criteria are similar to those formerly provided for by Article 12(1)(b) Brussels II-bis, save that jurisdiction had to be accepted 'expressly or otherwise in an unequivocal manner'.

1.78. The powers to prorogue jurisdiction are narrower under the Convention than under Brussels II-ter in that they are only available where there are existing matrimonial proceedings.[161] In contrast, under Article 10 Brussels II-ter

---

[160] Note also the application of the 1996 Convention to refugee children and children whose habitual residence was in a third State before their displacement, discussed in Chapter 4 at 4.103 et seq.

[161] For discussion of the Article 10 of the Convention, see N. Lowe, M, Everall and M. Nicholls, *International Movement of Children: Law Practice and Procedure* (2nd ed. by N. Lowe, M. Nicholls) Lexis Nexis, Family Law, 2016, 5.92–5.94 and 5.101.

(discussed in Chapter 4),[162] the parties' freedom to choose the forum in which proceedings concerning matters of parental responsibility can be exercised, subject to various conditions, whether or not there are existing matrimonial proceedings or parental responsibility proceedings. The application of Article 97(2)(a) is discussed in detail in Chapter 4 at 4.94 et seq.

ii) Transfer of Jurisdiction

1.79. The second exception under Article 97(2) concerns transfer of jurisdiction. Under Brussels II-bis, the equivalent of Article 97(1)(a)[163] had no provisos, which meant that the court of a Member State in which the child was habitually resident had no power to transfer jurisdiction to a non-EU Hague Convention State under the Regulation and also could not do so under the 1996 Convention.[164] A good example was an English decision, *West Sussex Council v. H*.[165] In this case, an English local authority had brought care proceedings concerning a girl of Albanian nationality who had been born and lived all her life in England, and who was therefore considered to be habitually resident there, notwithstanding that she had no regularised status in the UK. The girl had been abandoned by her Albanian mother, while her father had no parental responsibility. The maternal grandparents wanted the child to be brought to Albania. It was held that there was no power to transfer the proceedings to Albania under the Regulation, since it was a non-EU Member State. But it was also held that there was no power to make a transfer under Article 8 of the 1996 Convention (to which Albania is a party) since under Brussels II-bis, once it was found that the girl was habitually resident in England, jurisdiction could **only** be taken under the Regulation. Although that interpretation had been criticised[166] as being incompatible both with the Charter of Fundamental Rights of the European Union and the UN Convention on the Rights of the Child, however inconvenient it may have been, it was surely the right interpretation.

1.80. Article 97(2)(b) Brussels II-ter, addressing the concerns caused by the above interpretation of Brussels II-bis,[167] provides that where the other

---

[162] See Chapter 4 at 4.42 et seq.
[163] That is, Article 61(a) Brussels II-bis.
[164] A lacuna identified by T. KRUGER and L. SAMYN, 'Brussels II bis: successes and suggested improvements' (2016) 12 *Journal of Private International Law* 132.
[165] [2014] EWHC 2550 (Fam).
[166] See H. SETRIGHT, D WILLIAMS, I. CURRY-SUMNER, M. GRATION and M. WRIGHT in *International Issues in Family Law The 1996 Hague Convention on the Protection of Children and Brussels IIa*, Jordans, Family Law, 2015, para. 5.85.
[167] In the Impact Assessment accompanying the Commission's Proposal to recast Brussels II-bis (SWD (2016) 207), at pp. 115–116, the Swedish expert identified the issue addressed in *West Sussex County Council v. H*, namely that neither Article 15 of Brussels II-bis nor Article 10

State involved is a Contracting State to the 1996 Convention, but which is not bound by the Regulation, then 'with respect of a transfer to or from that State, Articles 8 and 9 of the Convention shall apply'. Article 8 permits, subject to a number of conditions, a Contracting State, having jurisdiction, to request another Contracting State to assume jurisdiction where it considers that it would be better placed to assess the best interests of the child. Article 9 permits a Contracting State, not having jurisdiction, to request a Contracting State with jurisdiction that they be authorised to exercise jurisdiction where it considers that it would be better placed to assess the best interests of the child.[168]

iii)   *Lis Pendens*

1.81. The third exception provided for by Article 97(2) concerns *lis pendens*. This issue is discussed in detail in Chapter 5 (see 5.58 et seq). Suffice to say here that Article 20 Brussels II-ter (like Article 19 Brussels II-bis) makes provision for dealing with the position where parallel proceedings are brought before courts of different Member States between the same parties and involving the same cause of action, namely, by giving jurisdiction to the court first seised and requiring the court second seised to stay the proceedings. But Article 20 only applies as between courts of Member States bound by Brussels II-ter and not, therefore, between a court of a Member State and court of a State not bound by the Regulation.

1.82. The non-application of the *lis pendens* provisions to courts of a State Party to the 1996 Convention that were not bound by the Regulation proved problematic under Brussels II-bis. This was illustrated by an English case, *Re X*,[169] in which the father brought proceedings concerning the children in England and Wales (and a Member State for these purposes), while the mother brought proceedings in Russia (which, like the UK, was a party to the 1996 Convention). The Russian court decided that the Russian proceedings were first in time. The question arose as to whether, given that the children were found to be habitually resident in England and Wales at the commencement of proceedings there, could the English court nevertheless stay the proceedings in accordance with Article 13 of the 1996 Convention? It was held that it could not, since it was clear that under what was then Article 61(a) Brussels II-bis, it was mandatory to apply the Regulation rather than the 1996 Convention if the child who was the subject of proceedings was habitually resident in a Member State.

---

of the 1996 Hague Convention would be available if the other State was not an EU Member State. This was because 'according to Article 61 of the Regulation, the 1996 Hague Convention should not apply, as the Brussels IIA Regulation takes precedence'.
[168]   For discussion of the transfer provisions under Brussels II-ter, see Chapter 5.
[169]   [2021] EWCA Civ 1305, on which see N. Lowe, 'Operating Brussels II-ter in children cases involving third States' in *Festskrift till Maarit Jänterä-Jareborg*, Iustus Förlag, 2022, pp. 203, 214–215.

1.83. The inconvenient result of the undoubtedly correct application of Brussels II-bis in *Re X* was that neither the *lis pendens* provisions of Brussels II-bis nor those of the 1996 Convention could be applied. Article 97(2)(c) Brussels II-ter addresses this lacuna by providing:

> where proceedings relating to parental responsibility are pending before a court of a State Party to the 1996 Hague Convention in which this Regulation does not apply at the time when a court of a Member State is seised of proceedings relating to the same child and involving the same cause of action, Article 13 of that Convention shall apply.

1.84. In other words, in a case involving a court of a Member State and that of a State Party to the 1996 Convention that is not bound by the Regulation, the *lis pendens* provisions of the 1996 Convention apply. What this means is that under Article 13 of the Convention, the authorities of the Contracting State with jurisdiction must abstain from exercising that jurisdiction if, at the time of the commencement of proceedings, 'corresponding measures' have been requested from the authorities of another Contracting State having jurisdiction at the time of the request which are still under consideration.[170]

3. Applicable Law

1.85. Under Article 98, the 1996 Convention continues to have effect in relation to 'matters not governed by this Regulation'. An important consequence of this is, as Recital (92) makes clear, that the applicable law provisions in Chapter III of the 1996 Convention (which principally deal with the allocation, exercise and termination of parental responsibility)[171] continue to apply. According to Recital (92), where proceedings are before a court bound by Brussels II-ter, the reference to the rules of jurisdiction when applying the *lex fori* rule in Article 15(1) of the Convention[172] are to be 'understood as referring to 'the provisions of this Regulation'. This 'understanding' is to make it clear that when applying the applicable law provisions of the Convention, courts are still bound by the rules of jurisdiction as provided for by the Regulation.[173]

---

[170] For further discussion of Article 13 of the Convention, see N. Lowe and M. Nicholls, above n. 163, para. 5.96. For discussion of the not dissimilar *lis pendens* provisions under Brussels II-ter, see Chapter 5.

[171] For the application of which see N. Lowe and M. Nicholls, *The 1996 Hague Convention on the Protection of Children*, Jordans, 2012, Chapter 4.

[172] Article 15(1) provides that in exercising their jurisdiction under the provisions of Chapter II of the Convention, the authorities shall apply their own law.

[173] This point should surely have been in the text of Brussels II-ter rather than in a Recital. In any event, the normative value of this Recital has been questioned since EU law does not contain provisions on the law applicable to parental responsibility; see C. González Beilfuss, above n. 42, p. 141.

E. RELATIONSHIP WITH OTHER EU REGULATIONS

1.86. Brussels II-ter does not deal with its relationship with other EU Regulations, but this omission can be problematic since cases can concern issues relating to divorce, parental responsibility and maintenance, which in turn requires the application of different rules as set out by different Regulations.[174] This is well illustrated by *R v. P*.[175] In this case, a husband and wife, both Romanian nationals, lived in the UK, where they had a child before separating. The husband returned to Romania, but the wife and child remained in the UK. The wife issued proceedings in Romania seeking a dissolution of the marriage, an order that the child should reside with her and that she should have sole parental responsibility, and an order that her husband should pay maintenance for the child. The Romanian court held, on the basis of the spouses' common nationality, that it had jurisdiction under Article 3(1)(b) of what was then Brussels II-bis to hear the divorce petition, but did not have jurisdiction to hear the residence and parental responsibility application. However, considering that the issue of the child's maintenance was strongly connected to the determination of parental responsibility and the child's residence, the Romanian court made a reference for preliminary ruling on whether it had jurisdiction under the Maintenance Regulation. The CJEU ruled that the Romanian court had jurisdiction over this matter under Articles 3(a) and 5 of the latter Regulation, regardless of the fact that it did not have competence under Brussels II-bis to determine the issue of parental responsibility. It observed:

> that where there is an action before a court of a Member State which includes three claims concerning, respectively, the divorce of the parents of a minor child, parental responsibility in respect of that child and the maintenance obligation with regard to that child, the court ruling on the divorce, which has declared that it has no jurisdiction to rule on the claim concerning parental responsibility, nevertheless has jurisdiction to rule on the claim concerning the maintenance obligation with regard to that child where it is also the court for the place where the defendant is habitually resident or the court before which the defendant has entered an appearance, without contesting the jurisdiction of that court.

1.87. Another inter-Regulation issue is the meaning of 'related proceedings' for the purpose of Article 13 of the Maintenance Regulation by which any court other than the court first seised may stay its proceedings where 'related

---

[174] For a detailed discussion of the relationship between Brussels II-ter and the Maintenance, Succession and the Matrimonial Property Regulations, see M. WILDERSPIN, above n. 11, paras 11-017–11-103 (pp. 451–468).
[175] CJEU, 15 September 2019, *R v. P*, C-468/18.

actions are pending in the courts of different Member States'.[176] Actions are deemed to be related 'where they are so closely connected that it is expedient to hear and determine them together to avoid the risk of irreconcilable judgments resulting from separate proceedings'. This issue was explored by the UK Supreme Court in *Villiers v. Villiers*,[177] albeit in the context of a problem between England and Wales, and Scotland. At the time of the litigation, UK domestic law applied the same jurisdictional rules in maintenance cases to inter-UK cases as under the Maintenance Regulation.[178] In *Villiers* the husband and wife were married in England, but lived in Scotland until they separated, after which the wife returned to England. The wife petitioned for divorce in England, while the husband did so in Scotland. However, the wife consented to her petition in England being dismissed (thereby enabling the husband's petition to proceed in Scotland), but immediately issued further proceedings in England, *inter alia*, for interim maintenance. Were the Scottish divorce proceedings a 'related action' within the meaning of Article 13 of the Maintenance Regulation? The majority held that they were not, since the maintenance claim and determining marriage status were distinct actions. The minority view, adopting a broad, common-sense approach, was that the divorce and maintenance proceedings should be viewed as 'related actions'. While it remains to be seen how the CJEU might resolve a similar conflict, some guidance might be drawn from the case law on Article 30 of Brussels I-bis and its predecessors, which establishes that 'related' actions have an autonomous meaning and might not necessarily involve the same parties.[179]

IV. RELATIONSHIP WITH STATES THAT ARE NOT BOUND BY BRUSSELS II-TER

1.88. Formerly, States that were not bound by Brussels II were generally referred to as 'third States' but unlike Brussels II-bis,[180] no Article[181] in Brussels II-ter refers to such States in that way. It is tempting to think of such States, however they may be described, as non-EU Member States, but that overlooks the

---

[176] A similar problem arises with regard to the relationship between Article 18 of Council Regulation (EU) No 2016/1103 of 24 June 2016 (the Matrimonial Property Regulation) and Article 18 of Council Regulation (EU) No 2016/1104 of 24 June 2016 (the Registered Partnership Property Regulation).
[177] [2020] UKSC 30.
[178] Schedule 6 to the Civil Jurisdiction and Judgments (Maintenance) Regulations 2011, since amended, following the UK's departure from the EU.
[179] See, e.g., ECJ, 6 December 1994, *Tatry*, C-406/92.
[180] That is, Articles 12(4) and 61.
[181] But the term is referred to in Recitals (25), (88) and (91).

Chapter 1. History and Scope of Brussels II-ter

position of Denmark, which, as previously discussed[182] and alone of Member States, has never been bound by or subject to the Brussels II Regulations, including Brussels II-ter. Brussels II-bis dealt with this issue by defining the term 'Member State' as 'all Member States with the exception of Denmark'.[183] However, Brussels II-ter leaves the term 'Member State' undefined and where it is sought to refer to what in effect are non-EU Member States and Denmark that are parties to the 1996 Convention, reference is made to States to which Brussels II-ter does not apply.[184]

1.89. In general terms, whereas on the one hand, provided the jurisdiction criteria are satisfied and provided the proceedings fall within its scope, Brussels II-ter applies regardless of where the parties or even the child are located, on the other hand, the recognition and enforcement provisions have no application between Member States bound by Brussels II-ter and those that are not. The former position is clearly established by the CJEU in *UD*,[185] while the latter position is equally established by the CJEU in *Sahyouni*.[186]

1.90. In *UD* a British man married a Bangladeshi woman in Bangladesh. They later came to England, where the woman was granted a spousal visa to remain there, which was valid for three years. However, when heavily pregnant, the couple returned to Bangladesh. The woman gave birth shortly afterwards and the child remained in Bangladesh. Eleven months later, the man returned alone to England. The woman claimed that she had been unlawfully kept in Bangladesh through coercion by the father. She brought proceedings in England seeking the child's return and the question as to jurisdiction was raised. Following a reference from the English court, the specific question was whether for the purposes of Article 8 Brussels II-bis (now Article 7 Brussels II-ter), physical presence was a necessary element of habitual residence. It was held that it was.[187] However, in that reference the UK government formally raised the issue of whether Brussels II-bis was intended only to apply cross-border situations inside the EU. The CJEU ruled that there was nothing in Article 8 that indicated that it was so conditional and that accordingly:[188]

> it must be stated that the general jurisdictional rule provided for in Article 8 ... may apply to disputes involving relations between courts of a single Member States and those of a third country, and not only relations between courts of a number of Member States.

---

[182] See 1.10 above.
[183] See Article 2(3) Brussels II-bis.
[184] Article 97(1)(b) and (2), discussed above.
[185] CJEU, 17 October 2018, *UD*, C-393/18 PPU.
[186] CJEU, 20 December 2017, *Sahyouni*, C-372/16.
[187] See the discussion in Chapter 4 at 4.22 et seq.
[188] Paragraph 41.

Intersentia

Given that the basic jurisdictional rules are repeated in Brussels II-ter in Article 3 (matrimonial matters) and Article 7 (parental responsibility), there is no doubt that the position as established in *UD* applies to Brussels II-ter.

1.91. In *Sahyouni*, the applicant applied for recognition of a divorce pronounced in Syria. The CJEU observed,[189] *inter alia*, that, as what was then Brussels II-bis, only applied between Member States, a divorce delivered in a third country fell outside its scope.

1.92. It goes without saying that by definition, the States under discussion are neither bound nor subject to Brussels II-ter.[190] Yet that is not to say that the Regulation has no impact. In particular, as already discussed (see 1.69 et seq above), Brussels II-ter has a number of provisions concerning the application of the 1996 Hague Child Protection Convention as between Member States bound by the Regulation and Hague Convention States not so bound.[191]

V. TRANSITIONAL PROVISIONS

1.93. Brussels II-ter only applies to legal proceedings instituted, authentic instruments formally drawn up or registered and agreements registered on or after 1 August 2022 (Article 100(1)). Legal proceedings instituted, authentic instruments formally drawn up or registered and agreements 'which have become enforceable in the Member State where they were concluded' before 1 August 2022 continue to be governed by Brussels II-bis, provided they fall within the scope of that Regulation (Article 100(2)).[192] This means that, contrary to transitional provisions under Brussels II-bis,[193] decisions given in proceedings instituted before the cut-off date will continue to be recognised and enforced under the old Regulation, even though they have actually been handed down after 1 August 2022. Article 100(1) does not define when proceedings are 'instituted', nor does it make reference to Article 17, which deals with issue of when a court is 'seised'.[194] Nevertheless, as one commentator has convincingly

---

[189] Paragraph 22.
[190] In the case of Denmark, Recital (96) makes this expressly clear.
[191] For further discussion of this issue, see N. Lowe, above n. 170.
[192] For examples of CJEU decisions under the transitional provisions, see CJEU, 15 November 2022, *Senatsverwaltung für Inneres und Sport*, C-646/20, discussed above at 1.32, 1.51 and 1.54; and CJEU, 16 February 2023, *Rzecznic Praw Dziecka and Others*, C-638/22 PPU, discussed in Chapters 6 and 9.
[193] That is, Article 64(2).
[194] Article 17 is discussed in Chapter 2 at 2.3 et seq. For the similar problem of interpreting the application of Article 67 of the European Withdrawal Agreement (Agreement on the Withdrawal of the United Kingdom of Great Britain and Northern Ireland from the European Union and the European Atomic Energy Community, OJ L29, 31.1.2020, p. 7 (2019/C 384 I/01), see Chapter 12 at 12.9.

argued in relation to the similar problem in Brussels II-bis,[195] equating 'the institution of legal proceedings' to when the court is 'seised' 'has at least the major advantage of being a solution uniform in the starting point and guaranteeing for a single mode how the Regulation entered into force for all Member States', albeit that the two provisions are differently worded.

1.94. Providing for the **exclusive** application of Brussels II-ter or Brussels II-bis according to which side of 1 August 2022 the institution of proceedings, etc. fall, seems clear and, of course, there can be no argument that Brussels II-ter should apply to proceedings, etc. instituted on or after 1 August 2022 as provided for by Article 100(1). But the continued application of Brussels II-bis may be questioned, particularly as it leads to some complications, which will now be discussed.

1.95. The continued application of Brussels II-bis to the recognition and enforcement of pre-August 2022 orders, etc. has a number of consequences. First, the former rules of *exequatur* continue to apply to the enforcement of what are now regarded as non-privileged decisions (that is, all orders, etc. other than access orders or return orders made under Article 11 Brussels II-bis).[196] Second, the grounds for refusal of recognition or enforcement are those provided by Articles 22 and 23 Brussels II-bis. While in the case of matrimonial matters, the grounds provided by Article 22 Brussels II-bis are the same as those provided by Article 38 Brussels II-ter, in the case of judgments relating to parental responsibility, there are some important differences between the former Article 23 and the current Article 39. For example, whereas under Brussels II-bis, it was **mandatory** to refuse recognition and enforcement in cases where it was established that there was a failure to give the child an opportunity to be heard, under the current Regulation, refusal is **discretionary** in proceedings that only concern the property of the child (see Article 39(2)(a))[197] or where serious grounds, such as urgency, must be taken into account (see Article 39(2)(b)). Furthermore, while the other grounds of refusal under Article 23 Brussels II-bis are similar, they are not identical to Article 39(1) Brussels II-ter. In particular, where the order is found to be irreconcilable with a later order, recognition and enforcement *must* be refused, whereas under Brussels II-ter, refusal is limited to the extent of that irreconcilability.[198] Third, in the context of parental child abduction, Article 11 Brussels II-bis continues to apply, which means that the 'override' provisions will have a wider scope of application inasmuch as they are triggered by a refusal to order the child's return based on *any* of the grounds mentioned Article 13 of the 1980 Hague Abduction Convention,

---

[195] P. MANKOWSKI in U. MAGNUS and P. MANKOWSKI (eds), *Brussels IIbis Regulation*, OttoSchmidt, 2017, pp. 474–475.
[196] Discussed in Chapters 8 and 9.
[197] Discussed in Chapter 8 at 8.122 et seq.
[198] Discussed in Chapter 8 at 8.101 et seq.

thus including, when based on the lack of effective exercise of custody rights, consent or acquiescence (as provided for by Article 13(1)(a)). In contrast, under Article 29 Brussels II-ter, the override provisions are only triggered where the refusal to return is solely based either on a grave risk of harm or of an intolerable situation pursuant to Article 13(1)(b) of the Hague Convention or on the child's objections to return, pursuant to Article 13(2).[199]

1.96. The requirement that to continue to be recognisable and enforceable the order, etc. must fall within the scope of Brussels II-bis seems obvious, but it does mean that the scope of that Regulation may still have to be determined even where the matter is resolved under Brussels II-ter – for example, determining whether return orders made under the 1980 Hague Abduction Convention fall within the scope of Brussels II-bis.

1.97. Article 100(1) and (2) is differently worded with regard to the **enforceability of agreements** inasmuch as under Brussels II-ter, such agreements must be registered in order to be enforceable,[200] whereas no such requirement is mentioned in Article 100(2). This difference reflects the different wording of the two Regulations. What this means is that provided a pre-August 2022 agreement is enforceable in the Member State of origin, it will continue to be so after that date, whether or not it had been registered.[201]

1.98. Wide though Article 100(2) may be, it does not cover all possible transitional issues. In particular, it does not expressly apply to requests made under Article 55 of Brussels II-bis to a Central Authority in another Member State to provide information about a child or to placements of a child in another Member State as provided for by Article 56.[202] Presumably, in each case, the rules provided by Brussels II-bis must be honoured.

1.99. Another issue, understandably not dealt with by the transitional provisions in Brussels II-ter,[203] is the position with regard to **cases involving the UK and a Member State that were instituted before 1 January 2021 including those still pending when the so-called 'transition period'**[204] **came to an end** and Brussels II-bis no longer applied as between the EU and the UK.

---

[199] The 'override provisions' are discussed in Chapter 6 at 6.96 et seq.
[200] Enforceable agreements are discussed in Chapter 10.
[201] Note: under Brussels II-ter, 'agreements' must be registered to be recognisable and enforceable; discussed at 1.55 above.
[202] This issue *is* covered by the European Withdrawal Agreement (see Article 67(3)(c)), discussed in Chapter 12 at 12.18. Under Brussels II-ter, 'cooperation in matters of parental responsibility' is governed by Chapter V, which is discussed in Chapter 11.
[203] At the time when Brussels II-ter was concluded, the UK was a Member State and had fully participated in the preceding negotiations.
[204] See Article 67 (2) and (3) of the EU Withdrawal Agreement (above n. 203). In the UK this period is known as the 'Implementation Period'; see European Union (Withdrawal) Act 2018, s.1A(6) (as inserted by the European Union (Withdrawal Agreement) Act 2020.

As is discussed in Chapter 12, these cases are governed by the **EU Withdrawal Agreement 2019**.[205] Suffice to say here that Article 67 of the Agreement provides for the continuing application of Brussels II-bis with regard to jurisdiction and consequent recognition and enforcement of judgments given in legal proceedings instituted before the end of the transition period, for the recognition and enforcement of authentic instruments formally drawn up or registered and court settlements approved or concluded before the end of the transition period, and to requests and to applications received by the Central Authority or other competent authority of the requested State before the end of the transition period.

VI. MONITORING AND EVALUTATION

1.100. Article 101(1) obliges the Commission to present to the European Parliament and to the EESC 'a report on the ex post evaluation' of the Regulation. That report should be **presented by 2 August 2032**, that is, ten years after the Regulation came into force. Where necessary, the report should be accompanied by a legislative proposal.

1.101. Whereas it is standard practice to require the Commission to review the operation of a Regulation, a novelty of this Regulation is Article 101(2), which places, **as of 2 August 2025, an obligation upon Member States to provide the Commission upon request, 'where available', information** on:

(a) the number of decisions in matrimonial matters or in matters of parental responsibility in which jurisdiction was based on the Regulation grounds;
(b) with regard to applications for enforcement of an order a decision as referred to in Article 28(1),[206] the number of cases where enforcement has not occurred within six weeks from the moment the enforcement proceedings were initiated;
(c) the number of applications for refusal of recognition of a decision pursuant to Article 40 and the number of cases in which the refusal of recognition was granted;
(d) the number of applications for refusal of enforcement of a decision pursuant to Article 58 and the number of cases in which the refusal of enforcement was granted;
(e) the number of appeals lodged pursuant to Articles 61 and 62, respectively.

---

[205] See 12.6 et seq.
[206] That is, an order for the child's return in an application under the 1980 Hague Abduction Convention.

1.102. As Article 101(2) says, the above information will be relevant to an evaluation of the operation and application of the Regulation, but without gainsaying the usefulness of such statistics, it remains to be seen how effective this provision will prove to be. The information required will be hard to collect and will need to be coordinated in the sense that it must relate to the same periods. It should be noted that the **obligation only extends to providing the information where it is available.**

CHAPTER 2

COMMON RULES ON COURT PROCEEDINGS

I. Seising of a Court: Article 17 50
   A. Historical Background and Scope of Application 50
   B. Rationale and Structure of the Rule. 51
   C. Proceedings Instituted by the Court's Own Motion 53
   D. Relevance of ADR Proceedings Pending the Full Seising of
       the Court 54
   E. 'Document Instituting the Proceedings or an Equivalent
       Document'. 55
   F. The Document is 'Lodged with the Court' 56
   G. Service on the Respondent 57
II. Examination as to Jurisdiction: Article 18. 58
   A. Historical Background. 58
   B. The Rationale of the Rule and the Principle of Mutual Trust:
       The Court must Always, of its Own Duty, Assess Jurisdiction 59
   C. Jurisdiction 'Under the Regulation' 60
   D. Assessment of Jurisdiction in Other Member States. 61
   E. Effects of a Decision on Lack of Jurisdiction 63
III. Examination as to Admissibility: Article 19 63
   A. Historical Background to and Rationale of the Rule. 63
   B. Scope of Application: The Respondent has not Appeared in
       Court and is not Resident in the Forum 64
   C. Duties on the Court: The Structure of the Rule 66
   D. Intra-EU Transmission of Documents According to the 2020
       Service Regulation 67
   E. Transmission of Documents Out of the EU According to the
       1965 Hague Convention 69

2.1. Chapter 2, Section 3 of Brussels II-ter provides rules which are common to both matrimonial and parental responsibility cases. The Section encompasses diverse topics, ranging from the seising of a court, examination as to jurisdiction and examination as to admissibility, as well as rules on *lis pendens* and the right of the child to be heard (although the latter is only relevant in parental responsibility cases). This chapter is limited to examining the first procedural steps which need to be taken when a cross-border claim is filed, that is, the rules on seising of the court and the court's determinations that follow thereafter. Other topics will be discussed later on in Chapter 5 (*lis pendens*) and Chapter 7 (hearing of the child) respectively.

2.2. The rules provided by Articles 17, 18 and 19 constitute the backbone of uniform procedural rules for national proceedings. National procedural law is, however, a matter of **exclusive competence of Member States** such that the EU lacks competence to impinge in these matters. On the other hand, a common and functional framework is needed to ensure a correct and swift implementation of the Regulation. It also helps to strengthen mutual trust in national legal systems. The following rules thus seek to strike a delicate balance between these competing needs.

I. SEISING OF A COURT: ARTICLE 17

A. HISTORICAL BACKGROUND AND SCOPE OF APPLICATION

2.3. The rules on seising of a court have not been substantially changed, except for the addition of Article 17(c) in Brussels II-ter, which is discussed below (at 2.12), they are the same as previously provided by Article 16 Brussels II-bis. Article 16 was also identical to Article 11(4) Brussels II, which indeed was adopted as the model for Article 30 Brussels I and its successor, Article 32 Brussels I-bis.[1] Accordingly, as the four instruments (Brussels I, Brussels I-bis, Brussels II and Brussels II-bis) all use the same rule, framed exactly in the same terms, case law developed by the CJEU in relation to any of these instruments may be used to interpret the current Article 17.

2.4. Determining the moment in time when the court is seised will be relevant **in several situations**. The most important one is in relation to *lis pendens*, that is when two sets of proceedings, either identical or related one to each other, are pending in different Member States, as the application of the chronological rule provided by Article 20 requires ascertaining when a court is seised (see Chapter 5). There are, however, other situations where the Regulation connects effects to the seising of the court. For example, with regard to continued jurisdiction (so-called *perpetuatio jurisdictionis*) for the case where the child is lawfully relocated after proceedings have been instituted in the State of the child's habitual residence as envisaged by Article 7(1); or in relation to continued jurisdiction

---

[1] Article 11(4) Brussels II instead departed greatly from the previous Article 21 of the Brussels Convention, which had given rise to multiple problems in civil and commercial matters.

over abducted or retained children pursuant to Article 9(b)(iv); or in relation to the operation of transfer of proceedings under Article 12; or in relation to the procedure envisaged by Article 29 in abduction cases; or, of course, in relation to transitional application of the Regulation (Article 100).

B. RATIONALE AND STRUCTURE OF THE RULE

2.5. **Two opposite approaches can be found in national procedural laws**, depending on whether the documents instituting the proceedings must first be served on the defendant and then deposited by the court or, conversely, first deposited by the court and then served on the defendant. Simplifying the two models, the rules on the seising of a court may be described as, on the one hand, the serve-and-file approach (the former) and, on the other hand, the file-and-serve approach (the latter).[2]

2.6. Given such wide difference in national laws, it was deemed impossible both to elaborate on a single uniform rule, as well as to harmonise national laws into a common standard. A different path was thus taken. Article 17 acknowledges the divergences as to the definition of seisin in national laws of the Member States and reflects these divergences in **two alternatives**, each tailor-made for a different type of national procedure. However, the two alternatives do not imply referring to (diverging) national laws; instead, two procedures, different one from each other yet both euro-autonomous, have been provided for. It should be noted that **service of the instituting document** on the respondent **is never the relevant moment** for the seising of the court.

2.7. Under Article 17, a court shall be deemed to be seised:

a) at the time when the document instituting the proceedings or an equivalent document is **lodged with the court**, provided that the applicant has not subsequently failed to take the steps he or she was required to take to have service effected on the respondent;

b) if the document has to be served before being lodged with the court, at the time when it is **received by the authority** responsible for service, provided that the applicant has not subsequently failed to take the steps he or she was required to take to have the document lodged with the court.

In other words, Article 17 provides for **two different ways** for the seising of a court, which are put on an **equal footing**, requiring the same actions – lodging

---

[2] Such unofficial definitions were first introduced by A. BRIGGS, 'Decisions of British Courts during 2005 Involving Questions of Public or Private International Law' (2005) 76 *BYIL* 641, 655, when commenting upon UK decisions on *lis alibi pendens* and uncertainty as to dates.

of the document instituting the proceedings and service thereof on the respondent – to be performed, but in a different order. The underlying rationale is to put parties who compete in terms of filing a claim in different jurisdictions on the same footing so as to avoid any procedural disadvantage (or abuse) one of them may suffer (or seek) under national procedural laws. For the purpose of international jurisdiction, what is relevant is the **first contact with the administration of justice**, be it with the registrar, if the document has to be lodged with the court, or with the office for serving of documents if, according to national rules, the document has to be served on the defendant before it is lodged with the court. In practice, however, determining these moments may not be easy, especially in Member States where lodging a document does not of itself immediately initiate proceedings under national law. In this regard, a rule prescribing national authorities responsible for service to note the date (and the time) that the instituting document was lodged with the court would have been useful.[3]

2.8. Either moment will be of relevance, whichever comes first, as long as the necessary subsequent step mentioned by Article 17 has also been taken by the applicant. The completion of the full procedure as outlined by Article 17 is mandatory in order for the rule to operate. This construction has been described by reference to the concept of **retroactivity**.[4] The court becomes seised retroactively at the date when the first act was completed, irrespective of the exact date when the second act is accomplished, as long as this actually takes place.

2.9. As the rule is meant to ensure protection against abuse of process, for the purposes of checking the compliance of the applicant, account should not be taken of delays caused by the judicial system applicable, but only of any **failure of the applicant to act diligently**.[5] In addition, as discussed below,[6] the timing between the two events may be suspended in view of pursuing an amicable settlement of the dispute.

2.10. It is for each court to decide, according to its own *lex fori*, which path is appropriate to ascertain the moment in time when it is seised. However, once that path is determined, the relevant moment for the seising of the court

---

[3] Such a rule is to be found in Article 32(2) Brussels I-bis.
[4] C. Kohler, 'Die Revision des Brüsseler und des Luganer Übereinkommens über die gerichtliche Zuständigkeit und die Vollstreckung gerichtlicher Entscheidungen in Zivil – und Handelssachen – Generalia und Gerichtsstandsproblematik' in P. Gottwald (ed.), *Revision des EuGVÜ/Neues Schiedsverfahrensrecht*, Verlag Ernst und Werner Gieseking, 2000, p. 25 talks of Rückwirkungslösung; see also P. Mankowski, 'Art. 17 Brussels IIter' in U. Magnus and P. Mankowski (eds), *Brussels IIbis Regulation*, OttoSchmidt, 2023, p. 253, para. 39.
[5] CJEU, 16 July 2015 (order), *P*, C-507/14, para. 37.
[6] See below 2.14 et seq.

will be determined according to the Regulation and not to national law.[7] As an example, the path listed under paragraph (a) is more fitting for filing family proceedings under German, Swedish and Dutch law, while the path envisaged by paragraph (b) is more appropriate under Italian, French and Belgian law.[8]

2.11. Reference to 'the time' when the court was seised, as expressed in the English version of the Regulation for both cases, should be considered as meaning 'at the date'. This is not only in line with the purpose of the rule, but also better reflects the notion embodied in other-language versions.[9]

C. PROCEEDINGS INSTITUTED BY THE COURT'S OWN MOTION

2.12. A different moment might come into consideration when proceedings are instituted by the court's own motion. This scenario had not been provided for under the previous Brussels II-bis rule and had consequently attracted some criticism.[10] This may occur, for example, in parental responsibility cases that arise with regard to abandoned children or unaccompanied migrant children. In such cases, Article 17(c) provides that a court shall be seised at the time when the decision to institute the proceedings is taken by the court or, where such a decision is not required, at the time when the case is registered by the court.

2.13. Surprisingly, in such cases there is no requirement that such a decision be served on any interested party. It is surely desirable that notice be given to any party whose interest is known to the court.

---

[7] At 2.17 et seq.
[8] So, and with references to national provisions, see P. MANKOWSKI, above n. 4, p. 258, paras 62–63.
[9] See 'alla data' and 'à la date' in the Italian and French versions. In this sense, see P. MANKOWSKI, above n. 4, p. 198, para. 10. However, reference to the day may not suffice to determine when the court is seised, for example, in *lis pendens* cases. This happened, for example, in CJEU, 22 June 2016, *M.H.*, C-173/16, where, on the very same date, a divorce petition was received by the registry of a court in England (at 7.53 am) and a judicial separation summons was also lodged at the registry of a court in Ireland (at 2.30 pm). While the chronological principle should probably also apply to these cases, the practical question arises, given that Member States do not always keep track of the precise hour where both acts (reception for service and lodging with the court of documents) are actually performed. The CJEU did not address this specific issue, the case being solved on the different level of applying the autonomous rule set by Article 16 Brussels II-bis for determining when the court is seised.
[10] P. MANKOWSKI, above n. 4, p. 246, para. 9, proposing that the relevant moment should be 'when the court is first concerned with the matter as evidenced by the record or the minutes of the court'.

D. RELEVANCE OF ADR PROCEEDINGS PENDING THE FULL SEISING OF THE COURT

2.14. The growing importance of **mediation** and other methods of **alternative dispute resolution**, which may be explored during court proceedings, has prompted the legislator to address the question of how such a situation impinges on the seising of the court. **Recital (35)** clarifies, in accordance with the ruling by the Court of Justice in *P*,[11] that a court is deemed to be seised at the time when the document instituting the proceedings is lodged with the court, even when such proceedings have been suspended with a view to finding an amicable solution before such document is served upon the respondent (and therefore without the respondent having knowledge of such proceedings being started), provided that the party who instituted the proceedings has subsequently taken the necessary steps to have service effected on the respondent.

2.15. In *P* a Spanish-Portuguese couple argued about custody rights over their common children, habitually resident in Portugal but on holiday in Spain at the moment of proceedings. The father filed a request for a provisional order on custody rights at the court in Madrid, as a preliminary request to divorce proceedings. Ten days later, however, before the document was served on his wife, he filed a request for a suspension of proceedings with a view to exploring the possibility of reaching an amicable settlement of the dispute with his spouse. The suspension was granted for a maximum of 60 days, lapsing from that same order. Some 40 days after that decision, which was never served on the mother (who was unaware of what was on-going in Spain), the mother filed a petition for custody rights before the Lisbon Family Court, also claiming that the children were unlawfully retained in Spain. The day after, the father resumed his Spanish proceedings and asked the court in Madrid to adopt provisional measures prohibiting the children from leaving the country and to fix a date for the hearing. The mother was summoned by phone to a hearing to take place 15 days later, and was served by return post of this application. At the hearing, the Spanish court rejected the contention that such court was the second seised and allowed the father's action to continue. The Portuguese court, accepting that the Spanish court was first seised, stayed and then dismissed the case in favour of the Spanish proceedings. The mother repeatedly appealed both decisions until the Supreme Court of Portugal decided to refer the case for a preliminary ruling by the CJEU.

2.16. The CJEU confirmed the view taken by both national courts and stressed that the mere lodging with the court is of itself sufficient for seising the court, provided that the applicant has subsequently not failed to take the required

---

[11] CJEU, 16 July 2015 (order), C-507/14, *P*.

steps to have service effected on the respondent. The Court further noted that while the staying of the proceedings is not mentioned by the provision, this fact may acquire relevance if it shows that the applicant is at fault, for example by omitting to take the necessary steps. However, in this case, at the stage when the staying of proceedings was sought and ordered, it was with a view to exploring the possibility of reaching an amicable settlement of the dispute. Given that Brussels II-bis (and Brussels II-ter even more so) attaches a particular weight to the amicable settlement of disputes, such a request and the subsequent staying of the proceedings could not be ascribed to the fault of the applicant.[12]

E. 'DOCUMENT INSTITUTING THE PROCEEDINGS OR AN EQUIVALENT DOCUMENT'

2.17. The expression 'document instituting the proceedings or an equivalent document' is to be found not just in Article 17(a) but also in several other rules of the Regulation, mainly with regard to grounds for refusing recognition (Articles 38(b) and 39(1)(b)), but also with regard to examination in respect of admissibility (Article 19(1)) and to the issuance of the certificate (Article 47(3)), and in the annexes. It should therefore be interpreted **consistently** through all the text and, as usual, **autonomously**, leaving no room for reference to national law when determining the meaning of the phrase 'the document instituting the proceedings'.

2.18. According to the Court of Justice's case law, regard must be made to *any document that will start a proceeding leading to a recognisable decision.*[13] But such a wide concept is subject to two requirements: first, the document must convey at the very least sufficient information to enable the other party to decide to take action; second, it must be served on the other party. However, this is the minimum requirement for the purpose of this rule[14] and one should avoid undertaking a more precise definition of these elements. Such an effort would be extremely difficult in the light of the variety of national forms such document may take; furthermore, any stricter definition would be frustrated by the fact that the seising of a court may be made also by any 'equivalent

---

[12] Above n. 11, para. 39. This view is equally apt for the application of Brussels II-ter. See in this regard *Practice Guide for the Application of the Brussels IIb Regulation* (2022) (hereinafter *2022 Practice Guide*), p. 97.
[13] See ECJ, 16 June 1981, *Klomps*, C-166/80, paras 8–11, with regard to Article 27 of the 1968 Brussels Convention.
[14] P. MANKOWSKI (above n. 4, p. 248, para. 16) points out that it is not required that the initial request presents a good arguable case or that it refers to any means of proof for the contentions it contains. Furthermore, it should not be necessary for the applicant longing for divorce to present a marriage certificate, since this is rather an administrative requirement and not an integral part of the initial application.

document'. In other words, it is not the external features of the document but the *function* that it serves – that is, being the first step of a proceedings leading to a recognisable decision – that will define whether the document is sufficient to seise the court for the purposes of the Regulation.

2.19. Careful consideration should be given to the case where some sort of **preliminary proceedings** are instituted with a view to bringing subsequent principal proceedings. This might be the case, for example, where one of the parties seeks an injunctive relief, or when preliminary proceedings to apply for legal aid are needed, or where an application for some kind of reconciliation procedure between the parties is lodged. As a general principle, the seising of the court for a preliminary proceeding will not be sufficient to establish the seising of the court with regard to the principal proceedings, as long as the **two proceedings are procedurally unrelated** one to each other.

2.20. However, the solution might be different where, under national law, the preliminary proceedings **must** precede the filing of the principal proceedings. The CJEU has, for example, clarified that where a mandatory conciliation procedure was lodged before a national conciliation authority, such a date should be considered as the date on which a 'court' is deemed to be seised.[15] Similarly, this may occur with regard to an application for legal aid, as long as the document needed for filing the proceedings meets the conditions required by Article 17 and discussed above at 2.18.

F. THE DOCUMENT IS 'LODGED WITH THE COURT'

2.21. The requirement that the document is 'lodged with the court' refers to the date and time when the instituting document, as described above at 2.18, is received by the court. In other words, **deposit alone is sufficient** for determining the moment of seising of the court and it is not a requirement that this effect is also envisaged under national rules. This means that, for the purpose of EU Regulations, it is irrelevant that under the competent *lex fori* the lodging of that document does not of itself immediately initiate the proceedings required.

2.22. The above principle has been clarified by the CJEU in *MH*.[16] The case concerned parallel matrimonial proceedings filed in the UK and Ireland. Mrs MH filed a divorce petition which was received by the registry of the

---

[15] CJEU, 20 December 2017, *Schlomp*, C-467/16, para. 58. This is now clarified in Recital (35), last sentence and in *2022 Practice Guide*, p. 97. See I. Kunda and D. Vrbljanac, 'Lis Pendens' in C. Honorati (ed.), *Jurisdiction in Matrimonial Matters, Parental Responsibility and International Abduction*, Giappichelli/Peter Lang, 2017, p. 226.

[16] CJEU, 22 June 2016 (order), *M.H*, C-173/16.

Family Law Court in England at 7.53 am on 7 September 2015 and date-stamped at 10.30 am of that same day. The petition was subsequently issued by the Family Law Court registry on 11 September 2015 and served on the other party on 15 September 2015. Mr MH lodged a judicial separation summons at the registry of the Irish High Court at around 2.30 pm on 7 September 2015. This was issued later the same day and served on Mrs MH on 9 September 2015.

2.23. According to the *lex fori* of each legal system, the divorce proceedings in England were deemed to be initiated on 11 September 2015 and pending from that day, while the judicial separation proceedings in Ireland were initiated as from 7 September 2015. However, the Irish Court of Appeal was doubtful that this construction was consistent with the wording of Article 16 Brussels II-bis and made a referral for preliminary ruling on the issue of whether the document is 'lodged with the court' when the court receives the document even though that event does not immediately commence the proceedings under the relevant national procedural rules.

2.24. The CJEU ruled that what was then Article 16 Brussels II-bis (and now Article 17 Brussels II-ter) contains an **autonomous definition** of the time when a court is deemed to be seised, which is determined by the performance of a **single act**, namely, depending on the procedural system under consideration, the lodging of the document instituting the proceedings, or the service of that document. Furthermore, Article 16(1)(a) (now Article 17(a)) requires the satisfaction not of two conditions (that is, lodging of the document *and* service of the same), but merely of one – the lodging of the document instituting proceedings or an equivalent document. The lodging of the document of itself renders the court seised, provided that the applicant has not subsequently failed to take the steps he was required to take to have service effected on the respondent. Any different rule under national law is irrelevant. Accordingly, once it has been established which of the two options (that is, Article 16 (1)(a) or (b) Brussels II-bis at the time of the decision, now corresponding to Article 17(a) and (b) Brussels II-ter) applies, depending on the nature of the internal law of the Member State concerned, when a court is seised can be objectively established solely on the basis of that time, **irrespective of any national procedural rule** intended to determine when and in what circumstances proceedings are initiated or are considered to be pending.[17]

G. SERVICE ON THE RESPONDENT

2.25. A similar construction must be given with regard to the requirement of service of the instituting document. As long as service has actually taken

---

[17] CJEU, 22 June 2016 (order), *M.H*, C-173/16, paras 25–28.

place, it is not the date of actual service that is relevant, but **the date when the document has been received by the authority** which, under the national rules, is responsible for such service. Cross-border service will normally be pursued in accordance to what is now the **2020 Service Regulation**,[18] which applies to all Member States, except Denmark.[19] The competent authority must be the one designated by each Member State in accordance with what is now Article 3 of the 2020 Service Regulation (formerly Article 2 of the 2007 Service Regulation).[20] The Hague Service Convention[21] or national rules will apply with regard to transmission for service of documents to be performed **outside the EU**.

2.26. Irregularities of service after lodging do not alter the seising of the court, as they might be cured at a later stage, even if this may undermine the respondent's right of defence. Such a possibility will be taken into consideration by the court when assessing the regularity and admissibility of the application pursuant to Article 19.

II. EXAMINATION AS TO JURISDICTION: ARTICLE 18

A. HISTORICAL BACKGROUND

2.27. Article 18 provides:

> Where a court of a Member State is seised of a case over which it has no jurisdiction as to the substance of the matter under this Regulation and over which a court of another Member State has jurisdiction as to the substance of the matter under this Regulation, it shall declare of its own motion that it has no jurisdiction.

2.28. In essence, this provision has remained unchanged through the different versions of the Regulation. Brussels II-ter only makes a minor amendment to the previous texts, with regard to the fact that the State shall have no jurisdiction 'as to the substance of the matter'. This latter clarification was not included in

---

[18] Regulation (EU) No 2020/1784 of the European Parliament and of the Council of 25 November 2020 on the service in the Member States of judicial and extrajudicial documents in civil or commercial matters (service of documents) (recast) (the 2020 Service Regulation). See below at 2.55.

[19] For further analysis on the instrument to be used for service of documents outside the EU, see below at 2.59.

[20] Regulation (EC) No 1393/2007 13 November 2007 on the service in the Member States of judicial and extrajudicial documents in civil or commercial matters (service of documents) (the 2007 Service Regulation), which repealed the previous Council Regulation (EC) No 1348/2000.

[21] That is, the 1965 Hague Convention on the Service Abroad of Judicial and Extrajudicial Documents in Civil or Commercial Matters, to which all EU Member States are parties.

Article 17 Brussels II-bis or Article 9 Brussels II. But these additional words only make explicit what was previously clearly implicit, bringing about no substantial improvement.

2.29. Article 18 compels the court to declare, by its own motion, that it has no jurisdiction where a) such court has no jurisdiction under the Regulation as to the substance of the matter **and** b) a court of *another* Member State has jurisdiction (as to the substance of the matter) under this Regulation. **Both requirements** have to be met for the rule to apply.

B. THE RATIONALE OF THE RULE AND THE PRINCIPLE OF MUTUAL TRUST: THE COURT MUST ALWAYS, OF ITS OWN DUTY, ASSESS JURISDICTION

2.30. The heading of the rule ('Examination as to jurisdiction') is misleading inasmuch as while on its face regard is made to the moment and the outcome of the court assessing its own competence, the rationale of the rule is more far-reaching and is deeply rooted in the essence of EU **judicial cooperation**. Its final aim is to safeguard the EU jurisdictional system, based on a distribution of competence among EU Member States which needs to be respected by all. The Brussels (I and II) system is a **closed and complete system** that must be respected and applied by all Member States. It thus reinforces and builds on the principle of mutual trust. This is done with regard to two different moments.

2.31. Article 18 firstly sets the seed of EU uniform procedural law, requiring any court which is seised of a matter which *prima facie* appears to fall under Brussels II-ter to analyse and **assess its own jurisdiction under the Regulation**. This operation must be done *ex officio*, without waiting for a formal request to be made by the parties. This also implies that any factual assessment integrating a head of jurisdiction should be made by the court on its own motion.[22]

2.32. This assessment must be carried out even when it is not required, or even forbidden, under national laws. **National procedural law** may, for example, impose time limitations or bar the exception of lack of jurisdiction. Similarly, national laws may limit appellate courts in reviewing international jurisdiction of a case challenged in a superior court. However, such national rules are subservient to Article 18, which, being an EU rule, will always prevail. Indeed, a flawless application of uniform rules on jurisdiction as provided by the Regulation serves the general interest to the administration of justice within the EU rather than the individual interests of the parties concerned or

---

[22] See, for example, the consequences of ascertaining habitual residence only relying on the parties' submissions in Chapter 3 at 3.52 et seq.

even of the particular Member State. The burden of correct interpretation and application of all rules, as well as of a careful screening of all circumstances which may ground international competence, is put entirely on the shoulders of the seised court. This also applies to **appellate courts**, which must always verify, by their own motion, that, at the time the lower court was seised, jurisdiction was given over that case.[23]

2.33. It should also be borne in mind that international competence **cannot be reviewed** at the stage of recognition and enforcement of the decision (see Article 69). In other words, the jurisdictional assessment made by the court seised in the State of origin will be finally binding for all Member States. The whole Regulation is strongly grounded on the principle of reciprocal trust that all courts will correctly apply jurisdictional rules.[24]

C. JURISDICTION 'UNDER THE REGULATION'

2.34. As a first step, the seised court is required to assess whether jurisdiction is provided 'under the Regulation'. Under Brussels II-bis, the effect of such a provision was to rule out the possibility of jurisdiction based on the appearance of the defendant/respondent. Following the introduction by Brussels II-ter of Article 10,[25] which allows for **a choice-of-court agreement** in parental responsibility cases, the concrete operation of this rule is partially reduced. However, it will still apply in matrimonial matters, where choice-of-court is not allowed, and in all cases where the conditions required by Article 10 are not met.

2.35. The rule raises some delicate **coordination issues** with regard to Article 6 and Article 14. Unfortunately, the issue, which had already been raised under Brussels II-bis, has not been clarified by the new provisions. These two rules provide for the so-called '**residual jurisdiction**' under national law.[26] According to the former, which applies in matrimonial matters, where a court has no jurisdiction 'pursuant to Article 3, 4 or 5', jurisdiction may be determined under national law. Article 14 provides a similar solution with regard to parental responsibility, giving precedence to Articles 7 to 11. The purpose of Articles 6 and 14 is to include national rules within the system of the Regulation, albeit on a secondary and residual level, which only come into consideration after seeking to apply the uniform rules. As national rules are therefore considered, albeit indirectly, as a part of the Regulation's system, the question arises as to how these

---

[23] For a case concerning the corresponding rule set in Article 19 of the Brussels Convention, see: ECJ, 15 November 1983, *Duijnstee*, 288/82, para. 15. See also P. MANKOWSKI, above n. 4, p. 266, para. 24.
[24] Among many others, see CJEU, 19 November 2015, *P*, C-455/15 PPU, para. 46.
[25] Discussed in Chapter 4 at 4.42 et seq.
[26] See, respectively, Chapter 3 at 3.67 et seq and Chapter 4 at 4.166 et seq.

provisions coordinate with Article 18, which generally refers to jurisdiction which is established 'under this Regulation'.

2.36. Given the general aim of Article 18 – namely, to safeguard the assignment of competences as provided by the Regulation with regard to all Member States – and that, on their proper construction, Articles 6(1) and 14 only come into consideration after it is ascertained that no other court within the EU can exercise jurisdiction under the Regulation, it is suggested that the seised court should stick to the following path:

a) at first determine if it has jurisdiction under the uniform rules provided by the Regulation for matrimonial matters (Articles 3–5) or for parental responsibility (Articles 7–11). If this is not the case, it should
b) determine whether any other Member State may exercise jurisdiction under any of the above mentioned criteria;
c.1) if another Member State court has jurisdiction under the Regulation, then it should declare its lack of jurisdiction, pursuant to Article 18;
c.2) if no other Member State court has jurisdiction under the Regulation, then it should determine if it can exercise jurisdiction under its own national rules, pursuant to Articles 6(1) and 14.

2.37. On this analysis, determining whether the court has jurisdiction '**under this Regulation**' is to be construed as meaning that jurisdiction is granted on Articles 3–5 for matrimonial matters, or Articles 7–11 for parental responsibility, with no regard to be given to national rules. The opposite construction, including assessing whether competence can be grounded on national grounds before that the possible competence of other Member States has been verified, would be inconsistent with the reading of Articles 7 and 11, as confirmed by the CJEU in *Sundelind*.[27]

D. ASSESSMENT OF JURISDICTION IN OTHER MEMBER STATES

2.38. It is also for the court seised to assess whether **courts in other Member States have jurisdiction**. As seen above (at 2.30 et seq), such an assessment aims to guarantee a consistent and workable functioning of the system as a whole, and not just from the point of view of the jurisdiction of the forum. Such an exercise may at times become **difficult and uncertain**, especially considering that some discretion is added to the system through the new additional provision on transfer of proceedings in parental responsibility cases. According

---

[27] ECJ, 29 November 2007, *Sundelind Lopez*, C-68/07.

to Article 13 Brussels II-ter,[28] a court which in principle does not have jurisdiction under this Regulation, but with which the child has a particular connection and is considered to be better placed to assess the best interests of the child in the particular case, may request a transfer of jurisdiction from the court of the Member State of the habitual residence of the child. This provision introduces some uncertainty as to whether another Member State may (or may not) exercise jurisdiction in the given case. In the light of Recital (37), which most appropriately clarifies that such a non-seised court should have the discretion to request a transfer of jurisdiction, but is under no obligation to do so, it is submitted that this possibility should be considered with great caution by the seised court.[29]

2.39. In any case, such an assessment of a future, prospective jurisdiction can **never be binding upon courts of other Member States**, which will need to make their own assessment. It may thus occur that the other court will also deny jurisdiction and refuse to hear the case, thereby leading to a negative conflict of jurisdiction and a denial of justice. Unfortunately, notwithstanding several pleas in the legal literature, a *forum necessitatis*, which was lacking in Brussels II-bis, has not been introduced in Brussels II-ter.[30]

2.40. A decision declaring lack of jurisdiction is not required to include any indication as to which court (in other Member States) may hear the case under the Regulation. However, notwithstanding that such an indication has no legal effect, it is suggested that the seised court should expressly state its reasons leading to the declaration on lack of jurisdiction and, possibly, give evidence of the grounds supporting the view that the case should be heard in another Member State. An express and consistent reasoning on this point would strengthen the perception of an integrated jurisdictional system and, possibly, provide the party with a more foreseeable access to justice. Furthermore, this will distinguish the case under Article 18 (where declaration of lack of competence is aimed to preserve the competence of another Member State) from cases where there is a negative conflict of jurisdiction and there is no court, either within the EU or in the forum, able to hear the case. In any case, the Regulation does not require the court lacking competence to transfer the case to the competent court of another Member State. It will in fact be for the interested party to bring the proceedings before the court of such other Member State.[31]

---

[28] Chapter 4 at 4.162 et seq.
[29] The opening of the draft rule that was discussed in the negotiations before the Council declares it applies 'without prejudice to Article 12' (on transfer of proceedings). This part was then removed and its content was added in Recital (37).
[30] On the lack of a *forum necessitatis* in Brussels II-ter (as opposed to other EU Regulations such as the Maintenance Regulation, the Succession Regulation and the Relationship Property Regulations), see further Chapter 3 at 3.85 et seq.
[31] *2022 Practice Guide*, p. 30.

2.41. There is obviously also no requirement that the court in the other Member State is already seised. However, when this is the case, the examination required by Article 18 will take precedence over Article 20 governing *lis pendens*. This latter provision will apply only when the seised court is *prima facie* convinced that it has jurisdiction.

E. EFFECTS OF A DECISION ON LACK OF JURISDICTION

2.42. Article 18 requires a declaration of lack of jurisdiction. The form and the effects of such a decision are questions of procedural law which, as such, are governed by the *lex fori*. In particular, it will be for the *lex fori* to establish if there is a *res judicata* effect between the parties.[32] However, it may be wondered whether a decision declaring lack of jurisdiction, although framed with regard to the case at hand, has a more general effect and implies that no (other) court in that particular Member State has jurisdiction at that particular moment.[33]

III. EXAMINATION AS TO ADMISSIBILITY: ARTICLE 19

A. HISTORICAL BACKGROUND TO AND RATIONALE OF THE RULE

2.43. Article 19 deals with the situation where the respondent who is habitually resident in a State other than the Member State where proceedings were instituted does not enter an appearance. In such circumstances, Article 19 gives the court power to stay proceedings effectively until it is shown that the respondent had sufficient notice of the proceeding to prepare his or her defence.

2.44. Article 19 is identically worded to Article 18 Brussels II-bis, which it replaces, except that Article 19(2) and (3) refers to what was then the new Regulation on service of documents, Regulation (EC) 1393/2007, which, ironically, has now been replaced by the 2020 Regulation.[34] As in other cases previously noted,[35] the rule is modelled on the corresponding rules of

---

[32] But see CJEU, 15 November 2012, *Gothaer*, C-456/11; and at Chapter 8.27.
[33] The question may be relevant with regard to matrimonial proceedings. For example, if a decision declaring lack of jurisdiction is grounded on the fact that the applicant is found not to have been habitually resident for the six months immediately before the application is made, as required by Article 3(a)(vi), and such a requirement is met at a later stage. In contrast, decisions relating to children never raise an issue of *res judicata* as such decisions are always *rebus sic stantibus* and never become final.
[34] See above, n. 18.
[35] See above 2.3 with regard to seising of the court.

the Brussels I Regulation and its successor, Articles 26 and 28 Brussels I-bis Regulation, respectively.

2.45. The rule only applies on the strict condition that the respondent is habitually resident in a State other than the one where the proceedings are instituted and does not enter an appearance (see below 2.48 et seq). The rule embodies one of the cornerstones of the right to **a fair trial** by aiming to safeguard the right of the respondent to be given the opportunity to an effective defence. While the rule aims at ensuring that such an opportunity was actually given, it does not oblige the respondent to appear in court. Consequently, there is no sanction against the respondent for failing to appear. In fact, where the respondent was properly served but nonetheless made a decision not to appear in court (which means that Article 19 does not apply), the court should undertake proper scrutiny that all jurisdictional rules have been respected pursuant to Article 18. The two rules (Articles 18 and 19) therefore provide a common minimum framework for the safeguard of judicial procedural rights and a fair trial.

2.46. A thorough and complete scrutiny of these safeguards ensures the proper operation of the Regulation in pursuit of its aim to promote the **free circulation of decisions**. The requirement that where a decision is given in default of appearance, the respondent is properly served with the document instituting the proceedings in sufficient time and in such a way as to enable him/her to arrange for his or her defence is also necessary in view of the recognition and enforcement of decisions, as clearly follows from Article 38(b).[36]

2.47. This is one of the very few instances where the Regulation sets the **same duty on the courts of two Member States**. While Article 18 requires the court of the State where the decision is originated to perform such examination at the first stage of the proceedings, Article 38(b) allows the court in the State of recognition to double-check this same requirement if proceedings are brought to oppose recognition or enforcement. In order to avoid inconsistencies between these two assessments, Articles 19 and 38(b) should be read in conjunction one with each other.

B. SCOPE OF APPLICATION: THE RESPONDENT HAS NOT APPEARED IN COURT AND IS NOT RESIDENT IN THE FORUM

2.48. Article 19 as a whole only applies when two conditions are met, both of which refer to the respondent. The first is that the respondent must **not have entered an appearance**. If the respondent has been served wrongly, at a wrong

---

[36] See below at Chapter 8.

address, in a language he or she does not understand, or lately, but nonetheless appears in court, Article 19 **does not apply**. All the rule is concerned with is that the respondent had knowledge of the proceedings in due time. Any irregularities in the serving of the introductory statement must be assessed by the court according to national rules and its own discretion. Similarly, if the respondent enters an appearance only in order to raise the objection that the court lacks jurisdiction, Article 19 does not come into consideration.[37]

2.49. The second condition is that the respondent must be **habitually resident in a State 'other than the Member State where the proceedings were instituted'**. This implies that habitual residence may be in *any* State, either a Member State or a third State.[38] The procedural safeguards guaranteed to citizens who are resident within the EU are thus extended to all. In contrast, if the respondent has his habitual residence within the forum State, the rule does not apply. The reason for this is that service of documents would then be an internal matter which is expected to cause less problems and difficulties.

2.50. Under this rule, it is the place where the respondent has his or her **habitual residence** that is relevant, not where the service of document should take place or has in fact taken place. Habitual residence is an autonomous notion to be interpreted consistently through the whole Regulation.[39] In this context, such a limitation can be problematic and can possibly lead to inconsistencies. It is certainly true that in most cases, the place where the document is served and the place of habitual residence will coincide. However, there are situations where the place of residence and the place where the service of the instituting document takes place are different, and service of documents can successfully be made in a place other than the respondent's habitual residence.

2.51. This may, for example, be the case with regard to international abduction of children, where the abducting parent is no longer at his or her place of habitual residence, where the service of document can successfully be made. Where the left-behind parent promptly files proceedings for custody over the child in the State of prior residence of the child and of the family as a whole, the habitual residence of the abducting parent will often still be in that State. However, such a parent will no longer be living there and the instituting document should be served in a different jurisdiction (for example, at the residence of the respondent's parents in his or her State of origin, or at the workplace of a person living in one State, but working in another). On the face of it, Article 19 does not oblige the

---

[37] P. MANKOWSKI, above n. 4, p. 274, para. 25, making the point that Article 19 aims at protecting a fair trial, not the rules on jurisdiction.
[38] A view reinforced by Article 19(3), which applies the 1965 Hague Service Convention; see below at 2.59 et seq.
[39] Below Chapter 3 at 3.30 and Chapter 4 at 4.8 et seq on autonomous interpretation of habitual residence for spouses and children, respectively.

court in the State of prior habitual residence of the abducting parent to examine the admissibility of the claim on custody filed by the left-behind parent. In fact, the requirement that residence of the respondent is in a different State is not met. However, failing to do so will give rise to a possible refusal of recognition and/or enforcement of the subsequent decision. In fact, Article 38(b) only gives relevance to the fact that the respondent has had the opportunity to have knowledge of the proceedings and to be able to arrange for his or her defence, irrespective of where the respondent has his or her habitual residence at the time the proceedings was instituted. Coordination problems between the two rules should be solved in light of the right to a fair process and Article 19 should be interpreted consistently.

C. DUTIES ON THE COURT: THE STRUCTURE OF THE RULE

2.52. With regard to the examination to be performed by the court in the above-mentioned situation of a respondent not entering an appearance, attention needs first to be drawn to the peculiar structure of the rule.

2.53. Article 19(1) is best regarded as defining the residual scope of the rule since it is subject to Article 19(2), which has priority, and to Article 19(3), which will apply when the situation envisaged by Article 19(2) is not met. The criterion that determines which paragraph is applicable is the legal instrument according to which transmission for service of the instituting document shall take place. Priority is given – as usual under general rules – to the Service Regulation. Although Article 19(2) refers to Regulation (EC) No 1393/2007 on the service in the Member States of judicial and extra-judicial documents in civil or commercial matters,[40] as said above and as further explained below,[41] the 2007 Regulation has since been superseded by the 2020 Regulation. When this instrument is not applicable, the Hague Convention of 15 November 1965 on the service abroad of judicial and extra-judicial documents in civil or commercial matters applies, as mentioned by Article 19(3). In effect, Article 19(1) only applies in the residual cases where neither the 2020 Regulation nor the 1965 Hague Convention applies, that is, where the other State is neither a Member State nor a Hague Convention State.

2.54. Bearing in mind this structure and the superseding 2020 Service Regulation, the proper order to apply the different provisions in Article 19 is as follows:

> 1. Where a respondent habitually resident in a State other than the Member State where the proceedings were instituted does not enter an appearance …

---

[40] Above, n. 20.
[41] Respectively, above at n. 18 and below at 2.55 et seq.

2. Article 19 of Regulation (EC) No 1393/2007 [now Article 22 of Regulation (EU) No 2020/1784] shall apply instead of paragraph 1 of this Article if the document instituting the proceedings or an equivalent document had to be transmitted from one Member State to another pursuant to that Regulation.

3. Where Regulation (EC) No 1393/2007 [now Regulation (EU) No 2020/1784] is not applicable, Article 15 of the Hague Convention of 15 November 1965 on the service abroad of judicial and extrajudicial documents in civil or commercial matters shall apply if the document instituting the proceedings or an equivalent document had to be transmitted abroad pursuant to that Convention.

1. … if neither Regulation (EC) No 1393/2007 [now Regulation (EU) No 2020/1784] nor the Hague Convention of 15 November 1965 on the service abroad of judicial and extrajudicial documents in civil or commercial matters is applicable the court with jurisdiction shall stay the proceedings so long as it is not shown that the respondent has been able to receive the document instituting the proceedings or an equivalent document in sufficient time to enable him or her to arrange for his or her defence, or that all necessary steps have been taken to this end.

D. INTRA-EU TRANSMISSION OF DOCUMENTS ACCORDING TO THE 2020 SERVICE REGULATION

2.55. As noted earlier, although Article 19(2) refers to Regulation (EC) No 1393/2007, that Regulation has been superseded by the 2020 Regulation, which entered into force on 22 December 2020 and applies from 1 July 2022. While a rule making reference to an already-outdated instrument is certainly inelegant, it does not affect the substance, as Article 63 of the 2020 Regulation repeals the 2007 Regulation as from the date of its application. Article 63(2) further explains that:

> 2. References to the repealed Regulation shall be construed as references to this Regulation and shall be read in accordance with the correlation table in Annex III.

Reference to Article 19 of Regulation (EC) No 1393/2007 should thus be read as a reference to **Article 22** of the 2020 Regulation, whose content is similar to the former, save for some stylistic adjustment.

2.56. Like its predecessor, the 2020 Regulation applies to all EU Member States, including Denmark.[42] When service of document is required within Member

---

[42] In accordance with Protocol No 22 of the Lisbon Treaty, Denmark is not a part to any of the measures taken pursuant to Title V of Part Three TFEU concerning the area of freedom, security and justice. Hence, Denmark is in principle not bound by the EU Service Regulation. However, the full content of the 1997 Regulation has been transposed in a bilateral agreement

States, transmission of all documents must be done in accordance to such an instrument, irrespective of where the respondent's habitual residence is.

2.57. As the 2020 Service Regulation is entirely devoted to the issue of transmission of documents, Article 22 is far more complex than what is provided for residual cases in Article 19 Brussels II-ter. It is not our intention here to provide comprehensive discussion of a rule which is structured in five paragraphs. Nevertheless, it is useful to reproduce Article 22(1), which reads as follows:

> 1. Where a document instituting proceedings or its equivalent has had to be transmitted to another Member State for the purpose of service under this Regulation and the defendant has not entered an appearance, judgment shall not be given until it is established that the service or the delivery of the document was effected in sufficient time to enable the defendant to enter a defence and that:
>   (a) the document was served by a method prescribed by the law of the Member State addressed for the service of documents in domestic actions upon persons who are within its territory; or
>   (b) the document was in fact delivered to the defendant or to the defendant's residence by another method provided for by this Regulation.

2.58. In order to attenuate the rigidity of this rule, Article 22(2) contemplates a derogation to paragraph 1 and gives discretion to the court to give judgment even if no certificate of service (or its equivalent) has been received. However, the court will make sure that the relevant document has been transmitted by one of the several methods provided for in the Regulation; that an adequate period has elapsed since the date of the transmission of the document (no less than six months); and that every reasonable effort has been made to obtain a certificate by the Member State. Article 22(3) justifies for provisional and protective measures in cases of urgency; Article 22(4) allows the court to relieve the defendant from the effects of the expiry of the time for appeal from the judgment, under the strict conditions provided for, with the only exclusion, provided for by Article 22(5), of judgments concerning the status or capacity of persons.

---

on the service of judicial and extra-judicial documents in civil and commercial matters signed on 19 October 2005 between the EC and Denmark (OJ EC 2005 L 300/55 of 17 November 2005; see also Council Decision 2006/326/EC of 27 April 2006 approving the said agreement). In accordance with the 2006 bilateral agreement, by letter of 22 December 2020 (OJEU L19/1 of 21 January 2021) Denmark has notified the Commission of its decision to implement the contents of the 2020 Service Regulation (above, n. 18). As such, the content of the 2020 Regulation is also applicable with regard to acts transmitted to or received from Denmark.

E. TRANSMISSION OF DOCUMENTS OUT OF THE EU ACCORDING TO THE 1965 HAGUE CONVENTION

2.59. When the instituting document needs to be served out of the EU, the corresponding transmission cannot be done pursuant to the Regulation. Reference must be made instead to the **1965 Hague Convention on the Service Abroad** of Judicial and Extrajudicial Documents in Civil or Commercial Matters. This is a successful Convention inasmuch as at July 2023, it is in force in 82 States (including all 27 EU Member States) and keeps attracting new signatory States.[43]

2.60. The case of the respondent not entering an appearance is addressed by **Article 15,** which, as seen above, derogates from Article 19 Brussels II-ter. The substance of paragraph 1 is similar to Article 22 of the 2020 Service Regulation and provides that:

> Where a writ of summons or an equivalent document had to be transmitted abroad for the purpose of service, under the provisions of the present Convention, and the defendant has not appeared, judgment shall not be given until it is established that –
>
> a) the document was served by a method prescribed by the internal law of the State addressed for the service of documents in domestic actions upon persons who are within its territory, or
> b) the document was actually delivered to the defendant or to his residence by another method provided for by this Convention, and that in either of these cases the service or the delivery was effected in sufficient time to enable the defendant to defend.

2.61. In the same way as already seen with regard to the 2020 Service Regulation, subsequent paragraphs give courts some leeway to derogate from this provision and to give a decision even if no certificate of service or delivery has been received. The conditions for such a rule to operate are similar to those provided by Article 22(2) of the 2020 Service Regulation. The same can be said of paragraph 3 on provisional and protective measures.

2.62. It is only when neither of the two instruments is applicable that **Article 19(1) comes into consideration**. This event will be quite rare in practice, given the large number of Contracting States to the 1965 Hague Convention.

---

[43] The status of ratifications table can be found at https://www.hcch.net/en/instruments/conventions/status-table/?cid=17. The full text can be found at https://www.hcch.net/en/instruments/conventions/full-text/?cid=17. See also '*Practical Handbook on the Operation of the Service Convention*', 4th edition, 2016, The Hague.

The rule seems to depart from the regime set by Article 22(2) and 22(3), although the substance is reproduced in a nutshell.

2.63. First, the court is obliged to **stay the proceedings** as long as it is necessary to establish that the aforementioned requirements for a fair trial are met. Unlike the EU-Hague Convention regime, the court is not barred from giving a decision, but it cannot dismiss the proceedings; in contrast, it must stay the proceedings until the situation is cleared. The order to stay the proceedings is inherently temporary and includes the power to give the applicant another chance to redress the initially ineffective service. As the rule does not mention how long the stay should be, this should be determined pursuant to national procedural law.

2.64. **Service of the document** in this case must be done in accordance with the **forum's national law**. By definition, when Article 19(1) comes into consideration, the document must be transmitted to the respondent in a State which is neither a Member State nor a party to the 1965 Hague Convention.

2.65. Full discretion is left to the court with regard to the assessment to be made, which includes the requirement that service was done 'in **sufficient time** to enable him or her to arrange for his or her defence' or, when this was not the case, 'that **all necessary steps have been taken** to this end'. As already mentioned, the rule is to be read in connection with the subsequent step of cross-border recognition and enforcement. Articles 38(b) and 39(1)(b), which provide the grounds for refusing recognition of a decision respectively in matrimonial and in parental responsibility matters,[44] will thus provide for some useful direction. In practice, any issue of non-appearance in court of the respondent will mostly be raised at the recognition/enforcement stage.

The same is true with regard to the notion of the '**document instituting the proceedings** or an equivalent document', such expression needing an autonomous interpretation consistent throughout the Regulation. Reference must thus also be made to Articles 17 and 18 with regard to seising of the court and examination as to jurisdiction, respectively.[45]

---

[44] Discussed in Chapter 8 at 8.90 et seq and 8.108 et seq, respectively.
[45] Above at 2.3 and 2.27 et seq, respectively.

CHAPTER 3

JURISDICTION IN MATRIMONIAL MATTERS

I. Introduction 72
   A. Historical Background. 72
II. The General Framework. 73
   A. *Favor Divortii* through Multiple, Alternative Criteria. 73
   B. Exclusive and Objective Criteria: No Choice of Court Allowed 75
   C. The Relevant Moment to Assess Jurisdiction 77
III. The General Ground for Jurisdiction in Divorce and Separation: Article 3. 78
   A. Jurisdiction Based on Habitual Residence 78
   B. Jurisdiction Based on Common Nationality 83
   C. The Problematic Definition of Habitual Residence of Spouses 84
      1) Autonomous Interpretation: No Reference to National Law 85
      2) How to Establish Habitual Residence of Spouses 88
      3) No Double Habitual Residence in Two Member States 92
      4) Manipulation of Factual Elements and the Courts' Duty to Ascertain the Relevant Situation 93
IV. No Transfer of Proceedings in Matrimonial Cases. 94
V. Jurisdiction on the Conversion of Legal Separation into Divorce: Article 5. 94
VI. Residual Jurisdiction: Article 6 98
   A. The Role of National Rules: Article 6(1) 99
   B. Protecting the Respondent Who is a National of, or Habitually Resident in, the EU: Article 6(2) 102
   C. The Lack of a *Forum Necessitatis* 104
   D. The Principle of Equal Treatment for EU Citizens Habitually Resident in a Member State: Article 6(3) 106

I. INTRODUCTION

A. HISTORICAL BACKGROUND

3.1. Jurisdiction in matrimonial matters is the oldest part of the Regulation, which has never been substantially modified. It dates back to Article 2 of the Brussels Convention of 1998 (an instrument which never came into force) and to Regulation No 1347/2000 (the so-called Brussels II Regulation, which was in force from 2001 to 2003). The subsequent Brussels II-bis Regulation made no modification to Article 3, except for changing the term 'court' to 'authority' so as to include any judicial or administrative authority with jurisdiction in matrimonial matters. In its 2006 Proposal[1] the Commission did suggest some amendments to the rules on matrimonial matters but, as is well known, this proposal was withdrawn given the impossibility of reaching the required unanimity in the Council.

3.2. One reason for not proposing to revise the provisions on matrimonial matters was allegedly the lack of real problems. The 2016 Commission Proposal[2] reported that:

> only limited evidence of existing problems (including statistics) was available at this stage [when submitting the proposal] to allow for a precise indication of the need to intervene and the scale of the problems, and for a fully informed choice of any considered option.

It thus concluded that 'for matrimonial matters the preferred policy option is retaining the status quo'.

3.3. The truth is that, as was already the case at the time of its first draft in 2001, jurisdiction in matrimonial matters represents a delicate compromise between opposing political standpoints: on the one hand, the strong political will of some Member States, aiming to preserve and guarantee their citizens' right to achieve freedom of status in an easy and uncontroversial manner, especially when living in other Member States providing for more stringent requisites to relinquish the matrimonial tie; and, on the other hand, the need to reduce the impact of the nationality criterion, which is now generally regarded as a weak connecting

---

[1] Proposal for a Council Regulation amending Regulation (EC) No 2201/2003 as regards jurisdiction and introducing rules concerning applicable law in matrimonial matters COM(2006) 399 final, referred to in Chapter 1 at 1.13, n. 30. This proposal initiated the process that eventually led to the Rome III Regulation.
[2] Proposal for a Council Regulation on jurisdiction, the recognition and enforcement of decisions in matrimonial matters and the matters of parental responsibility, and on international child abduction (recast) COM(2016) 411, 30 June 2016, (hereinafter 'the Commission's Proposal'), p. 3.

factor, and one that may be irreconcilable with EU law, which is based on the principle of non-discrimination on the ground of nationality. The final outcome, based on a wide range of alternative non-hierarchical criteria, clearly has its shortcomings and has been widely criticised for facilitating excessive forum shopping effect and thus increasing litigation in matrimonial matters.[3]

3.4. In addition to the above-mentioned considerations, at the time of recasting Brussels II-bis, the uncertainty on how to handle same-sex marriages played an important role. This being a very delicate and sensitive issue for some Member States, the risk was high that Member States would be divided as to how to address the matter. With these considerations in mind, and despite the many calls to search for better options for jurisdiction in matrimonial matters,[4] when recasting the Regulation, the political decision was taken not to alter anything in the whole chapter for fear that the necessary unanimity would not be reached in the Council.

II. THE GENERAL FRAMEWORK

A. *FAVOR DIVORTII* THROUGH MULTIPLE, ALTERNATIVE CRITERIA

3.5. Brussels II-ter seeks to implement the principle of free circulation of decisions in matrimonial matters and hence sets a framework allowing EU citizens to smoothly and easily achieve free status when their marriage breaks down and have the divorce decision automatically recognised in all EU Member States. In this respect, it is often said to embody a policy of *favor divortii*,[5] but this is only one side of the story. The rules in this chapter seeks to balance different needs: on the one hand, protecting the right to free circulation of the spouse who after the marital breakdown leaves the Member State where the couple had lived together; and, on the other hand, providing legal certainty for the other spouse who remains in such a State. Such balance is found by ensuring that there is a real link between the applicant and the Member State whose

---

[3] Among many, see, for example, the criticism and proposals by A. BORRÁS, 'Grounds of Jurisdiction in Matrimonial Matters: Recasting the Brussels IIa Regulation' (2015) *Nederlands Internationaal Privaatrecht (NIPR)* 1, 3–9; A. BONOMI, 'La competence international en matière de divorce. Quelque suggestions pour une (improbable) revision du réglement Bruxelles II bis' (2017) *Revue critique de droit international privé*, 207, 511–534 (515); E. PATAUT, 'Codifier le divorce international quelques remarques sur le projet GEDIP' (2020) 4 *Acta Universitatis Carolinae – Iuridica* 95–115.
[4] See scholars above at n. 3.
[5] See M. TENREIRO and M. EKSTRÖM, 'Unification of Private International Law in Family Law Matters within the European Union' in K. BOELE-WOELKI (ed.), *Perspectives for the Unification and Harmonisation of Family Law in Europe*, Intersentia, Cambridge 2003, p. 185.

courts have jurisdiction to give a ruling on the dissolution of the matrimonial ties concerned.[6]

3.6. To achieve this purpose, Article 3 provides seven different criteria, based either on habitual residence of one or both parties, or on common nationality, which are alternative to each other and have the same rank. It thus reads as follows:

> In matters relating to divorce, legal separation or marriage annulment, jurisdiction shall lie with the courts of the Member State:
>
> (a) in whose territory:
>   (i) the spouses are habitually resident,
>   (ii) the spouses were last habitually resident, insofar as one of them still resides there,
>   (iii) the respondent is habitually resident,
>   (iv) in the event of a joint application, either of the spouses is habitually resident,
>   (v) the applicant is habitually resident if he or she resided there for at least a year immediately before the application was made, or
>   (vi) the applicant is habitually resident if he or she resided there for at least six months immediately before the application was made and is a national of the Member State in question; or
> (b) of the nationality of both spouses.

3.7. In so doing, the Regulation permits the coexistence of several courts having jurisdiction, without any hierarchy being assigned to any of them. The question of a possible hierarchy, in particular between the criteria under para. (a), based on habitual residence of one or both spouses, and the criterion under para. (b), based on the controversial criterion of common nationality, was raised in the *Hadadi* case and referred for a preliminary ruling to the CJEU in 2009. The Court clearly ruled that all the grounds set out in the previous Article 3(1) are alternative and non-hierarchical, such that no ground has priority over another.[7]

3.8. The fact that any of these criteria may be triggered gives the **applicant the freedom to choose** which of the available fora may better serve his or her purposes. This approach raises some practical issues. First, it may lead to uncertainty as to the competent forum. Second, and most importantly, there is

---

[6] The point has been repeatedly stressed by the CJEU. See 13 October 2016, *Mikołajczyk*, C-294/15, paras 33, 49 and 50; 25 November 2021, *IB*, C-289/20, paras 35, 44 and 56; 10 February 2022, *OE*, C-522/20, para. 29.

[7] CJEU, 16 July 2009, *Hadadi*, C-168/08, paras 48–49, discussed further below at 3.25 (and also CJEU, 13 October 2016, *Mikołajczyk*, C-294/15).

concern that it has led to the unwelcome practice of the so-called 'rush-to-the-court', a consequence of the interplay between multiple heads of jurisdiction and the differences among substantive law regimes on divorce, legal separation and annulment existing in each Member State. The negative effect of forum shopping was to be reduced by the harmonisation of conflict-of-law rules on divorce;[8] however, no unanimity could be reached and Regulation No 1259/2010 (hereinafter 'Rome III') therefore resulted in an enhanced cooperation and is applicable only among 17 EU Member States, thus leaving room for significant divergences in the applicable law,[9] as this will eventually depend on the conflict-of-law rules applicable in each national forum.

3.9. Furthermore, it should be remembered that multiple and concurrent fora in matrimonial proceedings also affect jurisdiction on parental responsibility, maintenance obligations and matrimonial property, as the relevant Regulations in these fields all provide criteria to extend the competence of the court of dissolution of matrimonial ties also with regard to the aforementioned issues.[10]

B. EXCLUSIVE AND OBJECTIVE CRITERIA: NO CHOICE OF COURT ALLOWED

3.10. The criteria listed are **exclusive**. Formerly, this was expressly stated in the heading of Article 6 of Brussels II-bis. Although this heading has now been omitted, as it was considered both unnecessary and confusing,[11] the principle that such criteria are exclusive remains unchanged as it is founded on the structure of the Regulation and on the primacy of EU law. This means that the grounds

---

[8] According to Recital (9) of Regulation No 1259/2019, this instrument should 'prevent a situation from arising where one of the spouses applies for divorce before the other one does in order to ensure that the proceeding is governed by a given law which he or she considers more favorable to his or her own interests'.

[9] As of October 2023, the Regulation is binding on the following 17 States: Austria, Belgium, Bulgaria, Estonia, France, Germany, Greece, Hungary, Italy, Latvia, Lithuania, Luxembourg, Malta, Portugal, Romania, Slovenia and Spain. All other Member States apply their own private international law rules.

[10] See above, Chapter 1 at 1.2.

[11] See below at 3.68 et seq. A similar approach is taken in the Rome III Regulation, in accordance with the Commission's reasoning in its Proposal for a Council Regulation amending Regulation (EC) No 2201/2003 as regards jurisdiction and introducing rules concerning applicable law in matrimonial matters, COM(2006) 399 final, 17 July 2006, that such a provision may cause confusion and is superfluous. The deletion of the former Article 6 was also proposed by the Group Européen de Droit International Privé – European Group for Private International Law (GEDIP) since the 2017 Hamburg session (see the report at https://www.gedip-egpil.eu/).

set out by Articles 3, 4 and 5 are mandatory and exhaustive.[12] Consequently, whenever any of the grounds of jurisdiction provided under the Regulation apply, all national grounds of jurisdiction are superseded. Some residual room is left for the application of national rules, but only under very exceptional circumstances (which is also governed by Brussels II-ter: see Article 6, below at 3.67 et seq) that only arise when no other court in any Member State has jurisdiction over a claim under the Regulation criteria and the respondent is not a national of a Member State.[13]

3.11. The grounds for determining the jurisdiction of a Member State court are based on the principle of **objective connection** between one or both spouses and the forum State. Such relevant connection is identified either by the habitual residence or by the common nationality. However, in some cases, habitual residence is not sufficient in itself – for example, under Article 3(a)(ii), continued residence of one of spouses is additionally required, under Article 3(a)(v), the required length of 12 months of habitual residence must be proved and, finally, under Article 3(a)(vi), the required length of 6 months of habitual residence *and* nationality must be proved.

3.12. The Regulation leaves **no room** at all for the subjective criterion of party autonomy and the consequent **choice of court**. Indeed, the parties are not free simply to agree on the court where they want to divorce. Furthermore, competence based on the defendant appearing without contesting jurisdiction – so-called tacit prorogation – is not possible.[14] Although this has often been criticised in the legal literature,[15] the Commission's 2006 proposal providing for some limited room for party autonomy[16] was not taken up in the subsequent negotiations. The legislator's choice appears to be balanced by the high number of different fora that are provided by Article 3, all having equal footing, which therefore afford a wide range of possibilities on where to apply for divorce or separation. On the other hand, allowing parties to choose their forum would

---

[12] The term is used by A. BORRÁS, 'Article 6' in U. MAGNUS and P. MANKOWSKI (eds), *Brussels IIbis Regulation*, OttoSchmidt, 2017, p. 105, para. 10, criticising the use made by previous Article 6 of the term 'exclusive'.

[13] Article 6, discussed below at 3.67 et seq.

[14] M. WILDERSPIN, *European Private International Law: The Brussels II-b Regulation*, Oxford University Press, 2023, p. 134, para. 4.036.

[15] See scholars noted above n. 3; and also L. WALKER, 'Party Autonomy, Inconsistency and the Specific Characteristics of Family Law in the EU' (2018) 14 *Journal of Private International Law* 225, 241 et seq, arguing that this was not the result of a deliberate policy and promoting a more consistent approach among EU instruments in PIL family law based on party autonomy; and A. LIMANTE, 'Prorogation of Jurisdiction and Choice of Law in EU Family Law: Navigating through the Labyrinth of Rules' (2021) 17(2) *Journal of Private International Law* 334–360.

[16] Commission Proposal, above n. 1, Article 20a and 20b.

have achieved predictability, a much-needed aim which is frustrated by the current multiple fora.

3.13. It is worth emphasising that it is for the seised court to ascertain, by its own motion, that the connecting factor conferring international competence is given. When this is not the case, it is the court's duty to declare its lack of competence (see Article 18).[17]

3.14. It should finally be noted that the criteria for divorce only determines the international competence (jurisdiction) and not which court is competent within that Member State. This may be of relevance when assessing habitual residence of spouses. Given that habitual residence operates as a jurisdictional criterion, it is irrelevant whether the parties live separately or not, as long as they live in the same State. The local court is to be determined according to national procedural rules.

C. THE RELEVANT MOMENT TO ASSESS JURISDICTION

3.15. A difficult issue, upon which views differ, concerns **the relevant moment when a ground of jurisdiction should exist**. Although Brussels II-ter provides a uniform rule to ascertain the moment when the court is actually seised (see Article 17),[18] it does not specify whether jurisdiction is to be ascertained and has to exist at the moment the court is seised or at a later time (for example, at the time of the hearing or when the point is raised). As a general rule, under national procedural law of most (if not all) Member States, jurisdiction must be established *in limine litis*, that is, at a preliminary stage of the proceedings. This may imply that, in general, all factual and legal elements should exist at this moment. A similar solution might also be appropriate when ascertaining jurisdiction under the Regulation.[19] The *BM* decision,[20] where the CJEU clarified that habitual residence should exist **at the moment the application is made** in regard to the criterion under Article 3(1)(v) and 3(1)(vi) Brussels II-bis requiring that residence must exist 'immediately before the application was made', adds further weight to such a construction. The solution now applies to Articles 3(a)(v) and 3(a)(vi) Brussels II-ter.

3.16. Nonetheless, a different view may be inferred from the fact that, in contrast to Article 7, which governs jurisdiction in matters of parental

---

[17] Article 18 is discussed in Chapter 2 at 2.27 et seq.
[18] Article 17 is discussed in Chapter 2 at paras 2.5 et seq.
[19] M. WILDERSPIN, above n. 14, p. 141, para. 4.065, supporting this solution in general terms, although at para. 4.066 providing the opposite conclusion in relation to Article 3(1)(v) and (vi); see also M. NÍ SHÚILLEABHÁIN, 'Art. 3 Brussels IIter' in U. MAGNUS and P. MANKOWSKI, *Brussels IIter Regulation*, OttoSchmidt, 2023, p. 106 (para. 18).
[20] CJEU, 6 July 2023, *BM*, C-462/22. See below at 3.19, point 5.

responsibility,[21] Article 3 does not require that jurisdiction lies with that court 'at the time the court is seised'. While such starting point may be considered logical and inherent to the system, it is a matter of debate as to whether this should be automatically extended to all cases, so that **all factual elements should exist prior** to commencement of proceedings.

3.17. One could for example argue on the principle of economy of proceedings, in order to assume jurisdiction where the ground establishing jurisdiction was non-existent – or simply unclear – when the court was first seised, but is later clearly fulfilled. This may happen, for example, when it is uncertain as to whether habitual residence exists in the forum at the moment when the court is seised, but it is clearly existing later on. In other words, given the difficulty in ascertaining the exact moment in time when habitual residence exists, one could suggest a more flexible approach favouring **preservation of jurisdictional activity**. A too rigid approach requiring the court to declare a lack of jurisdiction on the ground that habitual residence did not exist at the time when proceedings were instituted, notwithstanding that habitual residence is now given in that same forum, would seem too formalistic and inappropriate in relation to a sound administration of justice. Furthermore, while the principle of *perpetuatio jurisdictionis* plays **no specific role** in matrimonial matters (as it is only specifically stated in respect of parental responsibility – see Article 7(1), discussed in Chapter 4), the aim of economy of proceedings, which is the underlying rationale of *perpetuatio jurisdictionis*, could be seen as a general policy for the whole Regulation and would similarly apply to the view offered above.

III. THE GENERAL GROUND FOR JURISDICTION IN DIVORCE AND SEPARATION: ARTICLE 3

3.18. Article 3 provides two separate set of criteria – namely, those based on habitual residence (Article 3(a)) and those based upon nationality (Article 3(b)).

A. JURISDICTION BASED ON HABITUAL RESIDENCE

3.19. Article 3(a) provides the following six alternative grounds of jurisdiction based on **habitual residence:**

- The **spouses'** habitual residence. While not expressly saying so, the rule clearly refers to the **common habitual residence**, given that habitual

---

[21] Discussed in Chapter 4.

residence of either spouse is expressly mentioned by Article 3(a)(iv). This is the most obvious and immediate ground of jurisdiction as it shows a strong connection to both spouses. The requirement is also satisfied if the spouses live in different places within the same State, something that is very likely given the high probability that at the time of the divorce/separation proceedings the couple no longer live together.

- The **last common habitual residence of the couple**, provided one of them **still resides** there. This amounts to a small deviation from the preceding rule, covering the case where one of the spouses has moved to a different country and is no longer resident in the previous common State. This criterion certainly gives an advantage to the spouse who remained in the same State after the breakdown, as it allows him or her to bring the divorce proceedings in the State of his or her own habitual residence. Nonetheless, it is highly predictable for both parties as it reflects a strong connection to the couple's joint life and, of course, is available for both of them. It should be noted that any previous habitual residence before the last common habitual residence is irrelevant, notwithstanding its length in time.
- The **habitual residence of the respondent**. This is the implementation of the well-known principle *actor sequitur forum rei*, which is widely accepted in general terms in many national and international instruments. While it needs no special explanation with reference to its procedural rationale, its use in matrimonial matters has been criticised.[22] In particular, the fact that jurisdiction is dependent upon the procedural role of the party using it (the claimant/respondent) is considered inappropriate for matrimonial matters, as such a connecting factor should better focus on the relationship between the parties and be neutral and independent of the parties' procedural role.
- The **habitual residence of either of the spouses**, in the event of a **joint application**. The criterion differs from the ones mentioned above, insofar as it allows the spouses a limited choice of forum, based on their common decision to file an application for divorce/separation. Under this letter's criterion, the current habitual residence of each of the spouses will amount to a ground of jurisdiction, provided the couple agree on filing a joint application. However, given that a 'joint application' is not defined, the exact scope of application of the rule remains uncertain. Bearing in mind the general reluctance to allow

---

[22] T. RAUSCHER, *Europäisches Zivilprozess und Kollisionsrecht EuZPR/EuIPR*, 4 ed. Vol. IV, *Brüssel IIa-Vo, Eg-Untvo, Huntverfübk 2007, Eu-Ehegütervo-E, Eu-Lp-Gütervo-E, Eu-Schutzmvo*, OttoSchmidt, 2015, p. 87, paras 31–32 promotes the use of 'einen rollenunabhängigen, nur für Ehesachen konzepierten besonderen Gerichtsstand'. According to the author, while this criterion obviously flows from the Brussels I tradition in civil and commercial matters, the *actor sequitur forum rei* principle should have no role in a modern PIL law in family matters.

choice-of-court agreements in matrimonial matters, it is submitted that the requirement should be construed as meaning that a joint application for divorce must be allowed not only by the procedural law of the *lex fori* but also by the law applicable to the divorce/separation, which must contemplate a joint divorce.[23] Joint applications for divorce are indeed a well-known procedure in some Member States.[24]

- The **habitual residence of the applicant**, where the **applicant** resided there for **at least a year** immediately before the application was made. This criterion has generated extensive discussion[25] as it exceptionally amounts to a *forum actoris*, albeit in conjunction with other conditions. The overall rationale for this (and the following) criterion is to provide for an easily accessible court for the spouse who moves to another Member State after the marriage breakdown. The place of the new residence of the applicant is therefore deemed relevant, but in order to safeguard the rights of the other spouse, it is not sufficient on its own. Indeed, habitual residence in the new State must be reinforced by the existence of other requirements – in particular, Article 3(a)(v) requires one year of residence.

In the past, the question was raised if habitual residence should exist for the whole one-year period before the application is lodged, or if habitual residence should be ascertained as existing at the end of the required timeframe, provided that (simple) residence started at least one year before application was made.[26] The point has been clarified by the CJEU in

---

[23] A different view is given by M. WILDERSPIN, above n. 14, p. 136, para. 4.047 suggesting that the rule should be given a broader interpretation so as to cover any divorce petition introduced by one party to which the other party consents. While this construction appears interesting and able to confer a wider *effet utile* to the rule, it also appears very close to a choice-of-court agreement, which is barred under Brussels II-ter. For a similar view, see also M. Ní SHÚILLEABHÁIN, *Cross Border Divorce Law: Brussels IIbis*, Oxford University Press, 2010, para. 4.09.

[24] In Italy, see the procedure for a 'divorzio consensuale' under Law No 70/1971.

[25] However, for the opposite view, see T. RAUSCHER, above n. 22, p. 90, paras 39–40, who notes that the parties' procedural role should be irrelevant and habitual residence of the defendant and of the claimant should be given the same weight.

[26] The issue was discussed in UK case law with regard to Article 3(1)(iv) Brussels II-bis, giving rise to opposite constructions. In *Marinos v. Marinos* [2007] EWHC 2047 (Fam), followed by *V v. V* [2011] EWHC 1190 (Fam), the courts held that the fifth and sixth indents of Article 3(1)(a) only require habitual residence at the date of the petition (launch of proceedings) provided that the applicant was resident (that is, not necessarily 'habitually' resident) for the required one year or six months. Conversely, in *Munro v. Munro* [2007] EWHC 3315 (Fam) and *Pierburg v. Pierburg* [2019] EWFC 24, the court held that habitual residence has to be established for the whole of the requisite one-year or six-month period. In Germany the majority of legal scholars (some of whom are discussed by R. HAUSMANN, *Internationales und Europäisches Ehescheidungsrecht*, C.H. Beck, Munich 2013, p. 20, para. 58) required habitual residence to exist from the beginning of the one-year or six-month period, so that the time needed to go from 'simple' to 'habitual' residence is not to be counted in such a time period.

the *BM* case[27] in the sense that habitual residence **must exist from the beginning of the required timeframe**. Consequently, it is not sufficient, as it may appear from a literal interpretation of the rule, that the applicant is habitually resident at the moment the application is made, but it is necessary that he or she is habitually resident there for the whole one year required by the rule. The advantage that the applicant is given to choose his or her forum is thus balanced out by the requirement that he or she shows the existence of a real link with such a forum.

The Court argued such a conclusion on multiple grounds. First, on a textual and systematic approach, the Court noticed that although Article 3 sometimes refers to simple residence, in the general scheme of that provision, the concept of 'residence' cannot be of a different nature depending on whether it is used in the second, fifth or sixth indent. The concept should always be understood as referring to 'habitual residence', as this is the only relevant connecting point for jurisdictional reasons. Simple residence does not come into consideration, as this would have the effect of weakening the criterion and jeopardising the uniformity of interpretation and application of the Regulation. Second, on a functional interpretation, the Court found that requesting habitual residence to run from the beginning of the given timeframe compensates for the fact that the applicant has the privilege of the *forum actoris* and guarantees the existence of a reasonable connection between such a forum and the applicant.[28] Finally, the proposed interpretation ensures legal certainty, as the criterion will be interpreted consistently in all Member States, while reference to simple residence would allow each court seised to apply national interpretation.[29]

---

[27] CJEU, 6 July 2023, *BM*, C-462/22. This case refers to the rule under Article 3(1)(a), sixth indent Brussels II-bis (which corresponds to Article 3(a)(vi) Brussels II-ter). However, the reasoning is extensible to the rule set by Article 3(a)(v) commented upon here.

[28] CJEU, 6 July 2023, *BM*, C-462/22, paras 32–33.

[29] The conclusion laid down in the *BM* decision was somehow advanced by CJEU, 25 November 2021, *IB*, C-289/20, in which the national court, which grounded its competence on Article 3(1)(a), sixth indent of Brussels II-bis, asked the CJEU whether a spouse may have two habitual residences. The CJEU did not directly address the question of whether habitual residence should exist during the whole six months prior to the application and focused on Article 3(1)(a) in general and the existence of habitual residence at the time of the application. However, from the passages quoted below, it may be inferred that habitual residence must be ascertained at the beginning of the six-month timeframe. The court argued 'it is common ground that IB, a national of the Member State of the national court seised, *satisfied the condition* – laid down in the sixth indent of Article 3(1)(a) of Regulation No 2201/2003 – *of having resided in that Member State for at least six months immediately before* lodging his application for the dissolution of matrimonial ties. It is also established that, since May 2017, IB has been carrying out, *on a stable and permanent basis, a professional activity of indefinite duration* in France during the week, and that he stays in an apartment there for the purposes of that professional activity. That evidence indicates that *IB's stay in the*

– The **habitual residence of the applicant**, where the applicant resided there for **at least six months** immediately before the application was made **and** he or she is a **national** of the Member State in question. This criterion is drafted upon the same lines just described under the fifth indent. The typical scenario envisaged by the rule is where the spouse moves 'back home' to the State of his or her own nationality. In this situation nationality plays no role as a self-standing connecting factor, but reinforces habitual residence by giving evidence of a (previous) real link with the State where the spouse has moved to. In fact, as a general rule, nationality shows institutional and legal ties, as well as cultural, linguistic, social, family or property ties with a given State.[30] Given such a relevant and prior connection, the requisite time of habitual residence is shortened to six months before the divorce, separation or annulment application. As clarified above in relation to the similar ground under Article 3(a)(v), it is not sufficient that habitual residence exists at the moment the application is made; it must already be established at the beginning of the six-month period.[31]

3.20. These last two grounds strike a balance between the need to have an available court for divorce to both parties (as part of the policy of *favor divortii*) and the general policy to provide certain and predictable fora.

3.21. It is often pointed out that the head of jurisdiction under Article 3(a)(v) and 3(a)(vi) give an advantage to the spouse remaining in the same State, as he or she will be able to access the courts straight away, whereas the spouse who has

---

territory of that Member State is stable and also shows, at the very least, *IB's integration into a social and cultural environment* within that Member State. Although such factors suggest a priori that the conditions laid down in the sixth indent of Article 3(1)(a) of Regulation No 2201/2003 might be satisfied, it is nevertheless for the referring court to ascertain whether it can be concluded, on the basis of all the factual circumstances specific to the case, that the person concerned has transferred his habitual residence to the Member State of that court' (at paras 59 and 60, emphasis added). See also D. Hodson and R. Bailey-Harris, 'The CJEU Casts Doubt on England's New Post-Brexit Divorce Jurisdiction Law' (2022) *International Family Law* 151.

[30] Based on such reasoning, the CJEU (10 February 2022, *OE*, C-522/20) considered that reference to nationality, as provided by Article 3(1)(a), sixth indent of Brussels II-bis, is not in conflict with the principle of non-discrimination on the grounds of nationality. The Court first recalled that the principle of non-discrimination requires that comparable situations must not be treated differently and different situations must not be treated in the same way unless such treatment is objectively justified. The Court then further found that the situation where an applicant who is a national of that Member State and who, because his or her marriage has broken down, leaves the shared habitual residence of the couple and decides to return to his or her country of origin is, in principle, not comparable to that of an applicant who does not hold the nationality of that Member State and who moves there after his or her marriage has broken down (see especially paras 29–34).

[31] See also above n. 28 confirming this conclusion on the basis of the decision in the *IB* case.

moved out of that State needs to wait for 6 or 12 months and, as clarified by the CJEU, he or she must be able to show habitual residence from the beginning of the required timeframe. However, given that the spouse who moves away could end up seising for divorce a court in a Member State that has no real connection to the other spouse or to their common life, the mentioned rule seems to strike a fair balance between opposing needs.

3.22. Finally, the *forum actoris* included in the last two grounds of Article 3(a) is only provided to protect the interest of the spouses and **cannot be triggered by a third party**. The system of multiple fora is meant to protect the rights of a spouse who has left the country of common habitual residence, while ensuring there is a genuine link between the party concerned and the Member State exercising jurisdiction. In *Mikołajczyk*,[32] a case where the daughter of one of the deceased spouses sought the annulment of her father's first marriage in Poland, the place of **her own** habitual residence, the CJEU held that a third party may not rely on a ground of jurisdiction linked to his or her own habitual residence. Indeed, the spouses had always lived in France and neither the spouses' common habitual residence nor the deceased father's habitual residence was in Poland.

B. JURISDICTION BASED ON COMMON NATIONALITY

3.23. Article 3(b) envisages only one ground for jurisdiction solely based on **nationality**. EU law generally regards any differentiation in treatment based on nationality with suspicion because of its discriminating effects for EU citizens.[33] Consequently, this connecting factor is generally rejected in EU Private International Law (PIL) instruments. Indeed, Article 3(b) is one of the very few cases within all EU private international law rules where nationality is used as a connecting factor.

3.24. Under Article 3(b), nationality must be common to both spouses, since giving relevance to nationality of only one of them would be to discriminate against the other spouse. The relevant nationality must be of a Member State. Indeed, as nationality is used as a ground for jurisdiction, it is only relevant if it is able to confer jurisdiction on a Member State's courts. As previously mentioned,[34] nationality should be enjoyed at the moment when the court is seised and/or the divorce claim is lodged (and not at the moment of marriage).

---

[32] CJEU, 13 October 2016, *Mikołajczyk*, C-294/15, para. 49, criticised by A. Borrás, 'Article 3' in U. Magnus and P. Mankowski, above n. 12, para. 11, finding this 'a very controversial answer'.
[33] See Article 18 TFEU.
[34] See above 3.15–3.17.

3.25. Several issues with regard to nationality have been resolved by the CJEU in the *Hadadi* case.[35] This case concerned a couple having a common double nationality (French and Hungarian) and who had been residing in France for all their married life. When the marriage broke down, the husband filed a petition for divorce in Hungary. A few months later, the wife did the same in France. The question arose as to whether the French court had a better case to hear the application as the couple were still habitually resident in France, while they had no effective connection with Hungary.

3.26. The CJEU pointed out that in a case of **common double nationality**, each nationality is equally relevant, as the Regulation does not require the existence of additional requirements, such as those necessary to determine the 'most effective' nationality. Determining that one nationality should prevail over the other for the purpose of jurisdiction would in fact imply giving weight to the place of habitual residence, with the result of an overlap of the two grounds of jurisdiction provided under Article 3(a) and 3(b). On the contrary, the Regulation is based on a number of alternative objective grounds with no hierarchy between them and each spouse may seise the courts of each of the Member State of nationality, at his or her own choice.[36]

3.27. On a different issue, it follows from the *Sundelind* decision[37] that in cases of spouses having a double nationality, national courts should not regard them as only having the nationality of the forum. On the contrary, the court must take into account the fact that the spouses also hold the nationality of another Member State and that therefore courts of that other State could also have jurisdiction to hear the case. Coordination among parallel proceedings which might be instituted in different Member States must be solved according to the chronological principle envisaged by the *lis pendens* rule.

C. THE PROBLEMATIC DEFINITION OF HABITUAL RESIDENCE OF SPOUSES

3.28. Brussels II-ter provides no definition on how the crucial notion of habitual residence should be interpreted. This is true both of habitual residence with regard to minors as well as with regard to spouses. However, while the CJEU has had a number of different occasions to provide guidelines in regard of minors,[38] only a few have been given with reference to habitual residence of spouses.

---

[35] CJEU, 16 July 2009, *Hadadi*, C-168/08.
[36] On the point of criteria being all on the same footing, see also above 3.7 et seq.
[37] ECJ, 29 November 2007, *Sundelind Lopez*, C-68/07, discussed below at 3.72 et seq.
[38] For Article 7, see further Chapter 4 at 4.8–4.30.

3.29. While the lack of express guidance leads to uncertainty in complex cases, it also allows the flexibility necessary to adapt the criterion to the multiple varieties of different cases. It is noteworthy that in all these years (more than 20 if one goes back to the original Brussels II Regulation) only a few, quite distinctive, referrals for a preliminary ruling on this notion have been made to the CJEU,[39] which clearly shows that while a particular problematic case may still arise, in general terms a flexible and fact-based criterion serves the needs of family litigation. Interpretative and systematic concerns might be more theoretical than practical.[40] Nonetheless, it is certainly true that habitual residence is one of the most discussed and litigated notions in national courts.

1) Autonomous Interpretation: No Reference to National Law

3.30. Some general guidance can be found in general principles. The first one is that, following the general and well-established guideline of the CJEU,[41] all terms used by Regulations and that do not refer to the law of Member States should be given a uniform and **autonomous interpretation**, to be achieved in light of the context of the provisions and of the objectives of each Regulation. Consequently, no reference should be made to national interpretation of similar grounds of jurisdiction provided for by the national law of the Member States. The question is different in regard to international instruments, such as the Hague Conventions in family matters. While the differences in context and structure between the Hague Conventions and the EU Regulations argue against an unchecked transposition of interpretation,[42] it should be kept in mind that these instruments share a general aim and approach – in particular when placing the best interests of the child at the forefront. As such, adequate consideration to the interpretation of habitual residence given by other superior

---

[39] CJEU, 25 November 2021, C-289/20, *IB v. FA*; CJEU, C-501/20, *MPA*, both of which referred for a preliminary ruling to the CJEU in December 2020. Both decisions are commented on below.

[40] T. RAUSCHER, above n. 22, p. 82, para. 21 points out a different degree of difficulty in handling the notion in States with different legal traditions.

[41] The principle is well established in private international law in family matters. With specific regard to habitual residence, see CJEU, 2 July 2009, *A*, C-523/07, para. 34; CJEU, 22 December 2010, *Mercredi*, C-497/10, para. 45. The rule commanding an autonomous interpretation goes back to the well-known *CILFIT* case (ECJ, 6 October 1982, *Srl CILFIT*, C-283/91, para. 19) is a 'golden rule' applicable to all EU law. On the principles of autonomous interpretation in EU private international law and specifically in family matters, see L. TOMASI, C. RICCI and S. BARIATTI, 'Characterisation in Family Matters for Purposes of European Private International Law' in J. MEEUSEN, M. PERTEGÁS, J. STRAETMANS and F. SWENNEN (eds), *International Family Law for the European Union*, Intersentia, 2007, pp. 341–388; C. RICCI, 'Habitual Residence as a Ground of Jurisdiction in Matrimonial Disputes Connected with the EU: Challenges and Potential', in 11(2020)1 *Civil Procedure Review*' 152 et seq.

[42] R. HAUSMANN, above n. 26, p. 16, para. 46. For a more cautious approach, see T. RAUSCHER, above n. 22, p. 82, para. 21.

courts when applying the Hague Conventions appears reasonable and consistent with the general goal of pursuing international harmony of decisions.

3.31. The need for an autonomous interpretation, clear-cut in principle as it may be, has nevertheless given rise to multiple misapplications by national courts, especially during the early years of implementation of the Regulation. No reference should be given, for example, to the national Bulgarian rules which consider as 'habitual' any residence lasting more than six months.[43] An additional difficulty has arisen in Lithuania, as the Lithuanian version of Brussels II-bis translated habitual residence as 'permanent residence' (*nuolatinė gyvenamoji vieta*), thus leading to misapplication by the national judiciary, which relied on the national notion. In 2016 the Lithuanian Supreme Court clarified that habitual residence under Brussels II-bis should not be linked to the national concept, but is an autonomous concept.[44]

3.32. In searching for an autonomous interpretation, a line of guidance may be drawn from definitions of the habitual residence of adults which were given both by the legislator and by the CJEU in different contexts of EU law. The assumption that 'individuals do not compartmentalise their lives into sections such as tax, social security and family' and thus 'it would make sense to simplify and converge approaches across legal fields rather than to needlessly complicate them'[45] appears sound and reasonable, although the specific aim and context of the instrument considered should also be taken into consideration.[46]

3.33. In general terms, for example, one could look at the domains of fiscal matters, social security and staff Regulations, where the CJEU has retained that habitual residence is 'where the habitual centre of their interests [is] to be found'[47] or, more precisely, 'in which the official concerned has established, with

---

[43] See (Bulgaria) County Court Sliven, Judgment No. 423/2010, 16 September 2010; (Bulgaria) County Court Blagoevgrad, Judgment No. 605, Case No. 47/2013, 19 February 2013, cited by A. LIMANTE, 'Establishing Habitual Residence of Adults under the Brussels IIa Regulation: Best Practices from National Case-Law' (2018) *Journal of Private International Law* 172, fn. 50. Similarly, no relevance was given in the UK to the notion of ordinary residence in the domains of immigration law or taxation law.

[44] Cf. the report presented by the Lithuanian Supreme Court on jurisdiction in family law matters in the EU, 'Tarptautinės ir Europos Sąjungos teisės taikymo sprendžiant jurisdikcijos nustatymo klausimą šeimos bylose apžvalga' in *Teismų praktika* (43) 2016; A. LIMANTE, above n. 43, 160–181 (esp. fns 31–32 for Lithuanian case law).

[45] T. KRUGER, 'Finding a Habitual Residence' in I. VIARENGO and F. VILLATA (eds), *Planning the Future of Cross-Border Families: A Path through Coordination*, CEDAM, 2020, p. 78.

[46] See under this respect the approach taken by the CJEU in the *MPA* case (CJEU, 1 August 2022, *MPA*, C-501/20) where the Court followed different analysis when determining habitual residence in regard to parents' matrimonial disputes, child's custody proceedings and child's maintenance claims.

[47] CJEU, 1 July 2004, *Wallentin*, C-169/03, para. 15, confirmed by the decision of 25 January 2007, *Finanzamt Dinslaken*, C-329/05, para. 23.

the intention that it should be of a lasting character, the permanent or habitual centre of his interests'.[48]

3.34. Further guidance could also be drawn from other Regulations in the field of judicial cooperation in civil matters, in particular the Maintenance Regulation and the Succession Regulation,[49] as such an approach would most usefully lead to a better coordination of rules on jurisdiction, thus simplifying the life of individuals resident in the EU. Along this line, mention is to be made of Recital (23) of the Succession Regulation, which provides that:

> In order to determine the habitual residence, the authority dealing with the succession should make an *overall assessment* of the circumstances of the life of the deceased during the years preceding his death and at the time of his death, *taking account of all relevant factual elements*, in particular the *duration and regularity of the deceased's presence* in the State concerned and the *conditions and reasons for that presence*. The habitual residence thus determined should reveal a close and stable connection with the State concerned taking into account the specific aims of this Regulation. (Emphasis added)

3.35. However, as an overall conclusion, given the multiple constructions that the CJEU has been offering through a very diverse case law and the fact that, when interpreting habitual residence for adults, the CJEU will give wide consideration to the scope and aim of the diverse instruments, it is suggested that one should refrain from searching an overall and uniform construction of habitual residence to be **valid for all EU instruments**. Instead, while certainly coordination and consistency between all instruments should be a general aim, the notion of habitual residence should nonetheless be tailored for the specific instrument and the specific situation to which it is referred.[50]

3.36. This same approach should be upheld in relation to the criteria elaborated for the **child's habitual residence**, which are centred on testing the

---

[48] CJEU, 25 November 1999, *Swaddling*, C-90/97, para. 29; see also 15 September 1994, *Magdalena Fernández*, C-452/93P, para. 22.
[49] Respectively Council Regulation (EC) No 4/2009 of 18 December 2008 on jurisdiction, applicable law, recognition and enforcement of decisions and cooperation in matters relating to maintenance obligations and Council Regulation (EU) No 650/202 of 4 July 2012, on jurisdiction, applicable law, recognition and enforcement of decisions and acceptance and enforcement of authentic instruments in matters of succession and on the creation of a European certificate of succession.
[50] For a similar conclusion, see B. HESS, 'Towards Uniform Concept of Habitual Residence in European Procedural and Private International Law?' (2021) *Polish Civil Procedure* 538, especially emphasising the different aim pursued by habitual residence as a connecting factor for choice of law and habitual residence as a ground for jurisdiction in international procedural law.

child's integration in his or her family and social life.[51] It is submitted that this test should be handled with caution, as such a notion is framed in view of the best interests of the child, a specific rationale which does not apply to adults.[52] Furthermore, while a child's habitual residence is generally mediated though the primary caregiver's residence and more frequently located into the specific place where the child is present, an adult may also be able to continue his or her social contacts and private relations when he or she is carrying out other activities in a different State and may, under specific circumstances, be able to continue his or her previous residence even when staying elsewhere. Furthermore, the specific nature of the proceedings grounded on habitual residence should be taken into account. While custody cases related to children require full proximity to all the circumstances, including social authorities, witnesses, friends and relatives which may be called to participate at some stage of the proceedings, proceedings on separation and divorce are much more focused on the parties themselves – two fully responsible adults. For all the above reasons, it is concluded that, while occasional reference to CJEU case law on children's cases may be of some help, any test elaborated with regard to children should not be regarded as the ultimate guideline in relation to adults.[53]

2) How to Establish Habitual Residence of Spouses

3.37. Guidance on this matter has been provided by the CJEU in two cases, *IB* and *MPA*. In these decisions, the Court, after recalling that habitual residence is essentially a question of fact,[54] made it clear that the adjective 'habitual' indicates that the residence must have a certain permanence or regularity and that the transfer of a person's habitual residence to a Member State shall reflect 'the intention of the person concerned to establish there the permanent or habitual centre of his or her interests, with the intention that it should be of a lasting character'.[55]

3.38. Following this guidance, it is clear that habitual residence of adults, like that of habitual residence of children, is primarily a **factual** criterion, to be

---

[51] A cautious approach may also be inferred from the *IB* decision (CJEU, 25 November 2021, *IB*, C-289/20) where the point was made that 'circumstances characterising the place of habitual residence of a child are clearly not identical in every respect to those which make it possible to determine the place of habitual residence of a spouse for the purposes of Article 3(1)(a)' (para. 54). See also the discussion in Chapter 4 at 4.13.

[52] B. Hess, above n. 50, at 535.

[53] Similarly, R. Hausmann, above n. 26, p. 16, para. 48. On a contrary note, see A. Limante, above n. 42, pp. 169–170, arguing that national case law has spontaneously followed the criteria set by the CJEU in the *A* and *Mercredi* decisions (for which, see below, Chapter 4 at 4.14 et seq).

[54] CJEU, 25 November 2021, *IB*, C-289/20, para. 52.

[55] CJEU, 25 November 2021, *IB*, C-289/20, paras 41 and 57; CJEU, 1 August 2022, *MPA*, C-501/20, para. 44.

assessed on the basis of a fact-finding and fact-weighing analysis to be carried out in each individual case. What needs to be demonstrated is an effective connection of the person concerned with a given State.

3.39. Habitual residence of adults will however differ from habitual residence of children, insofar as it will be found in the place where the person concerned has established, with the intention that it should be of a lasting character, the **permanent or habitual centre of his or her interests**. The 'integration' test required for children thus seems to give way to a 'centre-of-interests' test. Indeed, while the environment of a child is mostly a family environment, integration of an adult may be built on a 'significantly wider range of activities and diverse interests, concerning, *inter alia*, professional, sociocultural and financial matters in addition to private and familial matters'.[56] Under these circumstances, to require that all of these interests be focused in a single Member State in order to establish habitual residence would appear inconsistent with the main objective of Brussels II-bis (and Brussels II-ter), which is to allow the free circulation of persons and, in particular, to safeguard the rights of the spouse to relocate in a different Member State when, following a marital crisis, he or she has left the Member State of common habitual residence.

3.40. Given these premises, the centre of interests amounting to habitual residence for adults is based on **two elements**: (a) a physical and stable presence for a given amount of time; and (b) some kind of intention that such presence is not occasional and that the person concerned wants to establish the centre of his or her interests in such a particular place. These two elements will be examined separately.

3.41. Undoubtedly, **physical presence** is a necessary prerequisite of habitual residence. However, physical presence alone is not sufficient to establish habitual residence. An adequate **degree of stability** in a given State is required. In *MPA* the CJEU held that neither of the spouses, who worked in Togo as members of the EU Delegation to Togo, had a habitual residence in Spain, given that neither of them had been present in Spain, except for a few periods of leave or the birth of children; these events amounted to occasional and temporary interruptions in their everyday lives, which were irrelevant for the purpose of ascertaining habitual residence.[57] For the reasons explained above,[58] stability will thus replace the test of integration when establishing habitual residence

---

[56] CJEU, 25 November 2021, *IB*, C-289/20, para. 56.
[57] CJEU, 1 August 2022, *MPA*, C-501/20, para. 57. The Court also clarified that since posts in the delegations of the EU, such as that to Togo covered by the spouses, are deliberately requested by officials and other servants who so wish, it was doubtful whether the spouses did in fact intend, after their de facto separation, to leave Togo in order to transfer their habitual residence to the territory of Spain (at para. 59).
[58] Above at 3.39.

of adults, but this will not necessarily make things easier. While in the past stability was normally proved by the passing of a reasonable amount of time, the current, fast and constantly on-the-move art of living makes it necessary to downgrade the element of time and to focus on other factual circumstances which show sufficient settlement in a given place. While in controversial cases some court decisions endeavour to count the weeks (or even the days) which are spent in one jurisdiction or in the other, such practice is not always appropriate. A quantitative measurement alone is not sufficient. A qualitative measure should be used instead, and the reasons for the relevant person being in each State and the quality of the time there should be highlighted. In this regard, the state of mind and the intention to settle in a given Member State of the concerned person will also play a role (see further 3.44 below).

3.42. Furthermore, the **centre of interests** of the person concerned encompasses **all of his or her essential interests** relating to his or her professional, social and family life. Thus, while professional and financial interests will be of help in identifying such a centre, these factors alone should not automatically take precedence over the place where private and family interests are when their geographical location is not in the same Member State.

3.43. The relevant **factual elements** must be drawn from both professional and private life of the concerned person. According to Advocate General Campos Sanchez-Bordona in the *IB* case,[59] the following may be useful indicators: the fact that one is returning to the State of nationality (or of habitual residence before marriage); the fact that family members and friends are in such a State; the fact that one resides on a regular basis in that place; the fact that one has a rental agreement or owns a property or has taken steps to rent or own a property; and the fact that one has or is looking for stable employment in that place. The previous indicators are certainly not exhaustive, and other factors may also become relevant, such as available bank accounts, paying bills and utilities, having health insurance, having a general doctor, enrolling in sport and leisure activities, the habitual residence of one's own dependent children and the fact that this is the place where the concerned person will return after that work is carried out in a different State.

3.44. More difficult is the appraisal of and the weight to be given to the subjective element, i.e. the **intention** of the concerned party to settle in a given place. The relevance of the state of mind of the concerned person in establishing habitual residence in one Member State was recently confirmed by the CJEU in the *IB* case,[60] but unfortunately no further guidance was provided on this point, which is likely to mark a difference between the habitual residence of spouses and the habitual residence of children.

---

[59] See Opinion of 8 July 2021, C-289/20, para. 69.
[60] CJEU, 25 November 2021, *IB*, C-289/20, para. 57-58, on which see further below 3.50 et seq.

3.45. Different jurisdictions have different understandings on this point, but there are some common features. First, it is generally accepted that intention only becomes relevant when it shows itself in a tangible way.[61] Internal feelings and speculative life planning will not produce any legal effect if they do not manifest themselves in a material way. The need for a material dimension of intention carries with it the fact that the difference between the intention and the factual element is less clear-cut than it might seem at first glance.

3.46. Second, intention acquires significance mostly with regard to **recent relocations** to a Member State from a different Member State in which the spouses were previously habitually resident. Intention will therefore play a decisive role in those cases where, because of marriage breakdown, one of the spouses wishes to relocate elsewhere. Such a situation is common in international divorces/separations, often entailing the immediate transfer of residence in a different Member State of one of the partners.[62] An intention to relocate 'back home' to the Member State of nationality – or of habitual residence before the marriage – will be ascertained more easily and allow for habitual residence to be established also when factual elements are less decisive.[63] However, given that a double habitual residence is excluded (see below 3.49 et seq), a transfer of habitual residence is only possible when the **intention to abandon the previous place of residence** is also clear.

3.47. Proof of intention is not needed where several months of stay have elapsed and the intention to settle will be implied in the stay. It is in fact undisputed that **a lack of intention** to acquire habitual residence in a given State cannot prevent a finding that habitual residence is in such a State when a factual and objective assessment is sufficient to show this.

---

[61] Specifically on this, see CJEU, 2 April 2009, *A*, C-523/07, para. 40; 22 December 2010, *Mercredi*, C-497/10 PPU, para. 50. See, however, the different approach held by the Cour de Cassation, 14 December 2005 (referred to and commented upon by M. WILDERSPIN, above n. 14, p. 71, n. 131), attaching weight to the intention of a UK wife and mother who had moved to France for 18 months in order to follow her daughter's studies, but who had never intended to relinquish her habitual residence in the UK. The French court upheld this approach, notwithstanding the objective and prolonged connection with France.

[62] Preparatory work on both the 1998 Brussels Convention and the Brussels II Regulation shows that there was a strong concern for the situation of a spouse who, as a result of the breakdown of the marriage, transfers his or her residence to another Member State. The possibility of bringing divorce proceedings in a place which is the centre of interests of only one of the spouses was a *sine qua non* condition for acceptance of the 1998 Convention by a number of States. For a brief overview on the historical background, see Advocate General's Campos Sanchez-Bordona Opinion, 8 July 2021, C-289/20, paras 46–60.

[63] Such was the case in *IB*, where the French husband argued that he had relocated to France after the breakdown of the marriage; see below at 3.50. In contrast, see the facts underlying the *OE* case (CJEU, 10 February 2022, C-522/20), where, following the marital breakdown between a couple who were habitually resident in Ireland, the husband, an Italian national, relocated to Austria. The CJEU highlighted that such a situation was not comparable to the one of a former spouse 'going back home' (para. 33).

3.48. In other words, intention should not be overestimated. On the contrary, it plays a **residual role**, mostly limited to reinforcing or confirming a result already drawn from the objective analysis, especially in cases where the final outcome may seem uncertain. In light of the factual and objective nature of the criterion of habitual residence, which is necessary in order to achieve predictability and certainty, habitual residence cannot be determined, not even primarily, based on the criterion of intention.

3) No Double Habitual Residence in Two Member States

3.49. Double habitual residence is also excluded, as it would increasingly weaken the aim of determining predictable and objective grounds. National courts have sometimes reverted to the idea of a 'principal' habitual residence in complex situations where the family and professional life of one or both of the spouses was scattered across a few States.[64] The notion shows the difficulties in defining and applying habitual residence in complex cases, but the viability of a double habitual residence was clearly ruled out by the CJEU in *IB*.[65]

3.50. The *IB* case concerned an Irish-French couple having their common habitual residence in Ireland, where they lived together with their common children. During the course of their married life the French husband commuted regularly between Ireland and France, where he had his professional activity, an apartment, friends and leisure activities. When the marriage broke down, he increased his activity in France, spent more time there and finally filed a divorce petition before the French court, claiming to be habitually resident there. Following a factual assessment, the French court found that he had two residences: one, the family residence in Ireland; and the other, for professional reasons, in France. Clearly, the husband had not given up his residence in Ireland, where he maintained family ties and where he regularly stayed for personal reasons; on the other hand, his ties to France were neither occasional nor circumstantial and was the central location of his professional interests. Building on the *Hadadi* case,[66] pursuant to which double nationality led to a double head of jurisdiction, the French court made a reference to the CJEU for a preliminary ruling on the possibility of a spouse having a double habitual residence.

3.51. The reply of the CJEU that there is no such possibility is not surprising and is fully reasonable. While it may well be the case that a spouse has several residences at the same time, there shall be **only one habitual residence** for the purposes of Article 3(a). Allowing for multiple habitual residences would

---

[64] See, for example, Milan Tribunal, order 16 April 2014, (2015) *Rivista di diritto internazionale privato e processuale*, 162 et seq.
[65] CJEU, 25 November 2021, *IB*, C-289/20.
[66] CJEU, 16 July 2009, *Hadadi*, C-168/08; see 3.25 above.

undermine legal certainty because of the unpredictability it would cause, as well as leading to the determination of jurisdiction on the mere 'de facto' residence of one or other of the spouses. Such unpredictability would further affect jurisdiction on maintenance obligations and on the matrimonial property regime, given that Article 3(c) of Regulation 4/2009 and Article 5 of Regulation 2016/1103 provide the court seised for divorce with ancillary jurisdiction over, respectively, maintenance obligations and the matrimonial property regime.[67]

4) *Manipulation of Factual Elements and the Courts' Duty to Ascertain the Relevant Situation*

3.52. Finally, mention should be made of the **risk of manipulation** or **omission of the factual elements** building on the notion of habitual residence. Experience has shown how forum shopping can be achieved by the artificial creation of the required jurisdictional criteria. This can also occur when the parties are in agreement with each other.[68] The classic example of this is *Rapisarda v. Colladon*.[69] In this case a large number of Italian couples were divorced by the UK courts according to English law following the asserted habitual residence of one of them, at a time when the divorce process was much faster than under Italian law, which provides for a period of necessary separation before the divorce can be granted. It was later discovered that the residence of one of the spouses of the many couples was always at the same address in UK, which was in fact a P.O. Box in Berkshire. Two years later, when the deceitful scheme was discovered, all of the 180 divorce judgments were declared 'void' by the English High Court, which concluded that they were all obtained by 'using systematic fraud and forgery' and a 'conspiracy to pervert the course of justice on an almost industrial scale'.

3.53. The correct application of grounds of jurisdiction amount to a court duty.[70] Consequently, while relying on the parties statement and evidence is obviously frequent and very functional, the court seised should in all cases endeavour to search and investigate *ex officio* if the habitual residence of one of

---

[67] CJEU, 25 November 2021, *IB*, C-289/20, paras 47–48.
[68] R. CALABUIG, 'Cross-Border Family Issues in the EU: Multiplicity of Instruments, Inconsistencies and Problems of Coordination' in V. ABOU-NIGM and M. NOODT TAQUELA (eds), *Diversity and Integration in Private International Law*, Edinburgh University Press, Edinburgh 2019, p. 70.
[69] *Rapisarda v. Colladon (Irregular Divorces)* [2014] EWFC 35 and 179 other petitions; O. LOPEZ PEGNA, 'Collegamenti fittizi o fraudolenti di competenza giurisdizionale nello Spazio giudiziario europeo' (2015) 98 *Rivista di diritto internazionale* 397, 443–439; C. RICCI, 'Jurisdiction in Matrimonial Matters', in C. HONORATI (ed.), *Jurisdiction in Matrimonial Matters, Parental Responsibility and International Abduction*, Giappichelli/Peter Lang, 2017, p. 51–53; A. LIMANTE, above n. 43, p. 166.
[70] See in general Chapter 2 at 2.31.

the parties is in the forum. Moreover, special care and attention should be paid to checking the underlying factual elements submitted by the parties.

IV. NO TRANSFER OF PROCEEDINGS IN MATRIMONIAL CASES

3.54. Transfer of proceedings, which was introduced in Brussels II-bis and refined in Brussels II-ter in matters of parental responsibility,[71] is not applicable in matrimonial matters. No changes were made in this respect to the previous position under Brussels II-bis. Given the multiple criteria offered to the parties, coupled with the fact that the purpose of the transfer provisions is to confer jurisdiction on a court that does not have competence,[72] it was considered there was no need to envisage the possibility of transferring to a different court.

V. JURISDICTION ON THE CONVERSION OF LEGAL SEPARATION INTO DIVORCE: ARTICLE 5

3.55. Article 5 provides:

> Without prejudice to Article 3, a court of a Member State that has given a decision granting a legal separation shall also have jurisdiction to convert that legal separation to a divorce, if the law of that Member State so provides.

3.56. The origins of this provision date back to the 1998 Brussels II Convention, but it has scarcely been applied in practice, probably because of its unclear and ill-defined scope of application.

3.57. The *raison d'être* of this provision lies in the structural differences in the substantial law of Member States with regard to national divorce procedures. A so-called 'reflection time' is often required before a divorce can be granted, especially when this is not agreed by both parties and/or where there are common children. However, the relationship between actual separation and final divorce differs from State to State, both in terms of the required length of time and with regard to the necessity of a prior legal determination of the spouses' separation. Some Member States have different rules for divorce and for legal separation of spouses, as the two are different legal institutions, resulting in different effects

---

[71] Discussed in Chapter 5.
[72] Cf. in relation to the transfer provisions governing matters of parental responsibility, CJEU, 4 October 2018, *IQ*, C-478/17, para. 40, discussed further in Chapter 5.

on the matrimonial tie. Furthermore, in some of these States, separation is a necessary precondition in seeking a divorce, without which divorce cannot be rendered (this is the case, for example, in Italy and Ireland); in others, separation is a possible alternative, but each of the parties may seek a divorce from the outset without any need to go through a legal separation, which is an available option but not a requisite for claiming divorce (for example in France, Belgium and the Netherlands). Finally, some Member States completely ignore the idea of a **legal** separation, although such separation may be relevant to establishing a factual separation between spouses (for example in Germany and Austria).[73]

3.58. Article 5 provides continuing (sometimes also called 'derivative'[74]) jurisdiction in favour of the court that has previously declared the legal separation of spouses. The rule envisages the case where a Member State's court has declared a couple to be legally separated, but later, due to a change of factual circumstances – for example, the relocation abroad of one of the spouses – that court subsequently lacks jurisdiction to adjudicate on the divorce. The provision thus foresees an additional ground of jurisdiction, which complements those mentioned in Article 3,[75] and prescribes a continuation of jurisdiction for such a court, even when neither of the spouses have a connection with it at the time the divorce is filed. However, not all divorces following legal separation procedures fall within the scope of application of this rule. Indeed, the scope of application of this rule is quite peculiar and, in practice, very limited.

3.59. The rule only takes into consideration **legal separation** – in other words, separation that is formally declared by a public authority following some kind of legal proceedings. Although a possible requirement to show the irremediable breakdown of the union, factual separation is not relevant in this context.

3.60. It is unclear whether jurisdiction on separation should be established in the first place on the basis of Article 3. While some take this view, which follows from the rationale of the provision,[76] others stress the fact that jurisdiction is based on the procedural and substantial connection between the two sets of procedures and does not require the court to have established its jurisdiction

---

[73] Further details on a comparative overview on divorce and/or separation law in different Member States can be found in K. BOELE-WOELKI, F. FERRAND, C. GONZÁLES BEILFUSS, M. JÄNTERÄ-JAREBORG, N. LOWE, D. MARTINY and W. PINTENS, *Principles of European Family Law Regarding Divorce and Maintenance between Former Spouses*, Intersentia, Cambridge 2004, passim; and the Update Reports 2021 at https://ceflonline.ned.
[74] M. NÍ SHÚILLEABHÁIN, 'Art. 5 Brussels IIter' in U. MAGNUS and P. MANKOWSKI above n. 19, p. 118, para. 1.
[75] Arguing from the beginning of the provision, stating: 'Without prejudice to Article 3', M. NÍ SHÚILLEABHÁIN, 'Article 5' in U. MAGNUS and P. MANKOWSKI above n. 19, p. 118, para 6. This means that both parties always retain the choice to use any of the alternative criteria under Article 3.
[76] A. BORRÁS, 'Article 5' in U. MAGNUS and P. MANKOWSKI, above n. 12, p. 100, para. 5.

under the Regulation in the first place.[77] Both approaches make sense and it remains to be seen which view prevails.

3.61. Although a necessary relation between prior separation and subsequent divorce is common to different States, the rule envisages a very limited application, crafted around the crucial possibility of legal separation to be converted into divorce according to the national law of the Member State concerned. This raises two issues. First, the possibility of a '**conversion**' from separation to divorce does not depend on the Regulation, but on whether 'the law of that Member State so provides'. This expression is unclear. The most convincing interpretation is that it amounts to a double condition. On the one hand, it will be for the law applicable to divorce proceedings, eventually to be ascertained under the Rome III Regulation (in those Member States who are bound by it) or according to Member States national choice-of-law rules (in other cases), to determine whether under such a domestic law statute, the substantial conditions for divorce are satisfied and if a conversion is at all possible. If the applicable law does not allow for the possibility of a conversion, then this article is not applicable.[78] On the other hand, it will also be for the seised court, claiming to continue jurisdiction on divorce, to be able to take a decision based on the conversion of separation into divorce. This may be a problem in Member States that, while acknowledging the two sets of proceedings, will nevertheless consider them as two separate proceedings that are independent of each other.[79] In other words, in this respect Article 5 does not provide a uniform and autonomous ground of jurisdiction for divorce, but allows Member States

---

[77] R. HAUSMANN, above n. 26, p. 26, para. 75; T. RAUSCHER, above n. 22, p. 106, para. 6; M. Ní SHÚILLEABHÁIN, 'Art. 5 Brussels IIter' in U. MAGNUS and P. MANKOWSKI above n. 19, p. 119, para 8.

[78] R. HAUSMANN, above n. 26, p. 26, para. 75, A. BORRÁS, 'Article 5' in U. MAGNUS and P. MANKOWSKI, above n. 12, p. 100, para. 6.

[79] This is, for example, the situation under Italian law, where separation and divorce, notwithstanding that the former is a necessary legal step of the latter, constitute two different set of legal proceedings, each of them with a different object and nature. Italian legal literature generally considers Article 5 not to be applicable in the Italian legal system, on the assumption that under national law, the divorce proceedings are new proceedings and technically there is no 'conversion' from one to the other. See, for example, A. BONOMI, 'Il regolamento comunitario sulla competenza e il riconoscimento in materia matrimoniale e di potestà dei genitori' (2001) *Rivista di diritto internazionale* 298, 323 et seq. However, for a more flexible approach, see M. LUPOI, 'Il Regolamento n. 2201/2003 sulla competenza ed esecuzione della decisione in materia matrimoniale e genitoriale' in M. TARUFFO and V. VARANO (eds), *Manuale di diritto processuale europeo*, Giappichelli, Turin 2011; S. ZIINO, 'La giurisdizione sulle cause matrimoniali e sulle domande connesse secondo la normativa europea' (2014) *Rivista trimestrale diritto procedura civile* 546. Things may be different under the new rules (Legislative Decree n. 149 of 10 October 2022, which came into force in February 2023) which provide for the possibility to present from the outset an application asking for separation and divorce. On this point, see further case law, taking an opposite view, discussed at paras 3.65 et seq.

that envisage such a possibility under their own internal law to exercise their competence notwithstanding the competence of other fora provided for by Brussels II-ter.

3.62. Second, it is unclear what amounts to a 'conversion'. Based on a strict, literal, interpretation, this notion only seems appropriate to Ireland, under whose laws a judgment handed down for legal separation can be 'converted' *ipso jure* into a divorce if the legal separation has lasted three years. In this case, the judge grants the divorce and rules on its consequences. However, interestingly, a wider interpretation may be given so as to include in the scope of the provision cases where the decision on separation is a necessary precondition for the divorce decision ('wenn die Trennungsentscheidung eine Voraussetzung für das Schiedungsurteil darstellt').[80] This interpretation finds support in the Borrás Report on the original 1998 Brussels Convention, which states:

> The *conversion* of legal separation into divorce is fairly frequent in some legal systems. In some State separation is an *obligatory step* prior to divorce and a stated period of time must usually elapse between the separation and the divorce. That distinction is, however, unknown in other legal systems.[81] (Emphasis added)

3.63. This comment supports the idea that the term 'conversion' is used in a wider, non-technical, way to refer to all cases where separation is an obligatory step prior to divorce. Article 5 may thus be applicable in all of those Member States that in the circumstances at hand do not allow for divorce if it is not preceded by a legal separation.

3.64. The provision has rarely been applied across the EU. The requirement that 'conversion' is envisaged both by the applicable law and by the *lex fori* on the one hand, and the multiple jurisdictional grounds which the parties have at their disposal on the other hand, leaves little room for an autonomous application of this peculiar provision.

3.65. Nonetheless, among the few decisions, one, adopted in 2020 by an Italian court,[82] favours a more flexible interpretation and opens up new possibilities. A couple of mixed nationality, a Spanish woman and a man who was a national of the United Arab Emirates (UAE), had their last common residence in Italy. When the relationship broke down, the husband returned to the UAE, and the wife, who remained resident in Italy, claimed separation before the Italian court. Shortly after that the decision was given in 2017, the wife left Italy and relocated

---

[80] R. HAUSMANN, above n. 26, p. 26, para. 75.
[81] A. BORRÁS, Explanatory Report on the Convention (1998), para. 43.
[82] Tribunale Terni, 18 March 2020 n. 472, in 3(2020) *Rivista di diritto internazionale privato e processuale*, 675 seq. English summary at the EuFam II database, decision ITF20200305 http://www2.ipr.uni-heidelberg.de/eufams/index.php?site=entscheidungsdatenbank.

to Spain. After the requested period of separation had lapsed, the wife filed for a divorce before the Italian court.

3.66. The Italian court, while acknowledging the couple's lack of habitual residence in Italy, based its competence on Article 5 because legal separation had been declared by that same court a few years earlier. Referring to the above-mentioned passage of the Borrás Report, it argued that Article 5 applied in all cases where prior separation for a given lapse of time was a compulsory step for divorce under national law and pursued the aim of offering a unitary jurisdiction for the subsequent steps of the matrimonial proceedings. It also held that the law applicable to divorce was the Italian law pursuant to Article 9 of Regulation 1259/2010 (Rome III), according to which, where legal separation is converted into divorce, the law applicable to divorce is the law applied to the legal separation, which was the Italian law under Article 8 of that same Regulation.

VI. RESIDUAL JURISDICTION: ARTICLE 6

3.67. As noted above, Brussels II-ter makes a provision to preserve the application of a residual jurisdiction when no Member State otherwise has jurisdiction under the provisions of the Regulation. To this end, Article 6 *inter alia* provides:[83]

1. Subject to paragraph 2, where no court of a Member State has jurisdiction pursuant to Article 3, 4 or 5, jurisdiction shall be determined, in each Member State, by the laws of that State.
2. A spouse who is habitually resident in the territory of a Member State; or a national of a Member State, may be sued in another Member State only in accordance with Articles 3, 4 and 5.

3.68. Article 6 is the only provision dealing with matrimonial matters that has been changed to any real extent compared to the previous instruments. Following the Commission's 2016 Proposal,[84] which was only slightly redrafted during the Council's subsequent negotiations, Article 6 Brussels II-ter merges the previous Article 7 Brussels II-bis, including its heading, with the previous Article 6 Brussels II-bis. The latter's content has been reframed, with a different wording,[85] into Article 6(2) Brussels II-ter. This reconfiguration is reasonable, given that the two previous provisions complemented each other and were read in conjunction with one another under the previous text.

---

[83] Article 6(3) is discussed below at 3.88 et seq.
[84] COM(2016) 411.
[85] The reference to 'domicile' as applied to Ireland (and the UK) has been moved to Article 2(3).

A. THE ROLE OF NATIONAL RULES: ARTICLE 6(1)

3.69. Article 6(1) aims to clarify the role of **national rules** on jurisdiction in relation to the subject matter of the Regulation. It also defines jurisdiction in Member States with regard to cases which have a weaker connection with the EU and which may be termed as 'extra-EU disputes'. A parallel rule with regard to matters of parental responsibility is to be found under Article 14.[86] Generally speaking, national rules are seen with disfavour as they are unilaterally set by each Member State and may be based on criteria which tend to be exorbitant, such as the claimant's nationality or habitual residence. Nonetheless, given the lack of a rule on *forum necessitatis*, reference to such rules may be useful where the case presents a connection with the EU and there would otherwise be a risk of a denial of justice.

3.70. The rule is subject to two separate conditions: first, no court in any Member State may claim competence on the grounds of the Regulation (see 3.71–3.75 below); and, second, the respondent must neither be a national of nor habitually resident in a Member State (Article 6(2); see 3.79–3.84 below).

3.71. Article 6(1) clarifies the **mandatory and exhaustive nature** of the criteria set out by Articles 3–5, which apply irrespective of the nationality of the parties.[87] As it results from the structure of the Regulation, whenever any of the criteria set by **Articles 3–5** is satisfied, these **have to be applied** and national rules are displaced. In other words, EU national courts are bound to apply and respect the Regulation, not only when it confers jurisdiction upon the forum State, but also when it confers jurisdiction upon the court of any other Member State. This is further confirmed by Article 18, which directs a court to decline competence, whenever any such criteria gives competence to any other Member State's courts. Such a court is thus obliged to decline its competence and refer the case to courts of another Member State also when, under its own internal law, it would have competence.

3.72. The correct meaning and application of this rule has been clarified by the CJEU in one of the first decisions handed down on Brussels II-bis in the *Sundelind Lopez* case.[88] This case concerned a couple of Swedish and Cuban nationality who had been living together in France. Following the breakdown of the couple's relationship, the husband had returned to Cuba, while the wife maintained her habitual residence in France. The wife filed a divorce petition before the Swedish court on the basis of the Swedish national rule conferring jurisdiction upon the Swedish courts if the claimant is a Swedish citizen and

---

[86] See below, Chapter 4 at 4.166.
[87] On the characters of the criteria envisaged by Article 3, see above, 3.10 et seq.
[88] ECJ, 2 November 2007, *Sundelind Lopez*, C-68/07.

is resident in Sweden or has been resident there after reaching the age of 18.[89] When jurisdiction was declined both at first and second instance, an appeal was made to the Swedish Supreme Court, which referred for preliminary ruling to the ECJ.

3.73. The Court, applying what was then Article 7(1) Brussels II-bis, ruled that whenever the courts of a Member State have jurisdiction under Article 3 of the Regulation, courts of another Member State cannot base their jurisdiction on their national law. In that case, the French court had competence pursuant Article 3(1), second indent Brussels II-bis, since France was the place of the last common habitual residence of the couple and the wife was still there. This circumstance excluded the application of Swedish national rules pursuant to Article 7 Brussels II-bis.

3.74. Only when **none** of the criteria provided by Articles 3 to 5 of the Regulation **applies** (and when the respondent is neither a national of nor habitually resident in a Member State; see 3.79 below) is it possible – and indeed necessary – to revert to national rules. National rules on jurisdiction thus **play the role of a** *forum necessitatis*, which is otherwise lacking in Brussels II-ter.[90] They complete the jurisdictional system and allow for jurisdiction on matrimonial disputes in the peculiar case where there is a connection with the EU, but such a connection does not amount to a uniform ground of jurisdiction under the Regulation. In such a case, which would otherwise lead to a denial of justice, jurisdiction may be exercised by relying on national rules. It should be noted that national rules become applicable not by their own force, but because Article 6(1) so prescribes.[91] As such, any decisions that fall within the material scope of application of the Regulation must be recognised in all Member States (other than Denmark) on the basis of the Regulation, it being irrelevant that it was founded on national rules of jurisdiction.

3.75. The ambiguity in the formulation of this rule, which is centred on the position of the respondent spouse, led to some erroneous applications in the past. As the *Sundelind Lopez* case cited above shows, the provision should not be interpreted as meaning that where the respondent is neither a national of nor habitually resident in the EU, Brussels II-ter is not applicable. In fact, the Regulation applies **irrespective of the respondent's nationality and**

---

[89] See Chapter 3 Section 2 of Swedish Lag (1904:26 s. 1) om vissa internationella rättsförhållanden rörande äktenskap och förmynderskap (Law on certain international legal relations concerning marriage and guardianship).
[90] Below 3.85 et seq.
[91] C. CAMPIGLIO, 'Conflitti positivi e negativi di giurisdizione in materia matrimoniale' (2021) 3 *Rivista di diritto internazionale privato e processuale* 497, 505 and 519 says they are 'embraced' in the Regulation.

habitual residence, when other criteria conferring jurisdiction are met,[92] such as the habitual residence of the applicant and the additional requirements of Article 3(a)(v) or 3(a)(vi), or when the criteria set by Article 4 or Article 5 are met. For example, Article 6(1) does not apply when an applicant, who is a Member State national, brings proceedings against a third-State national who is habitually resident in the EU[93] (for example, a French man filing a divorce against his Swiss spouse, who is habitually resident in Italy). In this case any reference to national rules is excluded because competence can be grounded on Article 3(a)(iii).

3.76. However, there is one case where national rules on jurisdiction may be applicable even though a ground under the Regulation is theoretically available. As Recital (34) states, the Regulation is 'without prejudice to the application of public international law concerning **diplomatic immunity**'. What this means is that where one of the spouses is a serving member of the diplomatic body of a State (regardless of whether it is a Member State or not), the State in which the diplomat is carrying out his or her offices must not exercise its jurisdiction in matrimonial disputes, even if it is based on the Regulation. In such a case, Recital (34) states that 'jurisdiction should be exercised in accordance with national law in a Member State in which the person concerned does not enjoy such immunity'.

3.77. While the wording of Recital (34) is not free from some ambiguity, it should be understood that other Member States are allowed to apply their own national rules of jurisdiction when Articles 3–5 are not available in those Member States. In other words, if there is any ground for jurisdiction available under Brussels II-ter, the fact that under international customary law one Member State is prohibited from exercising jurisdiction does not permit the other Member State to derogate from the Regulation and apply its own national rules. This is possible only when the only jurisdiction envisaged by the Regulation (albeit available in theory) is barred by customary law.

3.78. As the CJEU clarified in the *MPA* case,[94] it is only the diplomatic immunity, within the meaning of Article 31 of the Vienna Convention, which is relevant. On the contrary, the status of civil servants of the EU enjoyed by two EU nationals seconded to a third State does not trigger the international immunity rules and therefore does not fall within the scope of application of Recital (34).

---

[92] See above Chapter 1 at 1.56. This is different from what happens in civil and commercial matters under Regulation No 1215/2012 (Brussels I-bis), which requires that the defendant has his or her domicile in a Member State for the general and special ground of jurisdiction to apply (but not for the so-called 'protective' or exclusive ground of jurisdiction).
[93] For a critical appraisal of this far-reaching protection of the third-State national who is a spouse of an EU national, see T. RAUSCHER, above n. 22, at p. 110, para. 4.
[94] CJEU, 1 August 2022, *MPA*, C-501/20.

B. PROTECTING THE RESPONDENT WHO IS A NATIONAL OF, OR HABITUALLY RESIDENT IN, THE EU: ARTICLE 6(2)

3.79. The application of national rules is limited by **Article 6(2)**, which aims to **protect the respondent spouse** who is a national of or is habitually resident in an EU Member State. Given the general dislike of applying national rules also in light of their discriminatory effect (see 3.69 above), the so-called 'EU citizen privilege' ensures that national rules on jurisdiction are not applied to EU nationals or non-EU nationals who are habitually resident in a different Member State. An EU national (or a person habitually resident in an EU Member State) can be sued in a State which is not the one of his or her nationality only on the basis of the agreed uniform grounds of jurisdiction.[95]

3.80. The rule puts both a defendant who is an EU national and a defendant who is habitually resident in the EU (and not an EU national) on the same footing. However, the two situations are quite different. While in terms of an EU national who is habitually resident outside the EU, the rule has the effect of limiting the effect of any reference to national rules of jurisdiction, the second part of the rule seems to be without a proper object. Any person who is habitually resident in the EU can only be sued in the courts of such a State pursuant to the general ground of competence set out in Article 3. In other words, there is no room for referring to Article 6, which only comes into consideration when **no other criterion applies** (see 3.74 above) and this part of Article 6(2) simply restates what is already clear under Article 6(1) – that is, that residual jurisdiction does not apply.

3.81. In any case, the rule only protects against being sued in a Member State **other** than in the State of one's own nationality (or in the State where one is habitually resident). An EU citizen (or a person habitually resident in a Member State) can in fact be expected to be subject to the jurisdiction of the State of his or her own nationality (or of habitual residence) if the national rules of such a State so provide.[96] Therefore, **national rules of the State of the respondent's nationality** are not subject to the rule envisaged by Article 6(2) and **can be**

---

[95] The rationale of the 'EU citizen privilege' has been questioned and, in the view of the present authors, is far from obvious. Among the critics, see those cited by A. BONOMI to the GEDIP Proposal of 2019 at the Katowice meeting cited below at n. 103.

[96] C. CAMPIGLIO, above n. 91, 523, making the point that a different construction expanding the protection against national fora also with regard to the rules of the State of nationality (or of habitual residence) of the respondent would make it impossible to seise a EU court in all divorces between EU citizens of different Member States who are habitually resident in a non-EU Member State. Referring to national rules is the only possibility to avoid a denial of justice. See also M. WILDERSPIN, above n. 14, p. 146, paras 4.091–4.095, arguing from a textual construction. The issue, which was controversial before, is now clarified by the decision in *MPA*, commented upon in para. 3.82 below.

applied to ground jurisdiction against such a respondent when no other ground under the Regulation is available.

3.82. The complex coordination of national rules on jurisdiction has been tested and clarified in *MPA*.[97] This case involved a couple of EU nationals, a Spanish wife and a Portuguese husband, married in Guinea Bissau and habitually resident with their children in Togo, where both of them were working as EU contractual agents. After the couple split up, they both remained habitually resident in Togo, but the Spanish wife sought a divorce, custody over the children and maintenance before the Spanish court. Finding that Articles 3–5 Brussels II-bis did not confer competence upon any Member State, the Spanish court reverted to national rules and found that it had competence through a rule that maintains Spanish jurisdiction to Spanish diplomats working abroad. The Portuguese husband contested the Spanish competence, and the case came before the CJEU.

3.83. Although the questions referred concerned multiple causes of action, in relation to divorce, custody of common children and maintenance, the following analysis is confined to jurisdiction in matrimonial matters. In this regard, the CJEU first found that the Spanish wife was not habitually resident in Spain as she had been only occasionally present on the territory and the legal fiction under Spanish law for individuals performing diplomatic tasks was irrelevant. Having considered that the spouses had different nationalities and thus no other fora was available in matrimonial matters under the Regulation, the CJEU proceeded to examine whether it was possible to use Spanish national rules to file a divorce against the Portuguese husband pursuant to what is now Article 6(1) Brussels II-ter (formerly Article 7(1) Brussels II-bis). Based on what is now Article 6(2) Brussels II-ter (formerly Article 6(b) Brussels II-bis), the CJEU gave a negative answer because such rule 'prevents the defendant in the main proceedings, who is a national of a Member State other than the one to which that court belongs, from being sued before the latter'.

3.84. However, what is even more interesting is the CJEU's clarification of what was until then a controversial question – namely, whether the preclusion under Article 6(2) also operates with regard to the national rules of the State of nationality of the respondent. The CJEU said:

> that interpretation does not mean that the spouse seeking the dissolution of matrimonial ties is deprived of the possibility of bringing his or her action before the courts of the Member State of which the respondent is a national, if Articles 3 to 5 of Regulation No 2201/2003 do not designate another place of jurisdiction. In such a case, Article 6(b) of that regulation [i.e. Article 6(2) Brussels II-ter Regulation] *does*

---

[97] CJEU, 1 August 2022, *MPA*, C-501/20.

not preclude the courts of the Member State of which the respondent is a national from having jurisdiction to hear the application for the dissolution of matrimonial ties, *in accordance with the national rules on jurisdiction of that Member State.* (Emphasis added)[98]

As mentioned above, this conclusion had already been reached by the legal literature and, in the absence of a more appropriate common rule providing a general *forum necessitatis*, seems the best solution that can be reached at the moment. Nonetheless, it should be remembered that the rule will not provide a solution in all cases, as will be explained in the following section.

C. THE LACK OF A *FORUM NECESSITATIS*

3.85. Article 6(2) does not tackle the real problem, which had already been pointed out under the former instruments – that is, the situation of a couple of **mixed nationality** (irrespective of whether at least one of them has EU nationality)[99] where both spouses are **habitually resident outside the EU**. Given that none of the criteria provided under Articles 3–5 is available, such a situation is in principle covered by national rules on jurisdiction. Yet, reference to national grounds of jurisdiction is not an optimal solution. In fact, this will result in a different access to justice among EU citizens and, moreover, will not always solve the problem. Lack of jurisdiction may occur, for example, when both spouses are habitually resident in a third country and the respondent is a national of a Member State. In such a case, Article 6(2) prevents resorting to national rules on jurisdiction of a Member State other than that of the State of the respondent's nationality. If such a State does not grant jurisdiction according to its own national rules and no reasonable court in a third country will try the application for a divorce, there will be a denial of justice.

3.86. As a 2007 study[100] showed, while a group of States have rules that confer jurisdiction on the grounds of nationality of at least one of the spouses (but seldom the claimant), for another group of Member States, nationality is not a ground of jurisdiction in matrimonial matters.[101] Other grounds of

---

[98] CJEU, 1 August 2022, *MPA*, C-501/20, para. 87.
[99] When both spouses have the nationality of a non-EU Member State and have their habitual residence outside the EU, the situation would appear not to have a reasonable link with the EU and a lack of jurisdiction of any EU court would appear justifiable.
[100] See the study for the EC Commission carried out by A. Nuyts, *Study on residual jurisdiction (Review of the Member States' Rules concerning the 'Residual Jurisdiction' of their Courts in Civil and Commercial matters pursuant to the Brussels I and II Regulations)*, General Report (final version, 3 September 2007), in particular p. 92.
[101] According to the study by A. Nuyts (above n. 100), this is the situation in Belgium, Cyprus, Denmark, Finland, Greece, Latvia, Malta, the Netherlands, Scotland and Spain (see the table at p. 97, para. 127).

jurisdiction may of course come into consideration (for example, a previous common habitual residence in a Member State, or the State where the marriage takes place), but this is less frequent than might be thought. In addition, some States do not have a national ground for jurisdiction in family matters and rely entirely on EU private international law rules.[102] Consequently there can be cases where an EU national who is habitually resident outside the EU might not have access to an EU court for a decision on his or her status. The situation is even more difficult when the action is filed against a partner having an EU nationality, because the applicant will not be allowed to use his own national fora against such a defendant pursuing Article 6(2) (but he may be able to use the national fora of the defendant's State of nationality – see above at 3.84). It is also worth remembering that a decision handed down from a third State will not be automatically recognised under Brussels II-ter, but must be recognised, if at all, under different national procedures (and possibly requirements) in each Member State. This hinders the free circulation of persons and conflicts with the major objectives of EU law.

3.87. As the above-mentioned situations are not at all rare, it is highly regrettable that it was not given adequate consideration. This could have been done by introducing a *forum necessitatis*, a solution which had been strongly supported by the legal literature,[103] but that was not contemplated by the 2016 Commission's Proposal or put forward in the Council's negotiations, given the political decision not to impinge in matrimonial matters. A rule on *forum necessitatis* is instead provided for by the Maintenance Regulation (Article 7), by the Succession Regulation (Article 11) and by the two Property Relationship Regulations (Article 11 in both). All these rules have a similar content providing competence when three conditions are met: (a) no EU court has jurisdiction under other rules set in the corresponding Regulation; (b) the dispute has nonetheless a sufficient connection to at least one Member State; and (c) the proceedings cannot reasonably be brought or conducted or would be impossible in a third State with which the dispute is closely connected. When all these

---

[102] See, for example, the laws in Spain and the Netherlands, which rely on the same grounds of jurisdiction used by the Brussels II-bis Regulation (see C. CAMPIGLIO, above n. 91, at 521).

[103] A. BONOMI, above n. 3, 522 et seq; C. GONZÁLEZ BEILFUSS, 'Choice of Court and Residual Jurisdiction in Divorce: A Plea for Reform That is Not Expected Any Time Soon?' (2021) 4 *Nederlands Internationaal Privaatrecht* 701. Mention should also be made of the proposal made by Group Européen Droit International Privé (GEDIP) on 15 September 2019 at the Katowice session for the introduction of a specific rule on *forum necessitatis*. The proposal and its general presentation by E. PATAUT is available at https://www.gedip-egpil.eu, under 'Katowice meeting'. On *forum necessitatis*, see in general R. CAFARI, '*Forum Necessitatis*: Judicial Discretion in the Exercise of Jurisdiction' in F. POCAR, I. VIARENGO and F. VILLATA (eds), *Recasting Brussels I*, CEDAM, 2012, p. 127 et seq; G. ROSSOLILLO, 'Forum necessitatis e flessibilità dei criteri di giurisdizione nel diritto internazionale privato nazionale e dell'Unione europea' (2010) 1 *Cuadernos de derecho transnacional* 403 et seq.

conditions are met, the EU court that has a sufficient connection to the dispute may, on an exceptional basis, hear the case. It should be noted that a *forum necessitatis* would imply the use of a greater discretionary power and therefore a lower degree of predictability and certainty. It is probably for such a reason that it was not introduced either in relation to matrimonial matters or in parental responsibility cases. It has been argued, however, that the existence of a *forum necessitatis* may be derived by the right to access to justice under Article 47 of the EU Charter on Fundamental Rights, especially where access to court is not available elsewhere.[104] It will then be for the CJEU to support such a construction when the occasion to address the issue will be offered.

D. THE PRINCIPLE OF EQUAL TREATMENT FOR EU CITIZENS HABITUALLY RESIDENT IN A MEMBER STATE: ARTICLE 6(3)

3.88. Article 6(3) implements the **principle of equal treatment** between EU nationals and non-EU nationals. The provision stems directly from the principle of non-discrimination among EU citizens which is provided by Article 18 TFEU. As such, it has its historical roots in the 1968 Brussels Convention in Civil and Commercial Matters,[105] and has since been transposed into both Brussels I and Brussels II Regulations, and their subsequent versions. Article 6(3) provides:

> As against a respondent who is not habitually resident in and is not a national of a Member State, any national of a Member State who is habitually resident within the territory of another Member State may, like the nationals of that State, avail himself of the rules of jurisdiction applicable in that State.

3.89. The rationale of the provision is to be found in the fact that national rules to be applied pursuant to Article 6 will, in most cases, make use of nationality as a ground for jurisdiction. The discriminatory nature of this criterion, which would otherwise prejudice nationals of other EU Member States who are habitually resident in a Member State, has been turned into giving them the advantage of **an additional ground for residual jurisdiction** by extending the availability of these criteria to all EU citizens who are habitually resident in the EU. On the contrary, national rules are not available to third-State nationals who are habitually resident in a Member State and who wish to sue a spouse who is also a non-EU national and is not residing in the EU.

---

[104] C. CAMPIGLIO, above n. 91, at 531; S. BARIATTI, 'Diritti fondamentali e diritto internazionale privato dell'Unione europea' in L.S. ROSSI (ed.), *La protezione dei diritti fondamentali. Carta dei diritti UE e standard internazionali*, Editoriale Scientifica, 2011, p. 417.

[105] See Article 4(2) of the 1968 Brussels Convention.

3.90. Unlike paragraphs 1 and 2, paragraph 3 requires that the claimant is (now) habitually resident in the EU. EU nationality alone is in fact not sufficient to trigger national rules under Article 6(3); it is also necessary that the claimant is habitually resident in the State whose national rules are considered.[106]

3.91. Summing up, the conditions for national fora to be applied under Article 6(3) are quite strict, namely:

- no court in the EU has competence under Articles 3–5 of the Regulation (i.e. the parties do not share a common EU nationality; the parties never had a common habitual residence in the EU; the respondent is not habitually resident in the EU; the claimant is not habitually resident or has just relocated in the EU);
- the claimant is an EU national and has moved his or her habitual residence to a Member State that is different from the one of his or her own nationality **less than** 12 months before filing its application;
- the respondent is not a national of a Member State; and
- the national rules of the State of habitual residence of the claimant confer jurisdiction in that specific case.

3.92. Where these conditions are satisfied, the EU spouse is allowed to make use of the national rules on jurisdiction of the State of his or her habitual residence to file an application for divorce against the other spouse who is neither an EU national nor habitually resident in the EU. Take, for example, the case of couple having (not common) Italian and Swiss nationality who live together in Switzerland. When the couple split up, the Italian spouse moves to France and sues the other spouse for divorce on the basis of Article 14 of the French Civil Code. This rule confers jurisdiction in civil cases to French courts, on the simple ground that the applicant is a French national. Under Article 6(3), such a rule may also be triggered in this scenario by the Italian spouse habitually resident in France.

---

[106] According to T. RAUSCHER, above n. 22, p. 125, para. 23, the ground for jurisdiction based on the claimant's nationality, sometimes in connection with the domicile or habitual residence, may be found in Bulgaria (Article 7 IPRG), Germany (§98(1)(1) FamFG), France and Luxembourg (Article 14 of both the French and the Luxembourg Civil Codes); Greece (Article 612 KPD); Austria (§76(2) JN), Spain (Article 22 LOPJ) and Sweden (3. Kap §2 Law 1904:26).

CHAPTER 4

JURISDICTION IN MATTERS OF PARENTAL RESPONSIBILITY

I.   Introduction 110
II. The General Rule on Jurisdiction: Article 7 111
     A. Background and Rationale of the General Rule 111
     B. The Meaning of 'Habitual Residence' 113
         1. The 'Integration Test' 113
             i)   The *A* Decision 113
             ii) The *HR* Decision 115
         2. Applying the Integration Test in the Case of Newborns and
             Very Young Children 117
         3. Some Key Elements in Establishing 'Integration' 118
             i)   Physical Presence 118
             ii) Duration of Residence 120
             iii) Intention 121
             iv) A Child can Only have One Habitual Residence at a Time. 122
         4. Overall Summary 122
III. Continuing Jurisdiction in Relation to Access Rights: Article 8 123
     A. The Basic Position and its Rationale 123
     B. The Scope and Conditions of Application of Article 8 124
IV. Choice-of-Court Agreements: Article 10 126
     A. General Framework and Historical Background 126
     B. The Reasons for Party Autonomy in Family Proceedings 126
     C. The Structure of the Rule, Covering Choice-of-Court and
         Prorogation 128
     D. Substantial Requirements 129
         1. The Child's Connection with the Prorogated Court 129
         2. Whose Consent is Required? 131
         3. Consent to Prorogation 133
         4. The Exclusivity of a Choice-of-Court Agreement 138
         5. Exercise of Competence must be in the Best Interests of the Child ... 139
     E. Formal Requirements 141
     F. Duration of Choice-of-Court Agreement: Article 10(3) 141
     G. Choice-of-Court Agreements in Connection with *Lis Pendens*
         and Transfer of Proceedings 143

	H. Choice of Court in Favour of a Third State that is a Party to the 1996 Hague Convention (and in Favour of One that is not) 145
V.	Jurisdiction Based on the Child's Presence: Article 11 147
	A. The Rationale of the Rule 147
	B. A Child with No Habitual Residence 147
	C. Refugee and Internationally Displaced Children 149
	D. Full but Time-Limited Jurisdiction. 151
VI.	Transfer of Jurisdiction: Articles 12 and 13 152
	A. Background and Structure of the Two Rules. 152
	B. The Rationale of the Rule and the Quest for Flexibility. 153
	C. What can be Transferred?. 154
	D. Transfer of Jurisdiction, not just of Proceedings. 154
	E. Article 12 and Transfer of Jurisdiction to Another Court 157
	1. The Child's Particular Connection with Another Member State. 157
	2. The Transfer is in the Best Interests of the Child 160
	3. The Other Member State's Court is 'Better Placed' to Assess the Best Interests of the Child 163
	F. The Operation of the Rule in Practice 165
	1. Who can Trigger the Transfer 165
	2. The Acceptance of the Receiving Court. 167
	3. Denial of Acceptance or Lack of Answer of the Receiving Court. 169
	G. Article 13 and the Request for Transfer of Jurisdiction 169
VII.	Residual Jurisdiction under Article 14 171
VIII.	Provisional and Protective Measures. 172
	A. Provisional and Protective Measures in Childcare Cases 172
	B. A Double-Track for Provisional Jurisdiction. 175
	C. A Uniform Ground for Provisional Jurisdiction. 178
	1. Measures must be Urgent. 179
	2. Measures must be in Respect of a Child 180
	3. The Territorial Link: The Child or Assets must be Located in the Forum 183
	4. Measures must be Provisional. 183
	D. Limited Territorial Effect 184
	E. Limited Effects in Time 189
	F. The Reciprocal Duty to Inform of Adopted Urgent Measures 190

I. INTRODUCTION

4.1. A major aspect of Brussels II-ter, as was true of its predecessors, is the provision of rules of jurisdiction and the consequent recognition and enforcement of decisions concerning the attribution, exercise, delegation, restriction or termination of parental responsibility.[1] The meaning of 'matters of parental responsibility' is discussed in Chapter 1.[2] Suffice to say here that such matters are broadly defined[3] as meaning 'all rights and duties relating to the person or property of a child which are given to a natural or legal person by a decision, by operation of law or by an agreement having legal effect including rights of custody and rights of access'.

4.2. The focus of this chapter is to examine the rules of jurisdiction with regard to matters of parental responsibility. Recognition and enforcement of such decisions will be discussed in Chapters 8 and 9 respectively.

II. THE GENERAL RULE ON JURISDICTION: ARTICLE 7

A. BACKGROUND AND RATIONALE OF THE GENERAL RULE

4.3. The general rule of jurisdiction in matters of parental responsibility is governed by Article 7(1), which provides that it lies with the court of a Member State in which the child is **habitually resident at the time the court is seised**. The rule thereby retains the *perpetuatio fori* principle, espoused by Article 8 Brussels II-bis,[4] according to which jurisdiction continues for the duration of the proceedings once it is established at the moment the court is seised.[5] This general rule is subject to Articles 8–10, which respectively concern: continuing

---

[1] See Article 1(b).
[2] At 1.35–1.44.
[3] Article 2(2)(7).
[4] A. Borrás, 'Article 8' in U. Magnus and P. Mankowski (eds), *Brussels IIbis Regulation*, OttoSchmidt, 2017, p. 113 et seq. and now T. Garber, 'Art. Brussels IIter' in U. Magnus and P. Mankowski (eds), *Brussels IIter Regulation*, OttoSchmidt, 2023, spec. at p. 59, para. 163. It should be noted that the *Commission's Proposal for a Council Regulation on jurisdiction, the recognition and enforcement of decisions in matrimonial matters and the matters of parental responsibility, and on international child abduction (recast)* COM(2016) 411 proposed a different construction of the rule. Article 7(1) in fact provided that, where a child acquires an habitual residence in another Member State following a lawful move, the authorities of that State shall have jurisdiction. This indeed is the position under Article 5(2) of the 1996 Hague Child Protection Convention. The proposal was dropped from the final version of Brussels II-ter. See further 4.129 for the use of transfer of proceedings in regard to the lawful change of the child's habitual residence.
[5] However, it should be noted that the *perpetuatio fori* principle applies only when the child lawfully relocates to another EU Member State. When, pending a proceedings but before any order is made, a child's habitual residence *lawfully* changes to the territory of a third State that is a Contracting Party to the 1996 Child Protection Convention, following Article 97(1)(a), the 1996 Hague Convention applies and the court of the Member State will ceases to have jurisdiction under Article 7 (see CJEU, 14 July 2022, *CC*, C-572/21). See further Chapter 1 at 1.70 et seq.

jurisdiction in relation to access;[6] jurisdiction in cases of the wrongful removal or retention of a child;[7] and choice of court.[8] Apart from different numbering, this general rule is the same as under Brussels II-bis.[9]

4.4. Article 7 (and its predecessors) reflects the general consensus of the international community to settle upon habitual residence as the appropriate connecting factor for determining jurisdiction in cross-border cases concerning children.[10] It is the principal connecting factor in the modern Hague Children Conventions[11] and, in particular, the 1996 Hague Child Protection Convention (which inspired the children content of the Brussels II Convention),[12] and the 1980 Hague Abduction Convention (which the Regulation complements). Habitual residence is also a key, but not exclusive, connecting factor in matrimonial matters under Article 3 of Brussels II-ter, which is discussed in Chapter 3.[13]

4.5. The choice of habitual residence as the principal connecting factor is based on the principle of proximity. As Recital (20) puts it:

> 'To safeguard the best interests of the child, jurisdiction should in the first place be determined according to the criterion of proximity.'[14]

The perceived advantage of habitual residence is that it provides the best means of identifying the forum with which the child has a real connection and in this respect is preferable to nationality and domicile. That, in turn, will identify the jurisdiction best placed to assess the child's best interests[15] when determining

---

[6] Discussed at 4.33 et seq.
[7] Discussed in Chapter 6 at 6.16 et seq.
[8] Discussed below at 4.42 et seq.
[9] See Article 8. The child's habitual residence was also the primary jurisdiction under Article 3 (1) Brussels II.
[10] For some discussion of the historical background, see, for example, B. HESS, 'Towards a Uniform Concept of Habitual Residence in European Procedural and Private International Law' (2021) 4 *Polski Proces Cywilny* 521 at 531–532.
[11] In fact, the Hague Conference pioneered using habitual residence as a connecting factor in its 1902 Convention on Guardianship and has used the concept in all its Conventions relating to family matters ever since.
[12] See, for example, Advocate General Kokott's Opinion 29 January 2009 in *A* (C–523/07), para. 24.
[13] The use of 'habitual residence' as a connecting factor is not, of course, unique to Brussels II-ter or to the Hague Children Conventions; it is also the jurisdictional tool in other EU Regulations such as those dealing with succession, maintenance, matrimonial property regimes and registered partnership regimes. For an overview of the use of 'habitual residence' in EU Regulations, see B. HESS, above n. 10, at 525 et seq.
[14] This Recital is in similar terms to Recital (12) Brussels II-bis, which was referred to by the ECJ, 2 April 2009, *A*, C–523/07, paras 12 and 35. See also ECJ, 23 December 2009, *Detiček*, C–403/09, para. 36.
[15] As Recital (19) says, 'the grounds of jurisdiction in matters of parental responsibility are shaped in the light of the best interests of the child and should be applied in accordance with them'.

disputes concerning the child's upbringing, since that is where the relevant evidence and expertise relating to the child's circumstances is most readily available. In effect, basing jurisdiction upon the child's habitual residence is the procedural application of the best interests of the child. But this test comes at the price of certainty and therefore predictability (especially if compared to the criterion of nationality). Although, as will be seen, the CJEU has done its best to set out the relevant factors in determining a child's habitual residence, it remains an open-ended, fact-specific concept that leaves the courts with considerable discretion.

4.6. Although in most cases, determining where a child is habitually resident is straightforward, the test is not always easy to apply and indeed the meaning of 'habitual residence' has generated considerable jurisprudence both in the Court of Justice and in national courts. The application is particularly problematic with regard to newborn and very young children.

4.7. As has been pointed out,[16] applying Article 7 involves two issues: defining the meaning of 'habitual residence' and determining which court is entitled to determine the existence of the habitual residence. With regard to the latter issue, it is clearly established that it is for the national court to determine the child's habitual residence 'taking into account all the circumstances specific to each individual case'.[17] It now remains to discuss the meaning of 'habitual residence'.

B. THE MEANING OF 'HABITUAL RESIDENCE'

4.8. 'Habitual residence' is not defined in Brussels II-ter, but has been the subject of a number of Court of Justice decisions in relation to its application to children.

1. The 'Integration Test'

i) The *A* Decision

4.9. The first and key decision is *A*.[18] A family, comprising three children, their mother and stepfather, left Sweden to spend time travelling in Finland. They did this over a summer, living a peripatetic lifestyle in caravans in various locations. After some months, during which the children did not attend school, the family unsuccessfully applied to the Finnish authorities for social housing. The parents

---

[16] By A. BORRÁS, above n. 4, p. 116.
[17] See ECJ, 2 April 2009, *A*, C-523/07, para. 44. For a critique of this position, see A. BORRÁS, above n. 4; see also at 4.13 below.
[18] ECJ, 2 April 2009, *A*, C-523/07.

then returned to Sweden, leaving the children in Finland ostensibly with the stepfather's sister. The welfare authorities decided, as a matter of urgency, to take the children into care on the basis of abandonment. The mother sought the children's return to Sweden and, having appealed, argued before the Finnish Supreme Administrative Court that, as the children were permanently based in Sweden, the case fell to that jurisdiction. The Supreme Administrative Court referred a number of questions to the then ECJ for preliminary rulings, one of which was the meaning of 'habitual residence' for the purpose of jurisdiction under what was then Article 8 Brussels II-bis.

4.10. The facts presented a classic dilemma, namely, determining the habitual residence of children permanently based in one Member State who are staying in another Member State for a short period and leading a peripatetic life. In deciding what the concept meant in this context, the Court considered that the established case law and in particular the establishment of the so-called 'centre of interest' test, which had been used in other areas of EU law in relation to an adult's habitual residence[19] could not be directly transposed to the context of an assessment of habitual residence of children.[20] Instead, having regard to what was then Recital (12) Brussels II-bis (now Recital (20) Brussels II-ter), the Court considered that regard had to be had to the fact that the grounds of jurisdiction are shaped in the light of the best interests of the child and, in particular, on the criterion of proximity.

4.11. With these points in mind, it was held that under Article 8, 'habitual residence' must be interpreted as meaning that:

> it corresponds to the place which reflects some degree of integration by the child in a social and family environment. To that end, in particular the duration, regularity, conditions and reasons for the stay on the territory of a Member State and the family's move to that State, the child's nationality, the place and conditions of attendance at school, linguistic knowledge and the family and social relationships of the child in that State must be taken into consideration.[21]

---

[19] See ECJ, 15 September 1994, *Fernández*, C-452/93P, referring to the place 'established, with the intention that it should be of a lasting character, the permanent or habitual centre of his interests' in regard to the residence of a EC official applying for expatriation allowance. This test is often referred to as 'the centre of interest' test and was also taken into account in regard to the Brussels Convention, see A. BORRÁS, Explanatory Report on the Convention, drawn up on the basis of Article K.3 of the Treaty on European Union, on Jurisdiction and the Recognition and Enforcement of Judgments in Matrimonial Matters, OJ 1998 C 221, p. 27, para. 32 ('the Borrás Report'). It was finally reiterated by the CJEU when considering the interpretation of habitual residence for adults under Article 3 Brussels II-bis in CJEU, 25 November 2021, *IB*, C-289/20, paras 40–42 and CJEU, 1 August 2022, *MPA*, C-501/20, para. 44. For further discussion of *IB*, see Chapter 3, at 3.49 et seq.

[20] Relying in this respect on Advocate General Kokott's Opinion 29 January in *A* (C-523/07), paras 33–38, discussed at 4.13 below.

[21] ECJ, 2 April 2009, *A*, C-523/07, para. 44.

Chapter 4. Jurisdiction in Matters of Parental Responsibility

These considerations will be revisited in the light of subsequent case law.

4.12. The key difference between what has become known as 'the integration test' and the 'centre of interest test' is with regard to intention. While not holding intention to be irrelevant, what the decision in *A* establishes is that **parental intention is not the pivotal factor** in determining the child's habitual residence.[22] The advantage of the integration test, as against the centre of interest test, is that it is more focussed on the situation of the child, with the purposes and intentions of the parents being only one of the relevant factors.[23] Its disadvantage is that it means that the concept of habitual residence, as espoused by the CJEU in *A*, is different for matters of parental responsibility under Article 8 and for matrimonial matters under Article 3.[24] That said, there is good reason to distinguish the habitual residence of children from that of adults since, on the one hand, the emphasis on intention is much less relevant in the former case,[25] while on the other hand, the 'best interests of the child', which Recital (19) combines with the habitual residence, is clearly unrelated to the habitual residence of adults.[26]

ii) The *HR* Decision

4.13. The integration test as laid down by the CJEU in the *A* decision was further explained in subsequent decisions and, in particular *HR*.[27] The mother, a Polish national, who lived and worked (on a contract of indefinite duration) in Brussels, had a child (who had dual Polish and Belgian nationality) by a man who was a Belgian national with whom she had been living in Brussels. Following the birth, the mother and child stayed in Poland (either at her parents' house or in an apartment she owned) on several occasions during her parental leave and subsequently during holidays and festivals, sometimes for periods of up to three months. After their relationship ended, the parents lived separately in Brussels. The child lived with the mother, and the father saw his daughter once a week. Wishing to settle in Poland with her daughter (now aged 18 months), the mother

---

[22] In the context of child abduction, there has been a global shift against determining a child's habitual residence primarily by reference to parental intention; see in particular *Office of the Children's Lawyer v. Balev*, 2018 SCC 18 (Can Sup Ct); and *Monasky v. Taglieri* 140 S Ct 719 (2020) (US Sup Ct).

[23] This point has been highlighted by the UK Supreme Court in *A v. A (Children: Habitual Residence) (Reunite International Child Abduction Centre Intervening)* [2013] UKSC 60 at para. [54], per Baroness Hale. Note, however, the reference to the 'centre of the child's life' in CJEU, 28 June 2018, *HR*, C-512/17, discussed further at 4.15 et seq.

[24] Note also the criticisms of the decision in *A* by A. BORRÁS, above n. 4, p. 117.

[25] See Advocate General Kokott's Opinion 29 January 2009 in *A* (C–523/07), para. 36, a point which A. BORRÁS, above n. 4, herself acknowledged.

[26] See B. HESS, above n. 10, 526.

[27] CJEU, 28 June 2018, *HR*, C-512/17.

Intersentia 115

applied to a District Court in Poland asking it to establish the child's place of residence as being at her own home in Poland and to put in place visiting rights for the father. The Court dismissed the application on the ground that the Polish courts lacked international jurisdiction to hear the case, since the child's place of habitual residence was in Belgium. The mother appealed, but at the same time made an application to a court in Brussels concerning parental responsibility over the child. However, that court stayed the proceedings pending the outcome of the proceedings initiated before the Polish courts. The Regional Court in Poland subsequently stayed the proceedings and sought a preliminary ruling on what factors should carry weight in determining the child's habitual residence on facts such as these.

4.14. In effect, the Regional Court sought a ruling on whether it could properly find the child to be habitually resident in Poland on the basis that child could be said to have some degree of integration into the social and family environment by reason of her mother's nationality and who had custody of her on a daily basis, speaking Polish, being christened in Poland and by her visits, lasting up to three months, to Poland during her mother's parental leave and during holidays. Alternatively, should Belgium be considered the child's place of habitual residence on the basis that the mother was employed there on the basis of an employment contract of indefinite duration and that it was where the child maintained regular but temporally limited contact with her father and his family?

4.15. In answering these questions, the CJEU said that for the purposes of the Regulation, a child's place of habitual residence is the place which, in practice, **is the centre of that child's life** and that it was for the national court 'to determine, on the basis of a consistent body of evidence, where that centre was located at the time the application concerning parental responsibility over the child was submitted'. Although this last observation seems reminiscent of the former 'centre of interest' test, it was clearly not intended to reign back on the 'integration test' established by the decision in *A*. To the contrary, in *HR* the Court was concerned with how that 'integration' might be established. In that respect, the Court considered that, having regard to the facts established by that court, the following, taken together, were **decisive factors**, namely that:

(i) from birth until her parents' separation, the child generally lived with those parents in a specific place;
(ii) the parent who, in practice, had custody of the child since the couple's separation continued to stay in that place with the child on a daily basis and was employed there under an employment contract of indefinite duration; and
(iii) the child had regular contact there with her other parent, who was still resident in that place.

By contrast, the following could *not* be regarded as decisive:

(i) the stays which the parent who, in practice, has custody of the child has spent in the past with that child in the territory of that parent's Member State of origin in the context of leave periods or holidays;
(ii) the origins of the parent in question, the cultural ties which the child has with that Member State as a result, and the parent's relationships with family residing in that Member State; and
(iii) any intention the parent has of settling in that Member State with the child in the future.

4.16. Although it was outside its remit to say so, it can be assumed that the Court considered the child to be habitually resident in Belgium. As the Court tellingly said,[28] the child's cultural ties or nationality 'cannot be given greater weight at the expense of objective geographical considerations without disregarding the EU legislature's intention'. Furthermore, note should be taken of its comment that the wish of the parent who, in practice, has custody of the child to settle with that child in that parent's Member State of origin in the future cannot, in itself, establish that the child's place of habitual residence is in that Member State.[29]

2. Applying the Integration Test in the Case of Newborns and Very Young Children

4.17. The meaning of 'habitual residence' was again considered in *Mercredi*.[30] This case involved another classic dilemma when determining habitual residence, namely, whether it can be established upon the basis of just a few days' factual residence in the State in question. In *Mercredi* the child (who was then two months old) was removed from the UK and brought by his mother to France on the island of Réunion, where he had been for four days when the proceedings was instituted. In the subsequent Hague abduction proceedings brought by the father, the French court refused to make a return order because the latter had no 'rights of custody' when the child left the UK. In the parallel custody proceedings, the French court granted the mother exclusive parental responsibility. In the meantime, the English court ruled that: (a) it had become seised of the case immediately following the father's institution of proceedings the day after the child had left the UK; (b) from that point on, the English court had 'rights of custody' and, because of the orders made, the father also had 'rights of custody'; and (c) at that time the child was 'habitually resident' in England. The mother appealed to the English Court of Appeal, which made a reference for preliminary rulings, *inter alia*, on the appropriate test for determining 'habitual residence'.

---

[28] At para. 60.
[29] At para. 65.
[30] CJEU, 22 December 2010, *Mercredi*, C-497/10 PPU.

4.18. The Court reiterated the *A* test. However, it added that in applying that test, the child's age is likely to be of particular importance and, in a case like *Mercredi*, where a newborn child is being looked after by the mother, it is necessary to assess the mother's integration in her social and family environment. To that end, relevant factors that should be taken into account include the duration, regularity, conditions and reasons for the stay in the State and reasons for moving there and, with particular reference to the child's age, the mother's geographical and family origins, and the family and social connections which the mother and child have with that State.[31] Although *Mercredi* departs from the general rule in directing the integration test to be conducted with regard to the caregiver, such a rule appears fully justified with regard to newborns. Unfortunately, what ranks as a 'newborn' for this purpose, and hence the actual scope of the *Mercredi* rule, is still to be established.

4.19. A problematic aspect of the Court's decision is its comment[32] that 'to distinguish habitual residence from mere temporary presence, the former must, as a general rule, have a certain duration which reflects an adequate degree of permanence'. This seems to import a test of 'permanence'. However, this reference to 'permanence' should not be construed as being forever or even necessarily indefinite, but in contrast to the idea of 'temporary' or 'instability'.[33]

3. *Some Key Elements in Establishing 'Integration'*

i) Physical Presence

4.20. In the case of *OL*[34] the issue raised was whether a child (even a newborn) can be habitually resident in a State in which he or she has never set foot. In *OL*, when the mother was eight months pregnant, the couple agreed that she

---

[31] In fact, in the subsequent domestic proceedings, the English court held (see *Mercredi v. Chaffe* [2011] EWCA Civ 272) that at the date the court became seised, the child remained habitually resident in England, but that by the time the merits of the case came to be determined, the right court to hear the case was the French court.

[32] CJEU, 22 December 2010, *Mercredi*, C-497/10 PPU, para. 51.

[33] Note the comment in CJEU, 12 May 2022, *WJ*, C-644/20, para. 67, where the Court said: 'the use of the adjective 'habitual' makes it possible to infer that residence must have a sufficient degree of stability, to the exclusion of a temporary or occasional presence'. See also the analysis by the UK Supreme Court in *A v. A (Children: Habitual Residence) (Reunite International Child Abduction Centre Intervening)* [2013] UKSC 60 at paras [51] and [80 vii]. In another UK Supreme Court decision, *Re R (Children) (Reunite International Child Abduction Centre and Others Intervening)* [2015] UKSC 35 at [16], Lord Reed remarked that it is 'the stability of the residence that is important, not whether it is of a permanent character. There is no requirement that the child should have been resident in the country in question for a particular period of time, let alone that there should be an intention on the part of one or both parents to reside there permanently or indefinitely'.

[34] CJEU, 8 June 2017, *OL*, C-111/17 PPU.

should give birth in Athens (Greece), where she could have the support of her parents' family, and that, subsequently, the mother would return to the marital home in Italy with the child. The couple accordingly travelled to Athens, where the mother gave birth, in February 2016. After the birth, the father returned to Italy. He subsequently agreed that the child should stay in Greece until May 2016, when he expected his wife and child to return to Italy. However, in June 2016 the mother decided, unilaterally, to remain in Greece with the child. In subsequent Hague return proceedings brought by the father, the Greek court made a reference for preliminary ruling asking whether physical presence was a necessary and self-evident prerequisite, in all circumstances, for establishing the habitual residence of a person and, in particular, a newborn child.

4.21. The Court ruled[35] that habitual residence requires some element of physical presence and that, consequently, in a situation in which a child was born in accordance with the common wishes of his parents in a Member State other than that in which the parents had their habitual residence before birth, and having resided with his mother continuously for several months, the initial intention of the parents that the mother should return with the child to the latter Member State cannot form a basis for the view that the child has his 'habitual residence' within the meaning of the Regulation. As it observed,[36] in the Regulation, the concept of 'habitual residence' essentially reflects a question of fact: 'Consequently, to take the position that the initial intention of the parents that a child should reside in one given place should take precedence over the fact that the child has continuously resided since birth in another State would be difficult to reconcile with that concept.'

4.22. That habitual residence necessarily involves an element of physical presence was confirmed by the CJEU in *UD*.[37] A British father married a Bangladeshi mother in Bangladesh. They later came to England, where the mother was granted a spousal visa to remain there, which was valid for three years. However, when heavily pregnant, the mother returned with the father to Bangladesh. The mother gave birth shortly afterwards and the child remained in Bangladesh. Eleven months later, the father returned alone to England. The mother claimed that she had been unlawfully kept in Bangladesh through coercion by the father. The mother brought proceedings in England seeking the

---

[35] Although the ruling specifically related to the application of what is now Article 29 Brussels II-ter (discussed in Chapter 6 at 6.105 et seq), the Court made it clear (see para. 41) that the concept of a child's habitual residence is uniform throughout the Regulation and that its ruling applies equally to what is now Article 7 Brussels II-ter. See also in this respect CJEU, 9 October 2014, *C v. M*, C-376/14 PPU, para. 54.
[36] CJEU, 8 June 2017, *OL*, C-111/17 PPU, para. 51.
[37] CJEU, 17 October 2018, *UD*, C-393/18 PPU. See also CJEU, 15 February 2017, *W and V*, C-499/15, at para. 61 – a case concerning a conflict of jurisdictions over matters of parental responsibility and maintenance.

child's return, and the question arose as to whether, for the purposes of what was then Article 8 of Brussels II-bis (now Article 7), physical presence in a Member State was a prerequisite of establishing habitual residence in that State, and whether coercion into giving birth in a third State and having to remain there had any bearing on that question.

4.23. The Court ruled that some physical presence *is* required to establish habitual residence for the purpose of the Regulation, since that 'is consistent with the criterion of proximity prioritised by the EU legislature, precisely in order to ensure that the best interests of the child are taken into account'.[38] It further ruled that, in the absence of such presence, the fact of coercion, even if it has the effect of the mother giving birth in a third State where she has been residing with the child ever since, has no bearing in establishing habitual residence. While the point is now undisputed, it is submitted that a **temporary interruption** of presence – such as for a long vacation, or a temporary move abroad – will not undermine the existence of habitual residence. These situations might in fact lead to a delicate factual assessment.

4.24. Although physical presence is a prerequisite of establishing habitual residence, presence alone is **not sufficient**. As the Court put it in *A*,[39] 'other factors must also make it clear that that presence is not in any way temporary or intermittent and that the child's residence corresponds to the place which reflects such integration in a social and family environment'. In this respect, a variety of factors will come into play, including the duration, regularity, conditions and reasons for the child's stay on the territory of a Member State and his or her nationality.[40] Furthermore, the relevant factors vary according to the age of the child concerned. In the case of newborn children, it is the caring parent(s)' integration that will be the key determining consideration. In the case of older children, their own views may be a relevant consideration.[41]

ii) Duration of Residence

4.25. Brussels II-ter does not lay down a minimum period of residence, though a possible inference from Article 8 is that habitual residence can commonly be

---

[38] See para. 63.
[39] ECJ, 2 April 2009, *A*, C-523/07, at para. 53.
[40] Research by A. LIMANTĖ and I. KUNDA, 'Jurisdiction in Parental Responsibility Matters' in C. HONORATI (ed.), *Jurisdiction in Matrimonial Matters Parental Responsibility and International Abduction*, Giappichelli/Peter Lang, 2017, p. 61, at pp. 70–71, found that Member State courts commonly look into the following factors: duration and regularity of the child's physical presence, the child's nationality, enrolment in school or kindergarten, enrolment in extra-curricular activities. registration for the purposes of receiving social benefits and for the purpose of healthcare and actual use of it, the child's family ties to a particular country, the languages spoken and at which level, and friends and other social connections.
[41] See 4.30 below.

expected to be established within three months' residence. However, **there is no fixed period by which integration can be established**. In this regard, context is everything, although in general terms, it has been well put[42] that where the child's presence is shorter, intention (discussed further below at 4.26 et seq) may play a greater role than where the period is longer. Another consideration is the degree of integration that the child had with the State that he or she has left, such that, again in general terms, the deeper that integration, the less fast integration in the new State will occur and vice versa.[43]

iii) Intention

4.26. **Intention alone is not sufficient** to establish habitual residence. The complete absence of physical presence (for whatever reason) means that a child cannot be considered habitually resident in that State and the intention of caring parent(s) cannot compensate for this.

4.27. This does not mean that intention has no part to play in assessing whether a child is sufficiently integrated in a State to be considered habitually resident there; on the contrary, it can play a **critical role** in determining whether a period of residence, particularly a short period, has reached the threshold of integration. As the Court noted in *A*, the intention of the parents to settle permanently with the child in a Member State can be taken into account where that intention is manifested by certain tangible steps such as the purchase or lease of a residence in the host Member State.[44] In short, as the Court stated in *OL*, while the intention of the parents cannot as a general rule by itself be crucial to the determination of the habitual residence of a child, it can constitute an **indicator** capable of complementing a body of other consistent evidence.[45]

4.28. An issue not yet considered by the CJEU, but which has been explored more generally in child abduction cases under the 1980 Hague Abduction Convention, is the relevance of **older children's views** when assessing their habitual residence. In view of the greater importance accorded to the voice of the child, it is submitted that such views are relevant (though not, *ipso facto*, determinative) and should be considered separately from those of the child's parents.[46]

---

[42] A. LIMANTĖ and I. KUNDA, above n. 40, p. 69.
[43] Note the observation of the UK Supreme Court in *Re B (A Child) (Reunite International Child Abduction Centre Intervening)* [2016] UKSC 4, at para. [38], per Lord Wilson, that this test does not require the child's full integration in the environment of the new State, but only a degree of it.
[44] ECJ, 2 April 2009, *A*, C-523/07, at para. 40.
[45] CJEU, 8 June 2017, *OL*, C-111/17 PPU, at para. 47.
[46] This was the UK Supreme Court's view in *Re LC (Children) (Custody: Habitual Residence) (Reunite International Child Abduction Centre Intervening)* [2014] UKSC 1, on which see

iv) A Child can Only have One Habitual Residence at a Time

4.29. Although it has still to be definitively decided, it seems clear that, as with adults,[47] a child can only have one habitual residence at any one time.[48] Moreover, such an interpretation would be in line with the established position under the 1980 Hague Abduction Convention.[49]

4. *Overall Summary*

4.30. The general rule of jurisdiction in matters of parental responsibility is that it lies with the court of the child's habitual residence. 'Habitual residence' has an autonomous meaning and is a factual notion. It is for the national court to establish the habitual residence of the given child, taking into account all the circumstances specific to each individual case.

4.31. According to the Court jurisprudence, a child's habitual residence corresponds to the place which reflects some degree of integration by the child in a social and family environment and is a place which, in practice, is the centre of that child's life. A list of relevant factors when determining habitual residence has been provided by the CJEU in some leading decisions (such as *A*, *HR* and *Mercredi*). Physical presence is prerequisite of habitual residence: a child (even a newborn) cannot be habitually resident in a Member State in which he or she has never been (*OL* and *UD*). Where the child has lived in different States, factors that will point to one State rather than the other being the place of the child's habitual residence will include the duration of actual residence, schooling, the intensity and quality of the child's personal relations, while the child's cultural or linguistic ties will be of less relevance. Parental intention cannot change this, nor

---

[47] J. CARRUTHERS, 'Discerning the Meaning of 'Habitual Residence of the Child' in UK Courts: A Case for the Oracle of Delphi' (2019/2020) 21 *Yearbook of Private International Law* 1, at 27–28; A. LIMANTĖ and I. KUNDA, above n. 40, p. 81; N. LOWE, 'The UK Senior Court's Contribution to the Global Jurisprudence on International Child Abduction' (2019) 135 *Law Quarterly Review* 114, at 128–129. The issue of hearing children more generally is discussed in Chapter 7.

[47] See CJEU, 25 November 2021, *IB*, C-289/20, discussed in Chapter 3 at 3.49 et seq.

[48] T. GARBER, above n. 4, p. 139, para. 52. See also the point made by J. CARRUTHERS, above n. 46, at 16 that in *HR* the CJEU regarded habitual residence as being *the* centre of the child's life. See also the analysis by A. LIMANTĖ and I. KUNDA, above n. 40, at pp. 82–83. In *Re L (Recognition of Foreign Order)* [2012] EWCA Civ 1157, the English Court of Appeal considered this to be position under Brussels II-bis.

[49] See e.g. in Australia, *In the Marriage of Hanbury-Brown v. Director General of Community Services* (1996) FLC 92-671; in England and Wales, *Re v. (Abduction: Habitual Residence)* [1995] 2 FLR 992; and in the US, *Friedrich v. Friedrich* 983 F2d 1396 (6th Cir 1993). But note the criticism of this blanket approach by R. SCHUZ, *The Hague Child Abduction Convention: A Critical Analysis*, Hart Publisher, 2013, 178–179; and by A. LIMANTĖ and I. KUNDA, above n. 40, p. 84.

does it matter whether the caring parent has been coerced into living with the child in a different State from that parent's 'home' State (see *UD*).

4.32. In the case of parental separation, no greater consideration should be given to the child's ties with the parent who looks after the child on a daily basis (*HR*). However, in the case of a newborn child, the integration in the social and family environment of the parent(s) looking after the child may play a significant role (*Mercredi*). It seems clear, but not yet definitively established, that a child can only have a single habitual residence at any one time.

III. CONTINUING JURISDICTION IN RELATION TO ACCESS RIGHTS: ARTICLE 8

A. THE BASIC POSITION AND ITS RATIONALE

4.33. As an exception to the general rule of jurisdiction conferred by Article 7, Article 8 (which is substantively the same as Article 9 Brussels II-bis)[50] provides that the court of the Member State of the child's former habitual residence retains a time-limited jurisdiction to modify an access order. Under Article 8(1), where a child **moves lawfully** from one Member State to another and becomes habitually resident there, the court that made a decision on access rights retains jurisdiction to modify it for three months following the move. The implication of this provision is that during this three-month period, the court of the **child's former habitual residence retains jurisdiction to the exclusion of the court of the new habitual residence**. However, this retained jurisdiction is only conferred in relation to the modification of access rights.[51]

4.34. This provision is subject to Article 8(2), which provides that the **retained jurisdiction ceases to apply if the holder of the access rights has accepted the jurisdiction of a court in the State of new habitual residence** by participating in proceedings there without contesting jurisdiction. This provision is generally interpreted as applying to the case where the holder of access rights chooses to seek a review of the access arrangements in the new State of habitual residence.[52] Whether participation in proceedings concerning **other** matters of parental responsibility concerning the child also triggers Article 8(2) has yet to be considered, but, given that Article 8 is an exception to the general rule of jurisdiction under Article 7, it is suggested that it should be applied restrictively,

---

[50] For extensive discussion of Article 8 Brussels II-bis, see e.g. A. BORRÁS, above n. 4, pp. 119 et seq.
[51] But note 4.41 below.
[52] See e.g. A. LIMANTĖ and I. KUNDA, above n. 40, p. 85.

with the effect that participation on **any issue** concerning parental responsibility would bring the continued jurisdiction to an end. This could happen, for example, if the moving parent has brought proceedings in the State of the new habitual residence, to which the other parent is responding.

4.35. The rationale of Article 8 is to allow the holder of rights of access to seek a court review of the access arrangements with a view to adapting them to new circumstances following the child's lawful move from one Member State to another without having to bring proceedings in the new jurisdiction. As the *2022 Practice Guide* comments, Article 8 'provides a guarantee that the person who can no longer exercise access rights as before, does not have to seise the courts of the new Member State'.[53] At the same time, Article 8 prevents someone taking a child to a new habitual residence and almost immediately making an application there to vary any access arrangements.[54] Unless the holder of the access rights agrees, the State of the new habitual residence does not have jurisdiction to entertain such an application for the first three months following the child's relocation there, which might be very inconvenient for the applicant.[55]

B. THE SCOPE AND CONDITIONS OF APPLICATION OF ARTICLE 8

4.36. The continuing jurisdiction under Article 8 is subject to five cumulative conditions. First, it only applies to **lawful moves**, that is, when the parent (or carer) is permitted to move with the child to another Member State.[56] If the move is unlawful, that is, where the child has been abducted, jurisdiction is governed by Article 9, which is discussed in Chapter 6. The application of Article 8 is also contingent upon the child **acquiring a new habitual residence** in a different Member State during the three-month period. If he or she does not, then the court of origin will have jurisdiction according to the general rule under Article 7, unless the child has also lost his or her habitual residence there. In that latter case, if the child has no habitual residence, then jurisdiction may be based on the child's presence, as provided for by Article 11.[57]

---

[53] *Practice Guide for the Application of the Brussels IIb Regulation* (hereinafter the *2022 Practice Guide*), European Union, 2022, at para. 3.2.4.1.

[54] However, it should be noted that Article 8 does not prevent bringing proceedings in respect of any other aspect of parental responsibility; see further 4.41 below.

[55] N. Lowe, M. Everall and M. Nicholls, *International Movement of Children: Law Practice and Procedure* (2nd ed. by N. Lowe and M. Nicholls), Lexis Nexis, Family Law, 2016, at para. 4.17.

[56] That is, where the other parent consents to the move, or the move has been sanctioned by a court or where no consent is required.

[57] *2022 Practice Guide*, paras 3.2.4.2.3. and 3.2.4.2.4. Article 11 is discussed below at 4.99 et seq.

4.37. Second, retained jurisdiction under Article 8 only applies to the modification of a **decision on access rights**, which must have been made **before the move**. In all other aspects of parental responsibility, including a shift in custody rights, a court of the Member State of the child's newly acquired habitual residence will have exclusive jurisdiction.

4.38. Third, Article 8 only applies in cases in which the court of origin has made a **decision on access rights**, which is **sought to be modified**. Given that a 'decision' is defined as a 'decision of a court of a Member State',[58] Article 8 has no application to the modification of an agreement. On the other hand, the reference to 'access' should be understood as applying broadly to include orders dealing with contact and visitation arrangements, however they are expressed. The *2022 Practice Guide*, for example, refers to the application of what is now Article 8 to 'access rights or other contact arrangements'.[59] On the other hand, jurisdiction of the State of previous residence is continued only to **modify** decisions.[60] What is meant by 'modify' in this context has yet to be determined. While it must surely cover altering the place, mode and frequency of access, it probably cannot be construed as retaining the jurisdiction to terminate contact as that would amount to a fundamental change as opposed to a modification of the decision.[61]

4.39. Fourth, the **holder of the access rights must continue to have his or her habitual residence in the Member State of the child's former habitual residence**. This latter condition should not be taken to limit Article 8 to applications made by holders of access rights. It equally applies where the 'moving parent' seeks to modify the decision.[62] In other words, the habitual residence requirement only governs jurisdiction and implies no limitation in regard to who is making the application. This interpretation makes sense, given that the object is not to force the holder of access rights to face litigation in the new State.

4.40. A fifth condition is that the holder of access rights must **not have accepted** the jurisdiction of the courts of the Member State of the child's new habitual residence. This condition derives from Article 8(2) and was discussed above at 4.34.

---

[58] Under Article 2(1), as discussed in Chapter 1 at 1.51 et seq.
[59] *2022 Practice Guide*, para. 3.2.4.1.
[60] It must be noted that when the access decision is not sufficiently clear or the necessary arrangement are not adequate, Article 54 grants the courts of the State of enforcement a limited power to make any further arrangement in order to organise the exercise of the right of access, as long as the essential element of the decision are respected.
[61] On this interpretation, when faced with an urgent need to protect the child from the actions of the person exercising access, the court of the child's habitual residence must use its powers to take protective and provisional measures as provided by Article 15 (which is discussed at 4.169 et seq).
[62] See A. LIMANTĖ and I. KUNDA, above n. 40, p. 84.

4.41. Retained jurisdiction only lasts for **three months after the move**, which means that in order for Article 8 to apply, the court of origin must be seised within this time. This period is calculated from the date on which the child was physically relocated from the State of origin, any previous event being irrelevant.[63] This should also not be confused with the date at which the child acquires a new habitual residence in such a Member State.

IV. CHOICE-OF-COURT AGREEMENTS: ARTICLE 10

A. GENERAL FRAMEWORK AND HISTORICAL BACKGROUND

4.42. Article 10 gives the parties some limited choice to bring proceedings in the forum they think will better serve their interests and thus provides flexibility in dealing with family crises. This is an important provision which has undergone major changes. The Commission proposed making various modifications to the previous Article 12,[64] but that proposal was in turn subject to multiple and substantial amendments during the Council negotiations. In the authors' view, the position finally adopted by Brussels II-ter is a clear improvement of the previous rule under Brussels II-bis, both on the Commission's proposal (referred to below at 4.48) and on the diverse drafts circulated in the Council.[65]

B. THE REASONS FOR PARTY AUTONOMY IN FAMILY PROCEEDINGS

4.43. Choice of court in family matters has always been a delicate issue. Party autonomy has now been recognised in regard to parental responsibility issues, while no similar provision has been introduced in regard to matrimonial matters, although this had been recommended by authoritative legal literature prior to and during the negotiating process. This may be explained by the fact

---

[63] This was clarified by CJEU, 27 April 2023, *CM*, C-372/22, at paras 29–33. In particular, the fact that the judgment which initially fixed the rights of access has become final on the date of the application for modification of that judgment is irrelevant. Thus, the court of previous habitual residence cannot rely against the holder of the rights of access on any 'force of *res judicata*' of the judgment which initially fixed those rights and the arrangements for them in order to find that the application made by the latter for the purpose of modifying those rights of access is inadmissible.

[64] See Proposal of the Commission, above, n. 4 and below at 4.48.

[65] See, for example, Council's note to the Delegations, 'Proposal for a Council Regulation on jurisdiction, the recognition and enforcement of decisions in matrimonial matters and the matters of parental responsibility, and on international child abduction (recast) – Revised text of Articles 1 to 11)' doc. ST 5572 2018 INIT of 26 January 2018, which still followed the approach proposed by the Commission and distinguished between two provisions.

that allowing some kind of (albeit limited) party autonomy in cross-border family disputes answers three different needs.

4.44. On the one hand, this is in line with a general trend allowing increasing room for party autonomy.[66] This is now a common experience which is confirmed by many European instruments, both in relation to choice of court and to choice of law and requires no further comment.

4.45. On the other hand, and with specific respect to Brussels II-ter, choice-of-court agreements serve the aim of procedural economy and **concentration of proceedings**, and thus counters one of the biggest shortcomings of the Regulation, i.e. fragmentation of issues arising out of a family dispute.[67] In fact, as noted earlier, Brussels II-ter is structured upon the assumption that matrimonial matters are separate and autonomous from parental responsibility matters, so that these will normally be settled in different fora. While matrimonial issues are brought before any of the courts mentioned by Article 3, the child's best interests dictate that proceedings concerning the child should be brought principally in the court of the child's habitual residence (Article 7). In reality, however, the two proceedings often arise at the same time and within the same family dispute. Concentrating the proceedings in one forum will then serve the interests of the parties, reduce the costs of justice and ensure consistency in the final settlement. The connection with matrimonial matters was clearer under Brussels II-bis (and in the Commission's first draft), where a specific provision allowed the parties to prorogate the forum of divorce or separation, so as to also hear claims on parental responsibility. Within such a framework, derogation from the general rule of fragmentation was seen as an exception, to be interpreted restrictively.[68] It remains to be seen whether the new rule, which is now drafted in more general terms, will be interpreted more extensively.

4.46. Furthermore, the rigidity connected with the (sole) criterion of the child's habitual residence needs to be tempered by some **flexibility** to cater for

---

[66] Already in 2005, the European Commission, 'Green book on applicable law and jurisdiction in divorce matters', 14 March 2005, COM(2005) 82 final, at points 3.3 and 3.6, proposed enlarging the possibilities for parties to choose both their court and applicable law. On the role of party autonomy in PIL family law, see, among many others, J. GRAY, *Party Autonomy in EU Private International Family Law*, Intersentia, 2021; C. GONZÁLES BEILFUSS, 'Party Autonomy in International Law' (2020) 408 *Recueil des Cours* 107.

[67] A strong tendency favouring a strict separation between divorce and parental responsibility is also present in the Hague Conference on Private International Law. Such a distinction is in fact to be found, even more dramatically emphasised, in Article 10 of the 1996 Hague Child Protection Convention. See P. LAGARDE, 'Explanatory Report on the 1996 Convention' (Permanent Bureau of the Hague Conference, 1998) (hereinafter 'the Lagarde Report') para. 61.

[68] This is again stated with reference to the current provision by the *2022 Practice Guide*, para. 3.2.6.1.

cases where, due to special circumstances, it is more appropriate for the claim to be heard in a different court. As mentioned before, under Brussels II-bis, this situation was dealt under a separate provision (Article 12(3)), which has now been merged into a single rule.

4.47. Finally, as the *2022 Practice Guide* mentions, Article 10 aims to promote 'the amicable dispute settlement at the level of access to justice but may inspire the parties to go further and to reach an agreement as to the substance of the case'.[69] Whether this will really be the case remains to be seen. No doubt, however, that a greater recognition of party autonomy in parental responsibility matters is a distinctive feature of Brussels II-ter[70] and a positive improvement in private international law in relation to children.

C. THE STRUCTURE OF THE RULE, COVERING CHOICE-OF-COURT AND PROROGATION

4.48. As mentioned above, the current rule removes the distinction made under Brussels II-bis between two different cases: the first, previously governed by Article 12(1) Brussels II-bis, where the court was already seised with a matrimonial claim and prorogation was meant to vest the court with jurisdiction on custody proceedings for the common children; and the second, governed by Article 12(3) Brussels II-bis, where no procedure was previously pending and the claimant sought to bring an 'independent claim' on parental responsibility before a court other than the one of habitual residence of the child. The need to distinguish between the two cases had been endorsed by the Commission's Proposal, which addressed the duality of the rule in the title, therefore changing the title from 'Prorogation of jurisdiction' to 'Choice of court for ancillary and autonomous proceedings'.[71] During the Council negotiations, the rule was

---

[69] See *2022 Practice Guide*, para. 3.2.6.1.
[70] This is especially to be appreciated with regard to the 1996 Hague Convention, where the corresponding provision, Article 10, envisages a limited possibility to prorogate the competence of the court for the divorce or the separation, and only where this is possible under the law of the forum.
[71] It has been noted that qualifying as 'ancillary' proceedings on parental responsibility that are brought in the context of matrimonial proceedings is contradictory and inconsistent with a Regulation that is structured on the two issues being separate and autonomous one from each other. Moreover, given the difficulties faced by many legal systems in terms of overcoming national provisions mandating courts to settle both issues at the same time, classifying parental responsibility claims as 'ancillary' to matrimonial disputes could reinforce the natural trend of national courts to attract the former to the latter. See C. Honorati, 'The Commission Proposals for a Recast of Brussels IIa Regulation' (2017) *International Family Law* 97, 101.

further split into two separate provisions.[72] Fortunately, at the last stage of the negotiations, the two provisions were reunited again into one under the title 'choice of court', and any reference to pending matrimonial proceedings was expunged from the final text.

4.49. Choice-of-court is now conceived as a free-standing situation, unrelated to matrimonial proceedings, which is grounded upon the needs of the parties and balanced with the best interests of the child. In this context, it should be noted that Recital (23) specifically refers to pending matrimonial matters as one of the cases where the need for a choice-of-court agreement may arise. In the authors' opinion, this is to be welcomed as it simplifies the reading and application of this important rule.

4.50. The rule now comprises four paragraphs which apply in all cases: the first paragraph addresses substantial requirements for a valid choice of forum; the second clarifies the formal requirements; the third spells out when such an agreement will cease its effect; and the fourth explains when such an agreement confers exclusive jurisdiction on the chosen court.

D. SUBSTANTIAL REQUIREMENTS

4.51. Under Article 10(1), a choice-of-court agreement is valid when three conditions are met: a substantial connection between the child and the chosen court; consent of the parties; and the assessment that exercise of jurisdiction will be in the best interests of the child.

1. The Child's Connection with the Prorogated Court

4.52. Under Article 10(1)(a):

> The courts of a Member States shall have jurisdiction in matters of parental responsibility where the following conditions are met:
>
> a) the child has a substantial connection with that Member State, in particular by virtue of the fact that:
>   i)   at least one of the holders of parental responsibility is habitually resident in that Member State;
>   ii) that Member State is the former habitual residence of the child; or
>   iii) the child is a national of that Member State;

---

[72] Article 10, 'Choice of court for ancillary proceedings', and Article 10a, 'Choice of court for autonomous proceedings'. See Proposal of the Commission, above n. 4.

4.53. This part of the rule draws on the former Article 12(3) Brussels II-bis and represents a compromise between allowing room for party autonomy and respecting a more restrictive approach with regard to choice-of-court agreements in family matters to be found in some Member States.[73]

4.54. Parties may choose a jurisdiction, but only to a limited extent. They may not agree on whatever court they wish, but have to choose a State with which the child has a **substantial connection**.[74] Examples of what a substantial connection may be is provided by the Regulation, namely, where the State concerned is that of current habitual residence of each of the two parents (or holders of parental responsibility), or of prior residence of the child, or of the child's nationality. However, the list is not a closed one, as shown by the expression 'in particular' at the beginning of the sentence, so other cases may arise in practice. Other relevant connections may be drawn from Article 12(4) on transfer of proceedings,[75] mentioning, for example, the place where property of the child is located, or which may arise in the given case, such as the nationality of one or both parents.

4.55. While a physical connection will, generally speaking, be more 'substantial', it may be queried if a 'legal' connection may also be relevant, such as **proceedings pending** in another State which involve the rights of the child. One could, for example, imagine the case of succession proceedings involving the rights of the child to be instituted or already pending in the State of habitual residence of the deceased. Formerly, under Article 12 Brussels II-bis, the CJEU clarified that, for the purposes of applying Article 12(3), previously pending proceedings was not a requirement.[76] However, while pendency of different proceedings on a related matter is not a positive requirement, there is nothing in Brussels II-ter

---

[73] See, for example, E. PATAUT and E. GALLANT 'Article 12' in U. MAGNUS and P. MANKOWSKI, above, n. 4, p. 161, para. 46.

[74] It should be noted that the solution adopted elsewhere is to allow only for a limited choice between courts clearly pre-identified by the legislator (see, for example, in relation to party autonomy for divorce and separation, as determined by Article 8 of the Rome III Regulation, or for party autonomy in relation to maintenance obligations, as determined by Article 4 of the Maintenance Regulation). The solution adopted in Brussels II-ter is more flexible and open-ended, since, provided the child has a 'substantial connection' with the State of the court seised and it is in the best interests of the child to do so, the parties are free to choose any court they wish.

[75] Discussed at 4.127 et seq.

[76] CJEU, 12 November 2014, *L v. M*, C-656/13, paras 45–52. The case concerned two children, previously resident in the Czech Republic with the father, who had been commuting between the father and the mother, who was resident in Austria where they also attended school. When the father seised the Czech court with custody proceedings and the mother entered an appearance in such proceedings, the Czech court, finding that the children were now habitually resident in Austria but had a substantial connection with the Czech Republic, asked the CJEU whether the conditions were met for a prorogation under Article 12(3). The clarification was needed in connection with Article 12(1), which instead required a previously pending divorce or separation proceedings.

preventing it from being a reasonable and logical ground for prorogating that court's competence to exercise jurisdiction over a child's connected rights, when the other conditions are also met.

2. *Whose Consent is Required?*

4.56. Article 10(1)(b) requires consent from 'the parties as well as any other holder of parental responsibility'. The term 'parties' is undefined, which is regrettable, since the term is open to different interpretations. The term may be read as referring to parties to the legal proceedings, or to parties to the choice-of-court agreement, or to both of these options depending on the sub-provision.[77] On a literal construction of the rule, it could be concluded that the latter is the correct answer, although this may lead to uncertainties in some cases. It is suggested that the term 'parties' has a different meaning depending on which sub-provision is involved. In the case of a proper choice-of-court agreement (under Article 10(1)(b)(i)), the consent needed is from the **parties to the agreement**. In the case of prorogation of the seised court (under Article 10(1)(b)(ii)), consent will be required from the **parties to the proceedings**. However, it should be noted that the time when the agreement is reached and the time when proceedings are filed may not coincide. Furthermore, the parties to the agreement may not be the same as those who later become parties to the subsequent proceedings. What is the position if the party signing a choice-of-court agreement is later deprived of parental responsibility? Will his or her choice of court become void, although it was valid when it was entered to? It is strange that the rule does not specify whether the parties to the choice-of-court agreement need to exercise parental responsibility rights over the concerned child.[78] While such a requirement may be considered implicit as it is inherent in the legal capacity to draft a choice-of-court agreement, it may become an issue if parental responsibility is subsequently lost (see below at 4.59).

4.57. Determining who is the holder of parental responsibility is a preliminary question which should be solved pursuing the conflict-of-law rules of the *lex fori* – an issue to be dealt within the EU by applying the 1996 Hague Child Protection Convention, and specifically Article 16 thereof, which calls for the application of the law of the State of the child's habitual residence.

---

[77] It should be noted that under previous Article 12 Brussels II-bis, the requirement was differently drafted with regard to prorogation of the court for divorce/separation (Article 12(1)(b)), referring to consent '*by the spouses* and by the holders of parental responsibility' and prorogation in proceedings 'other than those referred to in paragraph 1' under Article 12(3)(b), requiring consent 'by *all the parties to the proceedings* at the time the court is seised' (emphases added). The present rule, by merging the two different cases into one, adapts the requirement to the case that the 'parties' have settled an agreement for prorogation.

[78] The requirement was clearly set out by Article 12(1)(a) Brussels II-bis in cases where the spouses prorogated the competence of the divorce court.

4.58. In most cases, the relevant consent will be that of the child's **parents**, who will commonly each have parental responsibility, or by **other holder(s) of parental responsibility** when this is not the case. But in some systems, such as in Finland, the acquisition of parental responsibility by third parties is in addition to and not in substitution of the parents' existing responsibilities,[79] and consequently in such cases the consent of all the holders will be required.

4.59. It is unclear if a parent who is a party to the proceedings, but is deprived of parental responsibility, should nonetheless be required to give consent. The problem may arise in Member States in which a parent is a necessary party to care proceedings concerning the child, even when he or she no longer has parental responsibility. Requiring such a person's consent appears consistent with the wording of the rule requiring consent from 'the parties *as well as* any other holder of parental responsibility' (emphasis added), meaning that any party (to the proceedings – see 4.56 above) may also need to consent to the choice-of-court agreement, even when parental responsibility lies somewhere else. A further pointer to this being the correct interpretation may be found in Recital (23), which discusses the consent requirement of parties 'other than the parents' in a way that implicitly assumes that parents should always consent. Finally, such a solution may appear appropriate in view of the fact that a parent will always have a strong and legitimate interest in accepting or refusing the competence of a court which would be in charge of taking a decision impacting heavily on his or her own legal rights. In light of this, it would seem unfair to impose on him or her a decision taken by others without allowing him or her to express a view.

4.60. A **legal representative** will in principle be able to express consent on behalf of the represented parent, but only if there is a proved contact between the two and the parent was given all the relevant information. This will not be the case when the legal representative is appointed by the court of its own motion in the absence of the parent (see 4.70 below).

4.61. Separate consideration needs to be given to the position of the **Public Prosecutor** or to other public authorities having the standing to initiate a care proceedings under the *lex fori*. In *Saponaro*,[80] the CJEU highlighted that in some legal systems the Public Prosecutor is a mandatory part to proceedings concerning minors and represents the interests of the child. His or her opposition can therefore not be disregarded. However, in the absence of such opposition, the agreement of the Public Prosecutor may be regarded as implicit,

---

[79] See K. BOELE-WOELKI, F. FERRAND, C. GONZÁLES BEILFUSS, M. JÄNTERÄ-JAREBORG, N. LOWE, D. MARTINY and W. PINTENS, *Principles of European Family Law Regarding Parental Responsibilities*, Intersentia, 2007, p. 74.
[80] CJEU, 19 April 2018, *Saponaro*, C-565/18. For the facts of the case, see 4.65 below.

and 'unequivocal acceptance' by all parties may be held to be satisfied.[81] This reasoning of the CJEU has now been extended to any party, not just Public Prosecutors, and is codified in the second paragraph of Article 10(2), which, in regard to persons who become parties to the proceedings after the court was seised clarifies that 'in the absence of their opposition, their agreement shall be regarded as implicit'. As Recital (23) puts it, any party 'other than the parents who, according to national law, has the capacity of a party to the proceedings commenced by the parents, should be considered a party to the proceedings'. The rule will now also apply, for example, to social services having the standing to initiate a care proceedings, or to a child's guardian who is subsequently appointed by the court.

4.62. It should also be noted that, as a public authority in charge of safeguarding the minors' interests, it may well be presumed that the Public Prosecutor (as well as a child's guardian or legal representative) is always aware of the legal effects deriving from accepting the competence of the seised court, in regard to proceedings concerning a minor who is, by definition, habitually resident in a different Member State. Given that the consent to the court's competence by the Public Prosecutor will always be subsequent to the seising of the court, it is submitted that there should be no need for the court to make use of the warning required by Article 10(1)(b)(ii).

3. Consent to Prorogation

4.63. Substantial changes have been made by Brussels II-ter to the consent requirement for prorogation. Article 10(1)(b) now states that:

> the parties, as well as any other holder of parental responsibility have:
>
> (i) agreed freely upon the jurisdiction, at the latest at the time the court is seised; or
> (ii) expressly accepted the jurisdiction in the course of the proceedings and the court has ensured that all the parties are informed of their right not to accept the jurisdiction.

4.64. The most important change from the previous rule under Brussels II-bis is the **moment in time** when the choice-of-court agreement must be made. Previously, Article 12(3) Brussels II-bis required that the agreement be concluded 'at the time the court is seised'. Such a requirement proved to be unsatisfactory as it did not allow for **agreements concluded prior to the court being seised**. It also made no provision for when consent should be given in the course of proceedings. Article 10(1)(b) now gives an answer to both these issues.

---

[81] CJEU, 19 April 2018, *Saponaro*, C-565/18, para. 32.

4.65. A distinction is drawn between cases in which an understanding between the parties was made before or after the seising of the court. **Choice-of-court agreements** must be concluded prior to the seising of a court or, at the latest, at the time the court is seised. Stand-alone, express agreements are, generally speaking, quite rare in practice; however, prior agreements included in prenuptial or custody agreements can be found, particularly if American lawyers are involved. A more common experience is where an agreement is inferred by the **joint application, lodged by both parents**, possibly on behalf of their common child. This was the case in *Saponaro*, in which the parents acted on behalf of their child, habitually resident in Italy, and applied to the Greek court for the authorisation to renounce the inheritance of a deceased relative habitually resident in Greece.[82] The CJEU considered that by making a joint application to the same court, 'they demonstrated their willingness to seise that court and, in so doing, their agreement with the choice of court having jurisdiction. In the absence of other facts contradicting that finding, that agreement was to be regarded as "unequivocal", within the meaning of Article 12(3)(b)'.[83] Yet, attention should be paid to the extreme caution of the Court, which highlighted the lack of different contradictory facts.

4.66. An agreement concluded prior to the seising of the court is also of importance in those cases where the parties make an effort to deal with their dispute through **mediation**. In such cases, parties may be able to settle some of their issues out of court, and may wish to refer to a court those issues that they were unable to settle. Furthermore, and most importantly, even when an out-of-court agreement is reached, instituting legal proceedings may still be necessary in order to **incorporate the content of such an agreement** into a court decision for the purposes of making such an agreement legally binding and enforceable in all Member States. In both cases, parties may therefore agree upon which court should be seised, for example, choosing one which each of them considers to be neutral. The new provision offers leeway and a legal basis for this kind of situation and only requires the agreement to be entered into 'freely'. However, this adjective does not add much, since an agreement entered into under coercion would be null and void under any national law.

4.67. More relevant in practice are cases where a choice-of-court agreement is made **in the course of a proceedings already pending**, thus **prorogating the competence** of a court originally seised on a different matter. The typical case envisaged by the rule is where the applicant brings proceedings before a court lacking competence on parental responsibility, and the defendant enters an

---

[82] See CJEU, 19 April 2018, *Saponaro*, C-565/18, paras 24 and 25. On this decision, see also above 4.61.
[83] Now Article 10(1).

appearance without raising the exception of lack of competence. The legal effects of such a situation were unclear under the previous rule and led to divergent interpretations among national courts. The current rule improves the previous position by providing that competence must be accepted 'expressly or in an unequivocal manner'. A choice-of-court agreement can now only be accepted expressly, that is, by way of formally agreeing on the competence of the seised court (see also below at 4.72).

4.68. The CJEU was confronted with this issue a couple of times in the past, although it never explicitly addressed the point at stake. In *L v. M*,[84] two separate proceedings had been started in the Czech Republic for the custody of two minors commuting between Austria and the Czech Republic. Three days after the father had made an application to the Czech court for custody of the children, the mother made a separate application to the same court on the same subject. It appeared later on that this was done because she did not know where her children were. Once the mother was aware that the children were in Austria, she also applied to the competent court in Austria and clearly stated that she did not accept the international jurisdiction of the Czech courts. The father relied on the mother's application on the same subject matter (albeit in a different proceedings) to the Czech courts to assume there had been a valid prorogation under Article 12(3) Brussels II-bis.

4.69. The CJEU started by recalling that the rule on prorogation requires the existence of an agreement to be shown and that such an agreement should be express 'or at least unequivocal'.[85] It then found that this is manifestly not the case where **the court is seised on the initiative of only one of the parties** and the other party pleads lack of jurisdiction of the court seised. Even when this same party, who is the defendant/respondent in the first proceedings, at a later date brings separate proceedings for the same cause before the same court, **this will not amount to consent to prorogate competence** in the first proceedings. Such a conclusion appears to be supported by two considerations, which were also mentioned by the Court in *L v. M*. First, the best interests of the child can be ensured only by a concrete assessment, in each individual case, of whether the prorogation of competence sought is in accordance with the child's interests, and this can only be done with regard to a specific proceeding. Second, in accordance with what was then Article 12(2) Brussels II-bis (now Article 10(3) Brussels II-ter), prorogation of jurisdiction is only valid for the specific proceedings of which the court whose jurisdiction is prorogated is seised. The decision also shows how consent to prorogation of all parties must be unequivocal and should not be assessed in a formalistic way.

---

[84] CJEU, 12 November 2014, *L v. M*, C-656/1.
[85] See para. 56. The point was further reiterated by CJEU, 3 October 2019 (order), *OF*, C-759/18, para. 42–43.

4.70. Useful guidance may also be gained from the *Gogova* decision,[86] a case that addressed the issue of consent to prorogation given by a legal representative appointed by the court in the absence of the defendant. The Court took the opportunity to make it clear that the **requirement of consent** must be interpreted **strictly**, as prorogation is an exception to the general rule based on proximity.[87] It further pointed out that acceptance presupposes that, at the very least, the defendant is aware of the proceedings taking place before those courts. Consequently, an **absent defendant**, on whom the document instituting proceedings has not been served and who is unaware of the proceedings that have been commenced, **cannot be regarded as accepting that jurisdiction**. Furthermore, the consent of such a defendant cannot be derived from the conduct of a legal representative who was appointed by the court in the absence of the defendant and with whom the representative had had no contact. In the given circumstances, the defendant would not have had the information necessary to accept or contest the jurisdiction of those courts in full knowledge of the facts. While this conclusion leaves open the question of consent as expressed by a legal representative who was appointed by, and has contact with, the defendant, it clearly shows how cautious the CJEU is in finding the existence of consent and in principle refuses to accept that consent has been given when there is any uncertainty on the party's intention.

4.71. Notwithstanding this approach, national courts have in the past adopted **diverging practices**.[88] This might also be the result of a principle, which is common under the procedural law of many Member States, according to which lack of jurisdiction shall be contested *in limine lite*, i.e. within the first steps of the proceedings. Under several national procedural laws, not raising an exception is regarded as an acceptance of jurisdiction. The simple lack of opposition amounts to consent to prorogate the competence of a court which is in principle deprived of jurisdiction. However, this assumption appears to be ill-founded in the context of EU procedural law. Tacit prorogation is indeed often the object of a specific rule. Both Brussels I-bis on civil and commercial matters, and the Maintenance Regulation expressly provide that entering into an appearance without contesting jurisdiction amounts to a valid form of prorogation.[89] However, such a result

---

[86] CJEU, 21 October 2015, *Gogova*, C-215/15.
[87] See para. 41. The point was also made in CJEU, 19 April 2018, *Saponaro*, C-565/18, para. 27.
[88] See, for example, the different cases referred to by C. GONZÁLES BEILFUSS, 'Prorogation of Jurisdiction' in C. HONORATI (ed.), above n. 40, p. 193, mentioning cases from Spain and France, where the mere fact that jurisdiction was not contested was considered to amount to acceptance of that jurisdiction. Conversely, however, see the case law in UK, for example, *Bush v. Bush* [2008] EWCA Civ 865 and *Re L-R (A Child) (Jurisdiction: Habitual Residence: Acceptance of Jurisdiction)* [2014] EWCA Civ 1624. Note also *Re I (A Child) (Contact Application: Jurisdiction)* [2009] UKSC 10, in which the Supreme Court held that active participation and, *a fortiori*, initiation of proceedings are unequivocal acts of consent.
[89] See respectively Article 26 Brussels I-bis and Article 5 of the Maintenance Regulation.

cannot be inferred as a matter of interpretation, but is the effect of a specific rule. When the rule instead requires some kind of consent, as in the case of Article 10 (1)(b)(ii), it must be concluded that a positive statement or action is required, leaving no doubt that the party agreed on the choice of court.

4.72. Building on such an understanding, the new rule has removed the ambiguous reference to consent given in 'an unequivocal manner' and now only allows **the defendant to accept expressly** the competence of the seised court. A tacit prorogation – for example, entering an appearance with a defence on the substance of the case – is now clearly not possible.[90] Furthermore, in order to be sure that such acceptance is given with full knowledge of its consequences, an additional obligation is placed upon the court, namely, to inform all parties (including the claimant, who may have unwillingly seised the wrong court and irrelevant of the parties beig represented by a lawyer) of their right not to accept the jurisdiction of the court seised. The provision, which is modelled on a similar provision in Brussels I-bis[91] (also originating from the CJEU case law in civil and commercial matters), aims to ensure that acceptance is based on an **informed and free choice** of the parties and 'not a result of one party taking advantage of the predicament or weak position of the other party'.[92] Interestingly, according to Recital (23), such a verification is a duty on the court both when jurisdiction is based on a choice-of-court agreement (pursuant to Article 10(1)(b)(i)) and when it is based on acceptance of competence in the course of the proceedings (Article 10(1)(b)(ii)). However, such an extension is not supported by the textual wording of Article 10, which limits the court's duty to the latter case. Indeed, if there is an express agreement between the parties prior to the seising of the court, there should be neither the need nor the occasion for the court to remind the parties of the effects of such agreement.

4.73. In contrast to the rule under Article 10(1)(b)(i), the rule under Article 10(1)(b)(ii) does not set a time limit to when an agreement should be made. This leaves the option that a choice-of-court agreement is made also when proceedings are at **appellate stage**. It is uncertain however whether this is a uniform procedural rule under the Regulation, or whether this should be subject to the *lex fori*.

---

[90] *2022 Practice Guide*, para. 3.2.6.2.2. However, consent is assessed differently in relation to persons who become parties to the proceedings after the court is seised. In such a case, non-opposition is regarded as an implicit (tacit) agreement. See Article 10(2) and above 4.61.

[91] The rule is drawn from Article 26 Brussels I-bis, in regard to prorogation made by a weaker party, such as the policyholder, the insured, a beneficiary of the insurance contract, the injured party, the consumer or the employee. In such a case, before assuming jurisdiction, the court shall ensure that the defendant is informed of his or her right to contest the jurisdiction of the court and of the consequences of entering or not entering an appearance.

[92] Recital (23).

4. The Exclusivity of a Choice-of-Court Agreement

4.74. Whether or not a choice-of-court agreement is exclusive depends upon whether the agreement was made before or after the seising of the court pursuing Article 10(1)(b)(i) or Article 10(1)(b)(ii). In the latter case, as the competence of the seised court is strongly linked to the pending proceedings, it is no surprise – and very welcome from the point of view of clarity – that Article 10(4) **always makes jurisdiction prorogated in court exclusive**. This means that, from the moment that such acceptance is recorded in court, any other court, including the general court of the State of the child's habitual residence, is deprived of jurisdiction in that case. The rule also applies in the case of *lis pendens*. If the chosen court is the second court seised, the first seised court must declare its lack of competence.[93] However, it should be noted that no provision in Brussels II-ter mandates the court of the State of the child's habitual residence to declare its lack of competence when a (valid) choice-of-court agreements confers exclusive jurisdiction to another court. While respecting the exclusive nature of choice-of-court agreement is implicit in the Regulation, express guidance on such a delicate point would surely have been useful. The exclusive nature also has an impact on the chosen court, as this court will be precluded from transferring the proceedings to another court under Article 12(5)[94] (see also 4.92 below).

4.75. Exclusivity is not to be construed as referring to all parental responsibility matters, but is limited to the particular claim in the given proceedings.

4.76. Having said this, one should note that **exclusive jurisdiction** of the chosen court is **not the general rule**. By only referring to agreements conferring jurisdiction in relation to 'point (b)(ii) of paragraph 1', Article 10(4) clearly shows that choice-of-court agreements stipulated prior to (or at the time of) the seising of a court (that is, under Article 10(1)(b)(i)) are not included. However, this cannot be construed as meaning that the latter agreements cannot **also** confer exclusive jurisdiction on the chosen court. Indeed, in most cases the parties intend to choose the one and only court to which they may bring any future dispute. However, while exclusivity is the only possibility with regard to jurisdiction consented to *in court*, when the parties agree to a choice of court *prior* to the seising of a court, they are free either to make such jurisdiction exclusive, or to agree on the competence of an additional court while keeping the concurrent competence of the court of the State of the child's habitual residence.

4.77. The rationale of the rule is to safeguard each parent's freedom to choose where to bring a claim concerning parental responsibility in cases where choice of court is agreed (long) before the proceedings is brought and when

---

[93] See more in detail below at 4.90.
[94] *2022 Practice Guide*, para. 3.2.6.3.

the controversial issue is unknown. By making any prior choice of court non-exclusive, the legislator has, on the one hand, granted the parties the freedom to choose the court they consider better placed to solve their issues and, on the other hand, made this conditional on the actual consent of the parties that such a choice is still valid at the moment it comes into operation. Overall, therefore, the rule appears balanced and reasonable. Nonetheless, such a provision may lead to shortcomings if the parties are not aware of non-exclusivity. While one of them may erroneously rely on the prorogated court having sole jurisdiction, the other could lawfully seise the general court of the State of the child's habitual residence. Seising another court having jurisdiction under Brussels II-ter, notwithstanding a previous non-exclusive choice-of-court agreement, is a lawful use of the rules under the Regulation. Nonetheless, the seised court of the child's habitual residence, in light of the given circumstances, may find it appropriate to transfer the proceedings to the court previously chosen by the parties.[95]

5. *Exercise of Competence must be in the Best Interests of the Child*

4.78. Any agreement between the parties, even when aiming to confer competence to a court which has a substantial connection with the child, will **not by its own force be binding on the court**. Because the parties' interests may not be the same as the child's ones, Article 10(1)(c), requires the court to ascertain, by its own motion, if the exercise of such competence in the given case is in the best interests of that child. The terms of this third requirement are substantively the same as those under Article 12 Brussels II-bis[96] and confer a **wide discretion** on the court. The court is thus allowed to **refuse to hear the case** – in a similar way to what would be done under the *forum non conveniens* doctrine – whenever it considers that, irrespective of the child's substantial connection with the forum and of the parties' consent, it is not appropriate to exercise its jurisdiction based on the best interests of the child.

4.79. This additional condition makes it clear that prorogation is not to be applied mechanically – that is, merely because the other substantial and formal requirements are satisfied – but must be the result of a **specific and *in concreto* assessment** that the exercise of competence of that specific court, which is by definition different from the one of habitual residence of the child, will serve the best interests of the particular child in the circumstances of the given case. This assessment, which must be done at the time the court is seised, appears to be

---

[95] See 4.112 et seq below.
[96] The wording of Article 10(1)(c) Brussels II-ter is identical to the former Article 12(3)(b) Brussels II-bis. However, in the English version, Article 12(1)(b) Brussels II-bis referred to the 'superior' interests of the child, but that was regarded as an error in the text as it results from the first Practice Guide (*2014 Practice Guide*, p. 32, para. 3.2.6.2).

in line and consistent with the ECtHR jurisprudence on the best interests of the child, which requires all courts to apply rules only after taking into account the specific circumstances of the case.

4.80. While it is clear that what is meant is the need for a specific assessment drawn on the particularities of the case, it is less clear which elements a court should consider for the purposes of such an assessment. In the *Saponaro* case,[97] for example, the CJEU grounded its conclusion that the prorogated Greek forum was in the best interests of the child on the fact that the child had a substantial connection with Greece (in particular, because such a court was the one of the State of nationality of the child, of the residence of the deceased and of the place where the assets that were the subject matter of the inheritance were situated), that both parents agreed to the competence of such court and that the Public Prosecutor did not oppose it.[98] While this may have been convincing in that specific case, such a construction deprives the best interests test of much of its autonomous value, as this criterion will in the end overlap with the other two. Nonetheless, even where this is the case, the best interests criterion still retains an added value in the fact that the court will be required to give a tailor-made and circumstantial analysis of the situation.

4.81. The requirement of verifying that a choice-of-court agreement is in the best interests of the child shall be assessed in light of the exercise of jurisdiction. Insofar, it will not involve any assessment as to the possible outcome according to the law to be applied. As this same requirement is also a condition for the transfer of jurisdiction, some guidance may be drawn by the CJEU case law in that regard. However, this should be done with caution, given that the best interests requirement has undergone some major changes under Brussels II-ter since the relevant guidelines were given by the CJEU under Brussels II-bis (at 4.133, below).[99]

---

[97] For the facts of the case, see above 4.65.
[98] See CJEU, 19 April 2018, *Saponaro*, C-565/18, paras 36–39. In some legal systems public authorities, other than a Public Prosecutor, could also be called upon to act in the interests of the child.
[99] T. GARBER, 'Art. 10 Brussels II-ter' in U. MAGNUS and P. MANKOWSKI, *Brussels IIter Regulation*, OttoSchmidt, 2023, p. 180, para. 39 et seq. Mention should also be made of the opinion expressed by E. PATAUT and E. GALLANT, above n. 73, p. 165, para. 63, suggesting that the best interests of the child and the judicial discretion arising out of it may be used in order to 'open a bridge' between the rule on prorogation and the one on transfer of proceedings. In this regard, the distinguished authors suggest that 'it could be said that, where the court considers that international cooperation is preferred to a simple extension of its jurisdiction, it could refuse to hear the case on the basis of the best interests of the child test, suggesting that the holders of parental responsibility should seise the normally competent court. Such an interpretation would allow for a flexible and extensive interpretation of Article 12(3) Brussels II-bis without jeopardising the functioning of Article 15 [the rule on transfer of proceedings under Brussels II-bis]' (at p. 165, para. 53).

E. FORMAL REQUIREMENTS

4.82. In accordance with Article 10(2), any choice-of-court agreement which is made prior to court proceedings must be made in **writing**, dated and signed by the parties. This requirement is not only for the proof of the agreement, but also for its formal validity. The rule provides welcome clarity by removing any ambiguity connected to other forms of consent which were to be found under the previous Article 12 Brussels II-bis. Moreover, Article 10(2) attenuates the rigidity of the former rule by providing that other forms of communication – in particular, electronic means – are to be treated as the equivalent to 'writing' insofar as they constitute a durable record of the agreement. This means that, as is now common in several national legal systems, an exchange of emails will satisfy the formal requirement of being in writing. It would still be necessary, though, for such an agreement to be 'signed', possibly through some sort of electronic signature.

4.83. When the choice of court is not the result of a separate agreement, but of the acceptance by one party of the seising of a court by the other party, such acceptance needs to be collated by the court and **recorded in its records**. As this event will be incidental to the national proceedings, it will be governed by the *lex fori*. National rules and procedures therefore apply to the ways and means for collating and recording such consent. Nonetheless, the formal requirement that consent must be in writing and signed by the parties cannot be derogated, as it is founded directly on the Regulation.

F. DURATION OF CHOICE-OF-COURT AGREEMENT: ARTICLE 10(3)

4.84. As noted earlier, a choice-of-court agreement is in principle a derogation from the general rule of proximity. It is therefore contingent on the assessment of the best interests of the child in the specific case, a test to be performed by the court at the time it is seised (see above 4.78 et seq). It follows from the above that the duration of any choice-of-court agreement is **limited to the proceedings** for which such an agreement is made. This principle is set out in Article 10(3), which reads:

> Unless otherwise agreed by the parties, the jurisdiction conferred in paragraph 1 shall cease as soon as:
>
> (a) the decision given in those proceedings is no longer subject to ordinary appeal; or
> (b) the proceedings have come to an end for another reason.

4.85. The fact that competence must be verified and established in each specific case and with regard to the circumstances of the specific proceedings implies that – unless otherwise agreed by the parties – such competence will not continue after the concerned proceedings have been brought to an end. In other words, any prorogation of the court's competence is **temporary in nature**[100] and is bound to come to an end. The principle has been reaffirmed by the CJEU in several cases.[101]

4.86. The rule is not completely new, as it was previously to be found in Article 12(2) Brussels II-bis. However, this provision only referred to prorogation under Article 12(1) – that is, prorogation of the court before which proceedings for divorce or separation were pending.[102] It was therefore consistent with the aim to concentrate in such proceedings all issues arising from the couple's break-up, that such exceptional competence would be terminated upon the divorce proceedings being closed. The position is different with regard to the current rule, which, as previously noted (above at 4.48, and similarly to Article 12(3) Brussels II-bis), disconnects the choice-of-court agreement from the prorogation of the divorce/separation court. It is to be welcomed that, besides a general rule providing for the cessation of the effects of any prorogation agreement, **parties are now allowed to provide differently**, as is made clear by the beginning of Article 10(3). A different arrangement between the parties may be useful, for example, if it is expected that the decision to be taken by the prorogated court will need to be modified in the future and the parties wish to make sure that such future review of the situation is assessed by the same court. In all cases, any agreement of the parties aiming to continue the competence of the prorogated court must also be explicit and in writing, and, consequently, cannot be inferred from their conduct. Furthermore, such an agreement will, in any case, be subject to the scrutiny of the court that this is in the best interests of the child.

4.87. Article 10(3) provides welcome clarification with regard to when prorogated competence ceases. Previously, Article 12(2) Brussels II-bis made this dependant on the decision being 'final'. Such a condition was, however, equivocal because judgments on custody and access are always capable of being

---

[100] See E. Pataut and E. Gallant, above n. 73, p. 159, para. 38.
[101] See, for example, CJEU, 1 October 2014, *E v. B*, C-436/13, para. 40 and CJEU, 15 February 2017, *W and V v. X*, C-499/15, para. 68. In particular, in the latter complex case, the question was raised as to whether the Lithuanian court, which, in the course of divorce proceedings of the child's parents, had adopted a decision on parental responsibility (and also on maintenance obligations) in respect of a child who was resident in a different Member State (the Netherlands), retained jurisdiction to rule on an application for amendment of this decision, even though such a decision had become final and the divorce proceedings were closed. The CJEU held that such jurisdiction had in any event come to an end, since the decision granting the application for divorce and deciding on parental responsibility had become final.
[102] A similar rule did not expressly apply to prorogation under Article 12(3). It was the Court of Justice that extended the rule with the above mentioned decision. A similar provision is also to be found in Article 10(2) of the 1996 Hague Convention.

amended and are therefore never technically 'final'. Consequently, the provision created much uncertainty.[103] The term has now been replaced with a clearer reference to the moment when the decision 'is **no longer subject to ordinary appeal**'. Not only does this make the situation clearer, it also achieves uniformity throughout Member States. Furthermore, jurisdiction of the prorogated court will automatically **extend to appeal proceedings** which may be brought against the decision handed down by a first instance court.

4.88. The second case envisaged by Article 10(3) is when 'proceedings have come to an end **for another reason**'. This is an all-comprehensive clause including any other cause allowing for termination of proceedings under national law. It will be for the *lex fori* to determine when such a situation is verified. This will comprise, for example, the case where the application was withdrawn or the parties were inactive for some time.

G. CHOICE-OF-COURT AGREEMENTS IN CONNECTION WITH *LIS PENDENS* AND TRANSFER OF PROCEEDINGS

4.89. The greater attention paid by Brussels II-ter to party autonomy is also shown in the better coordination between choice-of-court agreements and other concurrent proceedings, such as *lis pendens* and transfer of proceedings. In both cases, the risk was that the rules laid down for these mechanisms for the coordination of proceedings would prevail over choice-of-court agreements and result in disregarding party autonomy. To avoid such a result, and drawing on the experience of Brussels I-bis, special rules have been introduced to uphold the effects of a choice-of-court agreement on *lis pendens* and on transfer of proceedings. However, these rules only apply when the competence of the chosen court is **exclusive**.

4.90. With regard to *lis pendens*, **Article 20(4) and (5)** reverses the general rule based on the chronological principle[104] and **gives precedence to the court seised on the basis of the choice-of-court agreement** pursuant to Article 10. Any court of other Member States, although previously seised, must stay the proceedings until such time as the court seised on the basis of the agreement declares its own competence, or lack thereof. Where such a court has established its own exclusive jurisdiction, the court first seised must decline jurisdiction in favour of the prorogated court.

---

[103] See, for example, T. KRUGER and L. SAMYN, 'Brussels II *bis*: Successes and Suggested Improvements' (2016) 12 *Journal of Private International Law* 132, 148.
[104] See Chapter 5 at 5.6 et seq. and, for references to the coordination to choice-of-court agreements, 5.14 and 5.15.

4.91. Similarly, with regard to **transfer of proceedings**, **Article 12(5)** provides that, where the parties have conferred **exclusive** jurisdiction under Article 10, that court cannot transfer the jurisdiction to the court of another Member State. On the face of it, the rule appears to limit the court's discretion to transfer to another court. In truth, however, in order for the rule to apply, the court must have **previously** assessed, pursuant to Article 10(1)(c), that exercising the court's jurisdiction is in the best interests of the child and should therefore be seen as only making clear what is to be expected by that court. This guarantees that the court will always be able to exercise its discretion at the moment it is seised and assess any change of circumstances that may affect the best interests of the child.

4.92. Transfer of proceedings is barred only when the parties have agreed to confer exclusive jurisdiction. A different solution may arise in relation to **non-exclusive choice-of-court agreements.** Given that in such a case jurisdiction is concurrent, it is submitted here that Article 12(5) does not apply and the prorogated court could avail itself of transfer of proceedings. This could be the case, for example, when, pending the proceedings, there is a change of circumstances that justifies a transfer to another court, or where a partial transfer of proceedings on a single issue which may be separated from the rest of the case would be appropriate.

4.93. Article 12(5) does not apply when the parties have agreed pursuant to Article 10(1)(b)(i) on a **choice-of-court agreement which is silent on whether jurisdiction is exclusive** and, later on, one of them seises the court of the State of the child's habitual residence. As noted above,[105] this is a legitimate use of the power conferred upon the parties by Brussels II-ter and the court of habitual residence is well seised. The rules on transfer of proceedings, although not expressly envisaging this scenario, may prove useful in governing the case properly and in the interests of the child. It should be noted that Article 13 also does not apply to such a situation. That provision allows a court not having jurisdiction to request, under specific circumstances, a transfer of jurisdiction from the State of the child's habitual residence. However, where the parties have agreed to confer jurisdiction on a court, that court theoretically has jurisdiction, thus excluding the application of Article 13. Article 12 applies instead, leaving the seised court of habitual residence the sole decision-maker as to the effects of the choice-of-court agreement.[106] Such a court may then consider that the court originally chosen by both parties serves the best interests of the child better than

---

[105] See above at 4.76, where it was emphasised that if the parties do not agree differently, the general rule is that choice-of-court agreements that are made prior to the proceedings being instituted are in principle non-exclusive.

[106] With regard to the question of whether choice-of-court agreements concluded under Article 10(1)(b)(i) should be construed as exclusive or not, see above at 4.76.

the one unilaterally seised, and may therefore give effect to the choice-of-court agreement concluded by the parties and transfer the case.

H. CHOICE OF COURT IN FAVOUR OF A THIRD STATE THAT IS A PARTY TO THE 1996 HAGUE CONVENTION (AND IN FAVOUR OF ONE THAT IS NOT)

4.94. Another innovation of Brussels II-ter is a greater attention to **coordination with the 1996 Hague Child Protection Convention**. So far as prorogation of proceedings is concerned, regard should be made to Article 97(2)(a).[107] According to this provision, where the parties have agreed upon the jurisdiction of a court of a State which is a party to the 1996 Hague Convention and not a EU Member State bound by the Regulation (that is, all Member States other than Denmark), Article 10 of that Convention shall prevail and apply. The rule is clear when the conditions for the application of the 1996 Hague Cnvention are met: that is, when the **child is habitually resident in a third State which is a party to the 1996 Hague Convention** (for example, Russia) **and** the parents agree to **give competence to a State that is also a party** to the 1996 Hague Convention (and not a Member State (for example, the UK)). Any EU seised court will have to stay or decline jurisdiction in favor of the prorogated UK court.

4.95. The child must be habitually resident in a Contracting State to the 1996 Hague Convention, but it is irrelevant whethere this is a EU Member State or a non-EU Member State. The rule is thus expressly meant to derogate from the general principle (provided for by Article 97(1)(a)) according to which Brussels II-ter prevails over the Convention when the child concerned has his or her habitual residence in a Member State. This means that a choice-of-court agreement in favour of a Contracting Party to the 1996 Hague Convention (for example, a UK or Swiss court) will be assessed pursuant to the 1996 Hague Convention rather than under Brussels II-ter, even where the child is habitually resident in the EU. This may be a disadvantage to the EU-resident child or parents because of the strict conditions under which a prorogation of competence is allowed under the 1996 Hague Convention, which only allows prorogation of the court of divorce/separation and only when such competence is provided for under the national law of the forum. Furthermore the 1996 Hague Convention sets no obligation to declare a lack of jurisdiction on courts of other States, thus allowing for greater uncertainty.

4.96. Article 97(2)(a), in contrast, is not applicable where the parties agree **to give competence to a court of a third State which is not a contracting party to**

---

[107] See above, Chapter 1 at 1.76 et seq.

the 1996 Hague Convention. The case obviously falls outside the Brussels II-ter Regulation, and the validity and the effects of any choice-of-court agreement will be governed by national private international law rules.

4.97. Article 97(2)(a) does not govern the opposite case where the parties agree to give **competence to a court of a Member State with regard to claims concerning a child habitually resident in a third State**. The situation may be different depending on whether the child is habitually resident in a State which is a party to the 1996 Hague Convention or not. In the former case, the Convention prevails according to Article 97(1)(a) and the choice-of-court agreement will be assessed pursuant to Article 10 of the Convention. However, the answer is less clear when the child is habitually resident in a third State which is not a Contracting Party to the Hague Convention. This situation was previously expressly dealt with by Article 12(4) Brussels II-bis, which also relaxed the requirements for prorogation by saying that jurisdiction of a Member State was deemed to be in the child's interest, 'in particular if it is found impossible to hold proceedings in the State in question'. This rule attracted opposing views: on the one hand, it was criticised for being obscure, inconsistent with the aim of proximity and in need of clarification;[108] on the other hand, it was praised for being a substitute to the lack of a rule on *forum necessitatis* and serving a real need for EU national parents living abroad with children.[109] The deletion of this rule, which was included in the Commission's proposal,[110] leaves the practitioners with no certain answer.

4.98. On the one hand, it could be argued under Article 97(1)(a) that the 1996 Hague Convention is still applicable, as the child is not resident in a Member State and thus apparently Brussels II-ter limits its scope of application. On the other hand, and more convincingly in the authors' view, it could be argued that Article 97(1)(a) derogates the general rule according to which habitual residence of the child in a Member State of the EU is not a condition for the application of Brussels II-ter.[111] Such a derogation is justifiable only when the conditions for the applicationn of the 1996 Hague Convention are given. If the child is habitually resident in a State which is not a party to the 1996 Hague Convention, the whole of Article 97 would be discarded, going back to the normal scope

---

[108] E. PATAUT and E. GALLANT, above n. 73, p. 166, paras 58–62.
[109] A. L. CALVO CARAVACA and J. CARRASCOSA GONZÁLEZ (eds), *Tratado de Derecho Internacional Privado*, Vol 2, cap. XV, Tirant Lo Blanch, 2020, pp. 2020 et seq.
[110] The rule still appeared in the first round of negotiations in the Council, but was deleted in subsequent negotiations.
[111] This is apparent from Articles 11 and 14, which apply only when, among other conditions, the child has no habitual residence in the EU, and was clearly stated by CJEU, 17 October 2018, *UD*, C-393/18 PPU, paras 32–41. Unfortunately, Article 97 is ambiguous in relation to this situation.

of application of Brussels II-ter and applying Article 10.[112] Accordingly, if the parties conclude a valid choice-of-court agreement in favour of the court of a Member State pursuant to Article 10, the chosen court will have competence over a child who has a substantial connection with this State (as required by Article 10(1)(a)), notwithstanding that his or her habitual residence is in a third State that is not a party to the 1996 Hague Convention. This would, for example, allow parents who are EU nationals habitually resident outside the EU (and not in a Contracting State to the 1996 Hague Convention) and who bring a claim for divorce or separation before a court of a Member State under Article 3 to also confer jurisdiction over parental responsibility of their common child, also habitually resident in a third State (which is not a party to the 1996 Hague Convention) in accordance with Article 10.

V. JURISDICTION BASED ON THE CHILD'S PRESENCE: ARTICLE 11

A. THE RATIONALE OF THE RULE

4.99. Article 11 is a rule inspired by a **policy of child protection** which comes into consideration only residually, in exceptional cases. The rule is similar to the one which was in the previous Article 13 Brussels II-bis, which was in turn inspired by Article 6 of the 1996 Hague Convention, but with some important differences.[113] The rule deals with the case where a **child is present** on the territory of a Member State, but his or her habitual residence cannot be established in **any** other State (whether in an EU Member State or a third State) and provides for a forum having general jurisdiction. Such a situation may occur in two different situations.

B. A CHILD WITH NO HABITUAL RESIDENCE

4.100. The first situation is where it is impossible to establish the habitual residence of a child anywhere. As a general principle, the mere presence of a person on the territory of a Member State is not considered enough to confer jurisdiction on the courts of that State, such a link being only occasional and

---

[112] In this sense, see A. LÓPEZ-TARRUELLA MARTÍNEZ, 'Análisis crítico e implicaciones prácticas de la competencia residual del Reglamento 2019/1111 en materia de responsabilidad parental' (2022) 14 *Cuadernos de Derecho Transnacional* 372. See also N. LOWE, 'Operating Brussels II-ter in Children Cases Involving Third States' in *Festskrift till Maarit Jäntera*, IUSTUS, 2022, p. 203 at pp. 205–207.
[113] Below at 4.106.

not in itself significant. Article 11 is an exception to this principle because, *ex hypothesis*, no other court will have jurisdiction over that child. The rule thus acts as a *forum necessitatis*[114] for cases which are of an exceptional nature.

4.101. In order for the rule to apply, the child's habitual residence must not be established anywhere. It is not sufficient to trigger Article 11 that the child's habitual residence is not in the territory of any EU Member State; it must **also not be possible to establish the child's habitual residence in any third State**. In fact, where a child is found to be habitually resident not in a Member State but in a third State, Article 14, which allows the court to residually apply national grounds of jurisdiction, will apply.[115] Article 11 in turn should apply only when the child has no established residence, for example, because he or she was born in a State where none of the parents is habitually resident, or if he or she was abandoned at birth or if the family has a peripatetic lifestyle.[116] Given the exceptional and residual nature of the rule and the weak connection expressed by the mere presence of the child on a territory, the rule should **not** be applied simply because **establishing habitual residence is particularly difficult and complex**, for example, because of the strong and well-balanced connections that the child shows with more than one State. On the other hand, Article 11 allows the jurisdictional system to be complete and have a forum for the protection of the child, without either leaving the child in a legal limbo or forcing the finding that habitual residence is in a given State.[117]

4.102. Building on the new possibility offered by Article 10, Article 11 will also not apply where there is a valid choice-of-court agreement. Although habitual

---

[114] A similar definition was given in relation to the parallel rule under Article 6 of the 1996 Hague Convention. See the Lagarde Report, above n. 67, p. 555.

[115] It may be noted that Article 11 and Article 14 may reach a similar conclusion and use the same connecting factor of the child's presence. However, the two rules operate differently: while Article 11 envisages a direct, uniform, ground for jurisdiction, Article 14 simply allows Member States to refer to their national rules, which may – or may not – provide for jurisdiction to be grounded in the child's presence. Article 14 is discussed below at 4.166 et seq.

[116] These cases are rare but not hypothetical. See, for example, *OL*, as decided by the CJEU (8 June 2017, C-111/17 PPU; see the facts of the case above at 4.20), or *Re F (Habitual Residence: Peripatetic Existence)* [2014] EWFC 26, where a child was taken all around the world by one parent. When he was brought to England, he was living in a tent when social services became involved. See further *2022 Practice Guide*, para. 3.2.7.

[117] See in this regard the criticism of M. WILDERSPIN in *European Private International Law: The Brussels IIb Regulation*, Oxford University Press, 2023, p. 212, para. 5-234 to the rule 'invented' by the UK Supreme Court in *Re B* [2016] UKSC 4. In that case the UK Supreme Court argued from the fact that habitual residence aims to protect the child and that a child should not be left in a legal limbo to conclude that habitual residence should not be considered lost until a new habitual residence is acquired in a different country. Such an approach is deemed contrary to the case law of the CJEU and 'ignores the fact that Article 11 makes provision, *inter alia*, for precisely this sort of situation' (at p. 213).

residence cannot be established, the only court with jurisdiction will be the one chosen by the parties (in most cases by the child's parents).[118] This solution is consistent with the understanding that this ground of competence is residual and does not apply when other grounds confer jurisdiction.

C. REFUGEE AND INTERNATIONALLY DISPLACED CHILDREN

4.103. The second case where Article 11 applies is the one concerning **refugee children and children internationally displaced** because of disturbances occurring in their Member State of (previous) habitual residence. This situation is different from the one just discussed because it *is* possible to ascertain the State of the child's habitual residence. However, in this second situation the link to this country is disrupted and appears no longer to be effective due to the child fleeing abroad and wanting to leave his or her home country for a longer time. Again the rule is modelled on Article 6 of the 1996 Hague Convention. Differently from the latter, however, where such a situation is the first object of the rule (and the abandoned child, considered by the second paragraph of Article 6, may be seen as an 'extension' of the previous one), Brussels II-ter (just like Article 13 Brussels II-bis) reverses the order of the rule and gives precedence to the unaccompanied child, while leaving the migrant and displaced child in the background. The reason for this reversal is unclear. Furthermore, and quite unfortunately, Brussels II-ter also greatly reduces its scope of application, as will be seen in the following paragraphs.

4.104. As the Lagarde Report on the 1996 Hague Convention explains, **Article 6 of the 1996 Hague Convention** is intended to provide protection for children:

> who have left their countries because of conditions which were arising there, and who often are not accompanied and, in any case, are temporarily or definitively deprived of their parents ... Such children often have need for their protection to be organised in a lasting manner ... They may indeed, for example, be led to apply for asylum.[119]

Article 6 clearly envisages a head of jurisdiction for migrant children coming to the EU on their own, with no parent or relative to take care of them and in a strong need for protection. It should be noted however that neither Article 6 of the 1996 Hague Convention nor Article 11 Brussels II-ter limit their scope to

---

[118] Such a situation was not covered by Article 12 Brussels II-bis. See, however, E. PATAUT and E. GALLANT, above n. 73, considering this case.
[119] Lagarde Report, above n. 67, p. 555, para. 44.

unaccompanied migrant children. Both rules are thus applicable also when the migrant child has moved with an adult having parental responsibility for him.[120]

4.105. Co-ordination with the 1996 Convention has, however, dramatically reduced the scope of application of Article 11 and jeopardised its effectiveness. In fact, as **Recital (25)** explains, the rule does **not apply to migrant minors** (including refugees) who are habitually resident outside of the EU and who leave their country as a consequence of political, social or economic difficulties. In these cases, Recital 25 says that Article 6 of the 1996 Convention always applies. Consequently, Brussels II-ter and the current rule only apply to 'refugee children or children internationally displaced because of disturbances occurring *in their Member State* of habitual residence' (emphasis added).[121]

4.106. According to Article 97(1),[122] the 1996 Hague Convention applies irrespective of where the child is habitually resident and irrespective of the fact that the child's nationality is of a Contracting State to the 1996 Hague Convention. On the face of Article 97(1), the only thing that matters is that the child is not habitually resident within a Member State (excluding Denmark). When this is the case, courts of Member States must give precedence to the 1996 Hague Convention and disregard Brussels II-ter. The rule aims to promote a better coordination with the Hague Convention, which is an innovative international instrument, having a more global scope of application. However, it appears ill-coordinated with other rules in the Regulation,[123] such as Articles 11 and 14, which also presuppose that the child is not habitually resident in a Member State bound by Brussels II-ter. As a matter of policy, it is debatable why the 1996 Hague Convention should apply instead of the Regulation with regard to children who were previously habitually resident in a State which is **not** a party to the Hague Convention or whose country of origin is uncertain.

4.107. Recital (25) explains that the application of this solution is based on Article 52(2) of the 1996 Convention, according to which the Convention 'does not affect the possibility for one or more Contracting States to conclude agreements which contain, *in respect of children habitually resident in any of the States Parties* to such agreements, provisions on matters governed by this

---

[120] T. GARBER, 'Art. 11 Brussels IIter' in U. MAGNUS and P. MANKOWSKI, *Brussels IIter Regulation*, OttoSchmidt, 2023, p. 192, para. 32.

[121] But the legitimacy of this Recital has been questioned by C. GONZÁLEZ BEILFUSS 'Regulation (EU) No. 2019/1111 (Brussels II-ter) and Third States: Relations with Other Instruments' in *Festskrift till Maarit Jänterä*-Jareborg, IUSTUS, 2022, p. 141.

[122] Which is also discussed in Chapter 1 at 1.69 et seq.

[123] For some criticism of how coordination with the 1996 Hague Convention is realised by Article 97, see B. CAMPUZANO DIAZ, 'The New Regulation (EU) 2019/1111: Analysis of the Improvements in the Relations with the Hague Convention of 19 October 1996 about Parental Responsibility' (2020) 12 *Cuadernos de Derecho Transnacional* 97.

Convention'. The subsequent paragraph 3 specifies that: 'Agreements to be concluded by one or more Contracting States on matters within the scope of this Convention do not affect, *in the relationship of such States with other Contracting States*, the application of the provisions of this Convention.'[124] However, this explanation is only partly convincing. It certainly says that **in respect of children habitually resident in a Contracting State,** such States are allowed to derogate to the Convention and thus apply Article 11 Brussels II-ter. This is further confirmed by Article 97(1)(a) Brussels II-ter, which says that the Regulation prevails over the Convention when the child is habitually resident in a Member State. However, reference to Article 52(2) of the 1996 Convention does not seem a conclusive explanation as to why the Convention should prevail over the Regulation in a situation where the child is habitually resident in a third State that is not a Contracting Party to the 1996 Hague Convention (or a national thereof). This is the case, for example, with regard to Afghanistan, Syria and most African States, which are commonly the country of origin of migrant children coming to EU and which are not Contracting States to the 1996 Convention. It is not immediately clear – and therefore not convincing – why, as a matter of principle, in these situations the legislators have chosen not to apply Brussels II-ter and to instead give precedence to the 1996 Hague Convention, given that the child will be present in a Member State and given the general primacy of EU Regulations over international conventions.

4.108. Whatever the underlying policy, the wording of the current rule is clear in being applicable **only to intra-EU cases** – that is, cases where children migrate and are displaced from one Member State to another EU Member State. This appears to be a quite extraordinary situation which will, more than likely, render Article 11(2) a dead letter.

D. FULL BUT TIME-LIMITED JURISDICTION

4.109. Although similarly based on the criterion of physical presence as Article 15, which confers limited jurisdiction to take provisional measures,[125] Article 11 is different from this rule in some respects. First, it is not subject to the requirement of urgency, and may also be activated in an ordinary, non-urgent situation. Article 11 may be used, for example, to designate a legal representative or a guardian in view of a prospective adoption of an abandoned child.[126] Second, the jurisdiction grounded in Article 11 is one of **full competence,**

---

[124] Emphasis added.
[125] Discussed below at 4.168.
[126] Lagarde Report, above n. 67, p. 555, para. 44.

enabling the court to take any decision on the substance of the case and not only on a temporary and territorially limited basis, as under Article 15.

4.110. On the other hand, the jurisdiction conferred by Article 11 is **inherently limited in time**, as it presupposes that the child has no habitual residence in any other State (or that such a link should be disregarded).[127] This means that, as soon as the child acquires a new habitual residence in one State (either within or outside a Member State bound by the Regulation), the criterion of presence will no longer suffice to ground jurisdiction. Given that habitual residence may be acquired in a relatively short time, Article 11 is likely to have a limited application.

VI. TRANSFER OF JURISDICTION: ARTICLES 12 AND 13

A. BACKGROUND AND STRUCTURE OF THE TWO RULES

4.111. The regime on transfer of jurisdiction has undergone some substantial changes compared to the previous Article 15 Brussels II-bis. The biggest difference affects the structure of the rule, which is now split into two rules dealing with different situations: on the one hand, the case where the seised court decides to transfer the proceedings to the court of another Member State (now governed by Article 12); on the other hand, the case where a court, not seised and not having jurisdiction under the Regulation, requests the transfer from the (already seised) court of the State of the child's habitual residence (Article 13). Such an approach reflects the position under Articles 8 and 9 of the 1996 Hague Convention.

4.112. The two situations were previously dealt under one rule, as set out by Article 15 Brussels II-bis. The limited practice experienced by the application of such a rule did not highlight a specific difficulty in this regard and, indeed, the Commission's Proposal followed the old unitary approach. However, during the Council negotiations, the decision was taken to split the regime into the two current provisions. Unfortunately, Recitals (25), (26) and (27) offer no explanation for such a radical change, the need for which does not appear to be supported by strong evidence. It still has to be seen whether this change will amount to a real improvement of the rule. The new rule brings about some minor changes to the procedure for the transfer of proceedings, making it more fluent and filling some gaps which had emerged under the former rule. Material requirements have, however, remained unchanged.

---

[127] See above at 4.22 et seq.

B. THE RATIONALE OF THE RULE AND THE QUEST FOR FLEXIBILITY

4.113. Transfer of jurisdiction (and of proceedings) amounts to an exception to the general rule based on the child's habitual residence. As previously explained,[128] Brussels II-ter is based on the fundamental principle that it is in the best interests of the child that any decision concerning him or her should be taken by the court which is closest to him or her. This is in general to be considered the court of the child's habitual residence. However, as is apparent from Recital (26), the legislator acknowledges that there may be situations where such a court might not be the most appropriate to deal with the case. In these cases, the court having jurisdiction under Brussels II-ter might want to consider if another court, while not having a general competence under the Regulation, might be the more appropriate in that specific case. The provisions thus aim to bring some flexibility to a system which, being structured around a one and only criterion – the child's habitual residence – appears to be too rigid.

4.114. It may be of interest to highlight how this same quest for flexibility underlies prorogation of proceedings.[129] Indeed, there is more than one parallel between the two provisions, for example, with regard to the requirements for the operation of the rule, be it the notion of the child's 'substantial connection' or the test of the new competence meeting the best interests of the child. Furthermore, both mechanisms require some sort of collaboration between the parties and the court, none of which can extend or transfer competence of its own motion.[130] The most evident difference between the two is that while prorogation is triggered by the parties (but requires confirmation by the prorogated court, which has to assess that this is in the best interests of the child), transfer of proceedings will generally – but not necessarily – be triggered by the court (although it will still need the support of at least one party, who will be required to resume the proceedings in a different Member State).[131] Interestingly, the two mechanisms are not cumulative, as the court whose jurisdiction is based on Article 10 is precluded from transferring jurisdiction elsewhere.[132] Article 12(5) expressly makes this point where the parties have agreed on exclusive jurisdiction.

---

[128] See above at 4.7.
[129] That is, Article 10, on which see above at 4.42 et seq.
[130] E. PATAUT and E. GALLANT, above n. 73, p. 176, para. 9, made a similar comment in relation to Brussels II-bis, stating that: 'The difference lies with the fact that Article 12(3) relies on party autonomy, whereas Article 15(1) relies on judicial cooperation. The bases of jurisdiction are therefore very different, but the main effect of both provisions is very similar: giving jurisdiction to a court that is not designated by any of the connecting factors of the Regulation.'
[131] This is true at least with regard to proceedings instituted between private parties. However, with regard to public law proceedings, the situation is more problematic. See below at para. 4.153.
[132] The issue of effects of choice-of-court agreements on transfer of proceedings is also dealt with above at 4.91.

As a general rule, and subject to specific circumstances, this will also be the case where prorogation was not agreed as exclusive (for example, when it was agreed upon before proceedings were pending pursuant to Article 10(1)(b)(1)). If the prorogated court has established that exercising jurisdiction is in the best interests of the child, it would be inconsistent to decide later on that it is in the best interests of the child to transfer elsewhere.

4.115. Because of their **exceptional nature**, the transfer provisions should be interpreted and applied restrictively.[133] In other words, the court normally having jurisdiction to deal with a given case must, in order to request a transfer to a court of another Member State, be capable of rebutting the strong presumption set by Brussels II-ter itself in favour of maintaining its own jurisdiction.

C. WHAT CAN BE TRANSFERRED?

4.116. The CJEU decision in *Child and Family Agency*[134] established that transfer provisions under what was then Article 15 Brussels II-bis had the same scope as the rest of the Regulation. The provisions were accordingly held to apply to the transfer of **public law proceedings**. This was the case even though a necessary consequence of such a transfer of jurisdiction to another Member State is that the authority of that State will need to bring a new set of proceedings that is separate from those brought in the referring State, pursuant to its own domestic law and, possibly, relating to different circumstances. There is no reason to doubt that the transfer provisions under Articles 12 and 13 Brussels II-ter should be similarly applied.

4.117. As in Article 15 Brussels II-bis, Article 12 Brussels II-ter permits a court having jurisdiction over the substance of the matter to request a **partial transfer** of proceedings. However, there is no express equivalent power in Article 13 with respect to requests for the transfer of proceedings by a court that does not have jurisdiction over the substance.

D. TRANSFER OF JURISDICTION, NOT JUST OF PROCEEDINGS

4.118. Although the rule on transfer of proceedings finds its roots in the Scottish tradition of *forum non conveniens*,[135] it is important to highlight the

---

[133] This point has been made by the CJEU on several occasions. See, for example, CJEU, 10 July 2019 (order), *EP*, C-530/18, para. 24; CJEU, 4 October 2018, *IQ*, C-478/17, para. 32; CJEU, 27 October 2016, *Child and Family Agency*, C-428/15, paras 47–48.
[134] Above n. 132.
[135] Among many others, see A. Arzandeh, 'The Origins of the Scottish *Forum Non Conveniens* Doctrine' (2017) 13 *Journal of Private International Law* 130. See also A. Arzandeh, *Forum (Non) Conveniens in England: Past, Present, and Future*, Hart Publishing, 2018.

novelty of the approach taken by the EU legislator. Like Article 15 Brussels II-bis, Articles 12 and 13 Brussels II-ter provide for a **transfer of jurisdiction** rather than just a transfer of proceedings.[136] Unlike under the *forum non conveniens* doctrine, the EU rules on transfer of proceedings, even though applicable to a particular set of proceedings, are meant to **shift jurisdiction** from one court having jurisdiction to potentially **any other Member State court which**, in principle, **does not have jurisdiction** under Brussels II-ter, but with which the child has a 'particular connection' in the given case. In other words, the transfer of jurisdiction provisions are not just rules on cooperation among the courts, but rather rules on jurisdiction.[137]

4.119. The requirement that the court receiving the transfer of proceedings must not have jurisdiction under Brussels II-ter is only expressly mentioned in Article 13. However, this follows logically from the fact that a transfer is only possible towards one of the closed list of courts mentioned by Article 12(4) (see below at para. 4.127), all of which will in principle not have jurisdiction under the Regulation. Furthermore, when interpreting Article 15 Brussels II-bis in *IQ*, the CJEU made the point that there can be no transfer of proceedings to another Member State court which is already competent under the Regulation, as this would undermine the rules governing the allocation of jurisdiction established by the Regulation.[138] Coordination between courts both of which having jurisdiction should be governed by the chronological principle under the *lis pendens* rule. The general terms used by the Court and the rationale underlying such decision may lead to the conclusion that this should be the same under Article 12 Brussels II-ter. However, the solution envisaged by the CJEU may appear too formalistic, and the issue be raised again in the future especially in light of the fact that, as will be seen below, in *IQ* the transfer was requested by the second seised court, a situation which is now dealt separetely under Article 13.

4.120. In *IQ* the Romanian mother of three minors habitually resident in the UK lodged an application for divorce before the Romanian court. She

---

[136] It was been noted that there is no real *transfer* of a proceedings, as the proceedings before the court of the second State are not a continuation but rather a new one which begin from start. The transfer is thus the 'coordinated termination of the proceedings before the court of the first State and the initiation of new proceedings along the same lines before the court of the second State that has assumed jurisdiction' (see T. GARBER, 'Art. Brussels IIter' in U. MAGNUS and P. MANKOWSKI, *Brussels IIter Regulation*, OttoSchmidt, 2023, p. 196, para. 11).

[137] See E. PATAUT and E. GALLANT, above n. 73, p. 176, para. 9.

[138] CJEU, 4 October 2018, *IQ*, C-478/17, para. 33, stating that: 'Article 15(1) ... allows the court that normally has jurisdiction ... to transfer its jurisdiction, over all or over a specific part of the case before it, *to a court that would not normally have jurisdiction in the matter* but which, in the circumstances of the particular case, must be considered to be 'better placed' to hear that case'. And further on (para. 39) that: 'Therefore, the court of another Member State with which the child in question has a particular connection and which is best placed to hear the case, ... cannot be the court that normally has jurisdiction as to the substance of the case on the basis of Article 8 or 12 of that regulation.' (emphasis added).

and her former husband validly prorogated the competence of the Romanian court under former Article 12(1) also applying for custody measures over the children. As the Romanian court handed down the decision on custody and access to the children, the mother, unsatisfied with the outcome, at first appealed against it before the Romanian Court of Appeal, and a few months later filed a claim for sole parental responsibility before the UK court on the ground that the children were habitually resident there. The UK court asked the Romanian Court of appeal to transfer proceedings, emphasising that the habitual residence of the three children had been in the UK for years, including during the entire proceedings before the Romanian courts, and that the UK court would therefore be better placed to hear the case under Article 15 Brussels II-bis.

4.121. On the referral of the Romanian Court, the CJEU offered a strict interpretation of the scope of application of transfer of proceedings, based on its exceptional nature. It thus excluded the application of the rule on transfer of proceedings, as the conditions for the operating of the rule, in particular concerning the child's particular connection with another Member State (see 4.126 below), must be interpreted strictly so that in no way can the court to which the proceedings is transferred be the one having jurisdiction as to the substance of the case on the basis of Article 7 or 10.[139] While the situation is thus settled where is a request for transfer under what is now Article 13, the question may need a different solution when it is the seized court considering a transfer under Article 12.

4.122. In the majority of cases, the transferring court will be the **general court of the State of the child's habitual residence**, grounding its competence in Article 7. On the face of it, Article 12 also leaves this option open to other courts, but this will rarely happen. As seen above,[140] the court basing … on its competence in Article 10 – that is, on the agreement of the parties, including the court for the parent's divorce/separation – will in most cases not be in a position to transfer the proceedings elsewhere, either because the parties may have agreed for an exclusive jurisdiction and transfer is then precluded by Article 12(5) or because of the best interests test making a further transfer quite unlikely for the court to decide. The only case where one could imagine a residual room for transfer from the prorogated court to another is where there is a change of circumstances in the course of the proceedings (for example, a change in the child's habitual residence or in the residential parent's habitual residence) calling for a different assessment of facts. Another court which could be in a position to transfer proceedings is the court of the place where the child is present, pursuant to Article 11. However, this ground is seldom used. In conclusion, it appears that the mechanism addressed by Article 12 will be a tool which is mostly in the hands of the general court of the child's habitual residence.[141]

---

[139] CJEU, 4 October 2018, *IQ*, C-478/17, paras 38–39.
[140] Above at 4.92.
[141] However, things are different with regard to Article 13. See below at 4.163.

4.123. On the other hand, neither Article 12 nor Article 13 confer jurisdiction on its own or in a mechanical way.[142] Both rules require several conditions to be met and, furthermore, a positive decision and action of the court exercising its jurisdiction under another rule of the Regulation. It should be noted that Articles 12 and 13 **do not apply to transfer of proceedings to a third State**. If such a third State is a Contracting State to the 1996 Convention, Articles 8 and 9 thereof will come into consideration in accordance with Article 97(2)(b).

E. ARTICLE 12 AND TRANSFER OF JURISDICTION TO ANOTHER COURT

4.124. The exceptional power of a seised court to transfer jurisdiction (and proceedings) to another Member State's court is subject to **three material conditions**: (i) the child must have a 'particular connection' with another Member State; (ii) the court of that Member State must be 'better placed' to hear the case; and (iii) a transfer to such court must be 'in the best interests of the child'. These conditions reflect those previously in force under Article 15 Brussels II-bis.

4.125. The transfer is **to a specific court or competent authority**[143] and not to the Member State as a whole. It is the responsibility of the transferring court to determine which local court in the other Member State is best placed to hear the case. This implies ensuring that such a court also has national competence. This may be a difficult task for the transferring court, especially if the parties to the proceedings are not involved in the transfer procedure and do not cooperate. The assistance of Central Authorities of the States involved or of the usual judicial networks will in such cases be of greatest help.[144]

1. The Child's Particular Connection with Another Member State

4.126. The first requirement is that the child has a 'particular connection' with a Member State other than the one having jurisdiction.

---

[142] This was mistakenly retained by the Austrian court in the *Povse* case decided by CJEU, 1 July 2010, C-211/10 PPU, para. 28.

[143] While the title of the rule refers to 'Transfer of jurisdiction to a court' and apparently envisages a relation between jurisdictional authorities, Article 2(2)(1) states that the term 'court' means 'any authority in any Member State with jurisdiction in the matters falling within the scope of this Regulation'. Article 12 may thus be construed as meaning that it is possible to transfer a case from a judicial authority to a public authority of a different Member State, when such authority, under its own rules, has the power to decide, for example, on the placement of a child.

[144] Reference may usefully also be made to the European Judicial Atlas (available at the E-Justice Portal https://e-justice.europe.eu/) which allows to identify the territorially competent court in each Member State and find contact details of it.

4.127. Article 12(4) clarifies what is to be considered a relevant connection and provides a **closed list** of cases (see 4.128 below). As confirmed by the CJEU, the list of factors is exhaustive. It follows that in any situation where those factors cannot be established, the transfer mechanism cannot apply.[145] On the other hand, the factors themselves are self-sufficient, given the legislative presumption that they are evidence – at least in essence – of a relation of proximity between the child and a different State. However, the requirement of a 'particular connection' should not be established in a formalistic way[146] and the mere existence of such factor will not be conclusive, because it will always be for the seised court to **compare the extent and degree** of the relation of 'general' proximity to the child that grounds the jurisdiction of the forum (and which will be particularly strong when competence is grounded in Article 7), with the extent and degree of the relation of 'particular' proximity mentioned by Article 12(4) and existing between that child and another Member State.

4.128. Under Article 12(4), a child shall be considered to have a particular connection with a Member States if that State:

(a) has become the State of habitual residence of the child after the court referred to in paragraph 1 was seised;
(b) is the former habitual residence of the child;
(c) is the State of the nationality of the child;
(d) is the habitual residence of a holder of parental responsibility; or
(e) is the place where property of the child is located and the case concerns measures for the protection of the child relating to the administration, conservation or disposal of that property.

4.129. Within the above list, the **State of the child's new residence** will in practice be of particular importance, especially since the rule on *perpetuatio fori*[147] in Article 7 has been retained. The Commission's 2016 Proposal, finding

---

[145] See CJEU, 27 October 2016, *Child and Family Agency*, C-428/15, paras 50–51; CJEU, 4 October 2018, *IQ*, C-478/17, para. 35; CJEU, 10 July 2019 (order), *EP*, C-530/18, paras 28–29. In the latter case, for example, concerning a child born in France with a strong French background, but habitually resident in Romania and with Romanian nationality, the Court held that the following factors were irrelevant, as they did not fall into the list under the previous Article 15(4): the child was born in France, her father was a French citizen, her blood relations in France were wide (including two sisters and a brother, a niece, her paternal grandfather, her father's current partner and their minor daughter, whereas the child concerned had no family ties on her mother's side in Romania), she attended a French school, her upbringing and mentality have always been French, and the language spoken at home between the parents and by the parents to the child has always been French. For the opposite view, according to which the list under article 12(4) is only demonstrative and a particular connection could also arise from other circumstances, see T. GARBER, above at n. 136, p. 201, para. 27 et seq.
[146] See *2022 Practice Guide*, 85, para. 3.3.1.
[147] Reference is to the principle according to which jurisdiction shall continue if it was established at the moment the court is seised. See above at 4.3.

support in some legal literature,[148] proposed the abolition of such a principle, with the implicit consequence that a lawful move of the child's habitual residence ended the competence of the seised court and automatically gave competence to the court of the child's new residence. However, the proposal was rejected, probably in the light of the possible manipulation of the connecting factor and of procedural efficiency. The rule on transfer of proceedings will now serve this case, as it gives the power and the discretion to the seised court to assess whether, under the specific circumstances of the case, it is appropriate to transfer the case to the new court. This is now reaffirmed in last sentence of Recital (21). Relevant factors for such a decision may be, for example, the reasons for the child's move, the stage of the pending proceedings or the position of the parties concerned. The CJEU has further clarified that transfer of jurisdiction is also possible with regard to proceedings for the modification of a decision on access rights pursuing Article 8.[149] However, when assessing such a case, the court should keep in mind that the special rule for continuing jurisdiction in the State of the child's previous habitual residence is drafted in the light of allowing the parent, who sees his or her child relocating to a different Member State, to seek a decision modifying his or her access rights without the need to access a court in a different State.

4.130. Transfer of proceedings could also be appropriate in the reverse situation where proceedings are brought before the court of the new habitual residence, but the child appears to (still) have a stronger connection with the **State of his or her previous residence**, for example, if the proceedings concerns access to the left-behind parent and the three-month time limit provided by Article 8 has expired. It should be noted that the particular connection required by the rule is with the child and not with the legal or factual issue at stake.

4.131. The State of the **child's nationality**, while rarely decisive on its own, may be relevant when such a State also is of one or both parents' nationality or where the grandparents or extended family live. This particular connection may be of value when the child is habitually resident in a different Member State, but following divorce/separation of the parents will possibly need to return 'back home' and be placed with someone of the wider family. The CJEU has also found that, in exceptional circumstances, a transfer of proceedings to the State of the child's nationality may also be appropriate when this is the State to which a child has been wrongfully removed, as it cannot be ruled out that that court may be better placed to ascertain all the factual circumstances relating to the life and needs of the child concerned and to take appropriate decisions with regard to that child, taking account of the criterion of proximity.[150] The solution offered by

---

[148] See T. KRUGER and L. SAMYN, above n. 103, 136.
[149] CJEU, 27 April 2023, *CM*, C-372/22, at paras 39–44. On this decision, see also above n. 63 in relation to Article 8.
[150] CJEU, 13 July 2023, *TT*, C-87/22, para. 66. As commented in the text, the CJEU gives a reading of the rule based on the sole perspective of the Regulation, but neglects the necessary

the CJEU raises concerns as it runs against a fundamental principle underlying the 1980 Hague Convention, according to which illegal transfer or retaining of the child should not allow the taking parent to bring custody proceedings in the State of refuge, thus drawing a procedural advantage from his or her illegal accomplishment. Similar considerations may also guide the decision to refuse transfer and give weight to the State of **habitual residence of the holders of parental responsibility**.

4.132. Finally, the State where **property of the child is located** will be appropriate when the proceedings concern measures related to these assets.

2. *The Transfer is in the Best Interests of the Child*

4.133. The existence of a particular connection within the meaning of Article 12(4) does not suffice for a transfer, as it only shows the relevant and necessary link, but not that such a court is also better placed to hear the case, or that exercising such competence would be in the best interests of the particular child. In order for a transfer of jurisdiction to be considered, Article 12(1) requires that:

> a court of another Member State with which the child has a particular connection would be better placed to assess the best interests of the child in the particular case.

4.134. This part of the rule has been substantially redrafted. Previously, Article 15 Brussels II-bis allowed a transfer when the other court with which the child has a particular connection 'would be better placed to hear the case, or a specific part thereof, *and where this is in the best interests of the child*'. Brussels II-ter adopts a different approach with regard to the role and impact of the best interests of the child in the transfer of proceedings. The issue therefore requires further investigation, particularly as this is one of the very rare cases where the legislator departed from the CJEU's guidance.

4.135. Since the transfer of jurisdiction is construed as a derogation from the general rule under Article 7 which is strongly based on pursuing the best interests of the child,[151] a transfer is also conditional on its being in the best interests of the child. Indeed, as an additional safeguard for the child, **both the transferring court (Article 12(1)) and the receiving court (Article 12(2))** must investigate whether the transfer of proceedings serves the best interests of

---

coordination with the aims underlying the 1980 Hague Convention. The responsibility of coordination is instead shifted to the court considering the transfer. In fact, when examining the conditions in respect of, first, the existence in the latter Member State of a court better placed to hear the case and, second, the best interests of the child, the court considering the transfer must take into consideration the existence of proceedings for the return of that child which have been instituted in that same State (para. 70).

[151] See the discussion on the rationale of habitual residence at 4.7 above.

the child. In other words, the assessment required by the rule is **double-proofed** by both courts, each of which must undertake a separate and independent evaluation.

4.136. One of the delicate questions arising under the previous Article 15 Brussels II-bis was whether the 'best interests' test is a **different test from the 'better placed' test** to be assessed separately, or whether both conditions may be examined together in a joint assessment. The question arose from the previous wording referred above at 4.134. Such a preliminary issue was discussed before the CJEU in the *Child and Family Agency* case.[152] Interestingly, in such a case both the Commission and Advocate General Wathelet supported the view that best interests is not a requirement per se, but a general precondition and the basis for all and any decisions regarding a minor. Indeed, it is a common understanding that this is a general criterion which must guide every decision concerning jurisdiction in matters of parental responsibility, whether a decision of principle or an exceptional one.[153]

4.137. However, the CJEU adopted a different interpretation and considered that best interests of the child is a third requirement, to be separately and autonomously tested and satisfied. According to the CJEU, the fact that a court may be better placed to hear a case does not necessarily imply that a transfer to such a court is always in the best interests of the child. Under the previous wording, it could have been agreed with such a statement, as this was consistent with the clear wording of the rule, which mentioned best interests as a separate condition. Yet, even then, the vague guidance that the Court gave on *how* to assess this requirement in concrete cases was less convincing. With sparing words, the Court held that the requirement that the transfer must be in the best interests of the child implies that:

> the envisaged transfer of the case to a court of another Member State is *not liable to be detrimental to the situation of the child concerned*. To that end, the court having jurisdiction must assess any negative effects that such a transfer might have on the familial, social and emotional attachments of the child concerned in the case or on that child's material situation.[154]

What was meant by the vague expression that transfer should not 'be detrimental to the situation of the child' was probably that the transferring court (*rectius* both courts) must assess the **impact on the child's immediate welfare**, in the short and medium term, of the transfer itself, i.e. the transfer's **immediate consequences** on the child. Such an assessment could be of most importance

---

[152] See above n. 154.
[153] In this sense, see Advocate General Wathelet's Opinion, delivered on 16 June 2016 to CJEU, 27 October 2016, *Child and Family Agency*, C-428/15, paras 70–72.
[154] CJEU, 27 October 2016, *Child and Family Agency*, C-428/15, paras 58–59 (emphasis added).

with regard to cases where the child is in foster care and, following the transfer of proceedings, he or she must be removed from that placement and returned to a different country.[155] This was indeed the particular issue underlying the case dealt with by the CJEU.

4.138. Whatever the right construction may be, this is one of the few cases where the EU legislator departed from the guidance offered by the CJEU and drafted a different wording. Article 12(1) now provides that the court must be 'better placed *to assess* the best interests of the child in the particular case' (emphasis added). The two requirements are now strongly connected and a better placed court (see below 4.141 et seq) is one which is in a better position to assess the best interests of the child.

4.139. The best interests of the child should be assessed '**in the particular case**', that is, bearing in mind the moment and the circumstances under which the case is brought and the purpose of responding to that need.

4.140. In any case, the assessment of the child's best interests test for the purposes of Article 12(1) and 12(3) should be limited to whether the transfer of jurisdiction serves those interests and should not involve whether the **final outcome of the dispute will be in the best interests of the child**. In other words, this test should not imply that sort of in-depth investigation of the complete situation, which is for the full-merits proceedings to ascertain.[156] Even less, should the transferring court consider whether the other court can avail itself of the options available to the transferring court or whether the child protection services have better competence, resources or efficacy. Indeed, the rationale supporting this provision is, as always, mutual trust among EU Member States.

---

[155] See, for example, *Re N (Children)* [2016] UKSC 15. This case concerned two young girls of Roma descent, born and resident in the UK and British-Hungarian nationals. They had been found in an extremely poor material and psychological situation and were placed with a foster family in the UK. This was the case when the UK social services started care proceedings. The High Court agreed to the request that the proceedings be transferred to Hungary, in consideration of the impossibility of the parents taking care of the girls in the UK and of the extended family residing in Hungary. On appeal, the Supreme Court determined that it is important to consider the 'transfer's immediate consequences on the children' and that the Court should have considered the consequences of the transfer on the girls, as this would have implied removing them from a current stable and balanced situation to put them into foster care in Hungary. The High Court also failed to consider whether the English court could achieve the same outcome as the Hungarian courts, without the need to transfer the case, which would also preserve the option of keeping the girls in their present home. For a further analysis, see N. Lowe and H. Setright, 'Transferring the Problem: How Article 15 of the Revised Brussels II Regulation Operates in the Public Law Context' (2017) *International Family Law* 13; C. Honorati and A. Limante, 'Jurisdiction in Child Abduction Proceedings' in C. Honorati (ed.), above, n. 40, pp. 209–210.

[156] See again Advocate General Wathelet's Opinion in CJEU, 27 October 2016, *Child and Family Agency*, C-428/15, para. 72.

3. *The Other Member State's Court is 'Better Placed' to Assess the Best Interests of the Child*

4.141. As previously mentioned, a better placed court is one which is in a better position than the seised court to assess the best interests of the child, having regard not to the final outcome of the substance of the case, but to the procedural efficiency of the proceedings. It will thus touch upon **a better assessment of the best interests of the child,** which will only focus on jurisdictional issues and leave aside any assessment related to the final outcome of the proceedings. It therefore implies a comparative approach under which the transferring court will determine whether a transfer would provide **a genuine and specific added value** compared to the possibility that the case remains before itself.

4.142. To that end, the court may take into account, among other factors, the **rules of procedure** of the other Member State, such as those applicable to the taking of evidence required for dealing the case.[157] Indeed, the different rules of procedure which are applicable under different legal systems may have a strong impact on the case and have often been challenged by the parties as a possible reason for a different court being better placed and therefore for grounding a transfer of proceedings.

4.143. The CJEU has acknowledged that **procedural rules** (but not substantial rules; see 4.146 below) may become relevant in determining which court is better placed. However, such an analysis is to be made with regard to **specific rules,** whose impact on the proceedings is to be assessed *in concreto*. Such an assessment should not be made in general terms, having regard to abstract rules or to the organisation of justice, within some Member States, an approach that could result in a procedural advantage for one or the other Member State. In contrast, the assessment must be made *in concreto*, with specific reference to the given case and to a particular rule. As the Court held in the *EP* case:

> the court with jurisdiction may take into consideration the rules of procedure applicable under the legislation of another Member State if they have a *specific impact* on the ability of the court of the latter Member State to deal with the case better, in particular by facilitating the gathering of evidence and testimony, and, in doing so, provide added value to the resolution of the case in the interests of the child. On the other hand, the view cannot be taken, in a general and abstract way, that the rules of law of another Member State, such as those referred to by one of the parties to the main proceedings, that is to say, the rules relating to the examination of the case in camera by specialised judges, constitute a factor to be taken into consideration when

---

[157] CJEU, 27 October 2016, *Child and Family Agency*, C-428/15, para. 54.

the court with jurisdiction assesses whether there is a court better placed to hear the case.[158] (Emphasis added)

4.144. Drawing on the examples of rules which should not be relevant and which were made by the CJEU in the *EP* case (such as specialised courts or *in camera* proceedings), other cases may be imagined where procedural rules may have an impact on the proceedings, but should not amount to making courts of another State to a 'better placed' court. For example, it is submitted that the rule – current in many but not in all legal systems – envisaging the appointment of a *guardian ad litem* or the mandatory presence of a **Public Prosecutor** in all cases concerning a child, would not be relevant. Similarly, any special facilities available in some Member States for the hearing of the child or practice in this field would also not make a court better placed to hear a case.

4.145. More generally, the 'better placed' test may be seen as referring to the **ability of a court to carry out its judicial functions in a better, more effective and faster way**. In this regard, judicial efficiency in the assessment of facts and of persons will be paramount. Other factors that may be taken into consideration could be the availability of relevant witnesses in the other Member State; the possibility to gather more information about the child and his or her family members in the other State where members of the extended family live; whether proceedings in the other Member State can be conducted in the first language of the family/child, therefore avoiding the need for interpreters and permitting the family to participate in judicial proceedings more effectively; the possibility of a family placement in another Member State so that the courts of such a Member State would be in a better position to evaluate all the circumstances; and, finally, there may be procedural advantages in the fact that there is judicial continuity between fact-finding and evaluation.[159]

4.146. In contrast, in assessing whether the other court is better placed, no reference should be made to the **substantive law** of that other Member State which would be applicable if the case was transferred to it. Doing so would be in breach of the principles of mutual trust between Member States.[160]

4.147. The Court's assessment should also include and balance out the **reasons against a transfer** and for retaining the competence of the forum. As such a

---

[158] CJEU, 10 July 2019 order, *EP*, C-530/18, para. 41.
[159] T. Garber, 'Article 12 Brussels II-ter', above n. 136, p. 203, para. 35, finds that the fact that the proceedings will be transferred to a court which will apply its own law should also weigh in assessing the best interests of the child, 'because there is a higher guarantee that decisions will be correct' and this 'means that the best interests of the child can be better taken into account'.
[160] See CJEU, 27 October 2016, *Child and Family Agency*, C-428/15, para. 57; CJEU, 10 July 2019 (order), *EP*, C-530/18, para. 39.

court is, at least in general, the court of the child's habitual residence, there is a strong presumption that such a court is the best-placed court. At this stage, however, it is mainly the procedural advantages that the court should weigh up. The most relevant factors of retaining the case being, of course, **time and judicial continuity**. Any transfer should be avoided when this would result in an excessive and undue delay. This could be the case, for example, if the proceedings have been pending for some time and most of the evidence has been heard and, possibly, a final determination can nearly be made. Similarly, it seems that a transfer would not be viable if the proceedings are at an appellate stage but the 'better placed' court would be a first instance court.[161] Further elements that could weigh against the opportunity of a transfer would include: an already made, complete and updated assessment of the current situation of the child; an updated understanding of the needs of the child, especially if he or she is/was taken into care by the local social services; a full knowledge of the ongoing situation in a foster family/children's house; a better assessment of the consequences of removing the child from such a placement.

4.148. Finally, the court should also take into consideration the **child's view on transfer** of proceedings. Not only is this a general and mainstream policy in all EU acts, but also any opposition to transfer by the child will affect the level of cooperation that may be achieved in that jurisdiction and impact on judicial efficiency and the final decision. While this is not expressly required by the rule, it is certainly something that the Court is bound to weigh up.[162]

F. THE OPERATION OF THE RULE IN PRACTICE

4.149. Paragraphs (1), (2) and (3) of Article 12 shed light on the practical implementation of the rule and give guidance to both the transferring and the receiving court on how to deal with a transfer. Overall the provisions set a clearer framework and timeframe for the operation of the rule which should facilitate a successful implementation of the rule and coordinate all parties involved.

1. Who can Trigger the Transfer

4.150. Pursuing Article 12(1) transfer may be triggered upon application of **one of the parties** or on the **court's own motion**. Whichever way the transfer is

---

[161] Such a question was referred for a preliminary ruling to the CJEU 4 October 2018, *IQ*, C-478/17. Unfortunately, the Court dismissed the case following a previous preliminary question and did not answer the question.

[162] For a case where two children strongly objected to the transfer of their case, see *Medway Council v. J.B. and Others* [2015] EWHC 3064 (Fam).

started, the first seised court will then stay the proceedings, or a part of it, and choose between one of the following two options:

(a) set a time limit for one or more of the parties to inform the court of that other Member State of the pending proceedings and the possibility to transfer jurisdiction and to introduce an application before that court; or
(b) request a court of another Member State to assume jurisdiction in accordance with paragraph 2.

4.151. The choice between one or the other is at the court's discretion, but the option under **Article 12(1)(a)** will in practice be more common. The envisaged procedure **relies on the cooperation of the parties** and seems appropriate when at least one of the parties agrees on transferring the proceedings and will therefore be active in the transfer procedure. The party will thus operate as a liaison between the two courts and allow a smooth development of the procedure. Within the set time limit, the party will need not only to inform the receiving court of a possible transfer, but also file a new proceedings before the receiving court, thus allowing such court to proceed with the child's best interests assessment required by Article 12(2) (see 4.155 below). The rule gives no indication on what a reasonable time limit may be. The *2022 Practice Guide* suggests that time 'should be sufficiently short to ensure that the transfer does not result in unnecessary delays to the detriment of the child and the parties'.[163]

4.152. Article 12(1)(b) is new. Although it may have a less frequent application, its introduction is welcome as it fills in a gap under Article 15 Brussels II-bis. There may be cases where the transferring court will not be able to rely on the parties, either because they are both against a transfer of proceedings or because there is only one party who is not in the position to do so, for example, because the case is instituted by a public childcare authority who would not have the *locus standi* to address a court in a different Member State. In such cases, where the seised court finds that a transfer of proceedings would be in the best interests of the child and that all other requirements are met, it will need to get in touch with the receiving court and **request such a court to assume jurisdiction**. Where the decision to stay the proceedings and request a transfer is subject to appeal under national law, the request to the court of a different Member State can be made only when such a decision is final (see Recital (26)).

4.153. A request may be done either directly,[164] through the Central Authorities of the Member States concerned, or through the liaison judges of the European

---

[163] *2022 Practice Guide*, p. 88, para. 3.3.3.
[164] Article 86(1) promotes direct contact among courts, provided the parties' rights and confidentiality are respected. Through the European Judicial Atlas, available at the E-Justice Portal (https://e-justice.europa.eu/), a court can identify the territorially competent court in

Judicial Network[165] or of the International Hague Network of Judges.[166] Direct contact is specifically mentioned by Article 86(2)(a) with regard to transfer of proceedings and should be favoured whenever the two judges speak or understand the same language. In order to avoid any delay or unnecessary procedural actions, the two judges should get in touch with each other before a request is made to assess whether a transfer would be in the best interests of the child.[167] However, the practical application of this rule may be problematic because of the procedural or public law of the requested State, which will often require someone else or, more likely, some public authority to seise the court in order to start a proceedings. As was stated by the UK Supreme Court in regard to a case started by a child care authority:

> The 'case' cannot be transferred in the same way that a case between parents or other private parties can be transferred. The proceedings in the other Member State will inevitably be different proceedings, with different parties, different procedures and possibly different substantive law. Indeed, there may not be proceedings in court at all, but only within the administrative authorities.[168]

4.154. Article 12(1)(b) also shows how transfer of jurisdiction is construed as a tool grounded in the cooperation between courts, which may be put into place even in the absence of any cooperation from the parties. Accordingly, Article 12 has deleted the previous requirement under the second paragraph of Article 15(2) Brussels II-bis, namely: 'A transfer made of the court's own motion or by application of a court of another Member State *must be accepted by at least one of the parties*' (emphasis added). The new rule in Brussels II-ter departs from such an approach and confirms that when the transfer is by the court's own motion, consent from the parties can be dispensed with.

2. The Acceptance of the Receiving Court

4.155. Once **the receiving court** is seised (under Article 12(1)(a)) or required to assume jurisdiction (under Article 12(1)(b)), it will proceed to independently

---

each Member State and find contact details, including names, telephones numbers and email addresses.

[165] EJN-civil national contact points for each Member State can be found at https://e-justice.europa.eu/contactPoint.do.

[166] Members of the Network are contact points within their jurisdiction and can provide information on various aspects of the law and procedure in their jurisdiction, including assisting with locating the competent authority. A list of the members of the International Hague Network of Judges is available on the Hague Conference website (www.hcch.net), under 'Child Abduction Section' then 'International Hague Network of Judges'.

[167] Such an approach is recommended by the *2022 Practice Guide*, p. 89, para. 3.3.4.2. See further below at 4.156.

[168] *Re N (Adoption: Jurisdiction)* [2016] UKSC 15, para. [34], per Lady Hale, on which decision, see further N. LOWE and H. SETRIGHT, above n. 155.

assess whether exercising such jurisdiction in the given case is **in the best interests of the child**. Although the rule is silent on the matter, it must be assumed that the transferring court will have transmitted to the receiving court all documents, reports and relevant elements which are necessary for the receiving court to be able to take a reasoned decision. Judicial cooperation and exchange of information appear greatly needed at this stage.

4.156. The best interests test to be performed by the receiving court mirrors the one already made by the transferring court.[169] This new assessment should **not be seen as a review of an assessment already made by the transferring court**, but as a double level of guarantee for the child, which finds its reason in the exceptional nature of transfer of proceedings. On the other hand, the receiving court should not view the request for transfer as a *fait accompli* that cannot be denied, or fear that the parties run into a denial of justice. The transferring court, which is already seised with the proceedings and has competence over it, will remain competent over the proceedings. Indeed, the exchange of views between the courts on the issue of transfer of proceedings is a good practice that should be promoted.[170]

4.157. Such an operation has to be done within the **time limit of six weeks** from the seisure/request.[171] The court will only accept jurisdiction on the positive outcome of such an assessment, thereby allowing the transferring court to decline its own jurisdiction and to complete the transfer of jurisdiction. Given that it is jurisdiction that is transferred, there is no specific duty on the transferring court to transfer the case file.[172] Nonetheless, whenever any relevant procedural activity has been carried out, this is certainly not precluded and it is submitted that it would be good practice to do so.

4.158. Transfer and acceptance of jurisdiction is limited to the **specific case**. Although there is no specific rule similar to the one on cessation of prorogation under Article 10(3), it is consistent with the exceptional nature of this provision that jurisdiction of the receiving court ceases as soon as the proceedings are terminated.[173]

---

[169] For the content of the best interests test performed by the transferring court, see above at 4.133 et seq.

[170] This is expressly provided by Article 86(2)(a), which refers to the cooperation and direct communication between courts for the purposes, in particular, of Articles 12 and 13. It should be noted that Article 15(6) Brussels II-bis previously provided that: 'The courts shall cooperate for the purposes of this Article, either directly or through the central authorities designated pursuant to Article 53.' It is a matter of regret that this provision has not been repeated in Brussels II-ter as it drew the court's attention to the much-needed cooperation in this specific case.

[171] Article 12(2).

[172] *2022 Practice Guide*, p. 90, para. 3.3.4.3.

[173] A similar conclusion is reached for Articles 8 and 9 of the 1996 Hague Convention; see Lagarde Report, above n. 67, at para. 56.

3. *Denial of Acceptance or Lack of Answer of the Receiving Court*

4.159. Until a formal acceptance by the requested court is received, the proceedings are stayed before the originally first seised court. In the interests of all parties to the proceedings, such a stay cannot be extended too long. For this reason, the requested court has a short timeframe to provide an answer (six weeks). The rule allows an additional week for the transmission of the answer to the transferring court. If an acceptance has not been received after seven weeks, the transferring court will resume the proceedings and continue to exercise its jurisdiction.[174]

4.160. The **seven-week time limit** runs differently depending on how the receiving court has been informed of the possible transfer. If this was done by the parties, in accordance to the procedure under Article 12(1)(a), the seven weeks run from when the time limit set by the first court for the parties (see above at 4.151) has expired – and not from the actual seisure of the receiving court. Where the transfer was directly requested by the transferring court in accordance with Article 12(1)(b), the seven weeks run from when the court has received the request. The rule does not consider a possible prorogation of such a time limit, but the transferring court may consider doing so when the circumstances may suggest this is the case.

4.161. Article 12(3) finally deals with the case where **no answer (or a negative answer) is given** by the receiving court. If, within the above-mentioned seven-week time limit, no answer has been received, or a negative answer following the best interests assessment is given, then the first seised court will resume the proceedings and continue exercising its competence.

G. ARTICLE 13 AND THE REQUEST FOR TRANSFER OF JURISDICTION

4.162. Article 13 is new and is modelled on Article 9 of the 1996 Hague Convention. It allows a court that does not have jurisdiction over matters of parental responsibility to request a transfer of jurisdiction to hear the case from the otherwise competent court (i.e. the court of the child's habitual residence, the court where the child is present or the court agreed upon by the parties). It should be noted that the rule **does not apply to cases of wrongful removal or retention** of a child. In particular, the State where the child has been brought or retained cannot ask for a transfer of jurisdiction from the State of habitual residence. This is to safeguard the system of rules on conflicts of competence in international abduction cases, as set by Article 9 and Chapter III of Brussels II-ter (discussed in Chapter 6).

---

[174] Article 12(3).

4.163. The substantial conditions for the operation of the rule are identical to those under Article 12 for the case of a transfer on the motion of the seised court and, more precisely, that: (i) the child has a 'particular connection' with the State of the requesting court; (ii) the requiring court is 'better placed'; and (iii) transfer must be 'in the best interests of the child'. For all these requirements, reference should be made to the discussion at 4.124–4.148 above. In particular, building on the clear wording of Article 13(1) and on the *IQ* decision, such court will be one not having jurisdiction under the Regulation, in particular not the court of the child's habitual residence and not the court whose competence has been the subject of a non-exclusive choice-of-court agreement under Article 10. Instead, the requesting court can only be one of those mentioned under Article 12(4), that is: the court of the State of the new habitual residence of the child in the case of lawful relocation after a court was seised; the court of the State of the former habitual residence of the child; the court of the State of the nationality of the child; the court of the State of habitual residence of a holder of parental responsibility; or the court of the State where property of the child is located if the case concerns measures for the protection of the child relating to the administration, conservation or disposal of that property. It should be noted that in all cases proceedings will be pending before a court lacking competence under the Regulation, a situation compelling such court to declare its lack of competence under Article 18. Coordination between the two rules require that such duty shall be postponed until the six-weeks time under Article 13(2) last sentence has elapsed. In all cases, for the rule to apply, such a court must be convinced – based on the information that the court may have gathered by its own motion – that it will be better placed to hear the case.

4.164. However, when the court is convinced that it is in the best interests of the child that a transfer of proceedings should take place, it may request the court of the Member State of the child's habitual residence to transfer jurisdiction. Nowhere in the rule is it expressly required that proceedings in such State be already pending. This however may be seen as an implicit requirement, as such court need to receive the request and, in a short timeframe, assess whether the best interests of the child justify such a transfer. As in other cases, communication may be made directly to the requested court if all details are already available, or be channelled via the Central Authority of the requested State.

4.165. Once the request is received by the court (alledgedly already seised with the proceedings), Article 13(2) allows for a short timeframe of six weeks to respond to the request. In that time, the seised court must separately assess if, in its own view, a transfer is in the best interests of the child.[175] It is only after such an assessment that the transfer will take place and the competence will shift to the requesting

---

[175] For the content of such an assessment, which will include the test of the court being 'better placed', see above at 4.133.

court. It is important to underline that a **lack of an answer** within the mentioned six-week timeframe is **not** be deemed **sufficient to confer jurisdiction** on the requesting court. The double assessment of the best interests of the child by both courts will guarantee that the derogation from the general presumption of competence laid down by the legislator is justified by the peculiarities of the case.

VII. RESIDUAL JURISDICTION UNDER ARTICLE 14

4.166. Article 14 has undergone no changes and has the same wording as in Brussels II-bis. The rule covers the case where **no court of any Member State has jurisdiction under Articles 7–11** and exceptionally allows each Member State to revert to its own national rules. Such a ground of jurisdiction is residual as it only applies when no other ground provided by Brussels II-ter is applicable in any Member State, and it parallels the similar ground provided by Article 6 with regard to matrimonial disputes.[176] Accordingly, Article 14 presupposes the **mandatory and exhaustive nature** of the criteria set out by Articles 7–11, which compels all EU national courts to respect the Regulation not only when it confers jurisdiction upon that State, but also when it confers jurisdiction upon the court of any other Member State.

4.167. Reference to 'national rules' of each Member State is ambiguous, as it does not expressly cater for **treaty-based rules** grounded in international conventions which may be in force in each Member State. This point was sometimes misunderstood by courts which reverted to national rules where the child was not habitually resident in a Member State, but in a Contracting State to the 1996 Hague Convention.[177] However, there is no doubt that international rules have precedence over national rules, and the point is now clarified in Recital (29), which explains that 'the term "laws of that Member State" includes international instruments in force in that State'.[178] Consequently, national courts, before reverting to national grounds for jurisdiction, should first verify if there is room for the application of international conventions, such as the 1996 Hague Child Protection Convention, the 1961 Hague Convention on the powers

---

[176] Article 6 is discussed in Chapter 3 at 3.68 et seq.
[177] See, for example, the decision by the Czech court of Nejvyšší soud, 23 Nd 64/2013, 29 May 2013 (to be found at the EUFAM database at http://www.eufams.unimi.it/2018/06/14/eufams-database-14-06-18/) applying Article 14 to a child habitually resident in Norway and on such grounds referring to the 1996 Hague Convention.
[178] The point was also stated by CJEU, 24 March 2021, SS, C-603/20 PPU, paras 61–64, pointing out that where a child has habitual residence in a non-EU Member State, jurisdiction must be determined in accordance with the applicable international conventions, such as, in the given case, the 1996 Hague Convention. Only in the absence of any such international convention must jurisdiction be determined in accordance with national law pursuant to Article 14 of the Regulation. For a clear assessment under Brussels II-bis, see R. HAUSMANN, *Internationales und Europäisches EhescheidungsRecht, Kommentar*, C.H. Beck, 2013, p. 214, para. 170.

of authorities and the law applicable in regard to the protection of infants or the Strasbourg Convention of 15 May 2003 on contact concerning children.[179]

Notwithstanding its apparently limited scope, the rule on residual jurisdiction provides a useful tool for the protection of **children who are resident outside the EU** but still have a connection to it. This may be the case, for example when they are children of parents with EU nationality and therefore themselves EU citizens. Furthermore, parents who are EU citizens may wish to revert to their own national courts to settle a matter on parental responsibility, notwithstanding that the family is settled in a third State. While nationality is not a ground for jurisdiction under EU private international law, it may be triggered in exceptional cases concerning third States based on national rules.[180] This was, for example, the case in the *MPA* decision concerning custody over two children having dual Spanish and Portuguese nationality and habitually resident in Togo. Having found that no other Member State had competence under the Regulation, the Court made it clear that it is open to every Member State to confer jurisdiction on its own courts on the basis of rules of national law, also when this implies departing from the criterion of proximity on which the provisions of the Regulation are founded or where the respondent father of the children concerned is a national of a Member State other than that of the court seised.[181]

VIII. PROVISIONAL AND PROTECTIVE MEASURES

A. PROVISIONAL AND PROTECTIVE MEASURES IN CHILDCARE CASES

4.168. The need for provisional measures in family crisis is undisputable. When a family experiences long-running disputes, the need to provisionally settle the

---

[179] However, the criterion is less clear than it seems at first sight, both because habitual residence under the 1996 Hague Convention is undefined and because the scope of application of this Convention is far from clear. On such delimitation problems, see Chapter 1 at 1.68 et seq.; and A. López-Tarruella Martinez, 'Análisis crítico e implicaciones prácticas de la competencia residual del Reglamento 2019/1111 en materia de responsabilidad parental' (2022) 14 *Cuadernos de Derecho Transnacional* 372 et seq.

[180] M. Herranz Ballesteros, 'Proyección de la competencia de las autoridades de los Estados miembros sobre menores residentes en terceros Estados: la experiencia española' (2020) 52 *Revista General de Derecho Europeo* 229 et seq, shows how Spanish courts have exercised jurisdiction based on Article 14 Brussels II-bis over a child habitually resident in a third State (not a Member State of the EU) when the applicant was habitually resident in Spain or a Spanish national. This occurred also when the defendant was domiciled in Spain.

[181] CJEU, 1 August 2022, C-501/20, *MPA*, paras 90–91. The complex case involved multiple actions: on divorce, on custody for children and on maintenance for the mother and the children. With each action being separately dealt with, the Spanish jurisdiction was established for custody and maintenance, but not for divorce. For the facts of the case and residual jurisdiction on divorce, see above Chapter 3 at 3.79 et seq.

situation with regard to children is common practice, either before or pending a final decision from the competent court. Measures taken in such a context of urgency with the aim of protecting the child may well, of course, have an impact on the final decision. Brussels II-ter, as previously under Brussels II-bis, offers multiple grounds for provisional and protective measures, adopting a **double-track approach**. Provisional measures may in fact be sought not only under Article 15 but also in the court having competence on the substance (see 4.172 below). However, Brussels II-ter is innovative with regard to the previous rules, both by substantially revising the former provision in Brussels II-bis and by introducing a new provision, Article 27(5), in the peculiar case of provisional measures which are taken in order to protect the abducted child upon his or her return to the State of habitual residence from the grave risk of harm mentioned in Article 13(1)(b) of the 1980 Hague Convention.

4.169. Article 15 Brussels II-ter builds on and replaces Article 20 Brussels II-bis, which in turn was modelled on Article 12 of the 1996 Hague Convention. However, the new rule marks a clear departure from the previous structure as it provides for a **uniform ground of jurisdiction**, instead of relying on national grounds of jurisdiction as was previously the case under Article 20 Brussels II-bis.[182] This is first shown by the different placement of the rule in Section 2, which concerns (jurisdiction on) parental responsibility. Previously, Article 20 Brussels II-bis was instead placed under Section 3, 'Common provisions'. The change is of relevance, especially since the place of the rule in the system of the Regulation was used by the CJEU to conclude that Article 20 Brussels II-bis was not a ground of jurisdiction and hence any measure based on such a rule could not benefit from the rules on the circulation of decisions.[183] The new function of Article 15 is further confirmed by the different wording the rule is given, according to which 'courts of a Member State *shall have jurisdiction* to take provisional, including protective, measures which may be available under the law of that Member State' (emphasis added), in contrast to the previous Article 20 Brussels II-bis, which informed that the rule 'shall *not prevent* the courts of a Member State *from taking* such provisional, including protective, measures in respect of persons or assets in that State *as may be available under the law of that Member State*' (emphasis added). Such a different perspective

---

[182] The point is now clearly made in the *2022 Practice Guide*, p. 48, para. 3.1.1.5.1. In the legal literature, see A. J. CALZADO LLAMAS, 'Vista de Las medidas provision ales y cautelares en los procedimientos de restitución de menores. Análisis del Reglamento (UE) 2019/1111 en conexion con el ordenamiento jurídico español' (2021) 12 *Cuadernos de Derecho Transnacional* 87, 99; A. BERNARDO SAN JOSÉ, 'Las normas de competencia internacional en materia de responsabilidad parental en el Reglamento (UE) 2019/1111 del Consejo de 25 de junio de 2019', (2020) 12 *Cuadernos de Derecho Transnacional* 1243–1289, 1283, who, however, does not considers this a novelty.
[183] On this relevant difference, see further below at 4.199 et seq.

is probably the answer to the restrictive approach given by the CJEU in the *Purrucker I* decision and, in the view of the Commission's first proposal, is aimed at reinforcing provisional justice and giving it full extra-territorial effect.[184] Unfortunately, the Commission's proposal has been limited by negotiations in the Council. In the end, the concrete effects of measures grounded in Article 15, notwithstanding the rule's different structure and wording, are not so different from those produced under previous Article 20 Brussels II-bis.

4.170. The rule further introduces welcome improvements with regard to better coordination between the court of provisional jurisdiction and the court exercising jurisdiction on the substance of the matter (at paras 2 and 3). Finally, it should be highlighted how Article 15 has a different wording and structure from other rules on provisional measures included in other EU regulations on judicial cooperation.[185] This implies that any case law and guidelines given by the CJEU with regard to provisional measures under such instruments should be treated with caution and not automatically applied to Brussels II-ter.

4.171. Following a distinction which is common in many national systems,[186] the title of the article refers to two different kind of measures: **provisional measures** (for example, orders temporarily anticipating the future settlement of the dispute) and **protective measures** (for example, orders aiming to preserve a situation in view of the final decision on the substance). Such a distinction is also embodied in the 1996 Hague Convention, which provides two distinct rules, with different regimes, for the two situations: Article 11 (urgent provisional

---

[184] The main difference with the Commission's Proposal (above n. 4) is not in the text of the proposed Article 12 (which, in spite of some linguistic tweaks, does not really differ from the current Article 15), but in the absence of what is now Article 2(1) on the definition of 'decision'. According to this definition, provisional measures granted under Article 15 are not eligible to be recognised under Chapter IV. The opposite intention of the Commission to include provisional measures in the regime of recognisable decisions was clearly evident in Recital (40) of the Proposal, which then read as follows: 'Where provisional, including protective, measures are ordered by an authority having jurisdiction as to the substance of the matter, their free circulation should be ensured under this Regulation. *The same applies to provisional, including protective, measures ordered in urgent cases on the basis of Article 12 of this Regulation by an authority of a Member State not having jurisdiction as to the substance of the matter.* Those measures should apply until a competent authority of a Member State having jurisdiction over the substance of the matter under this Regulation has taken the measures it considers appropriate' (emphasis added). This may be compared with Recital (30) of the current Brussels II-ter, having the opposite content. See again A. J. CALZADO LLAMAS, above n. 179, 99 and in more detail below at 4.200.

[185] Article 35 Brussels I-bis, for example, reads as follows: 'Application may be made to the courts of a Member State for such provisional, including protective, measures as may be available under the law of that Member State, even if the courts of another Member State have jurisdiction as to the substance of the matter.' Article 14 of the Maintenance Regulation, Article 19 of the Matrimonial Property and Article 19 of the Property of Registered Partnership Regulations, Article 19 of the Succession Regulation all have a similar wording.

[186] I. PRETELLI, 'Provisional Measures in Family Law and the Brussels IIter Regulation' (2018/2019) 20 *Yearbook of Private International Law* 117 et seq.

measures, with possible extra-territorial effects) and Article 12 (urgent protective measures, with effects limited to the forum). In contrast, under both Brussels II-bis and Brussels II-ter, the distinction between the two kind of measures is irrelevant, as both measures follow the same regime and share the same requirement of urgency. Any tentative categorisation between the two is therefore to be avoided.[187] Instead, attention should be drawn on the common feature of, and requirement for, both measures, i.e. the need of **urgency** in taking the measure (see below at 4.182 et seq). In light of the above, in the following paragraphs the expression 'provisional measures' and 'urgent measures' will be used as including both provisional and protective measures.

B. A DOUBLE-TRACK FOR PROVISIONAL JURISDICTION

4.172. Although there is no rule expressly saying so in Brussels II-ter, it is clear and undisputed that any ground conferring **jurisdiction on the substance** of a case will also confer jurisdiction to take any provisional measure which may be needed either before instituting the case or pending the case. In particular, provisional jurisdiction is inherent to the jurisdiction conferred to the court of the State of the child's habitual residence, to the court whose competence has been prorogated under Article 10 or to the court of the State where the child finds himself or herself, pursuant to Article 11.

4.173. Article 15 Brussels II-ter provides for an **additional ground** conferring provisional jurisdiction to a court which would otherwise **not have jurisdiction on the substance** of the case. Article 15(1) reads as follows:

> In urgent cases, even if the court of another Member State has jurisdiction as to the substance of the matter, the courts of a Member State shall have jurisdiction to take provisional, including protective, measures which may be available under the law of that Member State in respect of:
>
> (a) a child who is present in that Member State; or
> (b) property belonging to a child which is located in that Member State.

4.174. The exercise of provisional jurisdiction based on Article 15 is not linked to the existence of proceedings on the substance of the matter, in the

---

[187] A difficulty in drawing a clear dividing line between the different categories of protective measures is noticed in relation to the scope of Articles 11 and 12 of the 1996 Hague Convention. For more on this, see N. Lowe and M. Nicholls, *The 1996 Hague Convention on the Protection of Children*, Jordan Publishing, 2012, pp. 3.23 et seq.; H. Setright, D. Williams, I. Curry-Sumner, M. Gration, and M. Wright, *International Issues in Family Law The 1996 Hague Convention on the Protection of Children and Brussels IIa*, Jordan Publishing, 2015, paras 3.72 et seq.

sense that provisional measures may be requested from the court based on Article 15 either before or pending proceedings on the substance. Rules on coordination and *lis pendens* among the two set of proceedings are discussed in Chapter 5.[188]

4.175. However, the **ground** on which provisional jurisdiction is exercised is **not irrelevant**. In fact, as will be seen,[189] provisional measures taken by a court having competence on the substance of the matter benefit from the special regime of circulation of decisions provided by the Regulation, provided that the respondent was either summoned to the proceedings or, in the case where the decision was taken *inaudita altera parte*, he or she was notified before the measure is enforced.[190] In contrast, measures taken on the basis of Article 15 will never be eligible for recognition in other Member States and their effects will always be limited to the territory of the State where such measures were granted.[191]

4.176. The different regimes governing recognition of a provisional measure makes it necessary **to determine the ground on which such measure is taken** in any particular decision. This can either be expressly stated in the decision by making direct reference to the relevant provision (e.g. Article 7, 10 or 11) or it may be inferred from the reasoning, as, for example, where reference is made to the place of habitual residence of the child, the pending divorce proceedings or the presence of the child or other circumstances of fact which may support full jurisdiction. In light of the principle prohibiting a review on the substance of the decision (pursuant to Article 71), it is certainly good practice for the deciding court to make sure that the ground of jurisdiction is clearly ascertainable by anyone who will be reading the decision.[192]

4.177. However, there may be cases where such good practice is not followed and nothing is said in the decision, for example, because the decision itself is concise and short. It may also be the case that the place of habitual

---

[188] See Chapter 5 at 5.18.
[189] See below at 4.199 et seq.
[190] See Article 2(1), second paragraph, which reads: 'For the purposes of Chapter IV, "decision" does not include provisional, including protective, measures ordered by such a court without the respondent being summoned to appear, unless the decision containing the measure is served on the respondent prior to enforcement.'
[191] See below at 4.199 et seq. But note the special position of protective measures made in the context of abduction proceedings under Article 27(5), discussed at 4.179 and in Chapter 6 at 6.84 et seq.
[192] It is submitted that *ascertaining* the basis on which a court considered itself competent when issuing a decision does not imply a *review* of such decision and is not contrary to the principle prohibiting the review of jurisdiction of the court of origin. The point was made by Advocate General Sharpston in her Opinion in 20 May 2010, *Purrucker I*, C-256/09, para. 139.

residence of the child is ambiguous and not clearly definable, especially before full proceedings on the substance are instituted, and this may be difficult to ascertain in a summary proceedings, as is the one for provisional measures. In any such case, where there is doubt as to the ground conferring jurisdiction, the **presumption** is that jurisdiction is based on Article 15. In the *Purrucker I* case, the CJEU held that:

> where the substantive jurisdiction … of a court which has taken provisional measures is not, plainly, evident from the content of the judgment adopted, or where that judgment does not contain a statement, which is free of any ambiguity, of the grounds in support of the substantive jurisdiction of that court, with reference made to one of the criteria of jurisdiction specified in Articles 8 to 14 of that regulation, it may be inferred that that judgment was not adopted in accordance with the rules of jurisdiction laid down by that regulation.[193]

This may serve as a warning for the deciding court. Provisional measures which are meant to be recognised and enforced in a different jurisdiction must be supported by a well-drafted and appropriately worded decision. Failure to do so will undermine their efficacy and be a reason for refusing enforcement.[194]

4.178. In the context of **abduction proceedings**, the competence of the State of refuge to take provisional measures is governed by two separate rules, providing for different solutions. Measures which are directed **to protect the child from the risk of grave harm** upon his or her return to the State of habitual residence fall under Article 27(5) and benefit from a special extra-territorial effect which allows the measure to accompany the child when travelling to a different Member State.[195] All other provisional measures, in particular those aiming to rule on placement or access to the abducted child, fall under Article 15. In general, these measures are seen with disfavour as they may interfere with the competence of the court of the State of habitual residence. As such, they are limited both territorially and temporally. Having said this, attention should be drawn on Article 27(2) which directs the court in the State of refuge to adopt provisional measures in accordance with Article 15

---

[193] CJEU, 15 July 2010, C-256/09, *Purrucker I*, para. 76.
[194] Regretfully, Annex III, which provides the relevant certificate for the recognition and enforcement of decisions in parental responsibility matters does not raise sufficient attention on this point. No 9 of the certificate only requires to state whether provisional measures have been taken (yes, no and their description), but fails to ask on what ground such measures have been issued.
[195] See Chapter 6 at 6.84 et seq.

in order to safeguard the child's right to maintain relations with both his or her parents also in cases of abduction.

C. A UNIFORM GROUND FOR PROVISIONAL JURISDICTION

4.179. As mentioned above (at 4.169), providing a uniform ground for provisional justice marks a departure from the previous regime.[196] To better appreciate the changes, it is useful to briefly recall that Article 20 Brussels II-bis did not provide for a direct and uniform ground for provisional jurisdiction common to all Member States. Instead, it referred to 'national law', meaning that courts were allowed to use their own internal rules as a ground for provisional jurisdiction.[197] This of course caused disparity among Member States and undermined the predictability and consistency of provisional justice. However, disparity was partially reduced by the fact that Article 20 required such measures to be taken 'in respect of persons or assets in that State' and that the conditions under which such requirements are met had been further interpreted and explained by the CJEU.

4.180. Article 15 is to be construed as moving from a different perspective, with the idea of providing a uniform ground for provisional justice, thereby allowing for free circulation of provisional measures. While this ultimate goal was not achieved, the structure of the rule is clear. Reference to 'national law' now focuses on the type of provisional measures which may be available under internal law, and not on the possible ground of competence. The ground for jurisdiction is based on the presence of the child or on the location of the child's property on that Member State's territory.

4.181. While the above is a major novelty, the rest of the rule should be construed according to the previous case law of the CJEU. In particular, the

---

[196] The proposed impact of this new perspective was curtailed in the course of negotiations and the rule appears to be a compromise, balancing a reaction to and the implementation of the relevant CJEU case law.

[197] Article 20 was silent as to whether national rules should provide for national competence or for international jurisdiction. It seems that a rule providing for national competence in provisional and protective cases may also serve as a ground for international cases, as such a function is the effect of Article 20 itself. What is certain is that national rules may be complemented by rules derived from international conventions, such as Articles 11 and 12 of the 1996 Hague Convention, which may come into consideration and be especially useful where a national legal system lacks a rule on provisional jurisdiction. The technique of referring to national rules is not new. R. HAUSMANN, above n. 177, p. 253 notes that Article 20 has a similar function to Article 14 (now also Article 14 Brussels II-ter), in that it makes use of national grounds of competence for cases where common rules are not applicable. The only difference between the two is that residual jurisdiction applies when no court, in no Member State, has competence under the Regulation, while Article 20 applies in parallel to, but not as a derogation from, a court in another Member State having competence under the Regulation.

three cumulative conditions originally listed by the CJEU in *A*[198] in regard to Article 20 Brussels II-bis are still relevant, namely:

- the measures concerned must be urgent;
- they must be taken in respect of persons or assets in the Member State where the court seised of the dispute is situated; and
- they must be provisional.

These requirements will now be examined separately.

1. Measures must be Urgent

4.182. The requirement of **urgency** must be assessed autonomously, making no reference to national law. In light of the scope and the structure of Brussels II-ter, urgency must be construed as having regard to two aspects. On the one hand, the situation and needs of the child; on the other hand, the impossibility of bringing an action in a timely manner before the court which has competence on the substance under the Regulation.[199]

4.183. With regard to the situation of the child, urgency will be assessed in light of the child's physical, psychological and intellectual development and the need to prevent irreparable harm to him or her.[200] The effectiveness of the provisional or protective measures must also be considered.[201] In principle, when a child is in need, any judicial and public authorities of the place where the child finds himself or herself are under a specific duty to take action. However, the need for action must be balanced with the duty to respect the system of competences set out by the Regulation. The requirement for urgency must therefore also be assessed in the light of the possibility that protection is sought in the court having jurisdiction as to the substance. Such a court will always be the preferred venue and should have precedence over any other court. It is only when such a court is

---

[198] ECJ, 2 April 2009, *A*, C-523/07, para. 47. The same requirements were repeated in ECJ, 23 December 2009, *Detiček*, C-403/09, para. 3; and in CJEU, 15 July 2010, *Purrucker I*, C-256/09, para. 77.
[199] ECJ, 23 December 2009, *Detiček*, C-403/09, para. 42.
[200] A similar condition is to be found under Articles 10 and 11 of the 1996 Hague Convention. The Lagarde Report (above n. 67, at para. 68) brings the examples of the child's need for urgent medical treatment, or the rapid sale of perishable goods. The *Practical Handbook* on the 1996 Convention gives the example of the immediate need to suspend contact and/or to place the child in temporary accommodation where the child makes allegations of physical or sexual abuse against a non-residential parent whilst having contact with that parent outside the child's habitual residence. Both examples may be appropriate to Brussels II-ter too. However, in the context of an area of freedom, security and justice, urgency will particularly need to be assessed in the light of the possibility to seek the appropriate remedy in the court on the substance.
[201] ECJ, 2 April 2009, *A*, C-523/07, paras 59–60.

not in the position to act swiftly and effectively that the requirement of urgency is fully satisfied. Article 15 innovates on Article 20 Brussels II-bis in that it also imposes a duty to inform the court having jurisdiction on the substance and to coordinate with whatever action is taken by such a court, thus emphasising the priority of the assessment made by such a court over the one temporarily made by the court of provisional jurisdiction.

4.184. Urgency may derive from a sudden **change of circumstances** which require a quick reassessment of the family organisation. A change of circumstances, for example, always occurs in international abduction cases. However, in the *Detiček* case,[202] the CJEU clarified that the settlement of an abducted child in his or her new environment does not amount to a situation of urgency allowing the court in the State of refuge to take a provisional measure on custody matters based on Article 20 Brussels II-bis.

2. *Measures must be in Respect of a Child*

4.185. A major difference between Article 15(1) Brussels II-ter and Article 20(1) Brussels II-bis is the personal scope of application of the rule. The former provision referred to 'measures in respect of *persons* or assets in that State', whereas Article 15 Brussels II-ter now refers more strictly to 'measures taken in respect of *a child*' present in the territory, or to his or her property which is located there. The scope of application of the provision is on its wording thus restricted to the **sole (direct) protection of the child**. The different wording, however, is in practice less meaningful than it may appear at first reading.

4.186. The new drafting reflects the fact that the rule is now placed in the section on jurisdiction on parental responsibility (see 4.169 above) and is therefore not relevant to matrimonial proceedings. This is also consistent with the practice that emerged under Brussels II-bis, showing that provisional measures were mainly requested in cases concerning matters of parental responsibility, both in national courts and before the CJEU.[203] This outcome is not surprising, given that in matrimonial matters the scope of the Regulation is limited to the dissolution of matrimonial ties and does not include ancillary measures related to, for example, the reasons for divorce or the property consequences of the marriage.[204]

4.187. Within the domain of parental responsibility, however, the formal restriction to taking measures solely in respect of the child is a cause of concern and, if strictly construed, could create dangerous and unnecessary gaps. The

---

[202] ECJ, 23 December 2009, *Detiček*, C-403/09, para. 45 et seq. For the facts of the case, see below at 4.190.
[203] I. KUNDA and D. VRBLJANAC, 'Provisional and Protective Measures' in C. HONORATI (ed.), above n. 40, p. 234.
[204] See Recital (9) and above Chapter 1, at 1.26.

requirement is best construed as meaning that the **focus of the granted measure must be on the child** and not on other persons, in particular his or her parents. On the other hand, the requirement must not be interpreted restrictively, as meaning that measures must *exclusively* affect the child. Because of the obviously close and dependent relationship of a child to his or her parents, any measure taken in relation to a child will also affect one of if not both of the parents.

4.188. The decision to focus attention on the child, instead of referring to any 'person' as previously, addresses the previous uncertainties following from the former text and the connected case law. Reference to 'persons' to be located on the territory of the forum as made by Article 20 Brussels II-bis led to opposite interpretations: either that *any person* located in the forum would award provisional jurisdiction; or that *all persons* affected by the measure would need to find themselves in the forum. Both constructions proved to be unsatisfactory.[205] While the territorial link will be addressed below,[206] attention will be given here to the subjective requirement of the measure.

4.189. The ambiguity began with the *Detiček* decision, in which the CJEU found that the Slovenian court had no competence to make a provisional order to order a change of custody of the abducted child, *inter alia* because:

> such measure would be taken not only in respect of the child but also in respect of the parent to whom custody is now granted and of the other parent who, following the adoption of the measure, is deprived of that custody.[207]

4.190. The underlining assumption was that such a measure could not be covered by Article 20 because a new, provisional custody order would be taken in respect not only of the abducting mother and the child who were in Slovenia, but also of the left-behind father who was in Italy. This often-quoted passage and its underlying assumption was, it is submitted, a clear misunderstanding. Even under the previous wording, the rule could not be read as meaning that *all* persons involved by a provisional measure have to be in the forum themselves. Such a construction would have deprived the rule of any application, given that, by definition, the dispute arises in a disrupted family where cross-border issues are at stake. The situation in *Detiček* was peculiar because the CJEU was confronted with a conflict between two provisional measures on the child's custody, a prior one taken by the court of the State of habitual residence, and a subsequent one, taken by the State of refuge on the ground of Article 20.

---

[205] See some examples of the erroneous application of Article 20 by national courts which asserted jurisdiction to grant measures to be taken in respect of one parent, even if the child was located in a different State, as reported by I. KUNDA and D. VRBLJANAC, above n. 200, pp. 241–243.
[206] See below at 4.193 et seq.
[207] ECJ, 23 December 2009, *Detiček*, C-403/09, para. 51.

In *Detiček*, provisional jurisdiction was sought with the aim of circumventing and undermining the natural competence of the State of habitual residence, which had already been exercised with a provisional order on custody. The CJEU thus rightly reacted to such abuse of rules in order to safeguard the distribution of competences provided by the Regulation.

4.191. Measures for urgent protection may include orders directed to safeguarding the child's health and wellbeing, for example, if a child needs health treatment when finding himself or herself temporarily in a Member State other than the one of his or her habitual residence. However, provisional measures may also concern a different placement or access to the child measures in case of urgency – for example, if the principal caregiver is not able to perform his or her functions due to death or serious illness.

4.192. There may also be situations where the need for urgent measures appears to be directly related to a person other than the child, although the situation will also indirectly affect the child. An example is a situation with a background of **domestic violence**, where the mother (and the child) may be in need of urgent and protective measures against the abusive behaviour of her partner. While this situation will primarily put the integrity and emotional balance of the mother at risk, it will, undoubtedly although indirectly, also harm the physical and psychological wellbeing of the child. It is here supported the view that the best interests of the child require a flexible and broad interpretation, including the protection of all situations which may – albeit indirectly – affect and harm the child. Courts should move from the general understanding that evidence of a risk of domestic violence on the mother will always harm the child.[208]

---

[208] The point is now substantially supported in both the scientific and legal literature and under several legal systems (see, for example, Italy and Sweden), domestic violence against a parent is also considered a crime against the child. See also Opinion of the European Economic and Social Committee on Children as indirect victims of domestic violence, [2006] OJ C 325, pp. 60–64 which finds (at para. 2.3): 'Growing up in a climate of physical and psychological violence can have serious consequences for children. Children – even young children – feel very helpless and vulnerable in the face of the father's, stepfather's or mother's partner's violence and her powerlessness. They also sometimes feel responsible for what is happening. They often believe that the violence is their fault, or they try to intervene and protect the mother, and are then themselves abused. Although the effects on each individual child are different and not all children develop behavioural problems as a result of violence, and although there are no empirically established criteria for determining how great the risk is (if any) in each individual case, there do seem to be clear links … Growing up in a context of domestic violence can also have an impact on the children's attitude to violence and to their own violent behaviour. By observing their parents' behaviour or experiencing violence themselves, children can take on the adults' problematic behaviour patterns. The cycle of violence can lead boys to learn the role of perpetrator and girls to learn that of victim, and can mean that they themselves become perpetrators or victims of domestic violence when they are adults.' See also O. Momoh, 'The Need for Cross-Border Protective Measures in Return Proceedings' in K. Trimmings, A. Dutta, C. Honorati and M. Župan (eds), *Domestic Violence and Parental Child Abduction*, Intersentia, 2022, pp. 72–75.

It is a matter of regret that such a situation, which should be acknowledged and mainstreamed by EU institutions, has been overlooked and left unsolved by Brussels II-ter. The protection of the parent in need is thus left to the indirect protection granted through measures that are formally directed to the child.[209] Moreover no direction has been given by the legislator, not even in a Recital, and the implementation of a reasonable standard of protection is left to the discretionary action of courts.

3. *The Territorial Link: The Child or Assets must be Located in the Forum*

4.193. Article 15 Brussels II-ter further requires that the **child is located** in the State seeking to exercise provisional justice. Similarly, when the action concerns the property of the child, that property must be located in the State exercising provisional jurisdiction.

4.194. The fact that the child (or his or her property) must be located in the State effectively limits the application of the rule on provisional justice. Contrary to what was ruled under Article 20 Brussels II-bis in the *Detiček* case,[210] the fact that the parent, whose existing custody rights are affected by the provisional measure, is not in such a State will now be irrelevant.

4.195. The territorial link relates to the effectiveness of the prospective provisional measure, which is connected to the need for a prompt and immediate reaction, which in turn is only possible when the measure can be implemented immediately. In other words, the requirement that the child be located in the forum State is functional to the need that the measure will be enforceable in the territory in which it was made. Should this not be the case, such a measure would be useless, as, under the current system, provisional measures based on Article 15 do not produce effects outside the territory of the Member State in which such measure was taken.

4. *Measures must be Provisional*

4.196. As in other cases, the notion of what is 'provisional and protective' must be construed autonomously.[211] Under Brussels II-bis, no consideration had been given to its meaning. However, with regard to Article 24 of the Brussels Convention, the CJEU defined such measures as those which 'are intended to

---

[209] See the point made in the "Best Practice Guide – Protection of Abducting Mothers in Return Proceedings: Intersection between Domestic Violence and Parental Child Abduction' in K. TRIMMINGS A. DUTTA, C. HONORATI and M. ŽUPAN (eds), above n. 205, pp. 215 et seq.; and also the contributions of M. FREEMAN and N. TAYLOR, O. MOMOH, C. HONORATI and K. TRIMMINGS in the same volume.
[210] See above at 4.189.
[211] R. HAUSMANN, above n. 177, p. 232, para. 232.

preserve a factual or legal situation so as to safeguard rights the recognition of which is otherwise sought from the court having jurisdiction as to the substance of the case'.[212]

4.197. The passage just quoted above highlights an important feature of protective measures. However, given the peculiarities of provisional justice in family matters, as seen above,[213] this should be considered as no more than a indication, and should not necessarily limit the understanding of a wider notion of 'provisional' measures. As already noted, in the context of childcare provisional measures may usefully be sought to provide continuity and anticipate the settlement of a dispute in order to fill a gap of protection pending full-merit proceedings. It is suggested that 'provisional' should be construed as meaning that the measure is **temporary** in nature and is meant **not to undermine the final settlement** of the dispute, as made by the court having jurisdiction on the substance. In other words, the requirement is complementary to the rule provided in Article 15(3) stating that measures will cease to have effect when the decision on the substance will be taken.

4.198. The requirement is clear and the relationship between provisional and final measure appears consistent with the structure of the rule.[214] Nonetheless, the difference between the effect of a final and a provisional measure may in practice be less clear, as the following two considerations illustrate. First, the general principle applies according to which decisions in childcare are **always adopted** *rebus sic stantibus* – that is, so long as conditions have not substantially changed. As is well known, the situation in childcare is constantly liable to change and no decision lasts forever even when taken by a court having jurisdiction on the substance. Second, there may be cases where **a final decision is not issued** after all, either because the proceedings on the substance was never instituted, or because it was renounced and closed before a decision was handed down. In such cases the provisional decision will produce its effect for a long time. In other words, there may be provisional measures which produce final effects; and there may be final decisions whose effects last for some time only.

D. LIMITED TERRITORIAL EFFECT

4.199. As mentioned earlier (at 4.169), Article 15 was modelled on and resembles Article 12 rather than Article 11 of the 1996 Hague Convention. Like the former (and unlike the latter), provisional measures taken under Article 15

---

[212] ECJ, 10 November 1998, *Van Uden*, C-391/95, para. 37; ECJ, 26 March 1992, *Reichert and Kockler*, C-261/90, para. 34.
[213] See above at 4.172.
[214] As seen above at 4.184 in regard to the requirement of urgency.

have limited territorial effects. Such a departure from the general principles is not clearly stated in the text, but it is confirmed by Recital (30), according to which provisional and protective measures based on Article 15:

> should not be recognised and enforced in any other Member State under this Regulation, with the exception of measures taken to protect the child from a grave risk as referred to in point (b) of Article 13(1) of the 1980 Hague Convention.

4.200. Recital (30) clarifies and puts in clear language what should otherwise be construed – not without some difficulties – arguing from the rules on the definition of decision, as set out in **Article 2(1)**. Pursuant to such a provision, in fact:

> For the purposes of Chapter IV, 'decision' includes:
>
> ...
>
> (b) provisional, including protective, measures ordered by a court which by virtue of this Regulation has jurisdiction as to the substance of the matter or measures ordered in accordance with Article 27(5) in conjunction with Article 15.

Hence, arguing *a contrario* from this rule, since provisional measures ordered by a court not having jurisdiction on the substance and grounded in Article 15 are not mentioned, they are not 'decisions' for the purpose of Chapter IV. This is certainly not an example of good drafting and the result could have been stated more clearly – and possibly in a place where one would expect to find the exclusion of provisional measures from Chapter IV, that is, either in the Article on provisional measures or at the beginning of Chapter IV, but certainly not in Chapter I under the definition of 'decision'.

4.201. The rule codifies the solution given by the CJEU in the *Purrucker I* case where the question was raised as to the effects of a provisional measure granted under Article 20 Brussels II-bis. Limited territorial effects of urgent measures was not the apparent solution under the text of Brussels II-bis either. Indeed, in *Purrucker I*, the Commission and some Member States argued that measures within the scope of Article 20 should qualify for the system of recognition and enforcement provided for by Brussels II-bis. Such an argument was reinforced by pointing to the possibility of a removal of persons or assets on which the decision impinges after the court had ruled, or the possibility that the child might suffer an accident or illness requiring that authority be obtained from someone in another Member State.[215] Nonetheless, the CJEU, applying a systematic interpretation based

---

[215] CJEU, 15 July 2010, *Purrucker I*, C-256/09, para. 88.

on the preparatory documents, including the **Borrás Report** to the Brussels II Convention of 1998 and Brussels II Regulation,[216] and arguing from the identical wording of the rule in the three instruments, was convinced that measures based on Article 20 Brussels II-bis were not meant to circulate with the regime for recognition and enforcement provided by that Regulation and were confined to the State in which they were adopted. The reasons for the legislator adopting such an approach was apparently linked to the fact that Article 20 had a wider scope of application than the Regulation itself. Indeed, the provision covered provisional measures related to *any person* and *any asset* located in the territory of a State not having jurisdiction on the substance. The rule could therefore also cover matters falling outside the scope of that Regulation. Recognising extra-territorial effects to these measures would have therefore led to recognising and enforcing measures, the adoption of which could circumvent rules laid down in that same or in other EU Regulations (for example, at that time, Regulation No 44/2001).[217]

4.202. The Court's reasoning in *Purrucker I* is disputable and not fully convincing,[218] and it is not surprising that the Commission's Proposal aimed to reverse such an interpretation and, in line with Article 11 of the 1996 Hague Convention, to provide for a full circulation of provisional measures (at least as long as they are not ordered without the respondent being summoned or not enforced prior to service). However, this perspective was overturned in the course of negotiations at the Council without an explanation.[219] Although the current solution is now firmly confirmed by Brussels II-ter, its rationale should be questioned along the following lines.

4.203. A first line of reasoning of the CJEU is based on the working documents of a rule having similar text drafted for the 1998 Convention (which never

---

[216] Reference is made to the Brussels II Convention on Jurisdiction and the Recognition and Enforcement of Judgments in Matrimonial Matters, to its Explanatory Report (the Borrás Report) and to Council Regulation (EC) No 1347/2000 of 29 May 2000. For all such documents, see Chapter 1.
[217] For this reasoning, see CJEU, 15 July 2010, *Purrucker I*, C-256/09, paras 83–87. Other arguments were drawn on the differences between Article 20 Brussels II-bis and Article 11 of the 1996 Hague Convention (paras 88–90) and on the risk of circumvention of the rules of jurisdiction laid down by that regulation and of forum shopping (para. 91).
[218] See C. Honorati, 'Purrucker I e II ed il regime speciale dei provvedimenti provvisori e cautelari a tutela dei minori' (2011) 2 *Int'l Lis* 66.
[219] In the working document circulated to the Working Party on Civil Law Matters, named 'Revised text of Article 1-11' doc 5572/18 of 26 January 2018, Article 2 still did not exclude provisional measures from the definition of decision for the purposes of Chapter IV. The current text appears instead in working document 'Revised text of Chapters I to III', doc. 12855/18 of 10 October 2018. None of the documents published in this span of time refers to the reasons for such a change.

entered into force). While preparatory documents are a traditional tool of interpretation, referring to a Convention which never entered into force cannot nowadays be fully persuasive, especially given the different scope of application of the envisaged rule. The current rule is, in fact, more conveniently limited to a child (and his or her property) located in the State adopting the measure. There seems to be little room for taking decisions falling under other Regulations which may be in conflict with Brussels II-ter, a concern which had led to restricting the extra-territorial effects of provisional measures based on Article 20 Brussels II-bis.[220]

4.204. The strongest argument under Brussels II-bis was drawn from the lack of uniform rules on provisional justice and the fact that such measures were based only on national grounds of jurisdiction.[221] Under these circumstances, allowing provisional decisions to circulate freely under the Regulation could have the effect of undermining the uniform rules of competence set by that instrument. The argument based on overall consistency and the need that automatic recognition and simplified enforcement is linked to uniform grounds of competence of the State where the decision was taken is a powerful one. However, even before Brussels II-ter, the principle appeared to be not so strictly construed when one considers that full-merits decisions that are based on national grounds under Article 14[222] are nonetheless eligible to circulate under the Regulation, with no restriction. Moreover, unlike decisions grounded in Article 14, recognition and enforcement of provisional and protective measures in other Member States would not 'endanger' the system too long, as such measures always have temporally limited effects and cease to apply as soon as the court having competence as to the substance takes its own decisions (even where this is also a provisional measure). Whatever its force in the past, such an argument is deprived of any strength under Brussels II-ter, given that Article 15 clearly (although not expressly) provides an autonomous and uniform ground of jurisdiction for all Member States.

4.205. A more persuasive ground for limiting the effects of urgent provisional or protective measures taken by a court not having jurisdiction on the substance is to be found in the need to **avoid interfering with decisions taken by the court having jurisdiction on the substance** on that same matter. However, the correct balance between the two authorities is better and more usefully reached by providing that **any effect of the urgent measure ceases** as soon as the court of the Member State having jurisdiction as to the substance has taken the appropriate

---

[220] See above at 4.201.
[221] See above at 4.180.
[222] Discussed above at 4.166 et seq.

measures (as per Article 15(3), on which see below at 4.207).[223] Indeed, Brussels II-ter takes a step towards a wider recognition of extra-territorial effects of urgent measures with the introduction of the new Article 27(5) for abduction cases. Although this rule has a narrow and specific application, it shows that in principle there is no imperative reason to conclude that urgent measures should never produce effects out of the State which adopted them. While it is to be hoped that things may change in the future, for the time being the combined effect of Article 2(1) and Article 15 leaves no doubt that, outside the context of child abduction, urgent provisional or protective measures do not have extra-territorial effect.

4.206. An open question is whether measures falling within the scope of Article 15 may still **circulate in accordance with other national or international rules**. Such a possibility was expressly envisaged by the CJEU and by Advocate General Sharpston in *Purrucker I*.[224] However, such a conclusion rests on the assumption that Article 20 Brussels II-bis allowed the granting of urgent and provisional measures in matters not falling under the Regulation. Based on this understanding, Advocate General Sharpston concluded that 'recognition and enforcement of such measures are not governed by the Regulation. And [therefore], for matters not governed by the Regulation, pre-existing conventions remain applicable in relations between Member States'. Yet, for the reasons explained in the paragraph above, it is currently difficult to imagine a provisional measures taken in relation to a child located in a Member State and resident in another Member State that would not fall within the scope of application of Brussels II-ter. Certainly, recognition and enforcement of a measure falling under Brussels II-ter and with limited territorial effects under Article 15 could not be recognised under national rules or other international conventions.

---

[223] This conclusion was already reached by Advocate General Sharpston in her Opinion in 20 May 2010, *Purrucker I*, C-256/09 (para. 170), where she commented: 'I therefore see no danger of undermining the overall scheme of the Regulation or the general rule conferring jurisdiction on the courts of the Member State of the child's habitual residence if provisional measures taken in the circumstances set out in Article 20 are recognised or enforced in Member States other than that in which they were issued. As I understand that overall scheme, once it has been seised, the court having substantive jurisdiction remains competent at all times to take any appropriate measures. Any competence of another court to take provisional measures in the circumstances set out in Article 20 remains subordinate to that substantive jurisdiction … On the other hand, the efficacy of measures taken in those circumstances – which are, by definition, urgently necessary – would be potentially easy to avoid, pending such seisin, if their enforceability were to evaporate as soon as the child was taken across a national border.' As mentioned, the only reason in support of this conclusion was the 'deliberate intention on the part of the drafters' resulting from the preparatory documents of previous texts.

[224] CJEU, 15 July 2010, *Purrucker I*, C-256/09, para. 92 and Opinion of Advocate General Sharpston, para. 176.

E. LIMITED EFFECTS IN TIME

4.207. Article 15(3) is a crucial part of the rule. It mirrors Article 20(2) Brussels II-bis exactly. According to the provision:

> The measures taken pursuant to paragraph 1 shall cease to apply as soon as the court of the Member State having jurisdiction under this Regulation as to the substance of the matter has taken the measures it considers appropriate.

4.208. The rationale of the rule is to provide for **coordination between (provisional) decisions** taken by a court not having competence on the substance and (any kind of) decision taken by a court exercising a competence on the substance pursuant to Articles 7–14 Brussels II-ter. The rule is therefore meant to solve temporal conflicts that may arise between the two sets of decisions and ensuring that a provisional measure, taken because of urgency in a court not basing its competence on common rules set by the Regulation, will cease to have effect and will give way to a decision taken by the court with jurisdiction on the substance of the matter. On the other hand, the rule guarantees continuity of protection to the child concerned, ensuring that the settlement of a dispute concerning a child is always overseen by a court. Article 15(3) does not apply to pending proceedings, but only to decisions that have already been taken. The issue of *lis pendens* between two sets of proceedings on protective measures is dealt with by Article 20.[225]

4.209. The rule is **not to be construed by reference to the nature** of the two decisions, but to the ground on which each court has grounded its competence (see above at 4.172 et seq). Hence, the rule is not limited to the (probably most common) case where a final decision will prevail over a previously taken provisional decision, but also applies when the court having competence as to the substance has taken a provisional or protective measure. Furthermore, the content of the two decisions is irrelevant and the subsequent decision of the court having competence on the substance will always prevail, even if its content is similar or identical to the earlier order.

4.210. Article 15(3) clearly sets the **relation in time** between the two sets of decisions. The decision of the court having competence as to the substance must be subsequent to the provisional one. Article 15(3) does not apply in the reverse case where the court having competence as to the substance takes a decision first, whether on the substance or a provisional one, and, subsequently, because of a change of circumstances, the court of the State where the child is

---

[225] Discussed in Chapter 5 at 5.18 et seq.

temporarily located is required to take a provisional measure. In such a case, **the more recent decision** – that is, the provisional decision taken by a court not having competence on the substance – **prevails**, leaving the interested party with the option of filing a new case before the competent court. In an *obiter dictum* of the *Purrucker I* decision, the CJEU, while differentiating this case from that of a decision not complying with the conditions set by Article 20 Brussels II-bis, confirmed this approach for the cases falling under Article 20 Brussels II-bis (now Article 15 Brussels II-ter) and clarified that:

> a measure falling within the scope of that provision may, in the Member State of the court which has adopted the judgment, prevail over an earlier judgment adopted by a court of another Member State which has substantive jurisdiction.[226]

4.211. The effects ceasing in accordance with Article 15(3) are **any legal effects** which a 'normal' urgent and provisional measure would produce in the forum where it was taken. In principle, given that this kind of measure is not eligible for recognition and enforcement in other Member States, there will be no effects to cease in other Member States. However, the situation is different with regard to provisional measures taken **under Article 27(5)** by the Member State to which the child has been abducted (or retained in) upon ordering his or her return. Article 27(5) exceptionally allows this provisional measure to be recognised in other Member States, including the one where the child was previously habitually resident. Yet, Article 27(5) refers to Article 15, with the consequence that, also in this peculiar case, when the court of the State of habitual residence hands down its own measure, such a decision will prevail over the provisional one previously in force, which will cease to have effect according to Article 15(3). This construction is confirmed by **Recital (30)**, according to which:

> Measures taken to protect the child from such risk [the grave risk of harm referred to in Article 13(1)(b) of the 1980 Hague Convention] should remain in force until a court of the Member State of the habitual residence of the child has taken the measures it considers appropriate.

F. THE RECIPROCAL DUTY TO INFORM OF ADOPTED URGENT MEASURES

4.212. Article 15(2) and the second paragraph of Article 15(3) introduce a new reciprocal duty to inform the court or competent authority having jurisdiction

---

[226] CJEU, 15 July 2010, *Purrucker I*, C-256/09, para. 81.

on the substance of the matter about the taking of any provisional and protective measure on both courts concerned with the case. As **Recital (30)** explains:

> Insofar as the protection of the best interests of the child so requires, the court should inform, directly or through the Central Authorities, the court of the Member State having jurisdiction over the substance of the matter under this Regulation about the measures taken.

4.213. In practice, it may not always be easy for a court seised with an urgent matter and receiving information in a summary proceedings (as is often the case when considering whether to take provisional and protective measures) to ascertain which is the court having jurisdiction on the substance. In light of this, most conveniently, the rule directs the provisional court to inform the court or competent authority of the State of the (assumed) child's habitual residence, either directly or via the Central Authority. Only when it is clear from the results of the proceedings that another court has competence on the substance (for example, the court seised with the parents' divorce or separation) is the provisional court to direct information to such a court.

4.214. Article 15(2) appears to grant the court adopting provisional measures some **discretion** as to whether or not to inform the court having competence on the substance, as it makes giving any information conditional on the best interests of the child so requiring. In practice, however, such a discretion is more fictitious than real, as it is difficult to imagine a situation where, notwithstanding the need to urgently protect a child, the child's best interests are not served by the better coordination resulting from informing the court having the last word of the adopted provisional measures. In conclusion, it appears that this is a case where, despite the soft wording of the text, the provisional court should always inform the other court. This is also consistent with the wording of Article 86(2)(b), which expressly envisages direct communication and reciprocal cooperation in accordance with Article 15.

4.215. The intention of the legislator appears even more clearly when it is compared with the different wording of the similar duty set by the second paragraph of Article 15(3) on the court of the State having jurisdiction as to the substance. It would appear that a court would have a wider margin of discretion here, since the rule allows the court to do so 'where appropriate'. That this is a discretion and not a duty is confirmed by Recital (30), which informs that the failure to provide such information is not a ground for the non-recognition of the measure, which is meant to always take priority over the measure adopted in Article 15.

CHAPTER 5

COORDINATION OF PROCEEDINGS

I. *Lis Pendens* and Dependent Actions: General Notions 194
   A. Historical Background. 194
   B. The Legal Provision and the Chronological Principle. 195
   C. The Scope of Application of the Rule: No *Lis Pendens* between Proceedings on Matrimonial Matters and Parental Responsibility 198
   D. *Lis Pendens* between Proceedings on the Merits and Proceedings on Provisional Measures. 199
II. Common Procedural Issues. 201
   A. Ascertaining the Court First Seised. 201
   B. Duties of the First Seised Court: Establishing Jurisdiction and Deciding on the Substance 202
   C. Duties of the Second Seised Court. 204
      1. Staying the Proceedings. 204
      2. Declining Jurisdiction 208
   D. Cases where the Second Seised Court must Decide on the Substance. 210
   E. The Alternative of Considering a Transfer of Proceedings from the First Seised Court to the Second Seised Court 211
III. *Lis Pendens* in Matrimonial Matters Cases 212
   A. The Notion of Same Proceedings and the Case of 'False *Lis Pendens*' 212
   B. The Same Parties. 214
IV. *Lis Pendens* in Parental Responsibility Cases. 214
   A. The Same Cause of Action. 214
   B. Proceedings Related to the Same Child but Brought by Different Parties. 216

5.1. An integrated area of security, freedom and justice is not only built on common rules on jurisdiction, but also needs to rely on rules for coordination of proceedings. Given the multiple grounds of jurisdiction provided by the

Regulation both for matrimonial and parental responsibility matters[1] and the *forum shopping* possibility inherent to such a choice, it is acknowledged that parties may seek to solve their problems in different courts. It is therefore necessary to have rules coordinating multiple proceedings pending in different States.

5.2. The situation considered here is one where parallel or related proceedings are pending before **courts of two Member States**. It does not concern the case where one of the two proceedings is pending before a court of a non-EU State. This situation falls outside the Regulation and is governed by national rules on (international) *lis pendens*.[2] This will also be the case when the court of the Member State has assessed its competence according to this Regulation. However, Article 97(2)(c) reminds us that if such a third country is a party to the **1996 Child Protection Convention** and the two proceedings concern the same measures for the protection of a child, then Article 13 of that Convention shall apply.[3]

I. *LIS PENDENS* AND DEPENDENT ACTIONS: GENERAL NOTIONS

A. HISTORICAL BACKGROUND

5.3. Article 20 largely reflects the rule previously in force (Article 19 Brussels II-bis). Indeed, the first three paragraphs have the same content, apart from some minor changes,[4] while Article 20(4) and (5) are new. Furthermore, Article 19 Brussels II-bis was drafted in similar terms to those used in Article 27 Brussels I (Regulation No 44/2001) and established a mechanism for dealing with cases of *lis pendens* that is equivalent to that provided for by the latter article. On this

---

[1] Chapters 3 and 4 respectively.
[2] The solution results from the wording of Article 20, which refers to 'courts of different Member States'. Based on this, some Member State courts have applied internal rules to cases where a parallel proceeding was instituted in a third State. See, for example, Cass. it., order 4 February 2021 n. 2654, (2021) 5 *Famiglia e Diritto*, 473. However, a different approach is followed in civil and commercial matters. Brussels I-bis gives room for a wider application of EU rules, allowing Member State courts to give relevance to parallel proceedings pending in a third State and to stay the proceedings when they expect the foreign decision to be recognisable in the EU or when 'a stay is necessary for the proper administration of justice' (see Article 33 Brussels I-bis).
[3] Discussed in Chapter 1 at 1.83. It should be noted that Article 13 of the 1996 Hague Child Protection Convention refers neither to a situation of *lis pendens* nor of related proceedings, but to the situation where 'corresponding measures' for the protection of the person or the property of the child are requested in both proceedings.
[4] See in regard to Article 20(2) below at 5.22.

basis, when interpreting Article 20, account must be taken of the findings of the ECJ/CJEU with regard to Brussels I for the interpretation of Brussels II-bis.[5]

5.4. As under the previous instrument, Article 20 provides two different rules in regard to *lis pendens* in matrimonial matters (Article 20(1)) and parental responsibility matters (Article 20(2)). The same rule applies both with regard to the situation of *lis pendens* (i.e. when parallel proceedings, involving the same action, run in different States) and of related (or dependent) proceedings (when the two proceedings are introduced by actions which are not identical but related). In other words, the distinction between parallel and related proceedings, which is common under many national laws, is irrelevant in the context of EU proceedings. For the sake of brevity, in this Chapter reference will be made only to *lis pendens*, but it should be kept in mind that the same rule applies to related actions (see also below at 5.11 and 5.58 et seq).

5.5. Both notions must be given an **autonomous interpretation** in light of the purpose and structure of the Regulation.[6] It should be highlighted that in this context, rules on *lis pendens* aim to avoid having two decisions that are irreconcilable and therefore not being entitled to free circulation under the Regulation. As always, any reference to national law for construing these terms is to be avoided.

B. THE LEGAL PROVISION AND THE CHRONOLOGICAL PRINCIPLE

5.6. Article 20(1) relates to *lis pendens* and related actions in **matrimonial matters** and reads as follows:

> Where proceedings relating to divorce, legal separation or marriage annulment between the same parties are instituted before courts of different Member States, the court second seised shall of its own motion stay its proceedings until such time as the jurisdiction of the court first seised is established.

5.7. Article 20(2) relates to *lis pendens* and related actions in **parental responsibility** and is slightly differently worded:

> Except where the jurisdiction of one of the courts is based solely on Article 15, where proceedings relating to parental responsibility relating to the same child and involving the same cause of action are instituted before courts of different Member

---

[5] CJEU, 16 January 2019, *Liberato*, C-386/17, para. 38; CJEU, 6 October 2015, *A*, C-489/14, paras 27 and 28, recalling that Article 19 Brussels II-bis (which has the same wording of the current rule) is framed along the lines of Article 27 of Regulation No 44/2001, which replaced Article 21 of the Brussels Convention 1998.

[6] See CJEU, 6 October 2015, *A*, C-489/14, para. 28.

States, the court second seised shall of its own motion stay its proceedings until such time as the jurisdiction of the court first seised is established.

5.8. The two provisions have a common core which will be treated jointly (see 5.26 et seq below), but differ in some important respects, which will be dealt with later on (see 5.58 et seq and 5.70 et seq below).

5.9. For both situations, Article 20 lays down the well-known criterion of chronological order, which embodies the *'prior in tempore, potior in iure'* **principle**. Accordingly, the court first seised with the subject matter shall have precedence and exercise jurisdiction, while the second seised court shall stay the proceedings and ultimately declare their lack of jurisdiction. Thus, a simple – and allegedly *over*simplified – mechanism is put in place which is clear and effective, aimed at preventing parallel proceedings before the courts of different Member States and to avoid conflicts between decisions which might result therefrom.[7] The practical application of such a rule, including the duties incumbent on both courts, is discussed at 5.26 et seq below.

5.10. Although a rule commonly used in most legal systems, it may be doubted whether the chronological principle is really appropriate for international family law cases, especially in separation/divorce cases. In fact, as already mentioned, when coupled with the multiple fora available under the Regulation, with the diversity of substantial laws applicable to divorce proceedings and with the lack of uniformity in choice-of-law rules, the chronological criterion leads to an unwelcome 'rush to the court' (see Chapter 3 at 3.8). It is well known that by choosing one court or the other, the claimant (or both of them) may not only choose the law applicable to divorce (and therefore the conditions and the timing for breaking the matrimonial tie, especially with regard to the differences between separation and divorce), but may also acquire a powerful weapon for negotiating on the many and delicate issues that often come together with ending the couple's married life. This side-effect is questionable and unreasonable in the light of a legal community which seeks a fair and objective access to justice.

5.11. Furthermore, Brussels II-ter extends the chronological principle to **related or dependent** actions, that is, to proceedings which are closely connected to each other, but are not identical in their parts. The notion of 'dependent action' is not defined by the Regulation, nor has it ever been the subject of a preliminary interpretation by the CJEU. Some guidance may, however, be inferred by the similar provision in the Brussels I-bis Regulation, Article 30(3) of which explains that:

> Actions are deemed to be related where they are so closely connected that it is expedient to hear and determine them together to avoid the risk of irreconcilable judgments resulting from separate proceedings.

---

[7] CJEU, 6 October 2015, *A*, C-489/14, paras 29–30; 16 January 2019, *Liberato*, C-386/17, para. 43.

The guiding principle is thus built around the declared aim to avoid irreconcilable decisions. Even if it is not expressly mentioned by the legislator in family matters, this same rationale is likely to be the underlying notion of dependent actions in the context of Brussels II-ter. While neither providing a formal definition nor taking a theoretical stance on the definition of 'related' or 'dependent', the legislator has unequivocally considered as dependent actions relating to divorce, legal separation or marriage annulment. Besides these clear examples, other cases where two proceedings are related or dependent cannot be excluded. In all cases, it is here submitted that the mechanical application underlying the chronological principle, with the automatic priority given to the first seised court, is at odds with proceedings where the issues at stake may require to be dealt with in a different order.

5.12. Notwithstanding its drawbacks, and while the chronological principle certainly has shown its inadequacy in some divorce/separation cases, its success is clearly linked to its **simple and clear** application which avoids any discretionary assessment.[8] This is further helped by the (acceptably) clear rules set out by the Regulation on how to determine when a court is seised (see Article 17, which is discussed in Chapter 2 at 2.3).

5.13. The rule leaves **no room for discretion** for the courts. In particular, it does not allow for an assessment as to whether the **decision** to be issued by the first court **is recognisable** in the State of the second seised court. This may give rise to some perplexities when reflecting that *lis pendens* aims at avoiding irreconcilable decisions. One would think it neither logical nor necessary to stay or dismiss proceedings, when the parallel proceedings pending in another Member State appear to lead to a decision that will not be capable of recognition in the forum.[9] However, such a predicted future outcome is indeed complicated and would lead to uncertainty and unpredictability. The political choice was thus made to exclude any such assessment and to move from the presumption that all decisions rendered by EU courts will be eligible for recognition.

---

[8] P. MANKOWSKI, 'Art. 20 Brussels IIter' in U. MAGNUS and P. MANKOWSKI (eds), *Brussels IIter Regulation*, OttoSchmidt, 2023, p. 281 para. 6 underlines how a clear and workable rule was deemed better than an opaque, if doctrinally purer, rule, especially given that the aim was to prevent and avoid complex and prolonged arguments over the better or more convenient forum when there are competing jurisdictions within the EU.

[9] T. RAUSCHER, *Europäisches Zivilprozess- und Kollisionsrecht, EuZPR/EuIPR. Kommentar*, Band IV, 4. Aufl., OttoSchmidt, 2015, p. 243, para. 48 highlights how not even a potential contrast with public policy of the future decision will prevent the second seised court from staying the proceedings. Any potential cause for non-recognition of the decision should be addressed to and solved by the first seised court. If this turns out to be impossible and the decision laid down by the first seised court results in a limping marriage, with one of the parties still bound to the marriage in the second court's Member State while the other is not, the only possibility is to start a new proceedings in the second court's legal system as soon as the first one is over.

5.14. In order to attenuate some of the above-mentioned inconveniences, a new provision, **Article 20(4)**, has been inserted into Brussels II-ter. Again this rule has been drafted along the lines of Article 31(3) Brussels I-bis with regard to civil and commercial matters. According to Article 20(4), the chronological principle shall not apply and the rule is displaced when the parties have conferred **exclusive competence** upon a court under Article 10. In such a case, any other court, even if first seised, must stay the proceedings until such time as the prorogated court declares that it has no jurisdiction (as per Article 20(5)).

5.15. In other words, Article 20(4)-(5) has the effect of **reversing the rule on** *lis pendens* in favour of the prorogated (but second seised) court. The concrete impact of the new rule is, however, strongly reduced by the fact that prorogation is only allowed in parental responsibility cases, which in practice have been less critical, due to the pre-eminent role of the ground of jurisdiction based on the child's habitual residence. In the case of matrimonial proceedings, which more often trigger the filing in parallel courts, no prorogation is possible.

C. THE SCOPE OF APPLICATION OF THE RULE: NO *LIS PENDENS* BETWEEN PROCEEDINGS ON MATRIMONIAL MATTERS AND PARENTAL RESPONSIBILITY

5.16. Before discussing the conditions for (and the consequences of) *lis pendens*, it is useful to define what **cannot** fall under this regime. First, there can be **no *lis pendens* between matrimonial proceedings and parental responsibility proceedings**. This is an issue which frequently arises in national courts, as a typical family law case usually involves both a horizontal issue, relating to the parents status, and a vertical one, relating to measures concerning the couple's children. In some national legal systems,[10] the problem is felt even more sharply as national rules may require the court seised with separation or divorce to make provisions for the protection of children before or as a condition to separating/divorcing their parents. Nonetheless, following the general policy of EU Regulations to address specific legal topics and provide for private international law rules for each subject matter, different matters should be dealt with separately, each of them under its own private international law rules and grounds for jurisdiction. As is apparent from the structure of Article 20, which provides for different rules at para. (1) and para. (2), there can be no *lis pendens* between proceedings on matrimonial matters and proceedings on custody of the child/children born to the same parents, regardless of how these proceedings are connected one to each other under national rules.

5.17. A different situation is when both the proceedings pending in courts of different Member States involve different issues arising out of a typical family law

---

[10] See for example in Croatia, Lithuania, Poland and Romania.

case: divorce/separation, custody over children, maintenance for the children and/or the spouse, and, possibly, matrimonial property. In such a case, which is common in practice, each of these issues will be governed by its own rule on *lis pendens*: with regard to divorce/separation Article 20(1) will apply; with regard to custody Article 20(2); and with regard to maintenance *lis pendens* will be governed by Article 12 (for *lis pendens*) or Article 13 (for related actions) of the Maintenance Regulation. The theoretical complexity of this framework is greatly reduced by the fact that all of these rules apply the same procedural pattern and will result, in practice, in giving precedence to the same proceedings.[11]

D. *LIS PENDENS* BETWEEN PROCEEDINGS ON THE MERITS AND PROCEEDINGS ON PROVISIONAL MEASURES

5.18. A different matter is the question of *lis pendens* between **proceedings on the merits and** parallel proceedings, between the same parties and involving the same cause of action, **for provisional measures.**

5.19. In contrast to what happens in most national legal systems, the solution in such a case cannot be inferred by the nature of the proceedings. As the CJEU made clear in *Purrucker II*:[12]

> No distinction can be drawn on the basis of the nature of the proceedings brought before those courts, that is, according to whether they are proceedings for interim relief or substantive proceedings.

5.20. What is relevant is the **ground for jurisdiction** which is being used by the court in the proceedings for provisional measures. Provisional measures may be granted either by the court having jurisdiction on the substance of the case, based on Articles 3–14, or by a court which does not have jurisdiction on the substance of the case, on the basis permitted by Article 15. The latter provision makes it possible, under given conditions, to make use of national grounds of competence to establish international jurisdiction. However, in such a case, the decision shall not be able to circulate and will have limited territorial effects.[13]

5.21. As the rationale for *lis pendens* in the area of freedom, security and justice is to **avoid irreconcilable decisions** – which would in turn lead to

---

[11] The case where a claim related to parental responsibility is brought in a matrimonial proceedings as a related action is slightly different. In this case rules on *lis pendens* relating to the dissolution of marriage will apply (see CJEU, 16 January 2019, *Liberato*, C-386/17, para. 36).

[12] CJEU, 9 November 2010, *Purrucker II*, C-296/10, paras 72 and 73. For the relevance of the different grounds of jurisdiction which may be used to take provisional measures (so called double-track), see Chapter 4, at 4.172 et seq.

[13] For more detail on this, see Chapter 4, para. 4.200 et seq.

refusal of recognition – there needs not to be *lis pendens* each time one of the two proceedings leads to a decision which cannot be recognised. This is what happens for a decision that is founded on Article 15. In other words, *lis pendens* may be triggered only between two proceedings – for example, one on the merits and one on provisional measures – that are both founded on grounds of jurisdiction which may lead to overlapping competence on the case. This may happen because there is more than one court which can exercise jurisdiction on the substance according to the Regulation. If one court is seised with the substance of the case and the other court with a provisional measure, there will be *lis pendens* between the two proceedings.[14] But if one court is seised on the substance (and maybe also with a provisional measure) and the other court is seised with a provisional measure on the basis of Article 15, there is no risk of *lis pendens*. In this case, the decision on the substance (and also the decision on a provisional measure) issued by the court of the merits shall always prevail over the other measure issued by the court based on Article 15, even when the latter court is the first seised court.

5.22. This solution has now been expressly adopted by **Article 20(2)**, which makes it clear that with regard to parental responsibility cases, the *lis pendens* rule applies '[e]xcept where the jurisdiction of one of the courts is based solely on Article 15'. This means that whenever one of the two parallel sets of proceedings is based on Article 15, there is no cause for *lis pendens* and Article 20 does not apply. While such a limitation is expressly provided only in relation to parental responsibility cases, the same should also be extended – on the basis of existing CJEU case law – to matrimonial disputes. However, it should be noted that it is difficult to imagine provisional measures which are related only to the status of spouses.

5.23. This solution had already been envisaged under Brussels II-bis and was first clarified by the CJEU in *Purrucker II*.[15] The case concerned baby twins, S and M, born in Spain to a Spanish and German couple. Upon separation, the parents agreed that the German mother would relocate to Germany with both babies. On the given date, however, baby S was unable to leave the hospital due to medical reasons. The mother left with baby M for Germany while baby S remained in Spain. A few months later, the father sought a provisional order before the Spanish court for custody of both children. Shortly afterwards, following internal Spanish rules, he also filed proceedings on the substance. In the meantime, the mother started custody proceedings for both children before

---

[14] For example, take the case where proceedings for parental responsibility are pending before the prorogated court of the parents' divorce (pursuing Article 10), and then a provisional measure on custody is requested from the court of the child's habitual residence under Article 7. Both courts would have full jurisdiction and between the two proceedings there would be *lis pendens*.

[15] CJEU, 9 November 2010, *Purrucker II*, C-296/10.

the German courts. The question arose as to whether the German court was second seised and should stay the proceedings.

5.24. The Court recalled that the rules relating to *lis pendens* are intended to prevent parallel proceedings before the courts of different Member States and to avoid conflicts between decisions which might result therefrom. It followed that:

> *Lis pendens* within the meaning of Article 19(2) … can therefore exist only where two or more sets of proceedings with the same cause of action are pending before different courts, and where the claims of the applicants, in those different sets of proceedings, are directed to *obtaining a judgment capable of recognition in a Member State other than that of a court seised as the court with jurisdiction as to the substance of the matter*.[16]

5.25. As settled as it now is, the proposed approach gives rise to practical problems when the basis on which jurisdiction is grounded in what appears to be the first court is **not stated** in the decision and/or is **unclear from the reasoning**. In the *Purrucker* case, for example, the German court had difficulty in understanding the ground for jurisdiction used by the Spanish court.[17]

II. COMMON PROCEDURAL ISSUES

A. ASCERTAINING THE COURT FIRST SEISED

5.26. The chronological principle governing *lis pendens* requires ascertaining **when each court is seised** so as to determine which one is the first seised. Such a crucial determination is made by applying the autonomous rule provided by **Article 17**.

5.27. The details and practical operation of this rule are discussed in Chapter 2 at 2.5 et seq. Suffice it to say here that Article 17 seeks to strike a balance between the different approaches to be found under national procedural laws and sets out unique rules to determine in an objective and undisputable way when exactly a court is seised. It thus gives relevance to the moment when the document instituting the proceedings is either lodged with the court or is received by the authority responsible for service, whichever of the two comes first, as long as the necessary subsequent steps to institute the proceedings have also been taken by the applicant. A different moment might be of relevance where proceedings are

---

[16] CJEU, 9 November 2010, *Purrucker II*, C-296/10, para. 72.
[17] On the good practice to clearly state the ground of jurisdiction on which such measure is taken that national courts should follow when issuing provisional measures, see Chapter 4 at 4.176–4.177.

instituted on the court's own motion, such as when the decision to institute the proceedings is actually taken by the court or when the case is registered by the court. In all cases, a simple comparison between the two moments in time will show which is the first seised court. Each court must separately undertake this assessment.

5.28. **Practical problems** might arise when the two moments are close in time. In such a situation, the relevant moment when each court is seised, as ascertained by each court, might be unclear and difficult to determine. In practice, this will require the **cooperation of the parties**, or communication among the courts involved, either directly or through the Central Authority.[18]

It should also be mentioned that while the rationale of *lis pendens* is based on pursuing general interests, such as a sound administration of justice and promoting free circulation of decisions, in terms of practicalities, its application is dependent on one of the parties raising a *lis pendens* exception. A situation that might pave the way towards disregarding the rule.

B. DUTIES OF THE FIRST SEISED COURT: ESTABLISHING JURISDICTION AND DECIDING ON THE SUBSTANCE

5.29. Once it is established which is the first seised court, that court will have the full and sole power to deal with parallel proceedings. Not only does Brussels II-ter give such a court full (and mechanical) precedence over the second seised court, irrespective of the nature of the ground of jurisdiction being used or it being better suited to hear the case; the first seised court also has the final word on the establishment of its own competence. In contrast, the second seised court can only stay or, at a later stage, dismiss the proceedings (see below at 5.33).

5.30. The first seised court must therefore establish its competence. Following the principle that each court is the **sole judge of its own competence**, each court must separately and unilaterally assess competence from its own point of view. This is a necessary consequence of the basic rule prohibiting jurisdiction of the court of the State of origin being reviewed (see Article 69) and in this case operates both ways.[19] Furthermore, each court is not bound by what the other

---

[18] P. Mankowski, above n. 8, p. 299, para. 85 goes as far as suggesting that a burden should be put on the counsel at least in the second set of proceedings to provide information about the progress made or to be expected in the first proceedings to the second seised court. The European Judicial Network might also provide a proper basis for direct communication between the courts concerned. Cases tend to illustrate the potential of direct judicial communication and cooperation.

[19] See the principle stated in CJEU, 16 January 2019, *Liberato*, C-386/17, paras 45 and 51.

court decides. Once a court has determined that it is the first seised court and that it has competence over the case according to the Regulation, it can **proceed on the substance of the case**. Brussels II-ter sets no other duty on such a court. While a communication duty from court to court is formally not envisaged, it is certainly not forbidden and indeed highly recommendable. In fact, at least in complex situations, it serves the interest of a sound administration of justice and possibly avoids the arising of future difficulties and/or procedural abuses of the parties.

5.31. Brussels II-ter does not specify the meaning of the expression '**establish its own competence**'. Practice shows that in most cases there will not be a formal decision 'establishing' jurisdiction, but this will be inferred by the fact that the court continues on the merits and decides the case. The CJEU has indeed upheld an informal assessment making it clear that:

> it is sufficient that the court first seised has not declined jurisdiction of its own motion and that none of the parties has contested that jurisdiction before or up to the time at which a position is adopted which is regarded in national law as being the first defence on the substance submitted before that court.[20]

While such an informal way of establishing jurisdiction is sufficient for the first court to proceed on the substance of the case in light of the need to avoid negative conflicts of competence, it is submitted that a formal and final decision on jurisdiction would be more appropriate for the purposes of the second seised court dismissing the case pursuant to Article 20(3).[21]

5.32. Some uncertainty arises where a decision on jurisdiction is taken by the court of first instance, which is then **challenged before a superior court**. Should this situation amount to an established jurisdiction for the purposes of Article 20(3)? In light of the purpose of avoiding negative conflict of competence pursued by the rule, the second seised court should continue to stay the proceedings until the matter is clarified in the first seised court. In a complex English case, *EA v. AP*,[22] parallel proceedings on separation/divorce, parental responsibility and maintenance for the wife and for the children were pending before the Italian and the UK courts. The Italian first-seised court denied jurisdiction on the parental responsibility claim (while confirming it on the separate matrimonial matters claim), but this decision was challenged

---

[20] See CJEU, 6 October 2015, *A*, C-489/14, para. 34.
[21] See further at 5.48. For a similar conclusion, see T. RAUSCHER, above n. 9, para. 46, pointing out that this may happen through an interlocutory decision on jurisdiction or a final decision on the merits.
[22] [2013] EWHC 2344 (Fam). See also the further case law cited by CLARKE HALL & MORRISON on Children, LexisNexis, Looseleaf, Division 1, Chapter 8, para. 1037, n. 4.

in the superior court, the Corte di Cassazione. The second-seised UK court rightfully stayed the decision considering that the Italian jurisdiction had not been established until a final decision was rendered.

C. DUTIES OF THE SECOND SEISED COURT

1. Staying the Proceedings

5.33. In contrast, the second seised court only has procedural duties and is not allowed to determine the merits of the case until parallel proceedings are pending. This, however, may change if the first proceedings, for whatever reason, are terminated (see below at 5.39 et seq).

5.34. Brussels II-ter creates a **two-step approach** which is intended to deal with (positive) conflict of competences, while avoiding negative conflict of competences which would occur if both courts declare a lack of jurisdiction. Pending any formal establishment of jurisdiction (see above at 5.31) by the first seised court, the second seised court shall only, by its own motion, **stay its proceedings**. This is clearly a duty for the court. The CJEU has found that by refusing to stay its proceedings and exercising jurisdiction, the second court infringes the provisions of Article 20.[23] However, at this stage the court should **not dismiss** the case. Staying the proceedings – if necessary for all the time needed to come to a final decision in the first seised court – will guarantee that both parties will always have access to justice.

5.35. Following the principle according to which each court is the sole judge of its own competence, the second seised court should **refrain from assessing the competence of the court in the other Member State** where parallel proceedings are pending. This rule operates in both possible situations, i.e. either when the first court appears *prima facie* to be lacking competence,[24] as well as when the first court clearly appears to have jurisdiction.[25] In both cases, the only duty and power for the second court is to stay the proceedings.

---

[23] This was the case in *Liberato*, where the CJEU clearly stated that the second seised Romanian court violated the Regulation. See CJEU, 16 January 2019, *Liberato*, C-386/17, para. 38.
[24] T. RAUSCHER, above n. 9, para. 46 points out that also in the case where the first court wrongly founds its competence on the *lex fori*, this cannot be 'corrected' by the second seised court.
[25] I. KUNDA and D. VRBLJANAC, 'Lis Pendens and Dependent Actions' in C. HONORATI (ed.), *Jurisdiction in Matrimonial Matters, Parental Responsibility and International Abduction*, Giappichelli/Peter Lang, 2017, p. 217, refer the case of a Croatian court (County Court in Varaždin, 2 April 2014, P-3/14) which, having established that parallel proceedings had been first initiated in Germany, dismissed the petition, explaining that it was for the German court to exercise jurisdiction. The decision was reached on the circumstances alleged by the parties, according to which their habitual residence was in Germany. The authors rightly criticise the decision and emphasise that by deciding on its own jurisdiction and dismissing the case, the

5.36. The duty to stay and allow the first seised court to establish its own competence may lead to an **abusive exploitation** of the mechanism on *lis pendens*. Filing the first proceedings in a jurisdiction where proceedings are excessively lengthy, or very expensive, will prevent any other court from deciding on the merits of the dispute and will result in a disadvantage for the party seeking a quick definition of the matrimonial dispute. Even in this case, the second seised court can only wait for the first seised court to decide. In particular, the average excessive length of proceedings in a jurisdiction, or the excessive delay in ascertaining and establishing jurisdiction of the first court in the given case, cannot be a cause of exception to this rule. A decision on this point was given by the ECJ in the *Gasser* case.[26] Although given in the context of the 1968 Brussels Convention, the identical rationale and the identical structure of the rule requires that the same solution is given in relation to Brussels II-ter.

5.37. In *Gasser*, the second seised UK court contested the rule (the then Article 21 of the 1968 Brussels Convention) mandating a stay in favour of the first seised Italian court. In particular, the UK court argued that the rule should be discarded when the claimant brought proceedings in bad faith before a court (possibly lacking jurisdiction) for the purpose of blocking proceedings before the courts of another Contracting State, and the court first seised had not decided the question of its jurisdiction within a reasonable time.[27] The automatic operation of the *lis pendens* rule would grant the potential debtor (the claimant in the first proceedings) a substantial and unfair advantage which would enable him to control the procedure, or indeed dissuade the creditor from enforcing his rights by legal proceedings. Instead, the rule should be interpreted in conformity with Article 6 ECHR and be construed so as to preserve the right to a fair trial.

5.38. The ECJ gave a quick and concise answer to the grounds put forward, sharply stating that such a construction would be 'manifestly contrary both to the letter and spirit and to the aim of the Convention'.[28] The principle of mutual trust underlying the Convention, the need to ensure legal certainty and, for individuals, to foresee with sufficient certainty which court will have jurisdiction conflict with the idea of the second court unilaterally deciding when and if the

---

Croatian court second seised has in fact denied the German (first seised) court of its right to decide on its own. This is a prerogative of the first seised court, and all other courts should remain inactive until such a decision is rendered. The Croatian court should have stayed the proceedings and awaited the decision on jurisdiction by the German court.

[26] ECJ, 9 December 2003, *Gasser*, C-116/02.
[27] According to the UK court, a reasonable time for a decision on jurisdiction to be given would be within six months following the commencement of proceedings before the court first seised or a final decision on jurisdiction within one year following the commencement of those proceedings (see ECJ, 9 December 2003, *Gasser*, C-116/02, para. 60).
[28] ECJ, 9 December 2003, *Gasser*, C-116/02, para. 70.

first seised court should continue the proceedings. It is submitted that the same answer would still be appropriate today under Brussels II-ter.

5.39. In order for the *lis pendens* rule to apply, **both proceedings should be pending at the same time**. If one of the two proceedings has ended for whatever reason, there is no risk of conflicting decisions and the only proceeding left pending will continue. This may occur on procedural grounds, as the facts in the *A* case show.[29]

5.40. The *A* case concerned the divorce of two French citizens who were resident in the UK. When the husband lodged a request for judicial separation with the French court, the wife responded by filing a petition for divorce with the UK court. The UK court found that it was second seised and declined jurisdiction in respect of the divorce petition.

5.41. The proceedings before the French court continued with the adoption of a non-conciliation order on 15 December 2011. Time passed and the husband did not file the petition for separation, which is required by French procedural law. Instead, he filed a divorce petition, which was rejected on the grounds of the pending separation proceedings. Following French procedural law, when 30 months have elapsed from the making of the non-conciliation order, the provisions of the order expire and the proceedings are automatically terminated. This occurred at midnight on 16 June 2014. On 13 June 2014, the wife filed a new divorce petition with a UK court. On 17 June 2014, at 8.20 am local time, the husband filed a second divorce petition with a French court.

5.42. The husband applied to the UK court for his wife's divorce petition to be dismissed on the ground that the jurisdiction of the French courts had been unambiguously and incontrovertibly established. However, the Court of Justice rejected such an argument, stating that:

> a situation of *lis pendens* was existent until midnight on 16 June 2014. Once that date had passed, that is to say, at 00.00 on 17 June, since the proceedings before the French court first seised had lapsed as a result of the expiry of the provisions of the non-conciliation order made by that court, only the United Kingdom court seised on 13 June 2014 remained seised of a dispute falling within one of the areas referred to in Article 19(1) of Regulation No 2201/2003. The commencement on 17 June 2014 of divorce proceedings before a French court was subsequent to the commencement of the proceedings brought before that United Kingdom court. Taking into account the chronological rules laid down by that Regulation, it must be held that the effect of that sequence of events is that, subject to its being lawfully seised under the rules in Article 16 of Regulation No 2201/2003, the United Kingdom court became the court first seised.[30]

---

[29] CJEU, 6 October 2015, *A*, C-489/14.
[30] CJEU, 6 October 2015, *A*, C-489/14, para. 40.

The decision provides a good example of the mechanical application of the chronological rule (see above at 5.10 for some concerns regarding this). It also shows that the pendency of proceedings in another State does not prevent the useful filing of proceedings in a different Member State court. And, of course, this may prove useful if, for any reason, the first one is terminated. In the *A* case, the fact that another proceedings was already pending before a French court when the UK court was seised for the second time did not preclude that court from being properly seised.

5.43. Staying the proceedings is a duty of the court whenever the situation described above is clearly envisaged. However, it is unclear whether there should be a **formal *lis pendens* exception**, raised by one of the parties, in order for the court to acknowledge the *lis pendens* situation, or if this is an ***ex officio* duty** for the court. While the common practice is that courts will rely on the interest of one of the parties to bring such a situation to their attention, it cannot be excluded that in some cases the competence of the court is not formally challenged, and informal notice of a parallel proceedings filed elsewhere eventually arises at a later stage in the course of the proceedings. Under the previous text in Brussels II-bis, it would be assumed that it is always a duty of the court, also *ex officio*, to stay the proceedings from the moment that it receives notice of a parallel proceedings pending elsewhere, and when it assumes to be the second seised court. However, such a conclusion may now be questioned following the introduction of a new rule (Article 10) allowing – albeit only in parental responsibility matters – some room for prorogation of competence.[31]

5.44. Indeed, the behaviour of a party who, after successfully filing proceedings before the court of one Member State, appears in proceedings subsequently filed by the other party in a different Member State and does not contest the lack of jurisdiction may amount to a **tacit prorogation of competence of the second seised court**.[32] Such a situation was not envisaged under Brussels II-bis and has been newly addressed by Brussels II-ter. It therefore requires some further consideration. According to the second paragraph of Article 10(2), a lack of opposition by the person who appears in the proceedings (after the court was seised) shall be regarded as an implicit agreement to the court's competence. Accordingly, the court's competence may thus be prorogated by the unequivocal

---

[31] See Chapter 4, at 4.43 et seq.
[32] Take the case where a couple with children file for divorce. One of the parents first files a claim for parental responsibility in the State of residence of the child. When the other parent files a petition for divorce and a claim for parental responsibility in the State of their common residence, the first parent appears in the second seised court not only in relation to the divorce petition, but also argues on the substance of parental responsibility, claiming custody and possibly maintenance obligations. If such a party does not raise a *lis pendens* exception, and the claimant in the second seised court also has no interest in raising the issue, the question arises as to what the second court should do.

behaviour of the parties. This approach supports the view that if the claimant in the first seised court appears in the second seised court without contesting jurisdiction, such a behaviour amounts to a tacit prorogation and may fall under the provision of Article 20(5), thus reversing the duties of the two courts.

5.45. Furthermore, acceding to such a construction, which in all cases will need to be confirmed in practice, means that extreme caution should be used by the second seised court when the parties do not raise a *lis pendens* exception. The rationale underlying *lis pendens* serves not only the interests of the parties, but also the interests of a sound administration of justice, the pursuit of which should not rest entirely on the parties' behaviour.[33] While allowing some flexibility within the mechanical operation of *lis pendens*, which may be sensible and serve the interests of all, it seems reasonable that the second seised court should act with caution and take the necessary steps to ascertain that consistent behaviour is maintained by the parties in the first seised court. This may imply that both of them have taken what is necessary in the first seised court to terminate the proceedings in that forum before the second seised court can proceed on the merits. It should also be kept in mind that when assessing whether a valid prorogation under Article 10 is in place, the court must also assess whether this serves the best interests of the child.[34]

5.46. The only case where the second court can proceed on the substance, disregarding the fact that parallel proceedings has been previously filed, is when the parties have formally **prorogated the competence** of such court **and** made this **exclusive** pursuant to **Article 20(5)**. As previously mentioned (see above at 5.14 et seq), the effect of this new rule is to invert the duties incumbent on the courts. The first seised court will then stay the proceedings; the second seised court – which will base its jurisdiction on the parties' agreement – will assess its own competence and eventually proceed on the substance. In order to assess its own competence, the court must examine whether the formal and substantial requirements set by Article 10 are met. It should be recalled that prorogation is allowed only in parental responsibility cases and not in matrimonial matters.

2. *Declining Jurisdiction*

5.47. Only as a **second step** is the second seised court required to decline jurisdiction and dismiss the case. The first paragraph of Article 20(3) provides that: 'Where the jurisdiction of the court first seised is established, the court second seised shall decline jurisdiction in favour of the court first seised.'

---

[33] See also 5.28 above.
[34] See above, Chapter 4 at 4.79 et seq.

5.48. It is therefore only at this stage that the second seised court is allowed to close and dismiss the case. In order to avoid so-called negative conflict of competence – where neither of the seised courts settles the dispute between the parties – the greatest caution should be exercised when dismissing a case. Furthermore, declining jurisdiction amounts to refusing access to the seised court. For both reasons, declining jurisdiction should be a last-resort event and declared only when the second seised court is confident that the case is fully heard in the first seised court. For these reasons, a formal and final decision, either on jurisdiction or on the full merits of the case, should be required before a decision pursuant to Article 20(3) on dismissing jurisdiction is taken (see 5.31 above). In all other cases, it is suggested that the second seised court limits itself to staying the proceedings.

5.49. On the other hand, when a **formal decision** 'establishing jurisdiction' is taken in the first seised court, the second seised court should necessarily decline jurisdiction. This is a formal duty upon the court, which shall also act *ex officio*. Any assessment, including one on the potential lack of recognition of the future decision laid down by the first seised court, is surely excluded (see 5.13 above).

5.50. Where the second seised court declares its lack of competence in favour of the first seised court, the claimant/applicant in such proceedings is granted a special procedural right. The **second paragraph** of Article 20(3) provides that: 'In that case, the party who instituted proceedings before the court second seised may bring those proceedings before the court first seised.'[35]

5.51. This rule serves the purpose of granting access to justice to the party who has seised a court which in principle has competence under the Regulation, but in the given case is deprived of exercising such competence because of the need to coordinate with other jurisdictions. However, the rule does not amount to an independent ground of jurisdiction, displacing the system of rules on competence set out by Brussels II-ter. Hence, in order for the first seised court to hear the new claim brought by the respondent, such a claim must be independently grounded in one of the other heads of jurisdiction provided by the Regulation. With regard to matrimonial matters, this may also (but not necessarily) be founded on Article 4 (Counterclaim) or on Article 5 (Conversion of legal separation to divorce). With regard to parental responsibility cases, this might prove to be more difficult, with the result that the first seised court might lack competence to hear the new claim.

5.52. Article 20(3) is useful with regard to the court's first seised *lex fori* rules, which may have deadlines and rules barring a successful lodging of a

---

[35] It should be stressed that this rule applies only in the case envisaged by Article 20(3), i.e. when the second seised court declines jurisdiction and dismisses the case. It is **not** be applicable under Article 20(2), that is, when and until the second seised court stays the proceedings.

new claim at a later stage. For this provision to have a useful effect and not be merely declaratory, it should be understood that, following a decision declining jurisdiction by the second seised court, it should always be possible for the respondent to lodge a new claim in the first seised court and that this **cannot be precluded by internal procedural rules** which are consequently displaced. While such a construction is consistent with the need for a coordination of proceedings which must not jeopardise the citizens' access to courts, it may lead to uncertainties where the proceedings have reached the appellate court.[36]

D. CASES WHERE THE SECOND SEISED COURT MUST DECIDE ON THE SUBSTANCE

5.53. In principle, the second seised court should only decide on the substance of the case in exceptional circumstances. This may happen in two cases. First, this will occur when the **first court** dismisses the case **on the ground of lack of jurisdiction**. This is the case expressly envisaged by Article 20. The second seised court should wait until the decision in the first seised court is final and no longer challengeable.

5.54. The second circumstance is when the proceedings have come to an end in the first seised court. In this case the preclusive effect of *lis pendens* will no longer operate. If the decision is one **denying separation or divorce**, the second seised court will be free to (again) decide this claim. In fact, according to Recital (9), decisions refusing the dissolution of matrimonial ties are not covered by its provisions on recognition.[37]

---

[36] For contrasting views on the operation of Article 20(3) when the first seised proceedings are pending before the appellate court, see T. RAUSCHER, above n. 9, pp. 244–245, paras 53–54 (contrary) and U. SPELLENBERG, 'Article 20' in U. SPELLENBERG and D. HENRICH (eds), *Staudinger's Kommentar zum BGB, Internationales Verfahrensrecht in Ehesachen*, 14th ed., Sellier/De Gruyter, Munich 2005, para. 26 (in favour).

[37] See Chapter 1 at 1.26. Indeed, the Explanatory Report on the Brussels Convention (the Borras Report), OJ C 221, 16.7.98, para. 60 notes that during the negotiations on the Brussels Convention, there was much discussion as to whether the term 'judgment' covered only positive decisions or whether it also covered negative decisions adopted in a Member State. The Report further clarifies that, since the received mandate was to facilitate recognition and enforcement of divorces, legal separations and marriage annulments, the word 'judgment' refers only to positive decisions, that is, those that do grant a divorce, legal separation or marriage annulment. This understanding has followed through in subsequent versions of the Regulation and it should also be applied under Brussels II-ter. In other words, decisions refusing divorce, legal separations and marriage annulments fall outside of the scope of Brussels II-ter (see Recital (9) and *Practice Guide for the Application of the Brussels IIb Regulation*, 2022, p. 23).

E. THE ALTERNATIVE OF CONSIDERING A TRANSFER OF PROCEEDINGS FROM THE FIRST SEISED COURT TO THE SECOND SEISED COURT

5.55. Besides allowing the first seised court to take precedence and deal with the substance of the case, another option could be open to the two courts involved. Albeit this it is not expressly mentioned by Article 20, there must surely be the possibility of also **applying the rules on transfer of proceedings** to *lis pendens* cases. This would allow the proceedings to be held before a court that, although not the first seised, is deemed to be better placed in the specific circumstances. Making use of the rules on transfer of proceedings might help to **reduce the impact of the mechanical operation** of the chronological principle and therefore minimise the effects of a rush-to-the-court for the sake of securing the most favourable court. The first seised court should, if it considers that the second seised court, albeit formally not vested with the case, is better placed to hear the case and if the conditions for a transfer of proceedings laid down by Article 12 are satisfied, request that this court assume jurisdiction. Correspondingly, the second seised court could benefit from the now explicit possibility afforded by Article 13 and request a transfer of jurisdiction from the first seised court.

5.56. It is true that both rules on transfer of proceedings (Articles 12 and 13) in principle apply only when the court to which the proceedings are transferred does not have jurisdiction under Brussels II-ter. This condition is expressly stated in Article 13 and was held by the Court of Justice to be the proper construction of the former Article 15[38] (now Article 12). With regard to *lis pendens*, such a prerequisite will not be met at the outset because, by definition, both courts must have jurisdiction. However, when the first court has established jurisdiction, the second seised court will automatically be deprived of the power to hear the case. Hence, insofar as the condition for the operation of transfer of proceedings applies to a court which would otherwise not have the power to decide, the precondition is satisfied.

5.57. Transfer of proceedings only applies in parental responsibility cases.[39] Consequently, in cases concerning matrimonial matters, there are again no means to redress what in some cases is an inefficient way to coordinate parallel proceedings, as will be seen in the following paragraphs.

---

[38] See CJEU, 4 October 2018, *IQ*, C-478/17, para. 38–40 and further above Chapter 4 at 4.118 et seq.
[39] See Chapter 4 at 4.112 et seq.

III. *LIS PENDENS* IN MATRIMONIAL MATTERS CASES

A. THE NOTION OF SAME PROCEEDINGS AND THE CASE OF 'FALSE *LIS PENDENS*'

5.58. As mentioned earlier (at 5.5), Brussels II-ter provides an **autonomous definition** of 'same proceedings' for the purposes of *lis pendens*. The rule thus encompasses both the case of two proceedings which are identical – that is, they are between the same parties, have the same object and the same cause of action – *and* the case of related (or dependent) actions. Indeed, given the differences among national substantive laws, the latter will be the most frequent case. As the applicable rule is the same, there is no need to distinguish between cases involving the same cause of action and therefore amounting to a 'true' *lis pendens*, and cases where the two proceedings are only dependent or related to each other.[40]

5.59. This is of great importance for those Member States whose internal law acknowledges both legal separation and divorce. The two proceedings are generally construed as being different from each other. In fact, they do not have the same subject matter, nor do they have the same effect on the marriage tie. Legal separation allows the couple to live separately and simply attenuates such a bond; in contrast, divorce definitely resolves and dissolves the matrimonial tie between former spouses. All this becomes irrelevant in the framework of Brussels II-ter as the relationship between all such proceedings falls into the same pattern of dependent actions, sometime referred to as **false *lis pendens***.

5.60. According to Article 20(1), applications in matrimonial matters brought before the courts of different Member States are **not required to have the same cause of action**, provided that they concern judicial separation, divorce or marriage annulment. The rationale is to avoid having two decisions on the **same matrimonial tie** being made, thus leading to the **irreconcilability of decisions**. Such an interpretation is supported by a comparison between Article 20(1) and Article 20(2), which shows that the same cause of action is required only in regard of proceedings relating to parental responsibility. Consequently, a situation of *lis pendens*/dependent actions may exist either when two courts are seised of an

---

[40] The two situations are instead treated under different rules by the Brussels I-bis Regulation (see Article 29 and Article 30) and by the Maintenance Regulation (see Article 12 and Article 13). It should also be mentioned how both these latter Regulations use the term 'Related actions' instead of the term 'Dependent actions' used by Article 20 Brussels II-ter. Other versions use the same term through all the instruments (see for example the terms 'cause connesse' in Italian). For the finding that there is a 'notable difference' between 'dependent actions' for the purposes of Article 20 and 'related actions' within the framework of the other Regulations, see P. MANKOWSKI, above, n. 8, p. 283, para. 13.

application for divorce or when two courts of different Member States are seised with judicial separation proceedings in one case and divorce proceedings in the other. This construction is settled law and has been confirmed by the CJEU in several judgements.[41]

5.61. Notwithstanding it being settled law, such a provision opens up the way to several **problems** and, on an overall assessment, does not seem to lead to a satisfying settlement of disputes in matrimonial matters.[42] The truth is that the wide scope of *lis pendens* for matrimonial proceedings combined with the huge variety of different national rules in matrimonial matters has the effect of favouring bargaining strategies and delaying of proceedings which are neither in the interests of parties nor a sign of an efficient administration of justice. Member States which require legal separation generally consent to filing a divorce petition only after some time has elapsed since the separation decision is laid down. Separation proceedings already started in this State will preclude from filing divorce proceedings in another Member State. However, as soon as these proceedings are terminated and the *lis pendens* preclusion is over, each party can file for divorce in the other Member State, and the separation decision will have no effect.

5.62. Coordination problems are only partially reduced by the unification of the conflict-of-law rules in divorce, separation and annulment matters, as achieved by the **Rome III Regulation**. It is true that this instrument allows the parties to agree on the law applicable to their divorce and thus to choose the law which grants a faster and less troublesome divorce, but in order for a valid choice of law to be reached, the parties must be in agreement, something which is not always the case when the couple is experiencing a crisis. Furthermore, Rome III is based on an enhanced cooperation and does not apply to all Member States.[43]

It should be recalled that the scope of application of Brussels II-ter – and thus of the rule envisaged here – covers only the status of the spouses. It does not extend to further issues connected to the breakdown of the marriage.[44] In particular, the Regulation applies neither to the grounds for the breakdown of the marriage[45] nor to other measures that may be required in the frame of such proceedings, such as maintenance obligations in favour of the spouses or of

---

[41] See CJEU, 6 October 2015, *A*, C-489/14, para. 33; CJEU, 16 January 2019, *Liberato*, C-386/17, para. 35.
[42] For strong criticism of this construction, see T. RAUSCHER, above n. 9, p. 243, para. 48, who argues that what is required to the court – i.e the *petitum*, the judicial definition asked to the court – in the two proceedings on separation and on divorce is different.
[43] As of October 2023, the Regulation is in force in only 17 Member States: Austria, Belgium, Bulgaria, Estonia, France, Germany, Greece, Hungary, Italy, Latvia, Lithuania, Luxembourg, Malta, Portugal, Romania, Slovenia and Spain.
[44] See Chapter 1 at 1.26.
[45] See Recital (9) and Chapter 1 at 1.26.

common children or the property consequences of a marriage breaking down. Each of these issues will fall under its own Regulation and will be subject to its own *lis pendens* rule. This means that when a claim only for divorce is lodged in one Member State and, at a later stage, a claim for divorce, maintenance obligation and/or division of matrimonial property and/or damages because of a separation for fault is filed with the court of another Member State, such second seised court must stay/dismiss the claim on the status of the person, but will retain the claim on the other issues of maintenance, matrimonial property or damages.

B. THE SAME PARTIES

5.63. The actions in the parallel proceedings must be brought 'between **the same parties**', which means that the same physical persons have to be the parties in each proceeding. Their respective procedural role is irrelevant, as this will in most cases be reversed in each court.[46]

5.64. While the identity of the parties will normally not be an issue in matrimonial matters, it cannot be excluded that one set of proceedings may be instituted either by a third party or by a public body.[47] On a literal construction, this example shall not fall under Article 20, as the parties would be different. Nonetheless, a functional interpretation would require that such proceedings are considered related and the second seised court stays the proceedings as the risk of rendering irreconcilable decisions would be at its highest.[48]

IV. *LIS PENDENS* IN PARENTAL RESPONSIBILITY CASES

A. THE SAME CAUSE OF ACTION

5.65. Article 20(2) also provides an **autonomous definition** of how the notion of 'same proceedings' should be construed in proceedings relating to parental responsibility. The two proceedings must each concern **parental responsibility** and have the 'same cause of action', the provision **not** extending to merely related

---

[46] *2022 Practice Guide for the Application of Brussels IIb Regulation*, p. 34. The point had already been made in ECJ, 6 December 1994, *Tatry*, C-406/92, para. 31.
[47] For example, imagine the case of A instituting a divorce proceedings against B in one State, and then C instituting a proceedings for the annulment of marriage against B in another State, on the ground that B was already married to A (for this example, see D. KUNDA and D. VRBLJANAC, above n. 25, p. 236. Further examples are given in M. NÍ SHÚILLEABHÁIN, *Cross border Divorce Law. Brussels II bis*, Oxford University Press, 2010, para. 5.10.
[48] For the same conclusions, see D. KUNDA and D. VRBLJANAC, above n. 25, p. 237.

actions. The first term identifies the subject matter of the action and pursuant to Article 2(7) must be interpreted as including:

> all rights and duties relating to the person or the property of a child which are given to a natural or legal person by a decision, by operation of law or by an agreement having legal effect, including rights of custody and rights of access.[49]

5.66. More complicated is defining '**same cause of action**'. This term, too, must be construed autonomously and must not depend on national rules. However, its exact meaning is still unclear. It should be noted that the English version of Article 20 still refers only to the same 'cause of action', overlooking that other language versions also include the requirement of the **same object** of the proceedings. However, as has been made clear by the CJEU since 1987 with reference to the then Article 19 of the 1968 Brussels Convention,[50] also the English language version must be construed in the same manner as the majority of the other language versions which include both requirements.[51] Following that ruling, the 'cause of action' comprises the facts and the rule of law relied on as the basis of the action, and the 'object of the action' means the aim that the action has in view.[52] On this basis, legal literature has proposed that 'cause of action' is to be identified as what is the 'disputed matter',[53] or the 'central issue'[54] of the proceedings or the 'gleiche Grundlage'.[55] However, it is doubtful whether this will be helpful in controversial cases, as will be illustrated below.

5.67. Both the 'cause of action' and 'object' of the claim will generally be assessed on the basis of the assumptions made by the applicant/claimant in their introductory application. However, if either party to the proceedings subsequently modifies their initial application and the *lex fori* so permits, the

---

[49] For a wider interpretation of the notion, see Chapter 1 at 1.37 et seq.
[50] The point was stated in ECJ, 8 December 1987, *Gubisch Maschinenfabrik*, 144/86, para. 14 and was reaffirmed in ECJ, 6 December 1994, *Tatry*, C-406/92, para. 37.
[51] See the Italian, Spanish and French text, which use the wider expression referring to 'il medesimo titolo e il medesimo oggetto', 'la misma causa y el mismo objeto' and 'la même cause et le même objet'.
[52] See again ECJ, 6 December 1994, *Tatry*, C-406/92, at para. 38 and para. 40 respectively. In *Tatry* the ECJ concluded that an action for a declaration of non-liability brought by the shipowners, and another action brought by the cargo owners on the basis of a ship concerning a cargo transported in bulk and damaged, had the same cause of action. Furthermore, the second action had the same object as the first, since the issue of liability was central to both actions. Therefore, the action seeking to have the defendant held liable for causing loss (and ordered to pay damages) had the same cause of action and the same object as earlier proceedings brought by that defendant seeking a declaration that he was not liable for that loss.
[53] P. MANKOWSKI, above n. 8, p. 294, para. 60.
[54] A. MALATESTA, 'Art. 19' in S. CORNELOUP (ed.), *Droit européen du divorce. European Divorce Law*, LexisNexis, 2013, fn. 20.
[55] T. RAUSCHER, above n. 9, p. 239, para. 39.

modified and not the initial application should be relevant for determining the cause of the respective action.

5.68. Moving from theory to practice, it is to be understood that the two claims do not need to be formally identical, it being sufficient that they share the same 'hard core' of the case. One may assume, therefore, that there is *lis pendens* for the purposes of Article 20 between proceedings on custody over a child and a proceedings for access to the same child.[56] Although the final measure formally requested before the court will have a different content (custody as opposed to access), both proceedings imply the application of the same rule and share the hard core of regulating the parent/child relationship. However, things may be more controversial in other cases – for example, where a claim for changing the child's habitual residence is filed in one State and a parallel claim for access to the same child is filed in another State.[57]

5.69. In contrast, there will **be no** *lis pendens* for the purposes of Article 20 between proceedings for the placement of a child in a foster family and proceedings for access to that same child. Similarly, an application for the return of a child under the 1980 Hague Convention will not be the same cause of action as an application for parental responsibility.[58] Finally, as previously mentioned (see above at 5.16), matrimonial proceedings will never be considered as the 'same cause' as a parental responsibility proceedings and are also not 'related' to one another, regardless of what national law rules may otherwise provide.

B. PROCEEDINGS RELATED TO THE SAME CHILD BUT BROUGHT BY DIFFERENT PARTIES

5.70. It comes as no surprise that parallel proceedings must concern the **same child**. It is only when different decisions affect the same child that a situation of irreconcilability will arise. By contrast, the rule does not cover the situation where the same parents litigate for the same parental responsibility claim over their two children, and address a claim in relation to one child in one State and the other claim in relation to the other child in another State. This may happen if the two children have their habitual residence in different Member States – for example, because of their educational needs. In such a case, there is formally no *lis pendens* and the two proceedings could run in parallel. Indeed,

---

[56] Similarly, see T. RAUSCHER, above n. 9, p. 220, para. 40.
[57] In this case Article 20 would probably not require the second seised court to stay the proceedings (for this view, see D. KUNDA and D. VRBLJANAC, above, n. 25, p. 228), although the court may find it convenient to do so. Conditions and timing of access to the non-custodial parent will vary depending on the habitual residence of the child.
[58] See CJEU, 22 December 2010, *Mercredi*, C-497/10, para. 71.

the decision ending each proceeding would not be formally in conflict with the other. However, the courts may find it reasonable and sensible to unify the two proceedings and define the case in light of the best interests of the siblings if their situation is assessed together. This could be achieved by transferring one of the two proceedings before one of the two courts. Another option would be for one of the two courts to stay the proceedings using internal rules that make this discretionary on the court and then to resume the case when the other proceeding has come to an end, and decide giving due weight to the decision taken by the other court. In all cases, communication between courts will be expedient and most advisable.

5.71. In contrast to what Article 20(1) provides for matrimonial matters, the **parties to the parallel proceedings may be different** in each set. This is especially the case where one of the two sets of proceedings concerning the same cause of action is brought by a public or a childcare authority and the other set by one or both parents. In addition, grandparents may be a relevant party to one set of proceedings. In any of these cases, as long as the proceedings concern the same child, there will be *lis pendens*.

5.72. It should also be emphasised that parties are not already required to have parental responsibility rights. Indeed, this could be the object of the proceedings and it is not a requirement for the operation of the rule on *lis pendens*.

CHAPTER 6

INTERNATIONAL CHILD ABDUCTION

I. Introduction 220
   A. The Nature of the Issue and the International Instruments
      Involved 220
   B. The Background History of the Application of Brussels II-ter. 221
II. An Overview of the Application of the 1980 Hague Convention to
    Return Applications 224
III. Applying Brussels II-ter to Child Abduction. 226
   A. Jurisdiction: Article 9. 226
      1. The Basic Position and its Rationale 226
      2. The Context in which Article 9 Operates 227
      3. The Conditions upon which Courts of the Member State
         of Refuge Acquire Jurisdiction 228
      4. Agreement on Jurisdiction 231
   B. The Position where Application is made under the 1980 Hague
      Convention 232
      1. The General Position under Article 22 232
      2. Removal and Retention 233
      3. Wrongful Removal/Retention: Breach of Rights of Custody 236
IV. Expediting the Processing and Hearing of Return Applications 239
   A. Receipt and Processing of Applications by Central Authorities 239
   B. Concentrating Jurisdiction 240
   C. Expeditious Court Proceedings 241
      1. The Six-Week Timeframe 241
      2. When the Six-Week Timeframe Begins 242
      3. The Nature of the Timing Obligation 243
      4. Expeditious Enforcement 244
V. Alternative Dispute Resolution 245
VI. The Right of the Child to Express His or Her Views in Return
    Proceedings 247
VII. The Procedure for the Return of the Child 248
   A. Giving the Applicant the Opportunity to be Heard. 248
   B. Contact with the Left-Behind Parent. 249

| | C. Refusals Based on Article 13(1)(b) of the Hague Convention 251
| | D. Taking Provisional Measures to Protect the Child from Grave
| | Risk of Harm upon His or Her Return. 252
VIII. Enforcing Decisions Ordering the Return of the Child 255
| | A. The Enforcement Process in the Member State of Refuge. 255
| | B. The Enforceability of Return Orders 255
IX. Refusing to Order a Child's Return – The Override Mechanism:
| | Article 29 257
| | A. The Background to the Override Mechanism. 257
| | B. The Operation of the Override Mechanism 259
| | C. When the Mechanism Applies. 259
| | D. Certificating the Decision to Refuse the Child's Return 260
| | E. The Position Following a Refusal to Return: The Background 261
| | 1. The Position Following a Refusal to Return: The Scheme
| | under Brussels II-ter. 262
| | 2. The Nature and Object of Article 29(3) and (5) Proceedings . . . 264
| | 3. Decisions Entailing the Child's Return. 264
| | i) The Need for a Certificate and the Requirements for
| | Certification. 266
| | ii) The Effect of Certificated Decisions. 267

I. INTRODUCTION

A. THE NATURE OF THE ISSUE AND THE INTERNATIONAL INSTRUMENTS INVOLVED

6.1. Chapter III of Brussels II-ter deals with the issue of international child abduction, that is, where children are removed across international jurisdictional boundaries or retained there by one parent without the other's consent. The reasons for abductions vary enormously: commonly, they occur where one parent (usually the mother) decides unilaterally to return with her children to her home country following a breakdown of the relationship with her husband or partner, or where one parent takes the children on holiday with the other's consent but then decides not to return, although there are also situations where the abduction is deliberately intended to frustrate an unfavourable court order or where the abduction itself is violent. However the abduction is perpetrated, its effects on the children can be devastating. It is likely to be traumatic in the short term and potentially permanently damaging in the long term. As Advocate General Emiliou put it:[1]

---

[1] Opinion, 12 January 2023, *Rzecznic Praw Dziecka and Others*, C-638/22 PPU, para. 1.

Child abduction cases are unquestionably some of the most sensitive in which a court may have to adjudicate. They arise in particularly charged and emotional and legal context, in which the mutual resentment of the parents, their feelings towards their child or children and the fundamental rights of both sides – which revolve around the best interest of the child or children – are intertwined.

6.2.   The harmful effects of child abduction are reflected by Article 11 of the United Nations Convention on the Rights of the Child (UNCRC), which obliges State Parties to take measures 'to combat the illicit transfer and non-return of children abroad'. Globally, the principal international instrument dealing with abduction is the 1980 Hague Convention on the Civil Aspects of International Child Abduction (the 1980 Hague Convention), to which, at the time of writing, there are 103 Contracting States, **including all EU Member States**. However, with regard to applications for the return of the child made under the 1980 Hague Convention **as between Member States (except Denmark)**,[2] Brussels II-ter operates to complement and supplement the application of the 1980 Hague Convention.

6.3.   It is important to appreciate that the legal instrument(s) to be applied depends on the States involved: if both the State from which the child has been abducted (that is, the State of the child's habitual residence) and the State to which the child abducted (that is, the State of refuge) are Member States (other than Denmark),[3] then the 1980 Hague Convention as supplemented by Brussels II-ter applies; if only one of the States is a Member State but both are parties to the Convention, the Convention applies *simpliciter*. If one of the States is a Member State but the other is not a Contracting Party to the 1980 Hague Convention, then, unless the 1996 Hague Child Protection Convention is applicable, and in the absence of any bilateral arrangements, national private international rules apply. This chapter is solely concerned with the first of the above situations.

B.   THE BACKGROUND HISTORY OF THE APPLICATION OF BRUSSELS II-TER

6.4.   Neither the 1998 Brussels II Convention nor the original Brussels II Regulation (hereinafter 'the 2001 Regulation') affected the operation of the

---

[2]   Denmark is not bound by Brussels II-ter; see Recital (96) and the discussion in Chapter 1 at 1.10.
[3]   The *2022 Practice Guide for the application of the Brussels IIb Regulation*, EU, 2022 (hereinafter the *2022 Practice Guide*) refers to the two States as the 'Member State of origin' and the 'Member State of refuge' respectively. It should be noted that is not sufficient that the forum is a Member State or that the child is resident in a Member State; see C. HONORATI and A. LIMINATE, 'Jurisdiction in Child Abduction Proceedings' in C. HONORATI (ed.), *Jurisdiction in Matrimonial Matters, Parental Responsibility and International Abduction*, Giappichelli/Peter Lang, 2017, p. 96.

1980 Hague Convention even as between two Member States. Indeed, on the contrary, Article 4 of the 2001 Regulation required Member States to exercise jurisdiction 'in conformity' with it.[4] In contrast, Article 60(e) Brussels II-bis provided that in relations between EU Member States, the Regulation took precedence over the Hague Convention 'insofar as they concern matters governed by this Regulation'.

6.5. The background to this radical change began with a French proposal aimed at facilitating the exercise of cross-border rights of access, but which also included proposals concerning abduction.[5] That proposal was followed by a European Commission's proposal[6] designed to improve the original Brussels II Regulation, but which addressed the problem of child abduction through provisions on jurisdiction and on the return of the child. The two proposals were amalgamated into a new Commission proposal.[7] That proposal would have effectively disapplied the 1980 Hague Convention as between Member States by allowing courts of the State of refuge worried about ordering the child's return, at best, only to make provisional holding orders and even then only provided the exceptions akin to those set out in Article 13 of the 1980 Hague Convention applied, with the courts of the child's habitual residence then being free to make custody orders according to the merits.

6.6. The proposal attracted protracted debate[8] and over which Member States were split. Eventually, a compromise (brokered by Denmark which, ironically, was not party to the Regulation) was reached. That compromise was broadly

---

[4] This was in contrast to the supremacy accorded to the Regulation (see Article 37) over the European Convention of 20 May 1980 on Recognition and Enforcement of Decisions Concerning Custody of Children and on the Restoration of Custody of Children and the Hague Convention of 19 October 1996 on Jurisdiction, Applicable Law, Recognition, Enforcement and Co-operation in Respect of Parental Responsibility and Measures for the Protection of Children.

[5] Initiative of the French Republic with a view to adopting a Council Regulation on the mutual enforcement of judgments on rights of access to children, OJ 2000 C234/7 (see the proposed Article 11). It is said that these proposals were based on the French dissatisfaction with how Germany was applying the Hague Convention in relation to France; see for example, P. McELEAVY 'The Brussels II Regulation: how the European Community has moved into family law' [2002] *International and Comparative Law Quarterly* 884, 904–930.

[6] Proposal for a Council Regulation on jurisdiction and the recognition and enforcement of judgments in matters of parental responsibility, OJ 2001 C332/269.

[7] Proposal for a Council Regulation concerning jurisdiction and the recognition and enforcement of judgments in matrimonial matters and in matters of parental responsibility repealing Regulation (EC) No 1347/2000 and amending Regulation (EC) No 44/2001 in matters relating to maintenance, Brussels 3.5.2002 COM(2002) 222 final.

[8] See, for example, the debate between N. LOWE, 'Article 5(3) of the Draft EU Regulation on Parental Responsibility: Dealing with Child Abduction' [2002] *International Family Law* 36 and I. KARSTEN 'Article 5(3) of the Draft EU Regulation on Parental Responsibility: A Reply' [2002] *International Family Law* 42.

that applications for return of children wrongfully removed or retained would continue to be dealt with under the 1980 Hague Convention, but, in the event of a refusal to return, the court then had to notify the court of the requesting State which in turn had to notify the parties giving them the opportunity to pursue the custody claim which would be decided upon the merits. If that court then required the child's return, that order would be enforceable without further question.

6.7. The impact of Brussels II-bis on the operation of the 1980 Hague Convention[9] was more extensive than might have been contemplated at the time of the compromise. The basic scheme was to:

1. preserve the pre-eminence of the 1980 Hague Convention for dealing with applications for the return of abducted children, but nevertheless to give some direction on how that Convention should be applied as between Member States; and
2. govern the position in cases where a court refuses to make a return order under the Convention.

6.8. Notwithstanding that some viewed the relationship between the Convention and the Regulation as an uneasy one,[10] Brussels II-ter adopts the same strategy as before,[11] but with some important differences, including the following:

- clarifying that Brussels II-ter applies to return applications made directly to a court and not just those made via a Central Authority;
- providing more extensive provisions governing the timing of return applications and enforcement proceedings;
- adding provision for alternative dispute resolution;
- amending the provision for hearing the child;
- providing for the enforceability of a return order; and
- clarifying but also narrowing the scope of the 'override provisions'

---

[9] For an extensive commentary on Article 11 Brussels II-bis, see E. Pataut and E. Gallant, 'Article 11' in U. Magnus and P. Mankowski (eds), *Brussels IIbis Regulation*, OttoSchmidt, 2017, 131 et seq.

[10] See, for example, D. Martiny, 'New efforts in Judicial cooperation in European child abduction Cases' (2021) 4 *Polski Proces Cywilny* 501; and P. McEleavy 'The New Child Abduction Regime in the European Union: Symbiotic Relationship or Forced Partnership?' (2005) 1 *Journal of Private International Law* 5, 26.

[11] That is, it does not adopt the radical proposal by M. Hat'apka, 'Article 11 of the Brussels IIa Regulation: is there justification for return proceedings in the area of harmonised rules of jurisdiction and mutual recognition of decisions?' [2014] *International Family Law* 182 to abolish return applications altogether. See also J. Antomo 'Die Neufassung der Brüssel IIa-Verordnung' in T. Pfeiffer, Q.C. Lombach and T. Rapp (eds), *Europäisches Familien- und*

6.9. One result of these changes is that whereas under Brussels II-bis there was a single Article dealing parental child abduction, there is now a separate chapter governing the issue. Furthermore, there are special rules in Chapter IV dealing with the enforcement return orders made under the so-called 'override mechanism'.[12] This expanded coverage, as well as the inclusion of 'international child abduction' in the title of Brussels II-ter, reflects the importance that is attached to the issue.

II. AN OVERVIEW OF THE APPLICATION OF THE 1980 HAGUE CONVENTION TO RETURN APPLICATIONS

6.10. Before discussing how Brussels II-ter operates in conjunction with the 1980 Hague Convention, it is appropriate to provide a brief outline of the basic scheme of the Convention in relation to applications for the return of a child.[13]

6.11. In cases where it is alleged that a child has been 'abducted' from the State of the child's habitual residence to another State, applications may be made to the courts of the State of refuge under the Hague Convention to seek the child's return. As one commentary has observed,[14] the rationale of making applications to the State of refuge is that if a return order is granted, the court of that State is best placed to enforce it quickly and efficiently. The normal practice is for applications to be made via the left-behind parent's Central Authority, which transmits the request to the Central Authority of the State of refuge; however, Article 29 of the Convention permits applications to be made directly to a court of that State. The requested Central Authority, if satisfied that the application is 'well founded', has the responsibility for initiating or facilitating the institution of judicial or administrative proceedings with a view to obtaining the return of the child.[15]

Erbrecht, Nosmos, 2020, 13 (53 et seq.). Compare I. CURRY-SUMNER, 'The Revision of Brussels IIbis' [2015] *Nederlands Internationaal Privaatrecht* 1.

[12] Discussed at 6.96 et seq.
[13] For a detailed discussion of which, see N. LOWE, M, EVERALL and M. NICHOLLS, *International Movement of Children: Law Practice and Procedure* (2nd ed. by N. LOWE and M. NICHOLLS) Lexis Nexis, Family Law, 2016); R. SCHUZ, *The Hague Child Abduction Convention: A Critical Analysis*, Hart Publishing, 2013; and K. TRIMMINGS, *Child Abduction within the European Union*, Hart Publishing, 2013; T. KRUGER, *International Child Abduction Cases: The Inadequacies of the Law*, Oxford University Press, 2011; H. FULCHIRON (ed.), *Les enlèvements d'enfants à travers les frontières*, Bruylant, 2004; P. BEAMONT and P. McELEAVY, *The Hague Convention on International Abduction*, Oxford University Press, 1999.
[14] C. HONORATI and A. LIMINATE, above n. 3, p. 114.
[15] Article 7(f) of the Convention.

6.12. Once the court is satisfied that child has been 'wrongfully' removed or retained within the meaning of the Convention[16] then, under Article 12, **provided the application was brought within one year of the wrongful removal or retention**, it must order the child's return unless one of a number of narrow exceptions can be established. Under Article 13, a return may be refused if:

(a) the person, institution or other body having the care of the care of the person of the child was not actually exercising the custody rights at the time of removal or retention, or has consented to or subsequently acquiesced in the removal or retention;
(b) there is a grave risk that his or her return would expose the child to physical or psychological harm or otherwise place him or her in an intolerable situation;
(c) the child objects to being returned and has attained an age and degree of maturity at which it is appropriate to take account of his or her views.

6.13. Additionally, under Article 20 (rarely used in practice), a return order may be refused where this would not be permitted by the fundamental principles of the requested State relating to the protection of human rights and fundamental freedoms.

6.14. In cases where proceedings are brought **more than one year after** the wrongful removal or retention, Article 12 provides that a **return should still be ordered** 'unless it is demonstrated that the child is now settled in its new environment'.

6.15. It is worth stressing that when determining a Hague application, the court can only decide whether or not to make a return order and, if so, with what conditions (if any). **The Convention does not confer jurisdiction to determine the long-term future of the child**. Indeed, Article 16 forbids the court of the requested State from deciding on the merits of the rights of custody until it has been determined that the child is not to be returned under the Convention. Article 19 further provides that a decision to return the child is not to be taken to be a determination on the merits of any custody issue.[17]

---

[16] That is, the case falls within Article 3, namely, that the removal or retention was in breach of the applicant's rights of custody (which he or she was actively exercising) under the law of the State in which the child was habitutally resident immediately before the removal or retention.
[17] C. HONORATI and A. LIMINATE, above n. 3, p. 115 also point out that the return of the child does not necessarily imply returning him or her to the custody of the left-behind parent – it only means a return to the State of the child's habitual residence.

III. APPLYING BRUSSELS II-TER TO CHILD ABDUCTION

A. JURISDICTION: ARTICLE 9

1. The Basic Position and its Rationale

6.16. An important exception to the general rule of jurisdiction conferred by Article 7 concerns child abduction. Under Article 9, in the case of the wrongful removal or retention of a child and subject to any choice of jurisdiction pursuant to Article 10,[18] the courts of the Member State in which the child was habitually resident before the unlawful removal or retention retain jurisdiction until the child acquires a new habitual residence in another Member State **and** certain other conditions (discussed below) are satisfied. The retention of jurisdiction under Article 9 does not preclude applications being made to the State of refuge under the 1980 Hague Abduction Convention in conjunction with Article 22 of the Regulation for the return of a child wrongfully removed to or retained there,[19] nor, conversely, does it prevent the court with jurisdiction from requesting the transfer of the case to the court of refuge, pursuant to Article 12.[20]

6.17. Article 9 replaces Brussels II-bis Article 10,[21] which in turn was modelled on Article 7 of the 1996 Hague Child Protection Convention.[22] The underlying rationale of Article 9 is, in furtherance of the general aim of deterring parental child abduction between Member States, to ensure that the wrongful removal or retention of a child does not, *ipso facto*, have the effect of transferring jurisdiction, even if the child becomes habitually resident in the Member State of refuge.[23] This provision addresses what was once described[24]

---

[18] See further Chapter 4 at 4.42 et seq.
[19] See T. GARBER, 'Art. 9 Brussels IIter,' in U. MAGNUS and P. MANKOWSKI, (eds) *Brussels IIter Regulation*, OttoSchmidt, 2023, p. 161, para. 13.
[20] CJEU, 13 July 2023, *TT*, C-87/22. Transfer of jurisdiction is discussed in Chapter 4 at 4.111 et seq.
[21] For an extensive discussion of Brussels II-bis Article 10, see, for example, A. BORRÁS, 'Article 10' in U. MAGNUS and P. MANKOWSKI, above n. 9, pp. 122 et seq. For commentaries on Article 9 Brussels II-ter, see T. GARBER, above, n. 19, pp. 156 et seq.; and M. WILDERSPIN, *European Private International Family Law: The Brussels IIb Regulation*, Oxford University Press, 2023, pp. 185 et seq.
[22] For discussion of Article 7 of the 1996 Convention, see, for example, H. SETRIGHT, D WILLIAMS, I. CURRY-SUMNER, M. GRATION and M. WRIGHT, *International Issues in Family Law: The 1996 Hague Convention on the Protection of Children and Brussels IIa*, Jordans, Family Law, 2015, 9.23 et seq.
[23] See, in this respect, CJEU, 1 July 2010, *Povse*, C-211/10 PPU, paras [41]–[44] and re-iterated in CJEU, 13 July 2023, *TT*, C-87/22, para. 36.
[24] See M. TENREIRO, 'L'espace judiciaire européen en matière de droit de la famille, le nouveau règlement Bruxelles IIbis' in H. FULCHIRON (ed.), *Les enlèvements d'enfants à travers les frontières*, Bruylant, 2004, pp. 19, 27, cited and translated by A. BORRÁS, above n. 21, p. 124.

as one of the 'principal weaknesses' of the 1980 Hague Abduction Convention, namely, that the court of the State of refuge would have jurisdiction to hear the case on the merits once the Hague application for the return of the child has been refused. Like Article 7 of the 1996 Convention, Article 9 Brussels II-ter seeks to draw a balance between, on the one hand, not allowing an abductor to take advantage of his or her wrongful act to confer jurisdiction in the court of the State refuge and, on the other hand, not to eternally deprive that court of jurisdiction where the child remains there for a certain period of time.[25]

2. The Context in which Article 9 Operates

6.18. Article 9 only applies in the context of wrongful removals or retentions (the meaning of which is discussed at 6.33 et seq). In such cases, Article 9 provides that courts of the Member State of the child's former habitual residence retain jurisdiction until the child acquires a new habitual residence in another Member State **and** certain other conditions are satisfied. Before examining these conditions, some preliminary observations should be made. First, jurisdiction will only vest (if at all) in the Member State of refuge, upon the child becoming habitually resident[26] there, but, second, habitual residence alone will not be sufficient. Third, as is clear from the CJEU ruling in SS,[27] **Article 9 has no application to abductions to a third State** (in SS the third State involved was India). In such a situation, as the Court observed in SS,[28] the jurisdiction of the court seised has to be determined in accordance with the applicable international conventions or, in the absence of any such international convention, by its own national rules in accordance with Article 14.[29] Similarly, Article 9 does not apply to abductions to a Member State from a third State with jurisdiction having to be determined according to the rules set out by Brussels II-ter.[30]

---

[25] See A. BORRÁS, above n. 21, p. 124, in turn referring to the Explanatory Report on the 1996 Child Protection Convention by P. LAGARDE, HCCH, 1998, para. 46.
[26] The meaning of 'habitual residence' is discussed in Chapter 4 at 4.8 et seq.
[27] CJEU, 24 March 2021, SS, C-603/2 PPU. Contrary to the Opinion of Advocate General Rantos (Opinion, 23 February 2021, C-603/20 PPU), the CJEU rejected the contention that what was then Article 10 Brussels II-bis should be construed as meaning that the court of the Member State of the child's former habitual residence retains jurisdiction indefinitely in the event of a child becoming habitually resident in a third State following a wrongful removal or retention. See further N. LOWE, 'Operating Brussels II-ter in Children Cases Involving Third States' in Festskrift till Maarit Jänterä-Jareborg, Iustus Förlag, 2022, pp. 203, 208 et seq.
[28] CJEU, 24 March 2021, SS, C-603/2 PPU, para. 64.
[29] Discussed in Chapter 4 at 4.166 et seq.
[30] See T. GARBER, above, n. 19, p. 161, para. 11.

3. The Conditions upon which Courts of the Member State of Refuge Acquire Jurisdiction

6.19. Article 9 provides for two types of situations in which courts of the State of refuge can acquire jurisdiction. In the first, jurisdiction will be acquired where the child has acquired a habitual residence in another Member State **and** 'each person, institution or other body having rights of custody has acquiesced in the removal or retention'.

6.20. Article 9(a) requires **all holders of rights of custody** to have **acquiesced** in the removal or retention. Acquiescence is not defined in Brussels II-ter, but regard may be had to the jurisprudence on its meaning in Article 13(1)(a) of the 1980 Hague Abduction Convention, which provides one of the grounds for refusing to make a return order.[31] Unlike consent, acquiescence occurs after the removal or retention and basically amounts to an acceptance of the new situation. There has been debate about whether a distinction can be drawn between active and passive acquiescence,[32] and, if so, whether purely passive behaviour should qualify as acquiescence for the purposes of the Regulation.[33] That issue might eventually be resolved by the CJEU, but in the absence of a definitive interpretation, there seems to be force in the view that it is important to focus on the reality of the acquiescence and that in the absence of acquiescence being express, courts should be particularly cautious in finding it established.[34]

6.21. The second type of situation (provided for in Article 9(b)) is where the child has acquired a habitual residence in another Member State **and** has resided there for at least one year after the holders of rights of custody have or should have had knowledge of the child's whereabouts **and** the child is settled in his or her new environment **and one of the following conditions is met:**

- no request for a return has been lodged with the competent authorities in that period (**Article 9(b)(i)**);
- an application for a return lodged by the holder of rights of custody has been withdrawn and no new application has been lodged in that period (**Article 9(b)(ii)**);

---

[31] For a detailed discussion of this, see N. Lowe and M. Nicholls, above n. 13, paras 23.28 et seq.
[32] In the UK, the House of Lords abandoned making a distinction between active and passive acquiescence and instead focusing, except in exceptional circumstances, on the left-behind parent's subjective intentions; see *Re H (Minors) (Abduction: Acquiescence)* [1998] AC 72.
[33] For the view that it should not, see A. Borrás, above n. 21, p. 127; and H. Fulchiron, 'La lutte contre les enlèvements d'enfants' in H. Fulchiron and C. Nourissat (eds), *Le nouveau droit communautaire du divorce et de la responsabilité parentale*, Dalloz, 2005, pp. 223, 228.
[34] See A. Borrás, above n. 21, p. 127.

- an application for a return lodged by the holder of rights of custody was refused by a court of a Member State on grounds **other than** Article 13(1)(b) or (2) of the 1980 Hague Abduction Convention and that the decision is no longer subject to an ordinary appeal (**Article 9(b)(iii)**);
- no court was seised as referred to in Article 29(3) and (5) where the child was habitually resident before the unlawful removal or retention (**Article 9(b)(iv)**);
- a decision on rights of custody that does not entail the child's return has been given by the courts of the Member State where the child was habitually resident before the unlawful removal or retention (**Article 9(b)(v)**).

6.22. It has been observed[35] that the general idea underlying what is now Article 9(b) is that, after the child has spent a significant period of time in his or her new environment and has acquired a new habitual residence there, and if the holder of the rights of custody has either not asked for the return of the child or has given up the return proceedings that had been initiated, the removal/retention should cease to be considered temporary and that consequently jurisdiction should lie with the Member State of refuge. Yet, in order for Article 9(b) to apply, **in addition to the overall requirement** that the child has acquired a **habitual residence** in the Member State of refuge, **three separate conditions must be satisfied**, namely:

(1) one year must have elapsed after the holder of rights of custody knows or should have known of the child's whereabouts;
(2) the child must be settled in his or her new environment; and
(3) one of the conditions set out in Article 9(b)(i)–(v) is established.

6.23. The requirement (which hitherto has not been discussed by the CJEU) that the child must be shown to be 'settled in his or her new environment' should be noted. This requirement could either be viewed as complementing the overall requirement that the child be habitually resident in the State of refuge or as a separate requirement.[36] However, either way, this requirement needs to be satisfied. In the absence of a Regulation definition and CJEU case law on the meaning of 'settlement', it is possible to draw on the jurisprudence of the meaning of the term for the purposes of Article 12(2) of the 1980 Hague Abduction Convention. Under UK case law, for example, 'settlement' is regarded as involving both a physical element in the sense of relating to or being established in a community and an emotional constituent denoting

---

[35] See A. Borrás, above n. 21, p. 128.
[36] But query whether a child can be 'habitually resident' in a State in which he or she is not 'settled'?

security. 'New environment' encompasses place, home, school, people, friends, activities and opportunities, but not, per se, the relationship with the parent.[37]

6.24. Article 9(b)(iii) is new and applies in all cases where a **return order application is refused**, save where the refusal is made on the basis of Article 13(1)(b) (grave risk of harm) or Article 13(2) (child's objections) of the 1980 Hague Abduction Convention, **and is no longer subject to ordinary appeal** (that is, jurisdiction can be acquired notwithstanding that an extraordinary appeal is pending). While this provision is understandable, in that a refusal to return removes one of the objections to the Member State court of refuge acquiring jurisdiction, unlike most of the other conditions in Article 9(b), it is not rooted in the left-behind parent's inactivity. Outside the two grounds mentioned, Article 9(b)(iii) applies to all other cases of refusal, including those refused under Article 12(2) (the settlement ground) and Article 20 (the public policy ground) of the 1980 Hague Abduction Convention. The reason for excluding refusals based on Article 13(1)(b) and 13(2) is because they trigger the 'override mechanism' provisions whereby the parties have the opportunity of having a decision on the substance of rights of custody determined by a court of the Member State in which the child was habitually resident before the wrongful removal or retention.[38]

6.25. Under **Article 9(b)(iv)**, where all the other conditions are satisfied, jurisdiction will pass to the Member State of refuge if no court is seised under the override mechanism (that is, that at the time of the refusal, there were no proceedings pending in a court of the Member State in which the child was habitually resident before the wrongful removal or retention, or that the parties did not seise such a court within three months of being notified of the refusal).[39] This provision is wider than Article 10(b)(iii) Brussels II-bis (which is replaced), which only applied where the court in the Member State of the child's previous habitual residence closed the case before or after the court of refuge had made the non-return order.[40]

6.26. The final condition, as provided by **Article 9(b)(v)**, substantively replaces Article 10(b)(iv) Brussels II-bis. The rationale of this provision is that while the courts of the Member State of habitual residence retain priority over the courts of the Member State of refuge, that priority is lost once the former court

---

[37] *Cannon v. Cannon* [2004] EWCA Civ 1330 (England & Wales) and *Souci v. Souci* 1995 SC 134 (Scotland). In Australia, see *Director General, Department of Community Services v. M and C* (1999) 24 Fam LR 315.
[38] The override mechanism is discussed at 6.96 et seq.
[39] See respectively Article 29(3) and (5), discussed at 6.108 et seq.
[40] See the comment by M. WILDERSPIN, above, n. 21, p. 194, para. 5-164.

makes a decision on custody that does not require the child to be returned.[41] However, as the ECJ held in *Povse*,[42] given the general policy of deterring child abduction such that the unlawful removal of a child should not in principle have the effect of transferring jurisdiction, even if following the abduction the child has acquired an habitual residence in the Member State to which he or she has been taken, what was then Article 10(b)(iv) Brussels II-bis should be strictly interpreted. It was therefore held that it only applies if 'a judgment on custody that does not entail the return of the child' is a final one. It does not apply to an interim order.[43]

4. Agreement on Jurisdiction

6.27. Importantly, unlike Article 10 Brussels II-bis, Article 9 Brussels II-ter is subject to the parties' freedom (as per Brussels II-ter Article 10)[44] to agree that a particular court of Member State with which the child has a substantial connection should have jurisdiction. A 'substantial connection' for these purposes can be satisfied by the child being a national of the chosen Member State. But that choice must be freely agreed upon or expressly accepted and it must be in the interests of the child for the jurisdiction to be exercised.[45] In the case of child abduction, such agreements will rarely have been made in advance and, even if they have, are unlikely to be thought to be in the child's best interests to exercise jurisdiction. On the other hand, agreements either for a return or a non-return may more likely be made during the Hague return proceedings within the framework of a mediation between the parents. Pursuant to Article 10, and provided all conditions set forth in such rule are met, the parties are now authorised to derogate from retained jurisdiction under Article 9 and to confer jurisdiction on custody proceedings to the State of refuge.[46] In such cases, as Recital (22) suggests, where a non-return is agreed, and the child remains in the Member State of the new habitual residence, jurisdiction for any future custody proceedings should be determined on the basis of that new habitual residence.[47]

---

[41] Note may be taken of the English decision in *Re A, HA v. MB (Brussels II Revised: Article 11(7) Application)* [2007] EWHC 2016 (Fam) that a contact order does not entail the return of the child.
[42] CJEU, 1 July 2010, *Povse*, C-211/10 PPU.
[43] In CJEU, 1 July 2010, *Povse*, C-211/10 PPU, an Italian court's provisional order permitting the other to live with her daughter in Austria was held not to trigger Article 10(b)(iv).
[44] Article 10 is discussed in Chapter 4 at 4.42 et seq.
[45] See Article 10(1)(a) and (b).
[46] See further Chapter 4.
[47] Note Recital (22), which advises that Member States that have concentrated jurisdiction should 'consider enabling the court seised with the return application' to exercise an agreed jurisdiction on matters of parental responsibility. But query why this advice should be confined to States with concentrated jurisdiction?

B. THE POSITION WHERE APPLICATION IS MADE UNDER THE 1980 HAGUE CONVENTION

1. The General Position under Article 22

6.28. Under Article 22, where an application is made to a court of a Member State, either directly or with the assistance of a Central Authority, on the basis of the Hague Convention, by a person, institution or other body alleging a breach of rights of custody, for the return of child under the age of 16 wrongfully removed or retained in a Member State other than the Member State where the child was habitually resident immediately before the wrongful removal or retention, the court must apply Articles 23–29 and Chapter VI.

6.29. Although Article 22 essentially mirrors Article 11(1) Brussels II-bis, there are some important differences. First, the new provision makes it clear[48] that it applies both to return applications made directly to a court (as permitted by Article 29 of the Hague Convention) and to those made with the assistance of a Central Authority. Second, and reflecting the limited application of the Hague Convention, **Chapter III only applies to return applications of children under the age of 16.**[49] Nevertheless, it has been argued[50] that where a return order has been made, it will remain enforceable under the Regulation until the child becomes 18, but this interpretation seems doubtful. The final wording of Article 22 applies both the provisions of Chapter III (which are not a simple replica of the former Article 11(2)–(8)) and the general provisions on cooperation between Central Authorities under Chapter VI (see Chapter 11) and, by doing so, widens the impact of Brussels II-ter.

6.30. For applications falling within Article 22, the application of Chapters III and VI are mandatory, but are said to 'complement the Hague Convention'. What this means, as Article 96 makes clear, is that for return applications made between Member States, the Hague Convention continues to apply as complemented by Chapters III and VI.

6.31. Article 96 also applies Chapter IV to cases in which a return order made under the Convention in one Member State 'has to be recognised and enforced in another Member State following further wrongful removal or retention of the child'. This part of Article 96, which naturally flows from the definition

---

[48] Although Brussels II-bis could have been interpreted as applying to applications made to court, the clarity achieved by Brussels II-ter in this regard is welcome.
[49] See Article 22 and Recital (17); see also the comment by E. GALLANT in, 'Art. 22 Brussels IIter', U. MAGNUS and P. MANKOWSKI (eds), *Brussels IIter Regulation*, Otto Schmidt, 2023, p. 317, para. 9.
[50] See M. WILDERSPIN, above n. 21, pp. 297–298, para. 7-040.

of 'decision' in Article 2(1)(a)[51] and essentially replicates Article 1(3), which applies Chapter IV to return orders, means that a return order made in one Member State under the 1980 Hague Convention is itself enforceable in all other Member States under Brussels II-ter. Such a decision will circulate jointly with the specific certificate provided by Annex IV.

6.32. Chapter III only applies to **return** applications made under the Hague Convention. This means that **access** applications as between Member States cannot be made under Article 21 of the Convention. The general rule under Article 94 that the Regulation supersedes other Conventions is only derogated from, in the case of the 1980 Hague Convention, to the extent provided for by Article 96, namely, in respect of applications for the return of children wrongfully removed or retained from one Member State to another; for all other purposes, including access applications between Member States, the Regulation takes precedence. Indeed, right of access is expressly mentioned as a relevant part of parental responsibility in Article 2(2)(7) and different rules of Brussels II-ter are provided to deal (also) with access (see Article 8).

2. *Removal and Retention*

6.33. As already discussed (see 6.18), the special rule of jurisdiction under Article 9 only applies in cases of a child's wrongful removal or retention. Such a notion is also central to the operation of the 1980 Hague Abduction Convention. **In each case, including therefore where an application for the child's return is made under the 1980 Convention, courts are required to determine whether a 'wrongful removal or retention' has taken place within the meaning of Brussels II-ter.**[52] To determine that question, regard needs to be had to Article 2(11). The final arbiter of the application of Article 2(11) is the CJEU. Hence, while the jurisprudence developed under the Hague Convention is obviously relevant, it is not binding on the CJEU, whose task it is to determine the definition according to the Regulation. Nevertheless, it is suggested that in this regard, the CJEU should not search for an EU autonomous construction, but should instead consider the international character underlying the Convention.[53]

---

[51] Discussed further in Chapter 1 at 1.53.
[52] See CJEU, 5 October 2010, *J McB*, C-400/10 PPU; and the *2022 Practice Guide*, p. 121, para. 4.3.3.
[53] In this respect, regard might be had to the CJEU's comment in *TT* (CJEU, 13 July 2023, *TT*, C-87/22) para. [58] that while the provisions of the 1980 Hague Abduction Convention do not take precedence over the Regulation in relations between Member States in matters governed by it, they do 'have a close connection with those provisions such that they may have an effect on the meaning, scope and effectiveness of those provisions'. See also to similar effect CJEU, 16 February 2023, *Rzecznic Praw Dziecka*, C-638/22, para. 63.

6.34. Under Article 2(11), the removal or retention of a child is 'wrongful' where:

(a) such removal or retention is in breach of rights of custody acquired by decision or by operation of law or by agreement having legal effect under the law of the Member State where the child was habitually resident immediately before the removal or retention; and

(b) at the time of the removal or retention, the rights of custody were actually exercised, either jointly or alone, or would have been so exercised but for the removal or retention.

6.35. Article 2(11) Brussels II-ter replaces the same rule of Brussels II-bis, but, with the deletion of the latter's concluding words that 'Custody shall be considered to be exercised jointly when, pursuant to a judgment or by operation of law, one holder of parental responsibility cannot decide on the child's place of residence without the consent of another holder of parental responsibility', brings the definition, in this respect,[54] in the text into line with Article 3 of the 1980 Hague Convention.[55]

6.36. The meaning of wrongful 'removal or retention' was examined by the CJEU in *C v. M*,[56] in which, following divorce proceedings, a French first instance court determined that parental authority over the child concerned should be exercised jointly by the parents, but that the habitual residence of the child should be with the mother, with access being granted to the father. Notwithstanding this arrangement, the court also made a provisional order, permitting the mother to set up residence in Ireland. Following the refusal to stay this provisional order, the mother and child left for Ireland. Eight months later, a French appeal court overturned the original judgment and ordered the child to reside with the father, with access being granted to the mother. Having obtained a further order transferring exclusive parental authority to him and an order for the child's return, the father applied to the Irish court for a return order under the Convention together with a declaration that the mother had 'wrongfully retained' the child in Ireland. This litigation went to the Irish Supreme Court, which made a preliminary reference to the CJEU.

---

[54] But note: unlike Article 3 of the Convention, Article 2(11) does **not** expressly state that it is the law of State of the child's former habitual residence that determines whether rights of custody exist, though no doubt this is how it should be interpreted; see M. WILDERSPIN, above n. 21, p. 164, para. 5-040.

[55] Note: the former wording has been transferred to Recital (18). For the background to Article 3 of the 1980 Abduction Convention, see the Explanatory Report by E. PÉREZ-VERA, HCCH, 1982, paras 64 et seq.

[56] CJEU, 9 October 2014, *C v. M*, C-376/14 PPU.

6.37. The CJEU ruled that where a child has been removed from one Member State jurisdiction to another in accordance with a judgment which was provisionally enforceable in the Member State of origin, then, notwithstanding that that judgment was subsequently reversed upon appeal, the **removal** cannot be considered 'wrongful'. However, provided the child remained habitually resident in the State of origin, keeping the child in the requesting Member State, against a ruling fixing the child's residence at the home of the parent living in the Member State of origin, constitutes a wrongful **retention**. It is for the court of the Member State to which the child was taken to determine whether in all the circumstances, the child was still habitually resident in the Member State of origin immediately before the alleged wrongful retention. If not, the application for the return of the child under the Hague Convention must fail.

6.38. Implicit in this ruling is that 'removal' and 'retention' are separate concepts, the former occurring when the removal itself is in breach of rights of custody and the latter where retaining the child in another Member State jurisdiction subsequently becomes a breach of rights of custody. This may occur where an agreed period of stay is exceeded, or where a court order for the child's return is not obeyed. It is also implicit that an initially permissible removal cannot subsequently become a wrongful removal, but it can mutate into a wrongful retention.

6.39. The ruling does not go as far as to hold that not only are 'removal' and 'retention' separate concepts but also each occur on a specific occasion (that is, wrongful retention is not a continuing state of affairs),[57] but is consistent with this thinking. On the other hand, the decision in *C v. M* unequivocally establishes that a wrongful removal or retention under Article 2(11):

> presupposes that the child was habitually resident in the Member State of origin immediately before the removal or retention and that there is a breach of rights of custody attributed under the law of that Member State.[58]

6.40. Given this ruling, the distinction between removal and retention is important in order to determine the point in time at which the child's habitual residence should be assessed and, hence, for assessing whether the act was 'wrongful'.[59] This was well illustrated by *C v. M* itself, since the Irish court subsequently held[60] that in the eight months between the first instance ruling

---

[57] As established in the UK in *Re H, Re S* [1991] AC 476 and endorsed by the UK Supreme Court in *Re C and Another (Children) (International Centre for Family Law, Policy and Practice Intervening)* [2018] UKSC 8.
[58] CJEU, 9 October 2014, *C v. M*, C-376/14 PPU, para. 47.
[59] It is equally important in establishing jurisdiction according to Article 9. The meaning of 'habitual residence' is extensively discussed in Chapter 4 at 4.8 et seq.
[60] A finding which was upheld by the Irish Supreme Court; see *G (C) v. G (M)* [2015] IESC 12.

and the appellate decision, the child had become habitually resident in Ireland and, consequently, there had been no wrongful retention.[61]

6.41. An issue not yet determined by the CJEU, but one which is potentially important to the issue of retention, is whether, for the purposes of Brussels II-ter, there is a concept of 'anticipatory' or, as the UK Supreme Court has called it, 'repudiatory retention'. The issue arises where one parent evinces an intention to renege on an agreement to return a child *during* an agreed period of stay. In such a case, at what point does the retention become 'wrongful'? This question can be of crucial importance because if retention is only assessed at the end of the agreed stay, especially where that agreed period is a long one, the child's habitual residence is likely to have changed in the meantime, which means that the retention cannot then be 'wrongful'.[62] It remains to be seen whether the CJEU will agree with the UK Supreme Court, which held that under the Hague Convention, there is such a concept such that the retention becomes 'wrongful' at the point when it can be shown that the agreement has been repudiated even before the agreed date of return.[63]

3. *Wrongful Removal/Retention: Breach of Rights of Custody*

6.42. As Article 2(11)(a) states, in order to be 'wrongful', the removal or retention must be in breach of rights of custody. Under Article 2(9), 'rights of custody' 'includes rights and duties relating to the care of the person of a child, and in particular the right to determine the place of residence of the child'.

The key element of such rights is the right to determine the child's place of residence.[64] Having legal custody of a child might not in itself be sufficient to confer 'rights of custody' for the purposes of Article 2(11)(a). In any event, as the CJEU observed in *C v. M*,[65] a breach of access or accommodation rights does not amount to a breach of rights of custody.

6.43. Rights of custody can be acquired by decision, operation of law or by a legally enforceable agreement according to the law of the Member State where

---

[61] Yet, as the CJEU commented in 9 October 2014, *C v. M*, C-376/14 PPU, para. 66, the court is still bound under what is now Article 74 to recognise and enforce the appellate judgment of the court of origin unless an exception to doing so can be established under Articles 38 and 40; see Chapters 8 and 9.

[62] See, for example, the *Johnson* case (RÅ 1996 ref 52), which concerned a 'shuttle agreement' for three-year intervals, in which the Swedish Supreme Court held that after the first two years in Sweden, the child was habitually resident there.

[63] *Re C and Another (Children) (International Centre for Family Law, Policy and Practice Intervening)* [2018] UKSC 8, on which, see N. Lowe, 'The UK Senior Court's Contribution to the Global Jurisprudence on International Child Abduction' (2019) 135 *Law Quarterly Review* 114, 118–121. See also the Swedish Supreme Court decision. NJA 2012 s. 269.

[64] See also Recital (18), cited above at 6.35, n. 55.

[65] CJEU, 9 October 2014, *C v. M*, C-376/14 PPU, para. 61.

the child was habitually resident immediately before the removal or retention.[66] In determining this question, regard must be had to the applicable law provisions of the 1996 Hague Child Protection Convention, to which all Member States are Contracting Parties.[67]

6.44.   *McB*[68] establishes that notwithstanding Article 24 of the EU Charter of Fundamental Rights,[69] the Regulation must be interpreted as meaning that whether the removal or retention is wrongful 'is entirely dependent on the existence of rights of custody, conferred by the relevant national law, in breach of which that removal [or retention] has taken place'. Consequently, Member States are not precluded from requiring unmarried fathers to obtain an order from a court of competent jurisdiction to qualify as a person having 'rights of custody'. On the other hand, the clear import of *McB* is that under the Regulation, the concept of rights of custody only embraces *de jure* rights and **not** *de facto* or inchoate rights.[70] However, the better view[71] is that a **judicial order prohibiting relocation** of the child abroad without the consent of the court or the other parent (which in common law jurisdictions is also known as a *ne exeat* **order**) does amount to a right of custody because, in effect, it confers a right to decide where the habitual residence should be, though this has yet to be established by the CJEU.

6.45.   Although Article 2(11) is silent on who has rights of custody, the issue is addressed by Recital (18), which says for the purposes of Brussels II-ter, a person should be deemed to have 'rights of custody':

> where, pursuant to a decision, by operation of law or by an agreement having legal effect under the law of the Member State where the child is habitually resident, a holder of parental responsibility cannot decide on the child's place of residence without the consent of that person, regardless of the terms used under national law.

---

[66] Article 2(11)(a).
[67] See, in particular, Articles 16–18, which govern the position with regard to parental responsibility and on which see N. Lowe and M. Nicholls, *The 1996 Hague Convention on the Protection of Children*, Jordans, 2012, pp. 59 et seq.
[68] CJEU, 5 October 2010, *J McB*, C-400/10 PPU, para. 44.
[69] The Court rejected the argument that in providing for the child's right to have contact with both parents, the Charter precluded the Regulation being interpreted as preserving a Member State's freedom not to confer upon an unmarried or unregistered father any rights over his own child.
[70] Note the different position taken in the UK; see *Re K (A Child) (Reunite Child Abduction Centre Intervening)* [2014] UKSC 29 (on which, see Chapter 12 at 12.64), a standpoint not reflected in Member States and unlikely to be adopted by the CJEU.
[71] See C. Honorati and A. Liminate, above n. 3, p. 100, relying on the global jurisprudence on the application of the 1980 Hague Abduction Convention in this respect, in particular by the US Supreme Court in *Abbott v. Abbott* 560 US 1 (2010). For a similar standpoint taken in the UK, see *Re D (A Child) (Abduction: Rights of Custody)* [2006] UKHL 51.

In some legal systems which continue to use the language of 'custody' and 'access', the non-custodial parent might in fact retain responsibilities for important decisions concerning the child which go beyond a mere right of access.

6.46. Under Article 2(11)(b), rights of custody must not only have been in existence in the Member State of the child's habitual residence immediately before the wrongful removal or retention, but must also **have actually been exercised** either jointly or alone at the time, or would have been but for the removal or retention. There is no CJEU jurisprudence on this, although an analysis of decisions by national courts has led one commentary[72] to say that in principle, only actual abandonment of the child will lead to the conclusion that custody is not being actually exercised. As already noted, the critical issue is whether the parent is maintaining the right to determine the child's place of residence. So, for example, entrusting care of the child to grandparents or an educational institution, but maintaining control over major decisions does not exclude actual exercise of custody. Similarly, on this approach, it seems clear that missing some access visits or being in arrears with maintenance payments is not enough to establish the non-exercise of custody rights. But it is an interesting question as to whether never visiting the child, particularly if coupled with non-payment of maintenance, should be considered a non-exercise of such rights.

6.47. It is clear from the opening words in Article 22 that 'Where a person, institution or other body' applies for the return of a child under the Hague Convention, rights of custody can be held not just by a person, but also by an institution or other body.[73] However, one unresolved question under the Regulation is whether a court can have rights of custody. Under the Hague Convention, a number of common law jurisdictions hold the view that courts can have rights of custody as they can be considered as an 'other body',[74] but in the *Mercredi* case,[75] the ECJ declined to rule on whether a court can hold rights of custody for the purposes of the Regulation. However, the reasoning in the *McB* case that the 'wrongfulness' of the removal or retention 'is *entirely* dependent on the existence of rights of custody, conferred by the relevant national law' must surely lead to the conclusion that there is no autonomous

---

[72] See C. HONORATI and A. LIMINATE, above n. 3, p. 104 citing, *inter alia*, Austrian Supreme Court, 30 October 2003, No 8ob121/03g and Cour d'appel de Paris, 2 April 2013, No 3296. See also the Example in the *2022 Practice Guide*, p. 121 (para. 4.3.3.3).
[73] Compare Article 3 of the Hague Convention, which refers to 'rights of custody attributed to a person, institution or other body'.
[74] See, for example, in Ireland: *HI v. MG (Child Abduction: Wrongful Removal)* [2000] IR 110; the UK, *Re H (A Minor) (Abduction: Rights of Custody)* [2000] 2 AC 291; Canada, *Thomson v. Thomson* [1994] 3 SCR 351; Australia: *Secretary, A-G's Department v. TS* [2000] Fam CA 1692; and New Zealand, *Olson v. Olson, Re Family Court of New Zealand* 1994 FP 37/94.
[75] CJEU, 22 December 2010, *Mercredi*, C-497/10 PPU.

solution under the Regulation and the question of whether a court can have rights of custody will depend on the law of the Member State in which the child is habitually resident.

IV. EXPEDITING THE PROCESSING AND HEARING OF RETURN APPLICATIONS

6.48. As has been well said,[76] the Hague Convention is designed to be a 'hot pursuit remedy', yet the Convention itself provides relatively vague time targets.[77] Brussels II-bis sought to address that deficiency by introducing an obligation on the courts to dispose of return applications made under the Convention within six weeks. Although there had been some evidence that Hague return applications between Member States had speeded up following the introduction of this obligation,[78] the provisions were in need of clarity and of expansion. Brussels II-ter does just that: it provides for clear time targets for each level of court proceedings and addresses timing issues both with regard to Central Authorities processing applications and with regard to the enforcement process.

A. RECEIPT AND PROCESSING OF APPLICATIONS BY CENTRAL AUTHORITIES

6.49. Article 23(1) requires requested Central Authorities[79] to 'act expeditiously' in processing applications for the return of a child made by another Member State under the Hague Convention. In particular, Article 23(2) obliges them

---

[76] Per Thorpe LJ in *Re C (Abduction: Grave Risk of Physical and Psychological Harm)* [1992] 2 FLR 478, 488.
[77] Article 11(2) simply gives the applicant or the Central Authority of the requested State the right to request a statement of the reasons for the delay if the judicial or administrative authority concerned has not reached a decision within six weeks of the date of commencement of the proceedings.
[78] See N. Lowe and V. Stephens, 'A Statistical Analysis of Applications Made in 2015 under the Hague Convention of 25 October 1980 on the Civil Aspects of International Child Abduction', Prel. Doc. No.11B (revised February 2018) http://www.hcch.net/index_en.php?act=progress.listing&cat=7, which is analysed further by N. Lowe and V. Stephens, 'Operating the 1980 Hague Abduction Convention in the Context of BIIa: The 2015 Statistics' [2018] *International Family Law* 12. But this finding was not replicated in the 2021 Study, see N. Lowe and V. Stephens, 'A Statistical Analysis of Applications Made in 2021 under the Hague Convention of 25 October 1980 on the Civil Aspects of International Child Abduction', Prel. Doc. No.19B (2023).
[79] The meaning of 'requested' Central Authorities is not clear in this context. Presumably it means *any* Authority asked to act rather than that of the requested State. See M. Wilderspin, above, n. 21, p. 298, para. 7-043.

to acknowledge the receipt of the application within five working days of their receipt of it and, 'without due delay', to:

> inform the Central Authority of the requesting[80] Member State or the applicant, as appropriate, what initial steps have been or will be taken to deal with the application, and may request any further necessary documents and information.

6.50. Although this provision is welcome inasmuch as it is the first international attempt to focus specifically on the need for speed by Central Authorities when processing Hague applications, it represents a significant reining back on the earlier proposal[81] that Central Authorities should be obliged, where they initiate or facilitate the institution of court return proceedings under the Hague Convention, to ensure that the whole file prepared for the proceedings is complete within six weeks, except where exceptional circumstances make this impossible.

B. CONCENTRATING JURISDICTION

6.51. Some States limit the number of courts that are competent to hear applications made under the 1980 Hague Convention; others do not. However, it has become apparent that the Convention works best where jurisdiction is concentrated in a few courts which are familiar with and have expertise in dealing with Hague applications. One of the recommendations of the Fourth Special Commission to review the operation of the Convention specifically[82] 'calls upon Contracting States to bear in mind the considerable advantages to be gained by a concentration of jurisdiction to deal with Hague Convention cases within a limited number of courts'.

6.52. Under the Commission's 2016 proposal,[83] it would have been mandatory for Member States to ensure that the jurisdiction for the applications for a return of the child under the Hague Convention to be concentrated on a limited number of courts.[84] But that proposal understandably attracted opposition because it constituted too great an interference with Member States' autonomy. As a compromise, Recital (41) states that in order to conclude return applications

---

[80] As noted by E. GALLANT, above, n. 49, p. 319, n. 2.
[81] See Proposal for a Council Regulation on jurisdiction, the recognition and enforcement of decisions in matrimonial matters and the matters of parental responsibility, and on international child abduction (recast), COM(2016) 411, proposed Article 63(g).
[82] See 'Conclusions and Recommendations of the Fourth Meeting of the Special Commission to Review the Operation of the Hague Abduction Convention' (HCCH, 22–28 March 2001), Recommendation 3.1.
[83] Above, n. 81.
[84] See the proposed Article 22.

under the Hague Convention, as quickly as possible Member States should, consistent with their national structure, *consider* concentrating jurisdiction for those proceedings upon as limited a number of courts as possible.

6.53. Recital (41) suggests that abduction cases could be concentrated in a single court for the whole country or in a limited number of courts 'using, for example, the number of appellate courts as point of departure and concentrating jurisdiction for international child abduction cases upon one court of first instance within each district of a court of appeal'. In fact, even before Brussels II-ter came into force, jurisdiction in many Member States was already concentrated though the level of concentration varied.[85]

C. EXPEDITIOUS COURT PROCEEDINGS

6.54. Brussels II-bis broke new ground by introducing an obligation upon courts to dispose of return applications made under the Hague Convention within six weeks.[86] This obligation has been refined by Brussels II-ter, which provides **separate timing obligations for first instance proceedings and for appellate proceedings.**

1. The Six-Week Timeframe

6.55. The new timing provisions are governed by Article 24, by which courts must, in any event, act 'expeditiously' when seised of return applications and 'use the most expeditious procedures available under national law'. Article 24(2) further provides that a court at first instance must give its decision 'no later than six weeks after it is seised, except where exceptional circumstances make this impossible'. Similarly, under Article 24(3), a court of higher instance must, save where exceptional circumstances make this impossible, give its decision within six weeks once it is 'in a position to examine the appeal, whether by hearing or otherwise'.

6.56. Article 24 brings welcome clarity inasmuch as it was uncertain whether the former obligation included appellate proceedings. Providing for separate timeframes is also more realistic for, as statistical studies have repeatedly shown, Member States have struggled to meet the six-week obligation however it is interpreted.[87] Now, in the case of a single appeal, the previous six-week timeframe

---

[85] As C. HONORATI and A. LIMINATE, above n. 3, p. 114 found, jurisdiction is concentrated in Austria, Belgium, Bulgaria, Cyprus, the Czech Republic, Finland, France, Germany, Italy, Latvia, Lithuania, Romania, Slovakia and Sweden. Jurisdiction is also concentrated in Ireland.
[86] See Article 11(3) Brussels II-bis.
[87] See n. 78 above.

is at least doubled,[88] and is even further extended in the case of further appeals since, as Recital (42) makes clear, Article 24(3) applies the six-week timeframe both to a second or even a third appeal (in Member States where multiple levels of appeals are permitted). In fact, under the Commission's original proposal, only one appeal would have been permitted.[89] But that proposal was dropped and instead Recital (42) encourages Member States to 'consider' limiting the number of appeals under the Hague Convention to one.[90] What remains unclear, in the case of appeals, is precisely when the six-week period begins.[91]

6.57. As Recital (42) clarifies, the use of alternative dispute resolution mechanisms 'should not as such be considered an exceptional circumstance allowing it to exceed the timeframe. However, exceptional circumstances might arise while using such means or as a result of them'.

In other words, while the use of alternative dispute resolution mechanisms will not, per se, delay the six-week disposal obligation,[92] the consequences of using them can do so where more time is required to finalise a mediated agreement, as where, for example, the parties have reached an agreement but need some kind of legal procedure to make such agreement binding and enforceable. The *2022 Practice Guide*[93] adds that judicial vacations and lack of diligence by the defendant's representative should not be considered 'exceptional circumstances'.

2. When the Six-Week Timeframe Begins

6.58. So far as courts of first instance are concerned, Recital (42) states that the timeframe should begin 'at the moment that the court is seised'. 'Seised' must be interpreted in accordance with Article 17[94] such that, depending on the system applying in the requested State, the timeframe begins either when the document instituting the proceedings has been lodged[95] with the court, or when

---

[88] But for when the six-week period begins according to Article 24(3); see 6.58 below.
[89] That is, under Article 25(4) of the Commission's Proposal, above n. 81.
[90] In fact, multiple appeals in abduction cases are relatively unusual, see the 2021 Study, Prel. Doc. No 19B, above n. 78 and N. Lowe and V. Stephens, 'Operating the 1980 Hague Abduction Convention in the Context of BIIa', above n. 78. But note the CJEU's criticism of the introduction in Poland in 2018 of a new right of appeal on a point of law against a return decision before the Supreme Court in CJEU, 16 February 2023, *Rzecznic Praw Dziecka and Others*, C-638/22 PPU.
[91] See 6.59 below.
[92] Indeed, the obligation to invite the parties to consider mediation or other means of alternative dispute resolution does not apply if it 'would unduly delay the proceedings'; see Article 25, discussed at 6.69.
[93] *2022 Practice Guide*, p. 127, para. 4.3.6.1, citing CJEU, 7 November 2019, *K H K*, C-555/18 (see para. 55) and CJEU, 21 March 2013, *Novontech-Zala*, C-324/12, para. 21.
[94] See the discussion in Chapter 2 at 2.6 et seq.
[95] Telephone applications are not sufficient for these purposes; see CJEU, 22 December 2010, *Mercredi*, C-497/10 PPU.

the document instituting the proceedings has been served on the respondent, provided in each case, the applicant has not failed to take the second required step of either serving the document on the respondent or having the document lodged with the court.

6.59. For higher instance courts, Article 24(3) provides that the timeframe begins 'after all the required procedural steps have been taken and the court is in a position to examine the appeal'.

Recital (42) suggests that the required procedural steps:

> could include, depending on the legal system concerned, service of the appeal upon the respondent, either within the Member State where the court is located or within another Member State, transmission of the file and the appeal to the appellate court in Member States where the appeal has to be lodged with the court whose decision is appealed, or an application by a party to convene a hearing where such an application is required under national law.

But what is meant by the court is 'in a position to examine the appeal' remains to be established.

6.60. It is both helpful and realistic to spell out when the respective timeframes begin to run, though one consequence of this is that, bearing in mind the time needed to launch proceedings, at both first instance and on appeal, more than six weeks is effectively permitted at each court stage to conclude an application. In that respect, though, regard should be had to the power under Article 27(6) to declare a return order 'provisionally enforceable notwithstanding any appeal'. Although the six-week obligation does not apply to the required procedure for initiating proceedings both at first instance and upon appeal, as already seen, there is, under Article 24, a general obligation upon Member States to 'use the most expeditious procedures available' to meet the objective securing the prompt return of children wrongfully removed or retained in any Contracting State. Moreover, as discussed above,[96] Central Authorities must act 'expeditiously' in processing Hague applications. Further, as discussed below (see 6.63 et seq), under Article 28, authorities competent for enforcement must also act expeditiously.

3. *The Nature of the Timing Obligation*

6.61. Although it is clearly in the spirit of the Regulation that Member States should at least have in place procedures that court hearings will normally be completed within six weeks, **the obligation under Article 24(1) is to use the**

---

[96] See 6.49 above.

most expeditious procedures available. In the light of the procedural autonomy enjoyed by Member States, this does not require, of itself, States to introduce new procedures.

6.62. Brussels II-ter imposes no specific sanction for non-compliance with the time limits under Article 24. However, this does not mean that there are no sanctions for non-compliance.[97] A number of European Court of Human Rights rulings have found that rank failure to meet the then existing time limits under Brussels II-bis violated the ECHR.[98] There is also a sanction for **systemic breaches** of an EU obligation.[99] Although, at the time of writing, the Commission had not brought any 'defaulting State' before the Court under Brussels II-bis, on 26 January 2023, it issued a formal notice to Poland for what it considered to be a systematic and persistent failure of the Polish authorities to speedily and effectively enforce judgments ordering the return of abducted children to other EU Member States.[100] Given that Brussels II-ter provides more detailed timing provisions, the Commission might be more inclined to use the Article 258 TFEU procedure.

4. *Expeditious Enforcement*

6.63. Under Article 28(2), where a decision ordering the return of the child to another Member State is not enforced within six weeks of the initiation of enforcement proceedings, the party seeking the enforcement, or the Central Authority of the Member State of enforcement, has the right 'to request a statement of the reasons for the delay from the enforcement authority'.

6.64. This is the first time that a legislative attempt[101] has been made to address the enforcement process which can be notoriously lengthy. Although the right

---

[97] Although, given that the statistics (on which see N. LOWE and V. STEPHENS, 'Operating the 1980 Hague Abduction Convention in the Context of BIIA', above n. 78) show that some Member States consistently fall well short of the time targets, it is disappointing that this point is not expressly addressed.

[98] See, for example, ECtHR, 26 July 2011, *Shaw v. Hungary*, App No. 6457/09; ECtHR, 28 April 2015, *Ferrari v. Romania*, App No. 1714/10; and ECtHR, 1 March 2016, *KJ v. Poland*, App No. 30813/14.

[99] Under Article 4(3) of the Treaty on European Union (TEU), Member States must take all appropriate measures to ensure the fulfilment of their Treaty obligations (this obligation extends to national courts; see ECJ, 10 April 1984, *Sabine von Colson and Elisabeth Kamann*, C-14/83) and, in the event of a Member State's failure to do so, the Commission may start an infringement procedure under Article 258 TFEU (a procedure that does not necessarily come before the CJEU).

[100] INFR(2021)2001.

[101] But note CJEU, 16 February 2023, *Rzecznic Praw Dziecka and Others*, C-638/22 PPU, in which it was ruled that under Brussels II-bis the need for efficiency and speed which governs the reaching of a return decision equally applies to the enforcement of such a decision.

conferred by Article 28(2) is relatively weak, it is a step in the right direction and could open the door to human rights challenges under the ECHR.

V. ALTERNATIVE DISPUTE RESOLUTION

6.65. When the Hague Convention was being negotiated, mediation in family cases was not a generally developed practice and it was not in the drafters' contemplation. Indeed, at first sight, it might seem as if the positions of the abducting and left-behind parents would necessarily be too far apart for effective mediation. However, following pioneering work undertaken by the British NGO Reunite, it became apparent that mediation has an important role to play in abduction cases. Reunite's work and experience attracted global interest and, in due course, the Hague Conference published a *Guide to Good Practice on Mediation*.[102] It has been well observed[103] that even where the ultimate objective on a child's return is not achieved, mediation encourages dialogue between the parents and fosters contact with the child, and can help to promote acceptance of any subsequent court decision.

6.66. Although a number of mediation schemes specifically tailored for abduction cases have been developed in various Member States,[104] they are by no means available in all such States.[105] To address this inconsistency among Member States, Article 25 provides that, with some caveats (see below), in all return applications governed by Brussels II-ter, courts (but not the parties)[106] are expected, as early as possible and at any stage of the proceedings either directly or with the assistance of its Central Authority, to 'invite the parties to consider whether they are willing to engage in mediation or other means of alternative dispute resolution'. As Recital (43) states, the court should 'consider the possibility of achieving solutions through mediation and other appropriate means, assisted, where appropriate, by existing networks and support structures for mediation in cross-border parental disputes'. While this enjoinder presupposes that some mediation facilities should be available, Article 25 does not dictate what form these facilities should take.

6.67. The obligation on the courts to invite the parties to consider mediation, etc. is not an absolute one. According to Article 25, it will not arise if the invitation is considered: to be against the child's best interests; not appropriate in the particular case; or that it would unduly delay the proceedings.

---

[102] HCCH, 2011.
[103] See C. HONORATI, 'The Commission's Proposal for a Recast of Brussels IIa Regulation' [2017] *International Family Law* 97, 104.
[104] See the discussion in N. LOWE and M. NICHOLLS, above n. 13, paras 17.102–17.106.
[105] See C. HONORATI, above n. 103, p. 104.
[106] See E. GALLANT, above, n. 49, p. 322, para. 2.

6.68. With regard to the first exception, the mediation obligation is excluded only where it is thought to be **against** the child's best interests. **It is not a requirement that it must be shown that mediation is in the child's best interests** before the parties should be invited to consider it. Rather, the rule provides a general presumption that mediation – that is a less conflictual solution of the family crisis – serves the best interests of the child. However, the court has a discretion to rebut such a presumption when the specific situation so requires, for example, where because of the mother's vulnerability there are doubts as to whether a sufficiently balanced agreement can be reached. With regard to inappropriateness, the most obvious example, and one highlighted in Recital (43), is cases of domestic violence.

6.69. The greatest concern with regard to the use of mediation is that it could, either intentionally or unintentionally, delay the proceedings, which is contrary to the recognised need to reach speedy outcomes. As mentioned earlier,[107] the obligation upon the courts to reach a decision within six weeks is not interrupted by the use of alternative dispute mechanisms, but Article 25 goes further by providing that the courts will be justified in not raising the possibility of mediation at all if it is considered that, by so doing, proceedings would be unduly delayed. A clear danger of this provision is that it might be seen, particularly in States that do not have a well-developed mediation practice, as an encouragement particularly to lawyers not to offer mediation. In this regard it will be important that courts play a proactive role in suggesting and promoting mediation.

6.70. One problem of mediation is where the agreement goes beyond the return or non-return of the child and addresses other issues involving parental responsibility (such as access rights) or maintenance obligations and it is sought to embody that agreement in a court order in the State of refuge,[108] to make it enforceable. This raises the question of jurisdiction to make so-called 'package agreements', i.e. agreements encompassing different issues, each of which may have a different ground of jurisdiction. Recital (43) suggests that under 'certain circumstances', the Regulation should make it possible for parents who have reached an agreement not just on the return or non-return of the child, but also on other matters of parental responsibility:

> to agree that the court seised under the 1980 Hague Convention should have jurisdiction to give binding legal effect to their agreement, either by incorporating it into a decision, approving it or by using any other form provided by national law and procedure.

---

[107] See 6.57 above.
[108] Cf. embodying a package agreement in court order in the State of habitual residence, which is less problematic from the point of view of jurisdiction.

The Recital goes on to say that those States **which have concentrated jurisdiction**:

> should therefore consider enabling the court seised with the return proceedings under the 1980 Hague Convention to exercise also the jurisdiction agreed by the parties pursuant to this Regulation[109] in matters of parental responsibility where agreement of the parties was reached in the course of those return proceedings.

6.71. These points are useful, and seem apt even where abduction jurisdiction is not concentrated, but of necessity Recital (43) only deals with agreements on matters of parental responsibility falling within the scope of the Regulation. However, agreements may go beyond such matters as, for example, those dealing with maintenance or the protection of a parent. Accordingly, when concentrating abduction jurisdiction, consideration should also be given to conferring competence in a wide range of matters.[110]

VI. THE RIGHT OF THE CHILD TO EXPRESS HIS OR HER VIEWS IN RETURN PROCEEDINGS

6.72. Article 26 Brussels II-ter expressly applies Article 21 to return applications under the Hague Convention. Article 21 gives the child 'who is capable of forming his or her own views'[111] the right to express those views and have due note taken of them. Given the general application of Article 21, save perhaps for the sake of clarity and emphasis, there seems little justification for having this separate rule for abduction proceedings.[112] No doubt, however, the legislators had in mind the decision in *Aguirre*,[113] in which the certificate for a return decision had been issued, and hence enforcement required, despite the fact that the abducted child had not been offered an opportunity to be heard.

---

[109] That is, under Article 10, by which in certain circumstances (see Chapter 4), parties can make a binding choice-of-court agreement over matters of parental responsibility.

[110] Note the power to prorogate competence over maintenance pursuant to Article 4 of the 2009 Maintenance Regulation.

[111] As pointed out by E. GALLANT, above, n. 49, p. 323, para. 4, this wording is different from and an improvement on Article 11(2) Brussels II-bis, which qualified the obligation to hear the child with the words 'unless this appears to be inappropriate having regard to his or her age or degree of maturity'.

[112] It may be noted that whereas point 15 of Annex IV – on decisions ordering the child's return pursuant to the 1980 Hague Abduction Convention – requires the court in the State of refuge to state that the child has been given the opportunity to be heard, there is no similar requirement in Annex 1 in relation to decisions refusing a return under Article 13(1)(b) and/or 13(2) of the Convention. *Sed quaere?*

[113] CJEU, 22 December 2010, *Aguirre Zarraga*, C-491/10 PPU, discussed in detail in Chapter 7 at 7.31 et seq.

6.73. The issue of listening to children is extensively discussed in Chapter 7. Suffice to say that it is a matter for national law to determine how the child should be heard, and that in complying with this requirement, the court needs to guard against straying into considering the merits of the case, which is strictly forbidden by Article 16 of the Hague Convention, and to be mindful of avoiding undue delay.

VII. THE PROCEDURE FOR THE RETURN OF THE CHILD

6.74. An innovation of Brussels II-bis was to introduce uniform rules and common principles in Hague return proceedings between Member States. These common rules were in general inspired by a common level of protection of fundamental procedural rights and by the reciprocal trust in the standard of judicial procedures among Member States and because such rules integrated the provisions of the 1980 Hague Convention, which are silent in relation to most of these points. With some differences, these rules continue to be provided by Brussels II-ter.

A. GIVING THE APPLICANT THE OPPORTUNITY TO BE HEARD

6.75. Article 27(1) Brussels II-ter (which essentially replicates Article 11(5) Brussels II-bis) provides that a court cannot refuse an application to return a child 'unless the person seeking the return of the child has been given an opportunity to be heard'. Hitherto, this obligation has not been extensively considered by national courts[114] and not at all by the CJEU, but it is not without its problems, particularly where the return proceedings are not instituted by the left-behind parent, but by an authority. In some Member States the application for the return of the child is made by the Public Prosecutor, as requested by the Central Authority. While the Public Prosecutor is the procedural party to the return proceedings acting in the interests of the child, the left-behind parent, who has a personal and substantial interest in the return of the child, might not be a formal party to such proceedings. In this case it seems unfair that the return is refused without the parent being given the opportunity to

---

[114] But note the Spanish decision *Audiencia Provincial Baleares (Sección 4th)*, 22 December 2010, No 160, cited by C. HONORATI and A. LIMINATE, above n. 3, p. 120, which did consider the consequences of not hearing the left-behind mother.

be heard. It is therefore suggested that Article 27(1) be construed as giving the left-behind parent, **whether or not he or she is a party to the proceedings**, the opportunity to be heard. It has been suggested[115] that the term 'heard' should not be restrictively interpreted and that written testimony could satisfy the rule.

6.76. While such a requirement seems reasonable and fair, it may imply some undue delay, especially if the left-behind parent is not in the State of refuge and needs to be summoned at court. In this respect, note should be taken of Regulation No 2020/1783 on cooperation between courts of the Member States in taking of evidence in civil and commercial matters, (recast) under which a party can be heard in his or her home State via the use of videoconference or other communication technology.[116]

B. CONTACT WITH THE LEFT-BEHIND PARENT

6.77. At any stage of the proceedings, the court may, under Article 27(2), 'examine whether contact between the child and the person seeking the return of the child should be ensured, taking into account the best interests of the child'. This power must be exercised in accordance with Article 15, which means that it is limited to adopting provisional measures, *inter alia*, that the child has to be present in the Member State of refuge and the court must notify, in this context, the court or competent authority of the Member State of origin.[117]

6.78. Article 27(2) is new and was added during the negotiations on the Commission's proposals. It **plugs a gap** in the courts' powers under the Regulation to enable them to deal with the issue of contact during Hague proceedings[118] **and thereby avoids forcing the left-behind parent to bring costly and time-consuming fresh separate access proceedings**. As the Hague Conference's *Guide to Good Practice – Transfrontier Contact Concerning Children* observes,[119] an applicant under the 1980 Convention may wish to establish contact with the child pending any return decision, and any delay

---

[115] See E. GALLANT, above, n. 49, p. 326, para. 4.
[116] See Recital (53).
[117] Such notification can be made either directly to the court or competent authority or through the Central Authority: Article 15(2), discussed further in Chapter 4 at 4.212 et seq.
[118] On a strict interpretation of the 1980 Hague Convention, the court does not have jurisdiction to deal with this matter, as it is not a matter relating to the return of the child, but to parental responsibility. However, it should be noted that Article 27(2) does not expressly confer the power to make orders for contact, but only to consider whether to do so. Nevertheless, this is surely implicit; see M. WILDERSPIN, above n. 21, pp. 301–302, para. 7-058.
[119] HCCH, 2008, p. xxv.

in making that decision exacerbates lack of contact in the meantime and in turn could 'contribute to the alienation of the child from that parent, and may thereby increase the prospects of an Article 13b) defence succeeding'. It adds that in any event, 'preserving the continuity of the child's relationship with the applicant parent requires that the issue of contact be dealt with as quickly as possible. This may in turn help to ensure that the child is not re-abducted to the original State'. Preserving the continuity of contact is in line with Article 24(3) of the EU Charter of Fundamental Rights and Article 9 UNCRC.

6.79. Article 27(2) is narrow in the sense that only applies to contact between the child and the person seeking the child's return; it does not cover, for example, contact with grandparents, when they are not seeking the return of the child. Moreover, there is uncertainty as to whether Article 27(2) permits the court to make an access order after making a *final* return order, which might be relevant, for instance, where the child is being returned to an institution but the court wants to provide for some form of access to the left-behind parent (there is clearly no power to make contact arrangements between the child and the abducting parent). The reference in Article 27(2) to orders being made 'at any stage of the proceedings' suggests that there is such a power. On the other hand, bearing in mind that under Article 27(5) the power to make provisional (including protective) measures, which can include access,[120] can clearly be exercised following the making of a return order, Article 27(2) might simply be thought to provide a power to grant access as a temporary measure pending the return proceedings. The *2022 Practice Guide*[121] states that as 'the measures are of provisional nature they end with the return or non-return decision'. But whatever the position is, a provisional decision on contact issued under Article 27(2) is temporary in nature and is meant to be superseded by any subsequent decision on the substance by the court of the child's habitual residence. It has no extra-territorial effect and is neither recognisable nor enforceable in any other Member State.[122]

6.80. Welcome though this new power is, it poses the dilemma in terms of how courts can secure contact in the best interests of the child without straying into the forbidden territory of determining the substance of the case.

---

[120] See 6.85 below.
[121] *2022 Practice Guide*, p. 123, para. 4.3.4.
[122] Orders made under Article 15 generally do not have extra-territorial effect (see the discussion in Chapter 4 at 4.199 et seq); however, compare the position with regard to provisional, including protective measures under Article 27(5), discussed at 6.85 et seq.

C. REFUSALS BASED ON ARTICLE 13(1)(b) OF THE HAGUE CONVENTION

6.81. Article 27(3), which replaces Article 11(4) Brussels II-bis, provides that where a court considers refusing to return a child solely on the basis of Article 13(1)(b) of the Hague Convention,[123] it cannot do so:

> if the party seeking the return of the child satisfies the court by providing sufficient evidence, or the court is otherwise satisfied, that adequate arrangements have been made to secure the protection of the child after his or her return.

Like its predecessor, Article 27(3) is intended to reinforce the principle of immediate return by restricting the exception allowed for under Article 13(1)(b) of the Hague Convention to a strict minimum. The underlying fear is that, without this provision, too ready a reliance will be placed upon the Article 13(1)(b) exception to refuse a return.[124]

6.82. Article 27(3) goes further than Article 13(1)(b) of the Hague Convention by extending the obligation to return even if the requisite Article 13(1)(b) harm can be proved, if it is established[125] that adequate arrangements have been made to secure the child's protection after the return.[126] As Recital (45) helpfully explains, the type of arrangements that is envisaged in this context includes a court order from the Member State to which the child's return is contemplated prohibiting the applicant from coming close to the child, a provisional (including a protective) measure from that Member State allowing the child to stay with the abducting parent who is the primary carer until a decision on the substance of custody has been made in that Member State, or the demonstration of available medical facilities for a child in need of medical treatment.[127] Other examples mentioned in *2022 Practice Guide*[128] are the provision of secure accommodation

---

[123] Article 13(1)(b) permits the court to refuse to order the return of the child if there is a grave risk that the return would expose the child to physical or psychological harm.
[124] Although fears that Member States overuse Article 13(1)(b) are not borne out by the 2015 statistics; see the analysis by N. LOWE and V. STEPHENS, 'Global Trends in the Operation of the 1980 Hague Abduction Convention: The 2015 Statistics' (2018) 52 *Family Law Quarterly* 349, 364. Nevertheless, a growing number of refusals based wholly or in part on Article 13(1)(b) were recorded in the 2021 Study, see Prel. Doc. 19B, above n. 78.
[125] Note the observation by E. GALLANT, above, n. 49, p. 328, paras 11–12 that although the applicant has the burden of proof to show adequate protective arrangements are in place, the courts can make an independent assessment.
[126] See *2022 Practice Guide*, p. 124, para. 4.3.5.
[127] See also C. HONORATI and A. LIMINATE, above n. 3, p. 129 and the Austrian Supreme Court decision *Obe. ster Gerichtshof*, 28 August 2013, No 6 Ob 134/13/13v cited therein. Useful reference can also be made to the Hague Conference's *Guide to Good Practice on Article 13(1)(b)* (HCCH, 2020) paras 43 et seq.
[128] *2022 Practice Guide*, p. 125, para. 4.3.5.1.2.

for the parent and the child, the termination of criminal proceedings against the abducting parent and covering the abducting parent's living costs.

6.83. Establishing that procedures exist is not in itself sufficient; rather, it must be shown that concrete measures have been taken to protect the child in question and that they will be effective to secure his or her protection.[129] Article 27(4) provides that for the purposes of investigating the adequacy of any protective arrangements, the court may communicate with the competent authorities of the Member State where the child was habitually resident before the wrongful removal or retention' either directly[130] or with the assistance of Central Authorities, though Recital (45) advises that the court 'should primarily rely upon the parties'.

6.84. Article 27(3) only applies to refusals to return based **solely** on Article 13(1)(b) of the Hague Convention. While this clearly means that it does not apply to the application of other exceptions – for example, to refusals to return based on the child's objections[131] – the insertion of the word 'solely' could suggest that it does not apply where reliance is being placed on more than one exception.[132] However, that would surely be too narrow an interpretation. It is suggested that Article 27(3) should be interpreted as applying whenever the court is contemplating the application of the Article 13(1)(b) exception, regardless of whether it is also considering the application of other exceptions.

D. TAKING PROVISIONAL MEASURES TO PROTECT THE CHILD FROM GRAVE RISK OF HARM UPON HIS OR HER RETURN

6.85. Under Article 27(5), when the court of the Member State of refuge orders the child's return, it may also, where appropriate, take provisional (including

---

[129] This was clearly stated by the *Practice Guide for the Application of the Brussels IIa) Regulation*, EU Commission, 2014, p. 55, para. 4.3.3. It is implicit in the *2022 Practice Guide* (see p. 124, para. 4.3.5.1.1, referring to the court of refuge having to assess 'whether appropriate measures of protection have been put in place'). Note ECtHR, 21 May 2019, *OCI and Others v. Romania*, App No. 49450/17, in which it was held that what was formerly Article 11(4) did not mean that the State to which children have been wrongfully removed is obliged to send them back to an environment where they will incur a grave risk of domestic violence solely because the authorities in the State in which the child had its habitual residence are capable of dealing with cases of domestic child abuse.
[130] In accordance with Article 86, discussed in Chapter 11 at 11.39.
[131] See, for example, the English Court of Appeal decision, *Vigreux v. Michel* [2006] EWCA Civ 630 on the application of the former Article 11(4).
[132] It is not uncommon for reliance to be placed on more than one ground for refusal. According to the 2021 Statistics, above n. 78, 20% of cases governed by Brussels II-bis ending in a refusal were based upon on more than one ground.

protective) measures in accordance with Article 15 to protect the child from the grave risk referred to in Article 13(1)(b) of the Hague Convention, 'provided that the examining and taking of such measures would not unduly delay the return proceedings'.

6.86. Article 27(5) is new and confers an exceptional power to take protective measures. It reinforces the obligation to return the child even when there might be a risk in the return, but at the same time seeks to ensure that the return is actually safe. **It places a positive obligation on the court of the State of refuge to take steps to protect the child.** In other words, rather than expecting the State of habitual residence to take adequate arrangements or waiting for the left-behind parent to provide for sufficient evidence that such measures are in place, it has positively to collaborate in suggesting such measures to the State of habitual residence (either directly or via the Central Authority) or itself to take such measures as provisional orders. Article 27(5) can be seen as a further attempt to deter courts of the State of refuge from refusing to return the child because of a risk of grave harm. As Recital (46) puts it, such measures, which can include that the child continues to reside with the primary caregiver or how contact should take place after the child's return,[133] can be taken to minimise the risk of physical or psychological harm that might be caused to the child by the return and which would otherwise lead to a refusal to return. On the other hand, as the Recital says, such measures should not 'undermine the delimitation of jurisdiction between the court seised with the return proceedings under the Hague Convention and the court having jurisdiction on the substance of parental responsibility under this Regulation'.[134]

6.87. The drafting of the most appropriate protective measures will generally benefit from direct communication with the judicial or administrative welfare authorities in the State of habitual residence. Article 27(4) accordingly and appropriately suggests that the court of the Member State of refuge should consult the court or competent authorities of such a State, with the assistance of the Central Authorities or network judges, in particular within the European

---

[133] But the protection can be more detailed; see, for example, an English decision (applying the not dissimilar Article 11 of the 1996 Hague Child Protection Convention) *B v. B (Abduction: BIIR)* [2014] EWHC 1804 (Fam), in which the child was ordered to remain in the custody of her mother with the father being prohibited from molesting the mother and from coming within 100 metres of the mother's flat. Note might also be taken of the *Guide to Good Practice on Article 13(1)(b)* (HCCH, 2020) para. 43, which says that 'protective measures' can cover a broad range of existing services, assistance and support, including access to legal services, financial assistance, housing assistance, health services, shelters and other forms of assistance or support to victims of domestic violence. Although this comment is made in relation to the Hague Abduction Convention, it also seems apt for Brussels II-ter.

[134] A point underlined by the *2022 Practice Guide* p. 126, para. 4.3.5.2.

Judicial Network for civil and commercial matters and the International Hague Network of Judges. Welcome though this provision may be, any consultation should be pursued keeping in mind the need to avoid any delay in the decision and in returning the child.

6.88. **Orders made under Article 27(5) have extra-territorial effect**, which means they are recognisable and enforceable in all other Member States.[135] This rule gives teeth to the court's decision and is a real novelty in Brussels II-ter, given that, by definition, the provisional measures envisaged here are of relevance in another Member State – namely, that of the child's habitual residence to which he or she is returned. The need for such extra-territorial protective measures had clearly arisen in practice, as evidenced by the UK Supreme Court's questionable decision to apply the not dissimilar provision of Article 11 of the 1996 Hague Child Protection Convention in the absence of an equivalent provision under Brussels II-bis.[136] However, it should be borne in mind that if the respondent has not been summoned to appear (as may be the case where the left-behind parent is not a necessary part of the return proceedings), such a decision must be served on him or her prior to enforcement.[137] In any event, orders made under Article 27(5) are only temporary and remain in force until a court of the Member State of the child's habitual residence has taken measures that it considers appropriate.

6.89. The overall object of Article 27(3)–(5) is to restrict the use of Article 13(1)(b) of the 1980 Convention by the twofold strategy of restricting the power to refuse a return if it can be shown that there are adequate arrangements to protect the child upon his or her return and to give the courts of the requested Member State the power to make provisional (including protective) orders which have extra-territorial effect. These are useful powers, albeit that the jury is out as to how effective they may be.[138]

---

[135] See Articles 2(1)(b) and 15. This extra-territorial effect is exceptional and is confined to orders made to minimise the risk referred to in Article 13(1)(b) of the Hague Convention. On **all other occasions**, orders made under Article 15 **do not have that effect**. See further the discussion in Chapter 4 at 4.199 et seq.

[136] The UK Supreme Court had no qualms about using Article 11 of the 1996 Convention (see *Re J (A Child) (Reunite International Child Abduction Centre Intervening)* [2015] UKSC 75), but in doing so was open to the objection that it was acting contrary to what was then Article 20 Brussels II-bis; see the criticism by H. SETRIGHT, D WILLIAMS, I. CURRY-SUMNER, M. GRATION, M. WRIGHT, above n. 22, pp. 101–103 and M. WILDERSPIN, above n. 21, para. 7-071, n. 53. Note: Article 27(5) is wider than Article 11 of the 1996 Convention inasmuch as it is not conditional on the matter being one of 'urgency'.

[137] See Article 2(1), final paragraph.

[138] See the analysis of applications made in 2015 on the effect of Article 11(4) Brussels II-bis by N. LOWE and V. STEPHENS, 'Operating the 1980 Hague Abduction Convention in the Context of BIIa', above n. 78, pp. 16–17.

VIII. ENFORCING DECISIONS ORDERING THE RETURN OF THE CHILD

A. THE ENFORCEMENT PROCESS IN THE MEMBER STATE OF REFUGE

6.90. Article 28(1) obliges the 'authority competent for enforcement' to which an application has been made for the enforcement of a return order made under the 1980 Hague Convention 'to act expeditiously in processing the application'. An indication of what is meant by 'expeditiously' is provided by Article 28(2), inasmuch as it gives the party seeking enforcement or the Central Authority of the State of enforcement the right to request a statement of the reasons for delay in cases where the decision was not enforced within six weeks of the initiation of enforcement proceedings.[139]

6.91. The obligation to act expeditiously only applies to the enforcement of orders to return a child to another Member State and not to a third State, although there is nothing to prevent Member States from applying an expeditious process to the enforcement of all return orders. Article 28 does not directly oblige Member States to create a new enforcement process, but they could be penalised if there is a **systemic inability to enforce return orders quickly**.[140] It may be noted that the six-week period only begins to run from the initiation of enforcement proceedings, whereas the general duty to act expeditiously applies to the whole enforcement process.

B. THE ENFORCEABILITY OF RETURN ORDERS

6.92. Decisions ordering the return of the abducted child to his or her State of habitual residence do not, normally, pose an issue of enforceability or enforcement in other Member States. Such orders will normally be enforced in the same jurisdiction as the court making the return order, which is where the child is. Except to the limited extent discussed below, Brussels II-ter does not deal with enforcement of a return order by the Member State that made the order. However, there are unusual cases of so-called 'double abduction', that is cases where, pending or following the decision ordering the child's return, the

---

[139] Article 28(2) is discussed further at 6.63–6.64. Note also Article 56(4) which, in exceptional circumstances, permits the authority competent for enforcement to suspend enforcement proceedings where such proceedings 'would expose the child to a grave risk of physical or psychological harm' etc., see further Chapter 9 at 9.29 et seq.
[140] See further 6.62 above.

child is abducted from the State of refuge and relocated to a different Member State.[141] Given that Hague abduction proceedings do not directly concern the **substance** of parental responsibility,[142] there was a danger that return orders could be regarded as falling outside the scope of Brussels II-bis and therefore not enforceable under it. This doubt has been removed by Article 2(1)(a), which makes it clear that Chapter IV on recognition and enforcement applies to a decision ordering the return of an abducted child[143] to the State of his or her habitual residence pursuant to the Hague Convention and which has to be enforced **in a Member State other than the Member State where the decision is given**. As Recital (16) states, notwithstanding that such proceedings do not concern the substance of parental responsibility, return orders should benefit from recognition and enforcement under the Regulation without the need to bring fresh abduction proceedings, though without prejudice to the ability to do so.

6.93. Return orders made by a court in the State of refuge under the Hague Convention must be distinguished from those made by the court of State of the child's habitual residence under the 'override provisions'.[144] The former rank as non-privileged decisions, while the latter rank as 'privileged decisions', which is of particular significance with regard to refusing to recognise or enforce such orders.[145] Under Article 27(6), a return order made by a court of a Member State 'may be declared provisionally enforceable, notwithstanding any appeal, where the return of the child before the decision on the appeal is required by the best interests of the child'. Recital (47) suggests that national law may specify by which court the decision may be declared provisionally enforceable.

6.94. Providing decisions with provisional enforceability is a matter for national procedural law which varies greatly from Member State to Member State and made it impossible to agree on a common standard.[146] Under Brussels II-ter, provisional enforceability is grounded directly in the Regulation, thus allowing the court to grant it even when national rules do not provide for it. In other words, by conferring full discretion in the court as to the enforceability of a return

---

[141] See A. SCHULZ 'Das Vollstreckungssystem in der neuen Brüssel IIa-Verordnung' in C. BUDZIKIEWICZ, B. HEIDRHOFF, F. KLINKHAMMER and K. NIETHAMMER-JÜGENS (eds), *Standards und Abgrenzungen im internationalen Familienrecht*, Nosmos, 2019, 93, 108 and referred to by D. MARTINY, above n. 10, p. 516.

[142] See Recital (16) and note also Recital (5).

[143] Including any provisional and protective measures made with the return order in accordance with Article 27(5) in conjunction with Article 15 (discussed at 6.84–6.86 above): Article 2(1)(b).

[144] Discussed at 6.96 et seq.

[145] See Chapter 8 at 8.140 et seq and Chapter 9 at 9.57 et seq.

[146] For example, in the Italian legal system, all decisions are immediately enforceable, but the court can stay the enforceability if an appeal is lodged. In contrast, in Germany decisions concerning minors are never enforceable until they become final.

decision, Article 27(5) is of special relevance in those Member State which do not provide for the enforceability of a decision until it is final.

6.95. The rationale of this provision is to mitigate the harmful effects that a lengthy appeal process (particularly where up to three levels of challenge are permitted) could have on the child by delaying his or her return. Obvious examples include a return order made in the context of an abduction by the non-primary carer to a State with which the child has no connection and no familiarity, or where the child is at a crucial stage of his or her education in the State of habitual residence. Article 27(6) can also be seen in the general context of the attempts of Brussels II-ter to address the general problem of delay in determining Hague applications. However, understandable as this aim may be, Article 27(6) is problematic, not least because of the reference to the child's best interests, which is directed to whether a return order should be implemented immediately notwithstanding an appeal, but which could be misinterpreted as implying a welfare determination into the return decision itself. Nevertheless, as one commentator has noted,[147] there is concern that Article 27(6) could open up the possibility of 'a to and fro of the child between the two States'.[148] In that commentator's opinion, a binding decision of the appeal court in the State of refuge would have been a better solution.

IX. REFUSING TO ORDER A CHILD'S RETURN – THE OVERRIDE MECHANISM: ARTICLE 29

A. THE BACKGROUND TO THE OVERRIDE MECHANISM

6.96. A key innovation of Brussels II-bis was to introduce provisions dealing with the position following a refusal to return based on one the exceptions under Article 13 of the Hague Convention.[149] These collectively became known as the 'override mechanism'.[150] This mechanism was an integral part of the underlying strategy of Brussels II-bis on international child abduction to strengthen the return obligation under the 1980 Convention and to try to limit the possibilities opened by that Convention to refuse to order the return of the child.[151]

---

[147] D. MARTINY, above n. 10, p. 513.
[148] A classic example of consequential problems that can follow a removal pending an appeal is CJEU, 9 October 2014, *C v. M*, C-376/14 PPU, discussed at 6.36 above.
[149] Under Article 11(6)–(8) Brussels II-bis.
[150] It is referred to as the 'notwithstanding' return mechanism and as 'last word' procedure by E. GALLANT, above, n. 48, pp. 334 and 336, and as the 'second chance procedure', by, for example, T. KRUGER and L. SAMYN, 'Brussels II bis: successes and suggested improvements' (2016) 12 *Journal of Private International Law* 132, 158.
[151] E. PATAUT and E. GALLANT, above n. 9, 149.

6.97. Although, as mentioned at 6.6 above, this mechanism was of historical significance inasmuch it was the compromise that broke the deadlock between Member States and enabled the proposal to revise the Regulation to go ahead, research showed[152] that, in terms of children actually being returned notwithstanding the initial refusal, the mechanism had had a relatively small impact.

6.98. Despite these findings and other calls for the override mechanism to be abolished,[153] the Commission did not recommend its abolition probably on the basis, as one commentator put it,[154] that 'it provides an instrument for ensuring more effective protection of children and makes for European specificity'. No doubt too, it was thought important to maintain the policy of prioritising the return of abducted children.

6.99. Although Brussels II-ter maintains the override mechanism, unlike the Commission's Proposal,[155] it narrows its application. It also seeks to clarify its operation, not least in the common situation in which the left-behind parent simultaneously files two different sets of proceedings: one in the State of habitual residence, asking for a change in the child's custody or placement regime, and the other in the State of refuge, for the return of child. One of the legal challenges of international abduction proceedings of this understandable practice (given that the family crisis will normally not be confined to the abduction and will require a more general resolution of the child's future) is the need to put in place rules for coordinating the two proceedings. One of the purposes of the override mechanism is to ensure that within the EU, both courts cooperate, *inter alia*, by exchanging court documents, reports and findings, with a view to securing the best interests of the abducted child. An innovation of Brussels II-ter is that, unlike Brussels II-bis, it addresses the position where proceedings on the substance of rights of custody have already been filed in the State of the child's habitual residence and the case where this was not done separately (see below).

---

[152] See P. BEAUMONT, L. WALKER and J. HOLLIDAY, 'Not heard and not returned: the reality of Article 11(6)–(8) Proceedings' [2015] *International Family Law* 124; P. BEAUMONT, L. WALKER and J. HOLLIDAY, 'Conflicts of EU Courts on Child Abduction: The Reality of Article 11(6)–(8) Proceedings across the EU' (2016) 12 *Journal of Private International Law* 211. According to this research, out of the 63 known such proceedings Europe-wide heard between 1 March 2005 (when Brussels II-bis came into force) and 30 September 2015, only seven resulted in the child actually being returned.

[153] See, for example, T. KRUGER and L. SAMYN, above n. 150, p. 159; and I. CURRY-SUMNER, above n. 11, 1. Cf. L. CARPANETO, 'In-depth Consideration of Family Life v. Immediate Return of the Child in Child Abduction Proceedings within the EU' (2014) *Rivisita di dritto internazionale private e processuale* 931, 943 et seq.

[154] C. HONORATI, above n. 103, p. 107.

[155] See the Commission's proposed Article 26(2).

B. THE OPERATION OF THE OVERRIDE MECHANISM

6.100. The override mechanism is governed by Article 29 Brussels II-ter, the aims of which are as follows:

- to uphold and reinforce the competence of the State of the child's habitual residence, allowing such a court to have the last word on the matter of the child's custody;
- to prevent the court of the State of refuge from assuming jurisdiction following a refusal to return the child solely based on Article 13(1)(b) or (2) of the Hague Convention;
- to give the left-behind parent the opportunity of having a decision on the substance of rights of custody determined by a court of the Member State in which the child was habitually resident before the wrongful removal or retention; and
- to provide that if, following that adjudication, the court makes a decision entailing the child's return, then that decision is recognisable and enforceable as a 'privileged decision'[156] in another Member State, thereby overriding the initial refusal to order the return made by the court of the Member State of refuge.[157]

C. WHEN THE MECHANISM APPLIES

6.101. Article 29(1) confines the application of the override mechanism to decisions to refuse to order the return a child based 'solely' on Article 13(1)(b) (grave risk of harm) or Article 13(2) (child's objections) of the Hague Convention. In other words, it no longer applies to refusals based on the other so-called adult-centred exceptions (consent, acquiescence and non-exercise of rights of custody) under Article 13 of the Hague Convention or to refusals based on any other Article.[158]

6.102. There is logic in no longer providing that the adult-centred exceptions under Article 13 trigger the override mechanism inasmuch as, given the left-behind parent's position, there is no reason for the court of the child's habitual residence before the abduction to keep jurisdiction. However, it might also be wondered how often it will be appropriate to override a refusal based on the

---

[156] See Chapter 8 at 8.135 et seq.
[157] See Recital (48). But see Chapter 9 for discussion of when enforcement may nevertheless be refused.
[158] That is, Articles 3, 12(2) and 20, a point emphasised by the *2022 Practice Guide*, p. 133, para. 4.4.1.

grave risk of harm exception or indeed to override the child's objection. In any event, confining the mechanism to these two instances means that the elaborate mechanism, which will be discussed below, will not often be triggered and rarely applied.[159]

6.103. It is not clear what is meant by 'solely' relying on one of the two exceptions, which is a prerequisite under Article 29(1) to trigger the override mechanism. Read literally, where reliance is placed on more than one exception (as already noted, it is not uncommon for courts to rely on more than one exception when refusing a return order)[160] the override mechanism will not be triggered. But would that mean that when reliance is placed upon both the Article 13(1)(b) and (2) exceptions, the mechanism is not triggered? As discussed above (at 6.84), a similar problem of interpretation applies to the application of Article 27(3) and it is suggested that the same solution should be applied – namely, to apply the mechanism whenever a refusal is based in whole or in part upon Article 13(1)(b) and/or (2).

6.104. Note should be taken of Recital (48), which says that courts 'should refer explicitly to the relevant Articles of the Hague Convention on which the refusal was based'.[161] While this should mean that courts cannot avoid triggering the mechanism simply by not specifying the ground(s) upon which the refusal is based, there would appear to be nothing to prevent a court deliberately choosing to base the refusal upon a ground other than Article 13(1)(b) or (2) so as to avoid its operation.[162]

D. CERTIFICATING THE DECISION TO REFUSE THE CHILD'S RETURN

6.105. Where the court makes a decision (be it final or subject to appeal)[163] to refuse the child's return on the sole basis of Article 13(1)(b) or (2) of the

---

[159] According to the 2015 Statistics, above n. 78, there were only 22 refusals solely based on either Article 13(1)(b) and (2) as between Member States governed by Brussels II-bis, with a further four partially relying on the exceptions. According to the 2021 statistics, above n.78, there were 32 such refusals based wholly or in part on Article 13(1)(b) or (2). Nevertheless, as E. GALLANT, above, n. 49, p. 334, para. 8 notes, the reduction is explained by the desire to confine the mechanisms to 'the most contentious cases of refusal both in quantitive and qualitative terms'.

[160] See n. 132 above.

[161] See also the *2022 Practice Guide*, p. 134, para. 4.4.1, which says that the ground should be stated in the decision as well as in the Certificate (as per Point 7 of Annex 1). In the Commission's proposal, this requirement was included in the text.

[162] For an example of where this was done under Brussels II-bis, see the English decision *SP v. EB and KP* [2014] EWHC 3964 (Fam), in which reliance was placed upon Article 20 rather than Article 13(1)(b).

[163] ECJ, 11 July 2008, *Rinau*, C-195/08 PPU.

Hague Convention, it must **of its own motion** issue a certificate in the form set out in Annex 1. This certificate must be completed and issued in the language of the decision, but it can also be issued in another official language of the EU at the request of a party. However, there is no obligation for the court issuing the certificate to provide a translation or transliteration[164] of the translatable content of the free text fields.[165]

6.106. The purpose of the certificate is to inform the parties that: (a) they can seise the court of the Member State in which the child was habitually resident immediately before the wrongful removal or retention, within three months of the notification of the refusal, with applications regarding the substance of rights of custody; and (b) any decision resulting from the custody proceedings that 'entails the return of the child' is enforceable in any Member State.[166]

E. THE POSITION FOLLOWING A REFUSAL TO RETURN: THE BACKGROUND

6.107. Formerly, under Brussels II-bis,[167] in all cases following a relevant refusal to order the child's return,[168] the court had to transmit, either directly or through its Central Authority, a copy of the order and relevant documents to the court with jurisdiction or Central Authority in the Member State where the child was habitually resident before the wrongful removal or retention. In turn, unless the court of habitual residence was already seised by the parties, the court or Central Authority that received the information has, within three months, to notify the parties and, in effect, to invite them to bring custody proceedings. Following changes made during the negotiations among Member States,[169] the scheme under Brussels II-ter differs in a number of important respects. First, it confines the obligation of the court making the decision to refuse the child's return (on the basis of Article 13(1)(b) or (2) of the 1980 Convention) to transmit a copy of its decision, etc. if there are pending proceedings on the substance of rights of custody before a court of the child's habitual residence before the abduction. Second, where there are no such pending proceedings, the burden of submitting a copy of the decision, etc. is placed on the party seeking to seise the court of the child's habitual residence before the abduction to examine the substance of rights of custody. Third, the process of informing the parties of their

---

[164] That is, using the corresponding letters of a different alphabet or language.
[165] Article 29(2).
[166] Recital (49).
[167] See Article 11(6) and (7), discussed, *inter alia*, by E. PATAUT and E. GALLENT, above n. 9, pp. 143 et seq.
[168] That is, under any of the grounds provided for by Article 13 of the 1980 Hague Convention.
[169] The changes had not been included in the Commission's Proposal.

opportunity to bring proceedings in the court of the child's habitual residence to examine the substance of rights of custody is now done more efficiently via the certificate issued by the court when making its decision to refuse to return the child.

1. *The Position Following a Refusal to Return: The Scheme under Brussels II-ter*

6.108. Under Article 29(3), where, at the time of the decision refusing return, a court of the Member State in which the child was habitually resident before the wrongful removal or retention is already seised of proceedings to examine the substance of rights of custody, the **court making the decision to refuse the return of the child** must, if it is aware of those proceedings, and **within one month** of the refusal, transmit various documents directly or through the Central Authorities to the court of the child's habitual residence (see 6.109 below). The advantage of making it a court responsibility is that it better safeguards the interests of the left-behind parent and coordinates with the court of the State of origin's obligation when deciding on whether or not to use the override mechanism to take into account the reasons for non-return.[170] However, this obligation only arises if the court is aware of the pending proceedings. Brussels II-ter provides no mechanism for informing the court about these proceedings,[171] but given that at least one of parties must be aware of them, good practice would dictate that they should be formally asked whether there are such proceedings.

6.109. Under Article 29(5), where there are no pending proceedings on the substance of rights of custody in the court of the Member State in which the child was habitually resident immediately before the wrongful removal or retention, but one of the parties seises that court within **three months** of the notification of the refusal, the burden of submitting the required documents (see below) to that court falls on that party.

6.110. The documents that the court or party has to submit are:

- a copy of the decision; and
- the certificate issued; and, where applicable, a transcript, summary or minutes of the hearings before the court which refused the return of the child.[172]

---

[170] See Article 47(4), discussed at 6.121 below. See also CJEU, 19 November 2015, *P*, C-455/15, para. 52.
[171] The *2022 Practice Guide*, p. 134, para. 4.4.2 says that information about the pending case before the Member State of origin can be brought to its attention by the parties or *ex officio* in the course of cooperation and communication between the courts.
[172] It might be difficult for a party to obtain a transcript or minutes after the proceedings have terminated, especially if records are not maintained.

6.111. In addition to the above, the court obligation also extends to transmitting to 'any other document it considers relevant', which, as Recital (50) explains, refers to any documents which contain information that might have a bearing on the outcome of the proceedings relating to rights of custody, if such information is not already contained in the decision refusing return. Although there is no equivalent reference as far as the party obligation is concerned, according to Recital (51), this does not preclude the court seised with the 'rights of custody' proceedings from asking for additional documents which might contain information that might have a bearing on those proceedings if such information is not already contained in the decision refusing return. It should also be noted that the court of the Member State examining the substance of custody may, where necessary, 'require a party to provide a translation or transliteration … of the decision and any other document attached to the certificate'.[173]

6.112. The process of informing parties of their right to bring rights of custody proceedings in the court of the child's habitual residence immediately before the abduction has been streamlined. Under Brussels II-ter, this is done directly, via the certificate issued by the court making the decision refusing the return of the child and thereby avoids the additional obligation, previously imposed by Article 11(7) Brussels II-bis, upon the court that refused to return the child to notify the court or Central Authority of the child's pre-abduction habitual residence of that decision, and upon that court or Central Authority to notify the parties of their right to initiate rights of custody proceedings. This is a welcome improvement.

6.113. As the certificate makes clear, the parties have **three months** from being notified of the decision refusing the return of the child to seise the court. If no proceedings are initiated within this time limit, the override mechanism does not apply. This is a significant limitation compared with the previous scheme, which provided for no time limits, except the ordinary ones applying under national law. Given the normally multiple legal procedures that are initiated in international child abduction, coupled with high emotional involvement for all the parties involved and especially for the child, a tight time limitation appears sensible. On the other hand, once proceedings have been started within the three months, no time limit is expressed to apply to the determination of those proceedings. While this is understandable, given that such proceedings are full custody proceedings (see below) requiring the child's welfare to be thoroughly investigated, since time remains of the essence, it could perhaps be argued that, at the very least, courts should prioritise the hearing of such cases.

---

[173] Article 29(4).

2. The Nature and Object of Article 29(3) and (5) Proceedings

6.114. Both Article 29(3) and (5) proceedings are full welfare proceedings. This is clearly signalled by the reference in both paragraphs to a 'decision on the substance of rights of custody'. This is underscored by Recital (48), which states: 'In the course of these proceedings, all the circumstances should be thoroughly examined, taking into account the best interests of the child and including, but not limited to the conduct of the parents'.

Nevertheless, notwithstanding the requirement of certification that account needs to be taken of the reasons for and the facts underlying the prior decision to refuse the child's return,[174] it is important to stress that these proceedings are not a review mechanism of the court of the State of refuge's decision to refuse to return the child. The two proceedings are quite different – whereas the latter are solely concerned with whether to order the child's return, the former is a full merits hearing to determine the child's future, albeit that the final outcome might be similar to the Hague decision.

6.115. While Article 29(3) proceedings are clearly domestic law proceedings, there is some room for argument concerning the status of Article 29(5) proceedings. Could they be regarded, for example, as a special type of Regulation proceedings or even as Hague proceedings? The classification is not without significance, particularly if they are to be regarded as Hague proceedings, as courts may have to be guided by Convention policy and different rules on legal aid may apply. It is submitted the proceedings are best regarded as domestic proceedings, albeit that the foundation for any examination of the question of the custody of the child is through the gateway of Article 29(5).[175]

6.116. Under Brussels II-bis, the CJEU ruled in *RG*[176] that it is a matter for national law whether or not to create a specialised jurisdiction for Article 11(7)–(8) proceedings. Presumably, the same is true for hearing Article 29(3) and (5) proceedings under Brussels II-ter.

3. Decisions Entailing the Child's Return

6.117. Under Article 29(6), **any decision on the substance of rights of custody which entails the return of the child** made in the course of Article 29(3) or

---

[174] See Article 47(4), referred to at 6.119 below. Note also the ECtHR's ruling in ECtHR, 12 July 2011, *Šneersone and Kampanella v. Italy*, App No. 14737/09 that a domestic order under the Regulation scheme is subject to human rights considerations.
[175] See the analysis of what was then Article 11(7) Brussels II-bis in an English decision: *D v. N and D (by the Guardian Ad Litem) (Brussels II Revised: Article 11(7))* [2011] EWHC 471 (Fam), para. 39.
[176] CJEU, 9 January 2015, *RG*, C-498/14 PPU.

Article 29(5) proceedings is enforceable in another Member State in accordance with Chapter IV of Brussels II-ter. The wording of Article 29(6) differs from Article 11(8) Brussels II-bis (which it replaces) in two respects. First, unlike the former Article 11(8) of Brussels II-bis, which referred to any subsequent judgment which 'requires' the return of the child, Article 29(6) refers to decisions 'entailing' that return. No doubt the change of wording (made during the negotiations following the Commission's Proposal) is intended to bring Article 29(6) into line with Article 9(b)(v), which, as discussed at 6.26 above, is concerned with jurisdiction in cases of wrongful removal or retention of a child. It is perhaps a matter of debate as to whether any change of substance results from this change of wording.[177] The second change – namely, that rather than applying to any judgment requiring the child's return, Article 29(6) only applies to any decision **on the substance of rights of custody**, entailing the child's return – is arguably of more significance and calls into question the application a previous ECJ ruling, *Povse*,[178] on the meaning of Article 11(8) Brussels II-bis.

6.118. In *Povse* the ECJ ruled that orders requiring the child's return fell within the scheme even where the court with jurisdiction had not made a final decision on custody. In other words, it applied to return orders made pending a final hearing. The Court considered that such an interpretation was consistent with the need for expedition. It observed that confining the provision to return orders made in final custody proceedings 'would constitute a constraint which might compel the court with jurisdiction to take a decision on rights of custody when it had neither all the information and all the material needed for that purpose, nor the time required to make an objective and dispassionate assessment'. It rejected the argument that its interpretation might lead to the child being moved needlessly in the event of the court with jurisdiction ultimately awarding custody to the abducting parent. It reasoned that the need for the final order to be fair and soundly based, the need to deter child abduction, and the child's right (as per Article 24 of the EU Charter of Fundamental Rights) to maintain on a regular basis a personal relationship and direct contact with both parents, took 'precedence over any disadvantages which such moving might entail'.[179] Although some might think that the Court's reasoning was convincing, it has been argued[180] that this aspect of the ruling in *Povse* can no longer be considered good law under Brussels II-ter, as the requirement that the decision entailing a child's return must one **on the substance of rights of custody** means that it

---

[177] But note the analysis by M. WILDERSPIN, above n. 21, p. 316, para. 7-118.
[178] CJEU, 1 July 2010, *Povse*, C-211/10 PPU. Note the subsequent unsuccessful challenge under the European Convention on Human Rights: ECtHR, 18 June 2014, *Povse v. Austria*, App No. 3890/11.
[179] See paras 62–64.
[180] M. WILDERSPIN, above n. 21, p. 316, para. 7-117.

cannot apply to provisional orders. It remains to be seen whether Article 29(6) will be so interpreted.

6.119. The full meaning of 'decisions entailing the return of the child' has still to be explored by the CJEU. One possible area of difficulty concerns contact orders. In an English decision on the application of Article 11(8) Brussels II-bis,[181] it was held that the override mechanism was only triggered by decisions that determined that the child should live with a parent in the jurisdiction from where he or she was taken and not by a decision that the child should be made available to meet the parent there. It remains to be seen whether Article 29(6) will be similarly interpreted, but it may be that the change of wording makes a difference in this respect.

i) The Need for a Certificate and the Requirements for Certification

6.120. In order for the order entailing the return of the child to become recognisable and enforceable, it must be certified by the court of the Member State that made the order. Such orders qualify as 'privileged decisions' under the Regulation, which means that the scope for challenge is extremely limited.[182] However, a party is not bound to use the privileged decision route.[183]

6.121. The court that made the order entailing the return of the child shall, upon a party's request, issue a certificate.[184] However, under Article 47(3), a certificate may only be issued if:

(a) all parties concerned were given an opportunity to be heard;
(b) the child was given an opportunity to express his or her views in accordance with Article 21;
(c) where the decision was given in default of appearance, the person defaulting was served with the document which instituted proceedings or with an equivalent document in sufficient time and in such a way as to enable that person to arrange for his or her defence or it is established that the person defaulting accepted the decision unequivocally.

Article 47(4) adds the further requirement that the court must have taken into account in giving its decision the reasons for and the facts underlying the prior decision given in another Member State pursuant to Article 13(1)(b) or 13(2) of the Hague Convention.

---

[181] Re A, HA v. MB (Brussels II Revised: Article 11(7) Application) [2007] EWHC 2016 (Fam), para. 95.
[182] See further the discussion in Chapter 8.
[183] See Article 42(2). Why a party would not wish to use the 'privileged decision' route is unclear.
[184] Article 47(1). The certificate should be in the form set out by Annex VI: Article 47(1)(b).

6.122. Notwithstanding the above requirements, once issued, no challenges to the validity of the certificate, other than as a result of rectification made by the court of origin, are permitted.[185] As the CJEU emphasised under Brussels II-bis, the issue of a certificate in the Member State of origin is to be recognised and is to be automatically enforceable in another Member State, there being no possibility of opposing its recognition or enforcement.[186]

6.123. As Article 47(2) states, the certificate must be completed and issued in the language of the decision, but it may also be issued in another official language of the EU at the request of a party. However, there is no obligation on the court issuing the certificate to provide a translation or transliteration of the relevant content.

ii) The Effect of Certificated Decisions

6.124. Upon production of a copy of the decision entailing the return of a child which satisfies the conditions necessary to establish its authenticity[187] and the appropriate certificate, the order must be recognised in the other Member State, without any possibility of opposing its recognition unless and to the extent that irreconcilability with a decision referred to in Article 47 is found to exist.'[188] Similarly, provided the order is enforceable in the Member State in which is made,[189] it is enforceable in other Member States without any declaration of enforceability being required.[190] The net effect is that the order entailing the child's return overrides the initial refusal made under the Hague Convention.

6.125. Although it is open to a party to request partial enforcement of a decision, an order entailing the return of a child cannot be enforced without also enforcing any provisional measures, including protective measures, which have been ordered to minimise the grave risk of harm to the child referred to in Article 13(1)(b) of the Hague Convention.[191]

6.126. According to a CJEU ruling on the application of Brussels II-bis in the case of *Rinau*,[192] although it is a *sine qua non* that what would now be an Article 29(6) judgment backed by an Article 47 certificate can only be made

---

[185] Article 47(6). The rectification powers under Article 48 are discussed in Chapters 8 and 9.
[186] See CJEU, 22 December 2010, *Aguirre Zarraga*, C-491/10 PPU; and CJEU, 26 April 2012, *Health Service Executive and SC*, C-92/12 PPU.
[187] See further Chapter 8.
[188] Article 43, which in turn refers to Article 50.
[189] Note: under Article 47(5), the certificate only takes effect within the limits of the enforceability of the decision.
[190] Article 45(1).
[191] See Article 53(3).
[192] ECJ, 11 July 2008, *Rinau*, C-195/08 PPU.

following a decision not to return the child made by the requested State, once such a decision **has been made and communicated to the court of origin**, then, because of the need for speed:

- it was irrelevant for the purposes of issuing a certificate that the non-return decision had been 'suspended, overturned, set aside or, in any event, has not become *res judicata* or has been replaced by a decision ordering return, insofar as the return of the child has not actually taken place'; and
- given that the responsibility for properly issuing the certificate lies with the court of origin (viz that the child and the parties had been given the opportunity to be heard and the court had taken into account the requested court's reasons for and evidence underlined its non-return decision), once the authenticity of the certificate is not in doubt, opposing its recognition is not permitted and the requested court must therefore declare the enforceability of the certified decision and allow the child's immediate return.

6.127. In *Povse*,[193] another decision applying Brussels II-bis, the ECJ ruled, *inter alia*:

- A decision of a Member State with jurisdiction requiring the child's return falls within what would now be Article 29(6), even though that State's court has not made a final decision on custody. In other words, it applies to return orders made pending a final hearing.
- A subsequent judgment granting provisional custody rights made by a court in the Member State of enforcement and deemed enforceable under the law of that State does not preclude the enforcement of a certified order requiring the child's return.

It also ruled that enforcement of a certified judgment cannot be refused in the Member State of enforcement because, as a result of a subsequent change of circumstances, it might be seriously detrimental to the best interests of the child. Such a change must be pleaded before the court which has jurisdiction in the Member State of origin, which should also hear any application to suspend enforcement of its judgment. Yet, as will be discussed in Chapter 9, the position under Brussels II-ter is not so straightforward.[194]

6.128. Although the override mechanism can be said to enable the court of the child's pre-abduction habitual residence to 'trump' a non-return order (though it has always been the case that such a court can 'trump' a return order), as a

---

[193] CJEU, 1 July 2010, *Povse*, C-211/10 PPU.
[194] See the discussion of Article 56(4) and (6) in Chapter 9 at 9.29 et seq and 9.64–9.67.

matter of principle, given that the 1980 Hague Convention does not deal with jurisdiction after a refusal to return, it is clearly right to vest that jurisdiction in the court of the child's pre-abduction habitual residence. One problem of doing so is that the child and the abductor will not be present in that jurisdiction. But this argument has become less strong, particularly given the development of remote hearings in response to the COVID-19 pandemic. It has long been possible for both the child and abducting parent to be heard in the State in which they are staying by using the arrangements laid down in the Taking of Evidence Regulation.[195] Even so, given the relative paucity of cases and rarity of actual returns,[196] it might be questioned whether such an elaborate scheme[197] is justified.[198]

---

[195] Regulation (EU) 2020/1783 on co-operation between the courts of the Member States in taking evidence in civil or commercial matters (taking evidence) (recast).
[196] See the findings by P. BEAUMONT, L. WALKER and J. HOLLIDAY, 'Not heard and not returned: the reality of Article 11(6)–(8) Proceedings' above n. 152.
[197] In this respect, it might be observed that the final version of Brussels II-ter is more complicated than the Commission's proposed version.
[198] It might in any event, be queried whether the left-behind parent who had a custody order in their favour before the abduction, might be better advised to seek to enforce the order under Brussels II-ter since there are fewer grounds of refusal than under the Abduction Convention and the abolition of exequatur might be just as quick.

CHAPTER 7

THE HEARING OF THE CHILD

I. Introduction 271
   A. Background to the Position Taken by Brussels II-ter 272
   B. The Developing Position under the Brussels II Regulations 273
II. The Position under Brussels II-ter 275
   A. The Basic Obligation: Article 21 275
   B. Affording Children the Opportunity to Express their Views:
      Article 21(1) 276
      1. The Parameters of the Courts' Obligation. 276
      2. When the Obligation Arises 277
         i) Assessing a Child's Capability to Form His or Her Own
            Views 278
         ii) Providing a Genuine Opportunity to Express Views 279
         iii) The Means by which the Child is Heard 281
      3. Giving Due Weight to the Child's Views: Article 21(2). 281
      4. The Certification Requirement. 282
      5. The Effect of the Certificate. 283

I. INTRODUCTION

7.1. Reflecting the importance attached to **hearing children** in proceedings concerning them, **Article 21 Brussels II-ter** makes it an **express obligation** for the courts to give the child who is capable of forming his or her views a genuine and effective opportunity to express those views when exercising their jurisdiction **in all matters of parental responsibility**. It is important to note at the outset that Article 21 stops short of conferring, as some Member States wanted, a right to be heard upon a child; rather, it confers upon a child capable of forming views the right to have the opportunity to express them. This compromise was the outcome of lengthy discussion during the negotiations on the Commission's Proposal.

Intersentia   271

A. BACKGROUND TO THE POSITION TAKEN BY BRUSSELS II-TER

7.2. As has been widely observed, there has been, both within Member States and beyond, a decisive shift from the traditional position where children's views were decided solely based on the views of adults, that is, parents and professionals, to one where children are recognised as rights holders and therefore seen as active participants and actors in the family justice system rather than as passive victims of family breakdown.[1] International impetus to this change of approach was given by the **UN Convention on the Rights of the Child 1989** (UNCRC) to which all Member States are parties. Article 12 UNCRC places a general obligation on States Parties to 'assure to the child who is capable of forming his or her views the right to express those views freely in all matters affecting' them and for those views to be given due weight in accordance with their age and maturity, and a particular obligation for the child to be given the opportunity to be heard in any judicial and administrative proceedings either directly or through a representative or an appropriate body consistent with procedural rules of national law.[2] This obligation is underscored by Article 24(1) of the **Charter of Fundamental Rights of the European Union**, which gives children the right to express their views freely and for those views to be taken into account on matters that concern them in accordance with their age and maturity.[3] This right to express their views is part of and subject to the overarching principle expressed in both instruments that in all actions 'the child's best interests must be a primary consideration'.[4] As Recital (39) of Brussels II-ter states, these two instruments play an important role in the application of the Regulation.

7.3. Another international instrument to be born in mind is the **1950 European Convention on Human Rights** (ECHR), which again binds all Member States. Although it does not explicitly mention the right of the child

---

[1] See, for example, B. UBERTAZZI, 'Hearing of the Child' in C. HONORATI (ed.), *Jurisdiction in Matrimonial Matters, Parental Responsibility and International Abduction*, Giappichelli/Peter Lang, 2017, ch. 5; B. UBERTAZZI, 'The hearing of the child in the Brussels IIa Regulation and its Recast Proposal' (2017) 13 *Journal of Private International Law* 568; C. MOL, *The Children's Right to Participate in Family Law Proceedings*, Intersentia, 2022; M. MURCH, *Supporting Children When Parents Separate*, Policy Press, 2018, ch. 4; and N. LOWE and M. MURCH, 'Children's participation in the family justice system: translating principle into practice' [2001] *Child and Family Law Quarterly* 137.

[2] For a detailed analysis of Article 12, described as the most influential of the Convention's provisions, see L. LUNDY, J. TOBIN and A. PARKES 'The Right to Respect for the Views of the Child' in J. TOBIN (ed.), *The UN Convention on the Rights of the Child: A Commentary*, Oxford University Press, 2019, ch. 12.

[3] For an analysis of the Charter's application to child participation, see C. MOL, above n. 1, pp. 109–118.

[4] See Article 24(2) of the Charter and Article 3(1) UNCRC.

to be heard,[5] the European Court of Human Rights has, in the words of one commentator, 'incorporated the principles of Article 12 UNCRC into its analysis of Article 8 ECHR, by making the child's participation in any private law proceedings a procedural requirement under this provision'.[6]

7.4. A further international instrument to be noted is the **1996 European Convention on the Exercise of Children's Rights**,[7] to which 15 Member States are bound.[8] This Convention aims to supplement the UNCRC, *inter alia*, by providing procedural mechanisms by which the child can be heard in legal proceedings. Thus, while Article 6 provides that in proceedings affecting a child, the judicial authority, before taking a decision, must allow the child to express his or her views and give due weight to them, it also provides that the authority should ensure that the child has received all relevant information which, under Article 3, he or she has a right to receive.

7.5. Finally, it might be observed that the **Council of Europe's 2010 Guidelines on child-friendly justice** also promote children's right to be heard.[9]

B. THE DEVELOPING POSITION UNDER THE BRUSSELS II REGULATIONS

7.6. Given the above-mentioned international instruments, there was no need to make extra provision simply to impose an obligation upon the courts to give the child who is capable of forming his or her views a genuine and effective opportunity to express those views, though as is discussed below (see 7.8–7.9), there are clear advantages in placing that obligation in a regulatory framework. At all events, the original Brussels II Regulation of 2000 implicitly relied upon the wider international obligation and simply provided as a ground of non-recognition and enforcement of a judgment relating to parental responsibility the failure (except in cases of emergency) to give the child the opportunity to be

---

[5] In fact, the ECHR confers rights on 'persons' and, strikingly, makes no reference to 'child' or 'children'.

[6] C. FENTON-GLYNN, *Children and the European Court of Human Rights*, Oxford University Press, 2021, 289. In support of this comment, the author cites, *inter alia*, ECtHR, 2 February 2016, *NTS and Others v. Georgia*, App No. 71776/12; ECtHR, 3 September 2015, *M and M v. Croatia*, App No. 10161/13; and ECtHR, 11 October 2016, *Iglesias Casarrubios and Cantalapiedra Iglesias v. Spain*, App No. 23298/12. See also the analyses by B. UBERTAZZI, 'Hearing of the Child' above n. 1, pp. 163–168; B. UBERTAZZI, 'The hearing of the child in the Brussels IIa Regulation and its Recast Proposal', above n. 1, pp. 575–579; and C. MOL, above n. 1, ch. 4.

[7] ETS No 160.

[8] That is (as of 1 January 2024), Austria, Croatia, Cyprus, the Czech Republic, Finland, France, Germany, Greece, Italy, Latvia, Malta, Poland, Portugal, Slovenia and Spain.

[9] *Guidelines of the Committee of Ministers of the Council of Europe on child-friendly justice*, Council of Europe, 2010, paras 106 et seq.

heard 'in violation of the fundamental principles of procedure of the Member State in which recognition is sought'.[10]

7.7. More attention to hearing the child was paid in Brussels II-bis. As well as providing the same ground as previously for non-recognition and enforcement of a judgment relating to parental responsibility for failing to give the child the opportunity to be heard,[11] it also provided, in the case of an application for the return of a child under the 1980 Hague Abduction Convention as between two Member States (except Denmark), that it had to be 'ensured that the child was given the opportunity to be heard during the proceedings unless this appears inappropriate having regard to his or her age or degree of maturity'.[12] Additionally, Recital (33) stated that the Regulation recognised the fundamental rights and observed the principles of the Charter of Fundamental Rights of the European Union and, in particular, ensured the fundamental rights of the child as set out by Article 24 of the Charter.[13] However, as the *2022 Practice Guide* notes,[14] under Brussels II-bis there was 'no harmonised obligation for the courts of Member States exercising jurisdiction in parental responsibility matters to provide the child with an opportunity to express his or her own views'.

7.8. Brussels II-ter adopts a different approach. It imposes, through Article 21, **a general obligation upon the courts** of a Member State in all cases in which it is exercising jurisdiction in matters of parental responsibility **to afford the child capable of forming his or her views a genuine and effective opportunity to express those views and for those views to be given due weight in accordance with the child's age and maturity**. It applies this general right in return proceedings as between Member States under the 1980 Hague Convention[15] and defines the ground upon which recognition and enforcement of a decision relating to parental responsibility may be refused for failing to give the child the opportunity to be heard with reference to Article 21.[16] Brussels II-ter thus harmonises three aspects of hearing the child, namely, obliging the court to assess the child's capability to form his or her own views, affording the child a genuine and effective opportunity to express those views, and giving due weight to those views.[17] But over and above this, forcing courts to consider these three

---

[10] See Article 15(2)(b) and Article 24(2).
[11] See Article 23(b) and Article 31(2).
[12] See Article 11(2) and, in so providing, broke new ground; see further Chapter 6 at 6.72 et seq.
[13] The obligation to hear the child was also highlighted by the *Practice Guide for the Application of the Brussels IIa Regulation*, European Commission, 2016, Section 6.
[14] *2022 Practice Guide for the application of the Brussels IIb Regulation*, EU, 2022 (hereinafter the *2022 Practice Guide*), p. 188 (para. 6.2).
[15] See Article 26.
[16] See Article 39(2) and Article 41.
[17] See the *2022 Practice Guide*, p. 190, para. 6.3; and T. GARBER, Art. 21 Brussels IIter in U. MAGNUS and P. MANKOWSKI, *Brussels IIter Regulation*, OttoSchmidt, 2023, p. 310, para. 6.

elements helps to ensure that the key underlying aim of allowing the child to be involved in the proceedings with a view both of informing the court and the child is promoted.

7.9. The thinking behind making it **an obligation under the Regulation** to give the child a genuine opportunity to express his or her views is twofold. First, it was thought right as a matter of principle to highlight the importance of hearing children in **all cases on matters of parental responsibility** and not just (as in Brussels II-bis) in return applications in Hague abduction cases. As the Explanatory Memorandum to the Commission's Proposal pointed out,[18] if a decision is given without having heard the child, there is a danger that it may not take the best interests of the child into account to a sufficient extent. Second, there was the practical concern under Brussels II-bis that because of divergent rules governing the hearing of the child across Member States, those with stricter standards were encouraged to refuse recognition if the hearing of the child in the Member State of origin did not meet their standards.[19] Brussels II-ter seeks to do this by requiring courts to record both in their decision and in the accompanying certificate that where the child concerned was capable of forming his or her own views, he or she was given the opportunity to express those views in accordance with Article 21. In this way, while leaving it to each Member State to determine how the child's view should be heard, it nevertheless introduces a degree of homogeneity among Member States inasmuch as the same basic question relating to giving the child the opportunity to be heard has to be expressly addressed in all cases involving children. At the same time, because courts of other Member States cannot question the validity of the certificate,[20] the regime under Brussels II-ter ensures that recognition and enforcement cannot be refused on the mere fact that a hearing of the child in another country was done differently compared to the standards applied by the court before which recognition is sought.

II. THE POSITION UNDER BRUSSELS II-TER

A. THE BASIC OBLIGATION: ARTICLE 21

7.10. The basic obligation to afford the child the opportunity to express his or her views is set out in Article 21. Under Article 21(1), whenever a court of a

---

[18] Proposal for a Council Regulation on jurisdiction, the recognition and enforcement of decisions in matrimonial matters and the matters of parental responsibility, and on international child abduction (recast) COM(2016) 411, p. 4.
[19] Ibid., p. 15.
[20] See CJEU, 22 December 2010, *Aguirre Zarraga*, C-491/10 PPU. See further 7.23 et seq.

Member State is exercising its jurisdiction to hear a matter relating to parental responsibility, it must, in accordance with national law and procedure, provide the child, who is capable of forming his or her views, with 'a genuine and effective opportunity' to express those views 'either directly or through a representative or an appropriate body'. It should be noted that Article 21(1) gives children a right to be given the opportunity to express their view, but not a right to a hearing.[21] Where such an opportunity is afforded, then, under Article 21(2), the court must give due weight to the child's views in accordance with his or her age and maturity. As will now be discussed, the Article 21 obligation comprises a number of elements.

B. AFFORDING CHILDREN THE OPPORTUNITY TO EXPRESS THEIR VIEWS: ARTICLE 21(1)

1. The Parameters of the Courts' Obligation

7.11. Under Brussels II-ter,[22] the child's right to express his or her views only arises where a court is exercising jurisdiction in a matter relating to parental responsibility. A 'court' for these purposes means any authority in any Member State that has jurisdiction in matters falling within the scope of the Regulation.[23] As Recital (14) states, this term can include administrative authorities or notaries insofar as they have jurisdiction over a matter of parental responsibility. Although, as has been pointed out,[24] Article 21 is not addressed to those responsible for drawing up authentic instruments or agreements, recognition of such instruments or agreements may nevertheless be refused if the child capable of forming his or her views was not given the opportunity to be heard.[25] In any event, as Recital (71) notes, although the obligation to hear the child under Article 21 does not directly apply to authentic instruments and agreements, children should nevertheless be heard, pursuant to Article 24 of the Charter of Fundamental Rights of the European Union and Article 12 of UNCRC.

7.12. 'Parental responsibility' for these purposes is defined by Article 1(2)–(4) and includes rights of custody and rights of access, guardianship, curatorship and similar institutions, and the placement of a child in institutional or foster

---

[21] See the Court's comments to this effect in CJEU, 22 December 2010, *Aguirre Zarraga*, C-491/10 PPU, para. 62.
[22] Cf. the obligations under the UNCRC and the Charter of Fundamental Rights of the European Union, which have a wider application, but see further 7.20 below.
[23] See Article 2(2)(1).
[24] M. WILDERSPIN, *European Private International Family Law: The Brussels IIb Regulation*, Oxford Unversity Press, 2023, p. 251, para. 5-384.
[25] See the discussion in Chapter 10.

care, but excludes matters such as adoption, establishing or contesting of a parent–child relationship, and the name and forename of a child.[26] The court is obliged to apply Article 21 when considering (in the context of application concerning another Member State) whether or not to make a return order under the 1980 Hague Abduction Convention.[27]

7.13. Although, as noted earlier, the general underlying rationale of Article 21 reflects the importance attached to allowing a child to participate in proceedings involving him or her, it is important to consider the context in which the child's views are to be taken into account. In the context of proceedings concerning custody rights, a key objective is, as the *2022 Practice Guide* points out,[28] usually to assist in finding the most suitable environment in which the child should reside, whereas in child abduction applications under the 1980 Hague Convention, the purpose is often to ascertain the nature of the child's objections. In the former case, ascertaining the child's view is part of a full-blown welfare enquiry, while in the latter it is part of a summary enquiry to determine whether or not to order the child's return.

7.14. The obligation on courts of Member States to provide the opportunity for the child to express his or her views is to do so **in accordance with national law and procedure**.[29] In other words, Article 21(1) does not attempt to lay down a common procedure throughout Member States. This standpoint reflects Article 12(2) UNCRC and the former ground for non-recognition or enforcement of a judgment relating to parental responsibility under Article 23(b) Brussels II-bis. The divergent practice among Member States as to how children's views should be heard is further recognised by the provision at the end of Article 21(1) that allows children's views to be expressed directly or through a representative or other body.[30] In short, while Brussels II-ter places an obligation on courts to give the child the opportunity to be heard, it does not to dictate how this obligation should be discharged.

2. *When the Obligation Arises*

7.15. Under Article 21(1), courts must 'provide the child who is capable of forming his or her own views with a genuine and effective opportunity to express

---

[26] Discussed in Chapter 1 at 1.49 et seq.
[27] See Article 26. Child abduction is discussed in Chapter 6.
[28] *2022 Practice Guide*, p. 190, para. 6.3.
[29] This limitation was not included in the Commission's proposed Article 20. It is argued (see M. WILDERSPIN, above n. 24, p. 29, para. 1-122) that this limitation does **not** mean that it would be consistent with the Regulation for national law to fix a 'threshold age' as, to be compliant with Article 21, the court itself should have the opportunity to assess whether the individual child is capable of forming his or her own views.
[30] Again, this was not expressly stipulated in the Commission's proposed Article 20, which is discussed further below at 7.24.

[them]'. There are two elements to this obligation: first, it must be determined that the child concerned is capable of forming his or her own views; and, second, if satisfied that this is so, it must ensure that a genuine and effective opportunity is given to the child to express those views.

i) Assessing a Child's Capability to Form His or Her Own Views

7.16. With regard to the first and preliminary question, it should be noted that there is **no reference in this context to the child's age or maturity**. In this regard it has been well observed[31] that in deciding whether to hear a child, the 'court must assess the child's capability of forming their own views and not their maturity to form an opinion that should be taken into account for the decision'. It has accordingly been said that the 'capacity to understand' constitutes a **minimum level of self-awareness** and could extend to very young children.[32] As the *2022 Practice Guide* points out,[33] young children's views may be expressed by 'non-verbal means such as play, body language, facial expressions and painting. One commentary suggested[34] that in line with the view of the UN Committee on the Rights of the Child,[35] States should presume that a child has the requisite capacity and not vice versa, pointing out that it is not up to the child to first prove his/her capacity. The *2022 Practice Guide*, perhaps questionably, however, goes further, observing 'the court is not allowed to presume that the child is incapable of expressing his or her views'.[36]

7.17. Notwithstanding the above, practice will vary among Member States. Not all Member States will share the position taken in Germany, for example, that a three year-old child should generally be heard and that a four-year old has a right to be heard.[37] In this respect it needs to be remembered that the courts'

---

[31] See T. KRUGER and F. MAOLI 'The Hague Conventions and EU Instruments in Private International Law' in W. SCHRAMA, M. FREEMAN, N. TAYLOR and M. BRUNNING (eds), *International Handbook on Child Participation in Family Law*, Intersentia, 2021, pp. 69, 81. See also T. GARBER, above n. 17, p. 311, para. 9.

[32] C. HONORATI, 'The Commission's proposal for a recast of Brussels IIa Regulation' [2017] *International Family Law* 97, 101. This is in line with the more modern aim of hearing the child, namely, the child needs only to understand what the proceedings are all about in order to trigger the court's obligation to provide the opportunity to be 'heard' and not necessarily to be mature enough to have an opinion.

[33] *2022 Practice Guide*, p. 191 (para. 6.3.1), citing the UN Committee on the Rights of the Child General Comment No 12 (2009), para. 20.

[34] See B. UBERTAZZI, 'Hearing of the child' above n. 1, p. 161.

[35] In line with the UN Committee's General Comment No 12, above n. 33, para. 20.

[36] *2022 Practice Guide*, p. 191 (para. 6.3.1).

[37] See *OLG Hamm* (Higher Regional Court of Hamm) 26 August 2014, az. 11 UF 85/14, cited by B. UBERTAZZI, 'Hearing of the child' above n. 1, p. 161. For further analysis of the different positions taken by Member States, see B. UBERTAZZI, 'The Hearing of the Child in the Brussels IIa Regulation and its Recast Proposal', above n. 1, pp. 591–592. Note the position under Bulgarian law as explained in the *2022 Practice Guide*, pp. 195–196, para. 6.4.

obligation under Article 21(1) is subject to acting in accordance with national law and procedure. In other words, it is left to national law to determine when a child is too young to be considered capable of forming an independent view that should be heard.

7.18. Even where the court is satisfied that the child concerned is capable of forming his or her own views, the obligation to afford that child the opportunity to express them is not an absolute one. As Recital (39) says:

> while remaining a right of the child, hearing the child cannot constitute an absolute obligation, but must be assessed taking into account the best interests of the child.

7.19. Two examples of when it might be justifiable not to hear the child are provided by Article 39(2)(a) and (b),[38] namely, where the proceedings only concern the child's property (provided that giving such an opportunity was not required in light of the subject matter of the proceedings) and where there are serious grounds taking into account, in particular, the urgency of the case. With regard to the latter Recital (57) instances the case 'where there is an imminent danger for the child's physical and psychological integrity or life and any further delay might bear the risk that this danger materialises.'

7.20. Recital (39) also cites the example of cases involving agreements between the parties. Given that Article 21 does not apply to agreements (although in that context the obligation to hear the child can still be derived from the Charter of Fundamental Rights of the European Union and UNCRC),[39] the legislator presumably clearly had in mind court orders based on the parties' agreement. In many cases, if not most, it will be in the children's best interests for disputes over their upbringing to be amicably settled.[40] Even so, the appropriateness of this example of not hearing children might be questioned, at any rate, with regard to older children. Further, as the *2022 Practice Guide* says,[41] all the exceptions to the duty to hear the child 'should be interpreted very restrictively'.

ii) Providing a Genuine Opportunity to Express Views

7.21. The obligation under Article 21(1) is to provide children capable of forming their own views a **genuine and effective opportunity** to express them.

---

[38] These two paragraphs provide exceptions to the court's power to refuse recognition of a decision in matters of parental responsibility on the ground that it was given without giving the child who is capable of forming his or her views and opportunity to express those views in accordance with Article 21. Recognition is discussed in Chapter 8.
[39] See 7.2 and 7.3 above.
[40] In Hungary, for instance, an agreement between the parents is considered sufficient to represent the child's views; see B. UBERTAZZI 'The Hearing of the child in the Brussels IIa Regulation and its Recast Proposal' above n. 1, p. 591.
[41] *2022 Practice Guide*, p. 197, para. 6.5.

This requirement has many facets. An important consideration is the age of the child concerned.[42] Hearing very young children, for example, should clearly be conducted in a manner which befits their vulnerable state and in a protected environment.[43] In the case of older children, too, care needs to be taken to hear their views in a sensitive manner and in a safe environment, but over and above this, the following points have been well made:[44] the child should not be exposed to pressure or manipulation[45] and should have a genuine freedom in terms of whether or not exercise their right to be heard; the child should not be interviewed more times than necessary; the environment should be one in which the child feels respected;[46] and the child should be informed of the matters, options, possible decisions and their consequences.[47]

7.22.   An issue not covered by Brussels II-ter and therefore a matter of national law to determine is whether the parents or their lawyers have access to the minutes of any hearing of the child. If they do, this carries the risk of impeding the child's freedom to say whatever he or she feels. If they do not, this raises the objection that this would violate the right to a fair hearing contrary to Article 6 ECHR. Balancing the child's right to confidentiality with the parents' right to a fair hearing is far from easy.

7.23.   Echoing what the CJEU said in the case of *Aguirre*,[48] Recital (39) says that where the court decides to hear the child, it should take all measures which are appropriate to the arrangement of such a hearing, having regard to the child's best interests and the circumstances of each individual case. Where the child is abroad, as in the case of child abduction, Recital (39), again reiterating what was said in *Aguirre*,[49] states that the court of the Member State of origin must, so far as possible and always taking into consideration the child's best interests, use all means available to it under national law as well as the specific instruments of international judicial cooperation, including, when appropriate, those provided for by what was then the Taking of Evidence Regulation 2001.[50] It has been

---

[42]   A point emphasised by UN Committee on the Rights of the Child General Comment No 12 (2009), above n. 33, para. 34.
[43]   See C. HONORATI, above n. 32, p. 101.
[44]   See B. UBERTAZZI, 'Hearing of the child', above n. 1, p. 161.
[45]   The problem of a child being 'coached' by one parent against the other is a familiar one to family courts.
[46]   Cf. UN Committee on the Rights of the Child General Comment No 12 (2009), above n. 33, para. 42.
[47]   A point underscored by the 1996 European Convention on the Exercise of Children's Rights; see 7.4 above.
[48]   CJEU, 22 December 2010, *Aguirre Zarraga*, C-491/10 PPU, para. 66.
[49]   CJEU, 22 December 2010, *Aguirre Zarraga*, C-491/10 PPU, para. 67.
[50]   Council Regulation (EC) No 1206/2001 of 28 May 2001 on cooperation between the courts of the Member States in the taking of evidence in civil or commercial matters. This Regulation has since been superseded by Council Regulation (EU) 2020/1783 of the European Parliament

suggested[51] that as a general principle, the fact that it may not be possible to have the child present at the hearing 'only affects the mechanics of the process, but does not exempt judges from making a real effort to familiarise themselves with the child's position'.

iii) The Means by which the Child is Heard

7.24. It is left to **national law to determine the means** by which the child's view can be heard, but, as Article 21(1) provides,[52] those views may be made directly or through a representative or an appropriate body. As Recital (39) states, it is not the purpose of Brussels II-ter to 'set out whether the child should be heard by the judge in person or by a specially trained expert[53] reporting to the court afterwards, or whether the child should be heard in the courtroom or in another place or through other means'. Recital (53) makes the point that where it is not possible to hear the child in person and where the technical means are available, the court might consider holding a hearing through video-conference or other technological means. Remote hearings, as they have become known, have become more common and the technological means of doing so have developed considerably during the COVID-19 pandemic. However, a court should always take into consideration the best interests of the child and should not use the technology where it is inappropriate to do so.

3. *Giving Due Weight to the Child's Views: Article 21(2)*

7.25. Where a child is given an opportunity to express his or her views both in accordance with national law and procedure and Article 21(1), the court must, pursuant to Article 21(2), give 'due weight' to those views in accordance with the child's age and maturity.

7.26. Although as a generality it can be said that the older the child, the more significant his or her views are likely to be, there is no hard-and-fast rule. The child's views have to be individually assessed on a case-by-case basis. Without gainsaying the seriousness with which a child's views have to be

---

and of the Council of 25 November 2020 on cooperation between the courts of the Member States in the taking of evidence in civil or commercial matters (taking of evidence) (recast). According to the *2022 Practice Guide*, pp. 192–193, para. 6.3.2, the reference to the Taking of Evidence Regulation is intended to clarify that the hearing of the child 'falls within its scope for the purposes of the Regulation, irrespective of the national classification of the hearing as evidence, or another procedural institute'.

[51] See C. HONORATI, above, n. 32, p. 102.
[52] These alternatives were only implicit in the Commission's proposal as the final words of Article 21 were not included in the proposed Article 20.
[53] The importance of adequate training on how to communicate with a child for those professionals involved in the court process is stressed by the *2022 Practice Guide*, p. 198, para. 6.6.

considered, it is nevertheless only one consideration that the court has to take into account when arriving at a decision that it considers to be in the child's best interests. In other words, the child's views are not binding on the court.

7.27. In the Commission's proposal,[54] courts were to be required to 'document' their considerations concerning the weight placed on the child's views in their decision. This formal requirement has been dropped from the final version of Article 21.[55] Nevertheless it is clearly implicit in the requirement in Article 21(2) to give due weight to the child's view that a court must not only refer in its judgment to that view, but must also indicate what weight they put upon it. Indeed, in the context of any human rights challenges under the ECHR, it will be important to do so for, as the ECtHR Grand Chamber effectively said in *X v. Latvia*,[56] in order to demonstrate that a point that has been raised by one of the parties has genuinely been taken into account, the court must make a decision that is sufficiently reasoned on this point so as to enable the court to verify that these questions have been effectively examined. Although this comment was made in the context of child abduction, it clearly has a wider application and must equally apply to the requirement in Brussels II-ter to give 'due weight' to the child's views.

4. The Certification Requirement

7.28. As already noted, a key consequence of making it a general obligation under Brussels II-ter to afford the child the opportunity to express his or her views and to give due regard to it is to bring into play the certification process which is integral to recognition and enforcement. Recognition, enforcement and certification are discussed in detail in the following chapters. Suffice it to say here that certificated decisions given in a Member State concerning matters of parental responsibility[57] are recognisable without any special procedure being required[58] and, provided they are enforceable in the Member State that made it, are enforceable in any other Member State 'without any declaration of enforceability being required'.[59] In order to trigger these automatic consequences, the party seeking recognition and/or enforcement must produce both a copy of the decision and an appropriate certificate.[60] The party seeking

---

[54] See the final words of the proposed Article 20.
[55] This was motivated by the desire not to overburden the court with formal requirements under Brussels II-ter.
[56] ECtHR, 26 November 2013, *X v. Latvia* App No. 27853/09, para. 106.
[57] The same is true of decisions concerning matrimonial matters.
[58] See Article 30, discussed further in Chapter 8.
[59] See Article 39, discussed further in Chapter 9.
[60] See Articles 31(1) (recognition), 35(1) (enforcement of non-privileged decisions in matters of parental responsibility) and 47 (1) (enforcement of privileged decisions in matters of parental responsibility).

recognition/enforcement has a right, upon application to the appropriate court of origin of a Member State,[61] to obtain the required certificate.[62]

7.29. Although, as will be discussed in later chapters, the appropriate certificate differs according to the type of decision concerning matters of parental responsibility,[63] so far as hearing the child concerned, the certification requirement is the same. In each case, the court must certify whether or not the child concerned is capable of forming his or own views and, if so, whether or not he or she was given a genuine and effective opportunity to express his or her views.[64] If such a child was not given the requisite opportunity, then the court must set out its reasons for this. The court does not have to certify what weight it placed upon the child's views, although, as has been said,[65] its reasoning should be included in its decision.

5. The Effect of the Certificate

7.30. It is not possible to challenge the issuance of the certificate in the case of non-privileged decisions,[66] although there is scope for its subsequent rectification in the case of a material error or omission.[67] The position is similar in the case of privileged decisions, save that, as well as having the power to rectify the certificate, the court of origin must, upon application or its own motion, withdraw the certificate where it was wrongly granted.[68] On the other hand, the court of a Member State of enforcement (or in which recognition is in issue) has no such powers.

7.31. The inability of the court of the Member State of enforcement to question the certificate achieves a principal objective of Brussels II-ter – namely, it

---

[61] That is, that communicated to the Commission pursuant to Article 103.
[62] Under Articles 36 (non-privileged decisions) and 47 (privileged decisions).
[63] For decisions concerning matters of parental responsibility, the appropriate certificate is that using the form set out in Annex III, **except** where the decision is an order for return made in abduction proceedings under the 1980 Hague Abduction Convention, when the appropriate certificate is that using the form set out in Annex IV, or is a decision granting rights of access when the appropriate certificate is that using the form set out in Annex V, or is a decision on the substance of rights of custody entailing the return of a child (made in the context of the 'override provisions' pursuant to Article 29(6), discussed in Chapter 6) when the appropriate certificate is that using the form set out in Annex VI. The latter two decisions are classified as 'privileged decisions' for the purposes of Brussels II-ter; see, more generally, Chapter 8.
[64] Note that this is a more positive obligation compared with that under Articles 41(2)(c) and 42(2)(a) Brussels II-bis where a certificate should have been issued only if 'the child was given the opportunity to be heard, unless a hearing was considered inappropriate having regard to his or her age or degree of maturity'.
[65] See 7.27 above.
[66] See Article 36(3).
[67] See Article 37.
[68] See Article 48, discussed further below at 7.34.

prevents such a court from refusing to enforce an order because the hearing of the child in the Member State of origin did not meet its standards. On the other hand, it also means that the court of enforcement has to trust that the court of origin has properly discharged its obligation when issuing a certificate. It is clear from the CJEU decision in *Aguirre*[69] that no challenge to the propriety of the issuance of the certificate can be made in the court of enforcement, even where it can be shown that the court of origin falsely certified that it had given the child an opportunity to be heard. In other words, in such a case, the court of enforcement has no choice other than to recognise and enforce the decision.

7.32. In *Aguirre*, in the course of divorce proceedings, a Spanish court provisionally awarded the father rights of custody and the mother access to their daughter, on the basis that it was in the child's best interests to remain in Spain rather than to go to live with her mother in Germany as the mother wanted. The mother nonetheless left Spain and settled in Germany. Following an access visit, the mother retained her daughter in Germany. The father brought proceedings under the 1980 Hague Abduction Convention seeking his daughter's return to Spain, but, on appeal, the German court refused to make a return order on the basis of the child's objections.[70] There were further proceedings in Spain that resulted in the father being granted sole rights of custody and, notwithstanding that the child had not been heard,[71] in the issuance of a certificate pursuant to what was then Article 42(2) Brussels II-bis,[72] thereby triggering the overriding order entailing the child's return, which became binding on the German court. But when the father sought to have that order enforced, the German court stayed the proceedings and sought a preliminary ruling from the CJEU. The ruling sought was whether a court with jurisdiction in the Member State of enforcement could exceptionally oppose the enforcement of a certified judgment ordering the return of a child on the ground that the court of the Member State of origin had falsely stated in the certificate that it had fulfilled its obligation to hear the child before handing down its judgment and which was therefore contrary to Article 42, interpreted in accordance with Article 24 of the Charter of Fundamental Rights.

---

[69] CJEU, 22 December 2010, *Aguirre Zarraga*, C-491/10 PPU.

[70] The court, having heard the child, found that she was resolutely opposed to the return requested by her father; she categorically refused to return to Spain. The expert instructed by that court concluded following the hearing that the child's opinion should be taken into account in the light of both her age (she was then aged nine) and her maturity.

[71] The mother refused to travel to Spain with her daughter to attend the custody hearing and her request for the child to be heard by video-conference was rejected. The Spanish court apparently considered that the child had been given the 'opportunity to be heard'; see T. KRUGER and L. SAMYN, 'Brussels II *bis*: successes and suggested Improvements' (2016) 12 *Journal of Private International Law* 132, 158.

[72] Article 42(2)(a) stated, *inter alia*, that the judge of origin should issue a certificate only if 'the child was given an opportunity to be heard unless a hearing was considered inappropriate having regard to his or her age or degree of maturity'.

7.33. The Court ruled that even in the circumstances of this case, the court with jurisdiction in the Member State of enforcement cannot oppose the enforcement of a certified judgment on the ground that the court of the Member State of origin which handed down that judgment may have infringed the conditional requirements for issuing the certificate, since the assessment of whether there is such an infringement falls exclusively within the jurisdiction of the courts of the Member State of origin. In so ruling, the Court commented[73] that the clear division of jurisdiction between the courts of the Member State of origin and those of the Member State of enforcement, as clearly established by the earlier decisions of *Rinau*[74] and *Povse*,[75] rested on the premise that those courts respect, within their respective areas of jurisdiction, the obligations which the Regulation imposes on them, in accordance with the Charter of Fundamental Rights. In other words, the Regulation system rests upon the principle of mutual respect. As the Court put it:[76]

> The systems for recognition and enforcement of judgments handed down in a Member State which are established by [Brussels II-bis] are based on the principle of mutual trust between Member States in the fact that their respective national legal systems are capable of providing an equivalent and effective protection of fundamental rights, recognised at European Union level, in particular, in the Charter of Fundamental Rights.

According to the Court,[77] the party seeking enforcement must pursue legal remedies in the State of origin to challenge the lawfulness of a judgment certified pursuant to the Regulation. As it happened, in *Aguirre* itself, an appeal in the custody proceeding was still pending so that a challenge could be mounted then. But in many cases, it may not be at all obvious what the appropriate course of action is.[78]

7.34. The decision in *Aguirre* was controversial, with some taking the view that it was stretching mutual trust to breaking point.[79] Notwithstanding this criticism, far from stepping back from the decision in *Aguirre*, Brussels II-ter widens its

---

[73] See para. 59 of the ruling in CJEU, 22 December 2010, *Aguirre Zarraga*, C-491/10 PPU.
[74] ECJ, 11 July 2008, *Rinau*, C-195/08 PPU, para. 85.
[75] CJEU, 1 July 2010, *Povse*, C-211/10 CJEU, para. 73.
[76] See CJEU, 1 July 2010, *Povse*, C-211/10 CJEU, para. 70.
[77] See para. 71.
[78] See the criticism in this respect in L. WALKER and P. BEAUMONT, 'Shifting the Balance Achieved by the Abduction Convention: The Contrasting Approaches of the European Court of Human Rights and the European Court of Justice' (2011) 7 *Journal of Private International Law* 231, 243.
[79] For a particularly critical view, see L. WALKER and P. BEAUMONT, above n. 78. See also B. UBERTAZZI, 'The hearing of the child in the Brussels IIa Regulation and its Recast Proposal', above n. 1, pp. 599–600; and D. MARTINY, 'New efforts in judicial cooperation in European child abduction cases' (2021) 4 *Polski Proces Cywilny* 501, 510.

impact inasmuch as having to certify that the child has been heard in accordance with Article 21 applies to all decisions concerning parental responsibility and not just, as under Brussels II-bis, to judgments on rights of access and return orders made under the overriding provisions. **In all these instances, it remains the case that the court of the Member State of enforcement has no power to challenge a certificated decision.** However, Brussels II-ter does make two changes. First, the certificate has to be served with the decision.[80] Second, **in the case of privileged decisions** (that is, decisions granting rights of access and decisions on the substance of rights of custody entailing the return of a child, made in the context of the 'override provisions') **but not non-privileged decisions**,[81] Article 48 provides that the court of origin must, upon application or its own motion, withdraw the certificate where it was wrongly granted, having regard to the requirements, inter alia, of giving the child an opportunity to express his or her views in accordance with Article 21.

7.35. The continued application of the ruling in *Aguirre* places a premium on courts of origin acting with scrupulous diligence before issuing a certificate. It has been well said[82] that filing a certificate is not a simple 'tick-box' exercise. In the case of hearing the child, serious attention needs to be paid to whether he or she has been given 'a genuine and effective opportunity' to express his or her views. Nevertheless, it should be emphasised that a refusal to recognise or enforce a decision on matters of parental responsibility on the basis that a child had not been given the opportunity to be heard is only possible where there is no certificate saying that this opportunity had been given. Where there is such a certificate, the challenge must be, if at all, in the State of origin.

---

[80] This was the recommendation made by T. KRUGER and L. SAMYN, above n. 71, p. 158. In *Aguirre*, the certificate was served independently of any judgment.
[81] *Sed quaere?*
[82] See B. UBERTAZZI 'Hearing of the child', above n. 1, p. 175.

CHAPTER 8

RECOGNITION OF DECISIONS

I. Introduction 288
II. The Meaning and Effect of Recognition 290
    A. *Res Judicata* 291
    B. The Scope of Recognition 292
        1. Recognition of Unknown Legal Concepts 292
        2. Similar Terms Meaning Different Things 294
        3. The Scope of *Res Judicata* 297
III. The Procedure for Recognition 299
    A. Automatic Recognition 299
    B. Free-Standing Declaratory Proceedings on Recognition 300
        1. Positive Declarations 300
        2. Negative Declarations 301
    C. Recognition as an Incidental Question 302
        1. Rationale and Scope 302
        2. *Res Judicata* of Decisions on Recognition as an Incidental
           Question 304
    D. Stay of Proceedings. 305
        1. Background and Purpose 305
        2. Situations in which Proceedings May be Stayed 306
           i) The Judgment has been Appealed in the Member State
              of Origin 306
           ii) An Application for a Free-Standing Declaratory
              Judgment has been Submitted 307
        3. Scope 307
        4. Should Recognition be Stayed? 308
    E. Documents to be Produced. 308
        1. Purpose and Scope 308
        2. A Certified Copy of the Decision 309
        3. A Certificate Issued Pursuant to Article 36 309
        4. Translation or Transliteration 310
        5. Absence of Documents 311
IV. Partial Recognition 311

V. Refusal of Recognition 312
    A. General Comments 312
    B. Divorce, Legal Separation or Marriage Annulment 313
        1. Public Policy: Article 38(a) 313
        2. The Respondent was not Adequately Served 315
            i) Default Judgments: Article 38(b). 315
            ii) Inadequate Service. 315
            iii) The Defendant Must not have Accepted the Decision 317
        3. Irreconcilability with a Domestic Judgment: Article 38(c). 317
        4. Irreconcilability with an Earlier Foreign Judgment:
            Article 38(d) 318
    C. Parental Responsibility 318
        1. Public Policy: Article 39(1)(a) 319
        2. The Respondent was not Adequately Served:
            Article 39(1)(b) 320
        3. Non-Hearing of Person Concerned: Article 39(1)(c) 320
        4. Irreconcilability with a Domestic Judgment: Article 39(1)(d) 321
        5. Irreconcilability with a Later Foreign Judgment:
            Article 39(1)(e) 321
        6. Failure to Comply with the Procedure in Article 82:
            Article 39(1)(f) 322
        7. Failure to Hear the Child: Article 39(2) 322
    D. Limitations on the Right to Refuse Recognition 324
        1. Prohibition of Review of Jurisdiction of the Court of
            Origin: Article 69 324
        2. Differences in Applicable Law: Article 70. 325
        3. Non-Review as to Substance: Article 71 327
VI. The Special Regime for Privileged Decisions. 327
    A. Background and Scope 327
    B. Procedure. 328
        1. Free-Standing Proceedings or as Incidental Question 328
        2. Stay of Recognition 328
        3. Documents to be Produced 329
    C. Refusal of Recognition. 329

I. INTRODUCTION

8.1. The recognition of decisions in matrimonial matters and matters of parental responsibility within the EU is the cornerstone of Brussels II-ter and its predecessors. While the rules on jurisdiction generally attract more academic attention and generate more case law, the purpose of those rules is to create a level playing field in order to reach the level of mutual trust that is a prerequisite to recognition (and enforcement).[1]

8.2. The recognition of decisions serves the purpose of facilitating the free movement of persons, one of the four fundamental freedoms of the EU (together with the free movement of goods, services and capital). This could be seen in the first origins of EU competence in the area of judicial cooperation in civil matters, namely Article K.1 of the Maastricht Treaty,[2] which made it clear that judicial cooperation in civil matters[3] served the purpose of 'achieving the objectives of the Union, in particular the free movement of persons'. In the current legal basis for EU legislation in this area of the law, Title V of the TFEU on an 'Area of Freedom, Security and Justice', the connection to the free movement of persons has been omitted. However, it goes without saying that individuals contemplating a move from one Member State to another, who cannot be sure of the recognition of their divorce and/or decision giving them sole custody of the children, might think again. Today, this goal is expressed in Recital (3) Brussels II-ter, according to which '[t]he Union has set itself the objective of creating, maintaining and developing an area of freedom, security and justice, in which the free movement of persons and access to justice are ensured'.

8.3. Recognition (and enforcement) of decisions made under the Regulation is governed by **Chapter IV**. The structure of Chapter IV is complicated and one reason for its complexity is the decision, taken during the negotiations on the Commission's proposals, to keep the distinction between what is now referred to as 'privileged' decisions (that is, certified decisions granting rights of access and decisions entailing the return of children under the 'overriding mechanism' in child abduction cases; see 8.135 below) and all other decisions ('non-privileged decisions'). Another reason for its complexity is that Chapter IV continually changes its focus between recognition and enforcement (enforcement is discussed in Chapter 9) and between non-privileged and privileged decisions. A further complication is that enforcement of authentic instruments and agreements is dealt with separately in Chapter IV, Section 4 (authentic instruments and agreements are discussed in Chapter 10). Moreover, it is not self-evident that the term 'general provisions' is used for 'non-privileged decisions', whereas the term 'common provisions' designates rules that apply to both privileged and non-privileged decisions. The table below gives a general outline of Chapter IV.

---

[1] Cf. Recital (6) Brussels II-ter.
[2] Treaty on European Union (the Maastricht Treaty), OJ C191, 29.7.92, p. 1, 61. Article 220 of the EEC Treaty, which served as the basis for the Brussels Convention on jurisdiction and the enforcement of judgments in civil and commercial matters (a consolidated version of which can be found in OJ C27, 26.1.98, p. 1), was even earlier and dates back to the beginning of the what was then the EEC.
[3] Together with the other areas of cooperation included in the Article.

Chapter IV Recognition and enforcement

Section 1 General provisions on recognition and enforcement

Subsection 1 Recognition
Articles 30–33
Subsection 2 Enforceability and enforcement
Articles 34–35
Subsection 3 Certificate
Articles 36–37
Subsection 4 Refusal of recognition and enforcement
Articles 38–41

Section 2 Recognition and enforcement of certain privileged decisions

Subsection 1 Recognition
Articles 43–44
Subsection 2 Enforceability and enforcement
Articles 45–46
Subsection 3 Certificate for privileged decisions
Articles 47–49
Subsection 4 Refusal of recognition and enforcement
Articles 50

Section 3 Common provisions on enforcement

Subsection 1 Enforcement
Articles 51–55
Subsection 2 Suspension of enforcement proceedings and refusal of enforcement
Articles 56–63

Section 4 Authentic instruments and agreements

Articles 64–68

Section 5 Other provisions

Articles 69–75

II. THE MEANING AND EFFECT OF RECOGNITION

8.4. Recognition is not defined in Brussels II-ter. However, since there is a considerable degree of parallelism between Brussels II-ter and Brussels I-bis and its predecessors, upon which the rules of the former have largely been modelled, it is useful to look at case law and writing on Brussels I when interpreting Brussels II. In the explanatory report to the original Brussels Convention (the Jenard Report), the rapporteur says that '[r]ecognition must have the result of conferring on judgments the authority and effectiveness accorded to them in the

State in which they were given'.[4] This position has also been confirmed by the Court of Justice.[5] That sounds all fine and simple, but on closer examination the position is more complicated.

A. RES JUDICATA

8.5. Recognition normally[6] entails recognising that the foreign judgment establishes *res judicata*. *Res judicata* can mean two things: (1) it precludes new litigation on the same matter which has already been decided – this can be seen as the negative, or preclusive, side of the concept (in German: *negative Rechtskraft*); (2) the judgment has a conclusive effect and can be relied on should the matter decided become an incidental question in future proceedings – this can be seen as the positive side of the concept (in German: *positive Rechtskraft*). Another way of expressing this is to speak of a preclusive and a conclusive aspect of *res judicata*. An example of the latter would be a couple who have already divorced in Finland when one spouse brings an action in France for *prestation compensatoire*.[7] Under French law, such an action is precluded after the divorce and since the Finnish divorce must be recognised, the defendant can rely on it as a defence against the request for *prestation compensatoire*.

8.6. However, in the context of parental responsibility, the negative aspect of *res judicata*, even if theoretically accepted, has no role to play in practice. A spouse who is unhappy with a court decision in a matter concerning parental responsibility can always come back and seek a change in the original judgment claiming a change of circumstances – *rebus sic stantibus*. Only if it is obvious that nothing has really changed may a court, depending on the jurisdiction, refuse to hear the application on its substance. Nevertheless, in cases falling within the scope of Brussels II-ter, when there is a judgment on parental responsibility from one Member State and an application for recognition is made in another Member State, there will often have been a change in circumstances. On the other hand, the positive aspect of *res judicata* will be of fundamental importance to the holder of parental responsibility when taking decisions for the child concerning schooling, healthcare and when applying for various social benefits.

---

[4] Jenard Report, OJ C59, 5.3.79, p. 1, 43.
[5] ECJ, 4 February 1988, *Hoffmann*, C-145/86.
[6] There are exceptions to this principle. For instance, in the administrative law of most systems, a decision does not preclude new litigation on the same matter. If as a result of an administrative decision the parents oppose the placement of their child in the care of a public institution and this is tried in court, it does not preclude the parents from bringing an action again.
[7] *Prestation compensatoire* can be characterised as maintenance and as such falls outside the scope of Brussels II-ter. The incidental question of the recognition of the Finnish divorce judgment, on the other hand, does not fall outside its scope.

B. THE SCOPE OF RECOGNITION

8.7. As seen above (see 8.4), a judgment should be given the authority and effects it has in the Member State in which it was given. Although there is no reason to believe that this should not be the point of departure for Brussels II-ter, there are a number of questions that need to be addressed due to the differences in the legal systems of the Member States.

8.8. First, **not all legal concepts covered by the Regulation exist in all States** and it might pose difficulties for a Member State to recognise a legal concept that is unknown to its own law. For instance, marriage annulment is not known in all Member States. Second, **similar legal terms may mean different things**. The laws of Member States use various legal concepts expressing some form of parental responsibility – this term (as used in the official languages in which the Regulation is published) is not even used in many Member States – and the same term (as translated) might not mean the same thing while different terms are used to signify (more or less) the same thing. Third, when seeking to give a judgment the authority and effects that it has in the State of origin, one must ask oneself **what parts of the judgment that actually acquire *res judicata*?** If a divorce judgment contains a decision on fault by of one of the parties, is only the divorce decree binding in other Member States or is the finding of fault also binding? This question could become relevant as an incidental question in, for example, maintenance proceedings.[8]

1. Recognition of Unknown Legal Concepts

8.9. In the area of matrimonial matters, Brussels II-ter applies to 'divorce, legal separation and marriage annulment'. Following the public referenda in Ireland (1995) and Malta (2011), all Member States permit **divorce**, albeit on different grounds.[9] Things become more difficult with regard to **annulment** because not all Member States' laws feature such a concept. Neither Swedish nor Finnish law contains rules on marriage annulment. A marriage can only be dissolved through divorce.[10] A practical example would be the question of what marital

---

[8] If under the law applicable to maintenance the question of fault is relevant and this is not contrary to the public policy of the forum.
[9] There are now only two countries in the world where the laws do not contain a possibility for divorce: the Philippines and Vatican City.
[10] Both laws previously contained rules on annulment, but they were abolished in Sweden in 1974 and in Finland in 1987, *inter alia*, due to the infrequency of their use (two to three cases a year in Sweden). Today, a couple that has married in violation of rules preventing marriage (for example, a child marriage or a forced marriage) have a right to immediate divorce without observing the statutory 'cooling-off period' of six months and if they do not consent to divorce the public prosecutor has a right to file for divorce. However, on

status should be registered in Finland or Sweden for a person who was party to a marriage that was later annulled – 'unmarried' or 'divorced'?

8.10. The Commission's Proposal contained a provision dealing with the problem of enforcing a decision containing a measure or order that is unknown in the law of the Member State of enforcement, namely, that the courts of that State 'should adapt the decision to the extent possible to a measure or order that is known and which has equivalent effects attached to it and which pursues similar aims and interests', but subject to the condition that adaptation did not result 'in effects going beyond those provided for in the law of Member State of origin'.[11] However, this potentially useful provision was not incorporated into the final text of Brussels II-ter.

8.11. The inspiration for the proposed Article 33(2) appears to have come from Article 54 Brussels I-bis, which contains a rule on **adaptation**. Furthermore, Article 31 of the Succession Regulation also contains a rule on adaptation of rights *in rem*.

8.12. It is submitted that the absence of a similar rule in Brussels II-ter should not be interpreted *a contrario*. Adaptation is a general principle in private international law and a similar duty of adaptation in good faith must in the interests of mutual recognition and the effective application of EU law also be said to exist in the application of Brussels II-ter.[12]

8.13. The Borrás Report on the Brussels II Convention argues that, for example, an Austrian judgment for annulment could be treated as a divorce judgment in Sweden.[13] We would advise against a mechanical adaptation for such cases. Adaptation must be done with sensitivity. Being registered as unmarried rather than divorced could be of strong emotional and social importance to the individual, who could have a strong interest in the retention of the marital status attained in the country of origin by the annulment judgment. An adaptation that in practice would amount to a non-recognition could possibly be a violation

---

15 February 2023 the Finnish Parliament approved a government proposal (made in October 2021) to re-introduce annulment for forced marriages (but renamed 'upphävande/kumoaminen', which translates in English as 'repeal' rather than annulment). Under this legislation (which, at the time of writing, has not yet been brought into force), after the 'annulment', spouses will be registered as unmarried rather than divorced. The reason for this change is mainly symbolic so as to allow persons forced into marriage to avoid the social stigma that some people attach to divorce; see RP 172/2021 rd, 16.

[11] See COM(2016) 411, the proposed Article 33(2).
[12] G. Dannemann, 'Adjustment/Adaptation (*Anpassung*)' in J. Basedow, G. Rühl, F. Ferrari and P. de Miguel Asensio (eds), *Encyclopedia of Private International Law*, Edward Elgar, 2017, pp. 8–13. See also CJEU, 12 April 2011, *DHL Express France*, C-235/09, para. 58; and Chapter 9 at 9.79.
[13] Borrás Report, OJ C221, 16.7.98, p. 21, para. 57.

of Articles 20 and 21 TFEU as well as Article 7 of the Charter of Fundamental Rights of the European Union (cf. Article 8 ECHR).[14]

2. Similar Terms Meaning Different Things

8.14. Parental responsibility is widely defined in Article 1(2) Brussels II-ter (see Chapter 1 at 1.37 et seq) and includes, among other things, custody, guardianship and determination of the child's residence. The problem here is that concepts that are translated into the same word(s) might mean different things under different laws. The question is whether a legal concept in one law can be replaced with a legal concept in another law – that might go under the same name.

8.15. A decision on with which parent the child is to live could in one Member State mean just that and only that, whereas in another Member State it could entail giving more or less wide-ranging decision-making powers to the residential parent. A decision on joint custody could under the law of one Member State mean that the parents have the authority to take certain decisions without the consent of the other parent. The parent having sole custody under the law of one Member State may have the authority to take all decisions concerning the child without the other parent's consent and perhaps even without having to inform him or her. Under the law of another Member State, there might be limits as to what matters that can be decided without consent and a duty to keep the other parent informed.

8.16. Given that the same or similar concepts could mean different things depending on the applicable law, there is a great risk of misunderstandings. To avoid misunderstandings, a party may apply for a **certificate concerning decisions in matters of parental responsibility** contained in Annex III to Brussels II-ter, according to which the court of origin will have to specify which party has been given 'rights of custody' as defined in Article 2(2)(9) Brussels II-ter, which specifically points out the right to determine the residence of the child.

8.17. However, not all holders of custody have the right to determine the place of residence of the child; at least not if a substantial change is contemplated. In such a case the parent in question will *not* have rights corresponding to the definition of custody given in Brussels II-ter, but if the national judge does not tick the 'custody box' in the certificate, it would appear as if that parent had *no* rights of custody, which is also not correct.

---

[14] Cf. CJEU, 5 June 2018, *Coman and Others*, C-673/16 and CJEU, 14 December 2021, *Stolichna obshtina, rayon 'Pancharevo'*, C-490/20.

8.18. Moreover, even if one parent as holder of custody has the right to take all decisions on his or her own, he or she might have a legal obligation to inform the other parent of relevant events in the child's life on a regular basis. There is no box to tick in the certificate concerning the right to obtain information if that right follows from law. There is only a box to tick concerning other rights 'attributed according to the decision' (point 8). We would advise against getting involved in the almost philosophical question of whether a right stems from the decision or from the law on which it is based, but simply advise the judge to describe what other rights and duties follow from the decision, even if they are not explicitly stated in the judgment.

8.19. The above examples serve the purpose of illustrating the difficulty in translating/transplanting legal concepts from one legal system into another – Recital (18) Brussels II-ter also adverts to the differences in terminology. When recognising foreign judgments, it is necessary to look into what they actually mean. In order to facilitate this in practice, it is necessary that the judge tasked with filling out the form in Annex III uses the free space in point 6.1 of the certificate to explain what rights and obligations are given to the holder(s) of custody.

8.20. A further, complicating factor is that judgments do not exist in a vacuum; they are given against the backdrop of a particular national law. Many if not most judgments are written under the assumption that what follows from the law need not be said (depending on the legal tradition and perhaps even the style of the individual judge such information can be given orally to the parties or explained in the judgment or not at all).

8.21. To understand the way in which a foreign judgment will 'live on' in a new legal setting, it is necessary to turn to rules on applicable law. However, there are no such rules in Brussels II-ter, but there are under the 1996 Hague Child Protection Convention, to which all Member States are parties.

8.22. The point of departure is that 'the attribution or extinction' of parental responsibility by operation of law is governed by the State of the habitual residence of the child (Article 16(1) of the 1996 Hague Convention). However, if the child's habitual residence changes, according to Article 15(3), the law of the new habitual residence governs the 'conditions of application' of measures taken in the State of the former habitual residence – that is, **how parental responsibility is to be exercised.**[15]

---

[15] The *exercise* of parental responsibility is governed by the law of the child's habitual residence and if that changes, it is governed by the law of the State of the new habitual residence of the child; see Article 17.

8.23. It is of course **not always easy to distinguish between the existence of parental responsibility** (or some other term used in the judgment) **and its exercise.** The explanatory report (the Lagarde Report) to the Convention gives the example of the case where a guardian is appointed for the child in the country of its former habitual residence and under the law applied the guardian would have to ask a judge for authorisation to take certain decisions concerning the child, but under the law of the new habitual residence, the guardian could take these decisions without asking a judge. In this case the report holds that the non-requirement of authorisation is a question of the *exercise* of parental responsibility.[16]

8.24. For example, it would appear that a duty to inform the other parent about relevant events in the child's life that follow from the law of the child's original habitual residence, but not from that of the new habitual residence, is a question of the exercise of parental responsibility and that the duty to inform the other parent ceases after the relocation. However, if the duty to inform the other parent is expressed in the judgment itself, it could be seen as determining the existence of the obligation and it would remain unchanged. This delineation would appear to be rather fortuitous and the Lagarde Report concludes that 'no general formulation would allow all of the extremely diverse situations to be taken into account and ... all of these problems could only be resolved case-by-case by way of adaptation and, if this route were to turn out to be impracticable, by new measures to be taken by the authorities of the State of the new habitual residence'.[17]

8.25. If, at the time of judgment in the State of the child's original habitual residence, it is known that the child will move to another Member State – the judgment might even specifically authorise this – the judge could take the law of the anticipated new habitual residence of the child into account in accordance with Article 15(2) of the 1996 Convention. Although the applicable law will be that of the court making the order, it could, noting that the terminology for custody and access differs in the law of the Member State of the child's anticipated habitual residence is different, consider framing the judgment using the terminology of that latter State.[18] To this end, Article 79(d) Brussels II-ter stipulates that the Central Authorities of the two Member States may be of assistance.[19]

---

[16] See Lagarde Report, HCCH 1998, para. 91. See also the example given in the *Practical Handbook on the Operation of the 1996 Hague Child Protection Convention* (HCCH 2014), p. 97, para. 9.16.
[17] Lagarde Report, para. 91.
[18] See the *Practical Handbook*, above n. 16, p. 91, para. 9.2.
[19] The Central Authority's tasks under Brussels II-ter are discussed in Chapter 11 at 11.21 et seq.

3. The Scope of Res Judicata

8.26. The preclusive effect of a judgment differs between Member States. In some States it is only the operative part[20] of the judgment that acquires *res judicata*,[21] whereas for other States the *ratio decidendi* also acquires a preclusive effect.[22] The difference between the narrower and the wider understanding of *res judicata* corresponds to what in English is often described as the difference between **claim preclusion** and **issue preclusion**.[23] The former will bar a new action on the same matter between the same parties, whereas the latter (as per the House of Lords) 'may arise where a particular issue forming a necessary ingredient in a cause of action has been litigated and decided and in subsequent proceedings between the same parties involving a different cause of action to which the same issue is relevant one of the parties seeks to re-open that issue'.[24]

8.27. The importance of the difference is best illustrated by an example from the case law of the CJEU on Brussels I. In *Gothaer Allgemeine Versicherung*,[25] a Belgian court had dismissed a case on the basis that there was a choice-of-court clause that gave exclusive competence to the courts of Iceland. Thereafter the plaintiff brought the same action to Germany and the question was whether the finding of the Belgian court that the prorogation clause was valid was also binding on a German court. Given a narrow interpretation of the preclusive effect of *res judicata*, such as it is understood in German law, the finding that the prorogation clause was valid would not be binding on the German court but under the wider understanding that *res judicata* is given under French and Belgian law it would be. Concerning this question, the CJEU held that '[t]he requirement of the uniform application of European Union law means that the specific scope of that restriction must be defined at European Union level rather than vary according to different national rules on *res judicata*' and that 'the concept of *res judicata* under European Union law not only attaches to the operative part of the judgment in question, but also to the *ratio decidendi* of that judgment, which provides the necessary underpinning for the operative part and is inseparable from it'.[26] In the given case, *res judicata* also extended to the finding that the prorogation clause in favour of the Icelandic court was valid and was therefore also binding on the German court.

---

[20] In German law this is referred to as the *tenor*.
[21] For example, in German law.
[22] For example, in French and Belgian law.
[23] Claim preclusion is also referred to as 'cause of action estoppel' and issue preclusion as 'collateral estoppel' or 'issue estoppel'.
[24] *Arnold v. National Westminster Bank* [1991] AC 93 (HL), 105.
[25] CJEU, 15 November 2012, *Gothaer Allgemeine Versicherung and Others*, C-456/11. For a similar outcome to *Gothaer Allgemeine Versicherung* in English case law see *The Sennar (No. 2)* [1985] 1 WLR 490 (HL).
[26] CJEU, 15 November 2012, *Gothaer Allgemeine Versicherung and Others*, C-456/11, para. 40.

8.28. A paradoxical effect of *Gothaer Allgemeine Versicherung* is that a judgment could have a greater effect in another Member State than it does in the State of origin.[27] This would constitute a departure from what the Court of Justice stated in *Apostolides*, in which it held that 'there is however no reason for granting to a judgment ... rights which it does not have in the Member State of origin'.[28]

8.29. Under Brussels II-ter, the assumption must be that the Court will take the same position as it has when interpreting Brussels I. *Ratio decidendi* for a judgment that is necessary for the operative part and is inseparable from it will form part of the *res judicata*.

8.30. A practical example, drawing on *Gothaer Allgemeine Versicherung*, would be a prorogation agreement under Article 10. If the parties are in dispute over whether or not they have entered into a valid prorogation agreement and a court in the Member State to which the agreement purportedly gives exclusive competence to determine questions concerning the parental responsibility of a child finds that the agreement was not valid (e.g. because of undue pressure on one of the parties) and therefore dismisses the case, that finding would be binding on the courts of the Member State of the child's habitual residence if an action is brought there.[29] It would be barred from dismissing the case on the grounds of a valid prorogation agreement to another court.

8.31. The question is how far the Court's ruling in *Gothaer Allgemeine Versicherung* extends. Let us take the example of a court in Member State A that when ruling on an application for divorce also decides on the question of fault, as is relevant under the law of some Member States. If, in later proceedings for spousal maintenance in Member State B, under the applicable law, the same question of fault is relevant again, the question arises whether the decision on fault made by the court in Member State A, being a 'necessary underpinning for the operative part' is *res judicata* and the findings are therefore binding on the court in Member State B. The sweeping statements by the Court of Justice in *Gothaer* would indicate that this is the case, but such an interpretation would run contrary to what is said in Recital (9), according to which Brussels II-ter applies only 'to the dissolution of matrimonial ties [and that it] should not deal with issues such as the grounds for divorce'.[30] Against this background, caution should be exercised in relation to extending the scope of *Gothaer* this far.

---

[27] See also H. Roth, 'Europäischer Rechtskraftsbegriff im Zuständigkeitsrecht?' (2014) *Praxis des Internationalen Privat- und Verfahrensrechts (IPRax)* 136, 138, who speaks of 'gespaltene materielle Rechtskraft' (split *res judicata*).

[28] See ECJ, 28 April 2009, *Apostolides*, C-420/07, para. 66. Admittedly, that statement was made in a different context.

[29] And also, of course, binding on any other court in any other Member State.

[30] In Recital (10) Brussels II-bis, this was expressed in the following manner: 'The recognition of divorce and annulment rulings affects only the dissolution of matrimonial ties; despite

III. THE PROCEDURE FOR RECOGNITION

A. AUTOMATIC RECOGNITION

8.32. According to Article 30(1) (cf. Recital (54)) Brussels II-ter, **a decision given in a Member State – be it on matrimonial matters or on matters of parental responsibility – shall be recognised without any special procedure being required.** This is a provision that has remained virtually unchanged from the 1998 Brussels II Convention (Article 14) to the 2000 Brussels II Regulation (Article 14), Brussels II-bis (Article 21) and now Brussels II-ter. A similar provision was already to be found in the very first EU (then EEC) instrument on the recognition and enforcement of judgments, the 1968 Brussels Convention (Article 26) and is still to be found in all EU Regulations in force on the recognition and enforcement of judgments in civil matters.

8.33. A practical example of the meaning of this is that a person who wishes to remarry would only have to produce the divorce judgment (or, in the case of some Member States, an authentic instrument) in the State in which the marriage is to take place in order to prove that he/she is divorced and free to remarry.[31] The same applies in matters of parental responsibility where a parent who has been given sole custody of a child should be able to register the child in daycare or school without having to produce any other document than the judgment.[32]

8.34. In practice, people rarely carry foreign judgments around to prove personal status, but rely on information available in civil status registries. Therefore, Brussels II-ter, like all its predecessors, specifies in Article 30(2) that **in particular** no special procedure shall be required for updating one's civil status on the basis of a decision from another Member State on divorce, legal separation or marriage annulment.[33] To the extent that such matters are noted in civil status registries the same should apply to all decisions that are recognised under Brussels II-ter, including decisions on parental responsibility (but not on **parenthood** as that is excluded from scope of Brussels II-ter).[34]

---

the fact that they may be interrelated, the Regulation does not affect issues such as the fault of the spouses.'

[31] The *2022 Practice Guide for the Application of the Brussels IIb Regulation*, EU, 2022 (hereinafter *2022 Practice Guide*), p. 35.

[32] For other examples, see *2022 Practice Guide*, p. 98. Of course, under the law applicable to the exercise of parental authority, a parent with joint custody might be entitled to do so without the consent of the other parent.

[33] This has been said to be one of the most important innovations of the original Brussels II Convention; see M. Ní Shúilleabháin, *Cross-Border Divorce Law: Brussels II bis*, Oxford University Press, Oxford 2010, p. 243, para. 6.20, with further references.

[34] See Article 1(4)(a). Adoption decisions are excluded under Article 1(4)(b). See Chapter 1 at 1.49.

8.35. Article 30(2) specifies that only decisions in matrimonial matters that are final – that is, 'against which no further appeal lies under the law of that Member State' – are subject to automatic recognition. Since there is no similar statement made concerning decisions in matters of parental responsibility, the question of whether such a decision produces legal effects or not before becoming final would depend on the law of the Member State of origin.

B. FREE-STANDING DECLARATORY PROCEEDINGS ON RECOGNITION

1. Positive Declarations

8.36. Even though recognition is automatic, since the rules in the Regulation leave room for refusal, it is inevitable that at times the question of whether a particular judgment should be recognised or not can be in doubt. In such cases, whoever wishes to rely on the judgment has a legitimate interest in obtaining an authoritative answer to the question of recognition. Against this backdrop, **Article 30(3) Brussels II-ter gives an interested party the right to apply for a decision that there are no grounds for refusal of recognition.** When such a declaratory judgment is sought, the procedure provided for in Articles 59–62 is to be used, that is the same procedure that is to be used when a refusal of enforcement is sought (see below Chapter 9 at 9.38 et seq).

8.37. Almost identical rules are provided in Brussels I-bis (Article 36(2)), the Matrimonial Property Regulation (Article 36(2)), the Registered Partner Property Regulation (Article 36(2)), the Succession Regulation (Article 39(2)) and the Maintenance Regulation (Article 23(2)).[35] The Brussels Convention (Article 26) also contained such a rule.

8.38. This provision and its equivalents in other Regulations have not yet given rise to any case law from the CJEU. According to Recital (54) the definition of who is to be considered an interested party is left to national law. Where applicable, this concept could include public prosecutors, civil status registration authorities, social authorities or other child welfare authorities in the Member State in which recognition is sought.[36]

8.39. In most cases when a declaratory judgment is sought, there will be a dispute between the parties concerning the recognition of the judgment. In the

---

[35] But in the Maintenance Regulation only for judgments from a Member State not bound by the 2007 Hague Protocol on the law applicable to maintenance obligations (following Brexit this only applies to Denmark).
[36] See the Borrás Report, para. 65.

Brussels Convention, the existence of a 'dispute' was also a requirement. Possibly due to the difficulty of defining 'dispute', this was struck out in Brussels I-bis and has never been a requirement in the context of Brussels II, from the Brussels II Convention to the present Regulation.[37] Even where there is no dispute, a party might nevertheless want to forestall possible future dispute through a judgment that settles the matter of recognition once and for all. Furthermore, a party may wish to obtain a declaratory judgment to facilitate contacts with public authorities, for instance, to prove eligibility for child benefits available to holders of custody.

8.40. Member States' laws differ as to what sort of interest in a declaratory judgment an applicant must have in order to have standing and it could well be that under national procedural law, the person seeking a declaratory judgment might not have standing to do so. It is submitted that even though procedural law is largely left to Member States, such law may not hinder the effectiveness of the Regulation by making it generally impossible to obtain such a judgment.[38]

8.41. According to Article 30(4), local jurisdiction (venue) in the country in which recognition is sought shall be determined by the national law of that Member State. Member States are obliged by Article 103(1)(c) to communicate to the Commission which courts have jurisdiction. The courts and the authorities designated by the Member States can be found on the e-Justice Portal.[39]

2. *Negative Declarations*

8.42. Article 30(3) only applies to positive declarations on enforceability, whereas the predecessor to this rule, Article 14(3) of the Brussels II-bis

---

[37] The reference to 'dispute' is kept in the corresponding provisions in the Maintenance Regulation, the Succession Regulation and the Regulations on Matrimonial and Registered Partners Property Relations.

[38] (Unhappily) drawing the conclusion that the domestic law of the forum applies, see L.P.R. DE LIMA PINHEIRO, Art. 30 Brussels IIter' in U. MAGNUS and P. MANKOWSKI (eds), *Brussels IIter Regulation*, OttoSchmidt, 2023, p. 356, para. 7. For the same conclusion as is drawn in this book, but concerning similar provisions in the Matrimonial Property Regimes Regulation and the Property Regimes of Registered Partners Regulation, see P. FRANZINA, 'Article 36' in I. VIARENGO and P. FRANZINA (eds), *The EU Regulations on the Property Regimes of International Couples*, Edward Elgar, 2020, p. 342, para. 36.27. However, for the same opinion as expressed here concerning Brussels Ibis, see P. WAUTELET, 'Article 36' in U. MAGNUS and P. MANKOWSKI (eds), *Brussels Ibis Regulation*, 3rd ed., OttoSchmidt, 2016, p. 820, para. 20; and for the Succession Regulation, see I. PRETELLI, 'Article 39. Reconnaissance', in A. BONOMI and P. WAUTELET (eds), *Le droit européen des successions*, 2nd ed., Bruylant, Brussels 2016, para. 11.

[39] See https://e-justice.europa.eu/37842/EN/brussels_iib_regulation__matrimonial_matters_ and_matters_of_parental_responsibility_recast_.

Regulation, applied equally to positive and negative declarations.[40] The provision has been split in two in order to achieve symmetry with Brussels I-bis,[41] and the situation in which a party seeks a declaratory judgment that recognition of a judgment is to be refused is now governed by Article 40.

8.43. The reference to 'any interested person' found in Article 30(3) is not replicated in Article 40, which is completely silent on who has standing to make an application for a declaration of non-enforceability.[42] It is submitted that the two provisions should be interpreted equally and that no substantial difference is intended. It is also not necessary that an application for recognition of the judgment has been submitted beforehand in order to apply for a declaration of non-recognition.[43]

8.44. As for positive declarations, local jurisdiction (venue) is, according to Article 40(2), determined by the national law of the Member State in which a declaration for non-recognition is sought.[44]

C. RECOGNITION AS AN INCIDENTAL QUESTION

1. Rationale and Scope

8.45. The procedure for a declaratory judgment is free-standing and is not applicable where the question of recognition arises as an incidental question – that is, when the recognition of a foreign judgment is relevant for the outcome of the dispute with which the court seised is primarily concerned. Such situations fall within the ambit of Article 30(5), which allows a court to determine the question of recognition as an incidental question.[45]

---

[40] The Brussels Convention only had an explicit rule for positive declarations, which led to speculation as to whether it was possible to ask for a negative declaration or not; see P. WAUTELET, above n. 38, p. 821, para. 25.
[41] In Brussels II-bis, an application for a positive declaration is made according to Article 36(2) and for a negative declaration according to Article 45.
[42] The corresponding Article 45(1) Brussels I-bis speaks of 'any interested party'. Article 37 in the Commission's Proposal contained a reference to 'any interested party', but according to information given to us the Article was redrafted in order to not give an impression that recognition could only be refused after an application, but also *ex officio* by the authorities in the Member State in which recognition is sought. Whether *ex officio* refusal is possible would then be governed by national law.
[43] ECJ, 11 July 2008, *Rina*, C-195/08 PPU.
[44] Under Article 103(1)(c), Member States must communicate to the Commission which courts have jurisdiction. The courts and the authorities designated by the Member States can be found on the e-Justice Portal, above n. 39.
[45] Cf. Article 16 concerning the right to decide questions relating to parental responsibility *in substance* as an incidental question; see Chapter 1 at 1.43 et seq.

8.46. The rationale behind this rule is that if it did not exist, proceedings would have to be stayed and the interested party would have to bring separate proceedings – either for a positive declaration according to Article 30(3) or a negative declaration according to Article 40(1) – possibly in a different court.[46]

8.47. An example of when decisions to be recognised under Brussels II-ter could give rise to incidental questions is in the area of maintenance. Whether a party is divorced or still married will most often, depending on the applicable law, affect the level of spousal maintenance.[47] While the recognition of the maintenance decision would fall under the Maintenance Regulation, the question of marital status would be recognised incidentally according to Article 30(5). Furthermore, the question of with which parent the child should live and the manner in which access is to be exercised will affect the amount of child support to be paid. Article 30(5) only refers to courts, but in principle the provision should also be applicable in proceedings before an administrative authority.[48]

8.48. In *Matoušková*, the CJEU held that, where an issue of parental responsibility falls to be determined in the context of proceedings relating to succession, this issue cannot be resolved as an incidental question by the court having jurisdiction over the succession, but must instead be resolved by the court having jurisdiction in matters of parental responsibility.[49] The outcome was the same in *Mikołayczyk*, in which the validity of a marriage was raised as an incidental question in succession proceedings.[50] Again, the CJEU held that although this issue was raised as an incidental question in succession proceedings, it had to be determined, as a separate issue, by the court having jurisdiction in matrimonial matters (in that case, the courts of France, where the second wife was habitually resident) rather than the court that had jurisdiction over the dispute in the succession (*in casu*, Poland). These cases prompted the introduction of Article 16(3), which reverses the case law and gives the succession court jurisdiction as an incidental question, even if it does not have jurisdiction under Brussels II-ter.

8.49. Unlike the corresponding Article 36(3) Brussels I-bis that only speaks of 'refusal of recognition', Article 30(5) is neutral and refers to 'recognition'. Hence, **a court may as an incidental question decide both on the recognition and on the refusal of recognition of a foreign judgment.**[51]

---

[46] P. FRANZINA, above n. 38, p. 342, para. 36.31.
[47] See ECJ, 4 February 1988, *Hoffmann*, C-145/86.
[48] See the wide definition of 'court' in Article 2(2)(1) Brussels II-ter.
[49] CJEU, 6 October 2015, *Matoušková*, C-404/14.
[50] CJEU, 13 October 2016, *Mikołayczyk*, C-294/15.
[51] It has been argued that Article 36(3) Brussels I-bis is also applicable to recognition and not only refusal of recognition; see P. WAUTELET, above n. 38, p. 822, para. 27.

8.50. It goes without saying that **the question of recognition must be of some relevance for the outcome of the main issue of the case.**[52] If the question is completely unrelated to the main proceedings, it should be dismissed.

2. Res Judicata *of Decisions on Recognition as an Incidental Question*

8.51. Another question is **whether a decision on the recognition of a foreign judgment that has been taken as an incidental question becomes** *res judicata*. The general opinion on this matter appears to be that such decisions do not lead to *res judicata*.[53] This position corresponds to the statement in Article 16(2) that determinations **on the substance** of questions relating to parental responsibility only produce effects in the proceedings for which the determination was made.

8.52. One reason for considering decisions on recognition given as an incidental question as *res judicata* is that it would give the party opposing recognition an undue opportunity to challenge the decision if it were possible to raise the question again in declaratory proceedings under Article 40(1).[54] Furthermore, it would increase the risk of contradictory decisions and go against notions of procedural economy if the same question could be tried several times.

8.53. It should be borne in mind that a decision concerning the recognition of a decision from Member State A in Member State B is not the same question as whether the same decision can be recognised in Member State C. Such decisions cannot become *res judicata* outside the Member State in which they were taken. The requirement of **identity of actions**[55] **is not fulfilled** since the grounds for refusal of recognition under Articles 38 and 39 of decisions in matrimonial

---

[52] Many language versions of Article 36(3) Brussels I-bis, including the English version, maintain a requirement that the outcome of the proceedings 'depends on the determination of an incidental question'. There is no similar explicit requirement in Article 30(3) Brussels II-ter.

[53] See A. LAYTON and H. MERCER, *European Civil Practice*, Vol. 1, 2nd ed., Sweet & Maxwell, London 2004, p. 878, para. 26.011; P. FRANZINA, 'The Recognition and Enforcement of Member State Judgments: Arts. 36–38' in A. DICKINSON and E. LEIN (eds), *The Brussels I Regulation Recast*, Oxford University Press, 2015, p. 392, para. 13.93; E. D'ALLESSANDRO, 'Article 39 Recognition' in A.-L. CALVO CARAVACA, A. DAVÌ and H.-P. MANSEL (eds), *The EU Succession Regulation: A Commentary*, Cambridge University Press, 2016 p. 541, para. 13; U. BERGQUIST, 'Article 36: Recognition' in U. BERGQUIST, D. DAMASCELLI, R. FRIMSTON, P. LAGARDE and B. REINHARTZ (eds), *The EU Regulations on Matrimonial and Patrimonial Property*, Oxford University Press, 2018, p. 149, para. 36.31. However, for the opposite view, see P. WAUTELET, above n. 38, p. 823, para. 31; I. PRETELLI, above n. 38, para. 20. It should be noted that none of the comments concerns the question of the *res judicata* effect of recognition as an incidental question under Brussels II-ter, but the same question concerning the recognition under other EU Regulations.

[54] P. WAUTELET, above n. 38, p. 823, para. 31.

[55] See in general E. HARNON, '*Res Judicata* and Identity of Actions: Law and Rationale' (1966) 1 *Israeli Law Review* 539.

matters and matters of parental responsibility respectively are not uniformly applicable in all Member States. Both Articles refer to the public policy of the Member State in which recognition is invoked (see Articles 38(a) and 39(1)(a)). However, public policy is a national concept and not uniform throughout the EU, although the CJEU 'will review the limits within which the courts of a Member State may have recourse to that concept for the purpose of declining to recognise a judgment delivered in another Member State'.[56]

8.54. Moreover, recognition must be refused if the judgment made in Member State A is irreconcilable with an earlier decision given in a non-Member State, provided that it fulfils the conditions necessary for its recognition in the Member State in which recognition is invoked.[57] Rules on the recognition of third State judgments are not harmonised and depending on whether recognition is sought in Member State B or C, the decision from third State D could stand in the way of recognition of the judgment from Member State A or not.

8.55. It is therefore submitted that the ruling in *Gothaer Allgemeine Versicherung*, viz. that the *ratio decidendi* of a judgment given by a court of one Member State must also be binding on courts in other Member States, does not apply to judgments on the enforceability of a judgment in a particular Member States when this matter is raised as an incidental question.

D. STAY OF PROCEEDINGS

1. Background and Purpose

8.56. Article 33 gives a court a discretion to stay its proceedings in whole or in part either where: (1) an ordinary appeal against the decision to be recognised has been lodged in the Member State of origin; or (2) an application has been submitted that there are no grounds for refusal of recognition or that recognition is to be refused.

8.57. The roots of this provision go back to Article 30 of the Brussels Convention and there are similar provisions in Brussels I-bis (Article 38), the Lugano Convention (Article 30), the Maintenance Regulation (Articles 21(3) and 25), the Succession Regulation (Article 42) and the Matrimonial and Registered Partners Property Relations Regulations (Article 41).

---

[56] CJEU, 19 November 2015, *P*, C-455/15 PPU, para. 37. For the same position concerning public policy and the Brussels I Regulation, see also ECJ, 28 March 2000, *Krombach*, C-7/98, para. 22; and CJEU, 16 July 2015, *Diageo Brands*, C-681/13, para. 42.
[57] Articles 38(d) and 39(1)(e).

2. Situations in which Proceedings May be Stayed

i) The Judgment has been Appealed in the Member State of Origin

8.58. Under Brussels II-ter, a judgment can be enforced even if it has not become *res judicata*, that is, even if it can still be appealed. If the judgment has been appealed in the Member State of origin, there could be good reasons to await the outcome of that appeal before giving it effect in the country in which recognition is sought. For this reason, a court before which the appealed decision from another Member State is invoked has the power to stay its proceedings awaiting the outcome of the appeal.

8.59. Under Article 33(a), **proceedings may be stayed if an 'ordinary' appeal against the decision to be enforced has been lodged in the Member State of origin**. Since the distinction between ordinary and extraordinary appeals is unknown to the Irish and UK legal systems, the Brussels Convention was amended to take this into account when these two countries acceded to the Convention.[58] Later, in Brussels I-bis, the reference to 'ordinary' was taken out and there was no longer a need for such a special provision. The same applies to Article 25 of the Maintenance Regulation. However, in the Succession Regulation, 'ordinary' had found its way back but the reference to Ireland and the UK had been taken out – probably due to the fact that those two Member States had not exercised their right to opt into the Regulation and during negotiations had made it clear that they did not intend to do so, thus obviating the need for such a provision. Neither Ireland nor the UK was ever bound by any of the two Regulations on Matrimonial and Registered Partner Property Relations,[59] again doing away with the need for a special provision. However, the situation is different in respect of Brussels II-ter, which is binding in Ireland and Cyprus. To take account of this, Article 72 states that where a decision was given in either of those Member States,[60] any form of appeal shall be treated as ordinary appeal for the purposes of Chapter IV on recognition and enforcement.

8.60. Yet, with the exception of Cyprus and Ireland, Article 33(a) only authorises the court to stay proceedings if an **ordinary appeal** has been lodged in the Member State of origin. The term is not defined in Brussels II-ter, but the Court of Justice has given the concept an autonomous interpretation holding that 'ordinary appeal' refers to an appeal that must be lodged within a specified

---

[58] For an overview, see Schlosser Report, paras 195–204. The same holds true for Cyprus, which did not join the EU until 2004.
[59] Which are adopted under the mechanism of enhanced cooperation and are only binding in 18 Member States.
[60] The reference to the UK has become obsolete after Brexit.

time period[61] and that it cannot refer to 'appeals which are dependent either upon events which were unforeseeable at the date of the original judgment or upon the action taken by persons who are extraneous to the case, and who are not bound by the period for entering an appeal which starts to run from the date of the original judgment'.[62]

ii) An Application for a Free-Standing Declaratory Judgment has been Submitted

8.61. The second situation in which recognition may be stayed is referred to in Article 33(b), which empowers a court before which the question of enforceability is raised as an incidental question to **stay proceedings if the same matter is also brought as a free-standing action for a positive or negative declaratory judgment** – Article 30(3) and Article 40(1) respectively. Although the latter procedure for a negative declaratory judgment, unlike an appeal in the country of origin, cannot lead to a reversal of the judgment, it could lead to its non-applicability in the Member State in which recognition is sought. For that reason, there should be a possibility to also stay proceedings in such cases.

3. *Scope*

8.62. The various versions of this provision in other EU Regulations concerned with the recognition of judgments in civil law matters refer either to a 'court',[63] 'court or authority'[64] or 'competent authority'.[65] It is submitted that an authority entrusted with the keeping of civil status records, although it hardly falls within the definition of a 'court' given in Article 2(2)(1) Brussels II-ter, should also have the right to stay its 'proceedings' if the judgment from the Member State of origin has been appealed.

8.63. Recognition may be stayed even if an appeal does not have any suspensive effect on the enforceability in the Member State of origin.[66] An appeal that cannot lead to a reversal of the judgment, such as an application to the European Court of Human Rights, should not lead to a stay of recognition.[67]

---

[61] ECJ, 22 November 1977, *Industrial Diamond Supplies*, 43/77, para. 31, which interpreted the corresponding Article 30 of the Brussels Convention. This case is commented upon in T. HARTLEY, 'Procedure for Enforcement: Effect of Appeal in Judgment-Granting State' [1978] *European Law Review* 160.
[62] ECJ, 22 November 1977, *Industrial Diamond Supplies*, 43/77, para. 39.
[63] Article 25 of the Maintenance Regulation, Article of the 42 Succession Regulation and Article 41 of the Matrimonial and Registered Partner Property Relations Regulations.
[64] Article 38 Brussels I-bis.
[65] Article 21(3) of the Maintenance Regulation.
[66] P. WAUTELET, above n. 38, p. 832, para. 15.
[67] P. WAUTELET, above n. 38, p. 833, para. 16.

8.64. A prerequisite according to Article 33(a) is that an ordinary appeal *has* been lodged. It is not sufficient that the time limit for appeal has not expired and that an appeal might be expected.

4. Should Recognition be Stayed?

8.65. Article 33 clearly gives the court a discretion to stay proceedings. But it is not the task of the court in the Member State of enforcement to put itself in the shoes of the court in which the judgment has been appealed and undertake a parallel assessment. Instead, it must ask itself whether 'reasonable doubt arises with regard to the fate of the decision in the State in which it was given'.[68] In matters of parental responsibility, it would also have to decide what lies in the best interests of the child – to stay proceedings or not to do so, with the risk of subsequent modification of the decision by a court in the Member State of origin.[69]

8.66. The rule may be applied *ex officio* and is not dependent on a request by one of the parties. However, in most cases the only way for a court to know that the judgment has been appealed is that this has been brought to its attention by one of the parties.

E. DOCUMENTS TO BE PRODUCED

1. Purpose and Scope

8.67. The purpose of the standardisation of the documents required for recognition is to simplify the procedure. When a party seeks to invoke (rely on) a decision given in one Member State in another Member State, under Article 31(1), only two documents are necessary: (1) a certified copy of the decision; and (2) a certificate using the standard form set out in Annex II (matrimonial matters) or Annex III (parental responsibility). The system set up in Article 31 excludes any national requirements on documents needed to prove a matrimonial decision or decision on parental responsibility. The provision is, like all the other provisions on recognition and enforcement, only applicable to decisions from other Member States. However, it should be noted that the rules are also applicable to decisions in a Member State on the recognition or enforceability of a judgment from a third State if those decisions have been given in contradictory proceedings with a possibility to contest recognition.[70]

---

[68] ECJ, 22 November 1977, *Industrial Diamond Supplies*, 43/77, para. 33.
[69] L.P.R. DE LIMA PINHEIRO, above n. 38, p. 363, para. 3.
[70] See CJEU, 7 April 2022, *H Limited*, C-568/20 on this question under Brussels I-bis.

8.68. Article 31 applies when a party 'wishes to invoke in a Member State a decision given in another Member State', that is ask for a free-standing positive declaratory judgment under Article 30(3) or for a free-standing negative declaratory judgment under Article 40(1) or when the judgment is brought up as an incidental question under Article 30(5). The same requirements concerning documents also apply for the updating of the civil status records on the basis of a decision from another Member State on divorce, legal separation or marriage annulment.[71] Article 31 also applies to proving the content of a decision on costs (Article 73) or on legal aid (Article 74).

2. A Certified Copy of the Decision

8.69. The decision need not be produced in its original form.[72] A copy is sufficient, but it must be 'a copy of the decision which satisfies the conditions necessary to establish its authenticity'. Whatever those conditions are will have to be established by the Member State of origin – be it a formal stamp from the court that issued the judgment or in some other form.[73] Although not required, the original would, of course, also suffice.[74]

8.70. Normally, the judgment need not be translated. This is an important cost and time-saving provision, since the cost of translating an entire judgment can be prohibitive (and discriminatory since courts in some countries write longer judgments than others).

3. A Certificate Issued Pursuant to Article 36

8.71. In addition to a certified copy of the judgment, the applicant will need a certificate issued pursuant to Article 36. This certificate, which can also be used when seeking enforcement, should be in the form set out in Annex II for decisions in matrimonial matters and Annex III for decisions in matters of parental responsibility. Article 36 imposes a duty on the national court, as communicated to the Commission pursuant to Article 103(1)(b)[75] (normally the court that issued the decision) to issue a certificate. The certificate will not be

---

[71] Article 30(2).
[72] In some Member States, such as Sweden, the original never leaves the court. The parties are only given certified copies and a requirement to provide the judgment in its original form would be impossible to comply with.
[73] See Borrás Report, para. 103.
[74] U. BERGQUIST, A. FAYAD and E. HOVMÖLLER, *Bryssel II ter-förordningen, Rom III-förordningen, internationella äktenskapslagen och nordiska äktenskapsförordningen*, Norstedts Juridik, 2021, p. 130, para. 6.
[75] See https://e-justice.europa.eu/37842/EN/brussels_iib_regulation__matrimonial_matters_and_matters_of_parental_responsibility_recast_.

issued by the court *ex officio*, but only upon application by a party. There is no time limit before which an application must be made. The need for recognition in another Member State may not arise until several years after the judgment was given.

8.72. The certificate should contain the necessary information in order to recognise and, if necessary, enforce the judgment. It should also contain information on service and whether the judgment was given in default. Since this is the practically most important ground for refusal of recognition, this information facilitates recognition. In the case of decisions in matters of parental responsibility, the certificate must also contain information on whether the child or children were capable of forming their own views and, if so, were given the opportunity to express them that is required by Article 21 Brussels II-ter. Failure to give the child this opportunity constitutes a ground for refusal under Article 39(2).

8.73. As noted above (see 8.16), given the differences between the national laws of the Member States and the differences in meaning of the same terms, it is important that the rights concerning access and/or parental responsibility are described in as much detail as possible and taking into account the fact that the receiving court may not be familiar with the issuing court's legal system.

4. *Translation or Transliteration*

8.74. The Article 36 certificate will be drafted in the official language of the court of origin and the applicant is free to submit it in its original form. However, Article 31(2) entitles the receiving court or competent authority to request a **translation or a transliteration into its own language of the 'translatable content of the free text fields'** of the certificate. A translation or transliteration may be required if the court is unable to proceed without such a translation or transliteration,[76] that is, if it does not understand the language used. Transliteration refers to the change of the letters from one alphabet to another, for example, from Bulgarian Cyrillic letters or from the Greek alphabet into the Latin alphabet. However, it could be assumed that a judge who can understand Bulgarian or Greek will understand the text written in the original alphabet and will not need transliteration. Since the annex is translated into all official languages of the EU, there is no need for the translator to re-invent the wheel and translate the form itself.

8.75. Article 31(3) also entitles the receiving court or competent authority to **request a translation or transliteration of the entire decision** for which recognition or refusal of recognition is sought. This may, by way of exception, be

---

[76] See the *2022 Practice Guide*, p. 35.

needed if the certificate does not provide the necessary information. The provision foresees that a translation of the decision is made in addition to the translation of the certificate, and that will be necessary when the receiving judge or authority in the course of proceedings finds that a translation of the certificate is not sufficient.

8.76. Any translation or transliteration, be it of the certificate or the judgment, must be made in accordance with Article 91 Brussels II-ter. Article 91(1) provides that any **translation shall be into the official language of the requested Member State** and where there are several official languages in that Member State, into the official language designated by the law of that State. According to Article 91(2), translations of the Article 36 certificate may also be made into another official language of the EU that the requested Member State has communicated that it can accept.[77] Article 91(4) stipulates that any translation must be made **by an authorised translator**.

5. *Absence of Documents*

8.77. Article 32 specifies that if a certified copy of the decision and an 'Article 36 certificate' are not produced, the receiving court may either set a date for their production or dispense with it altogether if it considers that it has sufficient information to decide on recognition anyway, for example, through other equivalent documents. If so, the court may request translation of those other documents.

IV. PARTIAL RECOGNITION

8.78. Article 53 foresees the possibility of partial **enforcement** of a judgment (see below Chapter 9 at 9.72), whereas there is no corresponding provision pertaining to partial **recognition**. However, since reasons for non-enforcement and non-recognition of parts of a judgment are by and large the same, there is no reason why in the case of some judgments partial recognition should not be possible.

8.79. There may be several reasons why a judgment may only be partially recognisable **under Brussels II-ter**. First, **parts of the judgment might fall outside its scope**. For example, if in a judgment from Member State A it is determined that X is the father of a child and that he shall have joint custody together with the child's mother, only the part pertaining to custody must be recognised under Brussels II-ter, since parentage falls outside its scope.[78] If a judgment contains

---

[77] The languages communicated can be found at: https://e-justice.europa.eu/37842/EN/brussels_iib_regulation__matrimonial_matters_and_matters_of_parental_responsibility_recast_.

[78] See Article 1(4)(a).

decisions on both parental responsibility and maintenance, only the former can be recognised under Brussels II-ter. The latter is excluded from the scope of Brussels II-ter according to Article 1(4)(e), but can be recognised under the Maintenance Regulation.

8.80. Another reason why partial recognition may take place is that **one of the grounds for refusal applies in relation to a part of it but not all**. If, for example, in divorce proceedings, the matter of child custody was also decided and the child was capable of expressing his or her own views but was not given the opportunity to express them, recognition of the latter could be refused according to Article 39(2). However, this does not affect the duty to recognise the divorce.

8.81. Recognition of only a part of the judgment can take place because the court decides, *ex officio* or upon the request of the other party, that a part of it cannot be recognised. However, **a party may also choose to seek only partial recognition**, as in the case of a custody decision concerning two children when one of them has reached the age of majority since the judgment was given.

V. REFUSAL OF RECOGNITION

A. GENERAL COMMENTS

8.82. Although the main purpose of Brussels II-ter is to ensure mutual recognition of judgments within the EU (Recitals (2), (3) and (6)), there will be cases in which recognition should be refused. The Regulation contains rules on the refusal of recognition in Article 38 for matrimonial matters and in Article 39 for matters of parental responsibility. The rules on refusal of recognition are applicable regardless of whether the question arises as an incidental question (see Article 30(5)), in free-standing proceedings for recognition (see Article 30(3)) or for non-recognition (see Article 40(1)).

8.83. The grounds for refusal should be interpreted in a spirit that does not undermine the purpose of the Regulation.[79] Under Brussels II-bis, there were divided opinions as to whether these **grounds of refusal have to be raised by a party or whether the court can raise them of its own initiative**.[80] Recital (54) now clarifies that this question is left to national law.

---

[79] Cf. Jenard Report, p. 42.
[80] For *ex officio* application, see T. RAUSCHER, 'Art 22 Brüssel IIa-VO' in T. RAUSCHER (ed.), *Europäisches Zivilprozess- und Kollisionsrecht Band IV*, OttoSchmidt 2015, p. 272, para. 3. Against *ex officio* application: U. BERGQUIST, A. FAYAD and E. HOVMÖLLER, above n. 74, para. 4.

8.84. **The two lists of grounds for refusal are exhaustive** and no further grounds derived from national law may be invoked. It also does not constitute a ground for refusal if the court in the Member State of origin had violated the rules in the Regulation, for example, the rules on *lis pendens* (see Recital (56)).[81] Furthermore, Brussels II-ter explicitly stipulates (Article 69) that a misapplication of the rules on jurisdiction is not a ground for refusal (see below 8.124 et seq).

8.85. The rules on refusal of recognition in Articles 38 and 39(1) are mandatory. If the court finds the conditions for the application of one or more of the grounds of refusal are met, it must refuse recognition.[82] This follows from the wording of Articles 38 and 39 – 'shall be refused'. It could also be argued that Article 6 ECHR requires it.[83] In contrast, the ground for refusal in Article 39(2) – that is, if the child was not given an opportunity to express his or her views – is facultative.

B. DIVORCE, LEGAL SEPARATION OR MARRIAGE ANNULMENT

1. *Public Policy: Article 38(a)*

8.86. **Public policy** is a national concept, and it is for the courts of each Member State to define its content – Article 38(a) speaks of 'the public policy *of the Member State* in which recognition is invoked' (emphasis added). However, since recognition must be *manifestly* contrary to a State's public policy, the public policy exception **should be used only in exceptional cases**.[84] The CJEU 'will review the limits within which the courts of a Member State may have recourse to that concept for the purpose of declining to recognise a judgment delivered in another Member State'.[85]

8.87. The **prohibition of review as to the substance** (*révision au fond*) **in Article 71** reduces the instances in which public policy may be invoked to cases in which the **result** of recognition would be contrary to the public policy of the recognising Member State, not the underlying reasoning.

---

[81] See also CJEU, 16 January 2019, *Liberato*, C-386/17; and CJEU, 19 November 2015, *P*, C-455/15 PPU.
[82] Borrás Report, para. 67. See also M. SHÚILLEABHÁIN, above n. 33, p. 253, para. 6.36; T. RAUSCHER, above n. 80, 272, para. 3; and U. BERGQUIST, A. FAYAD and E. HOVMÖLLER, above n. 74, p. 141, para. 3.
[83] At least concerning lack of service and/or right of representation; see ECtHR, 20 July 2001, *Pellegrini v. Italy*, App No. 30882/96, para. 47.
[84] Jenard Report, p. 44. See also ECJ, 4 February 1988, *Hoffman*, 145/86, para. 21.
[85] CJEU, 19 November 2015, *P*, C-455/15 PPU, para. 37. For the same position concerning public policy and the Brussels I Regulation, see ECJ, 28 March 2000, *Krombach*, C-7/98, para. 22; and CJEU, 16 July 2015, *Diageo Brands*, C-681/13, para. 42.

The prohibition in Article 70 in refusing recognition of a decision in matrimonial matters because the law of the recognising State would not allow divorce, legal separation or annulment on the same facts further narrows the possible number of cases. For example, a divorce solely based on the mutual consent of the spouses must be recognised even in Member States that require more than consent. In this context, it is in and of itself irrelevant whether the court in the Member State of origin applied the law of an EU Member State or that of a third country.

8.88. It also follows from Article 69 that a misapplication of the rules of jurisdiction is not a reason to apply public policy, even when the error is blatant. Neither is the misapplication of any other rule of the Regulation a ground for refusal of recognition.[86] Only when recognition would 'result in the manifest breach of an essential rule of law in the EU legal order and therefore of in the legal order of that Member State' could the misapplication of the Regulation constitute a violation of public policy.[87]

8.89. Not only are there few cases in which the public policy exception can be invoked, but the grounds of refusal under Article 38(b)–(d) concerning default judgments and irreconcilable judgments further serve to reduce the need to do so. However, there are some circumstances, such as fraud, coercion or corruption, in which recognition could be refused. In such cases a review of the judgment will almost always be possible in the Member State of origin and if such proceedings have been instituted, it would be up to national law and the receiving court to decide whether it should stay its proceedings and await the outcome of review proceedings in the Member State of origin or proceed. Given the proximity to the evidence, it would in most cases be better to await the outcome of a review in the country of origin.[88] Indeed, if the allegations of fraud had been appealed in the country of origin and tried there, it would amount to a review of the substance to refuse recognition.

8.90. It could also be a violation of public policy if the reasons in the judgment have clearly been reused from similar judgments using the 'cut-and-paste' function of the judge's word processor and it is obvious that no individual concern was given to the particular case.[89]

---

[86] CJEU, 19 November 2015, *P*, C-455/15; CJEU, 16 January 2019, *Liberato*, C-386/17.
[87] CJEU, 16 July 2015, *Diageo Brands*, C-681/13, para. 50.
[88] Cf. CJEU, 22 December 2010, *Aguirre Zarraga*, C-491/10 PPU, which concerned an Article 11(8) judgment (now Article 29(6)) on the return of the child following a non-return decision after a wrongful removal/retention. For such decisions, there is *no* right of refusal.
[89] Concerning the duty under Article 8 ECHR to carry out meaningful checks in the context of the application of the 1980 Hague Child Abduction Convention, see ECtHR, 26 November 2013, *X v. Latvia*, App No. 27853/09.

2. The Respondent was not Adequately Served

i) Default Judgments: Article 38(b)

8.91. If a decision was given in default of appearance, recognition can be refused if the respondent was not properly served and has not unequivocally accepted the decision. It follows from its wording that Article 38(b) **only protects the non-appearing defendant**. If respondent entered an appearance, the provision cannot be applied. An appearance only to object against inadequate service does not count as an 'appearance'.[90]

8.92. It should be noted that Article 38(b) Brussels II-ter, unlike Article 45(1)(b) Brussels I-bis, does not contain the proviso that refusal of recognition is only possible if 'the defendant failed to commence proceedings to challenge the judgment when it was possible for him to do so'.

ii) Inadequate Service

8.93. The purpose of Article 38(b) is to protect respondents' right of defence and **should be read in conjunction with Article 19**, which obliges a court to stay proceedings, if the respondent does not enter an appearance, until it has ascertained that he or she has 'been able to receive the document instituting the proceedings in sufficient time to enable him or her to arrange for his or her defence, or that all necessary steps have been taken to this end'. Article 19 can be seen as the first line of defence, but if this for some reason has not held, Article 38(b) comes into play and will at least prevent recognition in other Member States.

8.94. Article 38(b) is applicable even if at the time the decision was given, the case had no intra-EU cross-border aspects. Hence, the provision protects a respondent who is habitually resident in the Member State of origin at the time when proceedings were instituted[91] or in a third country.

8.95. The provision **is only applicable to service of the document that instituted proceedings** or 'an equivalent document',[92] not to other documents

---

[90] Cf. ECJ, 24 June 1981, *Elefanten Schuh*, 150/80, a case under the Brussels Convention in which appearance to contest jurisdiction was not held to constitute tacit prorogation, that is, an acceptance of the court's jurisdiction. This is now explicitly stated in Article 26(1), last sentence Brussels I-bis.

[91] ECJ, 11 June 1985, *Debaecker*, 49/84, para. 13 (concerning the Brussels Convention).

[92] The Court's practice as to the meaning of this expression in the equivalent provision in the Brussels Convention would appear to be of little relevance in the context of matrimonial matters, since the case law concerns summary proceedings for payment of debts. See ECJ, 16 June 1981, *Klomps*, 166/80; and ECJ, 13 July 1995, *Hengst*, C-474/93.

that should be served on the respondent, such as summons to oral hearings or the judgment itself. A lack of service of such documents could in some cases be a ground for refusal under the public policy of the forum.[93]

8.96. If a defendant was not served with summons or other document that instituted the proceedings in time **and** in such a way that enabled that person to arrange for his or her defence, the decision does not merit recognition. The two requirements are cumulative and must both be fulfilled. According to the case law of the Court of Justice (on the Brussels Convention), the court in the Member State in which recognition is sought has the right to ascertain that these two requirements are fulfilled, even if the judgment to be recognised states that this is the case.[94] Each Member State may set its own standards. However, this may not amount to a review as to the substance.[95]

8.97. Under Brussels II-ter, there is **no fixed time which a respondent should be given for the preparation of his or her defence**. The Regulation does not seek to harmonise the different systems of service in the Member States.[96] Hence, the receiving court is not bound by rules in the Member State of origin and is free to find the time period insufficient, even if it was according to the law of the Member State of origin. What is an appropriate time period would appear to be dependent on the type of matrimonial proceedings and the law applied to them. If the only thing that the respondent has to do is to say yes or no to divorce in order to decide whether a cooling-off period should commence or not,[97] an appropriate time period could be relatively short. Where, however, divorce is dependent on factual circumstances pertaining to the breakdown of the marriage, which are to be either proven or disproven, more time might be necessary.

8.98. A further complicating factor is that divorce is often only part of a larger package of issues such as parental responsibility, maintenance and division of matrimonial property, where the latter two do not fall within the scope of this Regulation. Furthermore, only the Matrimonial Property Regulation contains a similar rule (Article 37). The Maintenance Regulation instead gives the respondent a possibility to apply for a review in the Member State of origin (Article 19). This lack of coordination between different Regulations is

---

[93] In England and Wales, see *Maronier v. Larmer* [2002] EWCA Civ 774 (CA), in which proceedings had been re-assumed after a delay of 12 years without the respondent being given proper notice. See X. Kramer, 'Enforcement under the Brussels Convention: Procedural Public Policy and the Influence of Article 6 ECHR' (2002/2003) 2 *International Lis* 16.
[94] ECJ, 15 July 1982, *Pendy Plastic*, 228/81.
[95] ECJ, 15 July 1982, *Pendy Plastic*, 228/81, para. 13.
[96] ECJ, 15 July 1982, *Pendy Plastic*, 228/81, para. 13.
[97] Under both Swedish and Finnish law, in the case of a joint application or if the respondent accepts the divorce, the court can divorce the couple immediately if there are no common children under the age of 16, but if one spouse does not accept the divorce, the cooling-off period is six months.

problematic and the receiving court will need to deal with each issue separately and apply the different Regulations accordingly.

8.99. The respondent not only has to be served in sufficient time but also **in such a way as to enable the arrangement of his or her defence**. The documents must be sufficiently clear and precise for the respondent to understand the matter, which means, *inter alia*, that he or she understands the language in which service took place. It should be noted in this context that Article 12(1) of the Service Regulation gives the respondent the right to refuse to accept service of a document that is not written in a language that he or she understands.[98]

iii) The Defendant Must not have Accepted the Decision

8.100. Even if the service was inadequate, the respondent loses the right to contest recognition on this ground if he or she **unequivocally accepts the decision**. Unequivocal acceptance does not have to be in the form of a formal declaration, but can take the form of actions by the respondent showing adherence to the decision. This could take the form of entering the new civil status in the civil registry, entering into a new marriage,[99] seeing the child in conformity with an access decision, entering an application for the division of matrimonial property, or applying for maintenance as an ex-spouse.[100]

3. *Irreconcilability with a Domestic Judgment: Article 38(c)*

8.101. Article 38(c) applies where a judgment from another Member State is irreconcilable with a judgment from the Member State in which recognition is sought. Theoretically, Article 20 on *lis pendens* makes this provision unnecessary and there should be no irreconcilable judgments from two Member States. However, as practice has shown, it does occasionally occur and if it does, the **domestic judgment trumps a judgment from another Member State irrespective of which judgment was first given**. The rule is outdated and encourages disrespect for the *lis pendens* rule.

8.102. Not all judgments falling within the scope of 'matrimonial matters' are irreconcilable. If a separation judgment was given in State A, a divorce judgment was later given in State B and recognition is sought in State A, there is no irreconcilability, since separation is a preliminary to divorce. But if the situation were the other way round and recognition in State B was sought for

---

[98] Regulation (EU) No. 2020/1784 of the European Parliament and of the Council of 25 October 2020 on the service in the Member States of judicial and extrajudicial documents in civil or commercial matters (service of documents) (recast), OJ L405, 2.12.2020, p. 40.
[99] Borrás Report, para. 70.
[100] U. BERGQUIST, A. FAYAD and E. HOVMÖLLER, above n. 74, pp. 145 f., para. 35.

the separation judgment from State A, recognition would have to be denied, since divorce supersedes separation.[101] Divorce is irreconcilable with marriage annulment and marriage annulment with legal separation and divorce. It might be thought that two judgments that both declare the couple divorced would not be irreconcilable, but the *date* of the judgment might be different and relevant for ancillary matters such as spousal maintenance, division of matrimonial property or succession, and the judgments would therefore be irreconcilable.

4. Irreconcilability with an Earlier Foreign Judgment: Article 38(d)

8.103.   Article 38(d) applies either when there are two judgments from Member States other than the one in which recognition is sought or from a Member State and a third State. Again, the *lis pendens* rule in Article 20 should prevent irreconcilability of judgments from two Member States, but that rule is not applicable vis-à-vis third States where the question of *lis pendens* is determined according to national law. The rule is only applicable when there is irreconcilability between two judgments from Member States or from a Member State and a third State. It is not applicable to the situation where there are two judgments from third States or a judgment from a third State and one from the Member State in which recognition is sought.

8.104.   A difference in comparison with Article 38(c) is that priority is given to the first judgment, irrespective of when proceedings commenced. If the judgments are from two Member States, it is the date upon which they are given which is decisive, since they are immediately recognisable in all other Member States without the need for any intermediary procedure. However, this is not the case with all judgments from all third States. In some cases, a court decision will first be required in the State in which recognition is sought. The question is then whether it is the date of the original judgment or the decision on recognition that should be decisive.[102]

C. PARENTAL RESPONSIBILITY

8.105.   Under Article 39, the grounds for refusal of recognition of decisions in matters of parental responsibility are to a large extent – *mutatis mutandis* – the same as the grounds for refusal of recognition in matrimonial matters. Article 39(1)(a) on public policy, (b) on inadequate service of respondent, (d) on irreconcilability with a later domestic decision and (e) irreconcilability

---

[101]   Borrás Report, para. 71.
[102]   See H. GAUDEMET-TALLON, M.-E. ANCEL, *Compétence et execution des jugements en Europe*, 6th ed., LGDJ, 2018, p. 645 f., para. 466, with further references to differing opinions.

with a later foreign decision have their counterparts in Article 38 (discussed at 8.86–8.104 above), and for those grounds of refusal, the discussion will only go into the peculiarities pertaining to parental responsibility here.

1. *Public Policy: Article 39(1)(a)*

8.106. As with the public policy exception in relation to decisions in matrimonial matters, this ground of refusal should be applied with the utmost restraint. However, there is one important difference – namely, that the receiving court is instructed to look primarily to **the best interests of the child**, not those of the receiving State in general. Recital (19) makes it clear that '[a]ny reference to the best interests of the child should be interpreted in light of Article 24 of the Charter of Fundamental Rights of the European Union ("the Charter") and the 1989 United Nations Convention on the Rights of the Child ("UNCRC") as implemented by national law and procedure'.

8.107. As each child is unique, what the best interests of the child are will vary from case to case. However, even though all children are individuals, they do not exist in a vacuum and the best interests of the child can vary according to his or her environment. It is also a concept that can develop over time. It is therefore difficult to exactly pinpoint the meaning of the concept. What can be said is that: (1) **the interests of the child should prevail over those of his or her parents** or other people in his or her environment, such as the extended family or members of a religious or ethnic group; and (2) **it is the best interests of the individual child that are to be ascertained** and not those of children in general.

8.108. However, having emphasised the importance of the **best interests of the child**, it should be pointed out that it **is not the only reason to refuse recognition on grounds of public policy**. The right to respect for private and family life contained in Article 8 ECHR (and Article 7 of the Charter) and the prohibition of discrimination in Article 14 ECHR (and Article 21 of the Charter) form part of the public policy of all Member States. Hence, a judgment that openly discriminates against a parent or the parents on the grounds of religion,[103] sexual orientation,[104] gender[105] or mental illness[106] would constitute a violation of public policy.

---

[103] ECtHR, 23 June 1993, *Hoffmann v. Austria*, App No. 12878/87; ECtHR 16 December 2003, *Palau-Martinez v. France*, App No. 64927/01; ECtHR, 12 February 2013, *Vojnity v. Hungary*, App No. 29617/07.
[104] ECtHR, 21 December 1999, *Salgueiro da Silva Mouta v. Portugal*, App No. 33290/96.
[105] ECtHR, 3 December 2009, *Zaunegger v. Germany*, App No. 22028/04; ECtHR, 30 November 2010, *P.V. v. Spain*, App No. 35159/09.
[106] ECtHR, 18 February 2020, *Cînţa v. Romania*, App No. 3891/18.

2. The Respondent was not Adequately Served: Article 39(1)(b)

8.109. Article 39(1)(b) corresponds to Article 38(b), except in that **adequate service should have been carried out in relation to 'the person in default' rather than 'the respondent'**.[107] The reason for this difference is that in some Member States, the question of parental responsibility can be introduced/raised *ex officio* by the court in divorce proceedings. What role the parties had in those proceedings is then without importance. Furthermore, if the question of parental responsibility was introduced into divorce proceedings by the respondent to those proceedings, then it is the applicant who must be served. Moreover, the relevant document that must be served is not 'the document that instituted the proceedings', but the 'equivalent document' that should have made the person in default in the matter of parental responsibility aware of the matter having been introduced into the proceedings. This question could also arise in the context of child welfare when the child is placed with a foster family or institution and the parents might not be parties to the proceedings in which the decision was taken.

3. Non-Hearing of Person Concerned: Article 39(1)(c)

8.110. Article 39(1)(c) has no parallel in Article 38. The rule protects not only the defendant but also **all persons, whether or not a party to the proceedings, whose parental responsibility has been infringed by the decision**. Such situations could arise when an earlier decision giving (aspects of) parental responsibility to a third person such as a foster parent or a child welfare authority is affected by the decision. Furthermore, since access rights are included in the concept of parental responsibility (see Article 2(2)(7)), the provision also addresses third-party holders of such rights, for example, grandparents, previous foster parents or step-parents.[108]

8.111. Unlike the other grounds of refusal, **this ground is not to be applied** *ex officio* but only upon application by a person claiming that his or her (or its in the case of a public body since these do not have gender in the English language) parental responsibility has been infringed by the decision. It is the lack of opportunity to be heard as such that constitutes the ground for refusal, not the fact that the outcome would have been different if the person in question had been heard.[109]

---

[107] It should be noted that the Italian version of the Regulation does not make a difference between Article 38(b) and Article 39(1)(b), using in both rules the same reference to the 'convenuto contumace'. However, other language versions, such as the German, French, Spanish and Dutch ones, show the same differences in wording as in the English version.
[108] T. RAUSCHER, 'Art 23 Brüssel IIa-VO' in T. RAUSCHER (ed.), above n. 83, p. 287, para. 18.
[109] T. RAUSCHER, 'Art 23 Brüssel IIa-VO', above n. 108, p. 287, para. 19.

4. Irreconcilability with a Domestic Judgment: Article 39(1)(d)

8.112. Article 39(1)(d) broadly corresponds with Article 38(c). However one difference is that whereas the former gives precedence to any judgment in matrimonial matters from the Member State of recognition, the latter only gives **precedence to a later judgment on parental responsibility** given in that Member State. This follows from the fact that judgments on parental responsibility never really acquire *res judicata* effects, since they may always be changed to reflect a change of circumstances (cf. Recital (56) last sentence). A later judgment therefore always supersedes an older judgment. This assumption is really only sound if the later decision is based on changed circumstances and not based on the same facts as the older decision, but then again, the rule is not discretionary. This provision, it would appear, would open the way for a circumvention of the override mechanism in Article 29(6) (see Chapter 6). In this context, it should be noted that it is the date of the judgment that counts, not the date on which proceedings were instituted.

8.113. The provision refers to the irreconcilability of a decision 'relating' to parental responsibility. That means that a decision on, for example, parental status that has indirect consequences for the question of parental responsibility can be held to be irreconcilable.[110] If the two judgments are only partially irreconcilable, there is no reason why the older judgment should not be recognised in part (see above 8.78 et seq on partial recognition). Consider the case of an older judgment from Member State A in which the mother is given sole custody of the child and the father is given certain access rights. The mother moves with the child to Member State B, lives with a new man for a few years, with whom the child forms a close bond, and then separates from him. If the now former stepfather successfully obtains access in Member State B, this could possibly be irreconcilable with the access rights of the child's biological father, but it does not change the fact that the mother has sole custody – a matter which may not have been addressed in the later judgment if the case only concerned access.

5. Irreconcilability with a Later Foreign Judgment: Article 39(1)(e)

8.114. Article 39(1)(e) corresponds to Article 38(d). Again, the difference is that **precedence is given to a later judgment**. Furthermore, it is clear from the wording that if the judgment is from a non-Member State, precedence is only given to a later judgment **if that State is the habitual residence of the child**.[111]

---

[110] Cf. Borrás Report, para. 73.
[111] This has not prevented some commentators from extending the requirement to judgments from other Member States; see, for example, P. GOTTWALD, 'Brüssel IIa-VO Art. 23', in T. RAUSCHER (ed.), *Münchener Kommentar zum FamFG*, 3rd ed., C.H. Beck, Munich 2019, para. 11; K. PARASCHAS, 'VO (EG) 2201/2003 Art. 23' in R. GEIMER and R. SCHÜTZE (eds), *Internationaler Rechtsverkehr in Zivil- und Handelssachen*, Beck-online, 2022, para. 45.

It is unclear whether the habitual residence of the child should be at the time the judgment was given or at the time recognition is sought. Since the basis for the rule is that other grounds of jurisdiction such as the child's nationality are regarded as less appropriate for the appreciation of the child's best interests,[112] we would interpret the rule as pointing to the habitual residence at the time the decision was taken.[113]

6. *Failure to Comply with the Procedure in Article 82: Article 39(1)(f)*

8.115. Article 82 (which replaces Article 56 Brussels II-bis) establishes a special procedure to be used when a child is placed in another Member State.[114] In such cases, the Central Authority of the Member State having jurisdiction shall transmit a request to the Central Authority of the Member State in which placement is contemplated. The Central Authority of the requested Member State must give its consent before placement can take place, see Article 82(5). If this is not the case, Article 39(1)(f) imposes on the Member State in which the child is to be placed a duty to refuse the recognition of such a decision.[115]

8.116. This provision was not included in the Commission's proposal for Brussels II-ter because such a ground of refusal was thought unnecessary following the proposed amendments to speed up the procedure.[116] The experience under Brussels II-bis was that Central Authorities were slow in answering such requests and because of the urgency of the matter decisions were taken without consent.[117] The proposal contained a time limit of two months, which was thought to alleviate this problem. However, in the negotiations, this time limit was changed to three months (see Article 82(6)) and Member States opted to keep this ground of refusal.

7. *Failure to Hear the Child: Article 39(2)*

8.117. According to Article 39(2), **recognition may be refused if it was given without the child being given an opportunity to be heard if that child is capable of forming his or her own views.** The rule is a natural pendant to

---

[112] Lagarde Report, para. 126.
[113] See also T. RAUSCHER, 'Art 23 Brüssel IIa-VO', above n. 83, p. 290, para. 26.
[114] Article 82 is discussed in detail in Chapter 11.
[115] The 'chapeau' in Article 39(1) states that recognition *shall* be refused. The procedure in Article 82 foresees consent from the Central Authority of the requested Member State, but if under the internal law of the requested Member State a court has the authority to override that lack of consent through a decision on the recognition of a foreign judgment, one can speak of a *right* to refuse.
[116] U. BERGQUIST, A. FAYAD and E. HOVMÖLLER, above n. 74, p. 150, para. 7.
[117] COM(2016) 411, p. 4.

Article 21, which imposes a duty on Member States to provide the child with an opportunity to express his or her views in proceedings concerning parental responsibility. This duty is reiterated in Article 26 concerning return proceedings after a wrongful abduction or retention (see Chapter 7 on hearing of the child). There is a duty of the court deciding on the substance to inform itself of the child's ability to form and express his or her views, taking his or her age and maturity into consideration.

8.118. Unlike the situation under Brussels II-bis, recognition cannot be denied when the child was given an opportunity to be heard. The rule does not require that the child actually was heard. While this allows for some flexibility in the different practices of Member States, it still leaves some issues open. The most important of these is the question of who is to be authorised to waive the child's right. It is difficult to see that this question can be answered by any other law than that of the forum. Whatever the case, the court of origin must state the reasons for not hearing the child in the decision and also in the required certificate (see Annex III, point 15.1.2). If no reasons have been stated at all, this ground for refusal comes into play.

8.119. Article 21 (and in the case of return proceedings Article 26, which refers to Article 21) only imposes a duty to hear the child if the child is capable of forming his or her own views, which will depend upon the child's age and degree of maturity. Whether the child has reached such a level of maturity is for the court of origin to decide and a review of its decision not to hear the child for this reason would amount to a review as to the substance, which is prohibited by Article 71 Brussels II-ter (see 8.132 et seq below). However, Article 71 only applies to situations where the court of origin has actually assessed the degree of maturity of the child and not cases in which it had simply omitted to hear the child.[118]

8.120. **Article 21 leaves the method in which the child is to be heard to the national law of the Member State of origin.** It is therefore not a reason to refuse recognition that the child has been heard in a different manner than would have been the case in the Member State in which recognition is sought – for example, via a child welfare authority rather than by a judge (cf. Recital (57)).

8.121. Unlike the grounds of refusal in Article 39(1), this provision is permissive in nature and does not oblige the requested court to refuse recognition if the child has not been given an opportunity to express his or her views. Cases in which recognition might not be refused could include those

---

[118] The duty to motivate judgments would oblige the court of origin to give reasons for not hearing the child; cf. CJEU, 23 October 2014, *flyLAL-Lithuanian Airlines*, C-302/13, para. 51 on this duty in general.

where it is clear that the judgment is in the best interests of the child regardless of the child's opinion in the matter and cases in which the child has not been heard and no reason has been given for this, but the age of the child makes it obvious that he or she could not have been capable of forming his or her own views.

8.122. Article 39(2) provides two exceptions to the power to refuse recognition due to a failure to give the child an opportunity to be heard. First, according to Article 39(2)(a), recognition should not be refused if proceedings only concerned the property of the child and hearing the child was not required in light of the subject matter, and, second, according to Article 39(2)(b) if there were serious grounds for not hearing the child, in particular, the urgency of the case. This provision gives the court of origin some discretion, but, again, Article 71 prohibits a review of the reasoning underlying the choice not to hear the child – if such reasoning was given. Although urgency is explicitly listed there may be other grounds for not giving the child the opportunity to be heard, such as if an abducting parent is concealing the location of the child.[119]

D. LIMITATIONS ON THE RIGHT TO REFUSE RECOGNITION

8.123. Articles 69–71 (previously Articles 24–26 Brussels II-bis) contain rules that reduce the possibility to invoke the grounds of refusal. These rules are applicable to both matrimonial matters and matters of parental responsibility.

1. Prohibition of Review of Jurisdiction of the Court of Origin: Article 69

8.124. **Article 69 prevents the review of the jurisdiction of the court in the Member State of origin that gave the judgment for which recognition is sought.** Since there is no ground of refusal in Articles 38 and 39 that explicitly addresses wrongful assumption of jurisdiction, the only ground of refusal that could have been used would have been the public policy exception. However, Article 69 makes it clear that public policy may not be used to review the jurisdiction of the court of origin.

8.125. The rule is absolute and not even manifest errors in the assumption of jurisdiction give right to a refusal of recognition.[120] Although the provision only addresses the rules on jurisdiction in Articles 3–14, a misapplication of

---

[119] See M. WILDERSPIN, *European Private International Family Law: The Brussels IIb Regulation*, Oxford University Press, 2023, p. 369, para. 8-186.
[120] Cf. CJEU, 16 July 2015, *Diageo Brands*, C-681/13.

the *lis pendens* provision in Article 20 similarly does not give a right to refuse recognition.[121] The corresponding rule in Brussels I-bis is Article 45(3). Brussels I-bis contains certain exclusive grounds of jurisdiction, and Article 45(1)(e) gives a right to refuse recognition if jurisdiction has been assumed in violation of those rules. However, Brussels II-ter does not contain exclusive grounds of jurisdiction and hence there is no corresponding rule giving a right of refusal. Article 6, which gives courts a right to apply domestic rules on jurisdiction in certain cases, is included in the scope of the rule and hence there is no right to refuse recognition even if jurisdiction (wrongfully) was based on national law.

8.126. Even though review of the jurisdiction of the court of origin is prohibited, **fraud** or **corruption** or other ways of **perverting the course of justice**, such as intimidation of a witness or a judge, are reasons to refuse recognition under the public policy exception. And if, for example, a court has erroneously assumed jurisdiction based on the false testimony of a witness, the reason to refuse recognition would be that basis and not the wrongful assumption of jurisdiction. It would therefore not be a violation of Article 69 to refuse recognition in such a case.

8.127. An example of this would be the *Berkshire Mailbox* cases (see also above 3.54) in which a large number of Italian couples (180!) registered the same post office box address in the UK in order to circumvent Italian divorce law and more quickly obtain a divorce under English law. Divorce proceedings in the UK, as in several other Member States, are written proceedings, and the veracity of the stated address had not been checked and all 180 couples were divorced. In the end, this scheme was discovered, and all divorce judgments were declared void by the High Court of Justice.[122]

2. *Differences in Applicable Law: Article 70*

8.128. Article 70 stipulates that **recognition of a decision in matrimonial matters may not be refused because the law of the Member State in which recognition is sought would not have allowed for divorce, legal separation or marriage annulment on the same facts**. The provision was first introduced in the Brussels II Convention to meet the concerns of Member States with liberal divorce laws. These States feared that the public policy provision would

---

[121] CJEU, 16 January 2019, *Liberato*, C-386/17. The same applied to the rule on transfer on jurisdiction under Article 15 Brussels II-bis, which was not referred to in Article 24; see CJEU, 19 November 2015, *P*, C-455/15 PPU.
[122] *Rapisarda v. Colladon (Irregular Divorces)* (2014) EWFC 35. See C. Ricci, 'Habitual Residence as a Ground of Jurisdiction in Matrimonial Disputes Connected with the EU: Challenges and Potential' (2020) 11 *Civil Procedure Review*, 151, 168 f.

be used in order to deny recognition of their judgments when divorce would not have been available in the receiving State under the same conditions.[123] On the other hand, a consequence of the provision is that recognition of legal separation and marriage annulment cannot be refused in those States whose internal laws do not contain rules on such matters (and those are States with liberal divorce laws).[124]

8.129. Article 27(4) of the 1968 Brussels Convention contained a right of refusal of a judgment from another Convention State if, as a preliminary matter, it had decided a question concerning, *inter alia*, the status of natural persons (e.g. divorce) in a way that conflicted with the choice-of-law rules of the State in which recognition was sought, unless the application of the law designated by those rules would have led to the same result. The 1988 Lugano Convention contained a similar rule. When the Brussels Convention was transformed into the 2000 Brussels I Regulation, this provision was not kept, nor did it find its way into the 2007 Lugano Convention.

8.130. There are no uniform rules on the law applicable to divorce within the EU that apply in all Member States. The Rome III Regulation contains choice-of-law rules for divorce and legal separation, but that Regulation only applies in 15 Member States.[125] Even so, the interest in mutual recognition of judgments and a desire to not make possible a review as to substance (on Article 71, see below at 8.132 et seq) have carried more weight than the interest in upholding national public policy.[126]

8.131. **Article 70 only applies to matrimonial matters and not to matters of parental responsibility.** Moreover, it only applies to the recognition of divorce if the law of the Member State in which recognition is sought does not allow for divorce, etc. on the same facts. It does not address the question of the case when the marriage itself is not recognised, for instance, because one or both spouses were under the age of 18. Such marriages are possible in many countries throughout the world, including some Member States, but are not legal and not recognised in some Member States. It remains to be seen if there is a right to refuse recognition of a divorce on the grounds of public policy if the underlying marriage is not recognised.

---

[123] Borrás Report, para. 76.
[124] U. MAUNSBACH, *Kommentar till Bryssel II-förordningen*, Karnov, Stockholm 2019, note 64.
[125] Council Regulation (EU) No 1259/2010 of 20 December 2010 implementing enhanced cooperation in the area of the law applicable to divorce and legal separation, OJ L343, 29.12.2010, p. 10. The Regulation is applicable in Austria, Belgium, Bulgaria, France, Germany, Hungary, Italy, Latvia, Lithuania, Luxembourg, Malta, Portugal, Romania, Slovenia and Spain.
[126] T. RAUSCHER, 'Art 25 Brüssel IIa-VO', above n. 83, pp. 292 f., para. 2.

3. Non-Review as to Substance: Article 71

8.132. Article 71 prohibits a court before which the question of recognition arises – either in free-standing proceedings according to Article 30(3) or 40 or as an incidental question according to Article 30(5) – **to review the judgment from another Member State as to its substance.** Such a rule is contained in all EU Regulations on the recognition and enforcement of judgments[127] – and this has been the case since the very first 1968 Brussels Convention (Article 29)[128] – and also in many other international Conventions, including, for instance, Article 27 of the 1996 Hague Child Protection Convention.

8.133. The court of a Member State in which recognition is sought may not 'substitute its own discretion for that of the foreign court nor refuse recognition if it considers that a point of fact or of law has been wrongly decided'.[129] The court deciding on recognition is not in the position of an appellate court.[130]

8.134. Article 71 prohibits the review as to the substance of the *judgment*, not the 'Article 36 certificate'.[131] The certificate may, after all, be issued by another court than that which decided the case. Even so, the CJEU has held that a court in the State of recognition is not competent to review the information in the certificate.[132]

VI. THE SPECIAL REGIME FOR PRIVILEGED DECISIONS

A. BACKGROUND AND SCOPE

8.135. Brussels II-bis had abolished all grounds for refusal of decisions concerning decisions relating to rights of access and judgments which, following the override mechanism after a refusal to return a child, require its return. The Commission's proposal did not contain special rules for such decisions

---

[127] Article 52 Brussels I-bis; Article 42 of the Maintenance Regulation; Article 41 of the Succession Regulation; Article 40 of both the Matrimonial Property Regimes and Registered Partner Property Regimes Regulations.
[128] See Jenard Report, p. 46.
[129] Jenard Report, p. 46. Part of the quote is in its turn a quote (and translation from French) from P. GRAULICH, *Principes de droit international privé: conflit de lois, conflits de jurisdictions*, Dalloz, 1961, p. 200, para. 254: 'Il [le juge] ne peut pas modifier ou corriger le jugement étranger. Il peut accorder ou refuser l'exequatur; il ne peut pas modifier ou corriger le jugement étranger.'
[130] U. BERGQUIST, A. FAYAD and E. HOVMÖLLER, above n. 74, p. 187, para. 1.
[131] See CJEU, 6 September 2012, *Trade Agency*, C-619/10, para. 35.
[132] CJEU, 22 December 2010, *Aguirre Zarraga*, C-491/10 PPU, para. 54. This goes against the case law of the CJEU concerning certificates under Article 54 of Brussels I; see CJEU, 6 September 2012, *Trade Agency*, C-619/10, para. 35.

(see the proposed Recital (33)),[133] but after lengthy discussions in negotiations, a special system was kept for these 'privileged decisions', as they are called. Under Brussels II-bis, one of the main differences between on the one hand decisions on access and decisions taken under the override mechanism and on the other hand all other decisions was that for the former the *exequatur* procedure was abolished (see below Chapter 9 at 9.4 et seq). Now that *exequatur* has been abolished for all decisions, the main reason for keeping this double track is a difference in grounds of refusal mainly pertaining to enforcement (see the overview given in Chapter 9 at 9.50).

B. PROCEDURE

1. Free-Standing Proceedings or as Incidental Question

8.136. Article 43 establishes that a privileged decision, just as all other decisions, is to be recognised without the need for any special procedure. As with ordinary decisions, **the question of recognition may be tried in free-standing proceedings** pursuant to Article 30(3) and 40 **or as an incidental question** pursuant to 30(5) (see Article 42(2), discussed above at 8.36 et seq).

2. Stay of Recognition

8.137. Article 44 gives a court a discretionary power to stay its proceedings in two different situations: (1) an application has been submitted alleging that the decision is irreconcilable with a later decision from the Member State in which recognition is sought or from a later decision which is recognisable there; and (2) when the person against whom enforcement is sought, in accordance with Article 48, has asked for the withdrawal of the 'Article 47 certificate' in the country of origin (see below). The place of Article 44 in a subsection dealing with recognition would indicate that the provision is only applicable in the context of recognition and not enforcement. However, since Article 44(b) speaks of 'enforcement', it is submitted that the entire provision is applicable both in the contexts of recognition and enforcement.

8.138. Concerning Article 44(b), a textual interpretation would indicate that a stay is only possible if a withdrawal rather than rectification of the certificate has been sought. Given the fundamental difference between rectification and withdrawal, it is submitted that the literal approach should be adopted. Withdrawal is sought when (it is alleged that) there is something wrong with

---

[133] COM(2016) 411, p. 27.

the underlying judgment, whereas rectification only indicates a discrepancy between judgment and certificate. In such cases the certificate may always be discarded in favour of the judgment itself.

3. Documents to be Produced

8.139. Article 43(2) specifies that a party who wishes to invoke a privileged decision from one Member State in another shall produce an authenticated copy of the decision and an Article 47 certificate. The latter are to be found in Annex V for decisions concerning rights of access and Annex VI for decisions under the override mechanism. The rules on translation and transliteration in Article 31(2)–(3) are also applicable (see above 8.74 et seq).

C. REFUSAL OF RECOGNITION

8.140. The major difference between the generally applicable rules and the rules for privileged decisions is that the grounds of refusal are narrower for the latter. Under Article 50, **the only ground of refusal is the existence of a later irreconcilable decision** relating to parental responsibility concerning the same child that was given in either the Member State in which recognition is invoked or is a recognisable decision from another Member State or the non-Member State of habitual residence of the child (see 8.114 above). The reasons for keeping this ground for refusal are discussed further in the context of enforcement (see Chapter 9 at 9.60).

8.141. In the context of enforcement, a court in the Member State of origin should issue a certificate which certifies that none of the circumstances (except the public policy exception, discussed above at 8.106 et seq)[134] that would have led to a right to refuse recognition under Article 39 exist. A court in the State of recognition does not have the right to refuse recognition if it holds the information in the certificate to be false. The only way for the party seeking to stop recognition (and enforcement) of a privileged decision in such cases would be to apply for a withdrawal of the certificate in the Member State of origin under Article 48.

---

[134] It is clearly impossible to certify that a decision does not violate the public policy of another State.

CHAPTER 9

ENFORCEMENT OF DECISIONS

I. Introduction 332
   A. The Distinction between Recognition and Enforcement 332
   B. An Overview of the Rules 332
II. The Procedure for Enforcement 333
   A. The Abolition of *Exequatur* 333
   B. Enforceable Decisions 334
   C. Authorities Competent for Enforcement 336
   D. Who can Apply for Enforcement? 336
   E. Documents to be Produced for Enforcement 337
   F. Suspension of Enforcement 338
      1. Enforcement Suspended in the Member State of Origin 338
      2. Other Grounds for the Suspension of Enforcement 339
III. Refusal of Enforcement 341
   A. Introduction 341
   B. Courts or Authorities Competent for Refusal of Enforcement ... 341
   C. The Procedure for Refusal of Enforcement 341
   D. Acting without Undue Delay 343
   E. Stays 344
   F. Grounds for Refusing Enforcement 344
      1. Overview of the Rules 344
      2. Legal Strategy: Negative Declaration on Recognition
         or Application for Refusal of Enforcement? 345
      3. Non-Privileged Decisions 346
      4. Privileged Decisions 346
      5. All Decisions 348
         i) Grave Risk that has Arisen after the Decision was Given 348
         ii) Grounds under National Law 349
   G. Appeals 350
IV. Partial Enforcement 350
   A. Reasons for Partial Enforcement 350
   B. Severability 350
   C. Costs 351
V. Adaptation 352

I. INTRODUCTION

A. THE DISTINCTION BETWEEN RECOGNITION AND ENFORCEMENT

9.1. As stated in Chapter 8, recognition means that the foreign decision precludes new litigation on a matter which has already been decided and that it can be relied on should the matter become an incidental question in future proceedings (see 8.5 above). Recognition is a *conditio sine qua non* for enforcement. Enforcing a decision means using public authority to coerce a party that is unwilling to comply with it. Enforcement will only be necessary if that party does not abide by the decision voluntarily.

9.2. Brussels II-ter is only concerned with the enforcement of decisions on matters of parental responsibility. Status decisions, to which decisions in matrimonial matters belong, are only recognised, not enforced.[1] Updating a civil status record in order to reflect the new civil status of a person after a divorce is, even if it requires action on behalf of the authority in charge of the record, an act of recognition and not of enforcement.[2] If a former husband or wife refuses to accept the divorce and a restraining order is required to keep him or her away from the former spouse, that is not enforcement of the divorce decision, but of the restraining order (which falls outside the scope of Brussels II-ter).

B. AN OVERVIEW OF THE RULES

9.3. Enforcement of decisions with regard to matters of parental responsibility made under Brussels II-ter is governed by Chapter IV, principally Section 1, Subsections 2, 3 and 4 (Articles 34–37 and 41), Section 2, Subsections 2 and 3 (Articles 45–50) and Section 3 (Articles 51–63). As noted in Chapter 8, the structure of Chapter IV is complicated because of its constantly changing focus between recognition and enforcement and the separate treatment of 'privileged decisions'. One further complication is that enforcement of authentic instruments and agreements is dealt with separately in Chapter IV, Section 4. This aspect of enforcement will be discussed in Chapter 10.

---

[1] But see further 9.11 below on costs in matrimonial decisions. Cf. **authentic instruments and agreements**, which **can** be enforced under the Regulation; see Articles 64–68, discussed in Chapter 10.

[2] In the negotiations for the Brussels II Convention, it was not self-evident to all Member States that automatic recognition also entails the updating of civil-status records. After lengthy discussions, it was agreed that this should require no special procedure and an explicit rule was added in Article 14(2) of the Convention – corresponding to Article 30(2) of Brussels II-ter. See the Borrás Report, OJ C221, 16.7.98, p. 27, paras 62 f.

II. THE PROCEDURE FOR ENFORCEMENT

A. THE ABOLITION OF *EXEQUATUR*

9.4. Where recognition of decisions has been automatic throughout the original Brussels II Convention and subsequent Regulations, without the need for any special procedure, enforcement originally required a court decision in the Member State of enforcement, establishing that the decision from another Member State was enforceable. This **procedure for the obtaining of a declaration of enforceability is commonly known as the *exequatur*[3] procedure** and is to be found in many international conventions as well as in several EU Regulations on the recognition and enforcement of decisions.[4] The purpose of the procedure is to give the State of enforcement an opportunity to verify that the decision fulfils the requirements for enforcement.

9.5. Since it acquired the competence to adopt Regulations and Directives in the area of cooperation in civil law matters through the Treaty of Amsterdam in 1999, the EU has set itself the task of abolishing the *exequatur* procedure in between Member States.[5] As a first step, in Brussels II-bis, the *exequatur* procedure was abolished in two specific instances, namely, the enforcement of access decisions and an order for a child's return made under the override provisions in connection with applications made under the 1980 Hague Abduction Convention.[6] These types of decisions are still treated separately in Brussels II-ter in that they are categorised as 'privileged decisions' and to which separate provisions apply (see Chapter 8).

9.6. Following the precedent set by Brussels II-bis and according to the plan set out in the 2001 Programme for the implementation of the principle of mutual recognition,[7] the abolition of the *exequatur* stage in the enforcement process has been applied to other areas, for example, maintenance obligations and, more generally, judgments in civil and commercial matters under Brussels I-bis. In this sense, Brussels II-ter continues the trend.

---

[3] From the Latin for 'let it execute'.
[4] Cf, by way of an example, Article 26 of the 1996 Hague Child Protection Convention as well as Articles 43 and 45–58 of the Succession Regulation, and Articles 42 and 44–57 of the Regulations on Matrimonial Property and the Property Regimes of Registered Partners.
[5] See Draft Programme of measures for implementation of the principle of mutual recognition of decisions in civil and commercial matters, OJ C12, 15.1.2001, p. 1, at p. 7. See also C. HONORATI, 'The Commission's Proposal for a Recast of the Brussels IIa Regulation' [2017] *International Family Law* 97, 109.
[6] Discussed in Chapter 6.
[7] Above n. 6.

9.7. In Brussels II-ter, *exequatur* has been abolished altogether, a change brought about by Article 34(1), which provides that:

> A decision on matters of parental responsibility given in a Member State which is enforceable in that Member State shall be enforceable in the other Member States *without any declaration of enforceability being required*. (Emphasis added)

9.8. Somewhat unnecessarily, the same point is reiterated in Article 45 in relation to the enforcement of privileged decisions.

9.9. The rationale for abolishing the *exequatur* stage is to save time and costs. The time for obtaining *exequatur* varied from Member State to Member State, and from case to case. It could take from a few days up to several months depending on the Member State and the complexity of the case. Moreover, the possibility to appeal a decision on enforceability could delay the procedure considerably, sometimes by up to several years.[8] Finally, the necessity to give an address for service within the area of jurisdiction of the court applied meant that a local lawyer usually had to be consulted, which entailed extra costs.

9.10. It is important to appreciate that the abolition of *exequatur* does not prevent applicants from seeking enforcement, nor does it prevent those opposing enforcement from applying for enforcement to be refused or for it to be suspended. The difference is that the grounds for a refusal or suspension of enforcement are not tried by a court in the framework of *exequatur* proceedings, but by the 'authority competent for enforcement' (see 9.18 below).

B.   ENFORCEABLE DECISIONS

9.11. As stated above, only decisions on parental responsibility can be enforced under Brussels II-ter. Nevertheless, even though mainly concerned with personal status, a decision in matrimonial matters could contain a decision on costs that could require enforcement.[9] The fact that Brussels II-ter contains no rules on enforcement in matrimonial matters could lead to the wrongful conclusion that a decision on costs would not be enforceable under Brussels II-ter. This question is discussed further below in 9.75.

9.12. It follows from Article 34(1) that only decisions that are enforceable in the Member State of origin are enforceable in other Member States. It is for the law of the Member State of origin to determine whether a decision is enforceable

---

[8]   COM(2016) 411, p. 4.
[9]   Ancillary questions concerning maintenance, custody, etc. that may have been decided within the framework of divorce proceedings are, strictly speaking, not matrimonial matters.

and to provide an answer to whether a decision is enforceable before the time period for launching an appeal has run out and whether an appeal has the effect of suspending enforceability or not.

9.13. Article 34(2) provides that for the purposes of enforcement in another Member State, the court of origin may **declare a decision granting rights of access provisionally enforceable** notwithstanding any appeal. **Brussels II-ter empowers a court to do so even if its national law does not provide for such a declaration of provisional enforceability.** There is no similar provision concerning other aspects of parental responsibility and hence any such declaration would have to be founded on the national law of the court of origin.

9.14. In *Bohez*[10] the CJEU held that the enforcement provisions under Brussels II-bis extended to the enforcement of penalty payments imposed by the Member State of origin to ensure the effectiveness of an order concerning parental responsibility (in this case an access order), provided that the amount of the payment has been finally determined by the State of origin. The penalty payment is ancillary to the principal obligation and serves the purpose of exerting financial pressure on the person with whom the child lives to cooperate in giving effect to the rights of access.[11] This ruling applies equally to Brussels II-ter, since the basic meaning of an 'enforceable decision' has not been narrowed by the Regulation.

9.15. In this context, it should be noted that under Brussels II-ter, for the purposes of Chapter IV on recognition and enforcement, Article 2(1)(a) extends the term 'decision' to include a decision made in one Member State ordering a child's **return** to another Member State under the **1980 Hague Abduction Convention** 'which has to be enforced in a Member State other than the Member State where the decision was given'. This could be the case if, for instance, the abducting parent has absconded with the child to yet another Member State following the return decision.

9.16. It follows from Article 2(1)(b) that the provisions on recognition and enforcement also apply to **provisional (including protective) measures made alongside a return order** made under the Hague Convention.[12] This inclusion of provisional, etc. measures made in the context of Hague Abduction proceedings in the category of enforceable decisions for the purpose of Regulation does not mean that such orders made in other types of proceedings are not enforceable decisions. On the contrary, such orders **are** enforceable, at any rate, provided

---

[10] CJEU, 9 September 2015, *Bohez*, C-4/14.
[11] CJEU, 9 September 2015, *Bohez*, C-4/14, paras 35–36 and 47.
[12] See Article 2(1)(b), which refers to provisional orders made in accordance with Article 27(5) in conjunction with Article 15. See further Chapter 6.

the court making them has 'jurisdiction as to the substance of the matter'.[13] If the court adopting a provisional measure does not have jurisdiction, that measure is not enforceable in any other Member State under Brussels II-ter.[14] The reason for making special provision in abduction cases is that the court ordering the return of the child will not have jurisdiction as to the **substance of the matter**.[15]

9.17. However, in all cases, provisional measures made 'without the respondent being summoned to appear' (that is, a without notice or *ex parte* order) are not enforceable 'unless the decision containing the measure is served on the respondent prior to enforcement'.[16]

C. AUTHORITIES COMPETENT FOR ENFORCEMENT

9.18. Article 52 requires a party seeking the enforcement of a decision made in another Member State to submit the application for enforcement with the 'authority competent for enforcement' in the Member State of enforcement. Member States are under an obligation to communicate to the Commission in accordance with Article 103(1)(d) which authorities are competent.[17]

D. WHO CAN APPLY FOR ENFORCEMENT?

9.19. Unlike Brussels II-bis,[18] the Regulation is silent on who can apply for enforcement but as a general proposition, it would seem that only '**interested parties**' can do so. This would be in line with Article 30(3), which provides that 'interested parties' can apply for a decision that there are no grounds for refusing recognition.[19] 'Interested parties' in this context includes not only the parties to the proceedings in which the decision sought to be enforced was made, but also the child concerned or any interested party acting in the best interests of the child, such as child welfare authorities or public prosecutors.

9.20. Under Article 51(2), **a party seeking enforcement does not have to have a postal address in the Member State of enforcement** and is only required to

---

[13] See Recital (59).
[14] See Recital (30).
[15] See Recital (5).
[16] See Article 2(1), final paragraph.
[17] Member States' notifications are available via the European Judicial Atlas: https://e-justice.europa.eu/37842/EN/brussels_iib_regulation__matrimonial_matters_and_matters_of_parental_responsibility_recast_.
[18] Article 28(1) Brussels II-bis required the application to be made by 'an interested party'.
[19] Discussed at Chapter 8 at 8.40.

have an authorised representative there if that is mandatory under that State's law 'irrespective of the nationalities of the parties'. This reverses the position under Article 30(2) Brussels II-bis, under which the applicant had to give an address for service within the area of the jurisdiction of the court applied to, or, where the law of the Member State of enforcement did not require the furnishing of such an address, appoint a representative *ad litem*. This follows the examples set by Article 41(2) of the Maintenance Regulation and Article 41(3) Brussels I-bis. The purpose is to limit as far as possible the formal requirements required for enforcement and the costs that will have to be borne by the party seeking enforcement.[20]

E. DOCUMENTS TO BE PRODUCED FOR ENFORCEMENT

9.21. According to Article 35(1), a party seeking the **enforcement of a decision** made in another Member State must provide the authority competent for enforcement with **an authenticated copy of the decision sought to be enforced together with an appropriate certificate** issued pursuant to Article 36 and to be found in **Annex III**. The certificate will not be issued automatically, but only upon application by a party. For further details on this, see Chapter 8.

9.22. Article 35(2) makes special provision with regard to the **enforcement of provisional (including protective) measures**. In such cases the certificate must certify that the decision is enforceable in the Member State of origin and, either that the court of origin has jurisdiction as to the substance of the matter or that it has ordered the measure when making a return order under the 1980 Hague Abduction Convention to protect the child from the risk referred to in point (b) of Article 13(1) of that Convention pursuant to Article 27(5) of the Regulation. Additionally, where the measure was ordered without the respondent being summoned to appear, the **certificate** must certify proof of service of the measure. The appropriate certificate with regard to provisional measures is set out in **Annex IV**.

9.23. Article 35(3) entitles the authority competent for enforcement to, where necessary, require the person seeking enforcement to provide a translation or a transliteration of the 'the translatable content of the free text fields of the certificate which specifies the obligation to be enforced'. It follows from Article 35(4) that a party may also be required to provide a translation or transliteration of the decision if the authority competent for enforcement 'is unable to proceed without such a translation or transliteration'.

---

[20] Cf. Recital (27) of the Maintenance Regulation.

F. SUSPENSION OF ENFORCEMENT

9.24. The grounds upon which enforcement proceedings may be suspended are set out in Article 56. These suspensory powers can be exercised in all enforcement proceedings with regard to matters of parental responsibility whether the decision in question is 'privileged' or not. **The power to suspend proceedings to enforce privileged decisions breaks new ground**, since under Brussels II-bis there was no power to stay such proceedings.[21]

9.25. In contrast to recognition proceedings and to the position both under Brussels II-bis[22] and under the Commission's proposals,[23] rather than referring to 'stays', reference is now made to 'suspending' enforcement proceedings. The terminology is now in line with that of the corresponding Article 44 Brussels I-bis. A possible explanation for the change in terminology is the abolition of *exequatur* proceedings (cf. Article 37 of Brussels I, which still used 'stay'). In terms of proper English terminology, *exequatur* proceedings are 'stayed', whereas enforcement is 'suspended'. It is unlikely that any difference was intended and not all language versions have changed.[24] Article 63 talks of 'stay' of proceedings for the refusal of enforcement.

1. Enforcement Suspended in the Member State of Origin

9.26. Under Article 56(1), the authority competent for enforcement or the court in the Member State of enforcement **shall** either of (1) its own motion, or (2) upon application of the person against whom enforcement is sought, or (3) of the child concerned (where applicable under national law),[25] **suspend the enforcement proceedings provided that the enforceability of the decision has been suspended in the Member State of origin.**

9.27. This is the only ground upon which the relevant authority or court can suspend on its own motion. This provision is new to Brussels II-ter. Even though it is important that authorities or courts react swiftly to loss of enforceability in the Member State of origin, there is no active responsibility on the authority or court competent for enforcement to 'investigate whether in the meantime enforceability has been suspended following an appeal or otherwise if there is no indication that this is the case'.[26]

---

[21] Namely, those under Article 40 Brussels II-bis, which were not then called 'privileged decisions'.
[22] See Article 35.
[23] See the proposed Article 36.
[24] For instance, the French version has changed from 'sursis à statuer' to 'suspension', whereas Italian uses 'sospensione' and German 'Aussetzung' in both Brussels II-bis and Brussels II-ter.
[25] If the child refuses enforcement, then the person against whom enforcement is sought and the child coincide; see CJEU, 26 April 2012, *Health Service Executive*, C-92/12 PPU.
[26] Recital (67).

2. Other Grounds for the Suspension of Enforcement

9.28. Under Article 56(2), the relevant authority or court has a **discretion**, upon application of the person against whom enforcement is sought or, where applicable under national law, of the child concerned, to suspend in whole or in part enforcement proceedings. It should be noted that **under Article 56(2), the competent authority cannot suspend enforcement of its own initiative.** Enforcement can be suspended where:

(a) an ordinary appeal has been lodged against the decision in the Member State of origin; or
(b) the time for such an ordinary appeal has not yet expired, in which case the suspension may specify the time within which any appeal is to be lodged (Article 56(3));[27]
(c) an application for refusal of enforcement has been submitted; or
(d) the person against whom enforcement is sought has applied under Article 48 for the withdrawal of a certificate issued pursuant to Article 47, that is, a certificate for a privileged decision.

9.29. Additionally, **Article 56(4)** provides that in exceptional cases, the relevant authority or court has a **discretion**, upon application of the person against whom enforcement is sought or, where applicable under national law, of the child concerned, or of any interested party acting in the best interests of the child concerned, to suspend enforcement proceedings 'if enforcement would expose the child to a grave risk of physical or psychological harm due to temporary impediments which have arisen after the decision was given, or by virtue of any other significant change of circumstances'.

9.30. However, enforcement must be resumed 'as soon as the grave risk of physical or psychological harm ceases to exist'. Yet if the 'grave risk' is of a lasting nature', then, under Article 56(6), enforcement may be refused (see 9.64–9.67 below), although before refusing enforcement, the relevant authority or court must 'take appropriate steps to facilitate enforcement in accordance with national law and procedure and the best interests of the child' (Article 56(5)).

9.31. Apart from providing discretionary grounds for suspending enforcement proceedings rather than designating them as grounds for stays, Article 56(2) does not break new ground and is uncontroversial. Article 56(4)–(6), on the other hand, does break new ground, though it was foreshadowed by the Commission's

---

[27] According to Recital (68), the time limit should only have effect for the suspension of the enforcement proceedings and should *not* affect the deadline prescribed by national law for lodging an appeal.

limited proposal that proceedings should be stayed 'where due to temporary circumstances such as serious illness of the child, enforcement would put the best interests of the child at grave risk'.[28] Article 56(4) has wider application, although the child's serious illness would be a good example of where the discretionary power could be triggered.

9.32. Recital (69) makes it clear that a serious illness of the child is not the only reason to suspend enforcement due to supervening circumstances, but that also 'manifest objection of the child voiced only after the decision was given' could constitute grounds for suspension – provided that the inattention to such objections would constitute a grave risk of physical or psychological harm for the child. The Recital makes it clear that the enforcement authority has a duty to try to overcome such impediments to enforcement, in accordance with national law and procedure.

9.33. The requirement that enforcement would 'expose the child to a grave risk of physical or psychological harm' is modelled on Article 13(1)(b) of the 1980 Hague Abduction Convention and no doubt reference can usefully be made to the developed jurisprudence on that latter provision. In any event, as its opening words make clear, suspension under Article 56(4) is intended to be exceptional. Furthermore, **the risk must be due to impediments arising after the decision or due to other significant changes**, which implicitly must also occur after the decision. In determining applications, **care needs to be taken not violate the prohibition in Article 71 on review on the merits of the decision sought to be enforced**. The passage of time in itself is not an impediment to enforcement.

9.34. Further grounds for suspension according to national law are permitted by Article 57 insofar as they are not incompatible with Articles 41 and 50 (grounds of refusal for non-privileged and privileged decisions) as well as Article 56. According to Recital (63), these grounds could include formal errors, prior enforcement of the decision, impossibility or *force majeure*, serious illness, imprisonment or death of the person to whom the child is to be returned, war in the Member State to which the child is to be returned or the fact that the decision does not have content that can be enforced under the procedural law of the Member State of enforcement. Since grounds of refusal under national law may not be contrary to Article 56, the child's opposition to enforcement can only be invoked if it constitutes a grave risk of physical or psychological harm to the child.[29]

---

[28] See the proposed Article 36(2).
[29] M. WILDERSPIN, *European Private International Family Law: The Brussels IIb Regulation*, Oxford University Press, 2023, p. 394, para. 8-291.

9.35. Article 57 is part of Section 3 of Chapter 4, which contains 'common provisions on enforcement', that is, provisions that are applicable both to non-privileged and privileged decisions. Hence, grounds for suspension under national law can also be invoked in respect of a privileged decision. This constitutes a departure from the Court's case law in *Povse*, in which it held that in relation to a decision taken under the override mechanism (which under Brussels II-ter is a privileged decision), the 'only rules of law of the requested Member State that are applicable are those governing procedural matters'.[30]

III. REFUSAL OF ENFORCEMENT

A. INTRODUCTION

9.36. Recital (62) makes it clear that **notwithstanding the abolition of *exequatur*, applications can still be made for a refusal of enforcement**, which should not jeopardise the respect for the rights of the defence. It is therefore possible to apply for refusal of enforcement and it follows from Article 41 that the grounds for refusal of recognition also apply to the refusal of enforcement (and then there are some additional grounds that are unique to enforcement; see 9.50 below).

B. COURTS OR AUTHORITIES COMPETENT FOR REFUSAL OF ENFORCEMENT

9.37. According to Article 58(1), Member States shall communicate to the Commission, the courts or the authorities that they have designated as competent to try applications for refusal of enforcement based on Article 39 pursuant to Article 103. Moreover, Member States shall also communicate the courts or authorities that they have designated as competent to try applications for refusal of enforcement based on other grounds that are permitted by Brussels II-ter.

C. THE PROCEDURE FOR REFUSAL OF ENFORCEMENT

9.38. **The procedure** for making such applications, both with regard to non-privileged decisions and privileged decisions, **is governed by Article 59**. Since

---

[30] CJEU, 1 July 2010, *Povse*, C-211/10 PPU, para. 73; M. WILDERSPIN, above n. 29, p. 391, para. 8-271.

Brussels II-ter requires a particular procedure for the refusal of enforcement, this may only take place within the framework of proceedings for refusal. The provision is silent on whether the court or authority responsible for enforcement of its own motion may examine grounds of refusal not invoked by the applicant. This would indicate that this is left to national law to decide.

9.39. Unlike recognition, it is only possible to apply for a decision on refusal of enforcement. Declaratory decisions on the enforceability of decisions are not provided for in Brussels II-ter. An application for refusal of enforcement will normally follow an application for enforcement, but there is nothing in Brussels II-ter that says that such an application cannot be made pre-emptively. In practice, however, if no enforcement has yet been sought, a party seeking to stop enforcement will normally bring an action under Article 40(1) for refusal of recognition. However, since some grounds for refusal are only available in relation to enforcement (see 9.51 below), a situation might arise in which a free-standing declaration of non-enforceability is sought.

9.40. Article 59(1) provides that the **procedure** for refusal of enforcement '**shall, in so far as it is not covered by this Regulation, be governed by the law of the Member State of enforcement**'. This is particularly relevant for time limits for the submission of documents, for example.[31] **It is not quite clear whether this also pertains to standing**. Either this is left to national law, as a question of procedure, or this right parallels the right to apply for suspension and is limited to the person against whom enforcement is sought[32] and, where permitted under national law, the child.[33]

9.41. Under Article 59(2), the applicant must provide the authority competent for enforcement or the court with a **copy of the decision and 'where applicable and possible, the appropriate certificate'**. But this requirement may be dispensed with if the authority or court already has them or if it is considered unreasonable to require the applicant to produce them (Article 59(5)). Usually, an application for refusal will follow an application for enforcement and to the extent that the requested Member State has appointed the same authority for both procedures, it will already have the necessary documents.

9.42. Applicants may be required to provide a translation or a transliteration of the translatable content of the free text fields of the certificate which specifies the obligation to be enforced (Article 59(3)) and, if it is unable to proceed without it, a translation or transliteration of the decision (Article 59(4)).

---

[31] M. WILDERSPIN, above n. 29, p. 396, para. 8-297.
[32] This could be a legal person in the form of a private or public institution unwilling to comply with a decision from another Member State.
[33] See Article 56(1).

9.43. As is the case when applying for enforcement,[34] Article 59(6) stipulates that a party seeking a refusal of enforcement does not have to have a postal address in the Member State of enforcement and will only be required to have an authorised representative there if that is mandatory under that State's law 'irrespective of the nationalities of the parties' (see 9.20 above).

D. ACTING WITHOUT UNDUE DELAY

9.44. Article 60 obliges the court or authority competent for enforcement to act 'without undue delay in procedures concerning the application for refusal of enforcement'. The purpose of this obligation is to prevent objections to enforcement from unduly delaying the enforcement. The provision is modelled on the corresponding Article 48 Brussels I-bis. This is a diluted obligation from that proposed by the Commission,[35] namely, that if the decision is not enforced within six weeks of the institution of enforcement proceedings, then the court of the Member State of enforcement had to inform the requesting Central Authority or the applicant if the proceedings were instituted without the Central Authority's assistance, about the delay, and the reasons therefore.[36]

9.45. This is not the first time that the EU has attempted to address the problem of delay in enforcement proceedings. As early as the Brussels Convention (Article 34), there was a provision instructing a court to decide on appeals against an *exequatur* decision 'without delay'. Similar provisions have appeared in all subsequent versions of Brussels I and Brussels II. In the end, the speed with which an application for refusal of enforcement will be decided is dependent on the resources that Member States are willing to allocate to their court systems and the way in which these are organised. It remains to be seen how effective this provision proves to be, but since its forerunners have proved to be of little effect, it would be wise to keep one's expectations down.[37]

9.46. Article 60 is narrowly worded and, as written, only applies to 'procedures concerning **the application for refusal of enforcement**'. This seems unduly narrow, though whether the need for expedition in conducting the enforcement process more generally can be inferred from Article 60 is a matter for conjecture. However, it is submitted that the general right in EU law to an effective remedy requires of Member States that they do not 'allow a final, binding judicial decision

---

[34] See Article 51(2), discussed at 9.20 above.
[35] The proposed Article 32(4).
[36] Article 28(6) contains a six-week time limit for the enforcement of decisions ordering the return of the child after a wrongful removal or retention.
[37] G. CUNIBERTI, 'Art. 61 Brussels IIter' in U. MAGNUS and P. MANKOWSKI (eds), *Brussels IIter Regulation*, OttoSchmidt, 2023, p. 484, para. 2.

to remain ineffective to the detriment of one party'[38] and that there is a general duty under Brussels II-ter to enforce decisions from other Member States with reasonable speed and effectivity.

E. STAYS

9.47. Article 63 allows the authority competent for enforcement or the court to which an application has been appealed to **stay proceedings for refusal of enforcement** for one of the following reasons:

(a) an ordinary appeal[39] against the decision has been lodged in the Member State of origin;
(b) the time for such an ordinary appeal has not yet expired – in such cases, the stay may specify the time within which any appeal is to be lodged (Article 63(2)); or
(c) the person against whom enforcement is sought has applied under Article 48 for the withdrawal of a certificate issued pursuant to Article 47.

9.48. The grounds for granting a stay mirror those that are to be found in Article 56(2)–(3) on suspension of enforcement. It is only logical that both enforcement and the procedure for the refusal of enforcement are suspended/stayed when the future enforceability of the decision is still uncertain. The **list of grounds is exhaustive** and there is no reference to national law, as is the case for suspension or refusal of enforcement in Article 57. As is clear from its wording, the possibility to stay proceedings is discretionary and the competent authority in the requested Member State will have to base its decision on a prediction of the likelihood that the judgment loses its enforceability in the Member State of origin.

F. GROUNDS FOR REFUSING ENFORCEMENT

1. *Overview of the Rules*

9.49. As was pointed out in Chapter 8, the complicated structure of Brussels II-ter when dealing with recognition and enforcement requires careful negotiation, and this is particularly so with regard to the grounds for refusing enforcement. It needs to be appreciated that Article 41, which states that the grounds for refusing recognition provided by Article 39 also apply to refusing enforcement of a decision in matters of parental responsibility, does not apply to

---

[38] CJEU, 16 February 2023, *Rzecznik Praw Dziecka and Others*, C-638/22 PPU, para. 84.
[39] See Chapter 8 at 8.59–8.60.

privileged decisions. On the other hand, Article 50, which permits refusals on the basis of a later irreconcilable decision, only applies to privileged decisions. A further complication is that Article 56(6), which permits refusals where the child would be exposed to a grave risk of physical or psychological harm of a lasting nature, applies both to non-privileged and privileged decisions. The same goes for Article 57, pertaining to grounds for refusal under national law. Lastly, an entirely separate provision is made by Article 68, which enumerates the grounds upon which enforcement of an authentic instrument or agreement on legal separation or divorce can be refused (see Chapter 10 below).

9.50. The following table summarises which Articles apply when.

Table 1. Summary of Articles Governing the Grounds of Refusal

Non-privileged decisions	Privileged decisions	Authentic instruments and agreements
Article 41 (applying grounds in Article 39)		
	Article 50	
Article 56(6)	Article 56(6)	
Article 57 (referring to national law)	Article 57 (referring to national law)	
		Article 68

Source: Produced by the authors.

9.51. As with recognition, in enforcement proceedings, including in applications for the refusal of enforcement, there is a general embargo against reviewing the jurisdiction of the court of origin in Article 69 and in Article 71 against reviewing the substance of the decision for of which enforcement is sought (see Chapter 8 above at 8.124 et seq and 8.131 et seq).

2. *Legal Strategy: Negative Declaration on Recognition or Application for Refusal of Enforcement?*

9.52. The choice between applying for a refusal of recognition according to Article 40 or for a refusal of enforcement will depend on who goes first – the person seeking enforcement of the decision or the person opposing it.

9.53. If an application for enforcement has already been launched, the only way to suspend enforcement is to apply for refusal of enforcement. Suspension of enforcement is only possible after an application for refusal of enforcement has been lodged (Article 56(2)(c)).

9.54. In the absence of an application for enforcement, the person opposing enforcement can either apply for non-recognition of the decision according to Article 40 or for a refusal of enforcement under Article 59 (nothing in the Regulation prohibits free-standing applications for refusal of recognition; see 9.15 above). The advantage of a successful application for non-recognition is that its effects go beyond non-enforcement. Not all consequences of a decision pertain to enforcement. On the other hand, certain grounds for refusal – namely, those that are found in Articles 56(6) and 57 – only apply to enforcement.

9.55. The differences can be illustrated by the following example. By a decision from Member State A, the parents have joint custody of the child who is to live with the father in Member State B. The mother remains in Member State A and has access rights. As part of a mediation agreement, the parties agree to continuing jurisdiction for the courts of Member State A. After some time, the mother brings new proceedings in Member State A in which she gains sole custody and the right to live with the child. In the event of a default decision due to service of those proceedings being insufficient to allow the father to arrange for his defence (a ground for refusal of recognition under Article 39(1)(b)), he would be best advised to apply for non-recognition, since a successful application would block not only the child from being physically transferred to Member State A but also any other effects of the decision giving sole custody to the mother. If she is considered to be the child's custodian in Member State B, this could, if the applicable law requires the consent of both holders of custody, create problems concerning the father's right to decide on schooling, medical care, obtaining travel documents, etc., even if he does not have to hand over the child. On the other hand, if he applies for refusal of enforcement, Article 57 would allow him to rely on grounds for refusal under national law – for instance, a rule or, more likely, a practice under national law saying that enforcement does not take place against the will of a child over the age of 16.[40]

3. *Non-Privileged Decisions*

9.56. Refusal of enforcement of non-privileged decisions concerning matters of parental responsibility can either be based on the grounds for refusal provided by Article 39 or by Article 56(6) or Article 57. The former grounds are discussed in Chapter 8, while the application of Articles 56(6) and 57 is discussed below at 9.64 et seq.

4. *Privileged Decisions*

9.57. Brussels II-ter breaks new ground by making provision for the enforcement of privileged decisions to be refused. Yet, unlike non-privileged

---

[40] Even if it remains to be determined by the CJEU whether such a rule or practice is compatible with Brussels II-ter, it is possible that he could convince a national court to apply this rule. The 1980 Hague Abduction Convention is not applicable to children over the age of 16.

decisions, there are only three grounds upon which a refusal may be based, namely, those provided by Articles 50, 56(6) and 57.

9.58. Under Article 50, enforcement of a privileged decision 'shall' be refused:

if and to the extent the decision is irreconcilable with a later decision relating to parental responsibility concerning the same child which was given:

(a) in the Member State in which recognition is invoked; or
(b) in another Member State or in the non-Member State of the habitual residence of the child provided the later decision fulfils the conditions necessary for its recognition in the Member State in which recognition is invoked.

9.59. Article 50 is written in the same terms as Article 39(1)(d) and (e), and the same considerations apply to its application in this context as for refusing recognition (see the discussion at 8.101 et seq). However, it may be pointed out that the references in Article 50(a) and (b) to 'the Member State in which *recognition* is invoked', if read literally, would not apply to 'enforcement' proceedings. Yet, clearly Article 50 is intended to apply in such cases – that is, where the decision is irreconcilable with a later decision given in the Member State in which refusal of enforcement is sought.

9.60. Even though the rule gives room for abuse,[41] the **reason why precedence is given to the most recent decision is that it is most likely to reflect the child's needs and interests at the time that enforcement is sought**. It departs from its predecessor, Article 47(2), subpara. 2 Brussels II-bis, which was interpreted by the CJEU as referring only to decisions from a Member State that had jurisdiction as to the substance.[42] The rule in Brussels II-ter explicitly applies irrespective of whether the decision comes from the Member State of enforcement, the Member State that issued the privileged decision or some other Member State. However, **it is important to recall that the decision must emanate from a Member State that had jurisdiction as to the substance**. The rule also applies to decisions from a third State if the child had habitual residence there and the decision can be recognised by virtue of, for example, the 1996 Hague Child Protection Convention or the national law of the Member State of enforcement.

9.61. **Article 50 is mandatory** and the court or authority competent for enforcement has no discretion. The latter decision must be enforced.

9.62. It is most likely that in practice Article 50 will be used in relation to access decisions, which by virtue of Article 42(1)(a) are privileged decisions. If, for example, following a lawful move from one Member State to another, the parent

---

[41] Seeing the danger of the rule being perceived as an invitation to courts to wrongly assuming jurisdiction: M. WILDERSPIN, above n. 29, p. 383, para. 8-244.
[42] CJEU, 1 July 2010, *Povse*, C-211/10 PPU, para. 76.

staying in the Member State of the child's former habitual residence does not avail himself or herself of the right given in Article 8 to modify a decision on access rights in the courts of that Member State, a later decision on access rights given in the Member State of the child's new habitual residence will take precedence.

9.63. Even so, cases in which Article 50 will be used can also be envisaged in relation to decisions taken under the override mechanism in Article 29(6).[43] If a court in Member State A to which a child has been abducted refuses the return of the child on the basis of Article 13(2) of the 1980 Hague Abduction Convention (the child objects to a return) and later a court in Member State B from which the child was abducted 'overrides' this decision and orders the child's return, a court in Member State A could still acquire jurisdiction by virtue of Article 10 following, for instance, a mediation agreement that the court confirms in a decision, whereby the parties agree that the child should stay in Member State A. If the parent in Member State B then changes his or her mind and seeks the enforcement of the override decision, recognition can be refused by virtue of Article 50.[44]

5. All Decisions

i) Grave Risk that has Arisen after the Decision was Given

9.64. Article 56(6) introduces a further ground for refusal of both privileged and non-privileged decisions, namely, where **enforcement would expose the child to a grave risk of physical or psychological harm of a lasting nature due to impediments which have arisen after the decision was given**, or by any other significant change of circumstances. As previously stated, given that the Article is contained in Section 3 on common provisions on enforcement – common as in common to privileged and non-privileged decisions – it is generally applicable.

9.65. As an example of when the provision can be applied, Recital (69) cites the case where the child, only after the decision was given,[45] manifestly objects to enforcement and those objections are so strong that disregarding them would entail a grave risk of physical or psychological harm for the child – for instance, if the child threatens to commit suicide if returned and this threat is to be taken seriously.[46] Another example would be if the child has fallen seriously ill after the decision was taken.

9.66. Unlike Article 50, the establishment of this ground vests a discretionary power to refuse enforcement which should only be exercised in exceptional

---

[43] Discussed in Chapter 6 at 6.95 et seq.
[44] This example is indebted to M. WILDERSPIN, above n. 29, p. 383, para. 8-243.
[45] Hence, the objections could not be taken into consideration by the court of origin.
[46] M. WILDERSPIN, above n. 29, p. 370, para. 8-193.

circumstances.[47] This exceptional power can be exercised by the court or authority competent for enforcement **upon application, but not on its own motion.**[48]

9.67. Article 56(6) is considerably narrower than a 'change of circumstances since the decision was given rendering enforcement manifestly contrary to public policy' ground contained in Article 40(2) of the Commission's proposal.[49] In that sense, the provision is to be welcomed. Even so, it remains to be seen how often this it is invoked; notwithstanding that this ground can only be exercised in exceptional circumstances, this new power opens up a fresh avenue for at the very least delaying enforcement and also, particularly in the context of abduction, threatens to undermine the principle of mutual recognition.

ii) Grounds under National Law

9.68. Article 57 provides that grounds for refusal of enforcement in national law of the requested Member State may be used to refuse enforcement. Recital (63) lists examples of grounds under national law that may be invoked, such as formal errors under national law, the action required by the decision has already been performed, *force majeure*, the serious illness of the person to whom the child is to be handed over, the imprisonment or death of that person, and the fact that the area to which the child is to be returned has turned into a war zone.

9.69. National grounds of refusal may only be applied to the extent that they do not conflict with Article 41, 50 or 56. This would exclude all grounds of refusal pertaining to the origin of the decision. Such grounds are harmonised and exhaustively enumerated in Article 39 (to which Article 41 refers).[50]

9.70. The relationship between Articles 56 and 57 is more complicated. If the child does not want to comply with the decision and has reached an age and level of maturity at which it is appropriate to take account of his or her views, this could be a ground for refusal of enforcement under national law of some States. However, Article 56(6), in combination with Recital (69), makes it clear that in such a situation, enforcement can only be refused if the child's objections are so strong that if they were to be disregarded, this would amount to a grave risk of harm for the child. Moreover, Article 57 cannot be used to reintroduce matters that were dealt with in the Member State of origin. If, in the decision to be enforced, the child's opposition to return was noted but not considered to be

---

[47] See Article 56(4), discussed at 9.29 above.
[48] G. Cuniberti, 'Art. 56 Brussels IIter' in U. Magnus and P. Mankowski, above n. 37, p. 477, para. 14.
[49] COM(2016) 411, which was heavily criticised by C. Honorati, above n. 5, 110–112.
[50] See *2022 Practice Guide for the Application of the Brussels IIb Regulation*, EU, 2022, p. 179.

sufficiently serious to motivate a non-return, Article 57 does not allow a court in the Member State of enforcement to substitute the assessment made by the court of origin for its own. Any opposition to the decision would have to take place in the Member State in which it was given.

G. APPEALS

9.71. Under Article 61, either party may challenge or appeal against a decision on the application for refusal of enforcement. According to Article 61(2), such challenges or appeals should be lodged with the authority or court that the Member State has nominated and communicated to the Commission pursuant to Article 103.[51] Pending the outcome of such an appeal, Article 63 allows enforcement proceedings to be stayed (see above at 9.47).

IV. PARTIAL ENFORCEMENT

A. REASONS FOR PARTIAL ENFORCEMENT

9.72. According to Article 53(1), a party seeking enforcement of a decision may apply for partial enforcement. There may be several reasons why a party would apply only for partial enforcement and, by and large, these are the same as apply to partial recognition (see Chapter 8 at 8.79) – the main reason being that **only parts of the decision fall within the scope** of Brussels II-ter. This would be the case of a decision ruling on divorce, and parental responsibility and other matters outside the scope of Brussels II-ter, such as the division of matrimonial property and maintenance to an ex-spouse and children. In such a case, only the part of the decision on parental responsibility would be enforceable under Brussels II-ter. Moreover, **if enforcement has been refused for one or several matters of a decision**, enforcement may nonetheless take place for the parts of the decision that are not affected by the refusal (Article 53(2)).

B. SEVERABILITY

9.73. Generally speaking, it is for the party seeking enforcement to decide whether to seek enforcement of the entire decision or only of parts of it. However, this would **depend on the severability** of the measures for which enforcement is

---

[51] See also Article 62 on further appeal. Under Brussels II-bis in *Re D (A Child) (Supreme Court Jurisdiction)* [2016] UKSC 34, no appeal was allowed to the UK Supreme Court, since that court had not been designated by the UK according to the Regulation.

sought. Some language versions give the indication that different claims can be enforced separately, whereas others, like the English version, use more general language.[52] It is submitted that if the matters for which enforcement is sought are interdependent, enforcement cannot be sought for only one of them. An example would be if enforcement is only sought for one sibling and it would be detrimental for the siblings to be separated. It should be possible to refuse partial enforcement in such a case, even if the separation would not be so harmful as to motivate refusal based on Article 56(6) – as it is, the separation could be most harmful for the child for which enforcement is not sought![53] Of course, it could also be the other way round and the enforcement of only parts of the decision could be motivated if one sibling has turned 18.

9.74. An explicit rule targeting the non-severability of a decision or, as it may be, decisions is to be found in Article 53(3). According to the provision, a decision ordering the child's return made according to the override mechanism in Article 29(6) cannot be enforced without also enforcing any provisional (including protective) measures which have been ordered to protect the child from the risk of the return exposing him or her to physical or psychological harm or otherwise placing him or her in an otherwise intolerable situation. If it were not for this rule, the left-behind parent who has been successful in obtaining a return order might seek to enforce only that order and not accompanying protective measures that he or she wishes to avoid.

C. COSTS

9.75. It follows from Article 73 that Chapter IV on recognition and enforcement applies equally to the enforcement of any order concerning costs taken following proceedings 'under this Regulation'. Strictly speaking, the rules on enforcement only apply to matters of parental responsibility and not to matrimonial matters. From this, one could deduce that a decision on **costs in a decision on matrimonial matters** is not enforceable. However, it is submitted that the general reference in Article 73 to all proceedings under the Regulation should be interpreted as meaning that the rules on enforcement are also applicable to such decisions.[54]

---

[52] In German 'Ansprüche', in Italian 'capi della domanda', in Swedish 'yrkanden', but in Dutch 'onderdele', in English 'matters' and in French 'points'.
[53] Seeing decisions on several children as different claims and as such subject to partial enforcement, at least in theory, see G. CUNIBERTI, 'Art. 53 Brussels IIter' in U. MAGNUS and P. MANKOWSKI, above n. 37, p. 465, para. 6. We would concur with the same caveat that this applies in theory but not always in practice. The same author questions whether the right to seek partial enforcement should exist in an instrument the purpose of which is to protect the interests of the child (at p. 464, para. 3).
[54] Of the same opinion and referring to German case law, see I. QUEIROLO, 'Art. 73 Brussels II-ter' in U. MAGNUS and P. MANKOWSKI, above n. 37, p. 531, para. 14.

9.76. A difficult situation arises in the case mentioned above where **only parts of the decision fall within the scope of Brussels II-ter**. In theory, only the part of the costs that pertains to matrimonial matters and/or parental responsibility should be enforceable under the Regulation. To the extent that it is possible to separate the costs relevant to matters within scope, only such costs should be enforced under Brussels II-ter and other costs would have to be enforced according to other rules, such as the Maintenance Regulation or the Matrimonial Property Regulation. In many (probably most) instances, this will not be the case and the decision on costs will not be specified for divorce, parental responsibility, maintenance, etc. In such cases it could be argued that the person seeking enforcement should be free to do so for all costs under Brussels II-ter (or under some other applicable rules), subject to the sole condition of non-duplication of recovery.[55]

V. ADAPTATION

9.77. As always, and in accordance with the principle of procedural autonomy of Member States, enforcement takes place according to the rules of the Member State of enforcement (Article 51(1)) and a decision given in one Member State, that is enforceable in that State, shall be enforced under the same conditions as a decision given in the Member State of enforcement. However, the case may be that the foreign decision contains provisions on enforcement measures that are unknown in the receiving Member State.

9.78. The Commission's proposal contained a specific provision requiring the Member State of enforcement to, to the extent possible, adapt the measure to an order known in its own law and 'which has equivalent effects attached to it and which pursues similar aims and interests'.[56] However, no such provision is to be found in Brussels II-ter as adopted, although such a provision is to be found in Article 54 Brussels I-bis.

9.79. In *DHL Express France*, the CJEU made it clear that the principle of sincere cooperation laid down in Article 4(3) TEU requires that Member States ensure judicial protection of an individual's rights under EU law.[57] In order to attain the objective attained by the measure to be enforced, Member States must take recourse to the relevant provisions of their own laws which ensure that the objective is attained in an equivalent manner.[58] This decision concerned the

---

[55] I. Queirolo, above n. 54, p. 531, para. 10.
[56] COM(2016) 411, p. 49 – proposed Article 33(2).
[57] CJEU, 12 April 2011, *DHL Express France*, C-235/09, para. 58.
[58] CJEU, 12 April 2011, *DHL Express France*, C-235/09, para. 56.

enforcement of an intellectual property right under the Trade Mark Regulation, but it is submitted that the Court's statements have general application and that the absence of an explicit rule in Brussels II-ter should not lead to the conclusion that adaptation is not possible.

9.80. The measure in question in *DHL Express France* was a penalty payment to be made to the enforcing party rather than to the State. To the extent that such penalty payments are ancillary to matters of parental responsibility,[59] an adaptation to a penalty payment to be made to the treasury of the enforcing State would in the opinion of these authors to a sufficient degree serve the purpose of ensuring enforcement and be an acceptable adaptation.

---

[59] Cf. CJEU, 9 September 2015, *Bohez*, C-4/14.

CHAPTER 10

RECOGNITION AND ENFORCEMENT OF AUTHENTIC INSTRUMENTS AND AGREEMENTS

I. Introduction 355
II. Scope 357
   A. The Definition of 'Authentic Instruments and Agreements' 357
   B. Drawing the Line vis-à-vis Private Agreements 358
   C. Drawing the Line vis-à-vis Decisions 359
   D. Agreements also Covering Matters Outside the Scope of
      Brussels II-ter (Partial Recognition and Enforcement) 360
III. Conditions for Recognition and Enforcement 361
   A. Jurisdiction 361
   B. Binding Legal Effect and/or Enforceability 362
   C. The Mandatory Certificate 363
   D. Hearing of the Child 363
IV. Procedure for Recognition and Enforcement 364
V. Grounds for Refusal 365
   A. Divorce and Legal Separation 365
   B. Parental Responsibility 366
   C. The Applicability of Articles 69–70 367
      1. Review of Jurisdiction 367
      2. Differences in the Applicable Law 368
      3. Non-Review as to Substance 368

I. INTRODUCTION

10.1. When the original 1998 Brussels II Convention was negotiated, there was discussion about whether the rules in the 1968 Brussels Convention containing a separate set of provisions concerning the enforcement of authentic instruments and court settlements should be duplicated or whether such provisions could be dispensed with altogether.[1] Since the laws of some Member States did (and still do) provide for authentic instruments in the area of parental responsibility, the decision was taken to include authentic instruments and court settlements in the scope of the Convention. The example given in the Borrás Report was agreements between parents on custody that under Finnish and Swedish law become enforceable after approval by the child welfare authorities.[2]

10.2. Instead of following the solution in the Brussels Convention and adding a separate title with provisions for authentic instruments and court settlements, these were included in the definition of a judgment and were therefore to be treated in the same way as a judgment.[3] A consequence of this was that unlike under the Brussels Convention – which only provided for the enforcement, not recognition, of such acts[4] – they could potentially become *res judicata* – provided of course that this was possible under the law of the country of origin. Moreover, the only ground for refusal under the Brussels Convention and its successors has been the public policy of the Member State of enforcement. This single ground for refusal was deemed to be insufficient, for instance, if the authentic instrument or court settlement related to parental responsibility and the child concerned had not been given an opportunity to be heard. Therefore, the same grounds of refusal as for judgments were made applicable.[5]

10.3. Article 13(3) of the Brussels II Convention remained unchanged when the Convention was transformed into the Brussels II Regulation. In Brussels II-bis, the provision was moved to Article 46 and into its own Section (containing just the one Article), but the only substantial change that had been made was that 'court settlements' had been changed to 'agreements between the parties'.

10.4. In the Commission proposal for Brussels II-ter, Article 46 was left substantially unchanged in the form of draft Article 55.[6] However, an important change was the introduction of a certificate, similar to the certificate used to facilitate the recognition and enforcement of judgments, in the draft Article 56. Nevertheless, in the course of negotiations, more changes were made.

---

[1] The Borrás Report, OJ C221, 16.7.98, p. 27, para. 61, erroneously refers to a title on *recognition* and enforcement of authentic instruments and court settlements in the Brussels Convention. Under the Brussels I regime, there has never been recognition of (the content in) such documents – only enforcement.
[2] Borrás Report, n. 1, para. 61.
[3] Article 13(3) of the Brussels II Convention.
[4] This has continued to be the case in the subsequent Brussels I Regulations.
[5] Borrás Report, n. 1, para. 62.
[6] See COM(2016) 411, p. 61.

The underlying reason for the need to expand the rules on authentic instruments and agreements was the trend amongst Member States to encourage non-judicial agreements concerning not only parental responsibility but also divorce.[7]

10.5. In Brussels II-ter, what was a single Article in Brussels II-bis has been expanded to an entire Section 4, covering Articles 64–68. The substantial changes compared to Brussels II-bis are: (1) definitions of authentic instruments and agreements; (2) the introduction of a mandatory certificate and rules for its rectification and withdrawal; (3) the requirement that agreements be registered with a public authority; (4) adapting the grounds for refusal to the specificities of authentic instruments and agreements, for instance, by the deletion of the protection of a defendant who has not entered into an appearance – a provision clearly unnecessary in the context of agreements; (5) making the rules on jurisdiction (at least indirectly, see 10.19 et seq) applicable also to authentic instruments and agreements.

II. SCOPE

A. THE DEFINITION OF 'AUTHENTIC INSTRUMENTS AND AGREEMENTS'

10.6. **Authentic instruments are defined in Article 2(2)(2)** as 'a document which has been formally drawn up or registered as an authentic instrument in any Member State in the matters falling within the scope of this Regulation and the authenticity of which: (a) relates to the signature and the content of the instrument; and (b) has been established by a public authority or other authority empowered for that purpose' – a definition that has been copied from Article 2(c) Brussels I-bis.[8]

10.7. In those Member States that have notaries, these could be a 'public authority or other authority empowered for that purpose', but in some Member States authentic instruments can also be registered by a court. All Member States are required by Article 103 to communicate to the Commission the authorities before which an authentic instrument may be drawn up or registered.

---

[7] See Council Document 7979/2/17 Rev 2 of 19 March 2018 with a compilation of Member States' replies to questions concerning the existence and effects of authentic instruments and agreements in the areas of matrimonial matters and parental responsibility. For the background to this, see also A. FRĄCKOWIAK-ADAMSKA, 'Intro to Arts. 64–68 Brussels IIter', in U. MAGNUS and P. MANKOWSKI (eds), *Brussels IIter Regulation*, OttoSchmidt, 2023, pp. 494 et seq, paras 6 et seq.

[8] In Brussels II-ter, 'in matters falling within the scope of this Regulation' has been added. The addition states the obvious.

10.8. An agreement is defined in Article 2(2)(3) as 'a document which is not an authentic instrument, has been concluded by the parties in the matters falling within the scope of this Regulation and has been registered by a public authority'. It is not easy to draw the line between an authentic instrument and an agreement that has been registered by an authority. Theoretically, an authentic instrument could take the form of a unilateral act expressed in a notarial deed, whereas an agreement would always require two parties and require mutual consent. However, as far as is known to these authors, there is no Member State that would give legal effect to an extrajudicial unilateral act in matrimonial matters or matters of parental responsibility. Since authentic instruments and agreements are governed by the same rules, the distinction lacks practical importance.

10.9. There are no formal requirements other than that the agreement must be registered by a public authority. However, there might be additional requirements under national law without the fulfilment of which the national authority will refuse to register the agreement. The Member State where recognition is sought may not impose any additional formal requirements or other requirements such as the parties having taken legal advice before entering into the agreement.

10.10. It should be noted that the term 'agreement' in this context only refers to agreements on the substance and not to choice-of-court agreements falling within the scope of Article 10.[9] Such agreements are subject to their own formal requirements in Article 10(2) and there is no requirement that they be registered with an authority.

B. DRAWING THE LINE VIS-À-VIS PRIVATE AGREEMENTS

10.11. Only if a particular document qualifies as an authentic instrument or a registered agreement will Articles 64–68 be applicable. If it falls below the 'lower threshold', which for instance would apply to **an agreement in which no notary had been involved and that had not been registered with an authority, then the agreement cannot be recognised or enforced under the rules of Brussels II-ter**, even if it is enforceable under the law of the Member State of origin.[10] Hence, the Regulation would not be applicable to a divorce resulting from a unilateral declaration such as *talaq* under Islamic law made by the husband (even if made before a religious court).[11] However, if this is possible, recognition and enforcement might still take place under national law.

---

[9] M. WILDERSPIN, *European Private International Family Law*, Oxford University Press, 2023, p. 114, para. 3-116.
[10] ECJ, 17 June 1999, *Unibank*, C-260/97 (concerning the Brussels Convention).
[11] CJEU, 20 December 2017, *Sahyouni*, C-372/16.

C. DRAWING THE LINE VIS-À-VIS DECISIONS

10.12. If the document in question goes above the 'higher threshold' and is considered to be a decision, the rules on the recognition and enforcement of decisions apply. The difference should not be exaggerated. As a point of departure, the procedure for recognition and enforcement of judgments also applies to authentic instruments and agreements, unless there are particular rules applicable to the latter (Article 65).

10.13. In *Senatsverwaltung für Inneres und Sport*, the CJEU ruled that a divorce following an agreement concluded by the spouses and confirmed by them before an Italian civil registrar was a decision and not an authentic instrument.[12] The Court noted that both the terms 'court' and 'judgment' were given wide definitions in the Regulation. Moreover, the Court emphasised the fact that the civil registrar had a duty to examine whether the consent of the spouses was valid, free and informed. **It is that substantive examination which distinguishes a decision from an authentic instrument or an agreement.** Other divorce agreements that have binding legal effects in the Member State of origin can be recognised as either authentic instruments or agreements under Brussels II-ter.[13] A paradoxical result of this judgment is that the Finnish and Swedish custody agreements entered into before a child welfare authority that first prompted the inclusion of authentic instruments and agreements into the original Brussels II Convention would be treated as decisions.[14]

10.14. The judgment has been criticised for giving 'decision' too wide an interpretation and thus minimising the scope of authentic instruments and agreements unnecessarily.[15] It has been pointed out that the examination by an Italian civil registrar does not go into the substance; no legal advice is required at any step of the proceedings and no hearing is carried out in order to ascertain whether the spouses' consent is true and valid. Such a decree should therefore not qualify as a decision.[16] On the other hand, the scrutiny carried out by the

---

[12] CJEU, 15 November 2022, *Senatsverwaltung für Inneres und Sport*, C-646/20. For further discussion of this decision, see Chapter 1 at 1.32 et seq and 1.51.
[13] CJEU, 15 November 2022, *Senatsverwaltung für Inneres und Sport*, C-646/20, paras 59–60.
[14] However, it should be noted that the Swedish legislator came to the same conclusion long before the judgment; cf. prop. 2007/08:98, p. 18 (a government bill containing a proposal for amendments to Swedish law caused by Brussels II-bis). Such agreements have to be *approved* by the Social Welfare Committee. Referring to such agreements as falling under Article 46 of Brussels II-bis, see U. MAGNUS, 'Art. 46 Brussels IIter', in U. MAGNUS and P. MANKOWSKI, above n. 7, p. 413, para. 5.
[15] E. BARGELLI, 'Reshaping the Boundaries between "Decision" and Party Autonomy: The CJEU on the Extrajudicial Italian Divorce' (2023) 8 *European Papers* 43, 49 f.
[16] BARGELLI, above n. 15, 47.

court before giving a judicial decision on divorce will in some Member States be minimal and even more superficial than that carried out by an Italian registrar. At any rate, the difference between the regime applicable to judgments and that applicable to authentic instruments and agreements is not that great.

D. AGREEMENTS ALSO COVERING MATTERS OUTSIDE THE SCOPE OF BRUSSELS II-TER (PARTIAL RECOGNITION AND ENFORCEMENT)

10.15. It goes without saying that only authentic instruments and agreements that fall within the substantive scope of Brussels II-ter can be recognised and/or enforced under the Regulation. In reality, **many agreements** – be they included in an authentic instrument or registered by an authority – **include matters falling both inside and outside the scope of Brussels II-ter**. An example of this would be a French divorce by mutual consent, which is countersigned by lawyers and registered with a notary. According to French law, such an agreement may (and to some extent must) include agreements on the marriage having broken down and therefore to be dissolved, on *prestation compensatoire* (spousal maintenance), on liquidation of matrimonial property (distribution of assets between the ex-spouses), on parental responsibility for any children and on child support.

10.16. As is the case for 'decisions',[17] only the provisions in the agreement concerning divorce and parental responsibility fall within the scope of Brussels II-ter, whereas any provisions concerning spousal and child support as well as the distribution of matrimonial property fall under the scope of the Maintenance Regulation and the Matrimonial Property Regulation respectively. Both these Regulations provide for the enforcement of authentic instruments and court settlements, but there are certain differences that will need to be taken into consideration when drafting the agreement and/or seeking recognition and enforcement. It will also be necessary to obtain different certificates for the different parts of the decision.[18] Neither of these two instruments allows for the recognition and enforcement of agreements[19] that are not court settlements or in the form of an authentic instrument.[20]

---

[17] See above Chapter 8 at 8.78 et seq and Chapter 9 at 9.72 et seq.
[18] M. WILDERSPIN, above n. 9, p. 402, para. 8-331.
[19] Under Article 2(3)(b) of the Maintenance Regulation, 'arrangements' that have been concluded with or authenticated by an administrative authority are characterised as authentic instruments.
[20] But then again, the distinction between a registered agreement and an authentic instrument is not an easy one to make; see 10.8 above.

Chapter 10. Recognition and Enforcement of Authentic Instruments and Agreements

III. CONDITIONS FOR RECOGNITION AND ENFORCEMENT

10.17. In order for an authentic instrument or agreement to be recognised and enforced under the rules in Section 4 Brussels II-ter, it must, apart from being an authentic instrument or agreement as defined in Article 2 and being within the scope of Brussels II-ter: (1) originate from a Member State that has jurisdiction;[21] (2) have binding legal effect and/or be enforceable in the Member State of origin;[22] and (3) be accompanied by a certificate using the form set out in Annex VIII or IX.[23] Moreover, even though it is not a requirement, recognition and enforcement may be refused if the child has not been given an opportunity to express his or her views.[24]

A. JURISDICTION

10.18. It follows from Article 64 that **for an authentic instrument or registered agreement to be recognised and/or enforced, it must originate in a Member State, which assumed jurisdiction in accordance with the rules in Chapter II.** In order to ensure the application of this requirement, the mandatory certificate can only be issued if the public authority or other authority that the Member State had empowered to draw up or register the authentic instrument or agreement had jurisdiction (see Article 66(2)(a)).

10.19. However, technically speaking, the rules on jurisdiction in Chapter II are only binding for courts. The concept of a court is defined in Article 2(2)(1) as 'any authority in any Member State with jurisdiction in the matters falling within the scope of the Regulation'. This would indicate that the concept goes beyond courts proper and also includes administrative authorities when they exercise jurisdiction. In the context of Brussels I-bis, the CJEU has made it clear that notaries are not included in the concept of a 'court'.[25]

10.20. However, the definition of court is different in Brussels II-ter from that in Brussels I-bis, and Recital (14) of Brussels II-ter explicitly includes 'other authorities, such as notaries' in the concept of 'court'. So, case closed; notaries are courts. Well, maybe not.[26] The reference to other authorities including notaries

---

[21] Article 64.
[22] Article 65.
[23] Article 66(5).
[24] Article 68(3).
[25] See CJEU, 9 March 2017, *Pula Parking*, C-551/15.
[26] M. WILDERSPIN, above n. 9, p. 111, para. 3-105, finds the first sentence of the Recital 'highly misleading' and that it 'is thus best ignored'.

Intersentia 361

refers only to such authorities and notaries that issue 'decisions' as defined in *Senatsverwaltung für Inneres und Sport* and by virtue of this can be included in the concept of a court.[27] The Recital then goes on and talks about '*[o]ther agreements which acquire binding legal effect … should be given effect in other Member States in accordance with the specific provisions on authentic instruments and agreements in this Regulation*' (emphasis added).

10.21. Moreover, in *Senatsverwaltung für Inneres und Sport*, the CJEU contrasted the situation with that in *Solo Kleinmotoren*,[28] in which the settlement in question was essentially contractual in nature, and the authority in question simply taking note of the legally binding settlement without examining the content.[29] Against this background, we conclude that authorities and notaries that draw up authentic instruments or register agreements that are not 'decisions' are also not 'courts'. This position appears to have been confirmed in the context of the Succession Regulation in the case of *WB*.[30]

10.22. As a consequence, it would appear that Member States are free to allow for divorces and agreements on parental responsibility to be agreed and drawn up before or registered by their notaries and other authorities, even if they would not have jurisdiction under Brussels II-ter if this is merely a registration of an agreement and the role of the notary or authority does not involve scrutiny and approval. These would then be effective domestically, but would not circulate freely in other Member States.[31]

B. BINDING LEGAL EFFECT AND/OR ENFORCEABILITY

10.23. Only authentic instruments and agreements that have 'binding legal effect' can be recognised and/or enforced in other Member States under the rules in Brussels II-ter. For such instruments or agreements concerning parental responsibility, there is also a requirement of enforceability (Article 65(2)). Article 46 Brussels II-bis required that such documents be 'enforceable', which leads to a discussion on whether that provision was also applicable to authentic instruments and agreements that did not contain any enforceable content, such as a decision on matrimonial status.[32] The change in terminology – and of course the explicit inclusion of legal separation and divorce in the Section – clearly

---

[27] CJEU, 15 November 2022, *Senatsverwaltung für Inneres und Sport*, C-646/20. See above at 10.13.
[28] ECJ, 2 June 1994, *Solo Kleinmotoren*, C-414/92.
[29] CJEU, 15 November 2022, *Senatsverwaltung für Inneres und Sport*, C-646/20, para. 57.
[30] CJEU, 23 May 2019, *WB*, C-658/17.
[31] M. WILDERSPIN, above n. 9, p. 408, para. 8-358.
[32] See J. FITCHEN, *The PIL of Authentic Instruments*, Hart Publishing, 2020, p. 355, with further references to positions for and against.

Chapter 10. Recognition and Enforcement of Authentic Instruments and Agreements

serves the purpose of making the rules applicable to authentic instruments and agreements concerning legal separation and divorce. Since these are matters concerning personal status, there will never be enforcement, only recognition.

10.24. Authentic instruments and agreements can in some Member States of origin lead to enforcement only after an act by a national court. The question then is whether 'enforceable' should be understood abstractly – the authentic instrument or agreement in question is **potentially** enforceable – or concretely. We would advocate a concrete interpretation.[33] An authentic instrument or agreement should not be more enforceable in other Member States than in the Member State of their origin.

C. THE MANDATORY CERTIFICATE

10.25. A novelty in Brussels-II-ter is the introduction of certificates, similar to those used for the recognition and enforcement of decisions. The form for the certificate concerning authentic instruments and agreements on matrimonial matters is found in Annex VIII and the certificate concerning parental responsibility in Annex IX. Article 66(5) makes it clear that **the use of a certificate is mandatory for cross-border recognition and enforcement of authentic instruments and agreements** in the EU.

10.26. The use of a certificate is not strictly mandatory when seeking recognition and enforcement of a decision – the court or competent authority in the receiving Member State may dispense with the production of a certificate if it considers that it has sufficient information even without it (see Articles 32(1) and 59(5)). One can only speculate over the reason for the difference, but it is not inconceivable that it follows from the greater diversity of the effects of authentic instruments and agreements compared to judgments. Perhaps the extra degree of control is introduced due to the novelty of the use of authentic instruments in an area previously reserved for courts. Moreover, notaries and authorities entrusted with drafting or registering authentic instruments and agreements are less used to rules on jurisdiction and there is much less transparency in relation to their reasoning than there is with courts.

D. HEARING OF THE CHILD

10.27. Article 21 of Brussels II-ter makes it **mandatory for courts** to provide a child that is capable of forming his or her own views a genuine and effective

---

[33] For a different opinion, see J. FITCHEN, above n. 32, p. 354.

opportunity to express them. The same applies in return proceedings (Article 26; see Chapter 7). There is no similar rule that binds notaries and other authorities that are involved in the drawing-up of authentic instruments or registering agreements concerning parental responsibility. However, not giving the child an opportunity to be heard is a ground for refusal of recognition and enforcement of authentic instruments and agreements just as it is for decisions (Article 68(3); see 10.41 below).

IV. PROCEDURE FOR RECOGNITION AND ENFORCEMENT

10.28. Article 65(1) refers back to Section 1 of Chapter IV for the **recognition of authentic instruments and agreements on legal separation and divorce**, that is, the rules applicable to non-privileged decisions. Hence, the divorce or legal separation will be recognised and enforced as if it were a court decision. It should be noted that marriage annulment is not covered by the scope of the section, since no Member State allows for the annulment of a marriage in the way of an authentic instrument or registered agreement.

10.29. These issues were discussed in Chapters 8 and 9, but briefly the reference to Section 1 means that the authentic instrument or agreement is recognised without the need for any special procedure (Article 30(1)). Any interested party may apply for a positive decision that there are no grounds for refusal of recognition (Article 30(3)) or a negative declaration that there are grounds for refusal (Article 40). The matter of recognition might also arise as an incidental question in court proceedings (Article 30(5)). A party who wishes to invoke the authentic instrument or agreement for the purposes of recognition must produce an authenticated copy of the document (Article 31) as well as the certificate issued in accordance with Article 66.

10.30. Article 65(2) is concerned with the **recognition and enforcement of authentic instruments and agreements concerning parental responsibility**. It refers back not only to Section 1 of Chapter IV, but also to Section 3 – common provisions on enforcement (see Chapter 9 above). Section 2 on the recognition and enforcement of privileged decisions does not apply and there is no such thing as a 'privileged authentic instrument or agreement'.[34]

---

[34] See M. WILDERSPIN, above n. 9, p. 407, para. 8-352, for a discussion on whether it would have been appropriate to treat authentic instruments and agreements concerning access in the same way as privileged decisions.

V. GROUNDS FOR REFUSAL

10.31. Where Brussels II-bis simply referred back to the same grounds for refusal as for judgments (decisions), **Article 68 Brussels II-ter contains a separate provision with grounds for the refusal of recognition or enforcement of authentic instruments and agreements**. No great change is intended, but Article 68 has been modified to fit authentic instruments and agreements.

A. DIVORCE AND LEGAL SEPARATION

10.32. Recognition of authentic instruments and agreements concerning divorce or legal separation is dealt with in Article 68(1). An obvious deletion has been point (b) of Article 38, which refers to decisions given in default of appearance. This cannot occur in the case of an agreement.

10.33. Point (a) of Article 68(1) concerns **the public policy of the Member State in which recognition is sought**. We do not want to repeat the discussion above in Chapter 8 and would only reiterate that the public policy exception is reserved for exceptional cases.

10.34. Points (b) and (c) of Article 68(1) refer to **irreconcilability with a decision, an authentic instrument or agreement** from the Member State in which recognition is invoked or from another Member State or a third State, provided that it can be recognised in the Member State of recognition and correspond to points (c) and (d) of Article 38. It would appear from the text that decisions on the one hand and authentic instruments and agreements on the other are placed on an equal footing and that decisions are not given precedence. This differs from the situation under Brussels I-bis and is a result of authentic instruments and agreements being recognisable under Brussels II-ter and not only enforceable.[35]

10.35. It is not particularly likely that there will be irreconcilable authentic instruments or agreements, since these require an agreement between the parties. If a party has obtained a decision from the Member State of origin nullifying the authentic instrument or agreement on the ground that it was the result of fraud, misrepresentation or the like, then the authentic instrument or agreement is no longer legally binding and cannot be recognised. It would therefore not be a case of irreconcilability, since it does not fulfil the condition necessary for recognition.

---

[35] Cf. ECJ, 2 June 1994, *Solo Kleinmotoren*, C-414/92 (concerning the Brussels Convention).

10.36. If the parties agree on legal separation in a Member State and later a party who does not want to wait for the period of separation to run its course obtains a divorce decision from a third State, the decisions of which are recognised in the Member State of recognition, the earlier agreement on legal separation will take precedence.

B. PARENTAL RESPONSIBILITY

10.37. Recognition and enforcement in matters of parental responsibility is covered in Article 68(2) and (3), which, *mutatis mutandis*, replicates Article 39.

10.38. Point (a) of Article 68(2) concerns **the public policy of the Member State in which recognition or enforcement is sought**. It corresponds to Article 39(1)(a).

10.39. Point (b) of Article 68(2) protects **the rights of a third party that is not party to the agreement.** It corresponds to Article 39(1)(c). In the context of authentic instruments or agreements, given the absence of judicial control, it is more likely than in the case of judgments that an agreement would infringe the parental responsibility rights of a third party, such as a former foster parent holding access rights.

10.40. Points (c) and (d) of Article 68(2) concern **irreconcilability**. This corresponds to Article 39(1)(d) and (e). Just like its counterpart in Article 39, it gives precedence to the later decision, since under the principle of *rebus sic stantibus* in matters of parental responsibility, there can always be a change of circumstances justifying a new decision, authentic instrument or agreement.

10.41. Article 68(3) allows the refusal of recognition or enforcement if **the child was capable of forming his or her own views, but was not given an opportunity to do so.** It corresponds to Article 39(2), but contains a few differences. First of all, there is no reference to Article 21 on hearing of the child for the simple reason that it is not applicable when an authentic instrument is drawn up or an agreement registered by an authority. There is no obligation under Brussels II-ter to hear the child, but may well be under national and international law.[36] Nevertheless, recognition **may** be refused if the child was not given an opportunity to be heard.

---

[36] For example, under French law, Article 388-1 of the Civil Code makes it mandatory to inform the child of its right to be heard and if he or she asks to be heard, the matter must be put before a court, and the consensual divorce (and any provisions concerning parental responsibility) becomes a court decision. Recital (71) also refers to Article 24 of the Charter and Article 12 UNCRC.

10.42. Another difference in relation to Article 39(2) is that the specific reference in point (a) to proceedings concerning only the property of the child, and in point (b) to serious grounds for not hearing the child (in particular, the urgency of the case) are not replicated. These two situations are not relevant to authentic instruments or agreements, since the holders of parental responsibility are not entitled to agree on the property of a third person, namely the child, and are also not relevant in cases of urgency in taking measures for the protection of the child.

C. THE APPLICABILITY OF ARTICLES 69–70

1. Review of Jurisdiction

10.43. Article 69 prohibits the **review of the jurisdiction of the court in the Member State of origin that gave the judgment for which recognition is sought**. However, notaries and authorities before which authentic instruments or agreements are drawn up or registered are not 'courts' (see above 10.19 et seq).

10.44. The question then arises as to whether it is possible to refuse recognition and enforcement if an authentic instrument or agreement has been drawn up or registered in a Member State that did not have jurisdiction under Chapter II. According to its wording, Article 69 is only applicable to the review of the jurisdiction of 'courts', not notaries and authorities. Moreover, Article 65 makes Section 1 of Chapter IV on recognition and enforcement applicable to the recognition of authentic instruments and agreements on legal separation and divorce, and Sections 1 and 3 applicable to the same in matters of parental responsibility. Article 69 is located in Section 5 of Chapter IV, which is not made applicable.

10.45. A literal reading would then lead us to the conclusion that a refusal of recognition or enforcement of an authentic instrument or agreement would be possible if the Member State in which recognition is sought held that jurisdiction had been wrongfully assumed and that this would be manifestly contrary to its public policy.[37] However, here a parallel could be drawn with the judgment of the CJEU in *P*.[38] In that case a Lithuanian court had wrongfully assumed jurisdiction based on Article 15 Brussels II-bis (corresponding to Articles 12–13 Brussels II-ter). In essence, the referring court wanted to know whether Article 24 Brussels II-bis (Article 69 Brussels II-ter), which only referred to the rules on jurisdiction in Articles 3–14, also prohibited a refusal of recognition based on the manifestly wrongful application of Article 15.

---

[37] See Article 68(1)(a) and 68(2)(a).
[38] CJEU, 19 November 2015, *P*, C-455/15 PPU.

10.46. Such a literal reading did not impress the CJEU, which recalled that a court in a Member State cannot refuse to recognise a decision from another Member State solely on the ground that it considers that EU law was misapplied in that decision.[39] Against this background, it is submitted that it is very difficult to conceive of a case in which a misapplication or non-observance of the rules on jurisdiction by a notary or authority when drawing up or registering an authentic instrument or agreement would fall within the limits of national public policy as defined by the CJEU.

10.47. Having said that, it is important to stress that the prohibition to review the jurisdiction only applies if the authentic instrument or agreement is accompanied by a certificate indicating that the rules of jurisdiction in Chapter II have been observed.[40] If there is no certificate, there is no right to recognition and/or enforcement under Brussels II-ter.[41]

2. *Differences in the Applicable Law*

10.48. Under Article 70, **recognition of a decision in matrimonial matters may not be refused because the law of the Member State in which recognition is sought would not have allowed for divorce, legal separation or marriage annulment on the same facts** (see Chapter 8 at 8.127 et seq). Here we have the problem that the rule according to its wording only applies to the recognition of 'decisions'. Again, we would assume that the principle of mutual recognition trumps a literal interpretation of this Article and submit that it should also be applied to authentic instruments and agreements in matrimonial matters.

3. *Non-Review as to Substance*

10.49. It follows from Article 71 that **under no circumstances shall a decision from another Member State be reviewed as to its substance**. Again, we have the problem that the provision only refers to 'decisions' and not to authentic instruments and agreements. Once again, we would submit that the principle of mutual recognition would trump a literal interpretation of this Article and that substantive review of authentic instruments and agreements is prohibited in the Member State in which recognition and/or enforcement is sought.

10.50. If, for example, a party to an agreement on parental responsibility claims that it is no longer in the best interests of the child, he or she would have

---

[39] CJEU, 19 November 2015, *P*, C-455/15 PPU, para. 46. See also concerning Brussels I, CJEU, 16 July 2015, *Diageo Brands*, C-681/13.
[40] This is mandatory under Article 66(2).
[41] See Article 66(5).

to go to court in the Member State that has jurisdiction and seek a judgment. If the argument is that he or she was coerced or fraudulently induced into entering into an agreement, then the correct thing to do is to challenge the agreement and apply for a withdrawal of the certificate in the Member State that issued it.

CHAPTER 11

COOPERATION IN MATTERS OF PARENTAL RESPONSIBILITY

I. Introduction 371
II. Central Authorities 374
    A. Designating and Resourcing Central Authorities 374
    B. The General Tasks of Central Authorities. 377
    C. Making and Dealing with Requests 378
        1. The Requests Mechanism 378
        2. The Specific Tasks of Requested Central Authorities 380
        3. Collecting and Exchanging Information about a Child 382
        4. Collection and Transmission of Information. 384
III. Cooperation between Courts and Competent Authorities 385
IV. Placement of a Child in Another Member State: Article 82 386
    A. Background. 386
    B. The Position under Article 82. 388
        1. The Scope of Article 82 388
        2. The Procedural Framework: the Recital (84) Guidance 391
        3. The Consent Requirement: the General Position 392
        4. The Position with Regard to Placements with Parents or
           Relatives. 393
        5. Obtaining Consent. 393
        6. Timing of Consent 396
        7. Recognition and Enforcement of Placement Orders. 396
        8. Costs. 398

I. INTRODUCTION

11.1. Chapter V of Brussels II-ter provides for cooperation in matters of parental responsibility. There are no comparable provisions concerning matrimonial matters.[1] Chapter V does not apply to the processing of return

---

[1] However, as pointed out by O. KNÖFEL, 'Intro to Arts. 76–84 Brussels IIter' in U. MAGNUS and P. MANKOWSKI (eds), *Brussels IIter Regulation*, OttoSchmidt, 2023, p. 549, para. 8, the

applications made under the 1980 Hague Abduction Convention even as between Member States.[2] Technically, this is because, as Recital (73) explains, such applications are not considered to be proceedings on the substance of parental responsibility. In any event, there was no need to make fresh provisions for such proceedings since there were already well-established cooperative provisions under the Convention (to which all Member States are a party).

11.2. Chapter V builds on the provisions first introduced by Part IV Brussels II-bis,[3] which, in turn, were inspired by Chapter V of the 1996 Hague Child Protection Convention.[4] Although Chapter V is primarily concerned with the role of Central Authorities, its reach goes beyond that, dealing, for example, with the implementation of decisions in matters of parental responsibility as between courts or competent authorities (see Article 81)[5] and, importantly, providing a regulated mechanism for the placement of children in another Member State (see Article 82).[6] Reflecting this wider application, the title of the Chapter is no longer tied to cooperation between Central Authorities. That said, it should be observed that a separate provision, Article 86, which falls under Chapter VI ('General Provisions'), deals with cooperation and communication between courts.[7] Further, Article 87 places an obligation upon Central Authorities with respect to the collection and transmission of information to a court or competent authority.[8]

11.3. As the Commission observed in the Explanatory Memorandum to its Proposal to recast the Regulation,[9] cooperation between Central Authorities

---

[1] Brussels II-bis Commission Proposal, COM(2002) 222 final, p. 19, contemplated the Central Authority system applying both to divorce and to parental responsibility.
[2] See Recital (73). The obligation to establish a Central Authority and its consequent duties under the 1980 Hague Abduction Convention are separately governed by that Convention – see Articles 6 and 7 respectively, discussed in detail by N. Lowe, M. Everall and M. Nicholls, *International Movement of Children: Law Practice and Procedure* (2nd ed. by N. Lowe and M. Nicholls), Lexis Nexis, Family Law, 2016, ch. 18.
[3] The original 2001 Brussels II Regulation contained no provisions on cooperation.
[4] For a general discussion of the background to cooperation between Central Authorities, see O. Knöfel, above n. 1, pp. 546–549; M. Župan, C. Höhn and U. Kluth, 'Central Authority Cooperation under the Brussels II-ter Regulation' (2020/2021) 22 *Yearbook of Private International Law* 183, at 184–185. For a discussion of the cooperation provisions of the 1996 Convention, see N. Lowe and M. Nicholls, *The 1996 Hague Convention on the Protection of Children*, Jordans, 2012, ch. 6.
[5] Discussed below at 11.34.
[6] Discussed below at 11.40 et seq.
[7] Discussed below at 11.35.
[8] Discussed below at 11.30.
[9] Proposal for a Council Regulation on jurisdiction, the recognition and enforcement of decisions in matrimonial matters and the matters of parental responsibility, and on international child abduction (recast) COM(2016) 411, p. 5.

in specific cases on parental responsibility is 'essential to support effectively parents and children involved in cross-border proceedings relating to child matters'. However, the results of a consultation conducted by the Commission[10] revealed a number of problems, not least that what was then Article 55 Brussels II-bis did 'not constitute a sufficient legal basis for national authorities in some Member States to take action because their national law would require a more explicit autonomous legal basis in the Regulation'. A major concern of parents was the lack of efficient cooperation between Central Authorities, which it was thought could best be resolved by clarifying the tasks so as to better support them. The consultation study also supported the inclusion of child welfare authorities into the cooperation system. Meeting these criticisms and generally **enhancing the cooperation provisions is a major plank of Brussels II-ter.**

11.4. It has been well noted[11] that, reflecting the growing appreciation of their practical importance, there has been a trend in Regulations generally and in the Maintenance Regulation in particular[12] to 'upgrade' and expand the cooperation provisions. This is true of the successive versions of Brussels II. The 2001 version had no cooperation provisions. Brussels II-bis had six Articles and one Recital. Brussels II-ter comprises nine Articles in Chapter V plus another two in Chapter VI, together with no fewer than 15 Recitals. Further evidence of the importance attached to this part of Regulation is the striking number of changes that were made to the Commission's Proposal[13] following the extensive discussion and negotiations between Member States. This resulted in both an expansion and rejigging of the provisions. In general terms, the changes introduced by Brussels II-ter aim to clarify who can ask for what assistance and information, from whom and under what conditions.

---

[10] See the *Study on the assessment of Regulation (EC) No 2201/2003 and the policy options for its amendment*, Deloitte, Coffey, 2015, prepared for the European Commission and referred to in the Commission's Explanatory Memorandum to its Proposal, pp. 5 and 9. See also the Final Report of the Study, Deloitte, Coffey, 2018, prepared for the European Commission.

[11] By M. ŽUPAN, 'Cooperation between Central Authorities' in C. HONORATI (ed.), *Jurisdiction in Matrimonial Matters, Parental Responsibility and International Abduction*, Giappichelli/Peter Lang, 2017, pp. 270–271. As Župan notes, there are a striking number of provisions in the Maintenance Regulation (Council Regulation (EC) No 4/2009 of 18 December 2008) on cooperation between Central Authorities: see Chapter VII, Articles 49–63. She also makes the point that the number of provisions dealing with Central Authorities has steadily increased in successive Hague Conventions dealing with children.

[12] See M. ŽUPAN, C. HÖHN and U. KLUTH, above n. 4, 185, citing, *inter alia*, I, CURRY-SUMNER, 'Transnational Recovery of Child Maintenance in Europe: The Future is Bright, The Future is Central Authorities', http//www.law.muni.cz/sborniky/Days-of-public-law/files/pdf/mep/Curry-Sumner.pdf.

[13] Above, n. 9.

II. CENTRAL AUTHORITIES

A. DESIGNATING AND RESOURCING CENTRAL AUTHORITIES

11.5. Under Article 76 (which is a simple replacement of Article 53 of Brussels II-bis), each Member State is obliged to designate one or more Central Authorities to assist with the application of the Regulation in matters of parental responsibility. Central Authorities are an integral part of the Regulation machinery to ensure cooperation between Member States and, in some cases, to directly assist individuals caught up in cross-border disputes. As is discussed below, they are, in essence, administrative bodies whose principal tasks are to: (i) communicate information on national laws and procedures and services available in matters of parental responsibility; (ii) take appropriate measures for improving the application of the Regulation; (iii) cooperate and promote cooperation among the competent authorities in their Member States to achieve the Regulation's purposes; and (iv) assist courts and competent authorities, and, in certain cases, holders of parental responsibility in cross-border procedures and to cooperate both in general matters and in specific cases, including promoting the amicable resolution of family disputes.

11.6. Unlike the Hague Conventions, which only permit multiple designations by 'Federal States, States with more than system of law or States having autonomous territorial units', under Brussels II-ter, Member States have an unfettered freedom to designate more than one Central Authority.[14] Where more than one Central Authority is designated, Article 76 requires the Member State to specify the geographical[15] or functional jurisdiction of each.[16] In these cases, communications should normally be sent directly to the relevant Central Authority with jurisdiction, but if it is sent to the wrong one, 'the latter shall forward it to the Central Authority with jurisdiction and inform the sender accordingly'.

---

[14] See M. Župan, above n. 11, p. 271.
[15] Formerly, under Brussels II-bis, the UK designated separate Central Authorities for England and Wales, Scotland and Northern Ireland.
[16] In this latter regard, Bulgaria has designated separate Central Authorities for dealing with matrimonial matters and matters of parental responsibility; Estonia has designated separate Central Authorities for the purposes of Articles 77(1), 79(c), (d) and (e) and 81, and for the purposes of Articles 79(a), (b), (f) and (g), 80 and 82; France has a separate Central Authority dealing with cross-border placements; Hungary has a separate Central Authority dealing with children removed abroad and vice versa; in Lithuania, a separate Central Authority communicates information on national laws, etc.; and in Slovakia, a separate Central Authority facilitates communication between courts. See the *European Judicial Atlas in civil matters* on the European Justice Portal at https://e-justice.europa.eu/37842/EN/brussels_iib_regulation__matrimonial_matters_and_matters_of parental_responsibility_recast.

11.7. Recital (72) asks Member States to consider designating the same Central Authority under the Regulation as under the 1980 Hague Abduction Convention and the 1996 Hague Child Protection Convention. The clear advantage of a common designation is that it can create synergies and allow the authorities to benefit from experience gained by the authorities in managing other cases under the Conventions.[17] Further, in operational terms, it removes any potential difficulties in determining which instrument should be applied where there are overlapping obligations such as discovering the whereabouts of a child.[18] A possible drawback of having combined functions is that it places greater pressure on the resources of the designated Central Authority.[19]

11.8. Recital (72) focuses on matters of parental responsibility and does not therefore mention designating the same Central Authority under the Maintenance Regulation as some States, such as Italy, do.[20] Again, such a common designation has the operational advantage of being better able to deal with potential difficulties in determining which instrument should be applied. Recital (72) is advisory only. The EU is not in a position to compel Member States to designate one and the same authority for Brussels II-ter and for the Hague Conventions; this is a matter of internal organisation for each Member State. In fact, Member States did not make any immediate structural changes to their Central Authorities pursuant to Brussels II-ter coming into force.

11.9. Although it is mandatory to designate a Central Authority, neither its location nor its structure is dictated by the Regulation, as this is a matter for national law. In most Member States, Central Authorities are located within the ministry responsible for justice, but it is by no means the only selected location.[21] Further, there is freedom to allocate work to different divisions within a Central Authority: in France, for example, one division deals with requests under Articles 78–81, while another unit deals with placements under Article 82. Member States must communicate to the Commission the names, addresses and means of communication for their designated Central Authorities.[22] They must also notify the Commission the official language or languages of the EU

---

[17] See the *2022 Practice Guide for the application of the Brussels IIb Regulation*, EU, 2022 (hereinafter *2022 Practice Guide*), p. 201, para. 7.1.1.
[18] See further below at 11.22 et seq.
[19] See M. Župan, C. Höhn and U. Kluth, above n. 4, p. 188. The question of resources is discussed at 11.10 below.
[20] A different solution in Germany is to locate the two different Central Authorities in the same building.
[21] M. Župan, C. Höhn and U. Kluth, above n. 4, p. 188, mention the justice ministry, family ministry, foreign affairs ministry, public prosecutor and the ministry justice and family. Details can be found in *The European Judicial Atlas in civil matters*, above, n. 16.
[22] Article 103(1)(f); and see *The European Judicial Atlas in civil matters*, above n. 16.

other than their own in which communications to the Central Authority can be accepted.[23]

11.10. To be able to perform their wide-ranging duties (discussed below) efficiently and promptly, it is clearly important that Central Authorities are adequately resourced. This is particularly so, as by Article 83, **assistance provided by them must be free of charge and each must bear their own costs in applying the Regulation.**[24] Although Brussels II-bis made no mention of the resources issue, the 2014 *Practice Guide on the application of Brussels II-bis* stated[25] that Central Authorities 'must be given sufficient financial and human resources to be able to fulfil their duties'. The Commission wanted to make that an obligation,[26] but that proposal was not approved. Instead, the compromise is to provide in Recital (72) that Member States 'should ensure that Central Authorities have adequate financial and human resources to enable them to carry out the tasks assigned to them under this Regulation'. While Member States understandably baulked at making it an obligation under the Regulation to provide Central Authorities with adequate resources, as that would seem to go beyond the EU's remit, it should not be assumed that this 'relegation' to a Recital signals a tolerance of inadequate funding. On the contrary, sufficient funding is vital to the proper discharge of the extensive duties imposed on Central Authorities by Brussels II-ter,[27] and the failure to do so could be considered a violation of the principle of effective application of EU law.

11.11. What 'adequate' resources comprise is not articulated, but on the basis of the *2022 Practice Guide* to Brussels II-ter,[28] it should include adequate training as regards the functioning of the Regulation and ideally the functioning of the 1980 Hague Abduction Convention and the 1996 Hague Child Protection Convention, joint training with the judiciary, lawyers and others involved in the functioning of the Regulation and the Conventions, and language training. The use of modern technology is clearly vital in order to facilitate efficient and speedy case management.

11.12. Replicating Article 58 Brussels II-bis, Article 84 provides that: (1) Central Authorities shall meet regularly; and (2) they will do so within the European Judicial Network (EJN), though, as Recital (86) says, this does not preclude other meetings from being organised.

---

[23] Articles 91(3) and 103(1)(h); and see *The European Judicial Atlas in civil matters*, ibid.
[24] But, as the *2022 Practice Guide* states (p.201, para. 7.1.1), **other** authorities may still claim costs, e.g. courts (for fees) and experts.
[25] *Practice Guide for the application of the Brussels IIa Regulation*, EU, 2014, p. 85, para. 7.5.
[26] See Article 61 of the proposed recast Regulation.
[27] See the comments by C. HONORATI, 'The Commission's proposal for a recast of Brussels IIa Regulation' [2017] *International Family Law* 97, 113, on the profound disparity between Central Authorities operating Brussels II-bis.
[28] *2022 Practice Guide*, p. 202, para. 7.1.1.

B. THE GENERAL TASKS OF CENTRAL AUTHORITIES

11.13. Under Article 77, the general tasks of Central Authorities are to:

(1) communicate information on national laws and procedures and services available in matters of parental responsibility and take measures that they consider appropriate for improving the application of the Regulation, and

(2) ... cooperate and promote cooperation among the competent authorities in their Member States to achieve the purposes of the Regulation.

11.14. Augmenting Article 77, Recital (74) states that Central Authorities should 'assist courts and competent authorities, and in certain cases also holders of parental responsibility, in cross-border procedures and cooperate both in general matters and in specific cases, *including for the purposes of promoting the amicable resolution of family disputes*' (emphasis added). This reference to the promotion of amicable resolution of disputes reflects the importance attached to the use of mediation or other means of alternative dispute resolution.[29]

11.15. The obligation in Article 77(1) is wider than that in Article 54 Brussels II-bis, which it replaces, in that it extends to providing information about different services available in matters of parental responsibility.[30] The obligation is a general one and is not intended to oblige Central Authorities to give legal advice in specific instances. As the *2022 Practice Guide* notes,[31] the information usually relates, *inter alia*, to the legal provisions on parental responsibility, existing provisional including protective measures, institutional or foster care and procedural issues such as seising a court, timeframes and possible appeals, and about enforceability.

11.16. The obligation in Article 77(2) to promote internal cooperation, etc. is new to Brussels II-ter, but there is a similar obligation under the 1996 Hague Child Protection Convention,[32] and it follows the lead given by the Maintenance Regulation[33] in recognising that apart from the Central Authorities, other national authorities have a role to play in the application of the Regulation.[34] What is meant by 'competent authority' in this context is not spelt out, but it

---

[29] See, for example, Article 79(g), discussed below at 11.27, and, in the context of international child abduction, Article 25, discussed in Chapter 6 at 6.65 et seq.
[30] See *2022 Practice Guide*, p. 204, para. 7.2.1.1.
[31] *2022 Practice Guide*, p. 204, para. 7.2.1.1.
[32] See Article 30. See also Article 7(1) of the 1993 Hague Convention on Intercountry Adoption.
[33] Council Regulation (EC) No 4/2009. See Article 50(1)(a) in particular.
[34] As O. Knöfel, above n. 1, p. 562, para. 3, says, the reference to 'competent authorities' was to clarify that Brussels II-ter applies to child welfare authorities as well as courts. See also M. Župan, C. Höhn and U. Kluth, above n. 4, p. 189 and the *2022 Practice Guide*, p. 204, para. 7.2.1.1.

clearly includes public authorities responsible for the institutional care for children.[35] It may be wondered why the Regulation does not require Member States to notify the Commission which authorities are competent for the purpose of Articles 80 and 82, according to the procedure set out by Article 103. Beyond providing that the EJN may be used,[36] Central Authorities are left to their own devices as to how promote internal cooperation.

C. MAKING AND DEALING WITH REQUESTS

1. The Requests Mechanism

11.17. As previously, Brussels II-ter facilitates the obtaining of advice, assistance and information from Central Authorities. **The basic mechanism for obtaining advice, etc. is the making of a request to the Central Authority to which the requested Authority is obliged to respond.** This means that those seeking aid have a right to obtain it.[37] This system (formerly referred to as the 'working method') is governed by Article 78, which effectively replaces Article 57 Brussels II-bis[38] with a more precisely worded scheme that addresses various lacunae under the previous regime.

11.18. Under Article 78(1), Central Authorities are, upon a request from a Central Authority of another Member State, under a basic obligation to 'cooperate in individual cases to achieve the purposes of this Regulation'. Requests can, in any event, be made by a court or a competent authority, which is a useful clarification of the previous position and means that both courts and welfare authorities can request the assistance of Central Authorities.[39] They can also be made by holders of parental responsibility,[40] but only in defined circumstances, namely, to seek information and assistance with respect to the recognition and enforcement, to facilitate agreement between the holders or with regard to the need to take measures for the protection of the child's person

---

[35] Note: for the purposes of what is now Article 82, a 'competent authority' must be one governed by public law; see CJEU, 26 April 2012, *Health Service Executive*, C-92/12 PPU, discussed at 11.67 et seq. According to O. KNÖFEL, above n. 1, pp. 562–563, para. 3, a competent authority is 'any office or agency which, according to its own law, has jurisdiction to entertain proceedings relating to parental responsibility in a Member State'.

[36] See Article 77(3), although this does not mention the Hague International Judicial Network, which is surely a matter of regret; see C. HONORATI, above n. 27, p. 113.

[37] This is in line with the ruling under the Maintenance Regulation in CJEU, 9 February 2017, *MS*, C-283/16, para. 40.

[38] However, it should be noted that the Correlation table in Annex X gives no equivalent to Article 57(1) and (2).

[39] See the Explanatory Memorandum to the Commission's Proposal, above n. 9, p. 16.

[40] Article 2(8) defines a holder of parental responsibility as 'any person, institution or other body having parental responsibility for a child'.

or property.[41] This restricted right means that individual holders of parental responsibility have no right to obtain assistance in discovering their child's whereabouts or with regard to the collection and exchange of information relevant in procedures in matters of parental responsibility. On the other hand, Article 78(5) expressly preserves the right of individual holders of parental responsibility to apply directly to a court of another Member State.

11.19.   As a general rule, the requesting court or competent authority has to submit a request to the Central Authority in its own jurisdiction. This is also true in the case of requests made by individuals, which have to be addressed to the Central Authority of the State of the applicant's habitual residence.[42] In effect, what Brussels II-ter does is to introduce a centralised way of communication via the Central Authorities.[43] This model follows the traditional diplomatic scheme, whereby requests are channelled via a single national entity which is the only one allowed to have contact with the similar entity in a foreign State. However, given the close cooperation built in the European judicial area, some room is made for direct contact between courts of different Member States.[44] In fact, this provision is without prejudice to the court's ability to make direct requests to another court, as provided for by Article 86.[45] However, it should be noted that this does not include other national authorities or individuals who can only apply to the Central Authority of their own State. Further, under Article 78(4), Central Authorities or competent authorities are not precluded 'from entering into or maintaining existing agreements or arrangements with Central Authorities or competent authorities of one or more other Member States allowing direct communications in their mutual relations'. Competent authorities should inform their Central Authorities of any such arrangement.[46] In any event, Recital (76) makes the point that **the obligation to proceed through Central Authority channels is only mandatory for initial requests.** Subsequent communications with the court, competent authority or applicant can take place directly.[47]

11.20.   In cases of **urgency**, this scheme may be displaced and direct contact is always possible, not just between courts but between others, such as national authorities and individuals. What ranks as an 'urgent case' is not specified in the text of the Regulation, but Recital (76) cites the example of the need to

---

[41]   See Article 78(2).
[42]   Article 78(3).
[43]   See M. Župan, C. Höhn and U. Kluth, above n. 4, p. 190.
[44]   Compare the scheme under the 1980 Hague Abduction Convention (Article 8), under which individuals can make applications either to the Central Authority of the child's habitual residence or to any other authority.
[45]   Discussed below at 11.39.
[46]   See Recital (77). At the time of writing, no such arrangements have been notified.
[47]   M. Župan, C. Höhn and U. Kluth, above n. 4, p. 190. Query the thinking behind this provision?

take measures for the protection of a child presumed to be at imminent risk. Obvious examples include the need to locate a child who has absconded from public care or where a family seek to avoid care protection proceedings by moving to another Member State.

2. The Specific Tasks of Requested Central Authorities

11.21. Articles 79 and 80 set out a number of specific tasks that Central Authorities must perform under Brussels II-ter. These replace and expand upon Article 55 Brussels II-bis. However, they are subject to the overall proviso that they do not impose an obligation upon Central Authorities to 'exercise powers that can be exercised only by judicial authorities under the law of the requested Member State'.[48] All the tasks set out by Articles 79 and 80 can be discharged by Central Authorities acting directly or through courts, competent authorities or other bodies.

11.22. Under Article 79(a), the requested Central Authorities **must** take all appropriate steps **to assist**, in accordance with national law and procedure, **in discovering the child's whereabouts** 'where it appears that the child may be present within the territory of the requested Member State'. This obligation only arises upon a request by a court or competent authority of another Member State.[49] Individuals cannot make direct requests and must seek assistance via their own court or Central Authority.

11.23. Although apparently new to Brussels II-ter, in practice many Contracting States acted on such requests under the more generally worded Article 55(a) Brussels II-bis.[50] This now express provision brings Brussels II-ter into line with the long-standing obligation both under the 1980 Hague Abduction Convention (see Article 7(a)) and under Article 31(c) of the 1996 Hague Child Protection Convention. The obligation under Brussels II-ter has a wide application, including, for example, discovering the whereabouts of runaway children or children whose families are fleeing from welfare authorities. Unlike the 1996 Convention, where the obligation is confined to discovering the whereabouts of children where they appear to be 'in need of protection', the obligation under the Regulation is phrased more generally, applying wherever the information is required for carrying out an application or request under this Regulation. Where the same Central Authority is designated to operate both these instruments, in operational terms any difference in wording or function should occasion no difficulty, but where different Authorities are designated, there could be difficulties in determining which instrument applies.

---

[48] Article 78(6).
[49] Article 78(2).
[50] See M. Župan, C. Höhn and U. Kluth, above n. 4, p. 191.

11.24. While Article 79(a) obliges Central Authorities to assist, **it does not regulate the means** of discovering a child's whereabouts. That remains a matter for national law. In fact, in discharging this obligation, Central Authorities can use a variety of means, agencies or bodies that have experience in locating children,[51] including the police, although in some States that may require bringing criminal charges. Other organisations that can usefully be alerted include Interpol and Missing Children Europe.

11.25. Under Article 79(b) and (f), requested Central Authorities must, upon a request by a court or competent authority of another Member State, take all appropriate steps to **collect and exchange information** relevant in procedures in matters of parental responsibility[52] and to provide such information and assistance as is needed by the courts and competent authorities to seek the child's placement abroad.[53] Under Article 79(d) and (e), requested Central Authorities must take all appropriate steps to **facilitate communication** between the courts, competent authorities and other bodies involved, in particular when assisting in the implementation of decisions in matters of parental responsibility,[54] and in connection with transfer requests, making provisional orders in cases of urgency and *lis pendens* issues.[55]

11.26. The two other tasks enumerated by Article 79 are ones that individual holders of parental responsibility as well as courts and competent authorities can request Central Authorities to discharge.[56] Under Article 79(c), requested Central Authorities must take all appropriate steps to **provide information and assistance** to holders of parental responsibility seeking the recognition and enforcement of decisions in the territory of the requested Central Authority, 'in particular concerning rights of access and the return of the child, including, where necessary, information about how to obtain legal aid'. This provision usefully extends the former obligation under Article 55(b) Brussels II-bis to include information about obtaining legal aid.

11.27. Article 79(g) obliges requested Central Authorities to take all appropriate steps to '**facilitate agreement between holders of parental responsibility through mediation or other means of alternative dispute resolution, and facilitate cross-border cooperation to this end**'. This obligation is part of a

---

[51] It is common practice to issue requests for information to solicitors, airlines, telephone companies and internet providers: see O. KNÖFEL, above n. 1, p. 568, para. 7.
[52] As provided under Article 80; discussed below at 11.29 et seq.
[53] Discussed below at 11.41 et seq.
[54] As required by Article 81, discussed below at 11.36 et seq.
[55] See also Recital (79), which makes the point that providing information for further direct communication such as contact details of child welfare authorities, network judges or the competent court might be sufficient.
[56] See Article 78(2).

consistent policy under the Regulation to promote amicable solutions wherever possible.

3. Collecting and Exchanging Information about a Child

11.28. Formerly governed by Article 55(a) Brussels II-bis, Article 80 Brussels II-ter now deals with collecting and exchanging information about a child. Requests under Article 55(a) had assumed growing and time-consuming importance. They could be made by individual holders of parental responsibility as well as courts and competent authorities. There was uncertainty about what information was required both when making and responding to the request. Furthermore, there was no time limit for responding. Article 80 addresses these issues. It provides a legal basis for providing information other than that relating only to the child (if that information is relevant in the requesting Member State) in matters of parental responsibility,[57] it introduces time limits for responding to request and it limits the right of individual holders of parental responsibility to make requests, but adds an obligation with regard to children exposed to a serious danger.

11.29. Under Article 80(1), upon a request with supporting reasons, the Central Authority of a Member State where the child is or was habitually resident or present, either directly or through the court, competent authorities or other bodies:

(a) **shall**, where available, provide, or draw up and provide a report on:
   (i) the situation of the child;
   (ii) any ongoing procedures in matters of parental responsibility for the child; or
   (iii) on decisions taken in matters of parental responsibility for the child;

(b) **shall** provide any other information relevant in procedures in matters of parental responsibility in the requesting Member State, in particular about the situation of a parent, a relative or other person who may be suitable to care for the child, if the situation of the child so requires; or

(c) **may** request the competent authority of its Member State to consider the need to take measures for the protection of the person or property of the child. (Emphasis added)

11.30. Only courts or competent authorities can request a report on the child's situation and on decisions taken in matters of parental responsibility under Article 80(1)(a) and (b), and in each case there is a **mandatory duty** upon the requested Central Authority to respond. On the other hand, individual holders of parental responsibility, as well as courts and competent authorities, can make

---

[57] It should be noted that the obligation to provide information in respect of a child involved in return proceedings brought under the 1980 Hague Abduction Convention is governed by Article 7(d) and (e) of that instrument.

a request with regard to the need for the protection of child's person or property under Article 80(1)(c), but the requested Central Authority **has a discretion whether or not to respond**.[58]

11.31. In all cases, requests must be made with supporting reasons and should, as Recital (81) says, 'contain, in particular, a description of the procedures for which the information is needed and the factual situation that gave rise to those procedures'. While this requirement does not preclude requests from being made where there are no existing legal proceedings, in such cases there will need to be a good reason for making the request as, for example, where child welfare agencies are contemplating whether to bring proceedings. In all cases requests and any supporting documents must be accompanied by a translation into the official language or one of the official languages or any other language that the requested Member State expressly accepts,[59] and, importantly, except where exceptional circumstances make it impossible, the requested information must be transmitted to the Central Authority or competent authority of the requesting Member State '**no later than three months following the receipt of the request**'.[60] According to Recital (85), the three-month timeframe should be regarded as the maximum timeframe and the competent authorities involved 'should strive to reply even more quickly'. The Recital also says that where the competent national authority cannot provide the information, it should explain why it cannot be provided. What it does not suggest is a timeframe for such a response.[61]

11.32. Article 80(2) creates a new obligation, namely:

> In any case where the child is exposed to a serious danger, the court or competent authority contemplating or having taken measures for the protection of the child, if it is aware that the child's residence has changed to, or that the child is present in, another Member State, shall inform the courts or competent authorities of that other Member State about the danger involved and the measures taken or under consideration. This information may be transmitted directly or through the Central Authorities.

11.33. This obligation, which was not in the Commission's proposals, is similar to that under Article 36 of the 1996 Hague Child Protection Convention,

---

[58] For examples of how these provisions may work, see the *2022 Practice Guide*, pp. 201–211, paras 7.2.3.3 and 7.2.3.4.
[59] Article 80(3).
[60] Article 80(4). The Commission's proposal was that the time limit should be two months.
[61] M. Župan, C. Höhn and U. Kluth, above n. 4, p. 193, argue that a provision corresponding to Article 53(2)(c) of the Maintenance Regulation should have been included in Brussels II-ter to the effect that there should be an immediate obligation to inform the requesting Central Authority and to specify the reason for the impossibility. The practicality of this suggestion can perhaps be debated.

except that it is confined to cases where the change of residence is to another Member State (the obligation under the 1996 Convention extends to a case where the child has become habitually resident or present in a non-Contractual State). The *Practical Handbook* on the 1996 Convention advises that it is a matter for the relevant authorities to determine whether in any particular case the child is exposed to serious danger. It cites the following possible examples: where the child has an illness requiring constant treatment, is exposed to drugs or an unhealthy influence such as a sect (to which one might add, is in danger of radicalisation), or where the child's carer was under the supervision of the authorities because of allegations of neglect or abuse, or where the child is an unaccompanied minor.[62] These seem apposite examples for the application of Brussels II-ter and are likely to be of increasing importance. Indeed, Article 80(2) is a potentially far-reaching provision[63] and, by having to alert local authorities to children considered to be in serious danger and to the measures either taken or being considered, can be seen as creating a duty upon the court to follow the welfare of such children, even where they relocate to a different Member State.

4. *Collection and Transmission of Information*

11.34. The mechanics of collecting and transmitting information in matters of parental responsibility, which the requested Central Authority is obliged to do under Brussels II-ter, is governed by Article 87. Article 87(1) provides an internal system of communication,[64] inasmuch as the requested Central Authority must transmit any application, request or the information contained therein to the court, the competent authority within its Member State or any intermediary as appropriate under national law and procedure.[65] In turn, the intermediary, court or competent authority which holds or is competent to collect, within the requested State, information required to comply with a request or an application made under the Regulation, must provide that information to the requested Central Authority at its request in cases where the requested Central Authority does not have direct access to the information.[66] The requested Central Authority must then transmit, 'as necessary', the information so obtained to the requesting Central Authority in accordance with national law and procedure.[67]

---

[62] *Practical Handbook on the operation of the 1996 Hague Child Protection Convention*, HCCH, 2014, para. 11.20.
[63] But note the comments in O. Knöfel, above n. 1, p. 579, para. 13.
[64] See M. Župan, C. Höhn and U. Kluth, above n. 4, p. 197.
[65] Article 87(1). This transmitted information may **only** be used by the recipients for the purposes of the Regulation: Article 87(2).
[66] Article 87(3).
[67] Article 87(4).

11.35. Although Article 87 replicates the essence of the obligation contained in Article 55 Brussels II-bis, it addresses the complaint that the former provision did not provide a sufficient legal basis for responding to requests by providing the necessary authority for doing so. The term 'intermediary', which is new to Brussels II-ter, is not defined in the Regulation. It was apparently intended to refer to lawyers involved in the proceedings concerning the child, but, on its wording, it could also include individuals, such as social workers or doctors, rather than institutions, who have relevant information. What Article 87 does not do is provide for any specific means of communication.[68]

III. COOPERATION BETWEEN COURTS AND COMPETENT AUTHORITIES

11.36. In a new provision, Article 81 Brussels II-ter[69] makes provision for cooperation between courts and competent authorities such that a court of one Member State may request the courts or competent authorities of another to '**assist in the implementation** of decisions in matters of parental responsibility given under this Regulation, in particular in securing the effective exercise of rights of access'.

11.37. Article 81 is modelled on, but is not identically worded to, Article 35(1) of the 1996 Child Protection Convention.[70] It underlines the importance that Brussels II-ter attaches to the need to establish and maintain contact between the children and their parents, which in turn is in line with Article 24(3) of the EU Charter of Fundamental Rights and Articles 9(3) and 10 UNCRC. 'Access' or contact is not confined to physical contact and embraces indirect contact by telephone or by the whole variety of internet platforms, but it will depend in the first place on what is ordered.

11.38. **Article 81 only permits a court to make requests**, but those requests can be made to another court **or** competent authority of another Member State.

---

[68] See the criticism in this respect in M. Župan, C. Höhn and U. Kluth, above n. 4, pp. 197–198.
[69] But it is a slight rewording of the Commission's proposed Article 64(3).
[70] Article 35(1) adds after 'securing effective exercise of rights of access', 'as well as of the right to maintain direct contacts on a regular basis'. This wording reflects Article 9(3) UNCRC. Brussels II-ter reflects the wording of Article 24(3) of the EU Charter of Fundamental Rights. Note also Article 7(f) of the 1980 Hague Abduction Convention, under which Central Authorities must cooperate with each other 'to make arrangements for organising or securing the effective exercise of rights of access'. It should be mentioned that in the Commission's proposal (see the proposed Article 64(5)), there was to be an obligation, as under Article 35(2) of the 1996 Convention, to 'gather information or evidence', and a discretion to make a finding, on the suitability of a person to exercise access and on the conditions under which access should be exercised. This is not included in the final version.

As Recital (82) states, Article 81 enables a court of a Member State that has already given a decision or is contemplating doing so, the implementation of which is to take place in another Member State, to request that the courts or competent authorities of that other State assist in the implementation of that decision. It cites as an example of the utility of this provision when making of a decision granting supervised access in another Member State. Another example might be in the context of organising indirect contact. A more detailed example (equally apt for the application of Brussels II-ter) is given by the *Practical Handbook* on the 1996 Convention,[71] namely, of an order envisaging contact handovers taking place at a neutral venue.

11.39. Direct judicial communication has long been an accepted practice when dealing with international child abduction under the 1980 Hague Abduction Convention. This practice has been effectively formalised for the purpose of Brussels II-ter by Article 86, which provides that the courts may cooperate and communicate directly with, or request information directly from, each other, '*provided that such communication respects the procedural rights of the parties to the proceedings and the confidentiality of information*'.

11.40. Under Article 86(2), the cooperation may be implemented by any means (which could include the EJN or, where appropriate, the International Hague Network of Judges) that the court considers appropriate and may concern in particular:

(i) **communication** for the purposes of Articles 12 and 13 (transfer requests) and for the purposes of Chapter III (child abduction)[72] and Chapters IV and V (recognition and enforcement); and
(ii) **information** in accordance with Article 15 (provisional orders in cases of urgency) and on pending proceedings for the purposes of Article 20 (lis pendens and dependent actions).

IV. PLACEMENT OF A CHILD IN ANOTHER MEMBER STATE: ARTICLE 82

A. BACKGROUND

11.41. There are different reasons why a court or competent authority might contemplate placing a child in another Member State. It could be to place a child with members of the wider family (for example, grandparents) in cases where it

---

[71] Above n. 62, Example 11 (1).
[72] For a summary of the role of Central Authorities in child abduction proceedings, see M. Župan, C. Höhn and U. Kluth, above n. 4, pp. 194–195. See also Chapter 6.

is not appropriate for the child to be with his or her parents. It could be to place a child in institutional or foster care with non-relatives in another Member State so as, for example, to take advantage of facilities not available in the child's State of habitual residence,[73] or which are nearest to the placing authority. Another example is of an unaccompanied child (whether a refugee or not) who has arrived in another Member State that can take care of the child.[74] The common characteristic of these 'placements' is that they are measures of child protection that are sought to be taken when, as the *Cross-border placement of children in the European Union*[75] study (hereinafter the '*Cross-border Study*') puts it,[76] 'a child has no one to look after him/her effectively or when a child needs special support due to a mental or physical illness/deficiency'. These measures are designed to be taken in the interests of the child. As the *Cross-border Study* observed,[77] while placements between individuals 'may be considered as a matter of "private law" or, rather, as a civil matter following the EU autonomous notion provided by art. 81 TFEU. On the other hand, the placement of a child in a foster family, institution or any other care solution may be defined as a measure of "social" protection and, therefore, as a matter of "public law"'. It is now clear that all such placements are parental responsibility measures that fall within the scope of the Regulation,[78]

11.42. The original Brussels II Regulation of 2001 made no provision with regard to the placement of children in another Member State. Such provision was first introduced by Article 56 Brussels II-bis, which in turn was modelled on Article 33 of the 1996 Hague Child Protection Convention and applied where a court in one Member State contemplated the 'placement of child in institutional care or with a foster family' in another Member State. The basic motivation for the provisions was the same for both instruments, namely, to avoid a receiving State being faced with a *fait accompli* with regard to a cross-border placement of a child.[79]

---

[73] In CJEU, 26 April 2012, *Health Service Executive*, C-92/12 PPU, for example, the child (who was habitually resident in Ireland) needed to be placed and remain in a secure care institution, but because no institution in Ireland was considered able to meet those needs, it was thought best to place her in a secure care institution in England.

[74] This is one of the examples cited by M. TARRAGONA in 'Cross-Border Child Placement' in C. HONORATI, above n. 11, pp. 293, 303. Note also the practice (referred to in the *Cross-border Study* (see n. 75 below, at para. 3) of placing German children in structures which are located in other Member States, but which are run by German citizens.

[75] Commissioned by the Policy Department for Citizens' Rights and Constitutional Affairs Directorate-General for Internal Policies, at the request of the JURI Committee and written by L. CARPANETO, EU, 2016, http://www.europarl.europa.eu/supporting-analyses.

[76] Ibid., para. 2.1.

[77] Ibid., para. 2.1.

[78] See ECJ, 27 November 2007, *C*, C-435/06, discussed in Chapter 1 at 1.24 et seq.

[79] See the Explanatory Report ('the Lagarde Report') to the 1996 Hague Child Protection Convention, para. 127.

11.43. When it was first introduced, Article 56 attracted little attention and was not specifically mentioned in the original Guidance on the Regulation (2005). However, it soon became apparent that in practice this provision was of some importance but was time-consuming for Central Authorities. It was more extensively dealt with in the 2014 *Practice Guide on Brussels II-bis*.[80] As practice developed, notwithstanding that certain aspects had been clarified by the CJEU in *Health Service Executive*,[81] it became clear that a number of issues relating to both the scope (did it apply to placements of children with another family member, such as grandparents?) and procedure (in particular, the absence of a consent mechanism and of any time limit when responding to a request) under Article 56 needed addressing. These and other problems were underscored by the *Cross-border Study*, which looked at the practice in 12 Member States, which confirmed that the application of Article 56 was by no means uniform and was in need of reform.

11.44. As discussed below, many of the practice issues identified as arising under Article 56 Brussels II-bis have been addressed by Brussels II-ter. However, a number of issues raised by the *Cross-border Study*, in particular those concerning jurisdiction, the power to amend placement orders, and the issue of costs have not been specifically addressed.[82]

B. THE POSITION UNDER ARTICLE 82

1. *The Scope of Article 82*

11.45. Placements of children from one Member State to another are governed by Article 82. Under Article 82(1):

> Where a court or competent authority contemplates the placement of a child in another Member State, it shall first obtain the consent of the competent authority in that other Member State.

---

[80] Above, n. 25. For legal analyses of Article 56 Brussels II-bis, see, for example, M. HERRANZ BALLESTEROS, 'El acogimiento transfronterizo en la propuesta de refundición del Reglamento Bruselas II bis' (2017) No 44 *La Ley Unión Eurpea*; and L. PINHEIRO, 'Article 55', in U. MAGNUS and P. MANKOWSKI (eds) *Brussels II bis Regulation*, OttoSchmidt, 2017, pp. 452–455.

[81] CJEU, 26 April 2012, *Health Service Executive*, C-92/12 PPU. For a valuable commentary on this decision, see A. DUTTA and A. SCHULZ, 'First Cornerstones of the EU Rules on Cross-Border Child Cases: The Jurisprudence of the Court of Justice of the European Union on the Brussels IIA Regulation From C to Health Service Executive' (2014) 10 *Journal of Private International Law* 1. See also M. WILDERSPIN, *European Private International Family Law. The Brussels IIb Regulation*, Oxford University Press, 2023, pp. 428 et seq, paras 9–027 et seq.

[82] Another suggestion by the *Cross-border Study* (above n. 75, pp. 75–76, para. 5.3.4) not taken up was to have specific provisions to protect runaway children.

Article 82 only applies as between Member States and not third States, but in the latter case, if the receiving third State is a party to the 1996 Hague Child Protection, then Article 33 of the Convention applies.[83] On the other hand, it has been pointed out[84] that Article 82 can apply in cases involving three Member States – that is, where Member State A is entitled to care for a child habitually resident in Member State B, but contemplates the placement of the child in Member State C.

11.46. Article 82(1) is wider than its predecessor inasmuch as it applies both to courts **and** to competent authorities and to 'placements' rather than 'placements in institutional care or with a foster family'. In both these respects, this wider application was agreed upon during the negotiations following the EU Commission's Proposal.[85]

11.47. What is meant by 'competent authority' in this context is not spelt out by Brussels II-ter, but having regard to the CJEU ruling in *Health Service Executive*,[86] with regard to the application of Article 56 Brussels II-bis to the obtaining of consent to a placement **from** a competent authority, it is clear that it must be an authority 'governed by public law'. An obvious example is a child welfare agency.

11.48. There is no definition in the Regulation of 'placement' for the purposes of Article 82, except that Article 82(2) does not include placement with a parent, while it is left to individual Member States to determine whether it applies to placements with close relatives (see further 11.58 below). As already noted, unlike Article 56 Brussels II-bis, Article 82 is not expressly confined to placements in institutional or foster care. On other hand, Recital (84) is so confined and this has led one commentator to say[87] that this makes it clear that the scope of Article 82 is no narrower than was the case previously, 'but it is unclear whether it is identical'. Further, given their exclusion from the Regulation generally,[88] it is clear that placements with a view to adoption and educational placements following a punishable act under national criminal law (but not educational placements for the protection of the child) fall outside Article 82.[89]

---

[83] For more on this, see N. Lowe and M. Nicholls, *The 1996 Hague Convention on the Protection of Children*, Jordans, 2012, paras 6.9 et seq.
[84] By O. Knöfel, above n. 1, p. 386, para. 4.
[85] Cf. the Commission's proposed Article 65(1), which essentially replicated Article 56(1) Brussels II-bis.
[86] CJEU, 26 April 2012, *Health Service Executive*, C-92/12 PPU, para. 95.
[87] M. Wilderspin, above n. 81, p. 428, para. 9-026.
[88] That is, under Article 1(4).
[89] See the chart on p. 215, para. 7.3.1 of the *2022 Practice Guide*. However, this does not mean that consent is not required, but that will be governed by different legislation. See further O. Knöfel, above n. 1, p. 578, para. 6 on the application of Article 82 to a short stay abroad.

11.49. Article 82 makes no reference to any jurisdictional requirement.[90] But, as the *Health Service Executive* case[91] establishes, it must nevertheless be the case that a court can only make recognisable and enforceable orders if it has jurisdiction according to the criteria set out by the Regulation and that competent authorities can only have *locus standi* over children habitually resident or present in the State.[92]

11.50. Brussels II-ter does not incorporate the suggestion in the *Cross-border Study*[93] that in cases of cross-border placements lasting more than one year, the courts of the Member State of origin should retain full jurisdiction as for the placement during the first one-year period following the move to the receiving State, but after that period, the courts of the receiving State should be recognised as having jurisdiction on the placement to check the adequacy of the solution of care provided. There can be different views on the merits of this suggestion: on the one hand, it addresses a problem that the Regulation does not directly deal with and does so in a simple and straightforward way; on the other hand, the 'solution' could be seen as being too rigid. At all events, the receiving competent authority is not powerless to act under Brussels II-ter. In cases of urgency, it can use the powers under Article 15 to take provisional (including protective) measures to protect the child (these powers are discussed in Chapter 4) and, in any event,[94] it could request a transfer of jurisdiction under Article 13 (as discussed in Chapter 4). These are more flexible remedies that might better suit the child's interests.

11.51. Another suggestion[95] of the *Cross-border Study* that has not been incorporated into Brussels II-ter is that there should be an express mechanism allowing for an adjustment of a cross-border placement order, where such an adjustment is necessary for the practical implementation of the order. As the *Study* pointed out, this would be a useful provision, given that, generally speaking, decisions concerning children and parental responsibility are held *rebus sic stantibus*, that is, in specific conditions and at a particular moment. This seemed a useful suggestion, but it was not taken up in Brussels II-ter.

---

[90] In this respect Article 82(1) differs from the Commission's proposed Article 65(1), which included the words 'having jurisdiction under the Regulation'.
[91] CJEU, 26 April 2012, *Health Service Executive*, C-92/12 PPU. See further below at 11.67 et seq.
[92] But note Recital (84), which refers to 'a decision on the placement of a child in institutional or foster care is being contemplated in the Member State of the habitual residence of the child'.
[93] Above n. 75, p. 66, para. 5.3.2.4.
[94] Indeed, in some cases the competent authority might have jurisdiction on the basis of Article 10, that is, based on the child's presence in cases where his or her habitual residence cannot be established. See further Chapter 4.
[95] Above n. 75, p. 73, para. 5.3.2.6, which draws on Article 11 of Regulation (EU) No 606/2013 on mutual recognition and protection measures in civil matters OJ L 181/4.

2. The Procedural Framework: the Recital (84) Guidance

11.52. It needs to be appreciated that **Article 82 provides the procedural framework** according to which such placements should be made. **It is not concerned with providing substantive provision governing the making of placements**, which, in any event, is not within the EU's remit to control. In other words, Brussels II-ter does not affect national law or procedure applicable to any placement decision made by the court or by a competent authority in the Member State contemplating the placement. Indeed, Brussels II-ter does not place any obligation on the authorities of the Member State having jurisdiction to place the child in the other Member State or further involve that Member State in the placement decision or proceedings.[96]

11.53. Notwithstanding that Brussels II-ter make no substantive provision for the making of placement decisions, Recital (84) provides useful guidance on what considerations should be taken into account when making such decisions, bearing in mind that the overarching principle is that the best interests of the child should remain the paramount consideration. The Recital emphasises that where a placement decision is being contemplated in the Member State of the child's habitual residence, the court should consider, at the earliest stage of the proceedings, what 'appropriate measures' it should take to ensure respect of the rights of the child, in particular the right to preserve the child's identity and the right to maintain contact with the parents, or, where appropriate, with other relatives, in the light of Articles 8, 9 and 20 UNCRC. In the Commission's Proposal,[97] mention was also be made of Article 24(3) of the EU Charter of Fundamental Rights (the right to maintain personal contact with the parents) and it was added that when considering solutions, 'due regard should be paid to the desirability of continuity in the child's upbringing and to the child's ethnic, religious, cultural and linguistic background'. This seems to be useful advice.

11.54. So far as 'appropriate measures' are concerned, Recital (84) makes the important point that where the court is aware of a close connection of the child with another Member State,[98] such measures could include, pursuant to Article 37(b) of the Vienna Convention on Consular Relations 1963,[99] notifying the consular body of that Member State. Such measures can also

---

[96] See Recital (84).
[97] See the proposed Recital (51).
[98] Such awareness might also be raised by information provided by the Central Authority of that other Member State. See Article 82(3), referred to in 11.56 below.
[99] Under this provision, there is an obligation on the competent authorities of the receiving State to inform the competent consular post without delay of any case where the **appointment of a guardian** appears to be in the interests of a minor or other person lacking full capacity who is a national of the sending State. See also the *2022 Practice Guide*, pp. 218–219, para. 7.3.2.

include making a request, as provided for by Brussels II-ter,[100] to that other Member State for information about a parent, a relative or other persons who could be suitable to care for the child, and, depending on the circumstances, requesting information on procedures and decisions concerning a parent or siblings of the child.

3. *The Consent Requirement: the General Position*

11.55. An important part of the procedural framework under Brussels II-ter is the consent requirement. Unlike Article 56 Brussels II-bis, which only required the court to 'consult', Article 82(1) Brussels II-ter requires a court or a competent authority **contemplating the placement of a child in another Member State, to first obtain the consent of the competent authority in that other Member State**. Additionally, under Article 82(5), placements should only be ordered or arranged by the requesting Member State **after** the competent authority of the requested Member State has consented to the placement. What this means is that there needs to be prior consent to the contemplated placement in general and to the specific placement or arrangement.[101] The consent required is that of the relevant 'competent authority'. As already noted, there is no definition of 'competent authority', but again relying on the CJEU ruling on the scope of Article 56 Brussels II-bis in the *Health Service Executive* case,[102] it is clear that it must be an authority 'governed by public law'. Apart from a court, an obvious example is the relevant child welfare agency, but it might be different for a proposed compulsory health placement. One may wonder why the Regulation did not require Member States to notify the Commission which authorities are competent for the purposes of Article 82, according to the procedure set out by Article 103.

11.56. In a new provision, which was added during the negotiations following the Commission's Proposal, Article 82(3) provides:

> The Central Authority of another Member State may inform a court or competent authority which contemplates a placement of a child of a close connection of the child with that Member State. This shall not affect the national law and procedure of the Member State contemplating the placement.

What this means is that, to the limited extent of informing of the child's close connection, it allows other Member States to intervene in the domestic family procedures of the Member State contemplating the placement, albeit that it does

---

[100] That is, under Article 80, discussed above at 11.28 et seq.
[101] Article 56(2) Brussels II-bis also required consent to the making of a judgment on placement.
[102] CJEU, 26 April 2012, *Health Service Executive*, C-92/12 PPU, para. 95.

not affect the latter State's law and procedure. This provision has not escaped criticism inasmuch as it is suggested that it may result in a whole new workload for Central Authorities and, on the basis that a 'close connection of the child to its State' effectively means nationality, that such Authorities are being asked to 'perform a sort of consular role'.[103]

11.57. Although Article 82(1) makes no mention of the need for prior consultation (unlike Brussels II-bis Article 56), Recital (83) states that 'a consultation procedure for obtaining consent should be carried out prior to a placement'. In any event, the need for prior consultation is implicit in Article 82(8), which permits Central Authorities or competent authorities to enter into or maintain existing agreements or arrangements with Central Authorities or competent authorities of other Member States 'simplifying the consultation procedure for obtaining consent in their mutual relations'.

4. *The Position with Regard to Placements with Parents or Relatives*

11.58. An uncertainty of the former procedure was whether it applied to placements with family members. This is resolved by Article 82(2), which provides that, in any event, **no consent is required where the child is to be placed with a parent**. Additionally, Member States have the discretion to decide that no consent is required in the case of placements with certain other categories of close relatives. These categories must be communicated to the Commission pursuant to Article 103. At the time of writing, Austria, Croatia, Cyprus, Ireland, Portugal and Slovakia have notified the Commission that no consent is required for placements with grandparents, uncles/aunts and certain siblings.[104] As the *2022 Practice Guide* points out,[105] these designations only have a unilateral effect such that while they must observed by another Member State contemplating a placement, there is no reciprocal obligation of the 'placing State' to adopt a similar position.

5. *Obtaining Consent*

11.59. Under Article 82(1), the Central Authority of the requesting Member State must, when seeking consent, 'provide a report on the child together with the reasons for the proposed placement or provision of care, information on any contemplated funding and any other information it considers relevant, such as the expected duration of the placement'. Further, pursuant to Article 82(4), the

---

[103] See M. ŽUPAN, C. HÖHN and U. KLUTH, above n. 4, p. 196.
[104] It should be noted that in Latvia, special rules apply to placements for less than three months with one parent's consent. For further details, see the European Justice Portal, above n. 16.
[105] *2022 Practice Guide*, p. 216, para. 7.3.1.1.

request and additional documents must be accompanied by a translation into the official language or one of the official languages or any other language that the requested Member State expressly accepts.[106]

11.60. The obligation to provide a report on the child, when seeking the consent of the requested Member State is new to Brussels II-ter and brings it into line with the requirement under the equivalent provision (Article 33 of the 1996 Hague Child Protection Convention).[107] As Brussels II-ter is silent on who should draw up the report and what it should contain, these matters are for national law to determine. However, in general terms, it will be for the court or competent authority seeking the placement to provide the report, which will in turn normally be written by a social worker. The report should contain at least basic details about the child's background, needs and his or her current situation. In the final analysis, the report should convey sufficient information to enable the requested authority to make an informed decision. There is no obligation under Brussels II-ter for the authority of placement to provide any follow-up report on the child, but that no doubt can be a matter for negotiation in any particular case.

11.61. Recital (83) makes some important additional points. First, it states that the report on the child should include 'the expected duration of the placement' and be 'supplemented by any other information which the requested Member State might consider pertinent such as any envisaged supervision of the measure, arrangements for contact with the parents, other relatives or other persons with whom the child has a close relationship, or the reasons why such contact is not contemplated in light of Article 8 of the European Convention for the Protection of Human Rights and Fundamental Freedoms'.

11.62. Second, the Recital deals with the issue of **time-limited consent** which had previously been the subject of the CJEU ruling in *Health Service Executive*.[108] The Court ruled that where the placement is contemplated for a brief period, the consent given to that placement cannot, upon the expiry of that period, have any effect, unless any extensions of that period have been authorised.[109] Consequently, an application for fresh consent is required for any subsequent extensions of the placement. By the same token, any decision on enforcement is strictly limited to the period of time stated in the judgment. To overcome the disadvantages associated with having to obtain a series of consents

---

[106] For details on this, see European Justice Portal, above n. 16.
[107] On which, see H. SETRIGHT, D WILLIAMS, I. CURRY-SUMNER, M. GRATION and M. WRIGHT, *International Issues in Family Law – The 1996 Hague Convention on the Protection of Children and Brussels IIa*, Jordans, Family Law, 2015, p. 216.
[108] CJEU, 26 April 2012, *Health Service Executive*, C-92/12 PPU. See further 11.67, below.
[109] Ibid., paras 134–146.

of short duration, the Court suggested[110] that the court of the requesting State should request consent for an adequate length of time, but without prejudice to being entitled, within the period covered by the consent, to reduce the length of the placement, according the best interests of the child. Reflecting this decision, Recital (83) states:

> where consent to placement has been given for a specified period of time, that consent should not apply to decisions or arrangements extending the duration of the placement. In such circumstances, a new request for consent should be made.

Although this is an important and pertinent point, one might question why the time-limited point is not included in the text of the Regulation.

11.63. The above provisions bring much-needed clarity to the required consent process. First, this means that **all requests for consent have to be channelled through the requesting Central Authority.** Second, they spell out that requests should include a report on the child and the reasons for the proposed placement or provision of care. This goes some way towards addressing the former uncertainty as to what information is required when making a request.

11.64. It is left to each Member State to determine the procedure for obtaining consent,[111] but as Recital (83) notes:

> in line with the case-law of the Court of Justice,[112] Member States should establish clear rules and procedures for the purposes of consent to be obtained pursuant to this Regulation, in order to ensure legal certainty and expedition. The procedures should, inter alia, enable the competent authority to grant or refuse its consent promptly.

This need for promptness is vital if the child's best interests are to be ensured – in particular, as Recital (83) makes clear, **the absence of consent should not be understood as consent and that without consent, the placement should not take place.** Both these points are important and it would surely have been better for them to have been included in the text of the Regulation. It is a matter of debate as to whether the latter comment in Recital (83) is intended to say that placements **cannot** be made without consent as opposed to that they ought not to be. It is a pity that this point is not made clearer, but the spirit of Brussels II-ter points to the former interpretation.

---

[110] Ibid., para. 140.
[111] Article 82(7). Note also Article 82(8), which preserves the right of Central Authorities to enter into or maintain existing agreements or arrangements with other Central Authorities simplifying the consultation procedure.
[112] That is, CJEU, 26 April 2012, *Health Service Executive*, C-92/12 PPU.

6. Timing of Consent

11.65. A major criticism of the position under Brussels II-bis was that no time limit was express for responding to requests. This lacuna is now filled by Article 82(6), which provides:

> Except where exceptional circumstances make this impossible, the decision granting or refusing consent shall be transmitted to the requesting Central Authority **no later than three months**[113] following the receipt of the request. (Emphasis added)

11.66. This time period applies both to the giving and the refusing of consent. Article 82(6) is supplemented by Recital (85), which makes the point that as time is of the essence, 'all competent authorities should strive to provide the reply' more quickly than the three-month 'maximum timeframe'. Welcome as this time provision is, the point has been made[114] that by leaving the consent procedure to national law, in cases where the Central Authority is not the authority that gives consent according that law, means that an additional burden falls on the national legislator to provide for the transfer of the request to the competent authority and still to comply with the time limit.

7. Recognition and Enforcement of Placement Orders

11.67. Recognition and enforcement of placement orders is not dealt with by Article 82. Instead, it is necessary to apply Chapter IV of Brussels II-ter, which is discussed in Chapters 8 and 9. Recognition and enforcement of placement orders was an issue addressed by the CJEU in *Health Service Executive*,[115] which was the leading decision on Article 56 Brussels II-bis. This case concerned an Irish child, SC, who was habitually resident in Ireland, but whose mother lived in England (which, at that time, was part of a Member State). SC had been subject of a care order made in Ireland in favour of the Health Service Executive (which is the statutory authority in Ireland with responsibility for children taken into care in Ireland). She was a vulnerable child with exceptional protection needs and had a history of absconding from where she had been placed. There had also been repeated episodes of risk-taking, violence, aggression and self-harm. Her most recent placement in a secure care institution in Ireland had failed; her situation rapidly deteriorated and on several occasions she attempted to take her own life. Clinical professionals

---

[113] Note: in the Commission's Proposal, the timeframe was to be two months; see the proposed Article 64(6).
[114] See M. Župan, C. Höhn and U. Kluth, above n. 4, p. 196.
[115] CJEU, 26 April 2012, *Health Service Executive*, C-92/12 PPU.

were all agreed that SC needed to remain in a secure care institution, but that there was no institution in Ireland that could meet her specific needs. The Health Executive considered that SC's care, protection and welfare needs could only be met in England, particularly as SC continually expressed the wish to be near her mother. With that in mind, the Executive requested by interlocutory application that the Irish High Court order SC's placement in a particular secure institution in England. The Executive informed the Irish Central Authority of the proceedings before the High Court in accordance with Article 56 and insisted that the required consent to the placement, pursuant to Article 56, be obtained from the Central Authority for England and Wales. The Irish Central Authority duly wrote to the International Child Abduction and Contact Unit (ICACU) (the administrative unit that carries out the day-to-day administration of the Central Authority's role in England Wales on behalf of the Lord Chancellor) seeking consent as required by Article 56. The latter responded by sending a letter from the secure care institution confirming that it was able to offer SC a placement. The Irish High Court subsequently made an interlocutory order placing SC in a specific secure institution in England (a 'secure care' order) with provision for regular reviews of the placement and of SC's welfare The order declared that the consent required by what was then Article 56(2) had been given by the ICACU. On the basis of this order, the Executive transferred SC to England.

11.68. Although the Irish High Court declared that all parties to the proceedings, except the child herself, were agreed that a secure placement met the child's specific needs, it nevertheless had a number of concerns, in relation to which it made a reference to the CJEU, including recognition and enforcement.

11.69. The CJEU held[116] that the placement procedure does **not** operate to override the normal rules of recognition and enforcement. In this respect, the ruling applies to the Article 82 procedure in Brussels II-ter. With regard to recognition, placement orders are to be recognised without any special procedure being required in accordance with what is now Article 30, which in turn embodies the fundamental principle of mutual recognition of judicial decisions as stated in Recital (3).[117] Recognition can only refused on one of the grounds exhaustively listed in Article 39, but that includes, in paragraph (1)(f), cases in which the Article 82 procedure has not been complied with.[118]

---

[116] See paras [100]–[106].
[117] Recital (3) Brussels II-ter embellishes Recital (3) Brussels II-bis (which had been described as the 'cornerstone for the creation of a genuine judicial area'; see CJEU 15 July 2010, *Purrucker 1*, C-256/09, para. 70).
[118] This ground would have been abolished under the Commission's Proposal; see the proposed Article 38 and the discussion in Chapter at 8.115–8.116. The general grounds for refusing recognition are discussed at 8.105 et seq.

11.70. The CJEU ruling has less relevance to the question of enforcement since, as is discussed in Chapter 9, the *exequatur* stage in the enforcement of **any** decision relating to parental responsibility has been abolished. Nevertheless, the CJEU ruling that the normal rules of enforcement apply to placement orders remains pertinent, even if these rules have changed. The appropriate procedure for seeking or opposing enforcement of placement orders under the Regulation is discussed in Chapter 9. Suffice it to say here that for enforcement purposes under Brussels II-ter, a placement order is a 'non-privileged' order.

8. Costs

11.71. As discussed at 11.10 above, there is a general provision under Article 83 that Central Authorities must bear their own costs when applying the Regulation,[119] However, the *Cross-border Study* proposed[120] making a specific provision with regard to placements such that each Central Authority or other authority of public law shall bear its own costs. However, the requesting Member State and the requested Member State are free to enter into an agreement concerning the allocation of charges. This proposal is not included in Brussels II-ter. Nevertheless, there is nothing to prevent Member States from entering into such an agreement.

---

[119] Assistance provided by Central Authorities pursuant to the Regulation must be free of charge: Article 83(1).
[120] Above n. 75, p. 75, para. 5.3.2.6.

CHAPTER 12

THE RELATIONSHIP BETWEEN THE EU AND THE UK

I. Introduction... 400
II. The Withdrawal Agreement..................................... 401
   A. General Application of the Agreement to Matrimonial Matters
      and to Matters of Parental Responsibility....................... 401
      1. The Overall Position...................................... 401
      2. The Territorial Scope of Article 67........................... 402
      3. 'Institution of Proceedings'................................. 402
   B. The Specific Application of Article 67........................... 403
      1. Jurisdiction... 403
      2. Recognition and Enforcement.............................. 404
      3. The Application to Child Abduction......................... 405
   C. The UK Perspective... 406
III. The Post-Transition Position..................................... 407
   A. Matrimonial Matters.. 408
      1. The 1970 Hague Convention................................ 409
      2. The Position where the 1970 Hague Convention does not
         Apply.. 411
         a) The Position in Member States........................... 411
         b) The Position in the UK.................................. 411
   B. Matters of Parental Responsibility.............................. 415
      1. The 1996 Hague Child Protection Convention................ 416
         i) The Position in Member States............................ 416
         ii) The Position in the UK.................................. 417
         iii) Some Critical Differences between Applying the 1996
            Convention and Brussels II-ter........................ 420
   C. Child Abduction... 423

I. INTRODUCTION

12.1. The UK is unique in being a **former Member State**. It formally left the EU on 31 January 2020 (which, in the UK, is known as 'exit day').[1] Accordingly, **the UK is neither bound by nor subject to Brussels II-ter**.[2] However, under the terms of the **European Withdrawal Agreement**[3] (hereinafter 'the Withdrawal Agreement'), provision was made for the continued application of EU law (principally so far as family law is concerned: Brussels II-bis) to the UK during what the Agreement refers to as the 'transition period'[4] (which, in the UK, is known as the 'implementation period').[5] This period ended on 31 December 2020.[6] In the UK, this is known as 'IP completion day'.[7]

12.2. As family law matters are not covered by the EU–UK Trade and Cooperation Agreement 2020,[8] and in the absence of any agreed particularised regime for family law, the Withdrawal Agreement is the only instrument that deals with family law issues following the UK's exit from the EU. Useful but non-binding advice on the operation of the Withdrawal Agreement has been issued by the EU Commission's 'Notice to Stakeholders on the Withdrawal of the United Kingdom and the EU rules in the Field of Civil Justice and Private International Law' (27 August 2020) (hereinafter 'the Commission Notice').[9]

12.3. Following the above events and arrangements, for the purposes of family matters, while the UK became a third State on 31 January 2020, it continued

---

[1] See the European Union (Withdrawal) Act 2018, s 20 of which defines 'exit day' as 31 January 2020 at 11 pm (GMT), which was midnight (CET).

[2] But that is not say that the UK is not affected by the Regulation. Like any other Contracting State to the 1996 Hague Child Protection Convention, it 'benefits' from Article 97; see further below at 12.23 and 12.46–12.47.

[3] Agreement on the withdrawal of the United Kingdom of Great Britain and Northern Ireland from the European Union and the European Atomic Energy Community, OJ L29, 31.1.2020, p. 7 (2019/C 384 I/01).

[4] See Article 2(e).

[5] See s 1A(6) of the European Union (Withdrawal) Act 2018 (as inserted by the European Union (Withdrawal Agreement) Act 2020.

[6] See Article 126 of the Agreement. Bearing in mind that Article 2(e) defines 'day' as a 'calendar day', the transition period could be regarded as having ended on 31 December 2020 at midnight according to the time operating in each individual Member State. However it should be noted that the Irish legislation, Part 19 of the Withdrawal of the United Kingdom from the European Union (Consequential Provisions) Act 2020, came into force with regard to the recognition of divorces, etc. at 11 pm on 31 December 2020, to coincide with the ending of the transition period in the UK: SI 2020/693, referred to by S. FENNELL, 'Brexit: Persistent Problems and Proposed Solutions: Family and Hague Law Cases' [2022] *International Family Law* 45.

[7] See s 39(1) of the European Union (Withdrawal Agreement) Act 2020, which defines 'IP completion day' as 31 December 2020 at 11 pm (GMT).

[8] Trade and cooperation agreement of 30 December 2020 between the European Union and the European Atomic Energy Community, of the one part, and the United Kingdom of Great Britain and Northern Ireland, of the other part, OJ L149, 30.4.2021, p. 10.

[9] EU Commission, Brussels, 27 August 2020 REV2.

to be bound by Brussels II-bis until 31 December 2020 and still is with regard to determining any proceedings pending, responding to requests received by the Central Authority[10] as of that date and to recognising or enforcing any judgment[11] made by a court of a Member States in proceedings in the transition period. This obligation is fully reciprocal, which means that courts of Member States are similarly bound to apply Brussels II-bis when determining proceedings brought by the UK under the Regulation before the ending of the transition period and with respect to the recognition and enforcement of a UK judgment made during that period. Similarly, a Central Authority of a Member State should apply Brussels II-bis to requests received from the UK during the transition period.

12.4. Insofar as the Withdrawal Agreement provides for the continued application of Brussels II-bis when determining cases concerning matrimonial matters or matters of parental responsibility that were pending as of 31 December 2020, it is of temporary and dwindling importance. However, with regard to the recognition and enforcement, the Agreement has long-term significance.

12.5. For **proceedings instituted after the end of the transition/implementation period (i.e. on or after 1 January 2021)**, the UK courts and those of Member States when dealing with the UK can no longer apply Brussels II-bis and, as noted above, the UK is neither bound by nor subject to Brussels II-ter. What this means is that when dealing with EU–UK cases, alternative means of dealing with them must be sought.

II. THE WITHDRAWAL AGREEMENT

A. GENERAL APPLICATION OF THE AGREEMENT TO MATRIMONIAL MATTERS AND TO MATTERS OF PARENTAL RESPONSIBILITY

1. The Overall Position

12.6. A formal agreement, the Withdrawal Agreement, was reached between Member States and the UK dealing with the many consequences of the latter's departure from the EU. Article 67 deals with matrimonial matters and matters of

---

[10] It should be noted that there are separate Central Authorities for England and Wales, Scotland and Northern Ireland.

[11] Article 2(4) Brussels II-bis defines 'judgment' as meaning divorce, legal separation, marriage annulment and judgments relating to parental responsibility. It should be noted that the term 'judgment' has been replaced by the term 'decision' in Brussels II-ter; see Chapter 1 at 1.18.

parental responsibility. This Article preserves, as between the UK and Member States, the application of Brussels II-bis with regard to legal proceedings instituted before the end of the transition period. It makes provision for the continuing recognition and enforcement of judgments made in legal proceedings under the Regulation and of authentic instruments formally drawn up or registered and court settlements approved or concluded before the end of the transition period.[12] Article 67 also provides for the continued application of the Maintenance Regulation,[13] which is an issue that often arises together with matters of parental responsibility.[14]

2. *The Territorial Scope of Article 67*

12.7. Article 67 provides for the continued application of Brussels II-bis as between the UK and Member States in situations involving the UK. As the Commission Notice says, the phrase 'situations involving the UK' is 'a formulation, which reflects the fact that the Withdrawal Agreement is based on reciprocal application and only applies in the EU-UK relationship'.[15]

12.8. The continued application of Brussels II-bis as provided for by Article 67 only applies as between the UK, which means England and Wales, Scotland and Northern Ireland,[16] and EU Member States, but does not include Denmark, which has never been a party to Brussels II-bis.[17]

3. *'Institution of Proceedings'*

12.9. For the purposes of jurisdiction, recognition and enforcement, Article 67 applies 'in respect of legal proceedings instituted before the end of the transition period'.[18] Although according to the Commission's Notice[19] the notion of

---

[12] It provides for the continuation of the cooperation provisions under Chapter IV with regard to requests and applications received by Central Authorities before the end of the transition period; see Article 67(1)(c), 67(2)(b) and 67(3)(a).
[13] Regulation (EC) No 4/2009.
[14] Maintenance falls outside the scope of this work, but for discussion of some the issues concerning the application of the Agreement, see E. JONES, 'Cross-border conflicts in the courts' [2022] *International Family Law* 113, 117–119.
[15] Above n. 9, para. 1.1, fn. 9.
[16] It does **not** apply to the Channel Islands, Isle of Man or Gibraltar and various Sovereign Bases to which the other parts of the Agreement can apply, as per Article 3.
[17] In other respects, the Agreement does apply to Denmark as per Article 2(b). It should be noted that as the Commission Notice (para. 1, n. 7) advises that while the EU Treaties provide for specific arrangements for the (non-)participation of Ireland in this part of the EU *acquis*, for the sake of simplicity, the notion of 'EU Member States' is used.
[18] See Article 67(1) and (2)(b).
[19] Commission Notice, para. 1.1. This is part of the general drafting strategy in Title VI of Part Three of the Withdrawal Agreement (of which Article 67 is a part) of using, where appropriate, the terminology of EU instruments in civil and judicial matters.

'proceedings instituted' is taken from Article 66(1) Brussels I-bis,[20] the same terminology is also used in the transitional provisions in Brussels II-bis.[21] However, as with those transitional provisions, when legal proceedings can be said to be 'instituted' is not defined, nor is reference made to Article 16 Brussels II-bis, which defines when a court is 'seised'. Notwithstanding this latter omission, there seems to be an obvious analogy between instituting legal proceedings and seising the court, and we submit that Article 67 should be interpreted by reference to the notion of 'seising' as given by each relevant instrument.[22] Applying Article 16 Brussels II-bis, this would mean (subject to the applicant not subsequently failing to have service effected on the respondent or to have the document lodged with the court) either at the time when the document instituting the proceedings or an equivalent document has been lodged with the court, or, if the document has to be served before being lodged with the court, at the time when it is received by the authority responsible for its service.[23] Nevertheless, the matter is not settled and there is the potential for different States to have different interpretations,[24] and such a clash could mean expensive parallel litigation, albeit that this is only likely to arise in a handful of cases. While the CJEU might be called upon to make a ruling in this respect either specifically on the application of Article 67 or on the analogous issue in the transitional provisions of Article 100 Brussels II-ter, any such ruling will not be binding on the UK, though the UK courts can and, in the authors' view should, have regard to it.[25]

B. THE SPECIFIC APPLICATION OF ARTICLE 67

1. Jurisdiction

12.10. Under Article 67(1), the EU rules on jurisdiction (in this case, those under Brussels II-bis) not only apply in respect of legal proceedings instituted before the end of the transition period but also to 'proceedings or actions that are related to such legal proceedings' pursuant to Article 19 of Brussels II-bis.

---

[20] Regulation (EU) No 1215/2012 on jurisdiction and the recognition and enforcement of judgments in civil and commercial matters (recast).
[21] See Article 64(1). The same wording is also used in Article 100(1) Brussels II-ter, which is discussed in Chapter 1 at 1.93 et seq.
[22] This is in line with our suggested interpretation of the similarly worded Article 100 Brussels II-ter; see Chapter 1 at 1.93.
[23] For the meaning of 'seising' under Article 17 Brussels II-ter, which is the sane as under Brussels II-bis, except that it also deals with proceedings instituted on its own motion; see Chapter 2 at 2.3 et seq.
[24] E. JONES, above, n. 14, p. 114.
[25] See s 6 of the European Union (Withdrawal) Act 2018, as amended.

This means that, as the Commission Notice advises,[26] the Agreement will continue to apply even if such related proceedings or actions are instituted after the end of the transition period.

12.11. According to the Notice, the inclusion of related proceedings or actions 'addresses situations where proceedings involving the same cause of action and between the same parties are brought in the courts of a Member State and the United Kingdom ("lis pendens") before and after the end of the transition period respectively (or vice-versa)'. The aim in these cases is to ensure that 'the EU rules on conflict of jurisdictions continue to apply where the court has been seised after the end of the transition period in an EU Member State or in the United Kingdom'.[27]

12.12. In fact, Article 19 Brussels II-bis does not refer to the concept of 'related proceedings', but, as was discussed in Chapter 5 in relation to its replacement by Article 20 Brussels II-ter (which is similarly worded in relation to legal proceedings), for these purposes at least, the distinction between parallel and related proceedings, which is common under many national laws, is irrelevant in the context of EU proceedings.[28] In essence, what the Agreement covers are parallel matrimonial proceedings and those relating to parental responsibility concerning the same child and involving the same course of action.[29]

2. Recognition and Enforcement

12.13. Article 67(2)(b) applies Brussels II-bis to the recognition and enforcement of judgments given in legal proceedings instituted, to documents formally drawn up or registered as authentic instruments, and to agreements concluded before the end of the transition period. In other words, **the continued application of Brussels II-bis is dependent on when the proceedings, etc. were instituted and not from the time of the decision.** This position reflects that under the transitional provisions under Article 64 Brussels II-bis. The inclusion of authentic instruments[30] and agreements as well as judgments is to be noted. This inclusion has more significance from the point of view of many Member States than from the UK's perspective, since in the latter jurisdictions, authentic instruments as such are unknown, while agreements (apart from parental responsibility agreements) are generally embodied in court consent orders. Unlike Brussels II-ter,[31] under the Withdrawal Agreement, 'agreements' have to

---

[26] Commission Notice, para. 1.1.
[27] Commission Notice, para. 1.1.
[28] See Chapter 5 at 5.4.
[29] For further discussion of these concepts, see Chapter 5 at 5.16 et seq.
[30] For the meaning of 'authentic instruments', see Chapter 1 at 1.54 and, in more detail, Chapter 10.
[31] See Article 100(1), discussed in Chapter 1 at 1.93.

be concluded but not necessarily registered. However, they must be enforceable in the State in which they were concluded.[32]

12.14. The continued application of Brussels II-bis to the recognition and enforcement of orders, etc. means that the grounds for refusal of recognition or enforcement are those provided by Articles 22 and 23 of that Regulation.[33]

12.15. With regard to the enforcement of judgments, etc. concerning matters of parental responsibility covered by the Withdrawal Agreement, there is a continuing need to apply for enforcement according to national law.[34] The only exceptions to this double-track regime are the enforcement of access decisions and of orders for a child's return made under the override provisions in connection with applications made under the 1980 Hague Abduction Convention, as provided for by Articles 41 and 42 Brussels II-bis.[35]

3. The Application to Child Abduction

12.16. In the context of parental child abduction, Article 11 Brussels II-bis continues to apply to applications made under the 1980 Hague Abduction Convention within the transition period. An important consequence of this is that the 'override' provisions (discussed in Chapter 6)[36] have a wider scope of application than they now do among Member States under Brussels II-ter, inasmuch as they are triggered by a refusal to order the child's return based upon **any** of the grounds mentioned in Article 13 of the 1980 Hague Abduction Convention rather than only where the refusal to return is solely based either on a grave risk of harm or of an intolerable situation or on the child's objections to being returned.

12.17. There remains uncertainty as to whether return orders made under the 1980 Hague Abduction Convention during the transition period are recognisable or enforceable under Brussels II-bis. The argument that they may

---

[32] As per Article 46 Brussels II-bis.
[33] As pointed out in Chapter 1, at 1.95, while for matrimonial matters, the grounds provided by Article 22 Brussels II-bis are the same as those provided by Article 38 Brussels II-ter, with regard to judgments relating to parental responsibility, there are some important differences between Article 23 Brussels II-bis and Article 39 Brussels II-ter, not least that under the former, it is mandatory to refuse recognition and enforcement in any case where a ground can be established, whereas under the latter, a refusal is discretionary in certain circumstances.
[34] Cf. Article 34(1) Brussels II-ter, which abolished the *exequatur* stage in the enforcement of **any** decision relating to parental responsibility. See Chapter 9. But it is to be noted that, as pointed out J in *NJ v. JB* [2023] EWHC 1762 (Fam) at para. 13, there is no longer any prescribed procedure for recognising or enforcing orders made under Brussels II-bis during the transitional period as the relevant secondary legislation, Part 31 of the Family Procedure Rules 2010, no longer applies to such orders.
[35] These Articles are referred to in Chapter 9.
[36] The 'override provisions' are discussed in Chapter 6 at 6.96 et seq.

not be is that since Hague abduction proceedings do not directly concern the **substance** of parental responsibility, return orders could be regarded as falling outside the scope of Brussels II-bis.[37] However, this will only be relevant in the unusual case of so-called 'double abduction', that is, where, pending or subsequent to the decision ordering the child's return, the child is abducted from the State of refuge and relocated to a different Member State.

C. THE UK PERSPECTIVE

12.18. Notwithstanding that in any event under international law the Withdrawal Agreement is binding on the UK, *inter alia*, with regard to the continued application of Brussels II-bis, national legislation was still required in order for it have domestic legal effect.[38] The legislation which does this is the European Union (Withdrawal Agreement) Act 2020, which applies throughout the UK – that is, England, Wales, Scotland and Northern Ireland.

12.19. The legislative position is complicated inasmuch as the 2020 Act amends the European Union (Withdrawal) Act 2018, which was passed to deal with the legal consequences of the UK's withdrawal from the EU. The net result is that the continued application of Brussels II-bis during what the legislation refers to as the 'implementation period' is provided for in section 7A of the 2018 Act as inserted by the 2020 Act.[39] Note, however, should be taken of section 6(1) of the 2018 Act (as amended), which provides that a UK court (a) 'is not bound by any principles laid down, or any decisions made, on or after IP completion day[40] by the European Court' and (b) 'cannot refer any matter to the European Court on or after' that date. It also provides that the Charter of Fundamental Rights is not part of domestic law on or after IP completion day. However, section 6(2) provides that UK courts 'may have regard to anything done on or after IP completion day by the European Court'. Although under this latter provision

---

[37] See the discussion in Chapter 6 at 6.92. This uncertainty has been resolved in Article 2(1)(a) Brussels II-ter, which makes it clear that return orders under the Hague Abduction Convention are recognisable and enforceable under the Regulation.
[38] See the Explanatory Report to the 2020 Act.
[39] The position is further complicated by the need to have regard to secondary legislation, i.e. in the case of England and Wales, to the Jurisdiction and Judgments (Family) (Amendment etc) (EU Exit) Regulations 2019 (SI 2019/519), reg 8 as substituted by reg 5 of the Jurisdiction, Judgments and Applicable Law (Amendment) (EU Exit) Regulations 2020 (SI 2020/1574) and, in Scotland, to Part 6 of the Civil and Family Justice (EU Exit) (Scotland) (Amendment etc) Regulations 2020 (SSI 2020/441), which replaces reg 6 of the Judgments (Family, Civil Partnership and Marriage (Same Sex Couples)) (EU Exit) (Scotland) (Amendment etc) Regulations 2019 (SSI 2019/104).
[40] That is, the day on which the implementation period ended according to UK legislation: 11 pm, 31 December 2020.

UK courts have a discretion as to whether or not to follow any new CJEU ruling, it can reasonably be expected that courts will give serious consideration to such rulings and will be cautious in departing from them.

12.20. During the transition period, there have been some important UK decisions on the application of Brussels II-bis. In particular, in *Re X*,[41] it was held, applying Article 61(a) Brussels II-bis, that Article 19, which governs *lis pendens*, had to be applied in preference to Article 13 of the 1996 Hague Child Protection Convention whenever the child concerned was habitually resident in a Member State. On the facts,[42] this meant that because the child was habitually resident in England and Wales, then, notwithstanding that there were prior proceedings in Russia (which is a non- EU Hague State), neither the *lis pendens* provisions of Brussels II-bis nor those of the 1996 Convention could be applied. However, although that will remain the position under Brussels II-bis and therefore under the Withdrawal Agreement (should the issue ever arise) Article 97(2)(c) Brussels II-ter addresses this lacuna by providing that in such circumstances, Article 13 of the 1996 Convention applies.[43]

III. THE POST-TRANSITION POSITION

12.21. As the Commission Notice advises,[44] with regard to legal proceedings instituted after the end of the transition period (i.e. on or after 1 January 2021), Member States will determine their international jurisdiction on the basis of the relevant EU instruments, which in the case of matrimonial matters and matters of parental responsibility now means (except for Denmark) applying Brussels II-ter. The UK, on the other hand, is not bound by Brussels II-ter and will apply its national rules to determine jurisdiction. However, the EU rules do not apply with regard to the recognition and enforcement of UK decisions made in proceedings instituted after the end of the transition period. Instead, Member States must apply any relevant international Convention or, if there is no applicable Convention, the national rules of the Member State in which recognition or enforcement is sought.[45] The UK will likewise apply any relevant

---

[41] [2021] EWCA Civ 1305. See also *Re A (A Child)(Enforcement of Foreign Order)* [2022] EWCA Civ 904, which provides an interesting example of the application of Article 23 Brussels II-bis with regard to the non-enforcement of judgments relating to parental responsibility. These grounds are now provided by Article 39 Brussels II-ter; see Chapter 8 at 8.105 et seq and Chapter 9 at 9.49 et seq.
[42] See further Chapter 1 at 1.82.
[43] See further Chapter 1 at 1.83.
[44] Commission Notice, para. 1.2.
[45] See Commission Notice, para. 3.2.

international Convention or, if there is no applicable instrument, its own national rules to the recognition and enforcement of post-transition decisions made by Member States. None of the EU provisions concerning judicial cooperation[46] apply as between Member States and the UK, and, as the Commission Notice advises,[47] such procedures will have to be initiated either according to national law on judicial cooperation with third States or, in some instances, relevant international Conventions.

12.22. Although in these respects the UK's position is no different from any other third State, given its previous status as a Member State, the impact of its exit from the EU is considerable (all the more so in view of the hitherto high volume of family law cases between Member States and the EU) and it will take time for this to be regularised. The remainder of this chapter is intended to provide guidance on the major aspects of the post-Brexit legal relationship between Member States and the UK in matrimonial matters and in matters of parental responsibility.[48]

A. MATRIMONIAL MATTERS

12.23. The impact of the UK's exit from the EU with regard to matrimonial matters is profound. In particular, as between Member States and the UK, divorces are no longer automatically recognised, which means there is a need of a formal procedure for recognition. Unlike matters of parental responsibility where the 1996 Hague Child Protection Convention provides broadly similar rules to those under Brussels II-ter and to which all Member States and the UK are bound, there is no alternative international instrument dealing with matrimonial matters comparable to the Regulation and to which all Member States are bound. The major international instrument is the 1970 Hague Convention on the Recognition of Divorces and Legal Separations (hereinafter the 1970 Hague Convention), but not all Member States are bound by it (see 12.24 below) and, in any event, it is not as comprehensive as Brussels II-ter; in particular, being a recognition instrument only, it has no *lis pendens* provisions (see 12.25 below). Furthermore, notwithstanding that the UK is a Contracting State to the 1970 Convention, it has its own domestic rules on jurisdiction on such matters (see 12.32 et seq below).

---

[46] That is, those formerly contained in Chapter IV Brussels II-bis (and now Chapter V Brussels II-ter discussed in Chapter 11.
[47] Commission Notice, para. 5.
[48] For a brief summary of the position between the UK and Italy, see M. DE SANNA, 'The updated Landscape for cross-border family law cases post-Brexit – particularly in relation to Italy – UK Cases' [2023] *International Family Law* 40.

1. The 1970 Hague Convention

12.24. The 1970 Hague Convention is a useful instrument facilitating the recognition of divorce and legal separation as between Member States that are Contracting States to the Convention and the UK.[49] But there are two important limitations. First, not all Member States are Contracting States to the Convention. At the time of writing, Cyprus, the Czech Republic, Denmark,[50] Estonia, Finland, Italy, Luxembourg, the Netherlands, Poland, Portugal, Slovakia and Sweden **are Contracting States**.[51] Austria, Belgium, Bulgaria, Croatia, France, Germany, Greece, Hungary, Ireland, Latvia, Lithuania, Malta, Romania, Slovenia and Spain **are not**. In other words, less than half the Member States are bound by the 1970 Convention. The point has been made[52] that it is open to the EU to authorise all remaining Member States to accede to it unilaterally as it did in relation to the 1996 Hague Child Protection Convention.[53]

12.25. The second crucial limitation is that even where the Convention does apply as between a Member State and the UK, since it is only an instrument of recognition, it does not contain any *lis pendens* provisions, which leaves so-called forum battles unresolved. As one commentator put it,[54] the removal in the UK of the *lis pendens* provisions under (what was then) Brussels II-bis is one of the greatest challenges for the UK–EU relations going forward (see further 12.42 below).

12.26. It is not intended here to provide a comprehensive discussion of the 1970 Convention, but merely to highlight the following. As the Preamble states, the 1970 Convention is designed to facilitate the recognition of divorces and legal separations obtained in Contracting States. To that end, Article 1 applies the Convention to 'the recognition in one Contracting State of divorces and legal separations obtained in another Contracting State which follow judicial or other proceedings officially recognised in that State and which are legally effective there'. Beyond this, there is no definition of divorce or legal separations and, it will be noted, it does not apply to annulments. It has been suggested[55] that by not

---

[49] See Example 1 in the Commission Notice, para. 3.2.
[50] Since Denmark has never been bound by the Brussels II Regulations, the position as between it and the UK has not been changed in this respect by the UK's exit from the EU.
[51] It should be noted that the UK only accepted the accessions of Estonia and Poland on 29 October 2020. For further details, see P. BEAUMONT, 'Some reflections on the way ahead for UK private international law after Brexit' (2021) 17 *Journal of Private International Law* 1, fn. 6.
[52] See D. HODSON, *The International Family Law Practice*, 6th ed., Lexis Nexis, Family Law, 2021, para. 3.131.
[53] See Chapter 1 at 1.69, n. 146.
[54] E. JONES, above n. 14, p. 117.
[55] D. HODSON, above n. 52, para. 3.138.

preventing the application in a Contracting State of rules of law more favourable to the recognition of foreign divorces, Article 17 could allow for recognition of same-sex divorces. On the other hand, as Article 1 makes clear, the Convention 'does not apply to findings of fault or to ancillary orders pronounced on the making of a decree of divorce or legal separation; in particular, it does not apply to orders relating to pecuniary obligations or to the custody of children'.

12.27. Under Article 2, subject to specified grounds for refusal (see 12.29 below), such divorce or legal separations must be recognised if,[56] at the date of the institution of the proceedings in the State of origin:

(1) the respondent had his habitual residence[57] there; or
(2) the petitioner had his habitual residence there and one of the following further conditions was fulfilled -
   a) such habitual residence had continued for not less than one year immediately prior to the institution of proceedings;
   b) the spouses last habitually resided there together; or
(3) both spouses were nationals of that State; or
(4) the petitioner was a national of that State and one of the following further conditions was fulfilled -
   a) the petitioner had his habitual residence there; or
   b) he had habitually resided there for a continuous period of one year falling, at least in part, within the two years preceding the institution of the proceedings.[58]

12.28. Although these grounds differ in some respects from those under Article 3 Brussels II-ter (which Member State courts are bound to apply), by the same token, jurisdiction to grant divorce or separation under the Regulation falls within the Convention criteria, such that UK courts will be bound to recognise them, provided the State concerned is a Contracting State to the Convention. Equally, divorces and legal separations, granted in the UK under its domestic rules of jurisdiction (see 12.32 et seq below) fall within the Convention criteria and must be recognised by Member States bound by the Convention.

12.29. Contracting States **may** refuse to recognise a divorce when, at the time it was obtained, both the parties were nationals of States which did not provide for

---

[56] It should be noted that the Convention does not prescribe the grounds of jurisdiction so that States remain free to choose other grounds that would fall outside the criteria required for recognition. However, this issue does not arise as between Member States and the UK, since in each case the relevant jurisdictional rules fall within the Convention criteria; see 12.31 below.

[57] See Article 3, which says: 'Where the State of origin uses the concept of domicile as a test of jurisdiction in matters of divorce or legal separation, the expression "habitual residence" in Article 2 shall be deemed to include domicile as the term is used in that State.'

[58] Article 2(5) has been omitted as it deals with the position where divorce is not available in the State of origin, which, unlike in 1970, is not the case in any Member State.

divorce and of no other State (Article 7); lack of adequate notice of the divorce or separation proceedings or providing inadequate opportunity to present his or her case (Article 8); incompatibility with a previous decision determining the spouses' matrimonial status (Article 9); or if recognition is manifestly incompatible with the public policy of the State of recognition (Article 10). The procedure for issuing proceedings for recognition or non-recognition is governed by national law.

2. *The Position where the 1970 Hague Convention does not Apply*

a) The Position in Member States

12.30. So far as **jurisdiction** to make decisions in matrimonial matters is concerned, Member States (apart from Denmark) must, regardless of whether or not they are Contracting States to the 1970 Hague Convention, apply Chapter II, Section 1 Brussels II-ter (which is discussed in detail in Chapter 3).

12.31. So far as **recognising a UK divorce** or legal separation is concerned, Member States that are not party to the 1970 Convention must apply their national law on recognition.[59] Ireland, which has a close connection to the UK, but which is not a party to the 1970 Convention, has passed specific legislation to facilitate the recognition of certain divorces, legal separations and marriage annulments granted in England and Wales, Scotland, Northern Ireland and Gibraltar.[60]

b) The Position in the UK

12.32. In the UK, **jurisdiction** to hear divorce, nullity or legal separation proceedings is governed in all cases by domestic law, which, in the case of England and Wales and Scotland, means applying the Domicile and Matrimonial Proceedings Act 1973 and, in the case of Northern Ireland, the Matrimonial Causes (Northern Ireland) Order 1978. Both these Acts have been amended by secondary legislation to take account of the UK's withdrawal from the EU.

12.33. So far as **England and Wales** is concerned, the relevant provision is section 5 of the Domicile and Matrimonial Proceedings Act 1973. Formerly,

---

[59] See the Commission Notice, para. 3.2.
[60] That is, s 126 of the Withdrawal of the United Kingdom from the European Union (Consequential Provisions) Act 2020, which was brought into force by Article 2 of the Withdrawal of the United Kingdom from the European Union (Consequential Provisions) Act 2020 (Parts 17, 18, 19 and 20) (Commencement) Order 2020 (SI No 693 of 2020) on 31 December 2020 at 11 pm to coincide with the ending the transition period in the UK. Note also s 125 of the 2020 Act, which provided for the continuing recognition of UK divorces, legal separations and nullity of marriage granted before the ending of the transition period.

section 5(2)(a) gave jurisdiction to entertain proceedings for divorce and judicial separation[61] if the court had jurisdiction under Brussels II-bis. This had to be changed following the UK's withdrawal from the EU. However, as one commentary explains,[62] the 'Ministry of Justice sensibly took the view that, on implementation of exit from the EU, there should be as much continuity as possible with the divorce jurisdiction used by England and Wales' under Brussels II-bis. However, rather than simply repeating what was then Article 3 Brussels II-bis,[63] the amended version contains two important differences.

12.34. Under section 5(2), as amended,[64] a court has jurisdiction to entertain proceedings for divorce or judicial separation[65] if (and only if) on the date of the application: both parties to the marriage are habitually resident in England and Wales, or were last habitually resident in England and Wales and one of them continues to reside there, or the respondent is habitually resident in England and Wales; or, in the case of a joint application, either of the parties to the marriage is habitually resident in England and Wales. Subject to the gloss discussed at 12.35 below, these grounds match those under Brussels II-bis and Brussels II-ter. Similarly, section 5(2)(f), by which jurisdiction can be taken if both parties are domiciled in England and Wales, is aligned with both Brussels II-bis and Brussels II-ter (under which special provision is made, in the case of the UK and Ireland, for jurisdiction to be based on domicile rather than nationality).[66] However, section 5(2)(f) goes further than the Regulations by providing that jurisdiction can be based on **either** spouse's domicile.

12.35. Another critical difference is with regard to section 5(2)(d) of the 1973 Act by which, as now amended, the court has jurisdiction where 'the applicant is habitually resident in England and Wales and has resided there for at least one year immediately before the application was made' or, by section 5(2)(e) where 'the applicant is domiciled and habitually resident in England and Wales and has resided there for at least six months immediately before the application

---

[61] Section 5(3) provided a similar position with regard to nullity of marriage proceedings.
[62] D. Hodson and R. Bailey-Harris, 'The CJEU casts doubt on England's new post-Brexit divorce jurisdiction law' [2022] *International Family Law* 151, 154, also published in [2022] *Family Law* 852, 855.
[63] Substantially repeated in Article 3 Brussels II-ter.
[64] That is, as amended by para. 7 of the Schedule to the Jurisdiction and Judgments (Family) (Amendment etc.) (EU Exit) Regulations 2019 (SI 2019/519).
[65] Jurisdiction in respect of nullity proceedings is governed by s 5(3) as amended by para. 8 of the 2019 Regulation and is the same as divorce, etc., except that there is an additional ground where either of the parties died before the application was made, namely, that either was at the time of their death domiciled in England and Wales or had been habitually resident in England and Wales throughout the period of one year ending with the date of death.
[66] See Article 3(b) and 3(2) Brussels II-bis, and Article 3(b) in conjunction with Article 2(3) Brussels II-ter. For these purposes, 'domicile' has the same meaning as under the relevant national law.

was made'. It has been argued[67] that this position is at odds with the apparent position taken by the CJEU in *IB*,[68] since confirmed by the CJEU in *BM*,[69] that habitual residence has to be established throughout the requisite periods and not mere residence followed by habitual residence on the date that the divorce proceedings are launched. Given this interpretation,[70] this difference of approach could lead to parallel proceedings with no common lis pendens provisions[71] to resolve the conflict.[72] This is a potentially serious conflict, given that under the Matrimonial Causes Act 1973, section 23(1), along with divorce jurisdiction, the courts in England and Wales also have jurisdiction over associated property and financial disputes between the parties.

12.36. The position in **Northern Ireland** is the same as in England and Wales.[73] However, the position in **Scotland** is different, simpler and, in some respects, more in line with Brussels II-ter. The relevant provision is section 7 of the Domicile and Matrimonial Proceedings Act 1973. This, too, formerly defined jurisdiction by reference to Brussels II-bis, but has been amended,[74] so as to give jurisdiction where either of the parties to the marriage is domiciled in Scotland on the date when the action is begun, or was habitually resident in Scotland **throughout the period of one year** ending with that date. This latter ground is unambiguous. It should be noted that there are only the two grounds of jurisdiction for divorce or legal separation.[75]

12.37. **Recognition** of divorces, annulments and legal separations (hereinafter 'divorces etc') granted in a Member State that is not party to the 1970 Hague Convention following proceedings instituted on or after 1 January 2021 is governed throughout the UK by Part II of the Family Law Act 1986. It is not

---

[67] See D. Hodson and R. Bailey-Harris, above n. 62, pp. 155 and 856 respectively.
[68] CJEU, 25 November 2021, *IB*, C-298/20, discussed further in Chapter 3 at 3.19, n. 28.
[69] CJEU, 6 July 2023, *BM*, C-462/22.
[70] See the discussion in Chapter 3 at 3.19.
[71] The position is different with regard to matters of parental responsibility; see 12.44 below.
[72] Although the UK courts are more relaxed than Member States about keeping jurisdiction by applying the forum non conveniens doctrine, which is a doctrine that places emphasis on consideration being given to which country is most appropriate for resolving the dispute between the parties; see the explanation by Lord Goff in *Spiliada Maritime Corporation v. Consulex Ltd* [1987] AC 470, 476; for further discussion, see *Butterworths Family Law Service* (Lexis Nexis, Looseleaf) Vol 2A, paras [201] et seq.
[73] See Article 49 of the Matrimonial Causes (Northern Ireland) Order 1978, as amended by para. 8 of the Schedule to the Jurisdiction and Judgments (Family) (Amendment etc.) (EU Exit) Regulations 2019 (SI 2019/519).
[74] By the Jurisdiction and Judgments (Family, Civil Partnership and Marriage (Same Sex Couples) (EU Exit) (Scotland) (Amendment etc.) Regulations 2019 (SSI 2019/104), Sch 1, para. 1.
[75] In the case of nullity, there is an additional ground where either of the parties died before the application was made, namely, that at the time of death, either was domiciled or had been habitually resident in Scotland throughout the period of one year ending with the date of death.

intended here to provide a comprehensive discussion of the 1986 Act,[76] but merely to highlight the following.

12.38. The 1986 Act makes a distinction between divorces, etc. obtained in a jurisdiction outside the British Islands[77] (which now includes, in this context, all Member States that are not parties to the 1970 Hague Convention) obtained by means of 'proceedings' and those that have been obtained other than by means of proceedings. The former is governed by section 46 and the latter by section 48. 'Proceedings' for these purposes are defined by section 54(1) simply as 'judicial or other proceedings'. Although this means that extra-judicial proceedings can qualify, case law[78] establishes that in order for there to be 'proceedings', there has to be some official or officially approved agency involved in the foreign procedure. While it remains to be seen to how a UK court will classify non-judicial divorces, particularly those by which divorce by mutual consent is obtained from a notary that are now permitted in certain Member States,[79] it seems inconceivable that such divorces will not be recognised in the UK.[80]

12.39. The significance of whether or not a divorce, etc. has been obtained by '**proceedings**' lies in the required conditions for recognition. In the case of divorce, etc. obtained by proceedings, section 46 of the Family Law Act 1986 provides that the validity of an overseas divorce, etc. will be recognised where: (a) the divorce, etc. '**is effective** under the law of the country in which it was obtained'; and (b) at the date of the commencement of proceedings, either party to the marriage was either **habitually resident or domiciled or a national** of the country in which the divorce, etc. was obtained.

12.40. In the case of divorce, etc. obtained **otherwise than by proceedings**, the criteria are stricter. Under section 46(2) of the Family Law Act 1986, the validity of a divorce, etc. will be recognised where: (a) it is effective under the law of the country in which it was obtained; **and** (b) **each party** to the marriage was domiciled in the country in which the divorce, etc. was obtained, **or** either party was domiciled in that country **and** the other was domiciled in a country under whose law the divorce, etc. is recognised as valid **and** neither party was habitually resident in the UK throughout the period of one year immediately preceding that date.

---

[76] For a more detailed discussion of the Act, see, for example, D. HODSON above n. 52, paras 3.144 et seq; *Butterworths Family Law Service*, above n. 73, Vol 5, paras [555] et seq.
[77] That is, England and Wales, Scotland, Northern Ireland, the Isle of Man and the Channel Islands.
[78] *Quazi v. Quazi* [1980] AC 744; and *Chaudhary v. Chaudhary* [1985] Fam 19.
[79] As in France (under Article 229-1 to 229-4 of the French Civil Code), Greece (under Article 1441 of the Greek Civil Code) and Spain (under Articles 82 and 87 of the Spanish Civil Code).
[80] Of clear relevance in this regard is CJEU, 15 November 2022, *Senatsverwaltung für Inneres und Sport* C-646/20, in which a divorce issued by a civil registrar in Italy was ruled to be a recognisable 'decision' for the purposes of Brussels II-bis. See further Chapter 1 at 1.32–1.33.

12.41. Even where the above criteria are satisfied, a court has discretion to refuse recognition where the overseas divorce, etc. is irreconcilable with a decision already in existence or there is no recognisable marriage of which a divorce or legal separation could be granted.[81] Recognition may also be refused in the case of a divorce, etc. obtained by means of proceedings if it was obtained without reasonable notice being given or where no reasonable opportunity to participate in the proceedings was given **and** recognition would be contrary to public policy.[82] In the case of a divorce, etc. being obtained otherwise than in the course of proceedings, recognition may be refused if there is no official certifying document **and** recognition would be contrary to public policy.[83]

12.42. Refusal to recognise a divorce, etc. is discretionary and will be exercised sparingly.[84] In the case of those obtained in a Member State, a refusal is likely to be extremely rare. Applications for a declaration that an overseas divorce, etc. is or is not entitled to be recognised may be made in England and Wales to the High Court or family court.[85] Applications may be made by either party to the marriage provided either of them is domiciled in England and Wales at the date of the application or has been habitually resident there for one year preceding the date of application.[86]

B. MATTERS OF PARENTAL RESPONSIBILITY

12.43. The impact of the UK's withdrawal from the EU is less profound with regard to matters of parental responsibility in the sense that the UK, like all Member States, is a Contracting State to the 1996 Hague Child Protection Convention. Although Brussels II-ter and the 1996 Convention are by no means identical, in general terms the basic scheme for jurisdiction, recognition and enforcement (but not the *exequatur* rules) is broadly similar. Consequently, unlike for matrimonial matters, the Convention provides, as between Member States and the UK, a comprehensive alternative means of dealing with cross-border issues concerning children and one that is not so very different from Brussels II-ter. Even so, for many, applying the 1996 Convention will be a new experience and it can be anticipated that jurisprudence concerning its application will develop, particularly, given the likely large volume of EU/UK cross-border

---

[81] See s 51 of the 1986 Act. The latter ground does not apply to annulments.
[82] Section 51(3)(a).
[83] Section 51(3)(b).
[84] D. HODSON, above n. 52, para. 3.172.
[85] Section 55(1)(d) and (e). Applications are made by petition and must comply with r 8.20 of the Family Procedure Rules 2010. Expert evidence may need to be commissioned; see the advice of the *Butterworths Family Law Service*, above n. 73, para. [638].
[86] Section 55(2).

cases. We now discuss, first from Member States' point of view and then from the UK's perspective, when the Convention applies and will then provide broad guidance[87] on how the Convention applies, particularly as between Member States and the UK.

1. The 1996 Hague Child Protection Convention

i) The Position in Member States

12.44. So far as Member States are concerned, following its withdrawal from the EU, the UK must be treated like any other third State that is a party to the 1996 Convention. So far as **jurisdiction** is concerned, courts of Member States must still apply Brussels II-ter even where the cross-border matter involves the UK, such as where the child is a UK national.[88] However, this is subject to the following:

- Contrary to the normally applicable principle of *perpetuatio fori*, jurisdiction, assumed under Article 7 Brussels II-ter on the basis of the child's habitual residence in a Member State, ceases to apply where the child's habitual residence is lawfully transferred during the proceedings from of a Member State to that of a third State which is a party to the 1996 Convention, which includes, of course, the UK.[89]
- Courts of Member States do not have jurisdiction to modify an access order as provided for by Article 8 Brussels II-ter where the child lawfully moves and becomes habitually resident in the UK.[90]
- Where the parties have agreed that a court in the UK has jurisdiction, Article 10 of the 1996 Convention applies. However, it should be noted that under this provision, the power to prorogue is limited to where there are existing matrimonial proceedings.[91]
- In the case of *lis pendens* – that is, where proceedings relating to parental responsibility are pending before a UK court at the time when a court of a

---

[87] For a detailed examination of the 1996 Convention, see, for example, N. LOWE, M. EVERALL and M. NICHOLLS, *International Movement of Children: Law Practice and Procedure* (2nd ed. by N. Lowe and M. Nicholls), Lexis Nexis, Family Law, 2016, chs. 5 and 9, H. SETRIGHT, D WILLIAMS, I. CURRY-SUMNER, M. GRATION and M. WRIGHT, *International Issues in Family Law: The 1996 Hague Convention on the Protection of Children and Brussels IIa*, Family Law, 2015; N. LOWE and M. NICHOLLS, *The 1996 Hague Convention on the Protection of Children*, Jordans, 2012; and D. VAN ITTERSON, *Ouderlijke Verantwoordelijkerd kinderbescherming*, Maklu, 2011. An updated commentary on the 1996 Convention can be found in CLARKE HALL & MORRISON *on Children*, Lexis Nexis, looseleaf, Division 1, ch. 8 and Division 5, ch. 5.
[88] See CJEU, 17 October 2018, *UD*, C-393/18 PPU, discussed in Chapter 1 at 1.90.
[89] See CJEU, 14 July 2022, *CC*, C-572/21, discussed in Chapter 1 at 1.170 et seq.
[90] Article 8 (discussed in Chapter 4 at 4.33 et seq) only applies as between Member States.
[91] Article 97(2)(a) Brussels II-ter, discussed in Chapter 1 at 1.77.

Member State is seised of proceedings relating to the same child and involving the same cause of action, no matter which court is first seised – Article 13 of the 1996 Convention applies.[92] This Article operates to prevent a court of a Member State from, as the Convention puts it, 'exercising' jurisdiction.

12.45. Provided that the matter falls within its scope (that is, it concerns 'measures directed to the protection of the person or property of the child'), courts of Member States must apply the Convention and not Brussels II-ter in relation to the **recognition and enforcement** of UK judgments[93] and to both receiving and making **transfer** requests.[94] Similarly, competent authorities must apply the Convention both to receiving and making **placement of children requests** involving the UK, and, more generally, cooperation between Central Authorities is governed by the 1996 Convention. In this respect, note should be taken of the fact that unlike in relation to Brussels II-bis, for operating the 1996 Convention the UK has designated a **separate Central Authority for Wales** in addition to those for England, Scotland and Northern Ireland.

12.46. As the decision in *CC*[95] well illustrates, courts of Member States can request a preliminary ruling from the CJEU on how Brussels II-ter should be interpreted in the context of the 1996 Convention. But whether the CJEU has *locus standi* to rule on how the 1996 Convention itself should be interpreted has yet to be established. Yet, even if it is ruled that it does, any ruling on how the Convention should be interpreted would not be binding on non-EU Hague States in general and the UK in particular, albeit that due account may be taken of any such decision.

ii) The Position in the UK

12.47. The UK formally signed the 1996 Convention in April 2003, but because of the lack of competence according to EU rules,[96] its ratification was delayed until Member States were collectively authorised to do so.[97] Ratification took effect on 1 November 2012. Because of the involvement of the EU, the 1996 Convention was implemented using the machinery provided for in section 2(2)

---

[92] Article 97(2)(c) Brussels II-ter, discussed in Chapter 1 at 1.83–1.84. Cf. the position with regard to matrimonial matters where there are no *lis pendens* provisions; see 12.35 above.
[93] As discussed in Chapter 1 at 1.57, Brussels II-ter has no application with regard to the recognition and enforcement of decisions made in a third State; see CJEU, 20 December 2017, *Sahyouni*, C-372/16.
[94] This provided for by Article 97(2)(b), discussed in Chapter 1 at 1.80.
[95] CJEU, 14 July 2022, CC, C-572/21, referred to at 12.46 above and in Chapter 1 at 1.70–1.74.
[96] Based on Opinion 1/13, in which the Court considered that the EU has exclusive competence concerning the accession of third States to the 1980 Hague Abduction Convention.
[97] See Council Decision 2008/431/EC of June 2008.

of the European Communities Act 1972,[98] namely, by specifying[99] that the 1996 Convention was to be regarded as one of the EU Treaties as defined by section 1(2) of the 1972 Act. As a result, the Convention became directly effective, which meant that there was no need to formally incorporate it into domestic legislation. Instead, all the necessary changes, including amendments to primary legislation (principally the Family Law Act 1986) were made by secondary legislation.[100]

12.48. Having ratified the Convention on its own behalf and not as a Member State meant that the UK's ratification was unaffected by its withdrawal from the EU. Nevertheless, the implementation process used at the time meant that steps had to be taken to ensure that the Convention continued to apply within the UK, notwithstanding the repeal of the European Communities Act by the European Union (Withdrawal) Act 2018. This was eventually achieved by the Private International Law (Implementation of Agreements) Act 2020, which amends the Civil Jurisdiction and Judgments Act 1982 and directly incorporates the Convention into domestic law.[101]

12.49. In the UK **jurisdiction** to hear cases concerning children is complicated. The major domestic legislation is the Family Law Act 1986. While that Act applies to custody and access proceedings, it only governs private law proceedings concerning children. Although the 1986 Act was primarily, but not exclusively, designed as a means of assigning priority of jurisdiction within the UK, it has a more general application and provides, at any rate for England and Wales and Northern Ireland, the jurisdictional rules in international cases. In that respect s 2 (for England) and s 19 (for Northern Ireland) of the 1986 Act[102] provide that courts of those territories should first apply the 1996 Convention to determine jurisdiction. It is also established[103] that the 1996 Convention should

---

[98] This was thought appropriate because it was only through the 2008 Directive that UK was able to ratify it at all.

[99] See the European Communities (Definition of Treaties) (1996 Hague Convention on Protection of Children etc) Order 2010 (SI 2010/232).

[100] That is, the Parental Responsibility and Measures for the Protection of Children (International Obligations (England and Wales and Northern Ireland) Regulations 2010 (SI 2010/1898) and the Parental Responsibility and Measures for the Protection of Children (International Obligations (Scotland) Regulations 2010 (SI 2010/213).

[101] See s 1 (2) and Sch 1 (which contains the full text of the Convention), inserting, respectively, s 3C and Sch 3D into the 1982 Act. For further background information, see N. Lowe, 'Living without the jurisdictional rules of Brussels IIa' in S. Gilmore and J. Scherpe (eds), *Family Matters (Essays in Honour of John Eekelaar)*, Intersentia, 2022, pp. 1075, 1077–1078.

[102] As amended by the Jurisdiction and Judgments (Family) (Amendment etc.) (EU Exit) Regulations 2019 (SI 2019/519). For further historical background to these rules of jurisdiction, see N. Lowe, above n. 101, pp. 1078 seq.

[103] See *Re A (A Child) (Habitual Residence: 1996 Hague Child Protection Convention)* [2023] EWCA Civ 659, applying the analysis in *A v. A (Children: Habitual Residence) (Reunite International Child Abduction Centre and others intervening)* [2013] UKSC 60. See also *London Borough of Hackney v. P and Others (Jurisdiction: 1996 Hague Child Protection Convention)* [2023] EWCA Civ 1213.

also be applied whenever the subject matter of the proceedings falls within the Convention's scope (that is, 'measures directed to the protection of the person or property of the child'[104]) even where the 1986 Act does not apply. The principal effect of this position is that the 1996 Convention is considered to provide the jurisdictional rules for care proceedings, at any rate, where the other State involved is also party to the Convention. The overall net effect of this position is that when dealing with child proceedings involving Member States, the courts of England and Wales and Northern Ireland, now apply the jurisdictional rules as provided by the 1996 Convention whenever they would have previously applied Brussels II-bis.

12.50. Given that the scope of the Convention is similar to that of Brussels II-ter (save that the former applies to kafala[105] and the latter to return orders made under the 1980 Hague Abduction Convention)[106] and the basic rule of jurisdiction is the child's habitual residence, the change of regime following the UK's withdrawal from the EU makes little difference in practice as to when orders relating to children may be made in England and Wales and Northern Ireland, save crucially they are made under the Convention and not the Regulation.

12.51. In Scotland, jurisdiction to make 'independent orders' concerning children is governed by Part III of the Family Law Act 1986. This makes no reference to the 1996 Convention, but instead primarily bases jurisdiction on the child's habitual residence in Scotland. However, Scotland is equally bound by the 1996 Convention[107] and in international cases will have jurisdiction to make protective orders concerning the child's person or property under that instrument in the same way as courts in the rest of the UK.

12.52. So far as UK courts are concerned, they must also apply the 1996 Convention to the following:

- **transfer** of jurisdiction;
- **prorogation** of jurisdiction;
- **taking any necessary measures of protection**; and
- **recognition and enforcement**.

---

[104] See Article 1(1)(a) of the Convention.
[105] *Kafala* is an Islamic concept akin to adoption. It is sometimes referred to as 'replacement protection'. As N. Lowe and C. Fenton-Glynn describe it; *Kafala* 'involves an individual a permanent commitment to the protection, care and education of a child but does not permit changing the child's family name or giving inheritance rights to the child, see 'Introduction an overview of adoption' in N. Lowe and C. Fenton-Glynn. (eds) *Research Handbook on Adoption Law*, Edward Elgar, 2023 p. 4.
[106] Compare the definitions of protective measures in Articles 3 and 4 of the Convention with that of matters relating to parental responsibility in Article 1(2), (3) and (4) Brussels II-ter.
[107] The Private International Law (Implementation of Agreements) Act 2020, which incorporated the 1996 Convention into UK domestic law, applies throughout the UK; see s 4.

12.53. The cooperative provisions as between Central Authorities and competent authorities are governed by Chapter V of the Convention. As noted earlier, the UK has designated for the purpose of this Convention a separate Central Authority for Wales, as well as for each of England, Scotland and Northern Ireland. Provisions concerning the placement a child in a foster family or institutional care are those provided for by the Convention (see Article 33).

iii) Some Critical Differences between Applying the 1996 Convention and Brussels II-ter

12.54. Although the rules of jurisdiction are similar, they are not identical and this has the potential to result in clashes. Happily, however, the major clash between the *perpetuatio fori* principle under Brussels II-ter and the loss of jurisdiction where the child's habitual residence changes to another Contracting State under the 1996 Convention has been resolved.[108] It is now clear that if, during proceedings before a court of a Member State, a child lawfully moves and becomes habitually resident in the UK, jurisdiction in the Member State court ceases. The same solution applies in the opposite circumstance where the child is lawfully removed to a Member State, while proceedings in the UK are pending. As soon as the child acquires habitual residence in a Member State, the UK jurisdiction will cease and the court in the Member State will acquire it.[109]

12.55. The key connecting factor in determining jurisdiction under both Brussels II-ter and the 1996 Convention is the **child's habitual residence**, but neither instrument defines the concept and, as discussed in Chapter 4, its meaning under the Regulation has been the subject of extensive jurisprudence. At time of its withdrawal from the EU, the UK's position was that the concept of habitual residence as explained by the CJEU in *A*,[110] namely, that it 'corresponds to the place which reflects some degree of integration by the child in a social and family environment', was equally applicable to the 1996 Convention.[111] However, since the UK is not bound by any subsequent CJEU rulings, nor are Member States bound by any UK court rulings, there is a danger that the future

---

[108] That is, by the CJEU, 14 July 2022, *CC*, C-572/21, referred to at 12.46 above and in Chapter 1 at 1.70–1.74.

[109] See *London Borough of Hackney v. P and Others (Jurisdiction: 1996 Hague Child Protection Convention)* [2023] EWCA Civ 1213.

[110] ECJ, 2 April 2009, *A*, C-523/07, discussed in Chapter 4 at 4.9 et seq.

[111] See *A v. A (Children: Habitual Residence) (Reunite International Child Abduction Centre and Others Intervening)* [2013] UKSC 60; and clearly accepted as applying to the 1996 Convention by the Court of Appeal in *London Borough of Hackney v. P and Others (Jurisdiction: 1996 Hague Child Protection Convention)* [2023] EWCA Civ 1213. See also *Warrington Borough Council v. T and Others* [2021] EWFC 68, in which it was held that foster care, albeit temporary, was not necessarily a bar to a finding of habitual residence.

application of 'habitual residence' may diverge. One potential clash, perhaps, is whether a habitual residence can be lost before another is gained. There has been a debate in the UK as to how readily a court should find a child in limbo in the sense that one habitual residence is lost before another is gained. There is authority for saying that a court should be cautious about making such a finding, but as a matter of fact rather than law.[112] However, the CJEU may disagree.[113]

12.56. With regard to making **provisional including protective measures**, whereas courts of Member States must apply Article 15 Brussels II-ter, those of the UK must apply Article 11 of the Convention. Although both Article 15 of the Regulation and Article 11 of the Convention give the courts jurisdiction to take such measures in cases of urgency based on the child's presence or the location of the child's property, a critical difference is that, except where they are taken in the context of return orders made under the 1980 Hague Abduction Convention,[114] such measures taken under the Regulation do not have extra-territorial effect, whereas those taken under the Convention do. Another difference is that under the Regulation, there is no equivalent power to that of Article 12 of the Convention to make provisional orders to protect the child whilst in the jurisdiction.[115]

12.57. As between courts of Member States and those of the UK, both must apply the 1996 Convention with regard to the powers to **prorogue jurisdiction**. Although both Brussels II-ter and the 1996 Convention allow for prorogation, the power to do so is narrower under the Convention, as Article 10 only permits it where there are ongoing matrimonial proceedings between the parents and the law of such State so provides, whereas under Article 10 Brussels II-ter, there is a free-standing power for parents to agree on another court of a Member State having jurisdiction, provided the conditions envisaged by that Article are met.[116]

12.58. With regard to the power to **transfer jurisdiction**, both the courts of Member States and those of the UK must use Articles 8 and 9 of the 1996

---

[112] See, in particular, the judgment of Lord Wilson in *Re B (A Child) (Reunite International Child Abduction Centre Intervening)* [2016] UKSC 4, but note equally the judgment of Baroness Hale and Lord Toulson and see the detailed discussion in CLARKE HALL & MORRISON, above n. 89, Division 5, paras [242] et seq.

[113] Lord Wilson's judgment is described as 'wrong' by M. WILDERSPIN, *European Private International Family Law: The Brussels IIb Regulation*, Oxford University Press, 2023, p 212, para. 5-234, but he arguably misinterpreted the judgment and overlooked the subsequent comment by Moylan LJ in *Re M (Children) (Habitual Residence: 1980 Hague Child Abduction Convention)* [2020] EWCA Civ 1105 at para. [61] that Lord Wilson's analysis did not replace the core guidance given by *A v. A* [1990] 2 AC 562 to the effect that the UK courts should apply the 'integration test established by ECJ, 2 April 2009, A, C-523/07, discussed in Chapter 4.

[114] That is, those made pursuant to Article 27(5); see further Chapter 6 at 6.86–6.89.

[115] For a discussion of these powers, see, for example, N. LOWE and M. NICHOLLS, above n. 89, pp. 44–45.

[116] See further Chapter 4 at 4.48 et seq.

Convention. Although Articles 12 and 13 Brussels II-ter are more clearly aligned with the 1996 Convention, the provisions are not identical. For example, under the Convention, but not the Regulation, a request can be made to a State to assume jurisdiction in a case where 'the authorities are seised of an application for divorce or legal separation of the child's parents, or for the annulment of their marriage'.[117] Moreover, although the Convention requirements that the requesting court must consider the court of another Contracting State to be 'better placed in the particular case to assess the best interests of the child' and for the requested court only to accept jurisdiction if it 'considers that this in the child's best interests' mirror those of Brussels II-ter, their meaning is a matter for interpretation and without an overarching court, there is clear potential for a divergence of view. Indeed, it was evident that the UK Supreme Court and the CJEU had different interpretations of the transfer powers under Article 15 Brussels II-bis, as, for example, on whether assessing whether the requested court was better placed to hear the case included an assessment of the substantive law that would apply.[118] Such differences may be perpetuated when interpreting the Convention. One matter where there seems to be alignment is that the transfer provisions under the Convention, like those under Brussels II-ter, apply to public law proceedings.[119]

12.59. Both the courts of Member States and those of the UK must apply the 1996 Convention with regard to **recognition and enforcement** of judgments relating to matters of parental responsibility. Under Article 23(1) of the Convention, measures taken by the authorities of a Contracting State must be recognised by operation of law in all other Contracting States; in other words, no legal proceedings are required for recognition in another Contracting State. This provision is akin to Article 30 Brussels II-ter. But unlike the Regulation, Article 24 of the Convention provides for advance recognition, by which an interested party can seek a ruling of whether measures taken in one State will be recognised in another Contracting State. This could be useful, for example, where one parent wants to know whether an access order will be recognised in the State to which the other parent will be moving.

---

[117] See Article 8(2)(c). Cf. Article 12 Brussels II-ter, which requires the child to have a particular connection with the proposed court as defined by Article 12(4).
[118] Compare CJEU, 27 October 2016, *Child and Family Agency*, C-428/15 and *Re N (Children) (Adoption: Jurisdiction) (AIRE Centre Intervening)* [2016] UKSC 15, for an analysis on which, see N. Lowe and H. Setright, 'Transferring the problem: how Article 15 of the revised Brussels II Regulation operates in the public law context' [2017] *International Family Law* 13.
[119] See *London Borough of Hackney v. P and Others (Jurisdiction: 1996 Hague Child Protection Convention)* 2023 EWCA Civ 1213, for the application of the Convention according to UK case law, and CJEU, 27 October 2016, *Child and Family Agency*, C-428/15 for the application of Brussels II-ter as per the CJEU; see also Chapter 4 at 4.116.

12.60. The fundamental difference between the Convention and the Regulation is with regard to enforcement. As discussed in Chapter 9, a key change made by Brussels II-ter is abolishing the need for an *exequatur* for all decisions. **This is not the case for measures taken under the Convention.** Instead, the scheme under the Convention is to require applications to be made in the Contracting State in which enforcement is sought for a declaration of enforcement or for registration for the purpose of enforcement.[120] Once declared enforceable or registered for enforcement, the measure can be enforced as if it had been made by the requested State. Enforcement takes place 'in accordance with the law of the requested State to the extent provided by such law, taking into consideration the best interests of the child'.[121] In other words, **in all cases, enforcement of measures taken under the Convention is subject to an enforcement process according to the national law in which enforcement is being sought.** In the UK, it is necessary for an order to be registered before it can be enforced and only the High Court in England and Wales or Northern Ireland and the Court of Session in Scotland has jurisdiction to register a measure taken in another Contracting State for enforcement.[122]

12.61. As under Brussels II-ter, recognition and enforcement can be opposed under the Convention. The grounds are similar but not identical and, unlike under the Regulation, where, upon establishment of a ground, refusal is generally mandatory,[123] under the Convention, a refusal is discretionary.[124]

C. CHILD ABDUCTION

12.62. So far as jurisdiction is concerned, it is clear, following the CJEU decision in *SS*,[125] that courts of Member States and, *a fortiori*, those of the UK, must apply Article 7 of the 1996 Convention rather than Article 9 Brussels II-ter.[126] Both these provisions preserve, **in cases of wrongful removal or retention**, the jurisdiction of the authorities of the State in which the child was habitually resident immediately before the removal or retention until the child

---

[120] See Article 26 of the Convention. Note that, unlike under Brussels II-ter, under the Convention there is no requirement for certificate to be attached; the order itself is sufficient proof of the measures taken.
[121] See Article 28 of the Convention.
[122] See reg 8 of the Parental Responsibility and Measures for the Protection of Children (International Obligations) (England and Wales and Northern Ireland) Regulations 2010 (SI 2010/1898); and reg 7 of the Parental Responsibility and Measures for the Protection of Children (International Obligations) (Scotland) Regulations 2010 (SSI 2010/213).
[123] Article 39 Brussels II-ter, discussed in Chapter 8.
[124] Article 23 of the Convention.
[125] CJEU, 24 March 2021, *SS*, C-603/20 PPU, discussed in Chapter 6 at 6.18.
[126] See N. Lowe, '*Operating Brussels II-ter in children cases involving third States*', in Festskrift till Maarit Jänterä-Jareborg, Iustus Förlag, 2022, pp. 203, 208

becomes habitually resident in another Contracting State **and** either each holder of parental responsibility has acquiesced in the removal or retention or, in the case of the Convention, the child has resided in that other State for at least one year after the holders of rights of custody have or should have had knowledge of the child's whereabouts and the child is settled in his or her new environment.[127]

12.63. What ranks as a 'wrongful removal or retention' for these purposes is spelt out by Article 7(2) of the Convention, namely, and in line with Article 3 of the 1980 Hague Abduction Convention and akin to Article 2(11) Brussels II-ter, where:

(a) it is in breach of rights of custody attributed to a person, an institution or any other body, either jointly or alone, under the law of the State in which the child was habitually resident immediately before the removal or retention; or

(b) at the time of removal or retention those rights were actually exercised, either jointly or alone, or would have been so exercised but for the removal of retention.

12.64. Given that there is no supranational court overseeing the interpretation of the 1996 Convention, there is the clear potential for diverging applications of Article 7. Member States will naturally look to the CJEU jurisprudence when considering such issues as the meaning of 'rights of custody' and what amounts to 'retention' and 'acquiescence', while the UK courts will apply the well-developed jurisprudence under the 1980 Hague Abduction Convention, *inter alia*, as established by its appellate courts and particularly by the Supreme Court. It is evident, for example, that different views are taken on whether the concept of rights of custody embraces de facto or inchoate rights as well as de jure rights.[128] It remains unclear whether the UK position that courts can have 'rights of custody'[129] or whether there is a concept of 'anticipatory' or, as the UK Supreme Court has called it, 'repudiatory retention', that is, where one parent evinces an intention to renege on an agreement to return a child **during** an agreed period of stay,[130] will be adopted by courts of Member States. It remains to be seen whether over time these interpretations of the 1996 Convention will converge, as is clearly desirable, or whether they will diverge further.

---

[127] See Article 7(1)(b). Under Article 9(b) Brussels II-ter, this last requirement is similar but more elaborate.

[128] Compare CJEU, 5 October 2010, *J McB*, C-400/10 PPU, which implies that it does not (see Chapter 6 at 6.44) with *Re K (A Child) (Reunite Child Abduction Centre intervening)* [2014] UKSC 29, in which the UK Supreme Court held that it did. The ruling in *Re K* was held to apply to Article 7 of the 1996 Convention in *B v. L (Removal to Poland: Unmarried Father; Rights of Custody: Declarations)* [2022] EWHC 2215 (Fam).

[129] See *Re H (A Minor) (Abduction: Rights of Custody)* [2000] 2 AC 291, which clearly held that it does, whereas in CJEU, 22 December 2010, *Mercredi*, C-497/10 PPU, the Court declined to rule on this point; see further Chapter 6 at 6.46.

[130] *Re C and Another (Children) (International Centre for Family Law, Policy and Practice intervening)* [2018] UKSC 8, discussed in Chapter 6 at 6.41.

12.65. All Member States and the UK are Contracting States to the 1980 Hague Abduction Convention and in that broad sense the UK's withdrawal from the EU makes no difference.[131] However, whereas when the UK was a Member State it operated, as against another Member State, the Convention as supplemented by what was then Article 11 Brussels II-bis, it now applies the Convention in its original form. Similarly, courts of Member States, when dealing with abductions to or from the UK, must also apply the 1980 Convention without any supplementation – that is, without regard to Chapter III Brussels II-ter.

12.66. The principal differences between Chapter III Brussels II-ter in return applications made between Member States and the UK and vice versa under the 1980 Convention are as follows:

- the specific timing provisions under Articles 23 and 24 Brussels II-ter[132] with respect to processing return applications under the 1980 Convention do not apply, although under Article 11 of the Convention, there is a duty to process return applications 'expeditiously';
- the procedure governing the return of a child under Article 27 Brussels II-ter[133] does not apply;
- the procedure (under Article 29 Brussels II-ter)[134] following a refusal to return a child under Article 13(1)(b) and (2) of the 1980 Convention ('the override provisions') does not apply;
- the right of the child to express his or her views in return proceedings and to give due consideration to those views (Article 26, applying Article 21 Brussels II-ter) does not apply, although a similar right is conferred by Article 12 UNCRC; and
- the promotion of alternative dispute resolution (under Article 24 Brussels II-ter) does not apply.

12.67. In practice, the non-application of the above provisions will not make much difference in the UK, at any rate, in the short term. The UK has a good record on the speed with which it processes and determines return applications under the 1980 Convention and generally meets the various six-week requirements.[135]

---

[131] The fear (see N. MOLE, 'Some Thoughts on the Impact of Brexit on the Rights of Children' [2017] *European Human Rights Law Review* 529, 532) that the UK's continued participation in the 1980 Convention as a 'third State' rather than as previously as an EU Member State, EU law might have prevented the Convention from continuing to apply as between Members States and the UK unless otherwise agreed, has proved unfounded.
[132] Discussed in Chapter 6 at 6.48 et seq.
[133] Discussed in Chapter 6 at 6.75 et seq.
[134] Discussed in Chapter 6 at 6.95 et seq.
[135] See N. LOWE and V. STEPHENS, 'A Statistical Analysis of Applications made in 2015 under the Hague Convention of 25 October 1980 on the Civil Aspects of International Child Abduction', Prel. Doc. No.11C (2018), UK National Report, http://www.hcch.net/

Its courts have a well-developed practice of hearing the child[136] and of not refusing a return on the basis of Article 13(1)(b) of the Convention if it is satisfied that adequate arrangements have been made to secure the child upon his or her return.[137] Its courts have powers to make interim orders, including securing the child's contact with person seeking the child's return.[138] In substantive terms, the major change is the non-application of the override provisions, but even in this respect the impact is relatively small, not least because UK courts do not often refuse returns, particularly on the basis of Article 13(1)(b).[139]

12.68. From Member States' point of view, it is a matter for speculation whether, in view of the new timing provisions under Articles 23 and 24 Brussels II-ter, return applications from the UK will be processed as 'expeditiously' as those from other Member States. Similarly, it may be wondered if Article 13(1)(b) of the Convention could be interpreted similarly to that provided for by Article 27(3) Brussels II-ter – that is, by preventing reliance on that exception to the duty to order the child's return if the court is satisfied that adequate arrangements have been made to secure the child upon his or her return, which is the position taken in the UK.[140] They must surely give the child the right to express his or her own views. But the powers to make arrangements to secure contact between the child and the person seeking the return, and, maybe, to make provisional orders more generally will depend on national law.

---

index_en.php?act=progress.listing&cat=7, analysed further by N. LOWE and V. STEPHENS, 'Operating the 1980 Hague Abduction Convention: The 2015 Statistics' [2018] *Family Law* 161.

[136] See *Re D (A Minor) (Abduction: Rights of Custody)* [2006] UKHL 51, *Re KP (A Child: Rights of Custody)* [2014] EWCA Civ 554 and the *2023 President's Guidance* which replaced the *2018 President's Guidance* [2018] Family Law 448, on which see N. LOWE and M. FREEMAN, 'Child Participation in Family Proceedings: England & Wales' in W. SCHRAMA, M. FREEMAN, N. TAYLOR and M. BRUNING (eds), *International Handbook on Child Participation in Family Law*, Intersentia, 2021, 171.

[137] See, for example, *Re C (Children) (Abduction: Article 13(b))* [2018] EWCA Civ 2834, *Re IG (Child Abduction Habitual Residence Article 13b)* [2021] EWCA Civ 1123 and the *2018 President's Practice Guidance on Case Management and Mediation of International Child Abduction Proceedings* [2018] Fam Law 448, 13 March 2018, para. 2.11(e).

[138] See s 5 of the Child Abduction and Custody Act 1985.

[139] See N. LOWE and V. STEPHENS, 'A Statistical Analysis of Applications', above n. 135.

[140] See the summary by Baker LJ in *Re IG (Child Abduction Habitual Residence Article 13b)* [2021] EWCA Civ 1123, para. 47.

INDEX

A

Abduction   1.1–1.2, 1.9, 1.15, 1.17, 1.20, 1.35, 1.53, 1.59, 1.64–1.67, 2.4, 2.51, 4.4, 4.17, 4.28–4.29, 4.178, 4.184, 4.205, 6.1–6.128, 7.7, 7.9, 7.12–7.13, 7.23, 7.27, 7.32, 8.3, 8.117, 9.5, 9.15–9.16, 9.22, 9.33, 9.63, 9.67, 11.1, 11.7, 11.11, 11.23, 11.39–11.40, 11.67, 12.15–12.17, 12.50, 12.56, 12.62–12.68

Abduction proceedings   4.17, 4.178, 6.72, 6.92, 6.99, 9.16, 12.17

Abolition of *exequatur*   9.4–9.10, 9.25, 9.36

Abuse   2.7, 2.9, 4.190, 9.60, 11.33

Access   1.3, 1.8, 1.37–1.39, 1.67, 1.95, 2.40, 3.21, 3.85–3.87, 4.1, 4.3, 4.33–4.35, 4.37–4.40, 4.47, 4.87, 4.120, 4.129–4.130, 4.178, 4.191, 5.10, 5.34, 5.48, 5.51–5.52, 5.65, 5.68–5.69, 6.5, 6.32, 6.36, 6.42, 6.45–6.46, 6.70, 6.78–6.79, 7.12, 7.22, 7.32, 7.34, 8.2–8.3, 8.25, 8.47, 8.73, 8.100, 8.110, 8.113, 8.135, 8.139, 9.5, 9.13–9.14, 9.55, 9.62, 10.39, 11.26, 11.34, 11.36–11.38, 12.15

Access application   1.67, 6.32

Access rights   4.33–4.35, 4.37–4.40, 4.129, 6.70, 8.110, 8.113, 9.55, 9.62, 10.39

Acquiescence (to removal or retention)   1.95, 6.20, 6.101, 12.64

Adaptation   8.10–8.13, 8.24, 9.79, 9.80

Address for service   9.9, 9.20

Adequate arrangements to secure the protection of the child (after return)   6.81–6.82, 6.86, 6.89, 12.67–12.68

Administration of child's property   1.48

Adoption   1.41, 1.49–1.50, 1.62, 4.109, 4.189, 4.201, 5.41, 7.12, 11.48

ADR *see* alternative dispute resolution

Advance recognition   12.59

Age (of the child)   1.18, 1.35–1.36, 3.72, 4.18, 4.24, 6.12, 6.28–6.29, 7.2, 7.7–7.8, 7.10, 7.16, 7.21, 7.25, 8.81, 8.117, 8.119, 8.121, 8.131, 9.55, 9.70

Agreement having legal effect   1.37, 4.1, 5.65, 6.34, 6.45

Agreements   1.23, 1.25, 1.33, 1.51–1.55, 1.73, 1.93, 1.97, 3.19, 4.42–4.98, 4.107, 6.27, 6.70–6.71, 7.11, 7.20, 8.3, 9.3, 9.51, 10.1–10.50, 11.19, 11.57, 12.13, 12.48

Alternative dispute resolution   2.14, 6.8, 6.57, 6.66, 11.14, 11.27, 12.66

Amicable (dispute) settlement   4.47

Amicable resolution of family disputes   11.5, 11.14

Ancillary measures   1.26, 4.186

Ancillary orders   12.26

Ancillary questions   9.11

Annulment   1.7, 1.22, 1.27, 1.34, 1.49, 1.52, 1.77, 3.6, 3.8, 3.19, 3.22, 5.6, 5.11, 5.60, 5.62, 8.8–8.9, 8.13, 8.34, 8.68, 8.87, 8.102, 8.128, 10.28, 10.48, 12.58

Anticipatory retention   6.41, 12.64

Appeal   1.71, 2.23, 2.58, 3.72, 4.17, 4.84, 4.87, 4.120, 4.152, 6.21, 6.24, 6.36–6.37, 6.53, 6.55–6.56, 6.59–6.60, 6.93, 6.95, 6.105, 7.32–7.33, 8.35, 8.56, 8.58–8.66, 9.9, 9.12–9.13, 9.27–9.28, 9.47, 9.71–9.71

Appearance   2.34, 2.43–2.46, 2.48, 2.52, 2.54, 2.57, 2.60, 2.65, 4.67, 4.71–4.72, 6.121, 8.91, 8.93, 10.5, 10.32

Applicable law   1.2, 1.4, 1.26, 1.68, 1.85, 3.8, 3.61, 3.64, 6.43, 8.16, 8.21, 8.25, 8.31, 8.47, 8.128–8.131, 9.55, 10.48

Application for refusal of enforcement   9.28, 9.39, 9.41, 9.44–9.46, 9.52–9.55, 9.71

Appropriate measures (to ensure respect of the rights of the child)   1.66, 11.5, 11.53–11.54

Area of freedom, security and justice   1.3, 5.21, 8.2

Area of justice and fundamental rights   1.12

Austria   3.8, 3.57, 5.62, 6.53, 7.4, 8.130, 11.58, 12.24

Authenticated copy of decision   8.139, 9.21

Authentic instruments   1.23, 1.51–1.55, 1.93, 1.99, 7.11, 8.3, 9.3, 9.50, 10.1–10.49, 12.6, 12.13

Authorised representative   9.20, 9.43

Authorised translator   8.76

Authority competent for enforcement   6.90, 9.10, 9.18, 9.21, 9.23, 9.26, 9.41, 9.44, 9.47, 9.61, 9.66

Automatic recognition   1.57, 4.204, 8.32–8.35

Autonomous interpretation and meaning   1.23, 1.31, 1.34, 1.51, 1.54, 1.87, 2.17, 2.24, 2.50, 2.65, 3.30–3.36, 4.30, 4.182, 4.196, 5.5, 5.58, 5.65–5.66, 5.63, 8.60, 11.41

B

Bangladesh   1.90, 4.22

Belgium   1.30, 3.8, 3.57, 3.86, 5.62, 6.53, 8.130, 12.24

Best interests of the child   1.12, 1.80, 2.38, 3.30, 3.36, 4.5, 4.10, 4.12, 4.23, 4.49, 4.51, 4.69, 4.77–4.81, 4.84, 4.86, 4.91, 4.93, 4.113–4.114, 4.124, 4.133–4.140, 4.134–4.135, 4.137–4.139, 4.141–4.148, 4.152–4.153, 4.155, 4.163–4.165, 4.192, 4.212, 4.214, 5.45, 5.68, 6.77, 6.80, 6.93, 6.114, 6.127, 7.9, 7.18, 7.24, 8.65, 8.106–8.108, 8.121, 9.19, 9.29–9.31, 10.50, 11.53, 11.62, 12.58, 12.60

Index

Better placed test 4.136–4.137, 4.143–4.146
Binding legal effect 6.70, 10.17, 10.20, 10.23–10.24
Borrás Report 1.34, 3.62, 3.66, 4.201, 8.13, 10.1
Breach of rights of custody 6.28, 6.34, 6.38–6.39, 6.42–6.47, 12.63
Bulgaria 1.27, 1.66, 3.8, 3.31, 5.62, 6.53, 7.17, 8.130, 11.6, 12.24

C

Cause of action estoppel 8.26
Central Authority 1.2, 1.66–1.67, 1.98–1.99, 4.164, 4.213, 5.28, 6.8, 6.11, 6.28–6.29, 6.49, 6.63, 6.66, 6.75, 6.86, 6.90, 6.107, 6.112, 8.115, 9.44, 11.6–11.9, 11.17–11.19, 11.22, 11.23, 11.26, 11.29–11.31, 11.34, 11.56, 11.59, 11.63, 11.65–11.67, 11.71, 12.3, 12.45, 12.53
Centre of interest (test) 4.10, 4.12, 4.15
Certificate (following a decision refusing the return of a child) 1.32, 1.51, 2.17, 2.58, 2.61, 6.31, 6.72, 6.105–6.107, 6.110–6.113, 6.120–6.128, 7.9, 7.28–7.35, 8.3, 8.16–8.19, 8.67, 8.71–8.77, 8.118, 8.134, 8.137–8.139, 8.141, 9.21–9.23, 9.28, 9.41–9.42, 9.47, 10.4–10.5, 10.17–10.18, 10.25–10.26, 10.29, 10.47, 10.50
Certificate for decisions in matrimonial matters 8.67, 8.71, 8.77, 8.131
Certificate for decisions in matters of parental responsibility 8.16, 8.67, 8.71–8.73, 8.76, 9.24
Certified copy of the decision 8.67, 8.69–8.70, 8.77
Change of circumstances 4.91–4.92, 4.122, 4.184, 4.210, 6.127, 8.6, 8.112, 9.29, 9.64, 9.67, 10.40
Child abduction 1.1, 1.9, 1.15, 1.17, 1.20, 1.53, 4.28, 4.205, 6.1–6.128, 7.13, 7.23, 7.27, 8.3, 11.39–11.40, 11.67, 12.16–12.17, 12.62–12.68
Children's home 1.41
Child's place of residence 4.13, 6.35, 6.42, 6.45–6.46
Child support 8.47, 10.15–10.16
Child's view 4.148, 7.9, 7.13, 7.24–7.27
Child welfare authorities 8.38, 9.19, 10.1, 11.3
Choice-of-court 1.77–1.78, 3.10–3.14, 3.19, 4.48–4.51, 4.53, 4.56, 4.59, 4.64–4.65, 4.67, 4.72–4.77, 4.81–4.82, 4.84–4.88, 4.89–4.93, 4.95–4.98, 4.102, 8.27
Choice-of-court agreements 3.19, 4.53, 4.65, 4.74, 4.76, 4.89–4.93, 10.10
Choice of forum 3.19, 4.50
Chronological principle 3.27, 4.119, 5.6–5.15, 5.26, 5.55
Civil registrar 1.32–1.33, 1.51, 1.54, 10.13–10.14
Civil status 1.26, 8.34, 8.38, 8.62, 8.68, 8.100, 9.2
Civil status registry 8.100
Claim preclusion 8.26
Collateral estoppel 8.26
Coercion 1.90, 4.22–4.23, 4.66, 8.89

Commission 1.7–1.8, 1.11–1.15, 1.50, 1.55, 1.100–1.101, 3.1–3.2, 3.12, 3.68, 3.87, 4.42, 4.45, 4.48, 4.97, 4.112, 4.129, 4.136, 4.169, 4.201–4.202, 6.5, 6.51–6.52, 6.56, 6.62, 6.78, 6.98–6.99, 6.117, 7.1, 7.9, 7.27, 8.3, 8.10, 8.41, 8.71, 8.116, 8.135, 9.18, 9.25, 9.31, 9.37, 9.44, 9.67, 9.71, 9.78, 10.4, 10.7, 11.3–11.4, 11.9–11.10, 11.16, 11.33, 11.46, 11.53, 11.55–11.56, 11.58, 12.2, 12.7, 12.9–12.10, 12.21
Concentration of jurisdiction 6.51
Concentration of proceedings 4.45
Conclusive effect of *res judicata* 8.5
Concurrent proceedings 4.89
Connecting factor 3.13, 3.19, 3.23, 4.4–4.5, 4.129, 12.55
Consent 1.32–1.33, 1.95, 4.51, 4.56–4.73, 4.77–4.78, 4.82–4.83, 4.154, 5.61, 6.1, 6.20, 6.35, 6.44–6.45, 6.101, 8.15, 8.87, 8.115–8.116, 9.55, 10.8, 10.13–10.15, 11.43, 11.45, 11.47, 11.55–11.67, 12.13, 12.38
Conservation of child's property 1.38, 1.42, 4.128, 4.163
Consultation procedure (for obtaining consent to placement) 11.57
Contact 2.7, 4.14–4.15, 4.38, 4.60, 4.70, 4.153, 4.167, 6.65, 6.77–6.80, 6.86, 6.118–6.119, 11.19–11.20, 11.37–11.38, 11.53, 11.61, 11.67, 12.67–12.68
Continuing jurisdiction 4.33–4.41, 4.129, 9.55
Contradictory proceedings 8.67
Cooling-off period 8.97
Cooperation among competent authorities 11.5, 11.13
Cooperation (and communication) between courts 11.2–11.3
Corruption 8.89, 8.126
Costs 4.45, 6.82, 8.68, 9.9, 9.11, 9.20, 9.75–9.76, 11.10, 11.44, 11.71
Counterclaim 5.51
Court competent for enforcement 9.27
Court first seised 1.81, 1.87, 4.74, 4.150, 4.159, 4.161, 5.6–5.7, 5.9, 5.11, 5.14, 5.21, 5.26–5.31, 5.36–5.38, 5.44–5.57
Court settlements 1.99, 10.1–10.3, 10.16, 12.6
Criminal law 1.41, 1.49, 11.48
Criminal proceedings 6.82
Croatia 11.58, 12.24
Curatorship 1.38, 7.12
Custody 1.37–1.38, 1.60, 1.71, 1.95, 2.15, 2.51, 3.36, 3.82–3.83, 4.1, 4.14–4.17, 4.48, 4.65, 4.68, 4.87, 4.120, 4.167, 4.189–4.190, 4.194, 5.16–5.17, 5.23, 5.65, 5.68, 6.5–6.6, 6.12, 6.15, 6.19–6.22, 6.24, 6.26–6.28, 6.34–6.35, 6.38–6.39, 6.42–6.47, 6.82, 6.99–6.101, 6.106–6.109, 6.111–6.115, 6.117–6.118, 6.127, 7.12–7.13, 7.32–7.34, 8.2, 8.14–8.19, 8.25, 8.33, 8.39, 8.79–8.81, 8.113, 9.55, 10.1, 10.13, 12.26, 12.62–12.64
Cyprus 1.2, 8.59–8.60, 11.58, 12.24
Cyrillic letters 8.74
Czech Republic 6.53, 7.4, 12.24

D

Danger (child's exposure to) 6.69, 6.92, 7.9, 7.19, 11.28, 11.32–11.33, 12.55
Death 1.34, 3.34, 4.191, 9.34, 9.68
Decision 1.17–1.18, 1.23–1.25, 1.32–1.33, 1.37, 1.46–1.48, 1.51–1.55, 1.65–1.67, 1.69, 1.79, 2.12–2.13, 2.15, 2.18, 2.24, 2.33, 2.40, 2.42, 2.45–2.47, 3.4–3.5, 3.15, 3.19, 3.55, 3.61–3.62, 3.65, 3.86–3.87, 4.1–4.3, 4.8–4.9, 4.12–4.13, 4.15, 4.19, 4.33, 4.37–4.39, 4.59, 4.66, 4.69–4.70, 4.84, 4.86–4.87, 4.93, 4.109, 4.112–4.113, 4.116, 4.119–4.120, 4.123, 4.129, 4.131, 4.136, 4.148, 4.152, 4.155, 4.167–4.169, 4.171, 4.175–4.177, 4.188–4.189, 4.197–4.198, 4.200–4.201, 4.203–4.205, 4.208–4.211, 5.11, 5.13, 5.20–5.21, 5.24–5.25, 5.27–5.28, 5.31–5.32, 5.34, 5.36, 5.42, 5.48–5.49, 5.52–5.54, 5.61, 5.65, 5.70, 6.15, 6.21, 6.24, 6.26, 6.31, 6.34, 6.39–6.40, 6.43, 6.45, 6.55, 6.59, 6.63, 6.65, 6.69–6.70, 6.72, 6.78–6.79, 6.82, 6.87–6.88, 6.90–6.95, 6.100–6.101, 6.105–6.108, 6.110–6.114, 6.117–6.128, 7.4, 7.8–7.10, 7.16, 7.26–7.31, 7.33–7.35, 8.2–8.3, 8.6–8.8, 8.10, 8.15–8.16, 8.18, 8.31–8.32, 8.34–8.36, 8.47, 8.51–8.56, 8.58–8.59, 8.65, 8.67–8.69, 8.71–8.72, 8.75, 8.77, 8.79, 8.81, 8.87, 8.91, 8.94, 8.96, 8.100, 8.104–8.106, 8.109–8.116, 8.118–8.119, 8.128, 8.135–8.137, 8.139–8.141, 9.1–9.5, 9.7–9.9, 9.11–9.19, 9.21–9.24, 9.26, 9.28–9.29, 9.32–9.35, 9.38–9.39, 9.41–9.42, 9.44–9.52, 9.54–9.65, 9.67–9.77, 9.79, 10.1, 10.12–10.16, 10.20–10.21, 10.23, 10.25–10.32, 10.34–10.36, 10.40, 10.46, 10.48–10.49, 11.38, 11.52–11.53, 11.60, 11.62, 11.65, 11.67, 11.70, 12.13, 12.17, 12.19, 12.29–12.30, 12.41, 12.46, 12.60, 12.62
Declaration on enforceability 8.42
Declaratory judgment 8.36, 8.39–8.40, 8.42, 8.45, 8.61, 8.68
Declaratory judgment (on enforceability) 8.36, 8.39–8.40, 8.42, 8.45
Declaratory judgment (on recognition) 8.36, 8.39, 8.42, 8.45, 8.61
Decline jurisdiction 4.90, 4.94, 5.47, 5.49
De facto rights of custody 6.44, 12.64
Default judgment(s) 8.89, 8.91–8.92
Definitions 1.15, 1.18–1.22, 3.32, 10.5, 10.13
Definition of agreement 1.18
Definition of authentic instrument 1.18, 10.6–10.10
Delay of enforcement 6.63, 9.44–9.45, 9.67
Denmark 1.5, 1.9–1.10, 1.18, 1.20, 1.58–1.59, 1.60, 1.62, 1.69, 1.75, 1.88, 2.25, 2.56, 3.74, 4.94, 4.106, 6.2–6.3, 6.6, 7.7, 12.8, 12.21, 12.24, 12.30
Dependent action 5.11
Dependent proceedings 5.4
Differences in applicable law 8.128–8.131
Direct contact between courts 11.19
Discrimination 1.30, 3.3, 3.88, 8.108

Divorce 1.4, 1.7, 1.22, 1.26–1.29, 1.31–1.33, 1.51–1.52, 1.54–1.58, 1.77, 1.86–1.87, 1.91, 2.15, 2.22–2.23, 3.5–3.6, 3.8, 3.12, 3.14, 3.19–3.21, 3.24–3.25, 3.36, 3.46, 3.50–3.52, 3.55, 3.57–3.58, 3.61–3.63, 3.65–3.66, 3.72, 3.75, 3.82–3.83, 3.85, 3.92, 4.45, 4.86, 4.95, 4.98, 4.120, 4.122, 4.131, 4.176, 4.186, 4.213, 5.6, 5.10–5.12, 5.17, 5.32, 5.40–5.42, 5.51, 5.54, 5.59–5.62, 6.36, 7.32, 8.2, 8.5, 8.8–8.9, 8.13, 8.31, 8.33–8.34, 8.68, 8.80, 8.87, 8.97–8.98, 8.102, 8.109, 8.127–8.131, 9.2, 9.49, 9.72, 9.76, 10.4, 10.11, 10.13–10.16, 10.22–10.23, 10.28, 10.32–10.36, 10.44, 10.48, 12.24, 12.26–12.29, 12.31–12.42, 12.58
Divorce by mutual consent 1.33, 10.15, 12.38
Documents to be produced (for recognition) 8.67–8.77, 8.139, 9.21–9.23
Domestic violence 4.192, 6.68
Domicile 4.5, 12.32–12.36
Double abduction 6.92, 12.17
Drugs 11.33
Duration of residence 4.25
Duty to inform of provisional and protective measures 4.183, 4.212–4.215

E

Educational placement 1.41, 11.48
EESC, see European Economic and Social Committee
EJN, see European Judicial Network
e-Justice Portal 4.125, 4.153, 8.41, 8.44, 11.6, 11.58, 11.59
Emancipation 1.35, 1.49–1.50
Enforcement 1.1–1.4, 1.6, 1.15, 1.23–1.24, 1.53, 1.55, 1.57–1.58, 1.60, 1.68–1.69, 1.73, 1.89, 1.95, 1.99, 1.101, 2.33, 2.46–2.47, 2.51, 2.65, 4.1–4.2, 4.177, 4.201, 4.204, 4.206, 4.211, 6.8–6.9, 6.48, 6.60, 6.63–6.64, 6.72, 6.88, 6.90–6.92, 6.122, 6.125, 6.127, 7.6–7.9, 7.14, 7.28, 7.30–7.34, 8.1, 8.3, 8.10, 8.32, 8.36, 8.59, 8.65, 8.67, 8.71, 8.78, 8.132, 8.135, 8.137, 8.140–8.141, 9.1–9.6, 9.8, 9.10, 9.11, 9.13–9.49, 9.51–9.61, 9.63–9.68, 9.70–9.73, 9.75–9.80, 10.1–10.2, 10.4, 10.11–10.12, 10.15–10.17, 10.23–10.27, 10.30–10.31, 10.37–10.38, 10.41, 10.44–10.45, 10.47, 10.49, 11.18, 11.26, 11.40, 11.62, 11.67–11.70, 12.3–12.4, 12.6, 12.9, 12.13–12.15, 12.21, 12.45, 12.59–12.61
England 1.79, 1.82, 1.87, 1.90, 2.22–2.23, 4.17, 4.22, 11.67, 12.8, 12.18, 12.20, 12.31–12.36, 12.42, 12.45, 12.49–12.50, 12.53, 12.60
Enhanced cooperation 3.8, 5.62
Erga omnes 1.47
Estonia 3.8, 5.62, 11.6, 12.24
European Council 1.11, 1.13, 1.68
European Economic and Social Committee 1.11, 1.14
European Judicial Network (EJN) 4.153, 11.12, 11.16, 11.40
European Withdrawal Agreement 12.1
Exclusive competence 2.2, 5.14, 8.27, 8.30

Exclusive jurisdiction 4.37, 4.50, 4.74, 4.76, 4.90–4.92, 4.122
Exclusivity (of choice-of-court agreement) 4.74–4.77
Exequatur 1.8, 1.95, 8.135, 9.4–9.10, 9.25, 9.36, 9.45, 11.70, 12.60
Exercise of custody rights 1.95, 6.46
Exercise of parental responsibility 1.48, 8.23–8.24
Existence of parental responsibility 8.23
Exit day 12.1
Ex officio 2.31, 3.53, 5.43, 5.49, 8.66, 8.71, 8.81, 8.109, 8.111
Ex parte 9.17
Expeditious enforcement 6.63–6.64
Expeditiously (duty to act) 6.90–6.91, 12.66
Explanatory Memorandum 1.12, 7.9, 11.3
Extra-judicial divorce 1.33
Extraordinary appeal 6.24
Extra-territorial effect (of provisional measures) 1.75, 4.169, 4.178, 4.205, 6.79, 6.88–6.89, 12.56

F
Failure to hear the child 8.117–8.122
False testimony 8.126
Final decision 4.148, 4.168, 4.171, 4.198, 4.209, 5.31–5.32, 5.34, 5.48, 6.118, 6.127
Finland 1.34, 1.62, 4.9, 4.58, 8.5, 8.9, 12.24
Force majeure 9.34, 9.68
Foreign judgment 8.5, 8.19, 8.21, 8.45, 8.49, 8.51, 8.103–8.104, 8.114
Formal errors 9.34, 9.68
Formal requirements (of choice-of-court agreements) 4.50, 4.79, 4.82–4.83, 9.20, 10.9–10.10
Forum 1.31, 1.47, 1.78, 2.38–2.40, 2.48–2.51, 2.64, 3.3, 3.8, 3.11–3.12, 3.17, 3.22, 3.27, 3.52–3.53, 3.69, 3.71, 3.74, 3.84, 3.87, 4.5, 4.42, 4.45, 4.50, 4.78, 4.80, 4.95, 4.97, 4.99–4.101, 4.118, 4.127, 4.147, 4.171, 4.188, 4.190, 4.193–4.195, 4.211, 5.13, 5.45, 8.95, 8.118, 12.25
Forum necessitatis 2.39, 3.69, 3.74, 3.84–3.87, 4.97, 4.100
Forum non conveniens 4.78, 4.118
Forum shopping 3.3, 3.8, 3.52
Foster care 1.38, 1.41, 11.15, 11.41, 11.48
Foster parent 8.110, 10.39
Four fundamental freedoms of the EU 8.2
France 1.7–1.8, 1.64, 3.8, 3.22, 3.25, 3.50, 3.57, 3.72–3.73, 3.92, 4.17, 5.62, 6.53, 7.4, 8.5, 8.48, 9.79–9.80, 8.130, 11.6, 11.9, 12.24
Fraud 3.52, 8.89, 8.126, 10.35
Free movement of persons 1.3, 8.2
Free space (of form) 8.19
Free-standing action (on recognition) 8.61
Free-standing decision (on recognition) 8.36–8.44
Free-text fields of certificate, *see* free space of form

G
Germany 1.6, 1.27, 3.57, 5.23, 7.17, 7.32, 8.27, 12.24
Gibraltar 12.31
Grandparents 1.39, 1.79, 4.131, 5.71, 6.46, 6.79, 8.110, 11.41, 11.43, 11.58
Grave risk of physical or psychological harm 9.29–9.30, 9.32–9.34, 9.49, 9.64–9.65
Greece 3.8, 3.86, 7.4, 12.24
Grounds for divorce 1.26, 8.31
Grounds for refusal of recognition (decisions) 1.95, 8.36, 8.53, 8.56, 8.105, 9.36, 10.29, 12.14
Grounds for refusal of recognition (authentic instruments and agreements) 10.31, 10.41, 10.45
Grounds for refusing enforcement 9.49
Guardian 1.44–1.45, 1.48, 4.61–4.62, 4.109, 4.144, 8.23
Guardian *ad litem* 1.48, 4.144
Guardianship 1.38, 1.62, 7.12, 8.14

H
Habitual residence 1.17, 1.28, 1.38, 1.70–1.74, 1.90, 2.4, 2.38, 2.49, 2.50–2.51, 2.56, 3.6–3.7, 3.11, 3.14–3.15, 3.17–3.22, 3.26, 3.28–3.53, 3.66, 3.69, 3.72–3.73, 3.75, 3.81, 3.86, 3.91–3.92
Hearing of the child 2.1, 4.144, 7.9, 7.22, 7.31, 8.117, 10.27, 10.41
Hungary 1.30, 1.66, 3.8, 5.62, 7.20, 8.130, 11.6, 12.24

I
Identity of actions 8.53
Illness 4.191, 4.201, 9.31–9.32, 9.34, 9.68, 11.33, 11.41
Impediments arising after the decision 9.33
Implementation period, *see* transition period
Imprisonment 9.34, 9.68
Inadequate service 8.91, 8.93–8.99, 8.105
Inaudita altera parte 4.175
Incidental question 1.42–1.43, 1.45, 8.5, 8.8, 8.45, 8.47–8.49, 8.51–8.55, 8.61, 8.68, 8.82, 8.132, 8.136–8.136, 9.1, 10.29
India 6.18
Indirect contact 11.37–11.38
Inchoate rights of custody 6.44, 12.64
Inform (duty to) 4.72, 4.150–4.151, 4.212–4.215, 6.49, 6.106–6.107, 8.15, 8.18, 8.20, 8.24, 8.117, 9.44, 11.5–11.6, 11.18–11.19, 11.31–11.32, 11.54, 11.56
Information (collect and exchange) 1.3, 1.15, 1.19, 1.64, 1.98, 1.101–1.102, 2.18, 4.60, 4.70, 4.145, 4.155, 4.163, 4.213–4.215, 6.49, 6.107, 6.111, 6.118, 7.4, 8.18, 8.20, 8.34, 8.72, 8.75, 8.77, 8.134, 8.141, 10.26, 11.2, 11.4–11.5, 11.13, 11.15, 11.17–11.18, 11.23, 11.25–11.35, 11.39, 11.54, 11.59–11.61, 11.63
Information and assistance (provision of) 11.18, 11.25–11.26
Inheritance 1.45, 1.48, 4.65, 4.80

Institutional care   1.41, 11.16, 11.42, 11.46, 12.53
Institution of proceedings   1.94, 4.17, 12.9, 12.27
Integration test   4.12–4.13, 4.15, 4.17–4.19
Intention   1.11, 1.36, 1.73, 2.57, 3.33, 3.37, 3.39–3.41, 3.44–3.48, 4.12, 4.15–4.16, 4.21, 4.25–4.28, 4.31, 4.70, 4.215, 6.41
Interested party   2.13, 2.40, 4.210, 8.36, 8.38, 8.46, 9.19, 9.29, 10.29
Interested person   8.43
International Hague Network of Judges   4.153, 6.87, 11.40
Internationally displaced (children)   4.103–4.108
Interpol   11.24
Intimidation of witness or judge   8.126
Interpretation   1.16–1.22, 1.30, 1.51, 1.73, 1.75, 1.79–1.80, 2.32, 2.65, 3.19, 3.30–3.36, 3.61–3.62, 3.65, 3.84, 4.29, 4.39, 4.59, 4.71, 4.121, 4.137, 4.192, 4.201–4.203, 5.3, 5.5, 5.11, 5.60, 5.64, 6.20, 6.29, 6.84, 6.103, 6.118, 8.27, 8.31, 8.60, 8.138, 10.14, 10.24, 10.48–10.49, 11.64, 12.35, 12.58, 12.64
IP completion day   12.1, 12.19
Ireland   1.10, 2.22–2.23, 3.50, 3.57, 3.62, 6.36, 6.40, 8.9, 8.59–8.60, 11.58, 11.67, 12.8, 12.18, 12.24, 12.31–12.32, 12.34, 12.36, 12.45, 12.49–12.50, 12.53, 12.60
Irreconcilable decisions   5.11, 5.13, 5.21, 5.64
Irreconciliability   8.101–8.102
Issue preclusion   8.26
Italy   1.40, 1.51, 1.56, 1.63, 3.57, 3.65–3.66, 3.75, 4.20, 4.65, 4.190, 11.8, 12.24

J
Joint custody   8.15, 8.79, 9.55
Judicial cooperation in civil matters   3.34, 8.2
Judicial cooperation in family matters   1.3

K
Kafala   1.38, 12.50

L
Lagarde Report   4.104, 8.23–8.24
Later judgment   8.112–8.114
Latvia   1.27, 1.66, 3.8, 5.62, 7.20, 8.130, 11.58, 12.24
Lawful move   4.35–4.36, 4.129, 9.62
Left-behind parent   2.51, 4.130, 6.11, 6.24, 6.75, 6.76–6.80, 6.86, 6.88, 6.99–6.100, 6.102, 6.108, 9.74
Legal representative   1.45, 4.60, 4.62, 4.70, 4.109
Legal separation   1.22, 1.27, 1.52, 1.55, 1.77, 3.6, 3.8, 3.55, 3.57–3.59, 3.61–3.63, 3.66, 5.6, 5.11, 5.51, 5.59, 5.61, 8.9, 8.34, 8.68, 8.87, 8.102, 8.128, 8.130, 9.49, 10.23, 10.28, 10.32–10.36, 10.44, 10.48, 11.4, 12.24, 12.26–12.28, 12.31–12.32, 12.41, 12.58
Lis pendens   1.81–1.84, 2.4, 2.41, 3.27, 4.74, 4.88–4.90, 4.119, 4.174, 4.208, 5.3–5.7, 5.13, 5.15–5.18, 5.21–5.22, 5.24, 5.43–5.45, 5.54–5.56, 5.58–5.62, 5.68–5.72, 5.84, 8.101, 8.103, 8.125, 11.25, 11.40, 12.11, 12.20, 12.23, 12.25, 12.35
Lithuania   1.30, 1.66, 3.31, 12.24
Local jurisdiction, *see* Venue
Locating children   11.24
Locus standi   4.152, 11.49, 12.46
Luxembourg   1.60–1.61, 12.24

M
Maintenance   1.4, 1.26, 1.45, 1.49–1.50, 1.86–1.87, 3.9, 3.34, 3.51, 3.82–3.83, 3.87, 4.71, 5.17, 5.32, 5.62, 6.46, 6.70–6.71, 8.8, 8.31, 8.37, 8.47, 8.57, 8.59, 8.79, 8.98, 8.100, 8.102, 9.6, 9.20, 9.72, 9.76, 10.15–10.16, 11.4, 11.8, 11.16, 12.6
Malta   1.63, 8.9, 12.24
Marriage annulment   1.22, 1.27, 1.34, 3.6, 5.6, 5.11, 5.60, 8.8–8.9, 8.34, 8.68, 8.102, 8.128, 10.28, 10.48
Matrimonial matters   1.1–1.2, 1.8, 1.13, 1.22, 1.26–1.34, 1.51, 1.56, 1.90, 1.95, 1.101, 2.34–2.37, 3.1–3.5, 3.17, 3.19, 3.52, 3.54, 3.68, 3.83, 3.86–3.87, 4.4, 4.12, 4.43, 4.45, 4.49, 4.186, 5.4, 5.6, 5.16–5.17, 5.32, 5.46, 5.51, 5.57, 5.60–5.61, 5.64, 5.71, 12.4, 12.6, 12.21–12.23, 12.30, 12.43, 8.1, 8.9, 8.32, 8.35, 8.48, 8.67, 8.71, 8.82, 8.87, 8.102, 8.105–8.106, 8.112, 8.123, 8.128, 8.131, 9.2, 9.11, 9.75–9.76, 10.8, 10.25, 10.48, 11.1
Matrimonial property   1.4, 3.9, 3.51, 5.17, 5.62, 8.37, 8.98, 8.100, 8.102, 9.72, 9.76, 10.15–10.16
Mediation   2.14, 4.66, 6.27, 6.65–6.70, 9.55, 9.63, 11.14, 11.27
Mental illness   8.108
Missing Children Europe   11.24
Modification   3.1, 4.37–4.38, 4.129, 8.65
Modify   4.33, 4.38–4.39, 9.62
Most expeditious procedures available   6.55, 6.60–6.61
Mutual recognition of decisions   1.3

N
Name   1.48–1.50, 7.12, 8.14
National grounds for jurisdiction   4.167
National grounds for refusal of enforcement   9.69
Nationality   1.79, 1.86, 3.3, 3.6–3.7, 3.11, 3.18–3.19, 3.23–3.27, 3.43, 3.46, 3.50, 3.65, 3.69, 3.71–3.72, 3.75, 3.79, 3.81, 3.84–3.86, 3.89–3.92, 4.5, 4.11, 4.13–4.14, 4.16, 4.24, 4.54, 4.80, 4.106, 4.128, 4.131, 4.163, 4.167, 8.114, 11.56, 12.34
National law   1.32, 1.41, 1.50, 1.52, 2.7, 2.10, 2.17, 2.24, 2.35, 2.64, 3.30–3.36, 3.61, 3.66, 3.73, 3.76, 4.61, 4.66, 4.88, 4.95, 4.152, 4.167, 4.179–4.180, 4.182, 5.4, 5.5, 5.31, 5.69, 644–6.45, 6.47, 6.55, 6.59, 6.70, 6.73, 6.93, 6.113, 6.116, 7.2, 7.10, 7.14, 7.17, 7.22–7.25, 8.20, 8.38, 8.41, 8.44, 8.83–8.84, 8.89, 8.103, 8.106, 8.120, 8.125, 9.13, 9.26, 9.28–9.30, 9.32, 9.34–9.35, 9.38, 9.40, 9.48–9.50, 9.55, 9.60, 9.68–9.70, 10.9, 10.11, 11.3, 11.9, 11.22, 11.24,

Index

11.34, 11.52, 11.56, 11.60, 11.66, 12.15, 12.21, 12.29, 12.31, 12.60, 12.68
Ne exeat order   6.44
Negative conflict of competence   5.32, 5.48
Negative declaration on enforceability   9.52–9.55
Negative *res judicata*   8.5–8.6
Neglect   11.33
Netherlands   1.30, 1.48, 3.57, 12.24
Newborn   4.6, 4.18, 4.20, 4.24, 4.31, 4.32
Non-judicial divorce   12.38
Non-privileged decisions   1.95, 6.93, 7.30, 7.34, 8.3, 9.35, 9.38, 9.49–9.50, 9.56–9.57, 9.64, 10.28
Northern Ireland   12.8, 12.18, 12.31–12.32, 12.36, 12.45, 12.49, 12.50, 12.53, 12.60
Notarial divorce   1.33
Notary(-ies)   1.33, 1.51, 1.54, 7.11, 10.7–10.8, 10.11, 10.15, 10.19–10.22, 10.26–10.27, 10.43–10.44, 10.46, 12.38

O

Obligation to inform   8.18
Official language   6.105, 6.123, 8.74, 8.76, 11.9, 11.31, 11.59
Operative part of judgment   8.26–8.27
Opportunity to be heard (for applicant)   1.95, 6.72, 6.75–6.76, 6.121, 6.126, 7.2, 7.4, 7.8, 7.9, 7.11, 7.14, 7.31, 7.35, 8.111, 8.117–8.118, 8.122, 10.2, 10.27, 10.41
Opt in   1.10
Ordinary appeal   4.84, 4.87, 6.21, 6.24, 8.56, 8.59–8.60, 8.64, 9.28, 9.47
Orphanage   1.41
Override mechanism   6.9, 6.24, 6.96–6.103, 6.108, 6.113, 6.119, 6.128, 8.112, 8.135, 8.139, 9.35, 9.63, 9.74

P

Parallel proceedings   1.81, 3.27, 5.4, 5.9, 5.13, 5.18, 5.24, 5.29, 5.32–5.33, 5.35, 5.43, 5.46, 5.57, 5.63, 5.70–5.71, 12.35
Parent-child relationship   1.49–1.50, 5.68, 7.12
Parental responsibility, meaning of   1.37, 1.40, 1.43
Partial enforcement   6.125, 8.78, 9.72–9.73
Partial recognition   8.78, 8.80–8.81, 8.113, 9.72, 10.15–10.16
Party autonomy   3.12, 4.43–4.47, 4.53, 4.89
Penalty payment   9.14, 9.80
Peripatetic lifestyle   4.9, 4.101
Perpetuatio fori   1.73, 4.3, 12.54
Personal status   1.35, 8.34, 9.11, 10.23
Person concerned   3.37–3.40, 3.42, 3.76, 8.110–8.111
Perverting the course of justice   8.126
Philippines   8.9
Physical or psychological harm to the child   9.34
Physical presence   1.90, 3.41, 4.20–4.24, 4.26, 4.31, 4.109

Placement of child (in another Member State)   11.41–11.42
Poland   1.27, 1.30, 3.22, 4.13–4.14, 5.16, 6.56, 6.62, 7.4, 8.48, 12.24
Police   1.24, 11.24
Portugal   1.63–1.64, 3.8, 5.62, 7.4, 8.130, 11.58, 12.24
Positive declaration on enforceability   8.36–8.41, 8.42
Positive declaration on recognition   8.36–8.41
Positive *res judicata*   8.5–8.6
Postal address in Member State of enforcement   9.20, 9.43
Practice Guide for the Application of the Brussels IIb Regulation   1.14
Preclusive effect of *res judicata*   8.27
Preparatory documents   4.201, 4.203
Presence (of child)   1.75, 1.90, 3.40, 3.41
Prestation compensatoire   8.5, 10.15
Principal connecting factor   4.4–4.5
Principle of proximity   4.5
Prior in tempore, potior in iure   5.9
Private divorce   1.16, 1.32
Prior residence   2.51, 4.54
Privileged decision(s)   1.95, 6.93, 6.120, 7.30, 7.34, 8.3, 8.135–8.141, 9.3, 9.5, 9.8, 9.24, 9.34–9.35, 9.38, 9.49–9.50, 9.57–9.58, 9.60, 9.62, 9.64, 10.30
Procedure for enforcement   9.4–9.35, 9.38–9.43
Procedure for recognition   8.32–8.77, 10.12, 12.23
Procedure for refusal of enforcement   9.38–9.43
Programme for the implementation of the principle of mutual recognition   9.6
Prohibition of review of the substance   8.87
Property (of the child)   1.38, 1.4, 1.6, 1.26, 1.37, 1.42, 1.48, 3.9, 3.19, 3.43, 3.51, 3.87, 4.1, 4.54, 4.128, 4.132, 4.163, 4.173, 4.180, 4.185–4.186, 4.193–4.194, 4.203, 5.17, 5.62, 5.65, 7.19, 8.37, 8.57, 8.59, 8.98, 8.100, 8.102, 8.122, 9.72, 9.76, 9.79, 10.15–10.16, 10.42, 11.18, 11.29, 11.30, 12.35, 12.45, 12.49, 12.51, 12.56
Prorogation   1.48, 1.77–1.78, 3.12, 4.48–4.50, 4.56, 4.63–4.73, 4.85–4.86, 4.94–4.95, 4.97, 4.114, 4.158, 4.160, 5.15, 5.43–5.46, 8.27, 8.30, 12.57
Protective measure   1.37, 1.48, 4.208, 4.209, 4.212–4.213
Provisional enforceability   6.94, 9.13
Provisional measure   4.171–4.172, 4.174–4.176, 4.190, 4.194–4.195, 4.197–4.201, 4.203–4.204, 4.208, 4.210–4.211, 5.21–5.22, 9.16–9.17
Public authority   1.32–1.33, 1.54–1.55, 3.59, 4.62, 4.153, 9.1, 10.5–10.9, 10.18
Public law   1.23–1.24, 1.41, 1.50, 4.116, 4.153, 11.41, 11.47, 11.55, 11.71, 12.58
Public policy   6.24, 8.53, 8.86–8.90, 8.95, 8.105–8.108, 8.124, 8.126, 8.128, 8.130–8.131, 8.141, 9.67, 10.2, 10.33, 10.38, 10.45–10.46, 12.29, 12.41
Public prosecutor   4.61–4.62, 4.80, 4.144, 6.75

Index

R
Radicalisation 11.33
Ratification 12.48
Ratio decidendi 8.26–8.27, 8.29, 8.55
Re-abduction 6.78
Rebus sic stantibus 4.198, 8.6, 10.40, 11.51
Recitals 1.15, 1.18–1.22, 1.45, 4.112, 8.82, 11.4
Recognition of decisions 1.3, 1.60–1.61, 8.1–8.2, 8.105, 9.4
Refugee children 4.103, 4.105
Refusal of enforcement 8.3, 8.36, 9.25, 9.28, 9.36–9.43, 9.44–9.48, 9.51–9.56, 9.59, 9.64, 9.68, 9.70–9.71
Refusal of recognition 1.95, 2.51, 8.3, 8.36, 8.49, 8.53, 8.56, 8.72, 8.75, 8.82, 8.85, 8.88, 8.92, 8.105, 8.125, 8.140–8.141, 9.36, 9.39, 9.52, 9.54–9.55, 10.27, 10.29, 10.31, 10.41, 10.45, 12.14
Refusing the dissolution of matrimonial ties 1.26, 5.54
Registered partnership 1.4
Registered partnership property 1.4
Related actions 1.87, 5.4, 5.6–5.7, 5.17
Related proceedings 5.2, 5.4, 12.10–12.12
Religion 8.108
Remote hearings 6.128, 7.24
Report (on the child's situation) 1.11, 1.13, 1.34, 1.100, 3.62, 3.66, 4.104, 4.201, 8.4, 8.13, 8.23, 10.1, 11.29–11.30, 11.59–11.61, 11.63
Representative *ad litem* 9.20
Repudiatory retention 6.41, 12.64
Request (for information) 1.41, 1.80, 1.84, 1.99, 1.101, 2.15–2.16, 2.31, 2.38, 4.93, 4.115, 4.117, 4.150, 4.152–4.153, 4.156–4.157, 4.159–4.160, 4.162–4.165, 5.40, 5.55, 6.11, 6.21, 6.49, 6.63, 6.90, 6.105, 6.121–6.123, 6.125, 8.5, 8.66, 8.74–8.77, 8.81, 8.115–8.116, 11.17–11.31, 11.34–11.36, 11.38–11.40, 11.43, 11.50, 11.54–11.55, 11.59–11.63, 11.65–11.66, 12.45–12.46, 12.58
Request for transfer of jurisdiction 4.162–4.165
Residence (of child) 1.17, 1.24, 1.28, 1.38, 1.70–1.74, 1.86, 1.90, 2.4, 2.38, 2.49–2.51, 2.56–2.57, 2.60, 3.6–3.7, 3.11, 3.14–3.15, 3.17–3.22, 3.26, 3.28–3.53, 3.65–3.66, 3.69, 3.72–3.73, 3.75, 3.81, 3.86, 3.91–3.92, 4.4–4.17, 4.19–4.41, 4.45–4.46, 4.48, 4.52, 4.54–4.55, 4.57, 4.74, 4.76–4.77, 4.79–4.80, 4.93, 4.95, 4.98–4.103, 4.105, 4.110–4.111, 4.113, 4.120, 4.122, 4.128–4.131, 4.147, 4.162–4.164, 4.168, 4.172, 4.176–4.178, 4.190–4.191, 4.211, 4.213, 5.15, 5.68, 5.70, 6.3, 6.5, 6.11, 6.16, 6.18–6.19, 6.21–6.22, 6.25–6.27, 6.35–6.37, 6.40–6.42, 6.44–6.46, 6.79, 6.86–6.88, 6.92–6.93, 6.95, 6.99–6.100, 6.102, 6.107–6.108, 6.112, 6.128, 8.14, 8.16–8.17, 8.22–8.25, 8.30, 8.114, 8.140, 9.58, 9.60, 9.62, 11.19, 11.32–11.33, 11.41, 11.53, 12.27, 12.35, 12.44, 12.50–12.51, 12.54–12.55

Residual jurisdiction 2.35, 3.67, 3.80, 3.86, 3.89, 4.167
Res judicata 1.47, 2.42, 8.8, 8.26–8.31, 8.51–8.55, 8.112, 10.2
Retention (of child) 1.64–1.65, 4.3, 4.162, 6.12, 6.14, 6.16–6.17, 6.19–6.22, 6.24–6.25, 6.28, 6.31, 6.33–6.41–6.47, 6.83, 6.100, 6.106–6.109, 6.117, 8.13, 8.117, 12.62–12.64
Return application 6.8, 6.29–6.30, 6.32, 6.48, 6.52, 6.54–6.55, 6.66, 6.72, 7.9, 12.66–12.68
Return of child 6.28, 6.99
Review as to the substance (*révision au fond*) 8.87, 8.96, 8.119, 8.134
Review of jurisdiction 8.124–8.127, 10.43–10.47
Review of the substance 8.89
Révision au fond (review as to the substance) 8.87
Right of child to express his or her views (in return proceedings) 6.72–6.73
Rigths *in rem* 8.11
Rights of custody 1.37–1.38, 4.1, 4.17, 5.65, 6.15, 6.19–6.22, 6.24, 6.28, 6.34, 6.38–6.39, 6.42–6.47, 6.99–6.101, 6.106–6.109, 6.111–6.112, 6.114, 6.117–6.118, 7.12, 7.32, 7.34, 8.16–8.17, 12.62–12.64
Rights of the defence 9.36
Romania 1.86, 12.24
Rush to the court 5.10

S
Same cause of action 1.81, 1.83, 5.7, 5.18, 5.24, 5.58, 5.60, 5.65–5.69, 5.71, 12.11, 12.44
Same parties 1.81, 1.87, 5.6, 5.18, 5.58, 5.63–5.64, 8.26, 12.11
Same-sex divorce 12.26
Same-sex marriage 1.13, 1.28–1.31
Scope of application 1.18–1.58, 1.96, 2.3–2.4, 2.48–2.51, 2.53, 3.19, 3.56, 3.58, 3.74, 3.78, 4.98, 4.103, 4.105–4.106, 4.121, 4.185–4.186, 4.201, 4.203, 4.206, 5.16–5.17, 5.61–5.62, 12.16
Scotland 1.87, 12.8, 12.18, 12.31–12.32, 12.36, 12.45, 12.51, 12.53, 12.60
Sect 11.33
Secure accommodation (for the abducting parent and the child) 6.82
Seising (of court) 49, 2.3–2.26, 2.65, 3.21, 4.62, 4.65–4.66, 4.72, 4.74, 4.76–4.77, 4.83, 11.15, 12.9
Self-harm 11.67
Separation 1.4, 1.7, 1.22, 1.27, 1.52, 1.55, 1.77, 2.22–2.23, 3.6, 3.8, 3.12, 3.19, 3.36, 3.46, 3.52, 3.55, 3.57–3.63, 3.65–3.66, 4.15, 4.32, 4.45, 4.86, 4.95, 4.98, 4.122, 4.131, 4.213, 5.6, 5.10–5.12, 5.17, 5.23, 5.32, 5.40–5.41, 5.51, 5.54, 5.59–5.62, 8.9, 8.34, 8.68, 8.87, 8.102, 8.128, 8.130, 9.49, 9.73, 10.23, 10.28, 10.32–10.36, 10.44, 10.48, 12.24, 12.26–12.29, 12.31–12.32, 12.41, 12.58
Serious illness 4.191, 9.31–9.32, 9.34, 9.68

Intersentia 433

Service   2.6–2.7, 2.14, 2.16, 2.24–2.26, 2.44, 2.49–2.51, 2.54–2.61, 2.63–2.65, 4.202, 5.27, 6.59, 8.72, 8.91, 8.93–8.100, 8.105, 8.109, 9.9, 9.20, 9.22, 9.55, 11.67, 12.9
Settled in his or her new environment (child has)   6.21–6.23, 12.62
Settlement (of child)   2.9, 2.15–2.16, 3.41, 4.45, 4.47, 4.171, 4.184, 4.197, 4.208, 5.61, 6.23–6.24, 10.1–10.3, 10.21
Six-week obligation/requirement (to dispose of return applications)   6.55–6.64
Sexual orientation   1.30, 8.108
Slovakia   1.27, 6.53, 11.6, 11.58, 12.24
Slovenia   3.8, 5.62, 7.4, 8.130, 12.24
Social services   4.61, 4.147
Spain   1.7, 1.30, 1.63, 3.8, 3.83, 5.23, 7.4, 8.130, 12.24
Spousal maintenance (or support)   8.31, 8.47, 8.102, 10.15
Standing (to apply for refusal of enforcement)   3.19, 4.49, 4.61, 8.40, 8.43, 8.45, 8.61, 8.68, 8.82, 8.132, 8.136 9.39–9.40, 9.54, 11.23
Status   1.6, 1.26, 1.32–1.33, 1.35, 1.48, 1.79, 1.87, 2.58, 3.2–3.3, 3.5, 3.78, 3.86, 5.16, 5.22, 5.62, 6.115, 8.9, 8.13, 8.34, 8.38, 8.47, 8.62, 8.68, 8.100, 8.113, 8.129, 9.2, 9.11, 10.23, 12.22, 12.29
Stay of proceedings   8.56–8.66
Stay of proceedings (for refusal of enforcement)   8.8, 8.24–8.26, 8.28–8.29, 8.31, 9.47–9.48, 9.51
Substantial connection   1.48, 3.60, 4.51–4.52, 4.54, 4.78, 4.80, 4.98, 4.114, 6.27
Substantive rules   1.2
Succession   1.4, 1.26, 1.44–1.45, 1.48–1.50, 3.34, 3.87, 4.55, 8.11, 8.37, 8.48, 8.57, 8.59, 8.102, 10.21
Summons   2.22, 2.60, 8.95–8.96
Supervised access   11.38
Suspension of enforcement   8.3, 9.10, 9.24, 9.28–9.35, 9.48, 9.53
Sweden   1.24, 1.27, 1.34, 1.62, 1.71, 3.72, 4.9, 6.53, 8.9, 8.13, 12.24

T
Tacit prorogation   3.12, 4.71–4.72, 5.44
Telephone (contact)   11.37
Temporary presence   4.19
Third State   1.17, 1.57, 1.70–1.73, 2.49, 3.78, 3.86–3.87, 4.22–4.23, 4.94–4.99, 4.101, 6.18, 6.91, 8.54, 8.67, 8.103–8.104, 9.60, 10.34, 10.36, 11.45, 12.3, 12.21–12.22, 12.44, 12.85
Time limit(s)   6.62, 6.113, 9.40, 11.28
Timing provisions   6.55, 6.62, 12.66, 12.68

Transfer of jurisdiction   1.76, 1.79–1.80, 2.38, 4.81, 4.93, 4.111, 4.113, 4.116, 4.118–4.124, 4.129, 4.133, 4.135, 4.140, 4.154, 4.157, 4.162–4.165, 5.55, 11.50
Transfer of proceedings   2.4, 2.38, 3.54, 4.54, 4.89–4.93, 4.112, 4.114, 4.117–4.119, 4.121, 4.123, 4.129–4.130, 4.134–4.135, 4.142, 4.148, 4.152–4.153, 4.156, 4.164, 5.55–5.57
Transition period   1.99, 12.1, 12.3, 12.6, 12.9–12.11, 12.13, 12.16–12.17, 12.20–12.21
Translation   6.105, 6.111, 6.123, 8.74–8.77, 8.139, 9.23, 9.42, 11.31, 11.59
Transliteration   6.111, 6.123, 8.74–8.76, 8.139, 9.23, 9.42
Transmission of information   1.64, 11.2, 11.34–11.35
Trusts   1.49–1.50

U
UK   1.10, 1.17, 1.58, 1.79, 1.86–1.87, 2.22, 3.52, 4.17, 4.94–4.95, 4.120, 4.153, 5.32, 5.37, 5.40–5.42, 6.23, 6.41, 6.88, 8.59, 8.127, 12.1–12.3, 12.5–12.9, 12.13, 12.18–12.25, 12.28, 12.31–12.60, 12.62, 12.64–12.67
Unaccompanied minor   11.33
Unborn child   1.36
Undue delay   4.147, 6.73, 6.76, 9.44–9.46
Urgency   1.95, 2.58, 4.9, 4.109, 4.168, 4.171, 4.182–4.184, 4.191, 4.208, 7.19, 8.116, 8.122, 10.42, 11.20, 11.25, 11.40, 11.50, 12.56

V
Validity of marriage   1.60
Vatican City   8.9
Venue   4.183, 8.41, 8.44, 11.38
Views of the child   7.2
Visitation   4.38
Visiting rights   4.13

W
Wales   1.82, 1.87, 11.67, 12.8, 12.18, 12.20, 12.31–12.36, 12.42, 12.45, 12.49–12.50, 12.53, 12.60
War   9.34, 9.68
Whereabouts of children (discovering of)   11.23
Withdrawal Agreement *see* European Withdrawal Agreement
Withdrawal of certificate   8.141, 9.28, 9.47, 10.50
Wrongful removal or retention   1.65, 4.3, 4.162, 6.12, 6.14, 6.16–6.17, 6.24–6.25, 6.28, 6.31, 6.33, 6.39, 6.46, 6.83, 6.100, 6.106–6.109, 6.117, 12.63

Milton Keynes UK
Ingram Content Group UK Ltd.
UKHW031125031224
452022UK00028B/517